China's Cultural Heritage
The Qing Dynasty,
1644–1912

SECOND EDITION

China's Cultural Heritage
The Qing Dynasty,
1644–1912

Richard J. Smith

RICE UNIVERSITY

Westview Press

BOULDER • SAN FRANCISCO • OXFORD

Published in 1994 in the United States of America by Westview Press, Inc., 5500 Central Avenue, Boulder, Colorado 80301-2877, and in the United Kingdom by Westview Press, 36 Lonsdale Road, Summertown, Oxford OX2 7EW

Library of Congress Cataloging-in-Publication Data
Smith, Richard J. (Richard Joseph), 1944–
    China's cultural heritage : the Qing dynasty, 1644–1912 / Richard
J. Smith. — 2nd ed.
        p.   cm.
    Includes bibliographical references and index.
    ISBN 0-8133-1346-5. — ISBN 0-8133-1347-3 (pbk.)
    1. China—Civilization—1644–1912.   I. Title.
DS754.14.S6   1994
951'.03—dc20
                                                                                                    94-948
                                                                                                    CIP

Printed and bound in the United States of America

     The paper used in this publication meets the requirements
(∞) of the American National Standard for Permanence of Paper
     for Printed Library Materials Z39.48-1984.

10   9   8   7   6   5   4   3   2

To Lisa
with gratitude for the love, the help,
and the humor

Contents

List of Tables and Figures   IX
Preface to the Second Edition   XI
Preface to the First Edition   XIII

1   **Introduction**   I

2   **The Qing Inheritance**   II

The Legacy of the Land, 12
The Historical Background, 26

3   **The Qing Political Order**   41

Imperial Rule and Metropolitan Offices, 44
Administrative Integration, 55

4   **Social and Economic Institutions**   69

Social Classes, 71
Forms of Chinese Socioeconomic Organization, 86

5   **Language and Symbolic Reference**   101

Distinctive Features of the Language, 102
Language and Culture, 115

6   **Thought**   129

The Chinese Mental World, 131
The Confucian Moral Order, 139
Daoist Flight and Fancy, 150

7   Religion   155

Official Sacrifices, 157
Buddhism and Religious Daoism, 165
Popular Religion, 174

8   Art   187

Attitudes Toward Art, 188
Crafts, 194
Painting and Calligraphy, 201

9   Literature   219

Categories of Classical Literature, 220
Vernacular Literature, 230

10   Social Life   245

Life-Cycle Ritual, 246
Amusements, 262

11   Tradition and Modernity, 1860–1993   277

The Challenge of the West, 277
Reform, Revolution, and China's Inherited Culture, 287

Appendix A: A Note on Chinese Names   299
Appendix B: Weights and Measures, Exchange Rates, and Costs   301
Notes   305
Bibliography   339
About the Book and Author   373
Index   374

Tables and Figures

Tables

2.1	North and South contrasts	18
2.2	Regional stereotypes	25
3.1	Central government revenue and expenditures (1899)	53
3.2	The examination system	61
3.3	Official salaries	66
4.1	The five degrees of mourning	87
4.2	Some estimates of tenancy	94
6.1	Early *yinyang* correlations	132
6.2	*Yinyang* and five-elements correlations	133

Figures

2.1	The Great Wall	17
2.2	Map of China	20
3.1	The Forbidden City	46
3.2	Manchu bannerman	49
3.3	The Qing bureaucracy	50
3.4	Examination halls	62
4.1	Mandarin squares	72
4.2	Status clothing	73
4.3	Agricultural life	76
4.4	A late Qing barber	80
5.1	Chinese characters (A)	104
5.2	Chinese characters (B)	105
5.3	Chinese characters (C)	107
5.4	Chinese characters (D)	108
5.5	Chinese characters (E)	108

5.6   Chinese characters (F)   109
5.7   Chinese characters (G)   109
5.8   Chinese characters (H)   110
5.9   Chinese characters (I)   110
5.10 Chinese characters (J)   111
5.11 Chinese characters (K)   111
5.12 Chinese characters (L)   117
5.13 Chinese characters (M)   119
5.14 Hexagrams   121
5.15 Trigrams   122
5.16 Diagrams from the *Yijing*   123
5.17 *Qian* and *Kun*   123

7.1   The Altar of Heaven   159
7.2   Arrangement of the *Shidian* sacrifice   161
7.3   Temple of Tianhou   165
7.4   Funeral procession   180
7.5   Grave   181
7.6   Ancestral temples   182
7.7   Ancestral tablets   183

8.1   Landscape garden   199
8.2   Sketches from the *Mustard Seed Garden Manual* (A)   205
8.3   Sketches from the *Mustard Seed Garden Manual* (B)   206
8.4   Sketches from the *Mustard Seed Garden Manual* (C)   207
8.5   Sketches from the *Mustard Seed Garden Manual* (D)   208
8.6   Types of calligraphy   216

9.1   Characters from *Dream of the Red Chamber* (A)   240
9.2   Characters from *Dream of the Red Chamber* (B)   241

10.1 Women with bound feet   250
10.2 A Manchu woman   251
10.3 House plan   252
10.4 Wedding processions   257
10.5 Amusements (A)   263
10.6 Amusements (B)   264
10.7 Amusements (C)   265
10.8 Gestures of respect   267

11.1 The deification of Mao   298

Preface to the Second Edition

I am pleased to have the opportunity to produce a new edition of *China's Cultural Heritage* for Westview Press. This revised and expanded version draws upon the enormous amount of new scholarship on Qing dynasty history and culture that has appeared in the past ten years. It also reflects my own rethinking of certain themes and arguments—a process encouraged not only by the ever-growing body of literature on late imperial China but also by a number of valuable scholarly reviews of the first edition and the helpful and encouraging comments of a host of friends and colleagues, many of whom have used the book in their courses. This edition also incorporates material from my recent work on Qing dynasty myth, ritual, divination, calendars, and almanacs (see the Bibliography) as well as from several ongoing research projects of mine, including a study of Ming and Qing dynasty maps as indices of evolving Chinese conceptions of the world.

Although this edition of *China's Cultural Heritage* has been revised substantially, it employs the same basic approach as the original work. It is intended to be selective rather than exhaustive, and although I have tried to include as much illustrative material as possible within space limitations, my focus remains steadfastly on topics that seem to be most relevant to Chinese conceptions of "Chineseness." My purpose in writing this book was, after all, to provide a framework for analysis, not a comprehensive history or an encyclopedic overview. Hence, Western readers may be disappointed by certain omissions, such as the absence of an extensive and systematic discussion of Chinese science and technology.

This point brings me to three main criticisms of the first edition. The first was that it was not sufficiently "historical." In the opinion of several reviewers, *China's Cultural Heritage* did not give adequate attention to the problem of change over time. Although my primary interest remains in what may be called (rather unfashionably at the moment) the "structure" of traditional Chinese society, I certainly agree that within certain basic cultural parameters China underwent a great deal of change in the Qing period, as in earlier times. In order to indicate this process more clearly, at the beginning of each chapter of the revised edition I have delineated the major historical trends of the Qing in the realms of institutions, language, thought, art, literature, and so forth. Nonspecialists should not be daunted by the allusive quality of these preliminary overviews.

The second criticism was related to the first. That is, some readers felt that the work did not give adequate attention to the enormous variety in Chinese culture across space as well as time. I have never denied this variety (which would, after all, be most difficult to do), but my interest has been and remains in cultural common denominators. In fact, part of my motivation for writing the book in the first place was to respond to the apparent move toward "disaggregation" in Chinese studies (advocated, for instance, by Paul Cohen in his historiographical critique of American scholarship on China). There is obvious value in local and regional histories, as well as in studies of what Cohen calls the "lower" levels of society, but the dialectic between holistic and particularistic studies must be sustained. How, after all, can we discuss dissidence, diversity, and change in China without an understanding of consensus, conformity, and continuity? What, in the end, makes the term "China" meaningful?

A third criticism was that *China's Cultural Heritage* did not contain enough "real" people, that the book was too abstract and impersonal. Culture is by definition a collective construction, and cultural analysis requires both generalization and detachment. Yet, having recently written a lengthy study of Chinese divination based on well over a thousand Qing dynasty biographies, I have come to appreciate more fully the value of using individual human beings to exemplify broader cultural views and phenomena. I trust that the infusion of additional flesh-and-blood people into this edition will give the book more "life" without burdening readers with too many names and dates.

Finally, I have decided to employ the *pinyin* romanization system for transliterating all Chinese names and terms. This is a pragmatic choice, not a political one. Although obviously not designed for the convenience of English speakers, *pinyin* is rapidly gaining currency in academic circles as well as in more popular writings on China. At the same time, however, a number of important Western works—including standard references and many valuable studies in Chinese history, philosophy, religion, art, and literature—still use the Wade-Giles system of transliteration. In recognition of this awkward but unavoidable situation, the index of this book includes Wade-Giles equivalents for all major *pinyin* entries.

Richard J. Smith

Preface to the First Edition

A major theme throughout China's imperial history has been the tension between the inherently divisive tendencies of a huge, geographically fragmented, and ethnically diverse land mass and the unifying impulses of a centralized bureaucratic empire administered by highly educated scholar-officials who shared a remarkably uniform cultural outlook. This book examines the interplay between these two contending influences during the Ch'ing [Qing] dynasty (1644–1912), a period remarkable for its expansiveness, cultural splendor, stability, and staying power. My thesis is that the Chinese of the Ch'ing [Qing] era, as in earlier periods, were obsessed with the concept of order (*chih* [*zhi*]) and that this preoccupation was expressed not only in their highly refined bureaucratic institutions and methods of social and economic organization but also in their philosophy, religious and secular ritual, standards of literary and artistic achievement, and comprehensive systems of classifying all natural and supernatural phenomena. This obsession was also evident in their cultural psychology—notably in their attitudes toward social conformity, consensus, collective responsibility, and their almost pathological fear of disorder (*luan*). But the effort to impose order on all aspects of the known world was at once China's greatest cultural strength and its most critical weakness, for the very factors that contributed to an unparalleled record of cultural cohesiveness and continuity also prevented a rapid and creative response to the challenges of the modern world in the nineteenth and twentieth centuries.

Although this book is interpretive rather than purely descriptive, it is not my purpose to drain the lifeblood from China's rich cultural tradition by subjecting it only to cold and detached analysis. This study is also intended as an exercise in appreciation, a sympathetic inside look at one of the world's most refined and impressive civilizations. Although it makes an intellectual argument, it also seeks an emotional response. For those with little prior knowledge of China, the book should promote greater understanding and a new respect for Chinese culture; and for fellow academic specialists, it should provide a fresh perspective on some familiar, but endlessly absorbing, cultural terrain. In all events, I hope it will encourage discussion, debate, and further analysis.

This book owes a great deal to students and colleagues, both of whom I have kept in mind and consulted at every stage of research and writing. I am especially grateful to three people: Allen Matusow, for urging me to undertake this study in the first place and for offering unfailing encouragement and valuable advice over a long span of time; John K. Fairbank, for his sustained scholarly interest, broad vision, and incisive criticisms; and K. C. Liu, for his inspirational example, limitless patience, and gentle guidance. Many other friends and colleagues, in a wide variety of disciplines, have read all or part of the manuscript and offered useful comments. These people are too numerous to mention individually, but their collective contribution is enormous and much appreciated. I would like to thank Rice University for its generous assistance in the form of summer research grants, the American Philosophical Society for its financial support of a related project, and the University of California, Davis, for sponsoring a productive summer spent as a visiting research scholar. Gratitude must also be expressed to the staff members of the East Asiatic libraries at Berkeley, Davis, Harvard, and Columbia for their efficiency and assistance. Finally, I would like to thank my wife, Lisa, and my son, Tyler, for once again cheerfully enduring the inconvenience involved in writing a book—most particularly Tyler, who competed with the typewriter for my attention but not for my affection.

Richard J. Smith

1

Introduction

$\mathcal{T}$his book focuses on the concept of "Chineseness." It asks, at least implicitly: How was a "Chinese" identity constructed in premodern times and by whom? What were the patterns of behavior, features of language, beliefs and values, systems of logic, symbolic structures, aesthetic preferences, material achievements, and institutions that came to be considered distinctively "Chinese"—at least by those who played the most visible and self-conscious role in their perpetuation? What, in other words, was the nature of traditional Chinese culture?

The notion of "culture" advanced here is a broad one. It encompasses not only artifacts and attitudes but also perceptions and prescriptions for social action. Of particular interest to me are the organizing principles of a given society. How do people categorize and interpret experiences and phenomena in order to create a coherent version of reality, and how, in turn, does their understanding of this "reality" influence their behavior?[1] Although the term "culture" is sometimes used in this book with respect to collective artistic, literary, and technical accomplishments, it refers fundamentally to classification—the naming and arranging of things, ideas, and activities into coherent systems of meaning. Viewed in this light, cultural analysis becomes the evaluation of these systems, their interrelationships, and their social manifestations. The trick, of course, is to avoid imprisonment by one's own set (or sets) of conceptual categories.[2]

Culture, however defined, is never static; it constantly undergoes transformations in response to new stimuli, whether generated from within or introduced from without. Ideas, values, and customs change, as do institutions, laws, and rituals. Even language changes.[3] Yet these transformations take place within frameworks of understanding that are often remarkably resilient—particularly in societies that have not faced fundamental challenges to their basic values and assumptions or to their sense of moral or material superiority. China has long been such a civilization. As a result, to this day modern scholars on both Taiwan and the Mainland can confidently, and with a surprising degree of consensus, speak of traditional China's "special characteristics" (*tezhi, tese*)—basic cultural attributes that endured for hundreds or even thousands of years.[4]

Historically, questions of Chinese cultural identity have been primarily the preoccupation of intellectual elites.[5] This is not to say that other elements of society, including peasants, lacked a role in either the construction or the articulation of traditional Chinese culture.[6] But they were seldom self-conscious about their contributions, and in any case the record of their views is frustratingly incomplete—particularly prior to the onset of systematic anthropological fieldwork in the early twentieth century.[7] For these and other reasons I have chosen an "elite" emphasis for this book. Furthermore, as Myron Cohen reminds us, "China's traditional elites were cultural brokers, for their high status in society was based upon nationally accepted standards [that were] also validated by local culture."[8]

The dominant social class of premodern China was the so-called "gentry" (*shenshi*)—a group formally defined as holders of official degrees earned by passing the prestigious civil-service examinations. This elite group, which together with their families constituted less than 2 percent of the entire population in late imperial times (that is, the last five or six hundred years of China's dynastic history), exerted a profound influence on Chinese social life and provided the pool of highly literate talent from which the majority of Chinese bureaucrats were drawn. We should, however, broaden this technical definition of elites somewhat to embrace the 15 percent or so of the population who probably qualified by virtue of their wealth, leisure, local influence, and participation in literati culture. Recent research has shown that not all elites in China had degrees and that as a group they were "much more diverse, flexible and changeable than earlier notions of gentry society suggested."[9]

Despite certain significant differences in their respective social backgrounds and specific interests,[10] local and especially national elites had a remarkably uniform cultural outlook, as well as a common stake in the protection, promotion, and perpetuation of China's ancient and glorious civilization. In the words of Joseph Esherick and Mary Rankin, "Gentry were the keepers of a particular set of cultural symbols that denoted refinement." Cultural displays by this group, such as the ability to compose verse in an elegant calligraphic hand, "set the lower limits to the gentry category by distinguishing gentry, with or without degrees, from others, such as village community leaders, who lacked the same cultural credentials."[11] How did this unique group of aspiring scholars, artists, poets, and administrators organize and explain the world around them? How did their conceptual structures and interpretations affect their behavior, and how, in turn, did these patterns of perception and behavior influence traditional Chinese society as a whole?[12]

In order to answer these questions I have chosen to focus on the Qing dynasty (1644–1912), the last imperial regime and a crucial bridge between traditional and modern life in China. The Qing was the largest consolidated empire in Chinese history and by far the most successful dynasty of conquest. On the whole, the Qing period witnessed the fullest development of traditional political, economic, and social institutions, as well as the greatest degree of regional integration within China proper. No dynasty was more "Confucian" in outlook or more self-consciously antiquarian. Furthermore, thanks largely to the systematic policy of sinicization undertaken by China's Manchu conquerors, and to the phenomenal peace and prosperity enjoyed by most Chinese during the reigns of the Kangxi (1662–1722), Yongzheng (1723–1735), and Qianlong (1736–1795) emperors, the Qing was a period of enrichment and "leisurely fulfillment" in material culture and the arts.[13] Contrary to stereotype, in many ways the Qing epitomized the best of China's cultural tradition, although ultimately the dynasty and the dynastic system itself fell victim to unprecedented internal pressures and erosion by Western technology and ideas in the late nineteenth and early twentieth centuries.

What did members of the Chinese elite have in mind when they spoke (or, more aptly, wrote) of "culture"? The core term in classical Chinese is *wen*. *Wen* conveys a wide range of meanings, most of which derive from the basic sense of "markings" or "patterns." *Wen* refers narrowly to Chinese writing and literature, but more broadly to a whole constellation of distinctive cultural attributes—art, music, ritual, and so forth—each of which, like literature, had an expressly moral component. *Wen* was the measure of a Confucian gentleman in traditional China, the mark of true "civilization." *Wen* did not, however, carry any of the primary meanings we associate with the Latin terms *civis* or *civitas*. Members of the Chinese elite did not consider themselves to be "citizens" in the classical Western sense, and although Chinese cities were often the source of gentry amusement, they were not really centers of culture in the way the elite defined it.[14]

Nor was culture simply a matter of individual preference and life-style. China was itself viewed primarily as a cultural entity. Although the frequently used term for China, *Zhongguo* (the "Central Kingdom"), implies an awareness of the country as both a political and geographical unit, a common alternative term, *Zhonghua* (the "Central Cultural Florescence") reflects a long-standing emphasis on the cultural basis of the Chinese state. Few Qing scholars would have disagreed with the following fourteenth-century definition of China:

> Central Cultural Florescence is another term for Central Kingdom. When a people subjects itself to the Kingly Teachings [i.e., Confucianism] and subordinates itself to the Central Kingdom; when in clothing it is dignified and decorous, and when its customs are marked by filial respect and brotherly submission; when conduct follows the accepted norms and the principle of righteousness, then one may call it [a part of the] Central Cultural Florescence.[15]

Barbarian conquest affirmed and reinforced this Sinocentric world view rather than shattering it.

How did the Chinese order their vast cultural world, which embraced "all under Heaven"? One useful, but seldom used, index is the famous Qing encyclopedia *Gujin tushu jicheng* (Complete Collection of Writings and Illustrations, Past and Present; hereafter *Tushu jicheng* or *TSJC*), presented to the throne in 1725 after decades of imperially commissioned collective labor. This massive and well-organized compendium, repository of "all that was best in the literature of the past, dealing with every branch of knowledge," was intended not only as a kind of moral and practical guide for the emperor and his officials but also as an expression of the unity and totality of Chinese culture. I have used the *TSJC,* together with a great many other official and unofficial compilations of the period, as a guide to the cultural concerns of the Qing elite.[16] Collectively, these sources attest to the extraordinary holism of the Chinese cultural vision—the conviction that "all strains of thought, all institutions, [and] all forms of behavior should embody and express a common set of values."[17]

Three related themes serve as the interpretive foundation of this book. All of these loom large in the Chinese documentary record, but they have received inadequate attention in the West. The first is cognition, the way the Chinese viewed the world around them. Despite the complexity of this outlook, with its intersecting Confucian, Buddhist, and Daoist elements and elaborate interplay between elite and popular conceptions of reality, we can identify at least one construct, or paradigm, that transcended ideology and class. Sometimes described as "complementary bipolarity," this viewpoint was expressed by the well-known, but much abused, concepts of *yin* and *yang*. These terms and their equivalents appear everywhere in the Chinese language and literature, yet too often they are taken for granted by Chinese scholars and either misunderstood or underestimated by scholars in the West.[18]

In traditional times, *yin* and *yang* were used in three main senses, each of which may be illustrated by the following excerpts from *Honglou meng* (Dream of the Red Chamber), China's greatest and most influential novel. In a colorful conversation with her maidservant, Kingfisher, Shi Xiangyun remarks: "Everything in the universe is produced by the forces of *yin* and *yang*. ... All the transformations that occur result from the interaction of *yin* and *yang*. ... When *yang* is exhausted, it becomes *yin*, and when *yin* is exhausted, it becomes *yang*. ... *Yinyang* is a kind of force in things that gives them their distinctive form. For example, Heaven is *yang* and Earth is *yin*; water is *yin*, fire is *yang*; the sun is *yang*, the moon is *yin*." "Ah yes," replies Kingfisher, "that's why astrologers call the sun the '*yang* star' and the moon the '*yin* star.'" After a lengthy discussion of several other such associations and correlations, Kingfisher ends the conversation by observing: "You're *yang* and I'm *yin*. ... That's what people always say: the master is *yang* and the servant is *yin*. Even I can understand that principle."[19]

Yin and *yang* were, then, (1) cosmic forces that produced and animated all natural phenomena; (2) terms used to identify recurrent, cyclical patterns of rise and decline, waxing and waning; and (3) comparative categories, describing dualistic relationships that were inherently unequal but almost invariably complementary. Virtually any aspect of Chinese experience could be explained in terms of these paired concepts, ranging from such mundane sensory perceptions as dark and light, wet and dry, to abstractions such as real and unreal, being and nonbeing. *Yinyang* relationships involved the notion of mutual dependence and harmony based on hierarchical difference. *Yin* qualities were generally considered inferior to *yang* qualities, but unity of opposites was always the cultural ideal.

Perhaps no other major civilization in world history has had such a pervasive, tenacious, and essentially naturalistic world view—an accommodating outlook contrasting sharply with the familiar religious dualisms of good and evil, God and the Devil, which are so prominent in the ancient Near Eastern and Western cultural traditions. The notion of *yinyang* complementarity, reinforced by certain Confucian intellectual predilections, no doubt contributed to the remarkable harmonizing tendencies of traditional Chinese thought—the obvious inclination on the part of Chinese scholars to value "similarity and convergence" over "difference and divergence."[20]

Much that is most distinctive about traditional Chinese culture can be explained by reference to *yinyang* conceptions and to the elaborate correlative thinking associated with these ideas. *Yinyang* polarities appear explicitly or implicitly in the description or evaluation of nearly every area of traditional Chinese life, from politics, cosmology, aesthetics, and mythology to ancestor worship, divination, medicine, and sex. All classes of Chinese literature employ *yinyang* terminology and/or symbolism, from the exalted Confucian Classics to popular proverbs. Steven Sangren's *History and Magical Power in a Chinese Community* (1987) provides an excellent example of how a full understanding of the hierarchical and asymmetrical "contrastive logic" of *yin* and *yang* provides valuable insights into the complex relationship between order and disorder in Chinese social life.[21]

The second major theme of this study is ethics, an abiding cultural concern, as a glance at any Chinese political, social, or philosophical tract will clearly indicate. Like the concepts of *yin* and *yang,* ethical terms pervade every area of traditional Chinese culture, including music and the arts. The modern Chinese philosopher Chang Tung-sun tells us that the most numerous terms in the Chinese language come from the related realms of kinship and ethics, and the index to Fung Yu-lan's well-known abridged history of Chinese philosophy states apologetically, "So much of Chinese philosophy is ethical that a complete list of 'ethical' references would be almost impossible."[22]

Yet it is not only the pervasiveness of ethical concerns in China that is striking. It is also the essentially nonreligious source of basic moral values. In sharp contrast to the way many other peoples have viewed their cultural traditions, the Chinese viewed their moral order as a human product. Although Confucian philosophers perceived a fundamental "spiritual" unity between the mind of Heaven (*tianxin*) and the mind of Man (*renxin*), the ethical system prevailing in China throughout the entire imperial era did not emanate from any supernatural authority. The major institutional religions of late imperial times—Buddhism and Religious Daoism—made no major contribution to the preexisting core of Confucian values, although they did play an important role in reinforcing secular norms.[23]

The relationship between secular values and traditional Chinese religion is reflected in the following inscription taken from a stele in the temple of the Consort of Heaven (Tianhou) in Foshan, Guangdong:

> When administrative orders from the national and local capitals attain their objectives, and when there is the Way of Man to provide effective principles and discipline, it is not necessary that spirits and gods play an impressive and prominent role [in government]. But when [such orders and the Way of Man] fail to effect justice, spirits and gods will be brought to light. ... As the ancients put it, in the age

of perfect government, spirits became inefficacious. It is not that the spirits are inefficacious; ... it is that when rewards and punishments are just and clear, the *yang* [human elements] function effectively, and the *yin* [spiritual elements] retreat into the background ... so there is no need for the efficaciousness [of spirits and gods].[24]

Supernatural authority might always be invoked in China, but in the ideal Confucian world it was considered unnecessary.

At the core of the orthodox Chinese ethical system in the Qing period were the so-called Three Bonds (*sangang*), explicitly identified throughout most of the imperial era with the *yinyang* notion of complementary inequality. The Three Bonds were those between ruler and subject, father and son, husband and wife. The nonreciprocal obligations owed by inferiors to superiors within this framework set the authoritarian tone of much of life in traditional China and gave concrete expression to two of the most powerful organizational symbols or metaphors in the Chinese sociopolitical vocabulary—the bureaucracy and the family. Undergirding both these symbols and these relations was an expansive, cosmologically based structure of ritual (*li*).

Ritual provides the third major theme of this book, in a sense uniting the other two themes with itself. Like art, ritual can be considered a kind of "language" that celebrates man-made meaning. It indicates the way a culture group represents its situation to itself, how it links "the world as lived and the world as imagined."[25] Of course, there are many different kinds and definitions of ritual, but in its broadest sense the term includes all forms of artificially structured social behavior, from the etiquette of daily greetings to solemn state ceremonies and religious sacrifices.

Such a broad definition accords well with traditional Chinese usage. Although the term *li* never completely lost either its original religious and mystical connotations or its close association with music as a source of moral cultivation, by late imperial times *li* had come to embrace all forms of sacred and secular ritual, as well as the entire body of social institutions, rules, regulations, conventions, and norms that governed human relations in China. *Li* has been variously translated as standards of social usage, mores, politeness, propriety, and etiquette, but no single term does justice to the wide range of its meanings and manifestations.[26]

Testimony to the enduring value of *li* in traditional China may be found in the venerated classic texts known as the *Yili* (Etiquette and Ritual), *Zhouli* (Rites of Zhou), and *Liji* (Record of Ritual), which together exerted a profound influence on the Chinese elite from the Han period through the Qing. These three works alone provided hundreds of general principles and guidelines, as well as literally thousands of specific prescriptions, for proper conduct in Chinese society. Furthermore, they inspired a huge number of supplementary ceremonial handbooks, which left few questions of ritual or etiquette to chance. For hundreds of years the Chinese commonly referred to China as "the land of ritual and righteousness" (*liyi zhi bang*), equating the values of *li* and *yi* with civilization itself.[27]

One measure of esteem for ritual in the Qing dynasty may be found in the *TSJC,* which devotes nearly 350 of its 10,000 *juan* (volumes) to *li*. This figure does not include the 320 *juan* devoted to the subcategory on religion (which overlaps ritual in subject material to a significant degree), nor does it take into account the prominent place occupied by the teachings of ritual (*lijiao*) and ritual institutions (*lizhi*) in subcategories such as music, Confucian conduct, classical and noncanonical writings, human affairs, social intercourse, family relations, official careers, examinations, government service, and political divisions. Indeed, very few of the *TSJC*'s thirty-two subcategories are devoid of references to *li*.

The observations of long-time Western residents in China provide yet another index of the importance of ritual in the Qing period. Even during the nineteenth century, when Chinese society seemed to be disintegrating in many areas, informed Westerners repeatedly remarked on the scrupulous attention still given to all forms of ritual by the Chinese. S. W. Williams spoke for many in asserting that "no nation has paid so much attention to ... [ceremonies] in the ordering of its government as the Chinese. ... The importance attached to them has elevated etiquette and ritualism into a kind of crystalizing force which has molded [the] Chinese character in many ways." Arthur H. Smith maintained that "ceremony is the very life of the Chinese," echoing John Nevius: "Politeness [in China] is a science, and gracefulness of manners a study and a discipline."[28]

No major aspect of Chinese life was devoid of ritual significance, and ritual specialists were ubiquitous at all levels of society. Everyone from emperor to peasant recognized the importance of ritual in preserving status distinctions, promoting social cohesion, sanctifying ethical norms, and transmitting tradition. Closely linked to both cosmology and law, ritual in China performed the function Clifford Geertz assigns to "sacred symbols" in synthesizing moral values, aesthetics, and world view. Perhaps no other single focus allows us to see so clearly the preoccupations of the Chinese people in late imperial times.[29]

Although this book is organized topically for clarity and convenience, it emphasizes the interrelationship of the parts of traditional Chinese culture to the whole.[30] Therefore, in addition to weaving a web of significance around the distinctive unifying themes of cognition, ethics, and ritual, I have tried to build an integrated structure of meaning through the sequential presentation of the topical material. Chapter 2, for example, indicates some of the ways in which China's physical endowment and historical experience shaped both the outlook and institutions of the Chinese in imperial times. The next two chapters analyze Qing institutions in some detail, illustrating the various ways in which traditional political, social, and economic organizations simultaneously reflected and reinforced the Chinese sense of order and cultural unity. The discussions of language, thought, and formal philosophy help us to understand certain distinctive patterns of perception and expression in China, and the chapter on religion underscores the complex interaction between Chinese ideas, values, and institutions. The following chapters on art, literature, and social customs are designed to show how shared symbols, organizing principles, aesthetics, and ethical values were manifested in various important areas of Chinese artistic and social life. By the end of these discussions, the reader should have a clearer understanding not only of the internal "logic" of the Chinese cultural system but also an appreciation for why it lasted so long and held together so well.[31]

Of course, as I have already indicated, it would be foolish to deny the diversity of traditional Chinese culture. China's immense size, regional variety, and ethnic cleavages present a picture of staggering political, social, and economic complexity. As caretakers of the largest consolidated empire in Chinese history, the Qing emperors oversaw (and tried to manage) a myriad of local cultures—each with its own distinctive styles of food, housing, clothing, speech, worship, entertainment, and so forth. Complicating matters were deep ethnic differences between the Manchu rulers and their subjects, both Chinese and non-Chinese, as well as hierarchical distinctions drawn by local populations—especially in commercialized urban areas—designed to differentiate themselves from various kinds of "outsiders."[32]

Urban and rural dwellers in China naturally had divergent viewpoints and lifestyles, but these differences paled by comparison to those based on social class. The most fundamental distinction in Qing times was between commoners and the elite: They wore different clothes, ate different foods, lived in different dwellings, and occupied different positions in the eyes of both society at large and the state. They even received markedly different treatment under the law. Yet Chinese society was not simply a two-tiered one. Instead of a single "little tradition" dominated by a "great" one (in Robert Redfield's famous formulation), there were many traditions, both above and below the principal social divide.[33]

David Johnson, coeditor of *Popular Culture in Late Imperial China* (1985) identifies at least nine distinct culture groups on the Chinese social spectrum. In an effort to do justice to the complexity of traditional Chinese society, and to illustrate the ways in which consciousness is influenced by "relations of dominance and subordination," Johnson proposes a model of late imperial China based on three crucial variables: education, legal privilege, and economic position. In his conceptual framework, the Chinese social spectrum ranged from the classically educated, legally privileged, and economically self-sufficient elite (the most dominant group) to illiterate and dependent commoners (the least influential). Intermediate groups reflect different combinations of these three variables—for instance, a person could be self-sufficient and literate but neither legally privileged nor classically educated.[34]

Of course, an elite woman could enjoy all three of these advantages and still be subordinated, if not actually oppressed. What about gender as a social variable in traditional China? Certainly women in the Qing period had a different world view than men—not least with respect to their self-image. A woman's subordinate status was, after all, reflected in (and reinforced by) not only legal statutes and informal social customs but also elite and popular literature, proverbs, handbooks on household ritual, medical texts, and even commentaries to the Kangxi emperor's Sacred Edict.[35] Yet we know that the circumstances for women in China were not necessarily the same empire-wide, even for those who had the same class status. Moreover, like disadvantaged men, women at all levels of Chinese society developed various strategies of empowerment, some of which simultaneously improved their lot and threatened the social status quo. An enormous amount of new research on Chinese women has vastly enhanced (and complicated) our understanding of late imperial China.[36]

Challenges to the social order took a number of different forms in the Qing dynasty. Some, such as marriage resistance, were localized and quietly subversive.[37] But class and ethnic tensions often led to large-scale violence. In fact, the Qing government waged a perpetual battle against bandits, rebels, feuding ethnic groups, warring clans, and other divisive elements in society, particularly during times of economic distress. Official propaganda, such as the imperially mandated lectures that formed part of the dynasty's widespread "community compact" system (*xiangyue*), repeatedly admonished people of all social classes to refrain from fighting and to promote harmony.[38]

Yet for all this sort of diversity and deviance in Qing China, the striking feature of the traditional culture as a whole was its unity across space and time. James Watson notes, for example, that "one need only read Eugen Weber's account of nineteenth century France to appreciate just how integrated Chinese society was during the late imperial era." Even peasant villagers "identified themselves with an overarching 'Chinese culture,' an abstraction they had no difficulty understanding."[39] Myron Cohen tells us: "In late traditional times there was in China a common culture in the sense of shared behavior, institutions, and beliefs," as well as "a unified culture ... [that] provided standards according to which people identified themselves as Chinese." Taking this Han or ethnic Chinese culture as a whole, he writes, "There can be no doubt that the historical trend in premodern times was toward increasing uniformity."[40] The task of this book, at least in part, has been to provide a detailed demonstration of these points.

The fate of traditional Chinese culture in modern times remains to be more fully explored. Unprecedented internal pressures and the devastating impact of Western imperialism during the latter half of the nineteenth century led in the twentieth to a fundamental reevaluation of China's inherited culture. Cultural iconoclasts assailed the Confucian political and social tradition and gravitated toward Western forms of art, literature, music, and recreation. Yet throughout the first half of the twentieth century, traditional Chinese patterns of perception, thought, belief, and behavior continued to have remarkable staying power, and even today we can see the obvious presence of tradition on both sides of the Taiwan straits.

❧ 2 ❧

The Qing Inheritance

*T*he most powerful influence on the character of the Qing dynasty was the dual inheritance of a vast and variegated land area and a long, unbroken cultural tradition. From the standpoint of geography, the diversity of China posed a formidable obstacle to national unification: Customs varied widely, and feelings of local affinity (*xiangtu qingyi*) ran deep. Nevertheless, since unification of the empire in 221 B.C., the Chinese elite had made a conscious and concerted effort to standardize customs (*tong fengsu*) and to integrate the country by means of a centralized bureaucracy and well-organized systems of propaganda, penal law, ritual, and formal education. Over time, the progressive sophistication of Chinese techniques of political, social, and intellectual control produced a powerful sense of China's cultural unity (*tongyi*), but regional differences in natural resources, climate, productivity, communications, population, ethnic groups, dialects, and life-styles continued to challenge this ordered outlook.[1]

"Outsiders" also posed a threat to the Chinese sense of order. Indeed, the political histories of China and its neighbors—especially those on the northern border—have always been dynamically and inextricably intertwined.[2] From earliest times, the boundaries of China waxed and waned in response to periodic bursts of either Chinese expansion or "barbarian" invasion. But who were the barbarians? At one level, the answer to this question is relatively easy, at least for imperial times: All those who did not consider themselves to be "the people of Han" (or an equivalent term) were by definition outside the pale of Chinese civilization and therefore "barbaric."

At another level, the answer is more complicated. One school of Confucian thought theorized that barbarians could become "sinicized" by adopting the language, moral values, rituals, and other features of Han Chinese culture,[3] and this view became the conventional one (see Chapter 6). Indeed, several dynasties of conquest, including the Qing, used the idea of "sinicization" repeatedly to justify their rule. But others saw the matter differently. Some believed, for example, that geography was destiny:

> Broad valleys and great streams are variously formed, and the people living there have different customs [*su*]. With respect to hard and soft, light and heavy, slow and quick, they are differently tempered; [they enjoy] different blends of the five flavors; their implements and weapons are differently fashioned; different clothing is suitable for them. ... The Chinese and the non-Chinese in the four quarters and the center all have their own characters which cannot be made to change.[4]

From this standpoint, the "cosmic breath" (*qi*) of a certain area determined whether its inhabitants lived like animals, "in nests and caves," or embraced the civilizing attributes of "ritual and right behavior." Not surprisingly, most Han Chinese believed that the harmonious "middle ground" they occupied was especially conducive to the production of sages and other worthies.

During the Qing dynasty, these issues became matters of acute political concern to China's Manchu rulers. Yet, individual emperors did not always agree on the relationship between their "racial" heritage, on the one hand, and their "cultural" rule of China, on the other.[5] All of the Manchu rulers, however, had a heightened sensitivity to any criticism of "barbarians" on the part of Han Chinese that might be construed as an attack on the legitimacy of Qing rule.[6]

Throughout their long reign, the Manchus took an aggressive stance toward most of China's "barbarous" frontier areas, particularly in the north. In 1683, Qing forces brought Taiwan under direct Chinese control after an extended period of Dutch and then rebel occupation, and in 1689 the Treaty of Nerchinsk stabilized and regularized China's border relations with Russia. During the eighteenth century, a succession of military expeditions, culminating with the famous "Ten Great Campaigns" of the Qianlong emperor from the 1750s to the 1780s, expanded direct Chinese rule into both Inner and Outer Mongolia, Central Asia (Chinese Turkestan; renamed Xinjiang, "New Territories," in 1768), and Tibet (Xizang). Two of these expeditions also brought Burma and Annam (Vietnam) under Chinese suzerainty.[7]

After 1800, the emphasis in China's foreign relations began to shift to the coast and the new maritime challenge posed by the West. As Jane Kate Leonard has pointed out, the Qing government's response to this challenge centered on traditional strategies for managing piracy and trade in what the Chinese referred to as the "Southern Ocean" (Nanyang).[8] Meanwhile, Qing Inner Asia began to come under the influence of Han Chinese culture. This process did not occur by design. Rather, as Joseph Fletcher puts the matter:

> The dynasty's need to make full use of Han Chinese talent, especially in the empire's non-Han territories, and to encourage Han Chinese settlers to people the Inner Asian frontiers, became evident to the Ch'ing [Qing] government only dimly and belatedly in the nineteenth century, after it was too late in Manchuria and Sinkiang [Xinjiang] to preserve the full territorial extent of the Ch'ing [Qing] realm. The Han Chinese expansion occurred in spite of the Ch'ing [Qing] government's efforts throughout the eighteenth century to prevent this expansion.[9]

THE LEGACY OF THE LAND

It is clear that no single factor, geographical or otherwise, can explain the "special character" (*tezhi*) of Chinese civilization. But Chinese and Western scholars alike long have recognized the close relationship existing between the land and the people in China. The following quotation is representative:

More people have lived in China than anywhere else. Upwards of 10 billion human beings have moved across her good earth; nowhere else have so many people lived so intimately with nature. A thousand generations have left their indelible impression on soil and topography, so that scarcely a square foot of earth remains unmodified by man. ... Few landscapes are more human.[10]

Fei Xiaotong, the well-known Chinese sociologist, places particular emphasis on China's rural foundations:

Only those who make a living from the soil can understand the value of the soil. ... [To] country people the soil is the root of their lives. In rural areas, the god represented in most shrines is Tudi, the god of the earth. Tudi is the god closest to human nature; Tudi and his wife are an old white-haired couple who take care of all the business of the countryside and who have come to symbolize the earth itself.[11]

Further, Fei writes:

Agriculture differs from both pastoralism and industry. Farmers are necessarily connected to the land, whereas herdsmen drift about, following the water and the grass, and are forever unsettled. Industrial workers may choose where they live, and they may move without difficulty; but farmers cannot move their land or the crops they grow. Always waiting for their crops to mature, those old farmers seem to have planted half their own bodies into the soil.[12]

China may be the only civilization on earth where historically the term "peasant" has not been one of contempt.[13] Since earliest times, the land has remained a paramount Chinese value, exalted in the classical literature, celebrated in popular mythology, and enshrined in the naturalism of *yinyang* cosmology.[14] Moreover, the Chinese have a "sense of place" that is extremely difficult for most modern Westerners to grasp. John Fairbank reminds us that the political-cultural center of Western civilization has moved steadily westward, "from Athens to Rome, then to Madrid, Paris, London and New York." But the corresponding movement in China has been a matter of only a few hundred miles—from Xian, below the loop of the Yellow River, to the lower Yangzi region (Hangzhou and Nanjing), and finally to Beijing. Thus, all the historic sites of Chinese history are clustered together. For Westerners, it would be as if "Moses had received the tablets on Mt. Washington, the Parthenon stood on Bunker Hill, Hannibal had crossed the Alleghenies, Caesar had conquered Ohio, Charlemagne's crowning in the year 800 was in Chicago, and the Vatican overlooked Central Park."[15]

Chinese travel accounts of the Qing period document in detail the enduring appeal of the landscape and its close connection with China's long and glorious past.[16] Listen to Kong Shangren, a Qing dynasty descendant of Confucius, as he describes a characteristically personal moment during his travels in Shandong province:

Suddenly, I stood face-to-face with Yellowstone Mountain—he who had angrily
blocked me before. But now that I have entered his domain, how could we not help
looking at each other with laughing faces? Stonegate [another mountain] flourishes
with an abundance of birds and animals while Yellowstone is of indigo rock streaked
with yellow patterns without a trace of growth. Yellowstone by no means imitates
Stonegate. In many ways, Yellowstone looks as if it has been painted by the brushstrokes of Huang Gongwang [1269–1354]. The more one looks, the more one falls in
love with it and it held me transfixed for a long while. A monk said, "further on is the
Grotto of Banners. When the Huang Chao Rebellion broke out in Lu [in 878], the
rebels occupied this very ridge." But I had no time to investigate it.[17]

Throughout the imperial era, geography remained a highly respected sphere of
scholarly activity in China. As a result, Chinese geographical writings were probably
unparalleled in premodern times for their systematic comprehensiveness. Of the four
major types of "monographs" in the dynastic histories under the general category of
governmental institutions (civil and military administration, geography, economy,
and law), geography usually ranks first in percentage of space. In the *TSJC,* geography is one of six main divisions, and its four subsections on the earth, political divisions, topography, and foreign countries together account for 2,144 out of the encyclopedia's 10,000 *juan*—second only to the division on human relations with 2,604.

This special concern with geography stemmed not only from its intrinsic attrac-
tions and the obvious relationship between geography and the practical concerns of
political control, military defense, and dynastic legitimacy but also from the fact that
many Chinese scholars found in the study of geography the key to a fuller understanding of both history and the classics.[18] Furthermore, geography had an aesthetic
dimension: Until the late nineteenth century Chinese cartographers routinely considered poetry, calligraphy, and painting to be integral features of their timeless
craft.[19]

Geographical writing flourished in China during the Qing period. Three of the
most distinguished geographers of the day were Gu Zuyu (1631–1692), Liu Xianting
(1648–1695), and Li Zhaoluo (1769–1841). Gu's famous *Dushi fangyi jiyao* (Essentials
of Historical Geography) is considered a masterpiece of careful and comprehensive
scholarship. Not only did he utilize more than a hundred Chinese geographical
works and all of the traditional dynastic histories (see Chapter 6), but he also traveled
extensively, gathering valuable information firsthand. Liu Xianting did the same. We
are told that he

> studied the topography of mountains and rivers, visited famous retired men, made
> heroes his friends, observed local customs, [and] assembled anecdotes widely. ... He
> discussed the changes in the ways of the universe and of the *yin* and *yang,* the grand
> strategies of the hegemons and kings, military arts, literature, institutions and
> regulations, and important points in various localities.[20]

Li Zhaoluo, who dutifully studied the geographical writings of Gu Zuyu, is best known for his dictionary of Chinese place-names, arranged by rhymes and subdivided by dynastic periods. It was first printed in 1837. Later editions of this work included a supplement of Qing dynasty place-names, also arranged according to rhymes and broken down into standard administrative subdivisions. Like Gu and Liu, Li became deeply involved in the compilation of local gazetteers. These historical and geographical compilations, often patronized by the government and always highly regarded, might center on a single administrative area or embrace the entire empire. The most noteworthy single achievement of this sort in the Qing period was the huge, imperially commissioned *Da Qing yitong zhi* (Comprehensive Gazetteer of the Great Qing Dynasty), patterned after a similar, but rather unsatisfactory, Ming publication.[21]

Compiled under the general direction of Xu Qianxue (1631–1694), with the able assistance of Gu, Liu, and many other competent scholars, the *Comprehensive Gazetteer* was first printed in the mid-eighteenth century. A later edition (1790) included additional information concerning new territories incorporated into the Qing empire as a result of the Qianlong emperor's Ten Great Campaigns. Organized by provinces (*sheng*), the gazetteer discusses each in terms of conventional categories such as boundaries, topography, official personnel, population, taxation, and famous statesmen. Under lower-level administrative divisions, it focuses on cities, educational institutions, topography, historical sites, passes, bridges, defenses, tombs, temples, noteworthy residents, famous travelers, local products, and so forth. At the end, the gazetteer devotes a large amount of space to China's colonial dependencies and to the countries and culture groups within the expansive sphere of China's tributary system of foreign relations (see Chapter 6). Such comprehensive gazetteers and their local counterparts were, and continue to be, invaluable sources of information on nearly every facet of traditional Chinese life.[22]

During much of the Qing period, the Chinese empire encompassed a vast area, estimated at 4,278,352 square miles. This included the eighteen regular provinces of China Proper (totaling 1,532,800 square miles), the Qing homeland of Manchuria (363,700 square miles), and the colonized "dependencies" of Mongolia (1,367,953 square miles), Chinese Turkestan (550,579 square miles), and Tibet (463,320 square miles). At its height, the Qing empire stretched from the northern tip of Sakhalin Island to Hainan Island in the south and from the Pacific Ocean to the Aral Sea. About half of this gigantic empire was quite mountainous, however, and only about 10 percent of it was regularly under cultivation. About 90 percent of the Chinese people lived on roughly 12 percent of the land.[23]

Throughout most of the imperial era, China's population hovered between 50 and 100 million. At the beginning of the Qing period, it probably stood at a little over 100 million. But during the extraordinary time of domestic peace and prosperity from the late Kangxi reign to the end of the Qianlong emperor's reign, the Chinese population skyrocketed until it reached an estimated 430 million people by 1850. This exponential increase in people created an increasingly unfavorable population-to-land ratio, monumental economic and administrative problems, and severe social strains. The implications of this situation for China's modern development were profound and sustained.[24]

Throughout its long history, China has been surrounded by formidable geographic barriers, which have impeded direct contact with other advanced civilizations. This geographic isolation unquestionably contributed to the unity and continuity of Chinese civilization and fostered a profound sense of cultural distinctiveness and superiority. China's eastern border was the awesome Pacific Ocean; to the south lay steaming and nearly impenetrable tropical jungles; to the southwest loomed the lofty plateau of Tibet and the towering Himalayas; and to the west and north were vast expanses of desert or grassland suited only for a harsh, essentially nomadic style of life. Significantly, China's closest neighbors were either sedentary peoples who openly sought to emulate Chinese culture—notably the Koreans, Annamese (Vietnamese), and Japanese—or pastoral peoples who periodically offered a military challenge to China but never presented a cultural threat. Until the traumatic nineteenth century, foreign visitors to China, including Europeans, regularly submitted to the humbling ritual of the Chinese tributary system (see Chapters 3 and 6), and often they adopted Chinese clothes and customs. Small wonder the Chinese perennially thought of themselves as the Middle Kingdom, the Central Cultural Florescence.

At the same time, however, China's massive size, huge population, and regional diversity posed formidable problems of administrative and cultural integration for the Qing government, creating a constant tension between centrifugal and centripetal forces. Two great geographical contrasts existed in traditional China. One was between the highly developed agricultural area of China Proper south of the Great Wall and the less productive but strategically important outlying regions of the empire known collectively as Inner Asia. The other was between North and South in China Proper (see Figure 2.1).

The Inner Asian regions on China's periphery had negligible economic value, but they provided a crucial buffer zone between China and border "barbarians" on horseback. The great expansive empires of Han and Tang (see next section) spent huge sums of money on military operations designed to pacify external invaders and stabilize China's frontiers. Similarly, security considerations rather than economic motives dictated the Qing conquests of Inner Asia in the seventeenth and eighteenth centuries.

For most of the Qing period, China's rulers did not even attempt to integrate their Inner Asian dependencies with China Proper. In fact, they made a conscious effort to maintain Manchuria as an exclusively Manchu tribal preserve and allowed considerable cultural and administrative leeway to the deliberately isolated colonized areas of Mongolia, Central Asia (Chinese Turkestan), and Tibet. Although each of these three regions was garrisoned by Qing troops, overseen by a military governor, and supervised by the Court of Colonial Affairs in Beijing, the Qing government granted local

Figure 2.1   The Great Wall. This massive structure, some three thousand miles in total length, symbolized the cultural divide between the sedentary agrarian peoples of China Proper and their nomadic neighbors on the northern steppe. Photo courtesy of the Peabody & Essex Museum, Salem, Mass.

tribal elites a large measure of political authority and allowed much of the indigenous governmental apparatus in these areas to remain intact. In Mongolia and Tibet, for example, Beijing supported the Lamaist religious hierarchy common to both regions, granted imperial titles to the hereditary ruling elites, and encouraged the preservation of their original tribal organizations and customs. Chinese Turkestan was by far the most ethnically diverse territory in Inner Asia; although governed like a huge garrison under the military governor in Yili, it too had native rulers and officials who enjoyed considerable cultural and administrative autonomy.[25]

Table 2.1   North and South Contrasts

North China	South China
Limited, uncertain rainfall	Abundant rainfall
Frequent floods and droughts	Adequate water year-round
Unleached, calcareous soils	Leached, noncalcareous soils
4- to 6-month growing season	9- to 12-month growing season
1–2 crops per year; relatively low yields; frequent famines	2–3 crops per year; high yields; prosperity
Major crops: gaoliang, millet, wheat	Major crops: rice and beans
Work animals: donkeys and mules	Work animal: water buffalo
Mud-walled houses with heated brick beds (*kang*)	Woven bamboo-walled and thatched-roof houses
Wide city streets	Narrow city streets
Smooth coastline with poor harbors; little fishing	Rough coastline with many harbors; much fishing
Foreign intercourse by land	Foreign intercourse by sea
Long-time residence; the nuclear area of Chinese culture	Populated mainly by southward migrations since Tang times
Comparatively uniform ethnic makeup	Numerous ethnic groups
Mandarin dialect (*guoyu*)	Many different dialects

SOURCE: Adapted from Cressey (1955).

Yet the Qing government's deliberate policy of segregating Inner Asia from China Proper was only partially successful. By the beginning of the nineteenth century, the expansion of Han Chinese into Inner Asia had begun in earnest, precipitated in part by severe population pressures. Sometimes illegally and sometimes abetted by the Qing authorities, Chinese farmers penetrated the Manchurian frontier and the grasslands of Inner Mongolia and began eking a living out of the stubborn soil of Qinghai (northeastern Tibet) and parts of Chinese Turkestan. Ironically, as Joanna Waley-Cohen has shown, the practice of exiling disgraced officials to the so-called New Territories (Xinjiang) of Chinese Turkestan helped to develop this strategic western frontier area and integrate it more fully into the rest of the empire. In 1884, Xinjiang became a Chinese province, and by the first decade of the twentieth century the regular Chinese system of field administration had been extended to the "three Eastern Provinces" of Manchuria. Nonetheless, the political and cultural integration of these areas was never complete, and in the waning years of the Qing dynasty, each one became a serious trouble spot.[26]

The other major geographic contrast was between North and South in China Proper, below the Great Wall. This contrast has been obvious to anyone who has ever traveled in China, past or present. The boundary between North and South is, of course, transitional; many geographical characteristics overlap or merge gradually from one area to the other. Still, striking and significant differences separate the regions north and south of the thirty-third parallel—a dividing line roughly marked by the Huai River in the east and the Qinling Mountains in the west.[27] These differences are represented in Table 2.1.

Such differences help account, in turn, for other contrasts between North and South. The greater strength of the lineage or "clan" system in South China, for example, may be explained at least in part by the requirements of a productive, labor-intensive southern rice economy based on extensive, cooperative waterworks. Similarly, the greater political instability of the South can be attributed not only to the simple fact of distance from the political power center of Beijing but also to the specific ethnic and other tensions arising out of the unique South China economic and social milieu (see Chapter 4).

In addition to the basic North-South division in China Proper, we can also identify several other regional divisions, based either on administrative (and often artificial) boundaries or on natural geographic factors such as soil and climate, mountain ranges, river and urban systems, linguistic and ethnic groups, and strategic defense areas. Traditionally, the Chinese have divided the realm below the Great Wall either into provinces (see Figure 2.2) and their administrative subunits or into a half dozen or so major geographic sectors that transcend provincial boundaries. One common division has been into the Northwest, Northern China, Southern China, the Southeast, and the Southwest. By and large, these designations correspond to major economic areas defined primarily by prominent river drainage systems.[28]

In traditional usage, the Northwest referred to the upper basin of the Yellow River, a relatively thinly populated area extending from the eastern border of Russian Turkestan to the Taihang Mountains—in other words, present-day Xinjiang, Gansu, Qinghai, Shaanxi (north of the Qinling Mountains), and Shanxi. Outside the riverine plains near the base of the loop of the Yellow River, agricultural activity in the Northwest has suffered from a chronic lack of adequate rainfall; but in those areas where rainfall has been sufficient, the rich, self-fertilizing soil known as loess produces abundant crops. Elsewhere in the Northwest livestock raising has prevailed, often undertaken by non-Chinese minority groups.

Northern China, also known as the Central Plain, included the lower basin of the Yellow River and the drainage areas of the Wei, Huai, and other rivers. It embraced the heavily populated provinces of Zhili (modern-day Hebei), Henan, Shandong, northern Anhui, and northern Jiangsu. Like the Northwest, Northern China was blessed with loess soil but cursed with light and unpredictable rainfall. Furthermore, Northern China had to contend with the peculiarities of the Yellow River floodplain. In most rivers of the world, a silt content of 5 percent is considered high, but the Yellow River has been known to carry as much as 46 percent, and one of its upriver tributaries, an astonishing 63 percent. In the absence of any tributaries for the last five hundred miles of its course, the Yellow River has continually built up its channel with sediment, so that now, as in Qing times, the bed of the heavily dyked river actually lies above the surrounding countryside in some places. Historically, and especially in times of dynastic decline when maintenance efforts slackened, the Yellow River repeatedly broke its dykes, flooding hundreds of square miles and affecting the livelihood of millions. In 1852, the eastward course of the river shifted from the south of the Shandong promontory to the north, a distance of several hundred miles!

20

Figure 2.2   Map of China. Adapted from Joseph Esherick and Mary Rankin, Chinese Local Elites and Patterns of Dominance. *Copyright © 1990, The Regents of University of California. Reprinted with permission.*

"China's Sorrow" demanded continual attention from the Qing government, but did not always receive it.[29]

Southern China, including the basins of the four major tributaries of the mighty Yangzi River (the Han, Gan, Xiang, and Yuan rivers), consisted of the provinces of Hubei, Hunan, Jiangxi, Shanxi (south of the Qinling Mountains), southern Anhui, southern Jiangsu, and northern Zhejiang. Although much of this region is hilly, it has been favored by adequate rainfall and an abundance of lakes, rivers, streams, and other waterways. Agriculture and inland fishing have always been extremely productive in these areas. The Yangzi plain, at the base of a 750,000-square-mile drainage area, is laced with canals and other navigable waterways.[30] Floods in this area are relatively infrequent, but they are often devastating when they occur. The famous flood of 1931, for example, was the most disastrous in world history, inundating some 34,000 square miles of land and affecting more than 25 million peasants.

The Southeast, like Southern China, is famous for its economic productivity. Traditionally the Southeast included the areas of southern Zhejiang, Fujian, Guangdong, Guangxi, Taiwan (made a province in 1885), and the island of Hainan. These ethnically and linguistically diverse regions—hilly, heavily terraced, and well irrigated—are fed by numerous rivers, among which the Xi (West) River is the most prominent. The people of the Southeast are renowned as the seafarers and adventurers of China. In Qing times, and more recently, thousands of sailors from coastal areas braved the open sea in small junks as well as oceangoing merchant vessels, while their less intrepid but no less enterprising fellow provincials worked the near-shore waters for oysters, shrimp, and prawns. The recent scholarship of John Wills, Chinkeong Ng, Dian Murray, and others has underscored the economic, social, and political importance of maritime China.[31]

The Southwest embraced three rather remote provinces: Yunnan, Guizhou, and Sichuan. In both Yunnan and Guizhou, large tracts of rugged mountains and high plateaus, deep gorges, and swift rivers have hindered transportation and agriculture. Sichuan, by contrast, supported a wide variety of profitable crops and other products despite its comparatively rough terrain; it was favored by a moist, temperate climate and endowed with a long-standing, ingenious, and highly effective irrigation system serving the fertile Chengdu plain. The "four streams" that give Sichuan its name (the Min, Lu, Suining, and Jialing rivers) are all south-flowing tributaries of the Yangzi.

A variety of models now exist for analyzing China's regional diversity in late imperial times.[32] One of the most influential of these has been G. William Skinner's notion of nine "macroregions." Like the traditional Chinese regional divisions outlined above, these macroregions transcended provincial boundaries. Each had a "core" area, consisting of "heightened economic activity in major cities, high population density, and comparatively sophisticated transportation networks for conveyance of food and merchandise," and a "periphery" of less populated and less developed areas. The peripheral zones isolated the core of any given macroregion from the cores of other macroregions and provided a "loosely policed area where illegal sects or bandit elements could develop in comparative freedom." Skinner thus provides a geographical framework for analyzing a wide range of political, social, and economic phenomena—from patterns of trade and transportation to the structure of imperial control and the spread of heterodox social movements.[33]

Skinner's scheme is somewhat controversial and assuredly requires further testing and refinement.[34] Nonetheless, it has proven to be an extremely productive way of looking at regional variety in China. Susan Nanquin and Evelyn Rawski, for instance, have employed his regional systems approach in showing how imperial policies and specific local conditions "produced very different social patterns" in eighteenth-century China.[35] Similarly, Keith Schoppa, Joseph Esherick, and Mary Rankin have used Skinner's approach to illustrate how regional variations in the social backgrounds of Chinese local elites affected their power, wealth, and status.[36] James Cole draws upon Skinner to explain the competition for social resources in the area of Shaoxing, and Stevan Harrell adopts a core-periphery approach in analyzing economic change in the vicinity of Taibei.[37] Esherick, Donald Sutton, and I have all benefited from Skinner's insights in our work on Qing dynasty popular beliefs, including shamanism and divination.[38]

According to Skinner's modified framework, the Northeast macroregion lies in an area that corresponds more or less with southern Manchuria. The North China macroregion embraces the provinces of Zhili (Hebei) and Shandong, while the Northwest covers the area south of the great loop in the Yellow River and extends westward. The Lower Yangzi macroregion includes southern Jiangsu, eastern Anhui, and northern Zhejiang. The Middle Yangzi occupies much of Jiangxi and virtually all of Hunan, Hubei, and Henan. The Southeast Coast extends from southern Zhejiang to northern Guangdong, while the Lingnan macroregion encompasses most of the rest of Guangdong and Guangxi. As its name suggests, the Yun-Gui macroregion consists of the provinces of Yunnan and Guizhou, and the Upper Yangzi macroregion focuses on Sichuan.[39]

Within these nine macroregions, there were a total of about fifty ethnic minorities—most of them quite distinct from the Han Chinese, or black-haired people (*limin*), who constituted about 94 percent of the total population of the realm. Most of these ethnic groups were concentrated in frontier provinces and in peripheral (as opposed to core) areas. The most statistically (and therefore politically) significant among them were the Zhuang (in Guangxi and Yunnan), the Hui or Muslims (Gansu and Shaanxi), the Uighurs (Xinjiang), the Yi (Sichuan and Yunnan), and the Miao (also known as Hmong; Guizhou, Yunnan, and Hunan). Some of these groups, such as the Uighurs and Hui, were supervised by officials appointed by the Court of Colonial Affairs, while others—especially the smaller and in general more "primitive" indigenous minorities of the Southwest—fell under the administrative authority of their own hereditary local chieftains (*tusi*).[40]

At times these tribal leaders oversaw standard units of jurisdiction and received regular official titles, preceded by the character *tu* ("native" or "local"). However, as with Qing policy toward ethnic minorities in the dependencies of Inner Asia, the government's concern was more with control and stability than with cultural integration. Assimilation was not normally a conscious administrative goal. As a result, the ethnic minorities under local chieftains in China Proper, like their Inner Asian counterparts, enjoyed a considerable degree of autonomy in their language, religious beliefs, customs, and government. Occasionally, however, minority peoples did suffer discrimination by both local Han Chinese and the state, and when they did, social conflict or outright rebellion sometimes ensued. Under these circumstances, Chinese officials might more readily advocate "sinicization of the barbarians" through education and other means in order to encourage social stability.[41]

The cultural assimilation of Han Chinese was always assumed but often difficult to achieve in practice. Regional differences in dialect, resources, population, and settlement patterns naturally contributed to different regional identifications and lifestyles. Although these differences were seldom as striking as those between Han Chinese and aborigines, Tibetans, Mongols, or Turkic peoples, in many respects the Cantonese, Hakkas (Kejia), and Hokkienese of South China were as distinct from one another as, say, Spaniards are from the French or Italians.[42]

In geographic terms, then, China was far less united than the base area of traditional Western civilization or even the subcontinent of India. Moreover, it lacked the convenient coastal communications of the Mediterranean. Divided into a complex patchwork of mountain and river systems, the vast Chinese empire presented formidable obstacles to itinerant merchants and other travelers, who had to rely on "route books" to guide them along the dynasty's roads and waterways. Works of this sort, which proliferated during the seventeenth and eighteenth centuries (and presumably facilitated the growth of interregional trade), delineated the structure of the dynasty's official relay system for transmitting official documents as well as other well-worn commercial paths.[43]

Although the Qing government helped maintain some major roads connected with its courier system, land transportation was at best costly and uncomfortable—especially in the outlying regions of the empire. Even in the North China plain the roads were deeply rutted and usually either dusty, muddy, or flooded. Springless two-wheeled carts, wheelbarrows, and sedan chairs provided the principal means of transport, cheap by day but expensive by the mile. The cost of transporting freight by land in many areas of China might be anywhere from twenty to forty times the usual standard for easily navigable rivers.[44]

The best communications in China could be found in the lower Yangzi River valley. More navigable waterways—including literally tens of thousands of miles of canals—existed in this region than in any comparable area of the world. The canals, varying in width from 10 to 100 feet, often widened into small lakes. Narrow roads followed alongside the principal waterways, serving as footpaths and towing paths for boats. Walled cities stood at the confluence of two or more canals, their size dictated by the economic and strategic importance of the intersecting waterways.[45] The Grand Canal provided the primary inland water communication between the vital lower Yangzi region and the north. Like the Yellow River into which it eventually flowed, the Grand Canal demanded, but did not always receive, regular upkeep from the Qing government.[46]

Prior to the late nineteenth century, when Shanghai emerged as a vibrant center of foreign trade, the primary commercial hub of China was Hankou, located on the Yangzi River at the nodal point of all but a few of the empire's long-distance transport routes. By 1800, this thriving city of about a million inhabitants radiated road and riverine "spokes" to all major regions of China as well as to eastern Central Asia.[47] Yet even in areas like Hankou, where well-developed communication routes encouraged extensive travel, regional identifications remained strong. One obvious reason was the centrifugal pull of Chinese localism (*xiangtu secai*). In the words of G. William Skinner,

> Native place was an essential component of a person's identity in traditional Chinese society. Strangers thrown into contact would in their initial conversational exchange invariably ascertain one another's native place as well as surname. A person's native county [i.e., district] commonly appeared on doorplates (and invariably appeared on tombstones) and was used in correspondence and belles lettres as a surrogate given name for prominent figures. The normative pattern was clear: a young man who left to seek his fortune elsewhere was expected to return home for marriage, to spend there an extended period of mourning on the death of either parent, and eventually to retire in the locality where his ancestors were buried. Even when these expectations were not realized, the son born to a sojourner inherited his father's native place along with his surname.[48]

Regional differences and local identifications naturally encouraged regional stereotypes. These stereotypes, which often found their way into the dynastic histories and local gazetteers as well as private writings, were derived from a wide variety of sources. Some reflected concrete geographical circumstances. The richly productive agricultural areas and well-developed commercial activities of South China, for example, encouraged the regional stereotype of southerners as greedy, shrewd, and sometimes unscrupulous. Northerners, by contrast, were viewed as upright and honest. Some regional stereotypes were based on historical and literary associations. Thus, the people of Hunan province were assumed to possess the sentimentality and emotionalism of their poetic countryman Qu Yuan (third century B.C.); the people of Sichuan, the love of music and adventure of their countryman Sima Xiangru (179–117 B.C.); and the people of Shandong, the frugality, simplicity, honesty, and sincerity of Confucius himself.[49]

Still other stereotypes were based on cosmological principles. According to the pervasive Chinese theory of the five elements, or activities (see Chapter 6), the element metal (*jin*) was associated with the direction west. People in West China were therefore believed to enjoy using weapons and to favor "cutting" (i.e., spicy) food. Since the South was associated with fire (*huo*), southern Chinese were naturally supposed to be fiery in temperament. Northerners, by contrast, were like water (*shui*)—cold, stern, slow, and straight. The east belonged to the element wood (*mu*), giving

Table 2.2 *Regional Stereotypes*

Province	Physical Trait(s)	Nonphysical Traits
Zhili (Hebei)	Tall, strong	Frank, honest, good-mannered, simple
Shandong	Tall, heavyset	Frank, honest, straight, simple, upright
Shanxi	Tall	Business-minded, simple, honest, resolute
Shaanxi	Strong, medium to tall	Honest, sincere, resolute, enduring
Gansu	Tall to medium	Enduring, honest, simple
Henan	Tall, strong	Honest, straight, mannered, violent temper
Jiangsu	Medium to small, delicate	Cunning, crafty, versatile, refined, luxury-loving, good in business
Anhui	Medium	Good in business, simple, frugal, clever
Zhejiang	Medium to small	Profit-hungry, scheming, not good as friends
Hubei	Medium to small	Scheming, unreliable
Hunan	Medium to small	Emotional, heroic, military, upright
Sichuan	Medium to small	Violent temper, too much talk
Fujian	Small to medium	Petty-minded, cunning, risk-taking, clannish
Guangdong	Small	Enduring, hard, culturally backward
Guizhou	Medium	Frugal, straight, poor, overdeveloped
Yunnan	Medium to small	Barbaric, enduring, frugal

SOURCE: Adapted from Eberhard (1965).

easterners the characteristics of growing, flourishing, and constantly changing. The center corresponded to the element earth (*tu*), considered by the Chinese to be stable, well balanced, and harmonious. Thus the people of Central China (variously defined) were solid and down to earth, without eccentricities.[50]

Multiple regional stereotypes were common, and occasionally they conflicted. But the striking feature of such stereotypes was their tenacity and widespread acceptance over time. Wolfram Eberhard's study of contemporary Chinese provincial stereotypes on Taiwan, for instance, indicates a remarkable affinity with Qing dynasty views.[51] According to this study, certain major traits can be identified for each of the eighteen provinces of China Proper. These traits are listed in Table 2.2.

By way of comparison, we might consider the Kangxi emperor's observations concerning the personality traits of his subjects:

> Sometimes I have stated that the people of a certain province have certain bad characteristics: thus the men of Fujian are turbulent and love acts of daring ... while the people of Shaanxi are tough and cruel. ... Shandong men are stubborn in a bad way; they always have to be first, they nurse their hatreds, they seem to value life lightly, and a lot of them become robbers. ... The people of Shaanxi are so stingy that they won't even care for the aged in their own families; ... and since the Jiangsu people are both prosperous and immoral—there's no need to blow their feathers to look for faults.

At another point Kangxi remarked, "The people of the North are strong; they must not copy the fancy diets of the Southerners, who are physically frail, live in a different environment, and have different stomachs and bowels."[52]

District gazetteers promoted more localized stereotypes. In general, the elite compilers of these works distinguished between residents who were comparatively docile and those who were potentially troublesome. Those in the former category (the vast majority of China's districts) tended to be described by stock phrases indicating the "absence of feuds," the avoidance of "involvement in lawsuits," and the habit of "never evading tax payments." Those in the latter category were labeled as "hot tempered," "frequently involved in feuds and lawsuits," and "militant." Such designations did not necessarily apply throughout any given province, however. In Hubei, for example, the residents of Huang'an district came to be described as "tough and daring," whereas in nearby Huanmei the local people were viewed as "soft and timid." Similarly, in Zhili, the natives of Xuanhua appeared in district gazetteers to be "militant and adventurous," while in Shunde they were "mild, inactive, and fond of learning the Confucian Classics."[53]

These regional, provincial, and local stereotypes unquestionably affected the outlook and policies of both the throne and local Qing officials, who were prohibited by law from serving in their home areas.[54] They also affected the conduct of Chinese personal and commercial relations—including what G. William Skinner describes as the "export" of entrepreneurial talent. Certainly it is no accident that fellow provincials from three neighboring counties in central Shanxi dominated the remittance banking business in China for over a century.[55] Regional and local stereotypes may even have influenced the subconscious self-image of individuals in China. Obviously, they posed an obstacle to nationwide social and political integration.

Given China's regional diversity and rampant localism, one may well wonder how China managed to thrive as a single political and cultural entity for so many millennia. Part of the answer lies in an examination of the general patterns of China's historical evolution.

THE HISTORICAL BACKGROUND

China's cultural development from Neolithic times through the Qing period may be viewed as a process, not always gradual, of expansion, incorporation, and progressive integration.[56] Some scholars, such as Ping-ti Ho, have emphasized the pristine origins and independent early development of Chinese civilization; but for most of Chinese history, foreign conquest and "barbarian" influences contributed significantly to the character and quality of Chinese culture.[57] The brief historical sketch that follows reflects a more or less traditional scheme of dynastic periodization. It highlights themes of particular importance to an understanding of Qing culture and relegates most references to new (often radically new) historical and philosophical interpretations to the notes.

China boasts a number of creation stories, most of which revolve around the idea of a cosmic alternation between disorder and order. Some are associated with the concept of *hundun,* an occasionally embodied form (variously represented as a large egg, a dumpling, a gourd, and so on) that operates spontaneously in various states of differentiation and shapelessness to produce all things. Others revolve around the idea of *yinyang* interaction (often understood in terms of the implicitly sexual union of Heaven and Earth), or the growth and disintegration of a dog-like creature called Pan Gu (this seems to have been a borrowed tale). The difference between these Chinese myths and the creation stories of many other cultures is that they do not involve a once-and-for-all event "requiring the causal presence of some 'extraordinary individual,' narrative persona, or hero of creation who stands outside the created order."[58]

Most traditional accounts of China's early history revolve around the so-called Five Rulers, an extraordinarily fluid category of culture heroes that sometimes includes the "Three Sovereigns," and which in any case refers to several different entities. These individuals are supposed to have lived in the period from 2852 B.C. to 2205 B.C., and although there has never been any agreement regarding the identity of the Five Rulers, much less their periods of reign, some names commonly appear in various texts: Fu Xi (also known as Bao Xi), Nü Gua (Nü Wa), Shen Nong, Huangdi (The Yellow Emperor), Zhuan Xu, Yao, Shun, and Yu. Of these figures, Fu Xi and Nü Gua are sometimes credited with being "the world's parents"; Shen Nong is usually viewed as "the inventor of agriculture"; The Yellow Emperor appears as a great warrior and "the initiator of civilization"; Zhuan Xu is "the emperor in whose hands Heaven was separated from Earth"; and Yao, Shun, and Yu are all considered "sage-heroes."[59]

Yu also receives praise in traditional Chinese lore for "controlling the floods" and founding China's first dynasty, the Xia (traditional dates, 2205–1766). A number of archaeologists have identified the Xia with excavations at the Erlitou sites near Luoyang in north central Henan, but the evidence is still tantalizingly incomplete. This much, however, we know: A distinctive Chinese culture had already begun to emerge in the broad Yellow River valley approximately seven thousand years ago. There, sustained by the rich and uniquely self-fertilizing loess soil, two major cultural complexes arose—one in the northwest and western part of the Central Plain and the other on the east coast and eastern part of the Central Plain.[60]

Eventually, by means of a still poorly understood process of diffusion, a dominant culture developed in North China that exhibited many of the traits that have come to be identified with Chinese civilization in its mature form: the cultivation of millet, rice, and other staple crops; the domestication of animals such as pigs and dogs; the use of silk and hemp for clothing; distinctive housing, food preparation, and artistic styles; divination; ancestor worship; and ideographic writing. Over a period of time, this northern Chinese culture base interacted with other Neolithic cultures scattered throughout various parts of East Asia, receiving enrichment without losing cultural hegemony. The result was the emergence around 1800 B.C. of China's first fully historic dynasty, the Shang (traditional dates: 1766–1122 B.C.).

Many aspects of Shang life show unmistakable Neolithic origins, but the Shang dynasty marks a dramatic new stage in China's cultural development. Building mainly on indigenous foundations, the Shang peoples in northern China developed a sophisticated sociopolitical system based on ancestor-related theocratic rule over city-states, as well as an advanced bronze technology, a highly refined writing system, and well-defined forms of social, economic, and military organization. Shang archaeological sites have been found in more than a dozen modern provinces, indicating the wide spread of Chinese culture by means of both trade and military expansion.[61]

The long-term cultural legacy of the Shang was primarily one of attitudes: an obsessive concern with ritual, a strongly bureaucratic outlook (especially evident in an abiding love of hierarchy, order, and classification), a consuming interest in the family and in ancestor worship, an aesthetically satisfying script, and the beginnings of *yinyang*-type art motifs and metaphysics. The Shang also provided concrete models for Chinese architecture, millet and rice agriculture, piece-mold bronze casting, jade working, and silk production and established precedents for the "protobureaucratic" control of large-scale labor resources, the strategic role for royal divination, and the "hierarchical dependency of young on old, female on male, ruled upon ruler."[62] In the Shang period we already find the emergence of a strongly authoritarian pattern in government and society—well before the establishment of large-scale, state-coordinated water-control projects in North China that enhanced "despotic" rule.

The Zhou dynasty (traditional dates: 1122–256 B.C.) replaced the Shang in what would become a familiar conquest pattern: As semi-barbaric "vassals" located on the margins of the Shang state, the Zhou people partook of Shang culture but also learned fighting skills from their contact with nomadic tribes to the north and west. Eventually they became powerful enough to conquer the Shang in about 1040 B.C. Traditional Chinese historiography describes the early (Western) Zhou as the Golden Age of China, a time of peace and prosperity under sage rulers such as the legendary King Wen (the Cultured King), King Wu (the Martial King), and the Duke of Zhou. Accounts of the period in the Confucian Classics describe an elaborate and undoubtedly idealized system of kingship, investiture, noble rank, lord-vassal relationships, fiefs, manors, knights, and serfs—similar in many ways to the feudalism of medieval Europe.

Significantly, however, China's knights (*shi*) seem to have been more literate and cultivated than their Western counterparts of a later period, and feudal ties in the Zhou were apparently based more on blood and pseudo-kinship than on contract and Western-style feudal principles. Moreover, when the Zhou kings invested their vassals with the "serfs" of a certain area along with the land, these people became, in a sense, more important than the territory itself. The result was that whole communities, composed of the descendants of a single lineage, "might be moved to another area and superimposed upon the local people to create another vassal state."[63]

Zhou feudalism seems to have been more highly centralized, at least in principle, than Western feudalism and governed more by the dictates of ritual and propriety day to day. Furthermore, the Zhou rulers developed a concept of political legitimacy unlike either the previous Shang system, based on the ability to communicate with deified ancestors, or the later Western doctrine of the "divine right of kings," which rested on birth alone. This distinctive Zhou notion became known as the Mandate of Heaven (*tianming*). It was predicated on the idea that Heaven, variously conceived as an impersonal deity or an abstract moral-spiritual force (see Chapter 6), bestowed the right to rule on the household of an ethically upright leader. A corresponding idea was that this "mandate" could be withdrawn if any ruler of the family line proved unworthy. This principle undergirded Chinese dynastic politics for the next three thousand years.

From a comparative standpoint, the most important feature of Zhou feudalism is that as a historical stage it never developed into capitalism—even though the system broke down in ways that are roughly comparable to the disintegration of feudalism in the late medieval West. The process began in China with the erosion of Zhou authority by barbarian invasions in the eighth century B.C. In 771 B.C. the capital at Hao fell and the Zhou ruling house had to move eastward to the area of modern-day Xian. Thus began the Eastern Zhou era, a time of unmistakable dynastic decline. During the so-called Spring and Autumn period (722–481 B.C.) more than a hundred small states (*guo*) emerged, each more or less independent of Zhou royal authority.[64]

Widespread fighting among these contending states proved disruptive and demoralizing—particularly as the struggles grew ever more intense and destructive in the Warring States period (403–221 B.C.). Mark Lewis argues that "ritually directed violence" during this time, in the form of sacrifices, warfare (including vendettas), and hunting, provided a form of cosmic legitimation of the ruler's authority in each state and thus helped to shape the character of the later Chinese imperium. At the same time, the incessant fighting of the period also produced what Lewis describes as the "sexual re-imaging" of Chinese politics. As the nature of warfare changed from limited battles between aristocratic armies to larger conflicts involving conscripted peasants, "the male collegiality of shared combat was replaced by the domination of husband over wife as the model of authority."[65]

Meanwhile, technological developments contributed to other important changes. The use of iron, for example, revolutionized warfare and facilitated transformations in agriculture, hydraulic engineering, and communications. Commercial activity and urbanization followed, remaking the old social order. New professions arose, and social mobility ensued. Land, once the sole possession of the king, became purchasable and transferable. Money circulated freely. Traditional values fell by the wayside or at least came under direct assault.[66] In the midst of the chaos and uncertainty, the search began for a means of restoring order and unity to China. This quest led to a flowering of Chinese philosophy as impressive as the roughly contemporary great age of Classical thought in the West.

Between the sixth and the third centuries B.C., a succession of brilliant and articulate Chinese thinkers offered a wide variety of solutions to China's pressing social and political problems. Confucius (c. 551–479 B.C.) and his followers—notably Mencius (c. 372–289 B.C.) and Xunzi (c. 300–235 B.C.)—advocated a return to the lost virtues of the early Zhou, to family-centered ethics, ritual, and social responsibility. The followers of Mozi (c. 470–391 B.C.) criticized the excessive ritual, lack of religious spirit, and particularism of Confucianism but shared many of the same general social goals and ethical concerns. By contrast, disciples of the legendary Daoist philosopher Laozi (sixth century B.C.) and his fully historical successor, Zhuangzi (c. 369–286 B.C.), sought release from social burdens; they were at heart individualists and escapists, concerned less with changing the world in an active way than with finding their special niche in the natural order. Related to the Daoists, at least in their interest in nature and natural process, were the followers of Zou Yan (c. 305–240 B.C.), who developed an elaborate cosmology based on *yinyang* principles and the five agents, or activities, associated with the elements of wood, metal, fire, water, and earth. Other schools of thought, such as the School of Names, contributed to the development of epistemology and ontology but left little long-term philosophical legacy in China.[67]

Not surprisingly, the various contending schools interpreted China's inherited mythology in different ways. Sarah Allen has shown, for instance, that although Warring States legends about culture heroes such as Yao, Shun, Tang (the founder of the Shang dynasty), and King Wu (the founder of the Zhou) display certain structural similarities—notably a mediated tension between "sagely" and hereditary succession to rulership—they convey significantly different versions of what subsequent generations came to consider China's "history." Some of these stories diverge in response to philosophical disagreements, but some of the differences have a social foundation. Thus, Mozi, reputed to have been from a class of prisoners or perhaps slaves, was at pains in his recounting of tales to emphasize the lowly social status of worthy ministers, whereas Mencius, of a more exalted background, took a greater interest in the role of elites.[68]

Ironically, it was the school of thought known as Legalism, which traditional scholars have considered barely a philosophy,[69] that exerted the most immediate and profound influence on Chinese society. Although derived from a wide variety of thinkers, including Guanzi (d. 645 B.C.) and Xunzi's student Han Feizi (d. 233 B.C.), Legalism developed into a rather narrow administrative approach emphasizing pragmatic government, universal and codified law rather than morality (contrary to the Confucian ideal), and state power as an end in itself. Guided by these basic principles and blessed with capable leadership, the Qin state—one of several major contenders for political supremacy during the late Zhou period—embarked on a systematic campaign of conquest that resulted in the fall of the Zhou ruling house in 256 B.C. and culminated in the subordination of all of China by 221 B.C.

The Qin dynasty lasted only fifteen years, but it left an enduring imprint on Chinese culture for the next two millennia.[70] Its sovereign, King Zheng, who adopted the title of emperor (*huangdi*) for the first time in Chinese history, brought unprecedented unity to China. Dismantling the vestiges of Zhou feudalism, including the practice of primogeniture, he instituted a nationwide system of freehold farming and imposed centralized, bureaucratic rule over the entire realm. At the same time, he initiated massive public works projects (including roads, waterways, and defensive walls)[71] and standardized weights, measures, coinage, axle lengths, and even the Chinese script. Less laudably, the first Qin emperor imposed rigid thought control on Chinese intellectuals and tried to suppress nonutilitarian works, including all but one of the major Confucian Classics. This policy, although not entirely successful, resulted in the destruction of great amounts of priceless literature and created countless later controversies over the authenticity of reconstituted texts.

Joseph Needham and others have argued that the crucial requirements of water management in North China, together with the need to provide widespread famine relief and to defend China against barbarian incursions, encouraged the unification and bureaucratization of the realm.[72] But the harsh policies and rapid changes introduced by the first Qin emperor proved to be too disruptive for the regime. Not only did they help stifle what might have been an emerging capitalism and stigmatize the idea of codified law, but they also generated empire-wide dissatisfaction, which quickly erupted into rebellion. Within four years of the first emperor's death, the Qin dynasty was overthrown.

The Han dynasty that followed (206 B.C.–A.D. 222) was one of the most glorious periods in all of Chinese history.[73] Indeed, later generations of Chinese proudly called themselves "the people of Han" (*Hanren*). The key to Han administrative success was the creation of an effective blend or balance of diverse cultural elements under the powerful and energetic emperor Wudi (reigned 141–87 B.C.). Wudi's government, for example, was fundamentally Legalist in structure but Confucian in spirit; the economy involved both state monopolies and private enterprise; Han foreign relations were marked by both aggressive expansion and strategic appeasement. Balance was also evident in the eclectic thought of Dong Zhongshu (179–104 B.C.), a highly influential Confucian court philosopher. Han art and literature reflected a creative blend of cultural influences—not only Confucian and Daoist, but also courtly and popular, foreign and native.[74]

During the four centuries of Han rule, China changed in a variety of ways. The political system, for example, required different mechanisms of control, systems of decisionmaking, and concepts of sovereignty at different times. Meanwhile, the population increased, land tenancy became more common, and the size of private estates grew. These changes were especially noticeable in the Later or Eastern Han period, which followed Wang Mang's usurpation of the throne from the Former (Western) Han rulers in A.D. 9. Wang's so-called Xin ("New") dynasty lasted for fourteen years and created several kinds of havoc. His radical economic reforms, designed to strengthen the state at the expense of private landowners and merchants, engendered widespread opposition, and his effort to recover the "original" Confucian Classics, which the first emperor of Qin had ordered destroyed, led to the "discovery" of editions that had been reportedly hidden away. Later generations of scholars—especially those in the Qing period—claimed that these works, written in an old-style script (*guwen*), as opposed to the so-called new characters (*jinwen*) of the Qin and Former Han, were in fact forgeries (see Chapter 6).[75]

Despite the unfortunate Wang Mang interregnum, and the decline of centralized state power that followed in its wake, the legacy of Han culture was enduring. As Kwang-Ching Liu has emphasized, the Han dynasty's conception of "ritual propriety and social morality" (*lijiao*; lit., the teachings of ritual) served as the foundation of state orthodoxy for most of the next two thousand years.[76] Furthermore, in its governmental structure, economic policies, social control mechanisms, foreign relations, educational system, scholarship, and artistic and literary accomplishments, the Han set the style and pattern for most later dynasties. Even the idea of Confucian eremitism as the loyalist alternative to serving a new regime seems to have been institutionalized in the Han.[77] Important changes took place over the next two thousand years, to be sure, but a Han scholar would have had comparatively little difficulty adjusting to life in any subsequent dynasty up to the late Qing—certainly less than, say, a Roman patrician in nineteenth-century Italy.

The fall of the Han in A.D. 222 ushered in an extended period of political disunity known as the Six Dynasties (222–589).[78] For much of this time, China was divided into two distinct areas, North and South, with the dividing line about the Huai River. The North suffered repeated barbarian invasions and chronic political instability, while the South remained immune from barbarian conquest and comparatively stable. During the first few decades of the Six Dynasties period, from 222 to 256, three large and powerful kingdoms battled for political supremacy. Their struggle, full of clever strategies and dark intrigues, became the inspiration for one of China's most famous novels in late imperial times (see Chapter 9).

Yet despite foreign invasions and political division, these were not China's Dark Ages, especially in the South. In fact, traditional Chinese culture flourished, receiving enrichment from Indian Buddhism, which spread rapidly in China during the centuries following its introduction from India during the later Han period.

Buddhism brought to tormented and disillusioned Chinese individuals the hope of escape from worldly suffering and sorrow. It introduced new ideas of reincarnation, karmic retribution, and the release of Nirvana and exerted a lasting influence on many aspects of Chinese philosophy, religion, art, literature, music, and architecture. At the same time, Buddhist monasteries began to play an important role in Chinese economic, social, and even political life, both North and South.[79] Among the many significant changes occasioned by the introduction of Buddhism was the establishment of Daoism as an institutional religion (as opposed to a more purely philosophical orientation; see Chapters 6 and 7). Although this new-style Religious Daoism drew upon the classical texts of Laozi and Zhuangzi, it developed primarily out of Chinese popular religion—an influence evident in its inclusion of home-grown deities, magical practices (including alchemy), and a fascination with immortality. Buddhism provided a structural model for this amalgamation of indigenous beliefs and practices—one that went well beyond the secret societies that had given Chinese popular religion a certain shape and focus in the Han dynasty.[80]

On the other hand, Buddhism was transformed by Chinese culture. Early attempts to translate Buddhist sutras invariably involved linguistic and social compromises. Familiar, but not necessarily equivalent, Chinese terms were initially used to translate Buddhist notions, and various attempts were made to match concepts (*geyi*) in order to establish parallels between Buddhist and indigenous Chinese sets of ideas. As a means of minimizing conflict between original Buddhist ideas and entrenched Chinese social values, passages in Buddhist sutras were sometimes altered or simply omitted. Over time, Buddhism became heavily "sinicized."[81]

The nearly universal acceptance of Buddhism by all levels of Chinese society by the sixth century, together with the strong memory of Han unity and glory, undoubtedly contributed to the political and cultural reunification of China in 589 by the Sui dynasty (589–618). During the Sui-Tang period (589–907), Buddhism received official patronage and became an integral part of state ritual and Chinese high culture generally.[82] But a series of politically inspired persecutions directed against the Buddhist religious establishment by Daoist-inspired emperors in the mid-ninth century helped undercut Buddhism's institutional power in China. Meanwhile, Confucianism, which had been used selectively by the Sui-Tang rulers as a convenient source of political theory and ritual precedent for the conduct of imperial affairs, witnessed an intellectual revival.[83] Thereafter, Buddhism continued to inspire, but never to dominate, Chinese intellectual life. Controlled by the state from above, it became appropriated by Chinese popular religion from below.

The intellectual vitality of the Tang was but one indication of the general growth and refinement of Chinese culture during this period. Like the Han, the Tang was expansive, cosmopolitan, creative, and self-confident. In the words of Michael Sullivan, "T'ang [Tang] culture was to the culture of the Six Dynasties as was Han to the Warring States, or, to stretch the parallel a little, Rome to ancient Greece. It was a time of consolidation, of practical achievement, of immense assurance."[84] The Tang also resembled the Han in the sense that a rebellion at mid-course produced significant changes in Chinese political, economic, and intellectual life. The Tang upheaval, known as the Rebellion of An Lushan (755–763), had far more dramatic consequences, however, than the Wang Mang rebellion.[85]

In government, the Sui-Tang examination system represented a major advance over the Han recruitment apparatus in opening channels of bureaucratic mobility. During the Tang period there were several regular examinations, which tested classical scholarship, law, calligraphy, mathematics, and literary skills. Of these, the literary examinations eventually became the most prestigious and the chief route to high government office. Although social origins, family connections, and proper "breeding" still gave distinct advantages to well-born candidates for official position, the Tang marks the beginning of a trend toward the replacement of aristocratic rule by "meritocratic" rule in Chinese government.[86] Meanwhile, the dynasty's self-conscious use of ritual as a form of legitimation indirectly contributed to this process by substituting the idea of the empire "belonging to one family" (*tianxia wei jia*) with the concept of the empire being "open to all" (*tianxia wei gong*). This doctrine did not, however, make Tang government in any sense "democratic." Indeed, Howard Wechsler argues that the ritual-related decisions made by the throne, including the choice to focus imperial worship on a single universal Heaven rather than multiple deities, ultimately had the effect of intensifying autocracy in China.[87]

Another Tang contribution to the character of Chinese government in late imperial times was its highly refined law code, which provided the general format of the law codes of subsequent dynasties down to the Qing, as well as many specific statutes. Tang law was overwhelmingly penal in emphasis and designed primarily to preserve the entire Chinese social order against acts of moral or ritual impropriety. It was only secondarily interested in defending the rights of an individual or group against another individual or group and not at all concerned with defending such rights against the state. As a result, law in the Tang and later periods usually "operated in a vertical direction from the state upon the individual, rather than on a horizontal plane directly between two individuals."[88] In all, it was an instrument of state power and control, not a source of individual autonomy.

After a brief period of disunity following the downfall of the Tang, the Song dynasty (960–1279) reestablished centralized rule over all of China.[89] Building on early Tang political institutions as well as late Tang intellectual developments and economic changes—notably the government's loss of control over both the land system and merchant activity after the An Lushan uprising and the southward movement of the population after the Huang Chao rebellion of 878–884—the Song carried Chinese material culture to new heights, combining remarkable administrative stability with unprecedented economic growth. Song China was the most populous and most urbanized country in the world, with more than 100 million inhabitants (120 million people around 1200) and more than fifty cities with populations in excess of 500,000. Song agriculture was probably the most sophisticated anywhere at the time; foreign and domestic commerce flourished; and great industrial enterprises, employing hundreds and sometimes thousands of workers, produced massive amounts of iron, steel, textiles, and other valuable commodities. In most respects, the Song level of economic development was not achieved by any European country until the eighteenth century.

The spectacular growth of the Song may be attributed to several related factors. One was certainly the stability of Song government and the state's unprecedentedly positive attitudes toward trade and economic development. Another was the loosening of traditional controls on merchants and the growth of new marketing centers. Yet another was the rapid expansion of credit facilities and the development of a sophisticated money economy. Population growth, urbanization, agricultural and industrial productivity, and commerce reinforced one another, and Chinese society as a whole benefited from a spate of inventions in virtually every area of science and technology, from biology, mathematics, chemistry, and medicine to hydraulic engineering, bridge building, shipbuilding, and architecture. Improvements in transport and communications, coupled with the expansion of education and the invention of printing (a Tang development), helped disseminate the new knowledge of the period.[90]

Although the Song was an age of great scientific and technological advancement, literature and the arts did not take a back seat to practical pursuits. Prose and poetry prospered, as did painting and calligraphy. The Song was also a time of rapid social change. The recent work of scholars such as Patricia Ebrey, Robert Hymes, and Valerie Hansen underscores the many important transformations in family, lineage, and religious life that unfolded during the period from 960 to 1279.[91] These changes were not necessarily progressive from a modern standpoint, however. The subjugation of women in later periods of Chinese history, for example, seems to be closely related not only to the Song social practice of footbinding but also to certain new currents in Song thought.[92]

For better or worse, the Song witnessed a flowering of Chinese philosophy almost as impressive as that of the Warring States period, although not nearly as wide-ranging. This development was an outgrowth of the social, economic, and technological changes outlined above as well as the product of a Confucian intellectual "revival" that had begun in the Tang with Han Yu (768–824). Known generally by Western scholars as neo-Confucianism, this multi-faceted philosophy was expounded by such brilliant and diverse thinkers as Shao Yong (1011–1077), Zhou Dunyi (1017–1073), Zhang Zai (1020–1077), Cheng Yi (1033–1107), Su Shi (1037–1101), the great synthesizer Zhu Xi (1130–1200), and his intellectual rival Lu Xiangshan (1139–1193). In the hands of these individuals, neo-Confucianism not only reasserted (and in many cases redefined) the ancient principles of Confucius and his more immediate successors but also buttressed these principles with cosmological and metaphysical speculations inspired by the very schools it was attacking: Buddhism and Daoism. Some Song thinkers, such as the reform-minded political adversaries Wang Anshi (1021–1086) and Sima Guang (1019–1086), were best known for their practical concern with statecraft and their comparative lack of interest in metaphysics; others, such as the broad-ranging scholar Shen Gua (1031–1095), made their primary mark in the history of Chinese science.[93]

What is striking about this burst of intellectual energy and inventiveness in the Song is that together with dramatic economic development, population growth, and urbanization, it did not produce far-reaching revolutionary change in China. We know, after all, that three simple Chinese inventions of the Tang-Song period—gunpowder, the magnetic compass, and printing—profoundly altered the contours of European history: Gunpowder weapons spelled the doom of European armored knights and feudal castles; the magnetic compass (and the axial rudder) enabled Europeans to discover the New World; and printing helped launch the Renaissance, the Reformation, and the Commercial Revolution in the West. Other Chinese inventions, coming in clusters to Europe, produced further important changes. Why did these inventions fail to transform China in a similar manner?[94]

The answer, in brief, is that by Song times, China's highly evolved political, social, and economic institutions could accommodate internally generated change without fundamental disruption. From an economic standpoint, despite some significant fluctuations in land tenure systems over time—including periodic experiments with nationalization of the land—the basic Han-style market economy prevailed for some two thousand years. In the eleventh century, however, China's per capita acreage began to decline, and, except for dynastic transitions, it continued (and continues) to do so. The result was that Chinese farming became increasingly labor intensive, discouraging the introduction of labor-saving devices.[95]

Intellectually, the establishment of the Jin dynasty (1115–1234) by the invading Ruzhen people, who drove the Song rulers from their capital at Kaifeng in the North to Hangzhou in the South, had a traumatic effect. In the view of James T.C. Liu, this event, together with Mongol pressure in the mid-thirteenth century, caused the Southern Song court to "turn inward" and establish a narrowly conservative orthodoxy, which was then, of course, reinforced by the civil-service examinations.[96] What is more, when the examination system finally became accessible to merchants in post-Song times, the Chinese state gave them every incentive to invest in education rather than commerce as a means of achieving upward social mobility.

In the end, government policy was decisive. By Song times, if not before, the highly centralized, bureaucratic managerial state possessed not only the political authority but also the institutional capacity to control, dominate, or at least channel major change of almost any kind, if it had the will.[97] It could establish monopolies, supervise trade, coopt inventions, and mobilize vast human and material resources in support of its own interests. It could also, of course, play an important role in unleashing the productive forces of society. Song economic growth was itself in large measure a product of unprecedentedly positive attitudes toward commerce on the part of the government. These attitudes did not, however, resurface during the final six and a half centuries of China's dynastic history.

The invasion of the Mongols and the founding of the Yuan dynasty (1279–1368) followed a pattern of nomadic conquest that had antecedents in both the Six Dynasties period and the Song.[98] It would later be repeated by the Manchus in the seventeenth century. This pattern involved the seizure of power in North China at a time of political disorder, the enlistment of Chinese as well as foreign advice and assistance, the conscious copying of Chinese administrative techniques and institutions, the use of both terror and appeasement in consolidating power, and the maintenance of an external base beyond the Great Wall in addition to military predominance in China Proper.

Mongol military rule tarnished the bright cultural image of the Song, stigmatized its policies, and brought both rising despotism and racial discrimination against Han Chinese. Yet the harshness and oppressiveness of Yuan administration could not stay the advance of traditional Chinese culture, which flourished in areas such as art, vernacular literature, and especially operatic drama. Confucian eremitism—a practice that reflected not only traditional-style loyalties to the previous dynasty but also the hard fact of diminished bureaucratic opportunities available to Han Chinese scholars—paid handsome cultural dividends.[99] Moreover, in time the Mongols became increasingly sinicized, as a comparison of the administrative attitudes and personal life-styles of Chinggis Khan (1155–1227) and his grandson Qubilai Khan (reigned 1260–1294) clearly indicates.[100] In testimony to the Yuan dynasty's patronage of Confucian scholarship in its later years, the civil-service examinations, which had fallen into abeyance, were reestablished in the early fourteenth century. Characteristically, however, the Mongols imposed a rigid orthodoxy on the content of the examinations, incorporating the commentaries of Zhu Xi into the official examination syllabus in 1313, where they remained until 1904.

When the Ming dynasty (1368–1644) expelled the Mongols, the long-standing issue of loyalty to the fallen regime acquired special meaning. Since all of China had never before succumbed to "barbarian" rule, late Yuan rebels placed particular emphasis on antiforeign themes in their propaganda and often used the banner of the Song dynasty as their justification for revolt. Perhaps this appeal to "native" sentiments, together with what John Dardess describes as a new sense of "public-service professionalism," made it easier for Confucian scholars to serve the new dynasty with their integrity and independence largely intact. Yet there remained significant numbers of Yuan loyalists who refused to join the Ming cause, and these individuals seem to have lived a life-style "very similar to that of Song loyalists during the first generation of Yuan rule." Scholars such as Yang Weizhen (1296–1370) and Dai Liang (1317–1383) considered themselves subjects of the Yuan and would not consider service with Chinese rebel leaders. In the words of Jennifer Jay: "What impressed these men the most about the Song loyalists, whom they wrote about extensively, was their loyalty to the collapsing dynasty and not their antiforeign sentiments about Mongol rule."[101]

The founder of the Ming, Zhu Yuanzhang, despite his hostility toward the Mongols, continued the Yuan dynasty's trend toward despotic rule by means of the early abolition of certain important institutional checks on imperial power, including the office of prime minister.[102] In the Ming, more than ever before, China's pyramidlike structure of civil, military, and censorial government, dating from Qin-Han times, dominated the Chinese world. In the words of a leading authority, "There was no group or force in society that served as a countervailing influence against the government, so that [Chinese] society was a single-centered rather than a multi-centered one."[103] Overall, however, Ming despotism neither stifled artistic and literary activity nor hindered economic growth. Indeed, by Ming times, the Chinese economy had once again become highly commercialized, with complex farm technology and sophisticated production methods. As late as the sixteenth century, and perhaps later, the Chinese economy was still the most sophisticated and productive in the world, and the Chinese probably enjoyed a higher standard of living than any other people on earth.[104]

What is more, contrary to stereotype, the Ming was a time of considerable vitality and diversity in Chinese intellectual life. The great scholar and Confucian activist Wang Yangming (1472–1529) was a towering figure in Chinese philosophy during the Ming era, but he did not stand alone. Thinkers such as the eccentric Wang Gen (1483–1541), founder of the so-called left-wing Taizhou school, and his colleagues, including Li Zhi (1527–1602) and Wang Ji (1498–1583), derived radical implications from Wang Yangming's notion of the mind-heart (*xin*) as the ultimate measure of Confucian morality. According to Chang Hao, the writings of these individuals were, from the very beginning, "marked by a degree of egalitarianism, nonconformism, and anti-establishmentarianism unprecedented in the Confucian tradition."[105] Over the long run, however, very few philosophers followed their iconoclastic lead.

Christian missionary contact with the Ming during the early seventeenth century brought some new Western scientific, technological, and religious knowledge to China, but it did little to alter the character of Ming intellectual life. Nor did it affect Chinese political, social, and economic institutions. The Jesuits, who succeeded in accommodating themselves in a deliberate way to the Chinese cultural and social milieu, were able to win a number of high-level converts and even to achieve some positions of responsibility within the Ming bureaucracy. But they depended completely on imperial support to maintain themselves and never came close to achieving any significant political power or intellectual influence. Later, their somewhat idealized accounts of China came to exert a small but significant impact on Enlightenment thinkers such as Voltaire, who is said to have written that the Chinese "have perfected moral science and that is the first of the sciences."[106]

For all the grandeur of the Ming, with its impressive public-works projects, economic growth, and cultural refinement, dynastic decline came inexorably, as it had come to all previous ruling houses. The pattern was a familiar one: reign by weak and self-indulgent emperors, official corruption and bureaucratic factionalism, the arrogation of power by eunuchs (a particularly acute problem in the Ming), fiscal irresponsibility, natural disasters, and the rise of rebellion.[107] Meanwhile, beyond the Great Wall, in the remote northeastern area of Liaodong, a tribal confederation of Tungusic peoples eyed the Middle Kingdom covetously. These warriors, who claimed descent from the Jurched (Ruzhen) founders of the Jin dynasty in the twelfth century, were the Manchus. They had long been tributaries of the Ming, but in the early seventeenth century, recently united under an able military leader named Nurgachi (1559–1626), they sought a different role.

In the early seventeenth century, Nurgachi and his son, Hong Taiji (1592–1643), built a formidable conquest force of about 150,000 well-trained soldiers, each belonging to one of eight fighting units distinguished by differently colored banners (*gusa* or *qi*). After Nurgachi's death, Hong Taiji refined this Banner fighting machine, built up a Chinese-style administration in Mukden (Shenyang), and in 1636 adopted the dynastic name Qing ("Pure"). By stages, the Banners incorporated Mongol and Chinese fighting men as well as a number of Korean, Russian, and other non-Manchu soldiers. Then, in 1644, after the rebel marauder Li Zicheng had taken the Ming capital of Beijing, the Manchus joined forces with Ming troops under Wu Sangui (1612–1678) to expel the insurgents, declaring that they had come to save China from rebel depredations.[108]

But while the Manchus sought to legitimize themselves as the protectors of China's cultural heritage, they also crystallized their image as "barbarian" conquerors by forcing the Chinese to shave the front of their hair and grow the Manchu-style queue (*bianzi*) as a sign of submission. And, as with the Song-Yuan transition, the problem of foreign rule added an extra dimension to the issue of fidelity to the fallen dynasty. Ming loyalists put up a fierce resistance to the Manchus and posed a much greater threat to the succeeding regime than did their Song counterparts.[109] Moreover, a great many more people of prominence were involved. The *TSJC*, for instance, contains more than five thousand biographies of noteworthy Ming loyalists, compared to fewer than seven hundred for the Song. Nevertheless, even such famous Ming supporters as Gu Yanwu (1613–1682), Huang Zongxi (1610–1695), Wang Fuzhi (1619–1692), and Lü Liuliang (1629–1683)—all of whom steadfastly refused to serve the Qing—encouraged their children, relatives, and students to give service to the new dynasty.[110]

Consolidation of Qing rule took several decades of fighting, but by the late 1680s—under the leadership of the dynamic Kangxi emperor—the Qing had eliminated or driven underground the last pockets of anti-Manchu resistance and had established a strong, stable regime. During this period of consolidation, the Jesuits easily transferred their allegiance to the Manchus, who, like the Ming rulers, greatly valued Western mathematical, astronomical, and calendrical skills. The Jesuits also made considerable headway in gaining high-level converts until a controversy between the various Catholic orders in China, centering on the proper interpretation of Confucian rituals, provoked papal interference. When this happened, the Catholic missionary effort became a political matter and not simply a religious one. The Yongzheng and Qianlong emperors responded by branding Christianity as "heterodox" and severely limiting the activities of all the Catholic orders in China, including the Jesuits.[111]

The expansive Kangxi, Yongzheng, and Qianlong reigns marked the apex of Manchu rule in China. Contemporary accounts of the eighteenth century suggest a prosperous society with abundant natural resources, a huge but basically contented population (an estimated 268 million people in 1776), and a royal house of great prestige, both at home and abroad. Small wonder Qing chroniclers of the period referred to their time as being "unparalleled in history."[112] Viewed from a nineteenth-century perspective (see Chapter 11), such claims sound like pathetic pride before the inevitable fall. In fact, however, they had substance, and there can be little doubt that for most of the imperial era, one reason for the astonishing staying power of traditional Chinese civilization was simply its ability to satisfy the needs of its vast population in ways that no other society on earth could match. A well-known study of modernization in China suggests:

> If a line is drawn in history at the seventeenth century or at practically any time during the previous millennium, the case could be argued, some believe convincingly, that no peoples can lay claim to higher incomes per capita or to a more equal distribution of opportunities to win a large share of such income, to higher levels of literacy, to more sophisticated arts and crafts, to more highly developed commerce, or to markedly more elaborate adornment of such marks of "civilization" as the fine arts of sculpture, painting, calligraphy, and music, the intellectual arts of philosophy and knowledge in its various forms (save that we know today as "science"), and the minor arts of cooking, gracious living in general, and humor, or the arts of governance and even war.[113]

This, in brief, was the Qing inheritance.

3

The Qing
Political Order

*T*he primary focus in this chapter and the next is on those political, social, and economic institutions that together played a key role in the ordering of Qing society. Later chapters will discuss in detail the philosophical and religious underpinnings of these institutions. Naturally enough, significant changes took place in nearly every area of Chinese institutional life in the two and a half centuries from the founding of the Qing to its demise in 1912. These changes are usually linked with specific reigns, as Chinese traditions of rulership made each emperor the "personification of an epoch"—particularly in late imperial times.[1]

During the first few years of Qing rule in China Proper, the Shunzhi emperor (r. 1644–1661) occupied the throne as a child under the regency of Dorgon (1612–1650), younger brother of Hong Taiji. When Dorgon died in 1650, various Manchu nobles scrambled to claim his inheritance, but the Shunzhi emperor, now thirteen, deftly managed to hold the fragile situation together and even to assert himself. Fond of Chinese literature, drama, and calligraphy, he favored Chinese officials over Manchus, and although personally attracted to Buddhism, he also befriended the Jesuit court astronomer Adam Schall von Bell. In his later years, however, the Shunzhi emperor's administrative judgment faltered; he became infatuated with one of his junior consorts and increasingly surrendered power to court eunuchs and Buddhist priests.

When Shunzhi died in 1661 (probably from smallpox), four senior Manchus assumed the regency for his young son, the Kangxi emperor (1662–1722). These men were openly scornful of Shunzhi for departing from Manchu ways and for relying too heavily on eunuchs. Under the leadership of a powerful general named Oboi (d. 1669), the regents attempted to tighten Qing administration by abolishing many eunuch offices, imposing heavy penalties for tax evasion, and employing draconian measures to starve out Ming loyalists on Taiwan. They also promoted Manchus to high bureaucratic positions in an effort to reverse the pro-Chinese policies of the Shunzhi emperor. The Kangxi emperor, however, shared his father's affection for Chinese culture and resented the high-handed behavior of Oboi. In 1677, at the age of fifteen, he cleverly arranged for Oboi's arrest on charges of arrogance and dishonesty, and from this point onward he took firm control of political affairs.[2]

Decisive and self-confident, the Kangxi emperor first precipitated and then suppressed the famous Revolt of the Three Feudatories (1673–1681). Soon thereafter he brought Taiwan under direct Chinese control (1683) and turned his military attention to China's northern frontiers. At court he checked eunuch power by relying on

41

both Chinese bondservants (*baoyi*) and Manchu nobles for the performance of various administrative tasks. As a ruler, Kangxi tended to be practical, frugal, tolerant, and conciliatory. Although notoriously disinclined to attack corruption (perhaps for fear of alienating a predominantly Chinese bureaucracy not yet fully reconciled to Manchu rule), he rewarded rectitude and tried to favor neither Manchus nor Chinese in official appointments. Intellectually, the Kangxi emperor was broadminded and intensely curious. He ardently promoted Chinese learning and the arts, but he also admired the scientific accomplishments of the Jesuits.[3]

Kangxi's death in 1722 precipitated a succession crisis from which his fourth son, Yinzhen, emerged as victor at the age of forty-five. He reigned as the Yongzheng emperor (1723–1735) and ruled in a rather feverish and chaotic way. Relying on elaborate but informal networks of administration, he paid extraordinary attention to the smallest details of government, writing endless notes to his officials in a "surging tide of scribbling" and allowing "no one group to monopolize a problem or manipulate information." Sensitive to persistent rumors that he had usurped the throne, the emperor remained suspicious of all potential rivals—including his brothers, several of whom he ordered arrested. But if the Yongzheng reign was marked by harshness and the growth of imperial autocracy, it was also distinguished by a powerful moral vision and a genuine commitment to meaningful administrative reform.[4]

The Qianlong emperor (1736–1796), who ascended the throne without incident at age thirty-five, deliberately sought to achieve a balance between the excessive severity of his father and the over-leniency of his grandfather. By and large he succeeded, although his desire to be judged a benevolent Confucian ruler led him to approach his father's reforms with a certain detrimental hesitation. Moreover, to his occasional dismay, Qianlong found that bureaucratic administration became ever more highly routinized. One reason, ironically, seems to have been the emperor's reluctance to reject the formal deliberations of his high metropolitan officials. Another was simply administrative overload. Beatrice Bartlett estimates, for example, that incoming provincial reports may have tripled over the course of the Qianlong reign and increased tenfold from the late Kangxi era.[5]

In the realms of both military affairs and patronage of Chinese culture, the Qianlong emperor exceeded the impressive achievements of his immediate forebears—and, one might add, most other rulers in Chinese history. But he also spent more money, and eventually he created severe fiscal problems for the state. Furthermore, in his later years Qianlong became increasingly careless, investing enormous power in a former imperial bodyguard named Heshen (d. 1799), who proceeded to embark on a heroic campaign of organized corruption. Although the full extent of Heshen's peculation remains to be determined, one Chinese historian, Li Jiannong, estimates the worth of his enormous personal estate as the equivalent of "ten times the seventy million tael annual income of the Chinese empire at the time."[6]

The Qianlong emperor formally abdicated the throne in 1795, but his second son, the Jiaqing emperor (1796–1820), did not personally assume the reins of power until the death of his father in 1799. Jiaqing was an intelligent, well-educated, and energetic emperor who immediately upon his accession to power at the age of thirty-nine initiated a series of reforms designed to rectify the administrative problems created by his father's late-reign dereliction of duty and his apparent protection of Heshen. As an essential first step, Jiaqing ordered Heshen to commit suicide. He then abolished the Secret Account Bureau (Miji chu), which Heshen had used to collect large fines (in some instances more than 100,000 taels) from servitors of the Imperial Household. A "drastic sweep" of top-level central government officials followed, along with various reforms in the imperial communications system.[7]

The Jiaqing emperor's other efforts to reduce expenditures and curb corruption met with far less success, however. By the early nineteenth century, population pressure, rising inflation, the increasing costs of river conservancy, and a myriad of other fiscal problems prompted him to hold his officials more closely accountable for cost overruns and to authorize deductions from their supplemental salaries (known as *yanglian*) in order to hold the line on administrative expenses. This measure only encouraged bureaucrats to resort to irregular means in order to make ends meet. Madeleine Zelin summarizes some of the unfortunate consequences:

> Deprived in large measure of their own legitimate sources of income, ... local officials began to resort to illegal surcharges, forced contributions, customary fees (*lou-kuei* [*lougui*]), manipulation of silver-copper ratios, and other devices for raising funds. Even the Chia-ch'ing [Jiaqing] emperor was forced to admit that local officials had no choice but to rely on *lou-kuei* [*lougui*]. Rather than allow them to extort from the people as they pleased, the emperor made the extraordinary recommendation that *lou-kuei* [*lougui*] be legalized and set up for its collection.[8]

From this point onward, rational fiscal administration deteriorated quickly. Informal networks of funding became the hallmark of the Chinese bureaucracy, and the acceptance of *lougui* became the mark of even virtuous officials. Corruption continued to be a problem, and the central government increasingly resorted to the sale of official titles (and even substantive offices) to cover its costs.

Clearly the dynasty was on a downward spiral. Nonetheless, it would be incorrect to claim, as some scholars have, that the Qing state no longer had the capacity for effective action. Research by Jane Kate Leonard and others has shown that Jiaqing's successor, the Daoguang emperor (1821–1850), was capable of dynamic and effective action—at least in spheres deemed essential to China's "national security." In late 1824, for instance, after flooding had destroyed the Grand Canal in northern Jiangsu and crippled the dynasty's grain transport system, the Daoguang emperor "undertook the disciplined supervision of canal-transport affairs," pursuing a flexible approach to crisis management that "was determined by changing realities in northern Jiangsu, rather than a mindless adherence to the regulations and traditions of the imperial ancestors."[9]

By the Xianfeng era (1851–1861), the Qing dynasty was on its knees, and the end appeared in sight. Foreign imperialism, domestic rebellion, and a series of succession crises over the next few decades combined to create unprecedented political and administrative problems for the imperial Chinese state. Yet the dynasty revitalized itself during the Tongzhi period (1862–1874) under the capable but conservative regency of the Empress Dowager, Cixi (1835–1908). Following the death of the Tongzhi emperor at the age of nineteen, she placed her four-year-old nephew on the throne to reign as the Guangxu emperor (1875–1908). Although often painted as a weak figure under the complete control of his domineering aunt, Guangxu seems to have been capable of bold, independent action, at least on occasion, in the later years of his reign. By this time, however, the dynasty was beyond redemption (see Chapter 11). When the Guangxu emperor died mysteriously in 1908 without issue, Cixi's infant grand-nephew, Puyi, became the Xuantong emperor (1909–1912) under a conservative regent, Prince Qing.[10] Three years later the dynasty fell.

Despite a flurry of desperate changes during the last decade of Manchu rule, the striking feature of the traditional Chinese state in Qing times was its capacity to accommodate change without fundamental disruption, to restore homeostatic balance. One crucial reason for this success was a highly evolved governmental structure that maintained central authority and at least the illusion of comprehensive rule, despite its superficiality and surprising administrative flexibility.

IMPERIAL RULE AND METROPOLITAN OFFICES

In its broad outlines, and in most specific respects, the government of the Manchus was patterned consciously on the Ming model. At the top stood the emperor, the Son of Heaven (*tianzi*) and supreme executive of the Chinese state. He was the mediator between Heaven and Earth—less than a god, but more than a mere mortal—the arbiter of all human affairs. He served, in the well-chosen words of John Fairbank, as "conqueror and patriarch, theocratic ritualist, ethical exemplar, lawgiver and judge, commander-in-chief and patron of arts and letters, and all the time administrator of the empire."[11] To play these roles effectively required a ruler of heroic talent and energy, and one of the most remarkable features of the Qing dynasty is simply that several such individuals managed to materialize in the seventeenth and eighteenth centuries.

The Qing emperors were more than simply the stewards of the Middle Kingdom; they also boasted universalistic pretensions as the rulers of "all under Heaven." This self-image can be traced in part to a long-standing Chinese conceit: the idea of a sage-king with all-encompassing moral authority who held sway over an "empire without neighbors." But it received powerful reinforcement in the Qing period from two more militant (and non-Chinese) conceptions of rulership, both of which shaped the identity and actions of China's Manchu monarchs to a significant degree. One was the idea of Inner Asian khanship—sustained historically by "fairly regular" engagements in battle, expressed in metaphors of slave ownership, and dependent upon tribal or lineage leaders for corporate support. The other was the Buddhist concept of a cakravartin ("wheel-turning") king—that is, a religious leader who by his worldly activism (including militant expansion of the empire) "moves the wheel of time and brings the universe closer to the ages of salvation." These two mutually reinforcing concepts invested Qing despotism with a distinctive Inner Asian flavor.[12]

Most Qing emperors labored long hours, from dawn to dusk. Memorials from high-ranking provincial and metropolitan officials, sometimes over a hundred a day, had to be read and acted upon. Emperors met every morning with officials and advisers to formulate domestic and foreign policies. During the rebellion of Wu Sangui in the 1670s, the Kangxi emperor handled as many as five hundred items of business a day and could not retire to bed until midnight. Both publicly and privately, the Qing rulers spoke often of the heavy burdens of their office and the enormous responsibilities involved in "giving life to people and killing people."[13]

Huge amounts of time were consumed by ceremonial activities, from mundane life-cycle rituals to solemn sacrifices of truly cosmic significance. The ritual role of the emperor was of special importance to the conduct of state affairs, for it was through his ritual responsibilities that the emperor legitimized his position, promoted confidence among his family members and within the bureaucracy, and inspired awe among the common people. He personally held countless inspections, audiences, and banquets; conferred titles on officials and gods; ratified agreements with foreign dignitaries; received tributary envoys from foreign states; sanctioned the Dalai Lama in Tibet and other religious figures within the realm; conducted state sacrifices to Heaven, Earth, and a host of lesser "deities"; prayed for relief from natural disasters; participated in the worship of his own and other imperial ancestors; oversaw the final stages of the civil and military examinations; and acted as the symbolic head of the imperial clan organization. These and other such ritual activities demanded painstaking and unwavering adherence to long-standing and carefully prescribed ceremonial requirements.[14]

Everything about the imperial institution was designed to foster a sense of awesome power and unapproachable remoteness. Ensconced in the walled, moated, and heavily guarded palace complex known as the Forbidden City, the Qing emperors carried out their daily tasks beyond the sight and sound of commoners. No buildings in the Inner (Manchu) or Outer (Chinese) cities of Beijing proper were permitted to rival those of the Forbidden City in size or splendor, just as no other individual in the entire empire was allowed to wear the special designs that graced the emperor's clothing and other items of personal use. The Forbidden City was itself a symbol of the emperor's unique position at the center of the universe and the apex of the world (see Figure 3.1).[15]

The emperor wrote in red, whereas his officials wrote in black. In audience, he alone faced south, while they faced north. Only the emperor could use the special term *zhen*, meaning "I," "myself." The characters of his personal name were taboo throughout the land, and any reference to the emperor or the imperial will was always separated from, and elevated above, the rest of the lines of any document in which it appeared. Imperial edicts were received with incense and ritual prostrations, and temples were built for the worship of His Majesty. All subjects performed the tra-

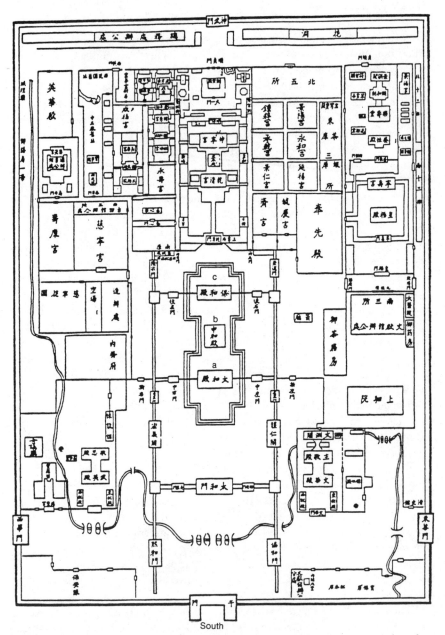

South

Figure 3.1   *The Forbidden City. In this diagram,* a *is the Hall of Supreme Harmony,* b *is the Hall of Central Harmony, and* c *is the Hall of Preserving Harmony. To the north of these Three Great Halls were three corresponding palaces that formed part of the Inner Court, where the Qing emperors lived and worked day to day. Source: Herman Koester, "The Palace Museum of Peking,"* Monumenta Serica *2 (1936–1937). Reprinted with permission of* Monumenta Serica.

ditional kowtow (three kneelings and nine prostrations) in the emperor's presence, but by design, few individuals saw him face to face. Contemporary accounts of the emperor's processions outside the Imperial City (i.e., through the Inner and Outer cities of Beijing) and his tours of the provinces attest to the careful cultivation of an imperial aura of sacred splendor and dignified isolation. In fact, the term *sheng* (lit., sacred) was conventionally and rather indiscriminately applied to nearly everything about the emperor, from his appearance and activities to his desires and personal attributes.

In the provinces, however, benign images of sacrality and dignity surrendered to more threatening images of severity and terror. Although the common expression "Heaven is high and the emperor is far away" generally referred to the absence of imperial intervention in most areas of Chinese everyday life, the potential for the emperor and his agents to take harsh and destructive action remained a persistent theme in local folklore. Legends such as the horrifying "Blood River" stories, which told of imperial retribution against arrogant lineage organizations, and tales concerning benevolent officials who were punished for interceding on behalf of local villagers in matters relating to imperial policy, perpetuated the idea of the emperor as a vengeful ruler prepared to destroy any group or individual foolish enough to challenge his authority.[16]

In theory, imperial power was absolute—as long as the emperor ruled by virtue. The Mandate of Heaven concept, which gave the people the right to rebel against oppressive rule and supported an "ethics of remonstrance" on the part of Chinese officials, encouraged monarchs to be responsible to their constituents. The emperor's sense of accountability to the people can be gauged by the tone of his prayers to Heaven in time of exigency. Consider the following excerpt from a long appeal for relief offered by the Daoguang emperor in the midst of a serious drought:

> Looking up, I consider that Heaven's heart is benevolence and love. The sole cause [of the drought] is the daily deeper atrocity of my sins. ... Hence I have been unable to move Heaven's heart and bring down abundant blessings. ... [I ask myself whether] I have become remiss in attending to the affairs of government; ... whether in the appointment of officers, I have failed to obtain fit persons; ... whether punishments have been unjustly inflicted; ... whether the oppressed have found no means of appeal; ... whether in persecuting heterodox sects the innocent have been involved; ... whether in the successive military operations on the western frontiers there may have been the horrors of human slaughter for the sake of imperial rewards. ... Prostrate I beg Imperial Heaven to pardon my ignorance and stupidity, and to grant me self-renovation, for myriads of innocent people are involved [in this drought because of me].[17]

The emperor's power was not only constrained by this general sense of accountability. It was also limited by his workload and personal abilities as well as by tradition, precedent, factionalism, and simple bureaucratic inertia. Even the most energetic and intelligent of the Qing emperors needed help in running the show.

Without able and efficient advisers at the top, the best-laid plans of rulers could easily become derailed. Beatrice Bartlett's careful study of imperial policy-making concludes that although China's eighteenth-century monarchs "retained all the powers that we ordinarily think of as imperial powers," they preferred to consult with their highest-ranking ministers and "tended not to exercise their decision-making authority alone." To be certain, the ministers remained dependent on imperial authorization of their objectives; but "ministerial cooperation was also essential to most imperial plans."[18]

Family obligations imposed another practical limitation on the ruler's power. Few emperors were inclined to alter the policies of their ancestors without careful consideration, and filial piety proved to be a formidable factor in imperial politics. The dedication of imperial sons to their mothers might simply take the form of extravagant and costly displays of indulgence (such as those of the Qianlong emperor, who took his mother on extended tours to South China and built lavish monuments to her).[19] But filial devotion might also allow empresses dowager to wield considerable influence in affairs of state.

The most dramatic illustration of this phenomenon in the Qing period was the rise to power of Yehenala, the biological mother of the young boy who became the Tongzhi emperor. When the Xianfeng emperor died in late 1861, Yehenala became the Empress Dowager Cixi, and with the support of the new emperor's brother, she engineered a coup d'état and assumed the reins of government directly. After the Tongzhi emperor's death, she manipulated the laws of dynastic succession in order to place her infant nephew on the throne and then adopted him as her son. This tactic solidified Cixi's position by forcing the Guangxu emperor to treat her with filial respect and deference. Even after the emperor attained majority, Cixi continued to play an active role in imperial politics, using the demands of filial piety as a tool in her ongoing struggle with her adopted son.[20]

Although the Qing emperors (and empresses) fully accepted the ritual symbolism and traditional values undergirding the Chinese imperial institution, they never completely abandoned their ethnic identity as Manchus. Indeed, they anxiously sought to preserve at least a measure of their cultural distinctiveness by prohibiting the Chinese practice of footbinding among Manchu women, by outlawing intermarriage between Manchus and Chinese, by maintaining a homeland base in Manchuria, and by keeping intact the native Manchu military system known as the Eight Banners (see Figure 3.2). In addition, the Manchus promoted certain tribal customs (such as shamanism), encouraged Manchu-style education among members of the imperial clan, and often gave Manchus preferential treatment in official appointments, under the law, in the examinations, and in many other areas.

The effectiveness and rigor with which these policies were pursued varied over time, but they served as a constant reminder to the Manchus of their precarious position as alien conquerors. This awareness tended to encourage them to ally with the most culturally conservative elements in Chinese society because they had originally justified their rule by proclaiming themselves to be the protectors of China's cultural

Figure 3.2   Manchu Bannerman. Photo courtesy of the Peabody & Essex Museum, Salem, Mass.

heritage. The alien origins of the Manchus and their cultural conservatism created insurmountable problems for the dynasty in the last decades of Qing rule.

The day-to-day personal and administrative needs of the Qing Inner Court were met by the Imperial Household Department—a kind of private minigovernment within the Forbidden City staffed primarily by imperial bondservants. Among the most important of its numerous subdepartments were the Office of Ceremonial and the Office of the Privy Purse.[21] Figure 3.3 indicates the relationship of the imperial, metropolitan, and provincial departments to be discussed.

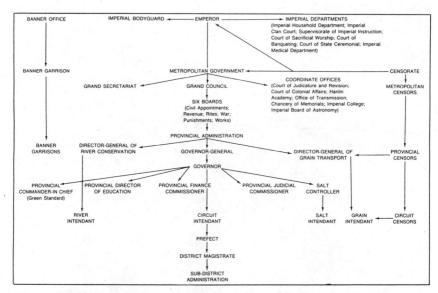

Figure 3.3   The Qing Bureaucracy. Source: Adapted from Yishan Xiao (1967) and Immanuel C.Y. Hsü (1990).

The Office of Ceremonial, as its name suggests, regulated the sacrificial and other ritual observances of the Inner Court. In addition, it managed the affairs of the imperial harem and controlled the eunuchs, who served in menial positions within the harem and elsewhere in the Forbidden City. Unlike the Ming emperors, who employed tens of thousands of eunuchs in various administrative capacities and who often surrendered substantial power to them, the Qing emperors retained only a few hundred and kept them under close supervision. As the Kangxi emperor once remarked: "Eunuchs are basically *yin* in nature. They are quite different from ordinary people. ... In my court I never let them get involved with government—even the few eunuchs-of-the-presence with whom I might chatter or exchange family jokes ... [are] never allowed to discuss politics." Still, by virtue of their closeness to the emperor and to imperial concubines, eunuchs in the Qing period, such as the notorious Li Lianying (d. 1911), might exert considerable political influence.[22]

The Office of the Privy Purse handled the Imperial Household Department's financial affairs. It derived revenue directly from the management of imperial estates in Manchuria and around Beijing, from the ginseng trade and other commercial operations, from the collection of customs revenue and foreign tribute, from loans to merchants, and from the expropriation of private property. These resources not only sustained the emperor, his family, and his entourage in proper imperial fashion but also provided occasional funds for charitable purposes, such as disaster relief, and for rewards to meritorious officials. In addition, the Office of the Privy Purse supplied money for military campaigns and for public-works projects. Its primary purpose, however, remained the maintenance of the imperial establishment and all its opulence.

Several other formal and informal Inner Court agencies attended to the emperor's personal, familial, and administrative needs. These included the Imperial Clan Court, the Department of the Imperial Bodyguard, and the Banner Office. As a general rule, administrative responsibility for the affairs of the Manchu ruling house and the multiethnic Banner military organization lay outside of the regular bureaucratic apparatus, creating an extra echelon of imperial government. At this level, the Manchu language gave the Qing rulers a special channel of privileged information regarding secret or sensitive matters of state.[23]

During the Qianlong reign and thereafter, the Grand Council emerged as the most important advisory agency within the Inner Court. It was established in the late 1720s as an auxiliary office to assist the Yongzheng emperor in conducting military operations. The prestigious grand councillors, ranging anywhere from four to twelve officials but usually averaging around a half dozen, met at least once a day with the emperor to discuss all aspects of imperial administration. As the emperor's most trusted bureaucratic assistants, the grand councillors read secret palace memorials, recommended policies, drafted edicts, and carried out the imperial will by issuing orders to other governmental agencies within the regular bureaucracy.[24]

The Outer Court consisted of various bureaucratic agencies inherited from the Ming dynasty. Of these, the Grand Secretariat occupied a position of paramount importance, at least until it was eclipsed as a formal advisory body by the Grand Council. Although located far from the emperor in a distant southeastern corner of the palace complex, the grand secretaries of the pre-Qianlong era were high-ranking dignitaries who straddled the Outer and Inner Courts. From the Qianlong reign onward, however, they had power only by virtue of their concurrent appointments. The Grand Secretariat's functions then became highly routinized and relatively unimportant from the standpoint of imperial policymaking—even after the Jiaqing emperor attempted to limit the power and scope of the Grand Council in the aftermath of the Heshen affair.[25]

Below the Grand Secretariat stood the Six Boards: (1) Civil Appointments, (2) Revenue, (3) Rites, (4) War, (5) Punishments, and (6) Works. These overlapping organs were responsible for the routine administration of the empire at the central governmental level. Each organization had its equivalent at lower bureaucratic echelons all the way down to the district or county. Even the Qing law code was divided into these six categories. The heads of the Six Boards had no authority to issue direct orders, however, and the lines of communication between them were often hopelessly crossed. The result, according to one highly critical Chinese historian, was that the autocratic Qing emperors "freed themselves completely" from the influence of the Six Boards.[26]

The Board of Civil Appointments was first among the Six Boards. It was responsible for most matters relating to the appointment, evaluation, promotion, demotion, transfer, and dismissal of officials in the 20,000-man metropolitan and provincial civil bureaucracy. Although Qing personnel administration was highly complex and not always bureaucratically "rational," on the whole the Board of Civil Appointments proved remarkably successful in establishing uniform standards for the appointment, evaluation, and discipline of both metropolitan and provincial officials. Particularly noteworthy as a control mechanism was the sophisticated Qing system of administrative sanctions embodied in the dynasty's *Chufen zeli* (Regulations on Administrative Punishment).[27]

The Board of Revenue, second in rank, held responsibility for empire-wide population and land registration; regulation of coinage; collection of duties, taxes, and grain tribute from the provinces; payment of salaries and stipends to officials and nobles; support of the military establishment; audits of central government and provincial treasuries and granaries; supervision of commerce, industry, state monopolies, and communications; and management of certain special administrative tasks relating to personnel and judicial affairs. Despite its wide-ranging bureaucratic scope and access to detailed economic information, the Board of Revenue—like the Qing government as a whole—confined its activities primarily to developing state revenue, promoting stability, and maintaining political power and control (see Table 3.1). As E-tu Zen Sun has recently shown, the board's limited ability to regulate and direct the private sectors of the Chinese economy determined its cooperative and conciliatory approach to the enterprises in which the state had a strategic stake.[28]

The Board of Rites, although ranked only third among the Six Boards, had extremely weighty responsibilities. One of its four major departments, the Department of Ceremonies, handled regular court ritual, the examination system, regulations regarding official dress and other marks of status, forms of etiquette between various ranks, and forms of written communication. The Department of Sacrifices oversaw state sacrifices, funerals, the dispensing of posthumous rewards, and, in conjunction with the Imperial Bureau of Astronomy, the editing of the Imperial Calendar (*Shixian li* or *Shixian shu*).[29] The Reception Department managed the highly ritualized tributary system of China's foreign relations, as well as the giving of gifts to officials and other miscellaneous activities. The Banqueting Department, as its name implies, was responsible for the preparation of food for banquets and sacrifices. Breaches of etiquette in any of these realms were punished by law.

Closely associated with the Board of Rites, and at times during the Qing period directly attached to it, were three "courts": the Court of Sacrificial Worship, in charge of all state sacrifices performed directly by the emperor or his appointed deputies; the Court of Banqueting, responsible for providing food and drink for special ritual occasions, including tributary feasts; and the Court of State Ceremonial, charged with the task of instructing guests at banquets in proper observances. A Board of Music also fell under the general direction of the Board of Rites, indicating the central importance of music to nearly all forms of Chinese ritual activity.[30]

The Board of War supervised various military rituals, but its major responsibilities were the instruction and maintenance of the Chinese constabulary known as the

Table 3.1   Central Government Revenue and Expenditures (1899)

Category	Millions of Taels
Revenue	
Land-poll tax	24.0
Wastage allowance (*huohao*)	2.5
Tribute grain commutation and allowance	2.5
Salt taxes	13.5
Likin tax (instituted in 1853 on goods in transit)	16.5
Customs	26.6
Native opium tax	1.8
Others	1.0
TOTAL	88.4
Expenditures	
Provincial administration	9.1
Foreign loans	24.0
Army	31.0
Navy	5.0
Customs administration and services	3.6
River conservancy	2.5
Frontier defense	2.0
Imperial household	1.0
Legations	1.0
Railways	0.8
Miscellaneous expenses	21.0
TOTAL	101.0

SOURCE: Adapted from Immanuel C.Y. Hsü (1990). This breakdown obviously includes sources of revenue and expenses that were not always as significant. Prior to the nineteenth century, for example, the central government received a far smaller share of its revenue from foreign customs and none at all from the likin transit tax. In the earlier period, however, the central government did not have to pay for railways, customs services (such as lighthouses), foreign legations, or foreign loans. Throughout the Qing period, military expenses consumed a large share of the central government budget, even when the dynasty had no appreciation of the need to acquire modern Western technology.

Army of the Green Standard. It handled the majority of regular military appointments, dismissals, and transfers, undertook the registration and periodic review of imperial troops, administered the military examinations, dispensed rewards and punishments, played a role in the making of military policy, and managed the dynasty's relay system of official communications. Although most matters relating directly to the Banner armies of the empire were beyond its purview, the Board of War remained responsible for the allocation of about two-thirds of the central government's total expenditures and for the deployment of Green Standard forces to suppress rebellion and maintain local control.[31]

The Board of Punishments provided a symbolic counterpoint to the Board of Rites, since law in traditional China was supposed to be invoked only after ritual had failed. The penal emphasis of Chinese law was reflected not only in the title of the Board of Punishments but also in the contents of the legal code, which was incorporated into the massive *Da Qing huidian* (Collected Statutes of the Great Qing Dynasty) and its supplements. The Board of Punishments often undertook its responsibilities in consultation with representatives from the Court of Revision and the Censorate. Together, these three offices were known as the Three Courts of High Adjudicature.

Routine legal matters flowed through one of the eighteen major departments of the Board of Punishments. These, like the departments in the Board of Revenue, were organized along geographical lines but had responsibilities and jurisdictions that extended beyond provincial boundaries. Various other offices within the Board of Punishments dealt with matters such as judicial review, revision of the legal code, and management of prisons.[32] Although the Chinese legal system had no "due process" in the Western sense, no trial by jury, and no formal representation by counsel, it did at least provide convicted persons with recourse to appeal.

Indeed, the Qing period witnessed the fullest elaboration of the Chinese appellate system—including all-important capital appeals—up to that time. Like so many other aspects of Qing administration, the system of appeals suffered from the pressures imposed by China's eighteenth-century population explosion; yet compared with other contemporary systems of justice, such as those of eighteenth- and nineteenth-century England and America, the Qing capital appeals system was, in Jonathan Ocko's words, "an admirable institution."[33] Even in the late nineteenth century, a time of precipitous dynastic decline, the Chinese criminal justice system "encompassed a broad range of sophisticated procedural and administrative measures designed to convict the guilty and acquit the innocent."[34]

The Board of Works was the lowliest of the Six Boards, yet its functions were vital. In general, the Board of Works maintained all public shrines and temples, imperial tombs, official buildings, military and naval installations, city walls, granaries, treasuries, public timberlands, official communication routes, and government-sponsored dykes, dams, and irrigation systems. In addition it provided military stores and other essential supplies (including copper coins) to appropriate governmental agencies. During most of the eighteenth century, the Board of Works operated quite efficiently. Recent studies conclude, for example, that the Qing state played a significant role in feeding the Chinese population and that the power of the government to affect the movements of the population, to distribute resources among regions, to regulate the use of land and water, and to control the circulation of grain "was a critical factor in the presence or absence of food crises and famines." By the nineteenth century, however, the cumulative effects of population pressure "rendered ineffective the power of the state to perform the same functions of regulation, or at least intervention, that it had apparently done so well in the previous era."[35]

The Six Boards, like all other regular bureaucratic organs (with the noteworthy exception of the Grand Council), fell under the close and continual scrutiny of the Censorate. This long-standing Chinese institution served as the "eyes and ears" of the emperor, providing him with secret information on the activities of civil and military officials at all levels. Although theoretically bound to guide and admonish even the emperor himself, in practice many censors became little more than imperial agents, tools of the autocracy. The dynastic record abounds with examples of noble and upright censors who sacrificed their careers and lives for their principles, but it also indicates that many censors became corrupted by power and ambition and embroiled in destructive factional politics. Moreover, the research of Gao Yihan suggests that the censorial system was not as active and independent outside the capital during the Qing era as it had been in earlier periods of Chinese history.[36]

One last metropolitan institution merits brief discussion: the Court of Colonial Affairs, mentioned briefly in Chapter 2. Unlike most Qing institutions, the Court of Colonial Affairs had no direct historical antecedent. Designed initially to oversee Qing relations with the Mongols, its responsibilities grew along with the expansion of the Chinese empire to embrace not only the areas of Tibet, Mongolia, and Chinese Turkestan but also the management of ethnic minorities within China Proper. In addition, the Court of Colonial Affairs handled China's "special relationship" with Russia, which had the status of neither a colonial dependency nor a tributary state. After 1860, under duress, the Qing government established an Office of Foreign Affairs, known as the Zongli Yamen, to oversee the regular conduct of China's relations with Western nations, including Russia. But this body was only an ad hoc graft on the existing administrative structure; it had no regular institutional status and was viewed by the Qing government as merely a subcommittee of the Grand Council.[37]

ADMINISTRATIVE INTEGRATION

The relationship between the governmental organs at the capital and those in the provinces was extremely complex and maintained by the unceasing flow of documents to and from the throne. Information from provincial officials arrived at Beijing via the imperial postal service in the form of rigidly formalized memorials and petitions. Routine memorials were received by the metropolitan Office of Transmission, which opened, checked, copied, and forwarded them to the agencies concerned and to the Grand Secretariat. The Grand Secretariat, in turn, drafted replies to these memorials for imperial approval. Special palace memorials, first used during the Kangxi reign, were transmitted directly to the emperor through the Chancery of Memorials and were supposed to be initially for his eyes alone. Although the palace-memorial system greatly increased the emperor's personal workload, it also provided him with information that could be used as a check on the regular bureaucracy or as a means of circumventing it altogether.[38]

The emperor also received valuable data from his frequent "business" audiences (*bijian*) with metropolitan and provincial officials. These highly structured, face-to-face encounters not only resulted in the mutual exchange of information but also enhanced the aura of the throne and reinforced bonds of loyalty. In any given interview the subject matter might range broadly. Typically the emperor began by asking about an official's family background and education. Often his questions revolved around examination experiences and scholastic issues. He might even ask officials to recite specific texts from memory—an exercise that usually revealed the prodigious mental powers of both parties. Although some conversations contained idle chit-chat, most focused squarely on administrative issues such as taxation, crops, local control, and especially the quality of other officials.[39]

The following short excerpt from one of Governor Chen Bin's four audiences with the Kangxi emperor in late December 1715 and early January 1716 reveals something of the tone of *bijian* encounters:

> [Emperor]: Do you have anything to say to me?
> [Chen]: On account of Your Majesty's immense grace, I, incompetent as I was, received the appointment as governor of Hunan. Since the province is vast and the responsibility is heavy, I am afraid I have failed in my duty and the people have suffered because of me.
> [Emperor]: How do you compare Hunan with Fujian?
> [Chen]: The people of Hunan rely entirely on their farmland for living ... [and their situation] is very difficult. Fujian province is very mountainous and its land is not sufficient for growing rice. People rely on fishing for their living. Neither province is easily governed. ...
> [Emperor]: Who is the financial commissioner of Hunan?
> [Chen]: Alin [a Manchu].
> [Emperor]: How is his performance as an official?
> [Chen]: He is very competent.
> [Emperor]: He is competent, all right, but I am not sure about his heart [honesty].[40]

Four days later, after receiving his new appointment as governor of Fujian, Chen Bin had his last audience with the emperor. Again, Kangxi asked him about provincial administration:

> [Emperor]: Do you know any good official who doesn't take money?
> [Chen]: Well, speaking of talent and ability, many officials possess such qualities. But offhand I don't dare mention anyone who doesn't take money. I will report to you in a palace memorial as soon as I discover any.
> [Emperor]: All right, [I expect] you [to] report ... on good ones as well as bad ones.[41]

The emperor added that he would not rely solely on Chen's opinions but would make further inquiries in order "to find out the truth." Clearly Kangxi understood how to encourage honest replies from his officials.

The large-scale ceremonial audiences known as *dachao* and *changchao*, which took place at the Hall of Supreme Harmony (Taihe dian) of the Forbidden City, lacked the intimacy of business audiences held in the Inner Court, but they performed another vital function—that of confirming symbolically a world view based upon "notions of order, coherence, hierarchy, and the focal sacrality of the Chinese emperor." In a very real sense, these grand and elaborate rituals, like those of imperial worship (see Chapter 7) contributed to what Angela Zito describes as "the symbolic construction of the King."[42]

Aside from the very general proclamations issued at large-scale audiences to announce joyous events, the imperial will was conveyed to the bureaucracy chiefly by means of edicts, court letters, oral instructions, rescripts, vermillion comments written by the emperor on memorials, and various general circulars. In analogous fashion, provincial officials sent down orders to their subordinates, commented upon petitions and reports, and circulated rules and regulations. At the local level, imperial "yellow posters" and other public announcements informed gentry and literate commoners of official policy. Government business at all levels had to be validated by official seals, which varied according to the department that handled their manufacture, the material used to make them, their design and style of script, their size, designated name, and of course the office to which they were assigned. Some editions of the *Collected Statutes* list twenty-five different official seals for the emperor alone.[43]

The so-called Beijing Gazettes (*Jingbao*) and their provincial counterparts provided a valuable source of information on public policy. Although issued by various publishers under different names, the Beijing Gazettes were alike in that they were supervised by the Communications Department of the Board of War and contained official documents released by the Grand Secretariat or the Grand Council. In the words of a well-informed foreign observer in nineteenth-century China, the Beijing Gazettes were "very generally read and talked about by the gentry and educated people in the cities." In the provinces, thousands of individuals found employment copying and abridging the gazettes for readers who could not afford to purchase complete editions. Circulated both officially and privately, the Beijing Gazettes provided a valuable means of horizontal communication in an empire where vertical communications were generally emphasized.[44]

The most exalted figure in the regular provincial administrative hierarchy was the governor-general (*zongdu,* sometimes translated viceroy). His jurisdiction encompassed at least one, usually two, and sometimes three provinces. Within this wide sphere he supervised and evaluated the work of civil and military officials, reported on provincial finances, and reviewed judicial cases. Below him stood the governor (*xunfu*), charged with the civil and military affairs of a single province. His responsibilities were similar to those of the governor-general, but he also held specific responsibility for overseeing the collection of customs duties, managing the salt administration, superintending the local examination system, and administering the grain tribute system.[45]

The provincial finance commissioner (*buzheng shi,* sometimes translated treasurer) served as a lieutenant governor, with primary responsibility for fiscal administration, the provincial census (taken every ten years), the promulgation of imperial commands, and a wide range of other administrative and judicial tasks. Most routine judicial responsibilities fell to the provincial judicial commissioner (*ancha shi*), who also helped manage the provincial postal system, evaluated officials, and helped supervise the local civil-service examinations. The educational affairs of a province were

generally supervised by a specially appointed officer from Beijing known as the director of education (*xuezheng*).[46]

The lower echelons of provincial administration were divided into a complex hierarchy of geographically based circuits (*dao*), prefectures (*fu*), independent departments (*zhili zhou*) or subprefectures (*zhili ting*), and districts or counties (*xian*). Each
circuit, consisting of two or three prefectures, covered from one-fifth to one-quarter
the area of a province. The intendant (*daotai*) of each had administrative duties similar to those of the governor-general and governor. Some provincial capitals also had
one or more intendants who performed specially designated functions in realms such
as communications, waterworks, military affairs, customs collection, grain tribute,
the salt monopoly, and so forth. After 1842, circuit intendants in newly established
treaty port areas (see Chapter 11) came to assume extremely important roles in diplomacy, intelligence-gathering, military reform, and economic modernization.[47]

At the bottom of the Qing bureaucratic ladder stood the district magistrate
(*xianzhi*), who had direct responsibility for from 100,000 to well over 250,000 people. Horribly overburdened, the magistrate functioned as a kind of mini-emperor,
playing the role of a "father-mother official" to his constituents, undertaking religious and other ritual responsibilities, dispensing justice, maintaining order, sponsoring public works, patronizing local scholarship, and all the while collecting taxes
for the state. In contrast to higher-level functionaries who "ruled other officials,"
magistrates "ruled the people." Reference works such as the *Fuhui quanshu* (Complete Book on Happiness and Benevolence)—of which we now have an excellent English translation—show us how magistrates learned to do their arduous and multifaceted work.[48]

The yamen (office) of the magistrate, which was always located within a walled
city, served as both his residence and workplace. Within this large compound, hundreds of regular administrative personnel and other functionaries might work: the as-
sistant magistrate, the district registrar, educational officials, jail wardens, clerks, and
runners, as well as private secretaries, personal servants, and family retainers. None of
these people, however, came close to matching the magistrate in prestige or power.
Private secretaries (*muyou*) usually enjoyed high status since most were degree holders
like the magistrate, but they did not hold formal positions and had to be content to
act in an advisory capacity. Clerks were usually commoners who had little hope of
obtaining degrees or official rank; they handled routine documentation in each of
the district yamen's six major departments corresponding to the Six Boards at
Beijing. Yamen runners were the lowest functionaries, socially disesteemed and officially classified as *jianmin* ("demeaned" people; see Chapter 4). They served as court
attendants, prison guards, policemen, and tax collectors. Although lacking in formal
authority, they often enjoyed considerable local power, and since they relied upon informal fees for their livelihood, they often found themselves in a position to gouge
the local populace.[49]

Subdistrict administration rested with a variety of institutions that had no formal
legal status. Each basic rural division (*xiang*), market town (*zhen*), and village (*cun*),

for instance, had its own locally "elected" headman or headmen. In order to exert more effective bureaucratic control over these units, however, and to cut across clan lines and other natural divisions in Chinese society, the Qing government also attempted to impose its own artificial administrative order on subdistrict urban and rural areas. These efforts included the tax-collection and registration system known as *lijia* and the similar local security system called *baojia*—both based on decimal groupings of mutually responsible families. The heads of these organizations, usually commoners with some degree of local influence, reported to the magistrate periodically and could be punished by him for inattention to duty.[50]

The effectiveness of such tax-collection and local control systems varied widely from place to place and from time to time during the Qing period. As a rule, however, from the eighteenth century on, district magistrates increasingly assigned local commoners known as constables (*dibao* or *difang*) to urban wards and rural subdivisions within the formalized *lijia* and *baojia* networks to assist or supplant the local heads of these organizations. These unsalaried agents of the magistrate often combined the roles not only of *lijia* and *baojia* headmen but also of yamen runners. They reported crimes, property disputes, fires, magical practices, and other suspicious activities; provided witnesses for inquests; assisted in public-works projects; helped collect taxes; and played a role in the official registration of individual households. Like yamen runners, local constables made their living by levying informal fees and sometimes by outright extortion. During and after the Taiping Rebellion (1850–1864), gentry-led militia organizations known as *tuanlian* (lit., grouping and drilling) began functioning as quasi-official subdistrict administrative organs, assuming not only *baojia* and *lijia* functions but also judicial functions. This development only enhanced the already considerable power of the rural-based gentry class.[51]

For all the state's effort to dominate Chinese society from the district capital and above, successful administration—especially in the countryside—depended on an informal alliance between officialdom and the rural-based gentry (see Chapter 4). Since a district magistrate's bureaucratic reach could not possibly extend directly to the hundreds of villages under his immediate jurisdiction even with the assistance of agents such as constables and runners, he had to rely upon the prestige and authority of the local elite to maintain order and stability. A symbiotic relationship thus developed. Gentry members in rural areas helped assure public security and acted as buffers between the peasantry and officialdom, while urban-based bureaucrats helped to further gentry interests through direct patronage, favorable treatment in taxation and other matters, and provision of official access to higher provincial authority. Just as a balance existed within the district yamen between the state interests represented by the centrally appointed magistrate and his personal secretaries on the one hand, and the local interests represented by clerks, runners, and constables on the other, so a balance existed between the district magistrate and the local gentry class.

The cultural common denominator of both officials and the gentry, and the primary source of their social prestige, was their preparation for, and success in, the civil-service examinations. By Qing times the examination system had become, in

Benjamin Elman's words, "a dominant force" in determining the character of traditional Chinese society.[52] Although lower degrees and even substantive offices might be purchased on occasion, especially in periods of administrative decline, on the whole the Qing examination system provided the major means of bureaucratic mobility and the primary avenue to wealth and power in China until the latter part of the nineteenth century. Women were not eligible for the exams, however; nor were Buddhist and Daoist clergy and various other social groups (see Chapter 4).

The system imposed rigid requirements on candidates for degrees. Success in the examinations demanded diligent application on the part of males from the age of five on. Beginning with primers such as the *Qianzi wen* (Essay of a Thousand Characters), students went on to memorize the so-called Four Books and Five Classics—a total of some 430,000 characters. By the age of twelve or so a precocious child might accomplish this feat. Training in calligraphy, poetry composition, and the difficult "eight-legged essay" style followed. In addition, aspirants for degrees had to familiarize themselves with a huge body of classical commentaries, histories, and other essential literary works. Enterprising private publishers produced collections of examination essays designed as a shortcut to study, but few candidates could afford to place sole reliance on such aids for their future well-being.[53]

The Chinese examination system consisted of an elaborate battery of tests at various levels (see Table 3.2). Success in the initial series of tests at the district level, held twice every three years, brought the *shengyuan* ("government student") degree and eligibility for the triennial examinations at the provincial level. Successful candidates at this level won the *juren* ("recommended man") degree and a chance at the coveted metropolitan *jinshi* ("advanced scholar") degree. Those who succeeded at the metropolitan level were ranked in order of excellence and invited to a special congratulatory banquet provided by the Board of Rites.

The last stage in the process was the more or less pro forma palace examination (*dianshi*), held for the top three classes of metropolitan graduates in the Hall of Preserving Harmony in the Forbidden City. The emperor generally presided over this affair with the assistance of various high-ranking civil officials who acted as "readers." In contrast to the brevity of the questions at lower examination levels, the emperor's questions were elaborate and florid in style. The responses of the candidates, in turn, were couched in the self-deprecating language and rigid form of a memorial to the throne. Following the announcement of the results of this examination, a series of banquets and ceremonies ensued, all of which enhanced the prestige of the *jinshi* graduates and served as reminders of status distinctions and obligations. The top *jinshi* were immediately appointed to the Hanlin Academy, where they performed various important editorial, pedagogical, and ritual functions for the emperor. Service in the Hanlin Academy virtually guaranteed metropolitan graduates of rapid promotion in the regular bureaucracy.[54]

The format for the examinations varied over time. For most of the Qing period the testing process at the top two levels consisted of three sessions, each lasting a full day (see Figure 3.4). One focused on classical texts; another emphasized certain types

Table 3.2   The Examination System

Levels of Examination

Preliminary Examinations
   District-level (*xiankao*)
   Prefectural-level (*fukao*)
   Examination for *shengyuan* degree (*yuankao*); district quotas
Provincial Examinations
   Examination for *juren* degree (*xiangshi*) after preliminary test known as *kekao*; district quotas
Metropolitan Examinations
   Major examination known as *huishi* for *jinshi* degree; provincial quotas
   Palace examination (*dianshi*)
   Further examination for specific official appointment (*chaokao*)

Successful Jinshi Candidates, 1890 (by Province)

Beijing	
Manchu Bannermen	9
Mongol Bannermen	4
Chinese Bannermen	7
The Provinces	
Jiangsu	26
Zhili	24
Shandong	22
Jiangxi	22
Fujian	20
Henan	17
Anhui	17
Guangdong	17
Hubei	15
Sichuan	14
Hunan	14
Shaanxi	14
Guangxi	13
Yunnan	12
Guizhou	10
Shanxi	10
Gansu	9
Taiwan	2
TOTAL	298

SOURCE: *NCH,* June 13, 1890; cf. Ping-ti Ho (1962). In 1702 a sliding scale of provincial *jinshi* quotas was instituted, based on the total of participants from each province in the three preceding examinations. This system became virtually frozen, with only minor adjustments during the latter half of the nineteenth century.

of discourse (*lun*); and the third addressed policy questions (*ce*). Except for a brief two-year period during the Oboi regency and another anomalous period from 1901 to 1905, by far the most important session (sometimes divided into two) was the one based on the Four Books and the Five Classics. Although policy discussions always played a part in the formal Qing examination process, they generally counted for lit-

Figure 3.4   Examination Halls. Candidates for the civil-service examinations were confined to these cramped "cells" during the testing period. Photo courtesy of the Peabody & Essex Museum, Salem, Mass.

tle. Moreover, "policy" was often broadly construed. The first policy question of the 1730 metropolitan exams, for instance, centered on the metaphysical attributes of the "Supreme Ultimate" (Taiji; see Chapter 6).[55]

Competition for degrees at all levels was ferocious. Tight government quotas limited the number of successful candidates in each examination. At the metropolitan level, for example, only about three hundred individuals could pass at any given time. Most provinces were allowed a quota of from fifteen to twenty *jinshi* per examination, although some received fewer than ten slots and others had as many as twenty-five. A certain quota was also set aside for Manchu, Mongol, and Chinese bannermen—usually in descending numbers for each group. At the lower levels of examination the quotas were less restrictive. About fifteen hundred *juren* degrees could be granted at one time, and as many as thirty thousand *shengyuan* degrees. Nonetheless, an aspirant for the lowest degree had only about one chance in sixty of success and only one chance in six thousand of ultimately attaining the *jinshi* degree. Candidates often took the examinations many times, and one could not normally hope to acquire the *shengyuan* degree before the age of twenty-four, the *juren* degree before the age of thirty, or the *jinshi* degree before the age of thirty-five.[56]

Furthermore, the best minds of the empire were not always successful, as many frustrated Qing scholars were quick to point out. Although the examination system did create a highly literate, culturally homogeneous elite, it placed a heavy premium on tradition, rote memorization, calligraphic skill, and literary style at the expense of creative thought and independent judgment. In addition, the examiners were often capricious and occasionally corrupt. Cheating scandals plagued the system.[57]

As if this were not enough, Chinese scholars also faced the problem of limited bureaucratic opportunities once they had earned a degree. By design, only a small fraction of the empire's total number of degree holders (over a million during much of the Qing period) could expect to gain one of twenty thousand or so official civil-government positions. *Jinshi* status almost automatically placed an individual in the middle stratum of the nine-rank bureaucracy, which ranged from metropolitan posts such as deputy commissioner in the Office of Transmission (rank 4A) or reader in the Grand Secretariat (rank 4B) to local offices such as circuit intendant (rank 4A), prefect (rank 4B), and district magistrate (rank 7A). But *juren* degree holders could be assured of only the most minor posts, and *shengyuan* had very few opportunities for regular bureaucratic employment. The vast majority of *shengyuan* languished as "lower-gentry" (see Chapter 4), enjoying certain gentry privileges to be sure but forced to "plow with the writing brush" by teaching in local schools or serving as family tutors. Many of these individuals became small tradesmen or entered other "demeaning" occupations in order to sustain themselves.[58]

Yet for all the frustrations of examination life, with its fierce competition and tightly controlled degree quotas, the lure of gentry status and the ultimate possibility of bureaucratic service—with its rich social and financial rewards—kept the vast majority of Qing scholars loyal to the system and the state. Officials, of course, had every reason to support the status quo. But the security-conscious Manchus, outnumbered perhaps 100 to 1 by the Chinese, made an unrelenting effort to ensure administrative control through an elaborate system of checks and balances inherited from the Ming and refined for their own purposes.

One important check on the Qing bureaucracy was the despotic power of the emperor, which reached its apex in the eighteenth century only to sink to its nadir during the nineteenth. Philip Kuhn's absorbing account of the "sorcery scare" of 1768 provides an excellent case study of how the Qianlong emperor used reports of evildoing in the provinces to shake officials out of their administrative complacency and their long-standing patterns of cronyism and self-protection. Yet it also reveals the formidable bureaucratic inertia that rendered his victories at best temporary and incomplete. As Kuhn puts the matter, although bureaucrats "might be picked off one by one by an enraged sovereign, their position as a group was quite secure, and they knew it."[59]

Another feature of the Qing check-and-balance system was the appointment of more or less equal numbers of Manchus and Chinese to head most top-level organs of government and the practice of appointing a careful mixture of Manchus and Chinese to oversee provincial administration. During the first few decades of Qing rule, the Manchus relied heavily on Chinese bannermen (*Hanjun*) to play a leading role in provincial administration, but increasingly thereafter regular Chinese civil officials and Manchus assumed their bureaucratic roles. Typically, a Chinese would serve as a governor, while a Manchu would occupy the position of governor-general.[60]

A third check was the use of Banner forces to maintain military control at the capital and in the provinces. Although outnumbered at least two to one by the 500,000-man Army of the Green Standard (an exclusively Chinese army), the multiethnic Eight Banners were carefully concentrated and positioned to assure them strategic superiority over Chinese forces in China Proper as well as in Inner Asia. Their principal task was, of course, the protection of Beijing and Manchuria, but the Banners also served as a check on the Army of the Green Standard, which was greater in absolute numbers but more fragmented in deployment.

Furthermore, military authority was carefully diffused. Although the governor-general and the governor exercised administrative jurisdiction over regular provincial military forces, they had no authority over Banner garrisons in the provinces, which were commanded by so-called Tartar generals (*jiangjun*). Governors-general and governors, for their part, shared responsibility for the Green Standard troops in their jurisdictions with a military officer entitled the provincial commander-in-chief (*tidu*). As with the civil bureaucracy, the system of shared responsibilities and overlapping jurisdictions contributed to administrative stability but often stifled initiative.[61]

Other Qing checks and balances included the effort to balance regular and irregular (i.e., purchased) bureaucratic appointments, the frequent transfer of officials (usually every three years or less), and rules prohibiting bureaucratic service in one's home area (for example, a district magistrate could not serve in his home district). Ironically, this "rule of avoidance" had somewhat opposite the intended effect, since officials in unfamiliar areas often found it necessary to rely on clerks, runners, constables, and others who had precisely the kinds of local ties and loyalties that the avoidance rule was designed to overcome.[62]

The problem of local ties and conflicting loyalties was evident at all levels of traditional Chinese government and society. As Tom Metzger has noted:

> For all its stress on loyalty and hierarchy, Chinese society has been characterized by a remarkably fluid pattern of betrayal and intrigue. Individuals frequently oscillated between cooperation with the centralized state bureaucracy and support for smaller, often more ascriptive groupings, such as lineages, clubs, cliques, or secret societies, inhibiting political centralization.[63]

Enmeshed in a huge and impersonal bureaucracy, and lacking either institutional or legal protection from imperial caprice, Qing officials—like the rest of Chinese society—sought comfort and security in particularistic personal relationships known colloquially as *guanxi* ("connections").

Many different types of *guanxi* existed in Chinese political and social life, and sometimes these overlapped or intersected to create especially powerful affiliations. The most common relationships included those based on lineage (*qinshu guanxi*), in-law ties (*yinqin guanxi*), family friendships (*shiyi guanxi*), shared home area (*tongxiang guanxi*), educational ties (*shisheng guanxi* or *tongxue guanxi*), and bureaucratic linkages (*liaoshu guanxi* or *tongliao guanxi*). Sworn brothers (*jiebai xiongdi*) enjoyed a special sort of *guanxi,* and even people with the same surname felt a certain affinity with one another. Most forms of *guanxi* implied a superior-inferior relationship in which the junior person owed loyalty, obedience, and respect, while the senior owed protection and assistance in advancement. Gift-giving from juniors to seniors, a reflection of the deep-seated Chinese social principle of "reciprocity" (*bao,* see Chapter 4), naturally solidified these bonds.[64]

Andrew Nathan points out that *guanxi* facilitated cooperation between individuals in traditional China not only by delineating status relationships but also by rendering the behavior of each party predictable, "both with regard to social formalities ... and with regard to potentially critical questions such as what one person had to ask of the other." Predictability and ease of intercourse, in turn, contributed to the establishment of trust. *Guanxi* as a system of "shared attributes" was thus highly formalized and extended well beyond what has been called the "old boy network" of acquaintances in the West. Furthermore, it implied a much stronger sense of responsibility, obligations, and indebtedness. No Qing official could afford to overlook *guanxi* in his political calculations, regardless of the issue at stake.[65]

The particularism of traditional Chinese society also helps explain the system of "organized corruption" within the Qing bureaucracy. To be sure, in part the extraction of revenue in the form of "gifts" from subordinates can be attributed to unrealistically low official salaries and high administrative costs (see Table 3.3). The tenure of most bureaucrats was short, and there were many expenses involved in preparing for an official career. But another factor was assuredly the institutionalized gift-giving that was characteristic of individuals who were related by some form of *guanxi* or who hoped to expand their network of useful acquaintances. Gift-giving was essential to bureaucratic advancement, but the line between voluntary gifts and extortion was not always easy to draw. Even apparently honest officials derived much of their income from presents. According to the records of one late Qing metropolitan official, over 30 percent of the 16,836 taels he received from 1871 to 1889 was in the form of gifts.[66] This amount, of course, would be mere pocket change to someone like Heshen.

Corruption within the bureaucracy was also encouraged by the central government's chaotic fiscal system—as confused as "tangled silk" in the words of a late Qing encyclopedia. Although the central government knew whether its prescribed tax and tribute quotas had been received from the provinces, it had no precise way of determining what sums beyond the quota had been collected and retained by provincial officials. This situation, together with the pressing fiscal needs and inadequate budgets of locally minded officials, fostered the widespread practice of "tax farming" (collecting extra revenue to cover costs or make a profit), which often led to abuse. Efforts by the energetic Yongzheng emperor to reform the cumbersome and corrupt Qing tax system enjoyed a measure of temporary success, but ultimately he failed to overcome deeply entrenched patterns of *guanxi.* Meanwhile, the comparatively small

Table 3.3   Official Salaries

Post	Annual Salary (taels)	Rice Stipend (shi)
Prince of the Blood	10,000	5,000
Duke (First Grade)	700	350
Earl (First Grade)	610	305
Count (First Grade)	510	255
Viscount	410	205
Baron	310	155
Civil official, Grade 1A-B	180	90
Civil official, Grade 2A-B	155	77.5
Civil official, Grade 3A-B	130	65
Civil official, Grade 4A-B	105	52.5
Civil official, Grade 5A-B	80	40
Civil official, Grade 6A-B	60	30
Civil official, Grade 7A-B	45	22.5
Civil official, Grade 8A-B	40	20
Civil official, Grade 9A	33.1	16.5
Civil official, Grade 9B	31.5	15.7

SOURCE: Immanuel C.Y. Hsü (1990). From the early eighteenth century on, Qing officials received a supplementary salary known as *yanglian* (lit., to nourish integrity). Thus, a governor-general (Grade 2A), whose salary was 155 taels, received in addition between 13,000 and 20,000 taels to encourage rectitude. Similarly, at the lower ends of the bureaucratic scale, a district magistrate (Grade 7A), whose salary was about 45 taels, would receive a supplement of from 400 to more than 2,000 taels, depending on the locality in which he served. Even so, unbudgeted administrative costs at all levels perpetuated the system of "customary fees" (*lougui*), which was regulated by local custom but often led to abuses.

amount of revenue received regularly by Beijing made the Qing government, in the words of Dwight Perkins, "an almost unbelievably weak [financial] instrument," especially in the nineteenth century.[67]

Another problem, common to all bureaucracies but especially acute in traditional China, was the double curse of massive paperwork and multifarious regulations. Officials could either drown in a sea of documents or be strangled by red tape. A bewildering variety of documents circulated within the Qing bureaucracy, each a reflection of the relative rank of the correspondents and the type of office involved. The requirements of bureaucratic protocol, and the system of shared responsibilities and overlapping jurisdictions at all levels of government, increased the volume of documents without facilitating the flow. Meanwhile, literal and tedious adherence to a vast number of minutely prescribed administrative rules and regulations imposed a crushing burden on Chinese bureaucrats.

Yet despite the elaborate checks and balances, particularism, corruption, paperwork, and overlegality of Qing administration, it would be wrong to dismiss the traditional Chinese state as nothing more than a ponderous, inflexible, and inefficient monolith. Notwithstanding the Manchu preoccupation with administrative control, it is clear that in practice Beijing allowed considerable leeway to local officials in the handling of affairs within their jurisdictions. Moreover, as a matter of principle many

Qing officials demonstrated what has been aptly characterized by Tom Metzger as a "pervasive moral commitment to flexibility."[68]

Administrative adaptations were often conceived in terms of, and legitimized by, the classical notion of "making adjustments to meet changing conditions" (*biantong*). Respected writers in late imperial China repeatedly emphasized that the essence of statecraft was in making allowances for "human situations." In the words of Wang Huizu (1731–1807), the well-known author of several extremely influential works on Chinese local government, "Law must distinguish between right and wrong, but the situation may allow moderation of the strict standard of right and wrong."[69] Because of this principle, it was always possible for an official to bend regulations in the interest of justice and in the best interests of the state.

Confucian morality remained the paramount consideration in traditional Chinese government—more important than either abstract law or technical specialization in the eyes of most scholar-officials. But Qing administration was not merely a matter of mouthing moral platitudes. Administrative handbooks, encyclopedias, and compilations on statecraft provided much concrete, practical, and valuable guidance for Chinese officials. What is more, in the evaluation of bureaucrats—whether through the annual process known as *kaocheng* or in the triennial reckonings known as *daji* (for provincial officials) and *jingcha* (for metropolitan officials)—the criteria for achievement were also concrete and practical. Personal integrity (*shou*) was important, to be certain, but so were an official's ability (*cai*) and administrative skill (*zheng*). And for all the Chinese government's stress on moral suasion, it also placed a premium on impartiality (*xu*), attention to detail (*xiang*), and carefulness (*shen*).[70]

Even emperors were evaluated posthumously in terms of specific administrative categories. One index is the organization of each major division of the *Shichao shengxun* (Imperial Injunctions of Ten Reigns), which collected various important edicts and decrees of the Qing rulers up through the Tongzhi reign and categorized them according to about forty areas of imperial concern. Taking the imperial injunctions for the Daoguang reign (1821–1850) as illustration, we can see that while considerable space is given to categories such as imperial virtue (*shengde*), imperial filial piety (*shengxiao*), and improvement of moral customs (*hou fengsu*), far more attention is devoted to such categories as military exploits (*wugong*), fiscal administration (*licai*), strictness of law and discipline (*yan faji*), and frontier administration (*ji bianjiang*).[71]

In all, then, Qing government represented a remarkably effective balance between the emperor and the bureaucracy, civil and military rule, central control and local leeway, formal and informal authority, morality and law, idealism and realism, rigidity and flexibility, personalism and impersonality. This balance gave Chinese government great strength and staying power, just as a similar set of balanced elements gave cohesiveness and continuity to Chinese social and economic life.

4

Social and Economic Institutions

$\mathcal{Q}$ing social and economic life naturally reflected many of the attitudes and assumptions underlying Chinese political behavior—notably a concern with hierarchical order, unity and social harmony, moral suasion, bureaucratic supervision, collective responsibility, and group consensus. It also reflected the same persistent tension between the universalistic demands imposed by the state through its laws, rules, and regulations and the powerful particularism of local customs, organizations, and personal connections (*guanxi*). Fei Xiaotong contrasts the "differential mode of association" (*chaxu geju*) in traditional China with the "organizational mode of association" (*tuanti geju*) in the modern West. The former, he maintains, is marked by "distinctive networks spreading out from each individual's personal connections." The latter involves the attachment of individuals to a preexisting structure, and then the formation of personal relationships through that structure.[1]

These two types of social organization reflect two different conceptions of morality, according to Fei. In the West, he says, "people in the same organizations apply universal moral principles to themselves and so regard each other as equals"—at least in theory. In traditional China, however, where society tended to be viewed as "a web woven out of countless personal relationships," each knot in the web became attached to a specific, particularistic ethical principle. In this "self-centered" but not "individualistic" society, relationships "spread out gradually, from individual to individual, resulting in an accumulation of personal connections." The result was that Chinese social morality made sense "only in terms of these personal connections."[2]

A central principle of traditional Chinese social relations was the concept of *bao,* or reciprocity. *Bao* covered all facets of social interaction and served as the rationale behind the highly refined system of gift-giving in China. In the words of the *Record of Ritual,* "Reciprocity is what the rules of propriety value. If I give a gift and nothing comes in return, that is contrary to propriety; if the thing comes to me, and I give nothing in return, that is also contrary to propriety."[3] The object in Chinese life was thus to keep one's obligations in balance, to avoid owing *renqing* (lit., human feelings) to another person.

Renqing covered more than mere sentiment. It referred to the concrete social expressions of "human feelings," such as the offering of congratulations and the giving of gifts on appropriate occasions. As a kind of "social capital" in Chinese interpersonal transactions, *renqing* occupied a position of crucial importance in the cultivation of *guanxi*. Favors dispensed (especially by superiors) required that gifts be given; gifts given implied that favors would be dispensed. The feelings of obligation in traditional Chinese society ran so deep that "even in a case of fulfilment of an official duty, if it happened to be beneficial to a particular person, he would be expected to cherish a sense of indebtedness to the person who was instrumental in the outcome."[4] Thus, for instance, an extremely close relationship was presumed to exist in Qing times between successful examination candidates and the examiners who passed them.

In Chinese economic life the cultivation of *guanxi*—particularly with officials— provided a significant measure of protection for merchants. But not all economic relationships in China involved *renqing*. To the extent that the terms of economic (as opposed to social) exchange were dictated by impersonal market forces, *renqing* had no place or purchase. In fact, Chinese businessmen often left their hometowns to do business far away precisely because it freed them from the particularistic pressures of *guanxi*. Villagers would walk miles to the local market town to do business in an impersonal setting, among relative strangers, rather than exchange goods directly with their neighbors.[5]

Although the particularistic principles of Chinese daily life proved remarkably resistant to change in late imperial times, social and economic conditions did not. In fact, as noted briefly in Chapter 2, during the late Ming dynasty a series of dramatic and far-reaching transformations began to take place in China. These changes included a huge influx of silver from foreign trade; increased urbanization, especially of the lower Yangzi River area (Jiangnan); the commutation of labor services into money payments; the growth of regional and long-distance trade; the emergence of a national market in bulk commodities; increased geographical mobility; the expansion of popular literacy; an increase in the size of the "gentry" (elite) class; the growth of lineage structures in both size and complexity; the professionalization of local managerial activities; and so forth.[6]

These changes contributed to transformations in the style of local politics, in patterns of personal and intellectual affiliation, and ultimately in modes of thought (see Chapter 6). They also created new opportunity structures that "altered the quality of gender relations and expanded the social roles actually assumed by women." By early Qing times,

> the increasingly urbanized society, especially of Jiangnan, saw greater sexual mingling in workplaces such as textile manufacturies, and in recreational sites such as teahouses and wineshops, where women appeared as both employees and customers. The cultural ideal of the sequestered women's quarters (*gui*) was ever more difficult to maintain in practice. Along with this, a new model of the worldly and refined professional courtesan arose ... [and a] new ideal emerged of the "companionate marriage," a love match between men and women who were similarly cultivated and shared aesthetic tastes. This in turn reflected an actual rise in female (and societywide) literacy rates. ... The fiction consumed by this growing reading public

exhibited a new sexual frankness, as well as the glorification of romantic attachments between men and women.[7]

Moreover, accelerated social mobility, a certain blurring of status distinctions, and the movement toward the relaxation of personal dependency bonds—symbolized and substantiated by the Yongzheng emperor's at least partially successful effort to emancipate various categories of "debased" peoples—"gave rise to urges both to reaffirm and reassess the moral imperatives implicit in social roles, especially those of gender."[8] The remarkable thing about these changes is that they occurred within an apparently rigid structure of political, social, and economic institutions. It is remarkable, too, that this structure remained fundamentally intact, despite these disruptions, during most of the Qing period (see also Chapter 10).

SOCIAL CLASSES

Chinese society in late imperial times was highly stratified, with status distinctions that were carefully preserved in the vocabularies of both ritual and law. At the top of the Qing social hierarchy stood two main groups of hereditary nobles: imperial clansmen and civil or military officials granted titles for conspicuous achievement. Members of these status groups received special allowances of property, food, and money, in addition to certain other social and economic privileges, depending on their rank. In a sense, some classes of bannermen outside of the Imperial Household might also be considered "noble" by virtue of special allowances and privileges. Their grants and stipends were quite meager, however, and allocated in a downward sliding scale that differentiated not only between different ranks but also between Manchu, Mongol, and Chinese bannermen of the same rank. By the nineteenth century, most of the once-esteemed Banner forces had been virtually abandoned by the court to become, in Pamela Crossley's apt appropriation of a well-worn Chinese phrase, "orphan warriors."[9]

Civil bureaucrats enjoyed enormous prestige, whether or not they possessed titular nobility. As indicated in Chapter 3, the nine-rank bureaucracy was divided into three strata—an upper level (ranks one through three), a middle level (ranks four through seven), and a lower level (ranks eight and nine). Each of these ranks had two classes, conventionally designated "A" and "B," and each rank had its own official dress, colored hat button, and other marks of status. Officials of the first rank, for example, wore a ruby button, a white crane embroidered on the breast and back of their official robes, and a jade girdle clasp set with rubies. At the other end of the bureaucratic scale, rank nine, officials wore a silver button, a white-tailed jay embroidery square, and a clasp of buffalo horn (see Figure 4.1). In addition to official titles and ranks, which usually graced formal papers, family records, ancestral tablets, and tombstones, the state also granted a variety of distinctions of merit, including the right to ride horseback within the Forbidden City and the right to wear a decorative peacock feather.[10]

Figure 4.1 Mandarin Squares. These bird designs adorned the official dress of bureaucrats holding Qing civil rank from 1 and 2 (top right and bottom right, respectively) to 3 and 4 (top left and bottom left, respectively). Source: Nakagawa (1800).

Figure 4.2   Status Clothing. Official ceremonial dress (left) and the costume of a lower degree holder (right). Source: Kiong [Gong Guyu] (1906).

Government statutes distinguished between ceremonial regulations appropriate for officials, for scholar-gentry, and for commoners. Although officials ranked above scholar-gentry on the Chinese social ladder, in fact the two groups overlapped significantly. In marriage and mourning ceremonies, for example, the ritual stipulations for the first group applied only to officials of the seventh rank and above; lower-ranking officials performed rituals appropriate to the second group, the gentry. Moreover, in public ceremonies at the local level, holders of the *jinshi* and *juren* degrees (the upper gentry) were generally considered equivalent in status to officials of the seventh rank and were therefore included in the first group.[11]

As is apparent, upper-degree holders had a social status at least as exalted as that of lower officials. Even lowly *shengyuan* and holders of various purchased titles such as *jiansheng* (student of the Imperial College) enjoyed social prestige and substantial privilege. As a class, both upper and lower gentry members were entitled to special terms of address, special clothing, and other badges of rank. Degree holders wore gold or silver brocades and fancy embroidery; by statute no commoners were permitted to wear these items (see Figure 4.2). Gentry members also received favorable legal treatment (including immunity from corporal punishment and exemption from being called as witnesses by commoners), official exemption from labor service or the labor service tax, and, above all, easy access to officialdom, which, of course, brought additional advantages and preferential treatment.[12]

One did not need a degree to have influence, however. *Guanxi* could be of decisive importance. Frederic Wakeman has shown by means of parable how elite cultural common denominators gave access to officials and thus provided the key to power holding and power wielding in traditional China. He posits a land dispute between "Mr. Wang, a wealthy but untutored peasant of Jiangsu," and Mr. Chen, a scholar "whose great-grandfather had been a ministry official sixty years earlier." Although Mr. Chen held no official degrees and was therefore not officially a member of the gentry class, "he had been tutored in the Classics as a youth and still spent three hours a day in his small study making modest marginal comments on a text of the *Book of Changes* in his own, rather elegant hand." One afternoon a week, "he would meet eight close comrades at a temple near the district capital. Wine would be heated and served, philosophical papers presented, and—as dusk came on—poems exchanged or a friend's painted scroll admired."

Politically astute, Mr. Chen used his personal connections with these men to resolve the impending law case. His first step was to find the appropriate "middleman"—one of the members of his poetry club who had gotten his examination degree in the same year as the local district magistrate and who thus enjoyed the relationship known as *tongnian* ("same year") *guanxi.* This friend was "most happy to introduce so cultivated a guest as Mr. Ch'en [Chen] to the official the following day over tea." The two men hit it off well:

> The magistrate was also enamored of the *Book of Changes* and impressed by Mr. Ch'en's [Chen's] theories about that classic. As Mr. Ch'en [Chen] was leaving, he asked if he might have the honor of presenting the magistrate with a small painting. ("The antique-dealer claimed it's a Sung [Song] scroll. It's not, of course. But it is quite a good forgery, and I thought Your Excellency might enjoy looking at such a trinket from so worthless a one as myself.") The official was happy to accept, and the two men parted on the best of terms.

When Mr. Wang "discovered that his opponent in the coming lawsuit was an acceptable guest at the judge's own home, he realized how foolhardy he had been and dropped the matter altogether." Later, he paid his own visit to Mr. Chen, "apologizing for having disturbed His Honor" and obsequiously remarking, "A great man does not remember the faults of a petty man" (*daren buji xiaoren guo*).[13]

The social life of the scholarly elite will be treated in greater detail in Chapter 10. For now it is sufficient to note the substantial outlays of money required by the extravagant gentry life-style, which often included lavish parties, large numbers of servants, and expensive hobbies such as the collecting of books and art. Fortunately for most of the Chinese elite, adequate financial resources were within easy reach. Chang Chung-li estimates that at times the gentry class enjoyed a per capita income about sixteen times that of commoners, and other scholars have written about the "huge disparity of income" between degree holders and the masses.[14]

Contrary to stereotype, the gentry class was not simply a landed elite. Although a majority of degree holders did live in rural areas and many were indeed landlords comfortably ensconced in country villas, by the early eighteenth century income derived from local managerial services (such as the mediation of legal disputes, supervision of schools and academies, management of public works and welfare projects, militia organization, and proxy remittance of peasant land and labor taxes to the district yamen clerks) began to replace landed wealth as the key economic underpinning of the gentry class—especially at the lower levels. And for those gentry who were primarily landlords, collusion with officialdom usually enabled them to pay taxes at much lower rates than those applied to middle-level or poor peasants.[15]

Below the scholar-gentry class stood three broad classes of commoners. According to long-standing Chinese usage, they were ranked under scholars (*shi*) in the following order: (1) peasants (*nong*), (2) artisans (*gong*), and (3) merchants (*shang*). Their proportions in society varied according to time and place. One early twentieth-century survey of eighteen districts in North China—an area encompassing 4.5 million people—indicates that about 3 percent of the population was composed of scholars, 2.5 percent of artisans, and 4 percent of merchants and that peasants made up the rest of the population. But a thriving commercial city like Hankou might have 30 percent merchants, 50 percent workers, 5 percent scholars, 5 percent peasants, and 10 percent "marginal elements."[16]

Within any given environment, individuals or families from each status group could be further subdivided according to specific occupation, income, life-style, and local prestige. Sometimes, for example, large property holders might be accorded polite terms of address and special privileges regardless of their education, and on occasion philanthropic commoners (*yimin*) came to be considered philanthropic officials (*yiguan*) because the government had accorded them certain privileges in acknowledgment of their generosity to the state. Similarly, upright elderly people might be officially recognized and socially honored as longevous commoners (*shoumin*) and eventually as longevous officials (*shouguan*). Thus, in certain local ceremonies, wealthy or aged commoners could hold positions of honor and respect right along with the educated elite.[17]

Although rated second on the traditional Chinese social scale, peasants—constituting at least 80 percent of the population in late imperial times—were often exploited and seldom well-educated. Working long hours on the land, at the mercy of the elements, their chances for meaningful social mobility were slim, and many lived on the barest margin of subsistence. In the absence of primogeniture, individual Chinese landholdings were constantly fragmented into small plots averaging at most twenty to thirty *mou* (c. three to five acres) per family in North China and perhaps twelve to fifteen *mou* (c. two to three acres) per family in the South (see Figure 4.3). Holdings of this size, adequate to support a family of five, might be located in several different areas near a given village—a practice that made it difficult for a family to farm the land efficiently.

Relatively few families of any status had landholdings of more than 120 *mou* (c. twenty acres)—the ceiling for economies of scale in the countryside—and good land

Figure 4.3   Agricultural Life. Plowing rice fields (left) and planting rice shoots (right). Source: Nakagawa (1800).

插苗

remained in short supply throughout the Qing era. At any given time, about 30 percent of China's peasant families were tenant farmers and another 20 percent or so were petty landowners who had to work rented land in addition to their own to make ends meet. In South China, tenancy was especially common, but even in some northern areas during the prosperous Qianlong period, at least one-quarter of the rural households were reportedly landless. Because of the relentless pressure on the land and a general shortage of capital, rents were high, and rural interest rates might approach 40 percent or more per year.[18]

Numerous local histories, official memoirs, and other accounts of the Qing period attest to the harshness and brutality of Chinese rural life. Listen to the residents of Tancheng, Shandong, describe conditions in their district during the early Qing: "Tancheng is only a tiny area, and it has long been destitute and ravaged. For thirty years now fields have lain under flood water or weeds; we still cannot bear to speak of all the devastation. On top of this came the famine of 1665; and after the earthquake of 1668 not a single ear of grain was harvested, over half the people were dying of starvation, their homes were all destroyed and ten thousand men and women were crushed to death in the ruins." The district magistrate of the area later remarked, "When I was serving in Tancheng, many people held their lives to be of no value, for the area was so wasted and barren, the common people so poor and had suffered so much, that essentially they knew none of the joys of being alive."[19] Under these conditions, peasants often found it necessary to practice infanticide, and many were forced to sell themselves or members of their families into prostitution or slavery.

It is true, of course, that the times were not always so bad, and peasant welfare obviously varied from place to place, even in the same period. The extension of specialized cultivation into previously underdeveloped agricultural areas during the early Qing brought new economic opportunities to peasant households in these regions. The cultivation of mulberry leaves, for instance—initially concentrated in the silk-producing provinces of Zhejiang, Jiangsu, and Guangdong—expanded rapidly into the new agricultural frontiers of Sichuan, Hunan, and Hubei. Similarly, Sichuan and Taiwan joined Fujian and Guangdong as major sugar cane–producing regions, and tobacco-growing moved northward from Jiangsu, Zhejiang, and Jiangxi to Shanxi, Shaanxi, and Sichuan.[20]

Whether out of ambition or exigency, growing numbers of small peasant producers turned to subsidiary occupations in order to supplement their family income. For them it was a short and relatively easy step from producing raw materials for the growing handicraft sector to becoming a part of that sector. In fact, small rural workshops and peasant homes dominated the processing of many goods, from wine, oil, sugar, and tobacco to cotton cloth, leather products, iron utensils, and other items of daily use. Cottage industry was also responsible for most of China's silk and tea production. To the degree that peasant women played significant roles in home industry and field labor, they enhanced their economic importance and presumably their status within the family.[21]

The term "peasant" thus covered a wide spectrum of rural inhabitants. Local conditions and individual economic circumstances obviously affected the outlook of farm laborers and determined in large measure the extent to which they participated in the ritualized activities and everyday indulgences of the elite. Peasants could not always afford the luxury of close adherence to gentry values, much less a gentry style of life.[22] Nonetheless, it is evident that many characteristic features of the elite viewpoint were closely mirrored in the rituals of Chinese peasant life. One striking indication is the general willingness of peasants to go deeply into debt in order to fulfill the ceremonial requirements of marriage and mourning. These performances "firmly linked China's common people to a national culture through their emulation of local elites."[23]

Artisans—or, more generally, workers—ranked third on the traditional Chinese social scale. Although lower in theoretical status than peasants, they often earned as much, or more, income per capita. In the words of a late Ming scholar (quoted by Gu Yanwu), "Agriculture gives a one-fold return on capital and needs the most labor of all, therefore fools do it. Manufacture provides a two-fold profit and requires a great deal of labor; clever fingers do it." Sidney Gamble's pioneering study of wages for artisans in the Beijing area from 1807 to 1902 indicates an enormous variation in rates of pay, but as a rule the daily income for unskilled laborers seems to have been between one and a half times and twice the cost of their food. Thus, for example, the daily payment for unskilled carpenters and masons in the period from 1877 to 1887 was 160 cash, 100 of which went for food.[24] Skilled laborers naturally earned more.

A wide variety of occupational groups fell under the general designation *gong*: craftsmen such as carpenters, masons, potters, metalworkers, coffin-makers, tailors, and jewelers; manufacturers of commodities such as silk, cotton, tea, paper, cooking oil, furniture, and candles; and service persons such as butchers, barbers, doctors, fortune-tellers, tool-sharpeners, cooks, maids, and marriage brokers (see Figure 4.4). Transport laborers were also considered *gong*, since even peasants avoided, if possible, this "degrading" form of manual activity. Artisans and laborers could be either independent operatives or regular employees of gentry families, merchant families, or the state. Most independent artisans and laborers joined occupational groupings known as "guilds," but these organizations had little in common with their namesakes in the West.[25]

Merchants occupied the lowest position in the formal four-class structure of traditional China, at least in theory. Stigmatized in the official literature as unscrupulous and parasitic, most Chinese merchants were chronically insecure. They lacked the power to command bureaucratic obedience and had little prospect of operating large-scale business without official support. Qing writers generally identified three main types of merchants: simple traders (*zuogu*), brokers (*yaseng*), and wealthy consignment merchants (*keshang*). Lowly street peddlers at one extreme of the commercial spectrum might barely make ends meet, but at the other end the great families of silk, tea, and salt merchants in the late imperial period often amassed huge fortunes and wielded substantial influence.

Figure 4.4   A Late Qing Barber. Here the barber shaves the front of the client's hair after curling the queue above it. Photo courtesy of the Peabody & Essex Museum, Salem, Mass.

Qing policies toward commerce were not as oppressive and intrusive as many scholars have claimed. For the most part, the Chinese government left local markets alone, encouraging self-regulation on the part of merchants. In the early Qing period the government issued brokerage licenses to individuals who assisted the state in regulating trade and tapping commercial wealth. These brokers also provided services for the merchants and used their licenses to control local resources for private gain. Later on, as the Chinese economy expanded, local elites assumed responsibility for collecting taxes in return for the privilege of overseeing the operation of local "benevolent markets"—once again out of economic self-interest. These were only two of several ways that elites could become more directly involved in the financial management of local communities. During the mid-nineteenth century, the Qing government's fiscal crisis compelled it to rely more heavily than in the past on commercial levies (notably the infamous likin [*lijin*] tax); yet once again the throne's response was to look to local merchant organizations for a way to manage the problem.[26]

As should be apparent, the line between scholars and merchants, so clean and clear in theory, became increasingly difficult to draw in practice. Throughout the Qing period, and especially during the nineteenth century, official and gentry families readily engaged in warehousing, moneylending, pawnbroking, and various lucrative wholesale and retail enterprises. Commercialization thus increasingly fused merchants and gentry into what Mary Rankin describes as "a vigorous, numerically expanding elite whose power rested on varying combinations of landownership, trade, usury, and degree holding." Ping-ti Ho writes that during the Qing "the social distinction between officials and rich merchants was more blurred than at any time in Chinese history except for the Mongol Yüan [Yuan] period."[27]

Moreover, rich merchants could always use their wealth to acquire exalted academic-bureaucratic status, either by purchasing degrees (and sometimes substantive positions) or by educating themselves (or their sons) to take the civil-service examinations. Commenting on the access to examination degrees available to merchants in Ming-Qing times, one Chinese scholar, Shen Yao (1798–1840), wrote somewhat hyperbolically: "While in the old days sons of scholars forever remained as scholars, in later times only sons of merchants could become scholars. ... China's center of gravity has tilted towards commerce, and consequently heros and men of intelligence mostly belong to the merchant class."[28]

In the absence of effective barriers to elite status, merchants had no incentive to challenge the existing Confucian social order. On the contrary, they upheld it, drawn by the maxim: "Commerce for profit and scholarship for personal reputation" (*gu wei louli ru wei minggao*). Frederic Wakeman writes:

> Emulating the gentry's status manner on a colossal scale, they [Qing merchants] consumed their capital conspicuously, dissipating the possibility of more productive investments and reaffirming the hegemony of the literati's high culture. There was a uniquely mad and millionarish quality to the "salt fools" ... who lavished fortunes on mechanized toys, Lake T'ai [Tai] rock decorations, and exotic pets, but this was just a magnified perversion of gentry fashion. And for all the squander, families like the Ma clan of salt merchants not only presided over one of the most famous literary salons of the eighteenth century and patronized many of the noted artists of the day, they also amassed private libraries of rare editions which were the envy of the Ch'ien-lung [Qianlong] Emperor.[29]

Through association and especially education, social mobility for all classes remained a distinct possibility in Qing China—certainly more so than in Tokugawa Japan. In the Ming-Qing period as a whole, over 40 percent of the upper-degree holders (*jinshi* and *juren*) reportedly came from families that had not produced an office holder or upper-degree holder in the preceding three generations. It is true that orthodox channels for social mobility were not as open in the Qing as in the Ming, but all classes in China continued to be attracted by the lure of the examinations until their abolition in 1905. Whose ambition would not be at least slightly stirred by the sight of a vermillion flag flying in front of a successful candidate's residence, his name emblazoned in gold for all the neighborhood to see?[30]

Even peasants and artisans hungered after the carrot of social mobility offered by the examination system. The vast majority, of course, had no real possibility of attaining the necessary formal education, which was overwhelmingly private in traditional China and beyond the financial reach of most of the population. Individual tutors, private schools (*sishu*), local academies (*shuyuan*), and Confucian school-temples (*xuegong*) were all closely associated with elite education and normally sustained either by private tuition, private subscriptions, or official subsidies. The families of scholar-officials and rich merchants were naturally the principal beneficiaries of these educational institutions.[31]

At the same time, however, some educational opportunities did exist for the poor and disadvantaged in Qing China—notably charitable schools (*yixue*) and community schools (*shexue*) established by philanthropic individuals or local groups, and sometimes by the government. Although designed in part as a rudimentary device for the ideological indoctrination of the lower classes (including ethnic minorities), such schools also provided the chance for latent academic talent to blossom. There were just enough Chinese-style Horatio Alger success stories to perpetuate a compelling social myth. In the words of Frederick Mote, "The belief in the active possibility of social mobility—perhaps even more than the actual statistical incidence of it—kept the different levels of cultural life coherent and congruent, if not truly identical in quality and character, for each level of life was an active model to be imitated by the one below it." The examinations thus served as a powerful vehicle for the preservation and transmission of China's Confucian cultural heritage.[32]

In addition to the four major classes discussed above, several other Chinese social groups warrant mention. One was the regular Buddhist and Daoist clergy, reported to number in the hundreds of thousands. By late imperial times, Buddhism and Religious Daoism had lost virtually all of the economic and institutional power they had once possessed; only a few prominent monasteries still claimed substantial landholdings and large numbers of clergy (four to five hundred). The great majority of the religious establishments in Qing China were small, poor, and weak (see also Chapter 7).

Lacking adequate financial resources, these institutions provided few social services, aside from sponsoring occasional religious fairs and feasts and putting up pilgrims for the night. Although a number of monasteries and temples boasted libraries and even printing facilities, they played no role at all in the Chinese educational system. In fact, Buddhist books were not even used in the regular curriculum of Chinese schools. The primary function of Buddhist priests and nuns in Chinese society was to undertake various ceremonies and sacrifices connected with ancestor worship and to attend to certain other religious and personal needs of males and females, respectively. Fees for these services, together with solicited and unsolicited donations from pilgrims and lay people, sustained the Buddhist and Daoist establishment. The larger monasteries and temples also derived food and rent from private landholdings.[33]

In China Proper, monks, priests, and nuns had little social standing and even less formal political influence. Aside from a few comparatively well-educated abbots (*fangzhang*), most clergy seem to have been illiterate and uninformed. The majority came from lowly origins. Not a few had originally been sold or given to monasteries as children. An edict issued by the Qianlong emperor in 1739 conveys the throne's low opinion of clerics:

> The ruling princes of old often issued decrees calling for the screening of [Buddhist] monks and Daoist priests. Certainly this was because there was indiscriminate mixture of the good and bad among the Buddhists and Daoists. Those among them who shut themselves [off] from the world to practice secretly the monastic discipline probably number but one or two in a hundred, while those who are idlers and loafers, joining the sangha [monastic community] under false pretenses just to seek for food and clothing, and those who are criminals ... fearing punishment and concealing themselves to escape the clutches of the law, are probably countless.[34]

Monastic rules were often strict and detailed, but apparently seldom followed. And if monastic discipline became intolerable, priests and nuns found it very easy to return to lay life. Given the social composition and protective environment of monasteries and temples, it is not surprising that they occasionally became havens for gamblers, thieves, and vagabonds, as well as rallying points for disaffected members of Chinese society. The colorful history of Baoming temple, on the outskirts of Beijing in the Western Hills, illustrates the way heterodox beliefs and practices could survive in "orthodox" institutional forms.[35]

Although ideologically willing to tolerate Buddhism and Religious Daoism as doctrines that "encourage what is good and reprove what is evil" (in the words of the Jiaqing emperor), the Qing government greatly feared the potential political power of organized religion. As a result, it imposed a number of restrictions on Chinese monastic life. Limitations were placed on the size of the clergy, the number of officially sanctioned monasteries and temples, and the scope of their religious activities. Abbots, monks, priests, and nuns were licensed by the Board of Rites and subject to indirect state supervision. The Qing government's administrative statutes contained a complete scheme of ecclesiastical gradations of rank and authority that conferred a kind of legitimacy on the religious establishment but at the same time subordinated the church to the state and officialdom. The principal supervisory officials of the church, chosen by the local Qing authorities from among the leading abbots of each district and prefecture, were known as religious superiors (*seng lusi* for Buddhists and *dao lusi* for Daoists). These individuals provided the major link between China's secular authorities and the formal priesthood.[36]

Another prominent but disesteemed social group in Qing China was the hereditary Army of the Green Standard. Unlike the Banner Army, which the Manchus originally intended solely as a fighting machine, the Army of the Green Standard by design undertook a variety of diverse and often nonmilitary responsibilities. In addition to meeting the needs of national defense and internal security, soldiers from the Army of the Green Standard provided an escort service for state funds, provisions, and prisoners; guarded granaries, tombs, and city gates; carried out government postal functions; and stood ready to undertake other designated tasks, such as providing labor for public-works projects. Unfortunately, the levels of pay, training, and general morale were low for common soldiers. Although officers of the middle grade and above were transferred regularly in the fashion of civil bureaucrats, the rank and file lived in a designated garrison area with their families for life. This arrangement had the advantage of placing soldiers in an environment where social restraints might operate to keep the men under control and where sons could learn military skills from their fathers. But it was precisely such a situation that bred vested interests and made it possible for underpaid and exploited soldiers to seek nonmilitary occupations in order to support their families.[37]

Officers for the Army of the Green Standard were supposed to be chosen from successful candidates for the military-examination system, which paralleled the civil-service examinations in both levels and degrees. But the military examinations tested physical prowess and required almost no literary ability. Although military degrees brought official gentry status, they were disesteemed by scholars and not necessary for promotion within the army itself. In fact, most officers in the Qing military were not products of the military-examination system, but rather, men who had come up through the ranks. They, like their more esteemed counterparts in the civil bureaucracy, were divided into nine ranks, each distinguished by colored hat buttons, embroidered "mandarin squares," and other official regalia.[38]

With the decline of both the Banner and the Green Standard armies by the end of the eighteenth century, mercenary armies known as *yong* (lit., braves) or *yongying* ("brave battalions") began to shoulder the dynasty's principal military burdens. These armies were organized along highly personalistic lines and usually commanded at the top by Qing civil officials. Comparatively well trained and well paid, *yong* and *yongying* recruits were heavily indoctrinated with Confucian morality. In the management and financing of such mercenary forces, local officials and their gentry advisers enjoyed considerable administrative leeway, but they were never beyond Beijing's reach. The throne's undiminished power of appointment and manipulation of empire-wide finances prevented the emergence of "warlordism" during the Qing period.[39]

At the very bottom of the Qing social ladder were several groups of "demeaned people" (*jianmin*), as distinguished from respectable commoners or "good people" (*liangmin*). Included in this lowly and statistically rather insignificant category were various slaves and indentured servants (such as the "tenant/servants" of Huizhou), entertainers, prostitutes, criminals, government runners, and certain regionally defined groups such as the Subei people of Shanghai, the shed people of the Yangzi Highlands (*bengmin*), the beggars of Jiangsu and Anhui (*gaihu*), the lazy or "fallen" people of Zhejiang (*duomin*), and the boat people of Guangdong (*danhu*). Members of these and related social groups suffered various forms of discrimination, from simple prejudice to unfavorable legal treatment. For much of the Qing period, demeaned people and their descendants could not take the civil-service examinations or intermarry freely with ordinary commoners.[40]

As a rule, the Qing legal code considered demeaned people to be subordinate as a class to ordinary commoners, just as commoners were subordinate to degree holders. It followed, then, that a crime committed by a demeaned person against a commoner had to be punished more severely than the same crime by a commoner against a demeaned person—just as a crime by a commoner against a degree holder brought more severe punishment than the same crime committed by a degree holder against a commoner. In accordance with the spirit of *li,* the relative class status of offender and victim was almost always a factor in determining penalties.[41]

Yet despite the depressed legal status of *jianmin* during the Qing period, a few opportunities for personal advancement did exist. Like lowly eunuchs at court, certain kinds of slaves and indentured servants came to acquire substantial power. This was certainly the case with imperial bondservants such as the rich and famous Cao Yin (1658–1712), reading companion and trusted informant of the Kangxi emperor. But it was also true of some indentured servants (*jiaren*) and permanent attendants (*changsui*) attached to Chinese officials, who, like yamen runners, used their close association with government authority to protect personal investments or peddle influence. Some such servants acquired so much illicit power that they became known as officials (*tangguan*) themselves.[42]

Women also might occasionally break the shackles of traditional Chinese society, despite the fact that there was no generally accepted place for women to display publicly the cultural accomplishments most prized by men. They could not, after all, take the civil or military examinations and were, for the most part, confined to the "inner" social space of the home (see Chapter 10). A common proverb of the Qing period stated baldly: "A woman is virtuous only if she is untalented." In the face of both social prejudices and institutional impediments, women had few attractive career choices.[43] Certainly none of the "six women's service positions" (*liupo*—brokers, matchmakers, sorceresses, "smooth-talkers," doctors, and midwives) brought any social prestige.

Nonetheless, a number of women became accomplished writers and painters in the Qing period, including the poets Cai Wan (1695–1755) and Wang Duan (1793–1839) and the famous landscape artist Chen Shu (1660–1736). Some women, such as Qin Liangyu (d. 1648) and Li Suzhen (d. 1855), led Chinese troops against bandits, rebels, or foreign invaders; and at least a few—notably Lin Puqing (1821–1877)—played active administrative roles. A number of women assisted their husbands in business, and others ran successful enterprises themselves. Recent research by a host of talented scholars has vastly enhanced our understanding of "women's culture" in late imperial China and the ways gender boundaries were constructed and contested.[44]

FORMS OF CHINESE
SOCIOECONOMIC ORGANIZATION

The social groups described in the preceding section operated day to day within a complex network of relationships. The context of these relationships ranged from the formal structure of the state and the informal structure of various nonadministrative urban and rural systems down to the clan and the nuclear family. The Qing government's attitude toward these informal institutions was characteristically ambivalent—at once supportive and suspicious—and always oriented strongly toward the concept of collective responsibility.[45]

Theoretically, the state had nothing to fear from the family (*jia*), which it touted as the model for Chinese society at large. After all, the emperor acted as the father (*fu*) of his subjects (*zi,* lit., children); district magistrates were designated "father-mother officials" (*fumu guan*); and the Chinese people as a whole were considered to be one large family (*dajia*). The problem with the family system from the Qing government's point of view was that it tended to compete for the loyalties of its members with the state and that it affected in fundamental ways the conduct of political as well as social and economic relationships.[46]

The philosophical and religious assumptions that lay behind the Chinese family system will be discussed more fully in subsequent chapters. For now, it should suffice to outline the fundamental features of the system. The organization of the Chinese family was hierarchical, authoritarian, and patrilinear:

> Among the characteristic roles were those of the family head (*jiazhang*)—the senior male and the family's formal representative to the outside world—and the family manager (*dangjia*), who was in charge of the family work and earnings. Although there was a clear distinction between these two roles, in small families the father would have both; with his advancing age and increasing family size the position of family manager was frequently taken over by one of his sons. Brothers had equal rights to family property, the dominant form of ownership, but were also obligated to pool their earnings as long as the family remained intact. The distribution of this property among them was a key element in family division (*fenjia*), which also involved the setting up of separate kitchens for each of the new and now economically independent families.[47]

The theme of Chinese family life (and social life generally) was subordination: the individual to the group, the young to the old, and females to males. Kinship terminology, which reflected specific status rights and nonreciprocal status obligations, was highly refined, with nearly eighty major kinship terms in general usage. The five basic degrees of mourning relationships (*wufu*), which extended outward in ever-

Table 4.1   The Five Degrees of Mourning

Degree and Duration	Representative Relationships
1. *Zhancui* (3 years)	Mourning by a man for his parents By a wife for her husband and husband's parents By a concubine for her "husband" (master)
2. *Zicui* (1 years or less)	By a man for his grandparents, uncle, uncle's wife, spinster aunt, brother, spinster sister, wife, son, daughter-in-law (wife of first-born), nephew, spinster niece, grandson (first-born son of first-born) By a wife for her husband's nephew and husband's spinster niece By a married woman for her parents and grandparents By a concubine for her "husband's" principal wife, his parents, his sons (by the principal wife or other concubines), and her own sons Lesser period of mourning for great-great grandparents within the second degree
3. *Dagong* (9 months)	By a man for his married aunt, married sister, brother's wife, first cousin, daughter-in-law (wife of a younger son or son of a concubine), nephew's wife, married niece, and grandson By a wife for her husband's grandparents, husband's uncle, husband's daughter-in-law, husband's nephew's wife, husband's married niece, and grandson By a married woman for her uncle, uncle's wife, spinster aunt, brother, sister, nephew, spinster niece By a concubine for her grandson
4. *Xiaogong* (5 months)	Includes mourning by a man for his grand-uncle, grand-uncle's wife, spinster grand-aunt, father's first cousin, etc.
5. *Sima* (3 months)	Includes mourning by a man for his great grand-uncle, great grand-uncle's wife, spinster great grand-aunt, married grand-aunt, grandfather's first cousin, grandfather's first cousin's wife, spinster first cousin of grandfather, etc.

SOURCE: Adapted from Chai and Chai (1967). The last two degrees are especially complex and have been considerably abbreviated in the above chart. In all categories, the linkage is through the male line, so that "cousin" means only a father's brother's son, not a father's sister's son or daughter. Also, in practice the actual wearing of mourning clothes was generally considered a duty juniors owed seniors, rather than the reverse.

widening circles, dictated ritual responsibilities within the family and also affected the legal decisions of the state (see Table 4.1).[48]

In the absence of a well-developed system of protective civil or commercial law, kinship bonds of blood, marriage, or adoption were the closest and most reliable ties in traditional Chinese society, even when the relationships were rather far removed from the nuclear family. For this reason, among others, nepotism was a common phenomenon in many urban and rural economic enterprises. We should not assume, however, that financial decisions were predicated only on good faith and benevolent paternalism. Even within the family, economic realities, including the diversification of family labor in response to ever greater competition for land, often made it necessary for households to draw up elaborate written agreements in order to provide for the smooth and efficient administration of family estates. The use of such documents within the family paralleled the employment of oral and written contracts in many other realms of Chinese social and economic life.[49]

Ideally, the Chinese nuclear family, which averaged a little over five persons in the Qing period, was a self-contained and self-sufficient social and economic unit. Extended families of three or more generations under one roof were comparatively rare in traditional China and confined almost exclusively to the well-to-do gentry class and rich merchants, who could afford to support a number of nonproductive family members and a large retinue of servants. Families with four or five generations living together enjoyed a great deal of social prestige and sometimes received ritual recognition from the state in the form of impressive memorial arches.

In both nuclear families and extended families, relatives were expected to live together in harmony. Responsibility for the care of the aged and infirm fell primarily on the family unit, which also disciplined and controlled its members. Social values were transmitted and reinforced by informal "family instructions" (*jiaxun*) of this sort:

> Follow parents
> Unite with brothers
> Love kinsmen
> Teach sons
> Provide for marriage
> Maintain the dignity of the women's apartments
> Punish malicious litigation
> Be warned against prostitutes and gamblers
> Establish a household head
> Repair the ancestral temple
> Establish ritual fields
> Preserve ancestral graves.[50]

More formal family rituals (*jiali*)—which the state encouraged elites and commoners alike to follow—reinforced these social values. The enormous strength of the Chinese family system lay precisely in its multifaceted relationship to both religious and secular life.[51]

One illustration of the complexity of this relationship can be seen in the practice of ancestor worship. By late imperial times, domestic ancestor worship had become virtually a cultural universal in China. Even kinship-renouncing Buddhist monks were required by law to observe mourning rites for their parents. Enriched by Confucian, Buddhist, and Religious Daoist ideas, ancestor worship buttressed the Chinese family system not only by cementing social relationships and reinforcing status obligations but also by fostering a profoundly conservative precedent-mindedness at all levels of society. Important decisions within the family, whether made by common peasants or by the emperor himself, required the "consent" of the ancestors, and all major social events were symbolically "shared" with them.[52]

The policies of the Qing government were closely linked to the practice of ancestor worship. On the one hand, the state used negative sanctions to maintain order by addressing the most compelling concerns of the ancestral cult. Rebel leaders, for example, stood the chance of having their entire families wiped out and their ancestral tombs destroyed. Punishments such as mutilation of the body (a gift from one's ancestors) and banishment (detachment from the family and natal community) were clearly designed as deterrents to the filial minded. On the other hand, the state actively supported ancestor worship as a matter of Confucian conviction. Officials were required to withdraw from duty for up to three years of mourning upon the death of a parent, and the Qing legal code even stipulated that criminals convicted of capital offenses might be allowed to receive a greatly reduced penalty and remain at home in order to continue family sacrifices if they were the sole male heirs of deceased parents.[53]

Confucian family values mitigated the law in other significant ways. Punishments, for example, were meted out within the family system according to the five degrees of mourning. These relationships were based on the superiority of the senior generation over the junior generation and of the male over the female. Thus, a son who struck or beat a parent (degree 1 relationship) was liable to decapitation, irrespective of whether or not injury resulted, but no penalty applied to a parent who beat a son (degree 2b) unless the son died. Likewise, a wife who struck her husband (degree 1) received a hundred blows of the heavy bamboo, but a husband who struck his wife (degree 2a) was punished only if he inflicted a significant injury—and then only if the wife personally lodged a complaint with the authorities. Perhaps the most astonishing feature of the Qing code was its stipulation that accusations—even if true—by subordinate members of a family against their superiors would entail legal punishment for the reporter. The false accusation of a father by his son was punished by strangulation, but a true report (except in the case of treason or rebellion) still brought a penalty of three years penal servitude plus one hundred blows of the heavy bamboo.[54]

Jonathan Spence's vivid reconstruction of the "Death of Woman Wang" illustrates some of the social variables that affected legal decisions in Qing dynasty China. In this famous case, a man named Ren killed his wife (née Wang) after she had had an affair with another man and run away from home. Ren then tried to blame the murder on a neighbor named Gao, who had earlier struck him in the face at a temple during an argument about woman Wang. Spence summarizes the disposition of the case by district magistrate Huang Liuhong:

> By Ch'ing [Qing] law, both Jen [Ren] and his father should have received the death penalty for falsely accusing an innocent person of a capital crime. But Huang found massive mitigating circumstances. In the first place, the father had known nothing about the crime; second, he was over seventy and Jen [Ren] was his only son; third, Jen [Ren] himself had no children, so the family line would certainly die out if he was executed; fourth, woman Wang had not followed the *tao* [*dao*] of a wife—she had

betrayed her husband and had deserved to die; fifth, Jen [Ren] had indeed been provoked in the temple by Kao [Gao], who should never have hit him.

The result was that Ren's father was exonerated, and Ren, instead of being executed, was sentenced to be beaten with the heavy bamboo and forced to wear a portable stock or cangue (*jia*) around his neck for a long (and humiliating) period of time. Gao was ordered to pay for woman Wang's funeral expenses in order to placate her spirit and teach him "not to hit people in the face when he lost his temper."[55]

The family relationships expressed in Chinese ritual and law naturally extended into the lineage (*zong*) or, more generally, clan (*zu*), both of which reflected the social assumptions and organizational principles of the Chinese nuclear family. A "lineage" may be defined as an agnatic (patrilinear) descent group with an especially strong corporate character; the less precise term "clan" refers generally to a corporate organization composed of descent groups in which the agnatic links between the constituent units are "extremely remote and most likely fictionalized."[56] For the sake of simplicity, however, I have chosen here to use the more general term "clan" to refer to both types of corporate kinship.

Chinese clans varied widely in size, structure, and influence, but the largest might number as many as ten thousand members and possess enormous corporate wealth. Clan organizations tended to be largest and most highly developed in the Southeast, well organized and widely distributed in the lower and central Yangzi provinces, and rather underdeveloped and thinly distributed in the northern provinces. Naturally enough, the social role of the clan differed substantially from place to place, but in both single-clan and multiclan villages, kinship organization invariably affected the leadership and general tenor of village life.[57]

Chinese clans, dominated in the main by prestigious gentry families but composed of all social classes, undertook social responsibilities that lay beyond the capacity of the nuclear or simple extended family. These responsibilities included providing welfare services, maintaining local order, encouraging economic cooperation, and securing educational opportunities for clan members. The educational role of the clan was particularly important, both in perpetuating the notion of social mobility and in encouraging orthodox social values. Although the conventional view has been that women stood outside the formal structure of Chinese extradomestic descent groups and that they did not exercise jural control over property and other resources, more recent research suggests that they were more than simply "passive reactors who lived in the shadows of an androcentric world."[58]

Clan charitable schools, sustained by revenue derived from clan property, gave poor but promising members the chance to acquire formal education. Part of the motive may have been Confucian altruism and the desire to give meaning to the Confucian dictum that "in education there are no class distinctions." More often than not, however, the motive was probably corporate self-interest. Success in the civil-service examinations did, after all, bring prestige and usually wealth to the clan as a whole, making the investment in worthy candidates from any social class a wise one. Significantly, a number of clans expressly stipulated that educational priority be given to orphans and other poor clan members. In all, charitable schools provided one of the best opportunities in traditional Chinese society for disadvantaged individuals to acquire a formal education.[59]

Clans did more than simply provide formal educational opportunities. They were also an important means of transmitting elite values to all classes of society within the clan. The principal devices were the clan rules (*zonggui*) compiled by the elite for the edification of all clan members. In the main they were Confucian in content, emphasizing family values, community harmony, ritual, respect, and self-control. Most compilations included quotations from the classics, neo-Confucian writings, imperial injunctions (*shengyu*), and other inspirational sources. Although the Qing government officially charged bureaucrats, gentry, and "virtuous and reliable" community elders with the task of periodically lecturing to the Chinese populace on the imperial injunctions as part of its *xiangyue,* or "community compact" system, it is clear that such exercises were often formalistic and ineffective, especially in the nineteenth century. Undoubtedly, regular lectures on the clan rules in clan meetings provided a much more effective channel for the communication of orthodox values to commoners, at least within the clan itself.[60]

Hui-chen Wang Liu has shown that orthodox Confucian values were often adjusted in clan rules to conform more closely to the realities of Chinese everyday life, especially the outlook of commoners. She finds, for example, that many clan rules represented a creative blend of Confucianism, Buddhism, Daoism, and folk religion. Some rules advised members to read Buddhist or Daoist religious tracts, others cited Buddhist authority for sanction, and still others went so far as to allow Buddhist images to be placed next to ancestral tablets in the clan shrine. Through such forms of accommodation, the clan rules—like vernacular literature—provided a convenient meeting point between elite and popular culture.[61]

Clan solidarity and adherence to clan rules were based in part on the clan's ability to impose on its members punishments ranging from reprimands, fines, and suspension of privileges to corporal punishment, expulsion, and even death (although only the state could legally execute individuals). Clan heads (*zuzhang*) used the public format of clan meetings to exert enormous social pressure on members, censuring deviant behavior and rewarding adherence to group norms. Meritorious deeds might be publicly announced, recorded in special "books of virtuous clansmen," or commemorated by clan petitions to the government for honorary plaques or arches. Such plaques and other honors were displayed conspicuously in the ancestral temple, where clan meetings generally took place.

Collective ancestor worship unquestionably provided a strong sense of tradition, group cohesiveness, and conformity within the clan. The ancestral temple, which was usually the largest and most impressive clan building, was more than a mere meeting place; it also served as a constant and powerful reminder of the link between the dead and the living, the past and the present. Tiered rows of spirit tablets, sometimes numbering over a thousand, were organized by generations on the clan ancestral altar. Around them were the honorific plaques and moral exhortations left by clan forefathers that inspired moral behavior and promoted positive ambition among their posterity.

In this environment many collective clan sacrifices and ceremonies took place on important occasions, such as the birth or marriage of clan sons, and on major festival days. These rites, and the clan feasts that followed, helped, in the words of C. K. Yang, "to perpetuate the memory of the traditions and historical sentiments of the group, sustain its moral beliefs, and revivify group consciousness. Through these rites and the presence of the group in its full numerical strength, the clan periodically renewed its sentiments of pride, loyalty, and unity."[62]

The state recognized the positive role of the clan in promoting orthodox values, providing social services, and maintaining local control. At the same time, however, it feared well-organized but nonofficial corporate entities. Thus, on the one hand, the Qing government willingly rewarded meritorious clansmen and exhorted clans to compile genealogies and to establish ancestral shrines, clan schools, and charitable lands (*yitian*). On the other hand, it sought whenever possible to make the clan system an adjunct of the official *baojia* local control apparatus by requiring officially sanctioned clan officers known as *zuzheng* (not to be confused with clan heads) to report on the affairs of their respective clans to the district authorities.[63]

Ultimately, the Qing government was as unsuccessful in imposing direct control over Chinese clans as it was in exerting control over Chinese villages. This is not surprising, since clans and villages were closely related and held together with ties and loyalties that were not totally susceptible to bureaucratic manipulation. Nonetheless, the throne and local bureaucrats never abandoned their effort to limit the political and economic power of clans and to supervise closely their social activities. For all the advantages of clan organization as a self-regulating control mechanism, the particularism of Chinese blood relationships could cause formidable political problems to the state. The massive Taiping Rebellion in the mid-nineteenth century, for example, which resulted in the loss of perhaps 20 million lives, had its origins precisely in the endemic clan conflict of South China.[64]

Many disputes between clans, and social tensions generally, stemmed from economic causes. Often at issue were questions of land ownership, water rights, and related agricultural concerns. Arable land remained a scarce and precious commodity in traditional China, and competition for it was fierce. Qing official land records distinguished several kinds of land, including private land, Banner land, military colony land, imperial estates, ritual land, and so forth. In practice, most of the land in China was privately owned and graded for tax purposes into more than twenty separate classes. The Qing system of land tenure, based on a general freedom to buy and sell land, varied from place to place, depending primarily on productivity. Factors such as soil and climate, transportation facilities, and proximity to markets affected terms of tenure, cropping practices, and the degree of reliance on subsidiary occupations.[65]

Since the tendency of the state was to leave governance of the economy as much as possible to the private sector—and since district magistrates generally proved willing to uphold written agreements—contracts delineating economic and social responsibilities usually assumed a written form in Qing dynasty China. Even in remote villages, written documents governed matters such as the sale and rental of property, the distribution of land rights, the hiring of labor, the pooling and redistribution of resources, and the sale and indenture of human beings. Thus, despite the weakness of the notion of the "rule of law" in China, there was still a respect for certain kinds of legal instruments. In the words of Myron Cohen, throughout the empire "men created, maintained, or severed relationships through contract, which was operative in family life ... as well as in the wider social setting. The use of contract for instrumental purposes must therefore be seen as a fundamental feature of Chinese behavior in general."[66]

Landlordism was especially prevalent in South China—not only because the land was more productive but also because so much property was corporately owned by wealthy clans. As we have seen, in the absence of primogeniture in China, private landownings were often quickly broken up (a process also governed by contracts); but wealth derived from corporately owned property permitted many clans to acquire and maintain their economic power. Naturally enough, this power could generate intense rivalries. Thus, the Qianlong emperor remarked in 1766:

> The ritual land attached to the ancestral halls in the eastern part of Guangdong has frequently caused armed feuds [between clans]. ... Ancestral halls are built and ritual land instituted normally for the purpose of financing the sacrificial rites and supplying the needs of the clansmen. If the land is used lawfully to consolidate and harmonize [kinship relations] ... it is not a bad practice at all. But if [it induces people] to rely on the numerical strength or financial power of their clans, to oppress their fellow villagers, or even worse, to assemble mobs and fight with weapons, ... [such a practice] surely should not be allowed to spread.[67]

The Qing government's response to such abuses of power was to tighten bureaucratic supervision of clans, to punish clan leaders, and even to redistribute clan land.

Chinese landlords, whether individuals, clans, or other corporate entities, extracted rents in money or in kind (see Table 4.2). These rents could amount to well over 50 percent of the yield, while official land taxes averaged only about 5 to 10 percent of the yield. In South China, fixed rents and generally longer leases encouraged farm improvements by tenants, but even in the North, increased inputs of labor allowed agricultural productivity to keep pace with population growth over the long run. Landlord exploitation varied according to place and time, but as a rule it was most acute in periods of dynastic decline and in areas where competition for land was most severe. Throughout most of the Qing period, absentee landlords were a distinct minority, and the physical proximity of peasants and elites, tenants and landlords, encouraged a certain rapport (*ganqing*) between them.[68]

Although direct social contact between elites and commoners was minimal, both groups operated day to day within the shared context of a flourishing rural market

Table 4.2   Some Estimates of Tenancy

			1920s and 1930s
		1880s	Tenant Households as a Percentage of
Province	Owners (%)	Tenants (%)	Peasant Households
Zhili	70	30	11
Henan			20
Shandong	60–90	10–40	20
Shanxi	70	30	16
Shaanxi			18
Gansu	70	30	18
Jiangsu	30–90	10–70	30
Anhui			43
Zhejiang	50	50	41
Hunan			41
Hubei	10–30	70–90	37
Jiangxi			39
Fujian	50	50	42
Guangdong			49
Gangxi			26
Sichuan			53
Guizhou	70	30	44
Yunnan			35
China as a whole			32.1

SOURCES: Chung-li Chang (1962) and Esherick (1981). For some estimates of the purchase price of land in Zhili and land rents in Henan during the 1810s, consult Naquin (1976), appendix 3.

system centered on one of forty thousand or more market towns distributed throughout China Proper. These market towns were linked, in turn, to higher-level markets and finally to major commercial cities. Each basic market town served as the nucleus of a marketing "cell" that typically included between fifteen and twenty-five villages, averaging perhaps one hundred households (about five hundred persons) each. This "standard marketing community," comprising an area of perhaps twenty square miles, allowed all villagers within two or three miles of the town easy access to its periodic markets, held every three days or so. In contrast to officially registered, licensed, and taxed markets at higher levels, lower-level markets generally supported only unlicensed petty brokers, who were self-regulated and self-taxed. Although most sellers (including peasants) at any standard market were likely to be itinerants, the standard market town normally possessed certain permanent facilities, including eating places, teahouses, wineshops, and at least a few shops selling basic items such as oil, incense and candles, looms, needles and thread, and brooms. Normally the town also supported a number of craftsmen and perhaps a few crude workshops for processing local raw materials.[69]

Standard marketing communities were, in the words of G. William Skinner, "the chief tradition-creating and culture-bearing units of rural China." Every few days, "the periodically convened local market drew to the center of social action representatives of households from villages throughout the system, and in so doing facilitated the homogenization of culture within the intervillage community." The standard market town was the major rural focus of extradomestic religious life, recreation, social interaction, and conflict resolution. The marketing community contributed to the integration of local social groups, the standardization of local weights and measures, and linguistic unity. In some respects the marketing system only reinforced China's inveterate localism, but in others it promoted the spread of elite culture throughout Chinese society.[70]

One important reason was the cultural predominance of the gentry in nearly every market town. Landlords (or their agents) regularly dealt with tenant farmers in market towns, and on market days various gentry leaders and aspirants to local leadership "held court" in their favorite teahouses, publicly dispensing wisdom and solving local problems, such as disputes among peasants from different villages. In Skinner's words, the gentry class provided "*de facto* leadership within the marketing community *qua* political system" to which virtually every peasant, petty craftsman, and petty trader in traditional Chinese society belonged. Local villages might well be administratively self-sufficient, as James Hayes has ably shown; but to the extent that villagers participated in the traditional standard market system, they could scarcely avoid exposure to gentry cultural influences.[71]

In higher-level commercial centers, and especially in walled cities, the urban ecology seems to have been characterized by two principal spheres of activity—one for merchants and the other for officials and gentry. Gentry and officials tended to reside and work in or near government yamens, Confucian school temples, and other educational centers, whereas merchants tended to be situated on or near major communication routes—locations determined more by transport costs than by convenience for consumers. Sharpening the distinction between merchant and scholar-official spheres of activity in Chinese cities was the general government prohibition against merchant shops being located too close to the local yamen lest they "spoil its dignity."[72]

In fact, however, the mutual commercial and cultural interests of well-to-do merchants and scholar-officials lessened the gap between the two spheres of activity in China's urban centers. Furthermore, although the style of life and range of diversions in Chinese cities could not possibly be matched in standard market towns, the lack of a sharp urban-rural dichotomy was a striking feature of Chinese culture in late imperial times. Even at the beginning of the twentieth century, "The integrative features of [China's] late imperial polity and society were still present ... and social changes had not yet produced an unbridgeable gap between modern urban centers and the countryside."[73]

Of course William Rowe has a valid point in asserting that Qing dynasty Hankou was in many ways more like an early modern European city than a traditional Chinese one and that the differences between Hankou life-styles and those of the surrounding rural areas were therefore comparatively great. Furthermore, he argues that Hankou shared "many social characteristics ... [with other] important commercial cities throughout the [Chinese] empire." Yet as Rowe himself acknowledges, Hankou had no place in the dynasty's regular administrative hierarchy and was unique (or at least unusual) in a number of other respects. On balance, most Chinese cities bore comparatively little resemblance to urban centers in the early modern West. One difference was certainly their cosmological symbolism, which was based solidly on *yinyang* and five elements correlations (see Chapters 6 and 7). Another was the absence in China of religious structures comparable in size and importance to those in Western cities. Yet another was the lack of class divisions in Chinese neighborhoods. Also significant is the fact that no Chinese building was obviously datable by a particular period style. "Time did not challenge time in the eyes of a wanderer in a city street in traditional China. ... No traditional Chinese city ever had a Romanesque or a Gothic past to be overlaid in a burst of classical renascence, or a Victorian nightmare to be scorned in an age of aggressive functionalism."[74]

In the Qing period as a whole, only about 25 percent of the gentry had permanent urban residences. Although in their capacity as officials members of the scholarly elite necessarily resided in urban areas, the majority came from the countryside and returned to the countryside upon retirement. With the exception of only a few commercial cities, such as Yangzhou, Hankou, and eventually Shanghai, no fundamental differences existed between urban and rural elites regarding basic family structure, housing, dress, eating and drinking habits, transport, and general cultural style. Many famous centers of learning were located in rural areas, as were great libraries and art collections. Just as there was no major gulf between the capital and the provinces in the cultural life of the Chinese elite, so there was no glaring cultural distance between the city and the countryside on the whole. Differences that did exist were primarily differences in degree or intensity rather than kind.[75]

We do see, however, a distinct set of contrasting elite attitudes toward urban-rural relations. In office, Chinese scholars tended to emphasize the civilizing functions of the city; out of office, they esteemed the purity of the rural sector. Institutionally, the elite served predominantly public interests in one capacity and primarily private interests in another. Thus a gentry member might become an upright and incorruptible district magistrate outside his native place, but then return home to the countryside to use his bureaucratic influence and social status to obtain preferential treatment in taxation and to protect kinship interests. As Frederic Wakeman remarks,

> Local social organization ... embodied contrary principles: integration into the imperial system and autonomy from it. The dynamic oscillation between these poles created the unity of Chinese society, not by eliminating the contradictions but by balancing them in such a way as to favor overall order. The balance was expressed in ideal terms as a Confucian compromise between Legalist intervention and complete laissez-faire.[76]

We can observe a similar balance in the Qing government's approach toward corporate organization in urban areas. Clan ties in Chinese cities were comparatively weak, since many, if not most, influential urban residents were sojourners. There were, however, other social entities that embodied similar organizational principles, performed similar services, and posed similar problems to the state. Quite naturally the Qing government tried to control them, but predictably with less than complete success—especially as its power waned dramatically in the nineteenth century.

The most important of these organizations were guilds and religious temple associations. Guilds went by a bewildering variety of names: *hang* (lit., lane), *huiguan* (local lodges or *Landsmannshaften*), *gongsuo* (public associations), *bang* (clique or subguild), and so on. Some were simply units of professional affiliation (trade, crafts, or services); others were business organizations based on geographical affinity (*tongxiang*); still others were primarily hostels for sojourning scholars, officials, or merchants from the same areas. Recent studies on Chinese cities not only reveal the great variety of associational arrangements that existed within these urban centers but also underscore the public (*gong*)—as opposed to either bureaucratic (*guan*) or private (*si*)—functions that they increasingly assumed in the nineteenth century.[77]

Guilds operated as self-governing corporate organizations, analogous in many respects to clans. Commercial guilds, for example, disciplined their members (individuals or businesses) through normative sanctions, fines, and the threat of expulsion; they sponsored business activity and regulated business practices; they mediated disputes among members; and they attempted, when possible, to resist excessive official pressure. Significantly, guild rules were often designed to preserve a stable economic environment by keeping outsiders out and limiting competition through control of prices and even regulation of quality. Guild revenues might be derived from contributions from corporately owned land and houses, rental income, interest from bank deposits, fines, dues, and levies.

Guilds performed a variety of important social functions. Some services were extended only to members, who joined the guild as a contractual act. These services included financial support for individuals and families that had fallen on hard times, family-style burial services and cemeteries for those who died away from home, and sponsorship of feasts and other celebrations. In addition, guilds and other associations—sometimes in combination—often provided services for the wider urban community, such as local policing, fire fighting, disaster relief, welfare (for orphans, the aged, and the poor), health care, education, and local defense. Their efforts paralleled and complemented clan-supported and independent gentry-supported social services in both rural and urban areas—services that were more extensive than generally supposed.[78]

The Qing government naturally applauded and encouraged the self-regulation and social service of guild organizations. At the same time, however, it made every effort to limit the scope of their power. One means of achieving this objective was to supervise certain spheres of Chinese economic activity and attempt to control them. The principal device was a system of formal and informal licensing that allowed Qing bureaucrats to extend monopoly rights to individual entrepreneurs or to guilds for a fee. Sometimes these monopolies were official and comprehensive in scope, such as the so-called Co-hong monopoly on foreign trade at Canton; other arrangements were local and contingent on personal ties and informal agreements. The monopoly mentality was widespread in Chinese economic life. In John Fairbank's memorable words, "The incentive for innovative enterprise, to win a market for new products, had been less than the incentive ... to control a market by paying for an official license to do so. The tradition in China had not been to build a better mousetrap but to get the official mouse monopoly."[79]

The Qing government relied on guild cooperation for the collection of commercial taxes, but guilds depended on official support for commercial success. Although the detailed regulation of much of Chinese trade and industry, as well as the adjustment of disputes within these spheres, fell to organizations of merchants and craftsmen, the guilds were licensed by the state, subject to bureaucratic supervision, and always susceptible to official exploitation. Even in the absence of official pressures, guilds frequently called upon the local Qing authorities to validate their rules and occasionally to assist in enforcing them. Undoubtedly, urban gentry members involved in trade acted periodically as intermediaries between merchants and officials, helping to bridge the gap between commercial and bureaucratic points of view.

Religious temples in cities and towns were often closely linked with guilds and other common-interest organizations such as *hui* (associations) and *tang* (lodges). These societies—whether bound by ties of kinship, surname, home area, profession, scholarly interest, religious outlook, or simply mutual aid—patronized a particular deity, or deities, who were thought to protect the group's special interests and to promote the general welfare of people living and working in the sphere of the deity's specific "jurisdiction." One common focus for such religious patronage was the local Lord of the Earth (Tudi gong). Devotion to this deity involved a degree of community participation as well as special interest: Neighborhood guilds, associations, and lodges often shared responsibility not only for local sacrifices and general upkeep of his temple or shrine but also for local security, neighborhood cleanup and ritual purity, and occasional entertainment such as dramatic presentations and feasts. Religious activity in these urban organizations transcended the particularism of Chinese society more effectively than did ancestor worship in clan organizations, but it was not free from risks.[80]

The state paid close attention to the religious activities of *hui* and *tang*. From the Qing government's standpoint (and often in fact), a thin line separated legitimate associations and lodges from the subversive secret societies that often went by the same generic names. In Qing times there was no Chinese equivalent for the Western term secret society. Traditionally, the expressions *jiaomen* ("sects") and *huitang* ("association lodges") were used to refer to potentially threatening politico-religious cults. In such usage, sects were identified primarily with peasant-based religious organizations in North China, while association lodges were linked more closely with politically oriented organizations in the South based on declassed elements from both urban areas and the countryside (see also Chapter 7).

In general, Chinese secret societies may be defined as associations whose policies were characterized by some form of religious, political, or social dissent from the established order. When dissent became disloyalty, members of such organizations were condemned as heretical (*xie*) and branded bandits (*fei*). The Qing code specified that leaders of "heretical organizations" were to be strangled and their accomplices to receive 100 blows of the heavy bamboo and banishment to a distance of 3,000 *li* (about 1,000 miles). Although some groups, such as the millenarian, anti-Manchu White Lotus sect, seemed especially threatening, heresy was a relative concept—in practice defined by the Qing government more in political and ritual terms than in ideological or theological terms. As a result, even the Longhua sect, which placed great emphasis on Confucian ethics, did not always escape harsh persecution by the state.[81]

It would certainly be a mistake to underestimate the subversive character of certain sectarian associations, notably those of the Triad and White Lotus type. Yet in traditional China, even the most heterodox organizations were susceptible to domestication. Philip Kuhn warns against distinguishing "too sharply between ... [orthodox and heterodox organizations] on grounds of supposed ideological differences"; and as if to underscore Kuhn's point, Frederic Wakeman suggests that the transformation of Zhu Yuanzhang from sectarian leader into founder and first emperor of the Ming dynasty may well have been "eased by certain ideological similarities between rebel heterodoxy and Confucian orthodoxy."[82] Perhaps such ideological affinities, including shared ritual symbols and assumptions, may help explain the endurance of the dynastic system in the face of frequent sectarian uprisings.

In any case, during the heyday of the dynasty, Qing social institutions operated for the most part in mutual interaction and harmonious balance. There was considerable geographic and social mobility as well as a substantial amount of elite-commoner rapport within the traditional land system and market structure. The markets and fairs that brought merchants from dispersed places to a common center "fostered cultural exchange among local systems within the trading area in question," while the travels of successful scholars to far-flung places "increased their social and cultural versatility and enlarged the cultural repertoire from which they could draw upon their return home." Within their wider local market community, peasants were exposed to customs, values, and exogenous norms originating not only in other villages like their own but also in cities—cultural elements "drawn not only from other little traditions but also from the great tradition of the imperial elite." In contrast to many other traditional "peasant communities," local systems in rural China were wide open when the dynasty was at its peak. Social and cultural integration in both the rural and urban sectors was substantial.[83]

But in periods of dynastic decline, local communities in China began to close up. Resistance to exogenous cultural influences arose, and economic closure ensued. Local society became increasingly militarized, and tensions increased between elites and commoners. A *sauve qui peut* mentality prevailed. Urban-rural and gentry-peasant friction increased as gentry power grew, and landlords began to flee the countryside

for the relative security of the cities, leaving rent collection in the hands of impersonal bursaries (*zuzhan*). The rapport that had existed between landlords and tenants
in better times could not possibly be maintained under such circumstances. Social
services probably declined in quality and number. The state used its coercive power
more ruthlessly and perhaps more arbitrarily. This was the unhappy situation Westerners encountered and described in nineteenth- and early twentieth-century China.
It was not invariably so.[84]

𝕝 5 𝕝

Language and
Symbolic Reference

𝓛ike Qing political and social institutions, the Chinese language exemplifies both the diversity and the unity of traditional Chinese culture. On the one hand, the spoken language was fragmented into at least a half dozen mutually unintelligible regional dialects (*diqu fangyan*), each of which had any number of local variants (*difang hua*). On the other hand, the standard written language could be understood by anyone who had mastered it, regardless of the dialect he or she spoke. On balance, the unifying features of the language outweighed the divisive features over time. This chapter is concerned primarily with the classical Chinese written script, the related system of "symbolic reference" embodied in the *Yijing* (Book of Changes), and the role played by both of these media in contributing to the cohesiveness, continuity, and special character of traditional Chinese civilization.

As with other realms of culture, the Chinese language did not remain static over the two and a half centuries of Qing rule. Although comparatively little research has been done on exactly how Chinese speech and writing may have changed under the Manchus, we know that during Qing times, as in earlier (and later) periods of Chinese history, the Han people appropriated a number of words, and perhaps even a few forms of grammatical usage, from other languages, both within and outside of China's borders. One of the most fascinating examples of this phenomenon is the so-called women's script (*nüshu*) of Jiangyong district in southwestern Hunan, which was used exclusively by Chinese women and included a great many non-Han lexical items in its basic syllabary of about 1,000 characters.[1]

Not surprisingly, several Manchu words, such as *sacima* (*saqima,* a pastry made of fried noodles, honey, and butter), found their way into the Chinese spoken and written language. Some scholars have even argued that Manchu usage may have influenced the popularity of certain grammatical forms in Chinese, such as passive voice. During the late nineteenth and early twentieth centuries, foreign terms began to pour into China on a scale unmatched since the introduction of Buddhism. The Chinese (with the help of Western translators) not only coined equivalent words but also "repatriated" a large number of terms initially written in Chinese characters (*Kanji*) by the Japanese, who had created these neologisms during the Meiji Restoration (1868–1912) to accommodate new ideas introduced from the West.[2]

On the whole, however, Chinese remained more resistant to the borrowing of alien terms than Japanese or any other "border" language. Manchu, for instance, acquired far more from Chinese than Chinese gained from it. Furthermore, although many Han bannermen initially learned Manchu as a matter of expediency, ever greater numbers of Manchus learned Chinese. Manchu remained the "official language" of the Qing dynasty, but by the eighteenth century it seems to have been rarely spoken, even at court. It persisted primarily in the written form of official documents and translations of various genres of Chinese literature, from the Confucian Classics to erotic novels.[3]

The *Yijing,* as one of the five Classics, was naturally among the first Chinese works translated into Manchu. Its cryptic system of sixty-four six-line symbols known as hexagrams (*gua*)—although not a language in the formal sense—nonetheless exerted a profound influence on Chinese thought and discourse throughout the imperial era. It explicated meaning through devices such as numerical symbolism, striking and often obscure metaphors, and words that were "indirect but hit the mark" (*yan qu er zhong*). During the Qing period a great many Chinese (and Manchu) scholars wrote tracts on the *Yi* that often read like dictionaries. Scholars argued endlessly over how to understand hexagram names (*guaming*) and how to interpret various numerological and other images in the text. Although interpretations of the work tended to follow scholarly fashions (see Chapter 6), the aim of most Qing scholars was not merely philological; in a very real sense they believed that the *Yijing* held the key to an understanding of the entire universe. For this reason they accepted unquestioningly the notion that Confucius had broken the bindings of his copy three times in assiduous study.[4]

DISTINCTIVE FEATURES OF THE LANGUAGE

A discussion of spoken Chinese need not detain us long. Of the various regional dialects in Qing China, the most widespread and significant was mandarin or *guanhua* (lit., the speech of officials). In Qing times at least 70 percent of the population spoke some version of this "official" dialect as their native tongue, as is still the case today. For this reason, among others, the Chinese words transliterated in this book have been rendered according to their mandarin pronunciation.

The other major regional dialects, in descending order of incidence, were (and still are): Wu (spoken in the provinces of Jiangsu and Zhejiang), Yue (also known as Cantonese), Xiang (Hunan dialect), Kejia (Hakka, spoken primarily in Guangdong, Guangxi, and southern Fujian), Southern Min (Amoy dialect, also known in more recent times as "native Taiwanese"), Gan (Jiangxi dialect), and Northern Min (Fuzhou dialect). According to a recent article by Xu Shirong, the differences among these dialects, taken as a whole, are roughly 20 percent in grammar, 40 percent in vocabulary, and 80 percent in pronunciation.[5] In addition, they vary in their use of tones (*shengdiao*) from four in mandarin to nine (or eleven, depending on how one counts) in Cantonese.

In the Qing period native speakers of mandarin predominated in most of North, West, and Southwest China. But even in areas where mandarin was generally not spoken (primarily the provinces of Zhejiang, Fujian, Guangdong, and Guangxi), scholars had every incentive to learn the mandarin dialect because it served as the lingua franca of Chinese administrators. During the Kangxi period, the emperor ordered the governors of Guangdong and Fujian to establish schools for instruction in mandarin so that officials coming from these areas would be able to communicate more effectively in audience, and eventually the entire Qing system of official schools was limited to candidates already fluent in mandarin. But neither these measures nor any others eliminated the problem of verbal communication at the local level. Since the rule of avoidance prohibited officials from serving in their home areas, they often did not speak the dialect of the region in which they served. Legal proceedings were thus conducted empire-wide in mandarin, with the awkward result that the remarks of Qing magistrates often had to be rendered by translators into the local dialect, and local testimony, in turn, into mandarin.[6]

Despite some regional peculiarities, the grammatical principles of spoken Chinese were (and are) the same, regardless of dialect. The basic semantic units (morphemes) of spoken Chinese are monosyllabic sounds, some of which have meaning by themselves and others of which have meaning only in combination with other monosyllables. For each syllable (with only a few exceptions), a written character exists, but a knowledge of the character is not, of course, necessary for comprehension of everyday speech. The common feature of all major Chinese dialects is that they are not inflected for person, tense, or number. Many words can function unchanged as nouns, verbs, or adjectives, depending on their position in a sentence. Thus, context and word order are of crucial importance.[7]

In mandarin, there are only a little more than four hundred individual sounds, resulting in a great number of homophones. Even with the use of four separate tones as a means of differentiation, there are still many words with precisely the same pronunciation and tone. (One playful linguist has written an entire short story using only words pronounced *shi*; see Figure 5.1.) Through the use of various linguistic devices, including the joining of related morphemes (such as combining *yi* with *fu*, both of which mean clothing, to form the standard compound for clothes, *yifu*), Chinese—like any mature spoken language—can express virtually any idea with full clarity. Nonetheless, the Chinese have long prized the ambiguity of their language, its musical rhythm and tone, and its marvelous capacity for rhymes and puns.[8]

Not surprisingly, Chinese scholars have traditionally devoted much attention to phonology. During the Qing period, phonological scholarship flourished, beginning with the study of rhymes in classics such as the *Shujing* (Book of Poetry) and the *Yijing*, but progressing to the study of phonetic changes in the Chinese language over time and in different regions and eventually extending to an analysis of the human voice itself. Most of the great phonological achievements of the Qing period were made by exponents of the school of learning associated with Dai Zhen (1724–1777) and Duan Yucai (1735–1815); but the critical questioning and careful scholarship of this school had its Qing intellectual antecedents in the work of Gu Yanwu (1613–

These are the first few sentences of a story (unpublished) composed by the well-known Chinese linguist Y. R. Chao. It consists entirely of characters pronounced <u>shi</u> (sounds like "shur") in the mandarin dialect. The text reads horizontally, from left to right. The tones appear to the right of each character. A literal translation follows.

石 (2) 室 (4) 詩 (1) 士 (4) 施 (1) 氏 (4) 嗜 (4) 獅 (1) 誓 (4)
食 (2) 十 (2) 獅 (1) 氏 (4) 時 (2) 適 (4) 市 (4) 視 (4) 獅 (1)
十 (2) 時 (2) 氏 (4) 適 (4) 市 (4) 適 (4) 十 (2) 獅 (1) 適 (4)
市 (4)

Stone Grotto poet, Shi by name, was fond of lions and swore he would eat ten lions. From time to time he went to the market to look at lions. When, at ten o'clock, he went to the market, it happened that ten lions [also] went to the market.

Figure 5.1   Chinese Characters (A).

1682), whose valuable writings include an extremely influential collection entitled *Yinxue wushu* (Five Books on Phonology).[9]

The study of phonology was only part of a broader scholarly interest in linguistics during the Qing. Although some noteworthy studies, such as Dai Zhen's *Fangyu shuzheng* (Commentary on the *Dialects*), were concerned primarily with speech and sounds, the major focus of Qing scholarship was on the classical written language, known as *wenyan wen* ("patterned words"). From Zhou times to the Qing, this literary language served as the primary vehicle for the transmission of China's entire cultural tradition. Throughout the imperial era, familiarity with the classical language in effect defined the Chinese elite. No attribute was more highly prized, none brought greater prestige or social rewards, and none was more closely linked with moral cultivation and personal refinement. In the minds of many, writing was "culture."[10]

The term *wenyan wen* refers to an extremely terse and evocative style of writing found in the great philosophical texts of the Zhou dynasty—notably the Five Classics of Confucianism; hence the term "classical Chinese." Considerable debate exists over the precise relationship between this ancient written language and the patterns of early Chinese speech, but it is safe to say that by Han times at the latest, and from that point onward into the twentieth century, a great social gap separated the "elegant" classical Chinese from the "vulgar" written versions of vernacular speech (*baihua wen*; that is, "unadorned words").

Although vernacular writing and classical Chinese both drew upon the same basic repository of characters (*zi*; written words), they employed them in very different ways. Derk Bodde provides an apt illustration. He compares a famous classical passage from the Confucian philosopher Mencius with a standard vernacular equivalent in order to show the great syntactical and stylistic differences that separate the two types of media. The classical text, for example, requires only twenty-four characters to express what the vernacular version says in thirty-eight. Moreover, these two ver-

Classical original from Mencius:

孟子見梁惠王惠王曰叟不遠千而來亦將有以利
吾國乎 Menzi jian Liang Huiwang. Huiwang yue: Sou buyuan qianli er
lai. Yi jiang you yi li wo guo hu? Mencius had an interview with King Hui of
[the state of] Liang. King Hui said: Venerable sir, you did not find a
thousand li [i.e., a long distance] far to come. Do you also [in addition to
taking the trouble to come here] have something of benefit to my country?

A vernacular rendering of the same:

孟子謁見梁惠王 惠王說老先生您不辭千里長途
的辛勞前來那對我的國家會有很大利益吧
Mengzi yejian Liang Huiwang. Huiwang shuo: Lao xiansheng nin buci
qianli changtu di xinlao qianlai, na dui wo di guojia hui you hen da liyi
ba?

Figure 5.2   Chinese Characters (B). Source: Adapted from Bodde (1991).

sions have a mere thirteen characters in common—five of which occur in proper
names. Aside from these names, the classical characters are monosyllables. By contrast, the vernacular equivalent employs five disyllabic compounds to provide the
clarity necessary for communicating the meaning in speech (see Figure 5.2).[11] The
great prestige of the classical language during imperial times derived in part from the
fact that it was not accessible through everyday speech. Learning it, in other words,
was not simply a matter of replacing spoken sounds with written characters; classical
texts had to be laboriously memorized.

In the Qing, as in earlier periods, Chinese characters had a magical, mystical quality, presumably deriving from their ancient use as inscriptions on oracle bones and on
bronze sacrificial vessels. Many Qing scholars traced Chinese writing to the revered
Yijing. So venerated was the written word that anything with writing on it could not
simply be thrown away but had to be ritually burned. One well-informed foreign observer during the late Qing wrote:

They [the Chinese] literally worship their letters [i.e., characters]. When letters were
invented, they say, heaven rejoiced and hell trembled. Not for any consideration will
they tread on a piece of lettered paper; and to foster this reverence, literary
associations employ agents to go about the street, collect waste paper, and burn it on
an altar with the solemnity of a sacrifice.[12]

These altars, known as Xizi ta (Pagodas for Cherishing the Written Word), could be
found in virtually every city, town, and village in traditional China.

The special reverence attached to Chinese writing may be illustrated in a variety
of other ways. During the Qing period an official could be degraded for miswriting a
single character in a memorial to the throne, and stories of the political and personal

consequences of using taboo or even vaguely suggestive characters are legion. During the Yongzheng reign, for instance, an official named Zha Siting (1664–1727) was imprisoned for selecting a classical phrase for the provincial examinations in Jiangxi province that contained two characters similar in appearance to those of the emperor's reign title if the top portions had been cut off. Qing authorities interpreted this phrase as an expression of Zha's wish that the emperor be decapitated. Zha died in prison, and orders were given for his body to be dismembered.[13]

In Qing popular culture, written characters had a special kind of magical potency, both positive and negative. On the one hand, prayers were often written and then burned as the most efficacious way of communicating with the gods. Protective charms, designed to be hung inside the home or workplace, often consisted only of a single character (or group of characters) with positive associations, such as "peace," "wealth," or "blessings." Auspicious "spring couplets" (*chunlian*), printed on red paper and displayed outside of virtually all Chinese households and businesses during the lunar New Year, had the same basic purpose. On the other hand, many Chinese believed that a piece of paper with the character "to kill" on it, or one that bore the word for a disease, a destructive animal, or an evil spirit, actually had the capacity to harm another person.[14]

The prestige of calligraphy as an art form enhanced the value of the written word in China. Quite apart from spring couplets, calligraphic inscriptions of one sort or another appeared everywhere in traditional Chinese society—from the outside of official buildings, temples, and commercial establishments to homes and landscape gardens. Deceased ancestors were almost always remembered with written tablets rather than images, and calligraphic scrolls adorned every gentry study. Esteem for the written word may even help explain the extraordinary reliance placed on written contracts of all sorts in Qing dynasty China, from agreements over the hiring of labor and the distribution of land rights to negotiations surrounding marriage, concubinage, and adoption.[15]

From a scholarly standpoint, Qing intellectuals looked upon the literary language as "a gateway to the classics," and they were profoundly devoted to it. In addition to works on phonology, the Qing period witnessed a proliferation of linguistic studies on ancient lexicons such as the *Shuowen jiezi* (Analysis of Characters as an Explanation of Writing), as well as the creation of new dictionaries and other etymological and philological research aids. One outstanding achievement was the imperially commissioned *Kangxi zidian* (Kangxi Dictionary), ordered in 1710 and completed about five years later. This work, which became the standard Chinese dictionary for the next two and a half centuries, begins with a quotation from the *Yijing*: "The Great Commentary says, 'In ancient times people knotted cords in order to govern. The sages of a later age used written documents instead to govern officials and supervise the people.'" This quotation testifies to the political importance attached to the written word in China from time immemorial.[16]

Chinese scholars have generally distinguished six major types of Chinese characters: (1) representations of objects (*xiangxing*); (2) indicative characters (*zhishi*),

Types of Characters:

1. Representations of objects (<u>xiangxing</u>): 人 ("person") 口 ("mouth") 日 ("sun") 月 ("moon") 子 ("child")
2. Indicative characters (<u>zhishi</u>): 上 ("up") 下 ("down") 至 ("arrive"; an arrow hitting a target) 高 ("tall"; the picture of a building)
3. Grouped characters (<u>huiyi</u>): 木 ("wood"), together with 斤 ("axe"), becomes 析 ("to split"; "to analyze")
4. Semantic-phonetic combinations (<u>xingsheng</u>): 言 ("words," the semantic element), together with 公 ("public," used here only for its phonetic value, pronounced <u>gong</u>), becomes 訟 ("litigation," pronounced <u>song</u>) (see also Figure 5.5)
5. "Borrowed" words (<u>jiajie</u>): 萬 ("scorpion," used for the word "ten thousand" because it had the same sound, <u>wan</u>)
6. "Transformed" characters (<u>zhuanzhu</u>): 布 ("cloth," used by extension to mean "money" since it was a unit of exchange)

Figure 5.3   Chinese Characters (C).

whose forms indicate meaning; (3) grouped elements (*huiyi*) that suggest meaning through the relationship of concepts; (4) semantic and phonetic combinations (*xingsheng*); (5) "borrowed" words (*jiajie*); and (6) "turned" or "transformed" characters (*zhuanzhu*). (For examples of each, see Figure 5.3.) H. G. Creel points out that many of the characters designated *jiajie* or *zhuanzhu* may also belong to one or more other word classes and that these two groups are themselves "so obscure that nearly two thousand years of discussion have not produced an agreement, among Chinese scholars, even as to the fundamentals of their application." Cheng Chung-ying contends, however, that the principles of phonetic borrowing and semantic extension expressed in these two categories reflect the inherent capacity of the Chinese written language for expressing deep, multidimensional philosophical meaning.[17]

By far the largest class of Chinese characters is that of semantic and phonetic combinations, sometimes called phonograms. Perhaps 90 percent of the lexical items in the *Kangxi Dictionary* are characters of this type. Each has a semantic indicator or "radical" (*bushou;* often originally the representation of an object) and a phonetic element, which can usually stand alone as an individual character with its own set of meanings. The phonetic element indicates the way a written word is probably pronounced, while the radical suggests the category of phenomena to which the word belongs. These categories include animals (humans and other mammals, reptiles, birds, fish, and mythical beasts such as dragons); parts of animals; minerals; natural phenomena and physical formations; structures; utensils; descriptives (colors, shapes, smells, and so on); and actions.[18] (For examples, see Figure 5.4.)

Not all 214 radicals are equally helpful in indicating the meaning of Chinese characters, but most provide fairly reliable and sometimes quite revealing clues. We find,

Some Radicals:

一 yi (one)	二 er (two)	大 da (great)
女 nü (woman)	山 shan (mountain)	弓 gong (bow)
心 xin (heart/mind)	水 shui (water)	火 huo (fire)
玉 yu (jade)	竹 zhu (bamboo)	羊 yang (sheep)
色 se (color)	虎 hu (tiger)	行 xing (movement)
車 che (cart)	門 men (door)	雨 yu (rain)
青 qing (green)	飛 fei (fly)	首 shou (head)
馬 ma (horse)	魚 yu (fish)	龍 long (dragon)

Figure 5.4   Chinese Characters (D).

Characters Pronounced Fang:

舟 ("boat" radical) plus 方 ("square," used as a phonetic)= 舫 ("barge" or "galley")

言 ("speech" radical) plus 方 ("square," used as a phonetic)= 訪 ("to ask" or "invite")

戶 ("door" or "household" radical) plus 方 ("square," used as a phonetic)= 房 ("room" or "house")

木 ("wood" radical) plus 方 ("square," used as a phonetic)= 枋 ("a type of wood")

Figure 5.5   Chinese Characters (E).

for example, that the "boat" radical (*zhou*), together with the phonetic element *fang* (lit., square), represents the idea of a "barge" or "galley" and is pronounced *fang*. The same phonetic joined with the "speech" radical (*yan*) means "to ask" or "to invite" (also pronounced *fang*). With the "door" or "household" radical (*hu*), it means "room" or "house" (again, pronounced *fang*); with the "wood" radical (*mu*), "a type of wood" (*fang*); and so forth (see Figure 5.5).

All sectors of Chinese society were attuned to the composition of written characters. Simply to look up a word in a dictionary like the *Kangxi zidian* required a knowledge of its radical, since all entries were categorized by radicals and listed by the number of strokes they contained in addition to the radical. Even in everyday speech an ambiguous-sounding name or concept might be clarified by reference to its constituent elements—for example, *shuangmu* ("a pair of wood radicals") to indicate the surname "Lin." In the case of Qing scholars, this sensitivity to the makeup of characters was heightened by their active interest in philology. Although most radicals and phonetic elements no longer looked like actual objects, the etymologies provided by ancient lexicons such as the *Shuowen jiezi* often encouraged scholars to think of them in this way. So did more "popular" etymologies, which served as mnemonic devices.[19]

田 <u>tian</u> (field)
富 <u>fu</u> (wealth)
累 <u>lei</u> (embarrassment)

Figure 5.6　Chinese Characters (F).

目 <u>mu</u> (eye)
自 <u>zi</u> (self)
見 <u>jian</u> (see)
貴 <u>gui</u> (honorable)
謝 <u>xie</u> (thanks)
射 <u>she</u> (arrow)
難 <u>nan</u> (difficult)
鞋 <u>xie</u> (shoe)

Figure 5.7　Chinese Characters (G).

The common denominator of scholarly and more popular forms of word analysis was the technique known as "dissecting characters" (*chaizi*). This process, which involved breaking characters down into their constituent elements, had a variety of applications in addition to philology. Fortune-tellers, for instance, commonly used *chaizi* as a means of "fathoming" the future. Clients would either select a character from a preexisting menu of possibilities or write one themselves, whereupon the diviner would derive an interpretation based on the relationship between the radical and the phonetic element of the chosen character, between that character and other characters with similar shapes and sounds, or between characters with common radicals.[20]

Word analysis of this type also found expression in games and riddles. For instance: "What raises its head in embarrassment and lowers it in wealth [contrary to expectations]?" Answer: The character *tian* ("field"), which is at the bottom of the word for "wealth" (*fu*) and at the top of the word for "embarrassment" (*lei*) (see Figure 5.6). Nicknames also grew from this fertile linguistic soil. The scholar Yuan Mei, for instance, came to be called "monkey" because his family name, Yuan, looked and sounded like the word for a certain kind of ape.[21]

A favorite technique in composition was the addition of strokes (*tianbi*) to a character in order to form a new one. By this means, a simple word such as *mu* ("eye") could be transformed into a more complex one, such as *zi* ("self"), *bei* ("shell"), *jian* ("see"), or *gui* ("honorable"). Reducing strokes (*jianbi*) reversed the process, as when *xie* ("thanks") became *she* ("arrow") or, with less precision, *nan* ("difficult") became *xie* ("shoe") (see Figure 5.7). Poets enjoyed composing verses using several characters with the same or related elements, such as the "water" radical, for visual effect, and writers who took pleasure in challenging others to "match couplets" were known to construct lines of as many as twelve characters, each with the same radical.[22]

Wang Baner:

板 ban (lit., board or slab)
木 mu (wood)
反 fan (return)

Figure 5.8   Chinese Characters (H).

士 shi (scholar)
工 gong (artisan)
才 cai (talent)

Figure 5.9   Chinese Characters (I).

Novelists, for their part, often paid close attention to the radicals and phonetic elements in the names of the people and places they wrote about. Thus, we find writers of "how to read" (*dufa*) books on vernacular fiction resorting to the technique of "dissecting characters" in order to explain the meaning of personal or family names. One example would be Wang Baner, grandson of Liu Laolao ("Grannie" Liu) in the novel *Honglou meng* (Dream of the Red Chamber). The late Qing commentator Zhang Xinzhi tells us that the character *ban* in his personal name expresses the idea of "springtime," since it is composed of the radical *mu* ("wood") and the phonetic element *fan* ("to return"), which together suggest "the return of the season of wood [i.e., spring]" (see Figure 5.8).[23]

Word analysis was even employed as a form of argumentation in late imperial China. Thus we find the social distinction between a scholar (*shi*) and an artisan (*gong*) explained in terms of the formation of their respective written characters. "The [person represented by the character] *gong*," we are told, "merely prepares human devices; therefore [the vertical stroke of the character] extends out neither above nor below [as in the character for 'talent' (*cai*)]"; whereas "one who has set his will on the *dao* [i.e., a 'superior man'] … extends out at the top [like the vertical line on the character for scholar]" (see Figure 5.9).[24] The persuasive power of such formulations cannot be appreciated without an understanding of the unique nature of the Chinese written script.

Although the *Kangxi Dictionary* boasts about fifty thousand characters, only a tenth or so had to be mastered for substantial literacy in Qing times. In fact, the major paradigmatic writings of the Zhou period are based on a core vocabulary of only about twenty-five hundred separate characters. Although the Four Books and Five Classics total well over four hundred thousand characters, the *Lunyu* (Analects) of Confucius, one of the Four Books, has only twenty-two hundred different lexical items and the classic known as the *Chunqiu* (Spring and Autumn Annals), only about a thousand.[25]

Facility in classical Chinese has never been simply a matter of recognizing large numbers of characters; rather it has been a matter of understanding fully the wealth

經 <u>jing</u>
尚 <u>shang</u>

Figure 5.10   Chinese Characters (J).

上 馬 <u>shangma</u>
馬 上 <u>mashang</u>
明 明 德 <u>ming ming de</u>
君 君 臣 臣 父 父 子 子 <u>jun jun chen chen fu fu zi zi</u>

Figure 5.11   Chinese Characters (K).

of accumulated meanings and associations a given term has acquired over time. Unfortunately for students of the language, some of the most common words in classical Chinese have the widest range of possible meanings. *Jing,* for example, can mean (among other things) "warp" (as opposed to "woof"); "longitude"; "vessels in a body"; "to manage, plan, arrange, regulate, or rule"; "to pass through, experience, or suffer"; "constant or standard"; "classical canon"; and even "suicide by hanging." *Shang* can mean "still or yet"; "in addition to or to add"; "to honor"; "to surpass"; "to proceed"; "to be in charge of"; and so on (see Figure 5.10). Philosophical terms often have literally dozens of meanings or shades of meaning.[26]

Complicating matters is the fact that in classical Chinese a great many words function in at least two, and often more, grammatical roles (nouns, verbs, adverbs, adjectives, and so on), depending on syntax. The expression *shangma,* for instance, might mean "to get up on a horse" or "a superior horse (or horses)"; whereas the reverse expression, *mashang,* could mean "on top of a horse" or, by extension, "immediately." The classical phrase *ming mingde,* "to illustrate (or exemplify) illustrious virtue," employs the character *ming* (lit., bright) in two different usages, first as a verb and then as an adjective. Similarly, in the Confucian axiom *jun jun chen chen fu fu zi zi* ("Let the sovereign be [i.e., act in the manner befitting] a sovereign; let the minister be a minister; let the father be a father; let the son be a son"), the first, third, fifth, and seventh characters function as nouns, whereas the identical characters in the second, fourth, sixth, and eighth places serve as verbs (see Figure 5.11).

This range of grammatical functions is by no means arbitrary, however.[27] Classical Chinese depends on rules of word order that are in several respects similar to those governing English. The standard sentence structure is subject-verb-object. Adjectives generally precede the nouns they modify, and adverbs precede the verbs they modify. Even the lack of inflection in classical Chinese creates no special grammatical problems as long as the context is clear. Unfortunately for the uninitiated reader, this is often not the case. Although grammatical devices exist in the classical language to indicate verb mood, noun number, and so forth, their use, in the words of one authority, "is not a matter of prescribed necessity."[28]

Furthermore, classical Chinese texts were not normally punctuated. Certain characters could be employed to indicate partial or full stops, questions, exclamations, and so on, but even they were sometimes ambiguous and not always used consistently and systematically. In the absence of clear-cut punctuation, the inherent ambiguity of written Chinese was amplified, with the result that even standard classical texts were often subject to a wide variety of possible grammatical readings. This necessitated heavy reliance on commentaries and lexicons. Such works were also useful in identifying and explaining the wealth of recondite historical and literary allusions in classical-style writing, as well as the huge number of specialized meanings acquired by certain characters in different philosophical or other contexts.[29]

In all, there was no real alternative to rote memorization and intensive tutorial assistance as a means of mastering the classical script. Beginning with specially designed Confucian primers such as the *Sanzi jing* (Three Character Classic) and the *Xiaojing* (Classic of Filial Piety), students recited passages aloud in rhythmic fashion with no initial appreciation of meaning. By stages, these texts were carefully explained, and students then advanced to more complicated materials. By memorizing vast amounts of diverse classical literature in this way, students internalized specific patterns of characters contained in a wide variety of paradigmatic sources—patterns that became indelibly etched in their consciousness. The same painstaking approach applied to the writing of Chinese characters. Over a long period of time, and with Herculean effort, the aspiring scholar eventually attained the necessary skills to chart his own scholarly path.[30]

The memorization of Chinese texts was facilitated by the rhythm and balance of the classical script. Each character, when pronounced, was monosyllabic, and each occupied the same amount of space in a text, regardless of the number of strokes it contained. Thus each character became a convenient rhythmic unit. This feature of the language naturally encouraged the Chinese, perhaps more than any other culture group, to think and write in terms of polarities. In the words of the world-famous linguist Y. R. Chao, "I venture to think that if the Chinese language had words of such incommensurable rhythm as *male* and *female, heaven* and *earth, rational* and [*ab*]*surd,* there would never be such far-reaching conceptions as *yin-yang,* [and] *ch'ien-k'un* [*qiankun*]."[31]

But *yinyang* and *qiankun* (the symbolic equivalents of *yang* and *yin* in the hexagrams of the *Yijing*) were only two of a huge number of such polarities. Many, if not most, of these polarities can be correlated directly with *yin* and *yang*—an expression of the central Chinese notion that ideas are complemented and completed by their opposites. Thus we find that the *Shuowen jiezi* defines *chu* ("going out") in terms of *jin* ("coming in") and *luan* ("disorder") in terms of *zhi* ("order"). Distance is *yuanjin* ("far-near"); quantity, *duoshao* ("much-little"); weight, *qingzhong* ("light-heavy"); length, *changduan* ("long-short"); and so forth. Possession (or existence) is expressed by the terms *youwu* (lit., have–not have, presence-absence); and in Chinese discourse of all kinds it is common to find juxtapositions such as ancient and modern (*gujin*), beginning and end (*benmo*), difference and similarity (*yitong*), loss and gain (*shide*), continuity and change (*yan'ge*). In these and other dualistic expressions we find a characteristic concern with the "relation of opposites" rather than with Western-style (Aristotelian) separate qualities and the "law of identity."[32]

Two things seem significant. The first is that for most polarities in Chinese, descriptions such as antithesis, contradiction, and dichotomy are misleading, since the terms involved usually imply either complementary opposition or cyclical alternation. The second is that the widespread use of such polarities—especially in classical prose and formal philosophy—suggests a distinctive attitude toward abstraction in which abstract ideas tend to be expressed in concrete terms ("instantiated") without dialectical resolution into a new abstract term as in the Indo-European linguistic tradition.[33]

One index of the prevalence of polarities in Chinese writing is their frequent use in the classical literature. In the first eighty characters of the Great Commentary of the *Yijing,* for instance, there are nearly a dozen prominent *yinyang*-style juxtapositions, ranging from man and woman (*nannü*), sun and moon (*riyue*), and Heaven and Earth (*tiandi*) to honorable and lowly (*zunbei*), activity and quiescence (*dongjing*), and good and bad luck (*jixiong*). A great many other such polarities are scattered throughout the classic, and indeed throughout all major works in the Chinese literary tradition. In imperial times, lists of polarities were compiled for ease of reference in composition, and Qing documents sometimes contain as many as six sets of polarities strung together for effect.[34]

Another indication of the importance of polarities is their frequent use as subject headings in encyclopedias such as the *TSJC.* In the subcategories on human affairs and social intercourse, for example, we find many headings such as love and hate (*haoe*), guest and host (*binzhu*), teacher and pupil (*shidi*), misfortune and fortune (*huofu*), and high and humble (*guijian*). In the subcategory on Confucian conduct there are literally dozens of common polarities, including righteousness and profit (*yili*), good and bad (*shane*), influence and response (*ganying*), substance and function (*tiyong*), knowledge and action (*zhixing*), names and realities (*mingshi*), and hard and soft (*gangrou*).[35]

Such polarities were not only semantically significant, they were also aesthetically attractive. Good prose demanded them. Consider the following three examples taken from the enormously influential compilation entitled *Jinsi lu* (Reflections on Things at Hand):

> In the changes and transformations of *yin* and *yang,* the growth and maturity of things, the interaction of sincerity and insincerity, and the beginning and ending of events, one is the influence and the other, the response, succeeding each other in a cycle.
>
> By calmness of nature we mean that one's nature is calm whether it is in a state of activity or a state of tranquility. One does not lean forward or backward to accommodate things, nor does he make any distinction between the internal and the external.

> The difference between righteousness and profit is only that between impartiality
> and selfishness. As soon as we depart from righteousness, we will be talking about
> profit. Merely to calculate is to be concerned with advantage and disadvantage.

Significantly, in the last example cited, the term "righteousness" (*yi*) was substituted
for the original term "humaneness" (*ren*) in order to employ a more satisfactory juxtaposition of ideas, namely, *yili*.[36] In translation, formulations such as those cited
above often appear unsubstantial and unsatisfying, but to the classical scholar completely conversant with the full range of meanings and associations of a given word,
term, or phrase, they were not only beautiful but also compelling.

The same emphasis on rhythm and balance that is manifest in the use of polarities
may be found in entire phrases of classical Chinese. In the *Wenxin diaolong* (The Literary Mind and the Carving of Dragons), considered by the great Qing scholar Ruan
Yuan (1764–1849) to be the very foundation of China's "literary laws," we find the
following passage in the section on parallelism:

> The "Wenyan" and "Xici" [Commentaries] of the *Book of Changes* embody the
> profound thought of the Sage. In the narration of the four virtues of the hexagram
> *qian* [i.e., *yang*], the sentences are matched in couplets, and in the description of the
> kinds of responses evoked by the dragon and the tiger, the words are all paralleled in
> pairs. When describing the hexagrams of *qian* and *kun* [i.e., *yin*] as easy and simple
> respectively, the passage winds and turns, with lines smoothly woven into one
> another; and in depicting the going and coming of the sun and moon, the alternate
> lines form couplets. Occasionally there may be some variation in the structure of a
> sentence, or some change in word order, but parallelism is always the aim.

This parallelism, in the view of the author, Liu Xie (c. A.D. 465–562), was as natural as
the endowment of living things with paired limbs.[37]

Of the four main types of parallelism distinguished by Liu Xie, the most esteemed
was the couplet of contrast. Liu provides an example: "Zhong Yi, the humble, played
the music of Chu; Zhuang Xi, the prominent, groaned in the manner of Yue." Both
parts of the contrasted couplet refer to spontaneous expressions of homesickness, and
each requires familiarity with a historical background naturally assumed by the author.[38]

Virtually all of the most influential forms of Chinese writing, from simple primers
to the most sophisticated poetry and prose, employed some type of linguistic parallelism, and a good "eight-legged essay" for the civil-service examinations could not,
of course, be written without it. Four-character phrases were especially common.
The great majority of Chinese fixed expressions, or aphorisms (*chengyu*), whether derived from the classics, poetry, or popular literature, consisted of four characters.
Such expressions are particularly prevalent in classics such as the *Shijing* and *Yijing*,
but they also are employed in many Chinese folk sayings. Indeed, the succinctness,
balance, and rhythm of the classical Chinese language made it eminently well suited

for popular proverbs, which helped bridge the gap between the mental world of the Confucian elite and the Chinese masses (see, for example, Figure 5.11).[39]

The use of balanced phrases in prose often required considerable stylistic manipulation in the form of either expansion through the addition of superfluous, or "empty" (*xu*), characters, or ruthless contraction. Succinctness was invariably esteemed. As Victor Purcell has observed,

> The rule is, if you can possibly omit, do so. The result may be that the meaning is quite hidden, but the reader is supposed not only to have an encyclopaedic knowledge to assist him in his guesswork, but to have unlimited time for filling in ellipses. This does not mean that the language has no words to fill in the ellipses, or that there are no words to convey tense, number or mood. It merely means that the spirit of the language is against their use.

Many other authorities, Western and Chinese, have made the same basic point.[40]

The brevity and grammatical flexibility of classical Chinese have been compared to modern telegrams and newspaper headlines, but the parallel can be taken no further. Rhythm, poetic suggestiveness, and economy of expression were not simply convenient means in China but rather literary ends. Chinese authors regularly and happily sacrificed precision for style, encouraging an intuitive as well as an intellectual approach to their work.[41]

Although Qing scholars distinguished between learning (*xue*) and thinking (*si*) and between erudition (*bo*) and grasping the essence (*yue*), neo-Confucian "rationalism" did not on the whole involve a conscious exaltation of reason over intuition. Indeed, Chinese thinkers often showed a marked preference for the latter—perhaps in part because the brevity, subtlety, and suggestiveness of the classical language encouraged an intuitive approach to the most profound understanding. A. C. Graham rightly observes that the Chinese have generally been most impressed by "the aphoristic genius which guides thought of the maximum complexity with the minimum of words, of which the *Tao-te ching* [*Daode jing*, The Way and Its Power] presents one of the world's supreme examples."[42]

LANGUAGE AND CULTURE

What else does the classical language tell us about traditional Chinese patterns of perception and thought? Certainly it provides important clues regarding elite social attitudes. We see, for example, that the classical language possesses an extraordinary number of kinship terms, indicating an intense and pervasive concern with family relationships. The early Chinese lexicon known as the *Erya*, which dates from the pre-Christian era, contains more than one hundred specialized kinship terms, most of which have no counterpart in English. Later works of a similar nature, including those by Qian Daxin (1727–1804), Liang Zhangju (1775–1849), and Zheng Zhen (1806–1864) in the Qing period, continued to place special emphasis on the highly refined nomenclature of family relationships. Even the works on local dialects by scholars such as Hang Shijun (1696–1773) and Qian Dian (1744–1806) devote inordinate attention to kinship terms and their variants. The great Qing encyclopedia *TSJC* includes two large subcategories—one on clan and family names and one on family relationships—that together account for 756 of the encyclopedia's total of 10,000 *juan*. Although not all of this material is related directly to kinship nomenclature, it does indicate the central significance of the family in traditional Chinese society.[43]

Chinese kinship terminology underscores the importance of social distinctions based on age and gender. A Chinese writer in traditional times (and in fact more recently) could never, for example, simply refer to another person as "cousin." He or she would have to employ a much more specific term that distinguished between male and female, designated paternal or maternal affinity, and revealed the relation's relative age. Thus, a male cousin on the father's side older than oneself would be referred to as *tangxiong*, a male cousin on the father's side younger than oneself as *tangdi*, a male cousin on the mother's side older than oneself as *biaoxiong*, and so on for five other types of cousins.[44]

Similar distinctions were obligatory for other members of both the male line, or *neiqin* (lit., inner relationship), and the female line, or *waiqin* (lit., outer relationship). This latter category was further divided into the subcategories of mother's kin (*mudang*), wife's kin (*qidang*), and daughter's kin (*nüdang*). These and other status distinctions were carefully preserved and expressed in the ritual vocabulary of the five mourning relationships discussed briefly in Chapter 4. In practice, of course, the ritual requirements of mourning might be modified or ignored, especially if they involved distant relatives or mourning for junior family members by their seniors. Although the rituals might not always be strictly observed, however, the relationships were seldom forgotten.

Other linguistic evidence may be adduced for the special importance of kinship identifications in Chinese society, as well as for the principle of the subordination of the individual to the larger social group. Derk Bodde writes, for example, that "the Westerner asserts his ego by placing his personal name first, then his family name" (John Jones rather than Jones John), whereas the Chinese does just the reverse (Sun Yat-sen rather than Yat-sen Sun). Further, Bodde notes, "The Westerner unthinkingly speaks and writes in terms of 'I' and 'you.'" The Chinese (in the past, much less now) tended to avoid such direct address by using instead indirect locutions in the third person, such as "humble person" (referring to oneself) and "sir" or "gentleman" (referring to the other person). Among the major honorific terms in traditional China—used both within and outside the family—were *ling* ("excellent" or "illustrious"), *zun* ("honorable"), *xian* ("virtuous"), *gui* ("exalted"), and *da* ("great"). *Yu* ("simple" or "stupid") and *xiao* ("small" or "inferior") were commonly used in self-deprecation. Naturally enough, usage varied according to the relationship. Thus, whereas a man might speak of his wife as "the demeaned one of the inner apart-

女 <u>nü</u> (woman; female)
奸 <u>jian</u> (villainous)
妨 <u>fang</u> (to hinder)
妒 <u>du</u> (to be jealous)
奴 <u>nu</u> (slave)
媚 <u>mei</u> (to flatter)
姦 <u>jian</u> (licentious)

Figure 5.12   Chinese Characters (L).

ments" (*jiannei*), a guest of the household would refer to her as "the honorable one of the inner apartments" (*zunnei*) or "your honorable wife" (*zunkun furen*).[45]

The question of the place of women in traditional Chinese society is an intriguing one. On first glance, the large amount of space devoted to women (*guiyuan,* lit., beauties of the female living quarters) in the *TSJC* (376 *juan*) would indicate a more exalted status than is generally supposed; and, as we know, a number of women during the Qing period, as in earlier times, achieved considerable distinction. But in the main, the individuals discussed in the encyclopedia are distinguished less by their personal accomplishments than by their exemplary Confucian virtues—notably female chastity. Of all the various subsections on women, by far the largest is "Widows Who Would Not Remarry" (*guijie,* 210 *juan*). By contrast, 7 *juan* are devoted to women writers (*guizao*), 4 to wise women (*guizhi*), and only 1 each to artistic women (*guiqiao*) and witty women (*guihui*).

It is also interesting to note the relatively large number of Chinese characters with the "female" radical (*nü*) that have decidedly pejorative connotations, including *jian* ("villainous"), *fang* ("to hinder"), *du* ("to be jealous"), *nu* ("slave"), *mei* ("to flatter"), and *jian* ("licentious") (see Figure 5.12). Of course, a number of very positive terms in Chinese also contain the *nü* radical, but most of these have to do with traditional female physical attributes, roles, and relationships. In speech these associations would not be apparent, as they are with, say, the English sound "sissy"; but as I have tried to indicate, Chinese culture as a whole paid far greater attention to the constituent elements of written words than did Western culture. Thus, such associations, both positive and negative, were never far from consciousness—at least not for the more literate members of Qing society.

There are other significant ways in which the Chinese language reflects basic cultural attitudes. Chang Tung-sun has pointed out, for example, that the language is extraordinarily rich in ethical terms and concepts, indicating China's long-standing preoccupation with moral values. Fung Yu-lan, for his part, suggests that the traditional use of expressions for the world, such as *tianxia* ("all under Heaven") and *ssu-hai chih nei* ("all within the four seas"), reflects a decidedly continental orientation very much unlike the outlook of the ancient maritime Greeks. And Chang Kwang-chih has employed a sophisticated analysis of early Chinese texts and terminology to support his contention that the Chinese are "probably among the peoples of the world most preoccupied with eating." Overall, however, the study of the Chinese language and its cultural implications is still in its infancy, especially in the West.[46]

The relationship between the classical Chinese language and formal philosophy, however, has been much discussed (and vigorously debated) by both Western and Chinese scholars.[47] Clearly Chinese language and thought enjoyed a mutually supporting, mutually enriching relationship. Yet one may argue that classical Chinese had an especially significant impact on the development of Chinese philosophy, not only because it endured so long as a living language (a point we shall take up later), but also perhaps because the characters themselves had such striking visual properties.[48]

While the ambiguity of the Chinese language may have encouraged an intuitive approach to understanding, it is possible that the ideographic origins of the script encouraged a preference for the concrete and descriptive over the abstract—at least in formal philosophical discourse. Although this hypothesis has been hotly contested, many scholars have observed that classical Chinese is relatively poor in resources for expressing abstractions. Thus, a word such as *zhen* ("true" as opposed to "false," *jia*) tended to be construed as "that which is true" rather than the abstract concept "Truth." (A. C. Graham aptly remarks that "Chinese philosophising centres on the Way rather than the Truth.") Similarly, *ren* ("human being[s]") tended to acquire the meaning of "a person" or "people" (general) rather than Man (abstract). "Hope" was difficult to abstract from the notion of "a series of expectations directed toward specific objects."[49]

Yet it certainly cannot be said that the Chinese lacked the capacity to think abstractly.[50] What can be said is that Chinese philosophers tended to express the abstract and general in terms of the concrete and the particular. The *Yijing*, as Cheng Chung-ying has observed, is an especially apt illustration of this particular attitude or orientation. In the highly refined symbolic system of the *Yijing*, philosophical principles are "embodied in concrete instances of things and their relations." Viewing the matter from a somewhat different perspective, we might say that universal or abstract principles have been most significant to the Chinese when realized or revealed in concrete things and particular contexts. This observation—which conforms with Chad Hansen's argument that Chinese theories of language, unlike those of the West, emphasize prescription rather than description—would help account for the practical orientation of so much of Chinese philosophy and for the general lack of speculation for speculation's sake in China.[51]

Another prominent feature of Chinese philosophy, already alluded to, may also be explained by reference to the classical language: the strong emphasis on what has been variously called relational, associational, analogical, or correlative thinking. Traditionally, Chinese thinkers have been less concerned with Western-style ontological categories (i.e., Platonic universals and Aristotelian essences) than with an analysis of relations among and between things, events, and concepts. Chu Yu-kuang believes that the emphasis on word relations in Chinese is "probably correlated with relational

仁者人也 <u>ren zhe ren ye</u>
義者宜也 <u>yi zhe yi ye</u>
政者正也 <u>zheng zhe zheng ye</u>

Figure 5.13   Chinese Characters (M).

thinking in many areas of Chinese life and culture." We have already noted Cheng Chung-ying's use of the *Yijing* as an illustration of Chinese relational thinking; other Chinese and Western scholars, such as Chang Tung-sun and Joseph Needham, also have used the ancient classic to make the same important point.[52]

China's *yinyang*-oriented "logic of correlative duality" (to borrow Chang Tung-sun's felicitous phrase) certainly differed from classical Aristotelian logic in the West. This does not, however, mean that the Chinese lacked the capacity to reason "logically." Many authorities—Westerners as well as Chinese—have demonstrated with abundant documentary evidence that logical rigor was possible, and even prominent, in certain types of Chinese philosophical discourse.[53] Nonetheless, it is true that the structure of the Chinese language, the aesthetics associated with it, and the penchant for relational thinking among the Chinese made some forms of argumentation far more appealing and persuasive than others. These factors help to explain, for example, the powerful Chinese preference for argument by analogy and the widespread use of numerical categories and correlations in all kinds of philosophical writing.[54]

Although *yinyang* dualism lay at the heart of Chinese relational thinking, most Chinese numerical categories involved groups of more than two. Most of these were odd (*yang*) numbers—notably threes, fives, and nines. Thus, we find in Chinese philosophical writing (and in daily discourse) repeated references to the "three sovereigns" (Fu Xi, Shen Nong, and Huangdi, in one common configuration), the "three teachings" (Confucianism, Buddhism, and Daoism), the "three obediences" (subject to sovereign, son to father, and wife to husband), the "three powers" (Heaven, Earth, and Man), the "three [types of womanly] dependence" (on father, husband, and son), and so forth. In all, more than three hundred different numerical correlations or associations were current in Qing times, ranging from groups of two or three (there were about seventy for the number three alone) to groups of one hundred or more. Such categories not only identified certain important relationships but also served as a convenient philosophical "shorthand." Like the concepts *yin* and *yang*, with which they were often correlated, numbers indicated hierarchy and precedence, expressed in a highly formalistic style.[55]

Correlational thinking, together with an emphasis on balance and rhythm (and the attractiveness of puns) in the Chinese language, helps to explain the popularity of four-character philosophical "definitions" of the following sort: *ren zhe ren ye* ("*ren* ['humaneness'] means to be human [*ren*]"); *yi zhi yi ye* ("*yi* ['righteousness' or 'duty'] means that which is appropriate [*yi*]"); and *zheng zhe zheng ye* ("*zheng* ['government'] means that which is correct [*zheng*]") (see Figure 5.13). Henry Rosemont argues that the advantage of such formulations is that they allowed a Chinese thinker to "maintain the semantic richness of his general terms and their relational representations yet unpack them when necessary—with or without logical explicitness—to elaborate one of their specific significations."[56]

This relational, or associational, process, so prominent in the classical language, was also central to the process of the *Yijing*—described by one modern Chinese authority as "the detection of analogous precepts, concepts and ideas in interrelated symbols, and a synthesis of them into more elaborate metaphysical or ethical notions."[57] In the following chapters we will take up the place of the *Yijing* in Chinese cosmology, ethics, divination, and popular religion, but here we are concerned with the classic as a supplementary system of Chinese language, or, to use Alfred North Whitehead's term, of "symbolic reference."[58]

The authority of the *Yijing* in late imperial China is seldom fully appreciated. Consider, however, the following quotation from the famous *Jinsi lu,* described by one scholar as "unquestionably the most important single work of philosophy produced in the Far East during the second millennium A.D.": "The *Yijing* is comprehensive, great and perfect. It is intended to bring about accord with the principle of [human] nature and destiny, to penetrate the causes of the hidden and the manifest, to reveal completely the nature of things and affairs, and to show the way to open up resources and to accomplish great undertakings." In a similar vein, the great Qing scholar Wang Fuzhi (1619–1692) wrote:

> It [the *Yijing*] is the manifestation of the Heavenly Way, the unexpressed form of nature, and the showcase for sagely achievement. *Yin* and *yang,* movement and stillness, darkness and brightness, withdrawing and extending—all these are inherent in it. Spirit operates within it; the refined subtlety of ritual and music is stored in it; the transformative capacity of ghosts and spirits emerges from it. The great utility of humaneness and righteousness issues forth from it; and the calculation of order or disorder, good or bad luck, life or death is in accordance with it.[59]

Throughout the Qing period, as Toda Toyosaburo's admirable research demonstrates, the *Yijing* remained a sacred work of nearly unchallenged scriptural authority, serving not only as a moral guide to action but also as a rich source of concepts and symbols.[60]

According to Confucius (as cited in the Great Commentary of the *Yijing*), "Writing cannot express words completely. Words cannot express thoughts completely. ... The holy sages set up images [*xiang*] in order to express the true and false completely." In other words, to the Chinese the six-line hexagrams of the *Yijing* represented symbolically the images or structure of changing situations in the universe and as such were believed to have explanatory value, if correctly interpreted. Like Chinese characters, these hexagrams were a distinctly visual medium of communication, concrete but ambiguous, with several possible levels of meaning as well as a great many accumulated allusions and associations. To a greater extent than most Chinese characters, however, the hexagrams came to acquire abstract significations.

*Figure 5.14   Hexagrams. Miscellaneous hexagrams with the character(s) for their "hexagram name" (*guaming*). Source: Xi Zhu (1979).*

The basic text of the *Yijing* consists of sixty-four hexagrams, each individually named and composed of six solid (*yang,* _____) or broken (*yin,* — —) lines in various combinations (see Figure 5.14), together with written decisions (*tuan*) and appended judgments (*xici* or *xiaoci*) for each. The decisions are short paragraphs that explain the overall symbolic situation represented by a given hexagram. The appended judgments characterize each of the six lines in turn and usually indicate a process leading from a beginning stage (line one, at the bottom of the hexagram), to a developmental stage (lines two through five), and on to an ending or transitional stage (line six). These lines also form a pair of individually named primary trigrams juxtaposed within each hexagram. There are eight possible primary trigram configurations (see Figure 5.15). According to the theory of the *Yijing,* the interpretation of various interrelated lines, trigrams, and hexagrams, and an appreciation of the changes they undergo and represent in certain concrete circumstances, will clarify the structure of human experience and, in the process of divination, illuminate the future.[61]

The so-called Ten Wings of the *Yijing,* traditionally (though falsely) attributed to Confucius, amplify the basic text and invest it with additional symbolism and multiple layers of meaning. Together, through the use of colorful analogies, metaphors, and other forms of imagery, these poetic commentaries elucidate the structure and significance of the hexagrams in terms of individual lines and constituent trigrams as well as other hexagrams. Further, they provide a moral dimension to the *Yijing* and a solid metaphysical foundation based on *yinyang* five-elements principles and an elaborate numerology. The metaphysics and numerology of the *Yijing* were communicated to all levels of society during the Qing period by means of fortune-tellers, alma-

*Figure 5.15   Trigrams. One arrangement of
the Eight Trigrams. Source: Xi Zhu (1979).*

nacs, and schematic devices such as the *Hetu* (River Chart) and *Luoshu* (Luo Writing)
(see Figure 5.16).

Although a fundamental assumption of the *Yijing* has always been the mutual interaction or interrelationship of all of its constituent hexagrams, the two most important points of symbolic reference in the classic were clearly the hexagrams *qian* ("the
creative") and *kun* ("the receptive") (see Figure 5.17). At the most basic level of symbolism, *qian* and *kun* represented Heaven and Earth in microcosm, as well as the generative power and potential of *yang* and *yin,* respectively. As *yinyang* conceptual categories, these hexagrams automatically assumed all of the attributes associated with
these two sets of relations, including the numerical correlations of odd and even (see
Chapter 6). In addition, *qian* and *kun* acquired the associations of their constituent
trigrams. Among *qian*'s various attributes were thus roundness, spirituality, straight-
ness, the color red, and the cutting quality of metal. By contrast, *kun* came to be associated with squareness, sagacity, levelness, the color black, and the transport capacity
of a large wagon.

Over time, *qian* and *kun,* and to a lesser extent the other sixty-two hexagrams derived from them, became rich repositories of diverse symbols, similar to variables in
symbolic logic. As substitutes for various classes of objects, the hexagrams, individual
trigrams, and even single lines had wide-ranging explanatory value. Fung Yu-lan
writes, for example, "Everything that satisfies the condition of being virile [*yang*] can
fit into a formula in which the symbol *qian* occurs, and everything that satisfies the
condition of being docile [*yin*] can fit into one in which the symbol of *kun* appears."
At the most fundamental level, then, if a man sought an understanding of the role
and place of, say, a ruler or a father (a *yang* relationship), he consulted the hexagram
qian and its associated commentaries; and if he sought an understanding of the role

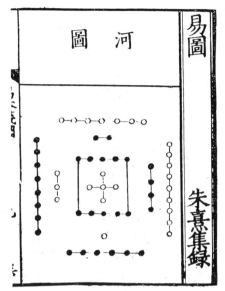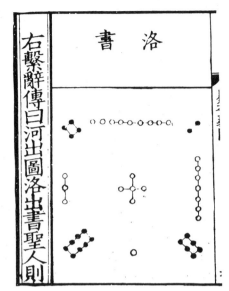

Figure 5.16   Diagrams from the Yijing. *The* Hetu *(left) and* Luoshu *(right). These charts were used for various numerological purposes. Source: Xi Zhu (1979).*

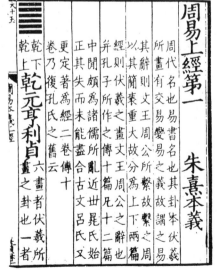

Figure 5.17   Qian and Kun. The first page of a standard Yijing *text for the hexagrams* Qian *(right) and* Kun *(left). The small characters immediately below the hexagrams refer to the two constituent trigrams of each; the larger characters represent the hexagram name and judgment. The other small characters are part of Zhu Xi's commentary to the text. Source: Xi Zhu (1979).*

or place of a subject or a son (a *yin* relationship), he consulted the hexagram *kun* and its commentaries.[62]

Naturally enough, the symbolism of the *Yijing* reinforced traditional Chinese social attitudes. Thus we find the following statement by Zhou Dunyi in the *Jinsi lu*:

> It is difficult to govern a family whereas it is easy to govern the world, for the family is near while the world is distant. If members of the family are separated, the cause surely lies with women. This is why the hexagram *kui* ["to part," number 38 in the traditional order] follows the hexagram *jiaren* ["family," number 37], for "When two women live together, their wills move in different directions." This is why Yao ... gave his two daughters in marriage to Shun in order to test him and see whether the throne should be given to him. Thus it is that, in order to see how he governs his empire, we observe the government of his family.[63]

Of course the process of consulting the *Yijing* for insight and guidance, whether in divination or in the course of general study, was usually far more complex than this example might suggest. The very structure of the *Yijing,* with its *yinyang*-style reconciliation of opposites, its cryptic language, multiple symbols, layers of meaning, and elaborate patterns of relationship among lines, trigrams, and hexagrams, militated against facile explanations except by the simpleminded. As the Kangxi emperor once remarked, "I have never tired of the *Book of Changes,* and have used it in fortune-telling and as a book of moral principles; the only thing you must not do, I told my court lecturers, is to make this book appear simple, for there are meanings here that lie beyond words."[64] Even with the aid of the major classical commentaries and some two thousand years of intensive scholarship on the *Yijing,* the interpretive possibilities of any hexagram were nearly inexhaustible—not only because it was assumed that the universe and human circumstances were in a state of perpetual flux, but also because a given hexagram never stood alone, in a vacuum. At the very least, consultation of one hexagram demanded consultation of its opposite.

The symbols of the *Yijing* were deemed useful for more than elucidating the nature of human affairs, although this was their primary function. They also served as evaluative categories. The Qing scholar Zhang Xuecheng (1738–1801), for example, used the symbolism of *qian* and *kun* in comparing the "round and spiritual" writing of the early Han historian Sima Qian (c. 145 B.C.–c. 90 B.C.) to the "square and sagacious" writing of his successor Ban Gu (A.D. 32–A.D. 92). Similarly, the author of the early Qing painting guide entitled the *Jiezi yuan huazhuan* (Mustard Seed Garden Manual) employed the vocabulary and numerical symbolism of the *Yijing* to describe the composition of plum trees. "The blossoms," he tells us, "are of the *yang* principle ... [and the] wood of its branches is of the *yin* principle. Its basic number is five, and its various parts and aspects are based on odd and even numbers [like the *Yijing*]. ... [The] branches symbolize the six lines [of the hexagrams] ... and the tips of the branches have eight knots or forks, symbolizing the Eight Trigrams."[65]

Qing scholars also used the *Yijing* to interpret China's greatest novels (see Chapter 9). The Daoist priest Liu Yiming (1734–1820), for instance, felt that *Xiyou ji* (Journey to the West) could not be appreciated fully without an understanding of the way different meanings attached to the same apparent hexagram symbolism in various parts of the novel. Wen Tong, a late Qing bannerman, developed the theory that several of the main characters in *Shuihu zhuan* (Water Margin) were related directly to hexagram images derived from the *Yijing*. And Zhang Xinzhi's well-known exegesis of *Honglou meng* (Dream of the Red Chamber) placed special emphasis on hexagram relationships in the analysis of personalities, as we can see plainly in the following passage on the four "sisters" of Jia Baoyu:

> Yuanchun corresponds to the hexagram *tai* [number 11], the hexagram of the first month, so she is the eldest sibling. Yingchun corresponds to the hexagram *dazhuang* [34], the hexagram of the second month, so she is the second oldest daughter. Tanchun corresponds to the hexagram *guai* [43], the hexagram of the third month, so she is the third oldest daughter. Xichun corresponds to the hexagram *qian* [1], which is the hexagram of the fourth month, so she is the fourth oldest daughter. But since all … are female, their *yang* lines are transformed into *yin* lines. Thus Yuanchun's *tai* is transformed into *pi* [12], Yingchun's *dazhuang* is transformed into *guan* [20], Tanchun's *guai* is transformed into *bo* [23], and Xichun's *qian* is transformed into *kun* [2]. This is one of the most important messages in the book, and I make comment on this in turn during the biographies of each of them.[66]

Yijing interpretations even influenced the shape of Chinese mythology. According to the Great Commentary, many fundamental features of traditional Chinese civilization, from writing and burial customs to administrative practices and agriculture, were inspired by certain relationships inherent in a dozen or so different hexagrams. Thus we read that the Yellow Emperor, Yao, and Shun "allowed their upper and lower garments to hang down [i.e., they ruled passively, by moral example], and the world was in order. They probably took this from the hexagrams *qian* and *kun*." And again: Shen Nong "split a piece of wood for a plowshare and bent a piece of wood for the plow handle, and taught the whole world the advantage of laying open the earth with a plow. He probably took this from the *yi* hexagram ['increase']."[67]

Chinese scientists often used the symbols of the *Yijing* to explain natural phenomena—especially since, in the words of the influential Song scholar Cheng Yi, the classic included all things, "from heaven, earth, the hidden [i.e., the supernatural] and the manifest [human affairs] to insects, plants, and minute things." Many considered the binary number system of the *Yijing* to be the basis for all mathematics, and most employed trigrams and hexagrams to categorize and evaluate various physical properties and natural processes. As scientific symbols, the hexagram *xun* ("the gentle," "the penetrating," "the wind") was commonly identified with the phenomenon of human respiration; *yi* ("the corners of the mouth," "nourishment"), with nutrition; and *guan* ("contemplation," "view"), with vision.[68]

Such identifications often went beyond simply equating natural phenomena with the "name" of a hexagram. Efforts were also made to explain the identification in terms of the attributes of the hexagram's constituent trigrams. Thus, the Ming scholar Wang Kui observed, "The upper eyelid of human beings moves, and the lower one keeps still. This is because the symbolism of the hexagram *guan* embodies the idea of vision. Windy *xun* [a trigram] is moving above, and earthly *kun* [also a trigram] is immobile below." His explanation of *yi* as a symbol for nutrition is similar, for although the two constituent trigrams of *yi* are different from those for *guan,* the lower one (*zhen,* "thunder") represented to Wang the movement of the lower jaw in eating, while the upper one (*gen,* "mountain") indicated immobility. These explanations do not, however, represent the conventional interpretations given to the constituent trigrams in either of the two examples cited.[69]

Whole hexagrams could be juxtaposed to indicate various "natural" relationships. As indicated earlier, *qian* and *kun* were widely employed to represent all kinds of *yinyang* relationships and attributes, as well as the generative powers these two terms implied. In similar fashion, the *yin* symbol *kan* ("the abysmal," "water") and the *yang* symbol *li* ("the clinging," "fire") served as scientific terms in a wide variety of realms, from chemistry to biology. In addition, many Chinese scholars viewed the trigrams and hexagrams of the *Yijing* not only as abstract formulations but also as "invisible operators," forces that actually caused or controlled situations. This also came to be believed of a few individual characters associated with certain specific hexagrams.[70]

Joseph Needham blames the *Yijing* for inhibiting the development of Chinese science (by which he means, of course, a Western model of historical development):

> I fear that we shall have to say that while the five-element and two-force [*yinyang*] theories were favourable rather than inimical to the development of scientific thought in China, the elaborated symbolic system of the *Book of Changes* was almost from the start a mischievous handicap. It tempted those who were interested in Nature to rest in explanations which were no explanations at all. The *Book of Changes* was a system for *pigeon-holing novelty* and then doing nothing about it. ... It led to a stylisation of concepts almost analogous to the stylisations which have in some ages occurred in art forms and which finally prevented painters from looking at Nature at all.[71]

Needham's judgment is perhaps too harsh, since China made many noteworthy scientific advances well after the *Yijing* had acquired the exalted status of a classic. Nonetheless, it is true that the great authority and convenient bureaucratic classifications of the work made it relatively easy for Chinese scholars to accept its symbols as irrefutable expressions of universal truths.[72]

Needham asserts that the negative influence of the classical Chinese language on Chinese scientific thought has been vastly exaggerated, and he argues correctly that the limits to China's scientific development must be attributed primarily to nonlinguistic factors. Yet there can be little doubt that the poetic Chinese language was not the most congenial medium for the expression of precise scientific ideas. Needham himself has remarked upon the "unfortunate" tendency of the Chinese in premodern times to employ ancient words for scientific concepts rather than to develop a new scientific terminology. Part of the problem was undoubtedly China's inability to draw upon Greek, Latin, and Arabic roots in the manner of Western (European) scientists, but it is also clear that the unique style of Chinese writing continued to be a hindrance, as did the convenient symbolism of the *Yijing*.[73]

Another limitation on the development of Chinese science may have been the tendency of scholars to create texts by amassing quotations from preexisting sources of authority and then organizing them in some sort of chronological or topical, but not necessarily analytical, order—what Derk Bodde describes as "composition through compilation"—rather than through a process of intellectual synthesis. This approach was not only a feature of most Chinese reference works; it was also characteristic of many philosophical and even "scientific" tracts. Prominent examples from late imperial times include the *Mengqi pitan* (Dream Torrent Jottings) of Shen Gua (1030–1094), one of China's greatest scientific minds, and Gu Yanwu's famous *Rizhi lu* (Record of Daily [Acquired] Knowledge). Although this traditional approach to the accumulation and dissemination of scholarly learning certainly did not prevent Shen, Gu, and others from developing creative ideas, on the whole it seems to have discouraged the intellectual habits of generalization and hypothesis.[74]

Robert Hartwell, in discussing traditional Chinese economic thought, reaches a similar conclusion. He remarks on the "amazing" propensity of writers in late imperial times to give equal treatment to statements of widely varying orders of abstraction and analytical significance. In his words:

> The Chinese normally did not distinguish ... between the relative worth of alternative modes of logical presentation. ... The failure to distinguish different orders of conceptualization severely limited the possibilities for integrating the separate ideas of economic doctrine into an explanatory system and precluded the broadening of abstraction essential to the progress of science. This was partly owing to the habitual use of the historical-analogical method ... [but] primarily the result of neglecting to search consciously for general hypotheses.[75]

However ill-suited classical Chinese discourse may have been in the realm of "scientific" exposition, it is clear that the written language did not provide particularly fertile soil for the independent growth of foreign ideas. Arthur Wright has discussed in detail the many problems of translation facing proponents of foreign concepts in China, from the Buddhist missionaries in the Six Dynasties period to the Jesuits and other Christian missionaries during the Qing. Time and again factors such as the semantic "weight" of Chinese characters—whether used as conceptual equivalents or merely in transliteration—tended to affect the meaning of the original foreign ideas. Thus, the classical Chinese script contributed to the cohesiveness and continuity of Chinese civilization by helping to "sinicize" alien and potentially disruptive doctrines.[76]

The classical language contributed to cultural continuity and cohesiveness in two other important ways. First, it established a direct linguistic link between the Chinese present and a distant, but not forgotten, Chinese past. Since the ancient classics and contemporary documents were all written in the same basic script, a Qing scholar had immediate intellectual access to anything written in China during the previous two thousand years. The language remained alive and well, part of a long-standing and still vital literary tradition and cultural heritage. Second, the script gave tremendous cultural unity to China across space. Because each Chinese character had the same basic set of meanings and associations, regardless of how it may have been pronounced, the literary language transcended local dialects, many of which were otherwise mutually unintelligible. There was thus no development in China comparable to the decline of Latin and the rise of national vernaculars in Europe. There was only the glaring fact that until well into the nineteenth century the Japanese, the Koreans, and the Vietnamese all continued to use classical Chinese as the principal means of written communication. This, of course, only fed China's already well-nourished sense of cultural superiority.[77]

𝕭 6 𝕰

Thought

*T*he most striking feature of traditional Chinese thought as a whole is its extraordinary eclecticism, its ability to tolerate diverse and sometimes seemingly incompatible notions with little sense of conflict or contradiction. In part, this remarkable integrative capacity can be explained by the powerful Chinese impulse to find unity in all realms of experience, human and supernatural. This tendency, in turn, may be traced to the long-standing Chinese idea of *yinyang* reconciliation of opposites—an outlook vividly expressed in late imperial times by the neat phrase *sanjiao heyi* ("the three teachings [of Confucianism, Daoism, and Buddhism] are united into one").[1] Thus, although the chapters on thought and religion in this book have been separated for convenience and clarity, in fact the two are inextricably related.

We should not, however, overestimate the fit between divergent strains of thought in Qing dynasty China. Even if we put "religion" aside for the moment[2] and focus solely on Confucian philosophy, it is clear that intellectual fashions changed significantly during the two and a half centuries of Manchu rule. These fashions, manifest in various separate "schools" of Confucianism, often invited powerful commitments based on regional identifications as well as patron-client and lineage ties.[3] What follows is a brief historical overview of the major Confucian schools and some of their primary intellectual exponents.

As had been the case during the Ming dynasty, the Qing rulers unwaveringly supported Zhu Xi's idealistic School of Song Learning—also known as the School of Principle (*lixue*)—as their official orthodoxy. Emphasizing loyalty to the sovereign, moral cultivation, and the power of positive example, Song Learning was distilled in the highly influential examination syllabus known as the *Xingli jingyi* (Essential Ideas of the School of Nature and Principle), commissioned by the Kangxi emperor in the early eighteenth century. The so-called Tongcheng School, centered in Anhui, embraced Zhu Xi's moral idealism but placed particular emphasis on literature as the vehicle of Confucian "faith."

Both of these schools were hostile to what they perceived as the overly empirical emphasis of the School of Evidential Research (*kaozheng xue*), whose iconoclastic advocates emerged as a "national elite" from the prosperous Yangzi River delta during the latter half of the seventeenth century. These creative *kaozheng* scholars—armed with sophisticated philological techniques and passionately committed to "seeking truth from facts" (*shishi qiu shi*)—devoted themselves primarily to textual criticism. Their research challenged a number of orthodox interpretations of the Confucian

Classics and even called into question the authenticity of certain received texts; and although the overall "subversive" effect of *kaozheng* scholarship is a matter of debate, there can be no doubt that it transformed Qing intellectual life in fundamental ways. Even exponents of Song Learning were affected.

During the eighteenth century Qing scholars routinely identified the School of Evidential Research with Han Learning—so named because its intellectual progenitors, Gu Yanwu (1613–1682) and Yan Ruoju (1636–1704), rejected Song-Ming sources in favor of earlier Han materials. Strictly speaking, however, Han Learning referred to a separate scholastic movement identified with the followers of Hui Dong (1697–1758) in Suzhou. Those who gravitated to Former Han sources were identified as members of the New Text School, while those who championed Later Han materials constituted a separate group. Technically, then, the term Han Learning applies only to this latter school.

The New Text School stood on the intellectual frontier between Song and Han Learning. It grew out of a late eighteenth-century revival of a much earlier controversy over the authenticity of certain versions of the Confucian Classics written in an ancient form of Chinese script known as *guwen* (see Chapter 2). These Old Text versions had been considered orthodox since the Later Han dynasty, when they replaced the set of classics written in the new-style script (*jinwen*) of the Early Han. But Qing *kaozheng* scholars such as Yan Ruoju began to uncover systematic evidence of forgeries in some of these Old Text versions, and these discoveries led to a fierce debate over issues such as the place of Confucius in Chinese history and the role of institutional change within the Confucian tradition.

The School of Statecraft, as its name implies, took practical administration as its central concern, avoiding the moralistic extremes of Song Learning as well as the scholastic extremes of Han Learning. It drew particular inspiration from the writings of men such as Gu Yanwu and Huang Zongxi (1610–1695), who had remained "committed to the welfare of the country in their scholarly pursuits." Although already an active intellectual force in the eighteenth century, Statecraft Learning rapidly gained momentum in the nineteenth as dynastic decline underscored the need for practical solutions to China's pressing problems.

Some Statecraft-oriented scholars, including Wei Yuan (1794–1856) and Gong Zizhen (1792–1841), had a deep and abiding interest in New Text scholarship. But it was not until the late nineteenth century that the progressive potential of New Text Confucianism became fully apparent. At that time, reform-minded exponents of New Text Learning—notably Kang Youwei (1858–1927) and his able student Liang Qichao (1873–1929)—moved to center stage in Qing political life. A central feature of Kang's spiritually inspired New Text approach was a "socio-moral pragmatism" that favored a free "ideological" interpretation of Confucianism over a literal and prosaic understanding.

Other schools of Confucian thought arose during the Qing dynasty, some championed by idiosyncratic individualists such as the avowedly anti-scholastic Yan Yuan (1635–1704) and his disciple Li Gong (1659–1733) and others espoused by eclectic thinkers such as Ruan Yuan (1764–1848) and Zeng Guofan (1811–1872). The syncretic tendencies of Chinese thought made it possible for a scholar-official like Zeng to esteem the literary and moral concerns of the Tongcheng School, and yet at the same time to recognize the merits of Han Learning, to gravitate toward the School of Statecraft in seeking solutions to the dynasty's administrative problems, and even to employ essentially Legalist methods in order to achieve idealistic Mencian aims. A distinctive feature of Zeng's thought, like that of many *kaozheng* scholars, was his emphasis on *li*—by which he meant not only rules of social usage, rituals, and ceremonies but also laws and institutions—as the common denominator of China's complex Confucian tradition.

Yet for all the diversity of Qing intellectual life, there was still a striking uniformity of outlook. Much of this uniformity can be explained by the educational common denominator of preparation for the civil-service examinations. The vast majority of Qing scholars read the same basic works, prepared for the examinations in the same basic way, and used the same set of evaluative terms and conceptual categories to express their ideas. The emphasis in private academies might differ somewhat from the curriculum in official schools, but the practical aim of elite education in Qing times remained success in the examinations, and the early patterns of rote learning directed to this goal left a deep impression on most scholarly minds.

Further, as Yü Ying-shih, Tu Wei-ming, and others have indicated, the differences between certain schools of Confucian thought have often been overemphasized. There were, for example, important affinities between Song Learning and Han Learning in the area of philology, between Song Learning and the School of Statecraft in the management of practical affairs, and even between Song Learning and Wang Yangming's intuitive School of the Mind (see Chapter 2) in the areas of both mental discipline and scholarship. New Text scholars, for their part, shared many administrative concerns with the proponents of the School of Statecraft, although their proposals for governmental reform were generally more radical. In all, as W. T. de Bary has suggested, the major polarities that existed in Confucianism between scholarship and public service, academic pursuits and self-cultivation, contemplation and activity, and aesthetics (or metaphysics) and practical concerns should be seen not as conflicting imperatives but as "dynamic unities," a source of both vitality and adaptability in Chinese intellectual life.[4]

THE CHINESE MENTAL WORLD

Before proceeding to a detailed discussion of Confucian philosophy, we may pause to consider the more general features of traditional Chinese thought. Among its most distinctive features—in addition to its harmonizing impulses—were an abiding concern with ethics and human relations; an interest in nature and natural processes; a deep sense of cultural distinctiveness and superiority; a profound awareness of and respect for tradition; a general preference for suggestiveness over articulation in philosophical discourse; an emphasis on the concrete over the purely abstract; and a heavy

Table 6.1   Early Yinyang *Correlations*

Yang	Yin
Heaven	Earth
Spring	Autumn
Summer	Winter
Day	Night
Big states	Small states
Important states	Unimportant states
Action	Inaction
Stretching	Contracting
Ruler	Minister
Above	Below
Man	Woman
Father	Child
Elder brother	Younger brother
Older	Younger
Noble	Base
Getting on in the world	Being stuck
Taking a wife, begetting a child	Mourning
Controlling people	Being controlled
Guest	Host
Soldiers	Laborers
Speech	Silence
Giving	Receiving

SOURCE: Adapted from the *cheng* attachment to the Mawangdui *Laozi* manuscript "B" (c. 250 B.C.); cited in Graham (1989).

reliance on bureaucratic classification, analogy, and the "logic of correlative duality" as a means of organizing and understanding the vast whole of human experience.

Attunement to natural processes in China encouraged an organismic view of the universe in which the cosmic forces of *yin* and *yang* continually interacted to produce the so-called five elements, or agents—wood, fire, earth, metal, and water (see Tables 6.1 and 6.2). These elements, in various combinations under various circumstances, became the material force (*qi*) of which all things, animate and inanimate, were constituted. In the words of *Reflections on Things at Hand,* "By the transformation of *yang* and its union with *yin,* the five elements ... arise. When these five material forces are distributed in harmonious order, the four seasons run their course." Like *yin* and *yang,* the five elements not only produced all matter but also dominated phases of time, succeeding each other in endless patterns of mutual interaction and cyclical alternation.[5]

The Chinese viewed the universe as a regular, self-contained, self-operating whole, spontaneously generated and perpetually in motion. Everything within the cosmos existed as part of an orderly and harmonious hierarchy of interrelated objects and forces in which "things of the same type" (*tonglei*) had a penchant for corresponding, resonating, and otherwise interacting with one another. Synchroneity (the coincidence of events in space and time) thus came to be stressed over simple causal-

Table 6.2 **Yinyang** *and Five-Elements Correlations*

A. Yin *and* Yang

Yang	Yin	Yang	Yin
Light	Dark	Activity	Quiescence
Hot	Cold	Life	Death
Dry	Moist	Advance	Retreat
Fire	Water	Expand	Contract
Red	Black	Full	Empty
Day	Night	Straight	Crooked
Sun	Moon	Hard	Soft
Spring-Summer	Autumn-Winter	Round	Square
Male	Female	South	North

B. Five-Elements (wuxing) *Correlations*

Correlation	*Wood*	*Fire*	*Earth*	*Metal*	*Water*
Domestic animal	sheep	fowl	ox	dog	pig
Organ	spleen	lungs	heart	liver	kidneys
Number	8	7	5	9	6
Color	green	red	yellow	white	black
Direction	east	south	center	west	north
Emotion	anger	joy	desire	sorrow	fear
Taste	sour	bitter	sweet	acrid	salty
State of *yinyang*	*yin* in *yang* (or lesser *yang*)	*yang* (or greater *yang*)	equal balance	*yang* in *yin* (or lesser *yin*)	*yin* (or greater *yin*)

NOTE: Like *yin* and *yang,* in Chinese thought the five elements were used to indicate both cosmic activities and conceptual categories. In either case, as with *yin* and *yang,* the pattern of movement was one of ceaseless alternation and cyclical change. The order of the elements and the process by which one displaced another varied according to different schemes.

ity as an explanatory principle. The harmonious cooperation and synchronic interaction of all things in the universe did not, however, arise from the commands of an external supreme will or authority. Rather, it proceeded from a natural unified cosmic pattern or process (the Way, or *dao*) that mandated that all things follow the internal dictates of their own natures.[6] Thus we find that even Pan Gu, the legendary "creator" in Chinese folklore, was never viewed as a Logos or demiurge, much less as the omniscient, omnipotent creator of the Semitic, Christian, and Islamic traditions. In fact, the Pan Gu story remains one of the weakest myths in a generally weak and unsystematic Chinese mythology.[7]

Lacking the idea of a personalistic creator external to the cosmos, the Chinese developed an approach to religious life that led them to reject both monotheism and theological absolutism. Although this approach strengthened diffused religions (such as ancestor worship, the worship of Heaven by the state, and the worship of patron gods in associations such as guilds), it weakened the prospects for institutional religion and kept China from developing a concept of evil as an active force in the personsified Western sense. The introduction of Buddhism and other alien belief systems in China, and the later development of an elaborate neo-Confucian metaphysics, did nothing to alter these basic features of Chinese religious life (see Chapter 7).[8]

Neo-Confucian metaphysics did, however, contribute the idea of a prime mover, or Supreme Ultimate (*taiji*), which generated the cosmic forces of *yin* and *yang* and also served as the source (and sum) of the ideal forms, or principles (*li*), around which material force coalesced to comprise all things. By late imperial times, elite interest in the metaphysical notion of *taiji* had waned considerably, but the concept remained an integral feature of official Qing ideology and was also solidly imbedded in the popular mind.[9]

Moreover, the use of *yinyang* as a conceptual paradigm continued unabated in all realms of traditional Chinese life. The idea of *yinyang* interaction generally sufficed as an explanation of cosmic creativity and change, and the specific evaluative terms *yin* and *yang* continued to be used to accommodate nearly any set of dual coordinates, from abstruse Buddhist or neo-Confucian concepts such as "perceived reality and emptiness" (*sekong*), "principle and material force" (*liqi*), and "substance and function" (*tiyong*) to such mundane but important polarities as light and dark, hot and cold, wet and dry, soft and hard, passive and active, male and female. It was a natural Chinese tendency to divide phenomena into two unequal but complementary parts.[10]

The important point to keep in mind is that *yin* and *yang* were always viewed as relative concepts. As creative forces they were continually in flux, each growing out of the other and each in turn "controlling" situations or activities. And even as specific evaluative categories they were never viewed as absolutes. The *Daode jing* (The Way and Its Power) underscores this basic point: "Being [lit., having] and non-being [lit., not-having] produce each other; difficult and easy complete each other. Long and short contrast each other; high and low distinguish each other. Sound and voice harmonize with each other; front and back follow each other."[11]

In the main, then, *yin* and *yang* were not things, but classifications of relations. Any given object or phenomenon might be designated *yin* in one set of relations and *yang* in another. Thus, in the vocabulary of painting and calligraphy, the brush was considered *yang* because it was the active instrument using ink (*yin*). Yet the brush could be considered *yin* in relation to the *yang* of the artist (or, for that matter, the artist's subject material); and although the ink was dark (*yin*) on the light paper or silk, it showed a *yang* aspect when considered in relation to the passiveness of the paper or silk. Similarly, although Heaven was fundamentally *yang* and Earth *yin,* at least some Chinese thinkers maintained that during the day both were *yang* and at night both were *yin.*[12]

One's philosophical outlook also affected the perception of *yinyang* relationships, for what one thinker saw as positive, another might see as negative. The great Han Learning scholar Hui Dong tells us, for example: "The way of change is that the unyielding [*gang,* i.e., *yang*] triumphs, the yielding [*rou,* i.e., *yin*] endangers. … But Daoists hold an opposite view, arguing that unyielding strength [*gangqiang*] brings death. Herein lies the difference between Confucians and Daoists."[13] To an extent, of course, Hui is correct in contrasting Confucian activism and Daoist passivity, as we shall see. But his stark statement obscures two important points. The first is that Confucians often placed a premium on "yielding" in social situations and promoted a view of government that was in many ways quite passive (*yin*). The second point is that circumstances were continually changing, and despite Hui's assertion that strength would always prevail, most Chinese—Confucians and Daoists alike—accepted the *Yijing*'s basic premise that change was a matter of *yinyang* alternation. Inevitably, *gang* would surrender to *rou,* even if only temporarily.

The idea of *yinyang* alternation was of course central to the traditional conception of time, which, following the usage of the *Yijing,* came to be seen as a kind of field or receptacle for human events. Indeed, the *yinyang* paradigm itself developed out of an early appreciation of the rhythms and regularities of cyclical change in nature—notably the twenty-four-hour cycle of light and dark and the seasonal fluctuation between the two poles of summer heat and winter cold. The Chinese word for time (*shi*) originally meant "the period of sowing," and it never totally lost its specific seasonal and cyclical connotations.

"Timeliness" was of central significance to the Chinese in all facets of daily life, at all levels. Two of the most important ritual acts of a new dynasty were to "regulate the calendar" and to "fix the time." Almanacs (*tongshu, liben,* etc.), based on the imperial calendrical model but designed for popular consumption, were ubiquitous and essential to the conduct of affairs in traditional Chinese society.[14] In everyday matters, the water clock divided the day and night into two-hour segments, while the lunar calendar marked the twelve months of the year (with intercalary adjustments to compensate for the 11-day difference between the lunar period of 354 days and the solar period of 365 days). Longer spans of time were conventionally measured in linear order by dynastic periods and by imperial reign names (*nianhao*) within each dynasty.

Overall, time in traditional China was usually viewed in cyclical rather than in linear terms.[15] Cycles might be as long as four Buddhist kalpas (each with a duration of more than a billion years) or as short as the common sixty-year and sixty-day cycles of the native Chinese tradition. Even dynastic periods were seen as macrocosms of the natural life cycle of birth, growth, decline, and death—comparable to the fourfold Buddhist cycle of formative growth, organized existence, disintegration, and annihilation. In contrast with the Christian, Islamic, and Judaic traditions, the world had no fixed starting point, although in Chinese popular culture human events were sometimes dated in successive years from the accession of the mythical Yellow Emperor in 2698 B.C.[16]

Shao Yong's widespread theory of recurrent and eternal 129,600-year cycles, originally inspired by Buddhism, provided a convenient means by which to reconcile a cyclical view of human experience with the pervasive idea of a golden age in China's past. According to Shao, the present cycle began at a date corresponding to 67017 B.C. and reached its peak at about 2330 B.C., during the reign of the legendary sage-ruler Yao. Human society was now in decline, however, and would continue to decline until the extinction of living creatures in around A.D. 46000. In A.D. 62583, the world would end, and a new cycle would then begin. Since dynastic history, as part of the total cosmic process, moved in a cyclical pattern, it followed that an identifiable *yinyang* alternation between order and disorder, prosperity and decline, was both natural and inevitable. Each situation contained the seeds of the other.[17]

But the Chinese also believed that historical circumstances depended on human action and that dynastic decline could thus be at least temporarily arrested by the concerted efforts of moral men. Such a phenomenon was known as a restoration (*zhongxing*, lit., rising at mid-course). Only a few such restorations had been recorded in Chinese history, but one did occur in the late Qing period, during the strife-torn reign of the Tongzhi emperor. Although most Chinese thinkers rejected the idea of historical progress in the sense of progressive improvement, they continued to be moved by a strong impulse to improve society by hearkening back to earlier historical models and times.[18]

History in China was written by scholars for scholars. As a moral drama it reflected predominantly Confucian value judgments. The history of any dynasty, which was always written by its successor, was more than just a narrative record; it was also a guide to proper conduct for the present and the future. The Qing scholar Zhao Yi (1727–1814) put the matter this way in the preface to his famous *Nianer shi zhayi* (Notes on the Twenty-two Dynastic Histories): "The [Confucian] Classics are the principles of government; the histories are the evidences [lit., traces] of government." In China, as Arthur Wright has observed, historical precedent acquired something of the power attached to law and formal logic in the West.[19]

The traditional Chinese dynastic histories followed a general model provided by the great Han historian Sima Qian. Although no two of the twenty-six formal histories (including the draft history of the Qing) are exactly the same, most consist of four major divisions: the imperial annals, chronological tables, monographs, and biographies. Of these, the monographs and biographies are especially helpful in indicating traditional categories of historical concern. Let us examine briefly the Ming History (*Mingshi*, compiled 1678–1739) and the Draft History of the Qing (*Qingshi gao*, compiled 1914–1927)—the last two traditional dynastic histories—with these concerns in mind.

Among the most significant monographs in each multivolume history are those on ritual, music, the calendar, astronomy, rivers and canals, food and commodities, law and punishments, the five elements, geography, literature, officials, chariots and costumes, the civil service, and the army. Among the most important shared categories of biography are those of dutiful officials, Confucian scholars, empresses, doctors, hermits, literary persons, eminent women, filial persons, and loyal subjects. Some differences are obvious—notably the special attention given to eunuchs, imperial relatives, and traitors in the *Mingshi* biographies and the new categories of monographs in the *Qingshi gao* relating to communications and foreign relations. These differences can be explained, of course, by the differing historical circumstances and problems of the two dynastic periods.[20]

Traditionally, China's foreign relations were not considered worthy of a special place in the dynastic histories, although discussions of "barbarians" could be found sprinkled liberally throughout the various major divisions, especially the biographies. This form of neglect bears testimony to the long-standing antiforeign prejudices of the Chinese, despite the important role aliens have played throughout much of Chinese history.

The Chinese view of other peoples, which evolved over many centuries of extensive contact with foreigners within China, on China's borders, and beyond, was based on the essentially unchallenged idea of China's cultural superiority to all other states. In general terms, the Chinese distinguished three major types of barbarian states, each defined by their geographical and cultural proximity to China. The closest group, known to modern scholars as the Sinic Zone states, consisted of nearby tributaries such as Korea, Annam (Vietnam), the Liuqiu Islands, and occasionally Japan; the next closest group, in the so-called Inner Asian Zone, consisted of tributary tribes and states of nomadic or seminomadic peoples on the fringes of the Chinese culture area; and the furthest group, or Outer Zone states, consisted of "outer barbarians" far from China in both physical distance and life-style. The further removed from the "civilizing influence" of Chinese culture, the more likely foreigners would be described by the Chinese as animals such as dogs and sheep, amenable only to policies such as beating, throwing them bones or food, and keeping them under a "loose rein."[21]

Throughout the imperial era, Chinese foreign policy varied according to China's strategic and administrative needs, the perception of an alien threat, the attitudes and activities of the barbarians themselves, and, of course, the whim of the emperor. In theory, at least, the Chinese view was passive: Barbarians were expected to gravitate to China solely out of admiration for Chinese culture. Force was to be used only as a last resort in the conduct of foreign relations. In fact, however, Chinese foreign policy in the Qing, as in other dynamic periods such as the Han and the Tang, was openly aggressive, although characteristically cast in terms of border defense.

Central to the ritualized Chinese world order was preservation of the age-old tributary system, which the Chinese viewed as an extension of their own internal social and political order. This system rested on the assumption of a hierarchical structure of foreign relations, with China at both the top and center. Relationships were based on feudal principles of investiture and loyalty, with China serving as the lord and other states as vassals. According to the tributary regulations of the Qing period, non-Chinese rulers were given a patent of appointment, noble rank, and an official seal for use in correspondence. They, in turn, presented symbolic tribute and periodic tribute memorials, dated their communications by the Qing calendar, and performed the appropriate ceremonies of the Qing court, including the kowtow. Loyal tributaries received imperial gifts and protection in return and were granted certain privileges of trade at the frontier and at the capital.

In times of military weakness, the Chinese were often obliged to buy off barbarians with tributary gifts and to make other compromises with the theoretical assumptions of the Chinese world order. In making peace with the foreign-ruled Jin dynasty in 1138, for example, the founder of the Southern Song had to accept the humiliating status of a vassal (*chen*). And even in periods of Chinese strength the tributary system proved to be quite flexible. John Wills shows, for instance, that during the Kangxi emperor's reign the Qing authorities were able to make pragmatic decisions based on domestic politics and strategic interests in dealing with foreign embassies from the Netherlands and Portugal—although he emphasizes that the facade of imperial authority over "strangers from afar" had to remain intact. In 1793, the Qianlong emperor displayed similar pragmatism in allowing Great Britain's special envoy, Lord George Macartney, to have an imperial audience, despite Macartney's refusal to perform the ritually required full kowtow (Qing official documents recorded him as performing it anyway). Further concessions followed the Opium War of 1839–1842. Yet, as John Fairbank has demonstrated, the tributary system showed remarkable staying power even after the Treaty of Nanjing (1842).[22]

In all, the Chinese were not overly concerned with the gap between theory and practice in foreign relations. Zhao Yi, for one, maintained that the practice of "true principle" in foreign affairs necessarily involved adjustments. "The teachings of true principle," he wrote, "cannot always be reconciled with the circumstances of the times. If one cannot entirely maintain the demands of true principle, then true principle must be adjusted to the circumstances of the time, and only then do we have the practice of true principle."[23] This convenient logic also applied to the employment of foreigners in Chinese civil and military administration, a phenomenon described by Fairbank as "synarchy."

As might be expected, the Chinese historical record abounds with praise for barbarians who "admired right behavior and turned toward Chinese civilization." Such conduct accorded perfectly with China's self-image of cultural and moral superiority. But all of China's barbarian employees did not serve the Middle Kingdom solely out of admiration. Some individuals were drawn by the prospect of financial and material rewards. Others submitted with large bodies of troops after defeat in battle or the deterioration of prospects in their homeland. A number came to China to render temporary service, returning home after a limited tour of duty. Although the general tendency was to measure barbarian devotion by the yardstick of cultural submission, Chinese policymakers recognized that personal, bureaucratic, and economic pressures and inducements necessarily complemented cultural controls.[24]

In the end, however, ethical and ritual concerns remained paramount to the Chinese. As Benjamin Schwartz points out, "A random perusal of discussions of barbarians in the various encyclopedias and other sources reveals again and again the degree of emphasis on the five relationships, the 'three bonds' ... and the whole body of *li* as providing the absolute criteria dividing barbarians from the men of the Middle Kingdom."[25] Although the Chinese notion of universal kingship was pre-Confucian and taken for granted by nearly all late Chou philosophical schools, no school of thought took ethics and ritual more seriously than the Confucians, for none placed greater emphasis on moral discipline and social order.

THE CONFUCIAN MORAL ORDER

Ping-ti Ho writes of the Qing: "In no earlier period of Chinese history do we find a deeper permeation and wider acceptance of the norms, mores, and values which modern students regard as Confucian." The Qing emperors ardently patronized Confucian scholarship and paid unprecedented homage to Confucius in official ceremonies, including two kneelings and six prostrations in Beijing, and the full kowtow—three kneelings and nine prostrations—in Qufu, the birthplace of Confucius. The education of Manchu princes followed carefully constructed Confucian lines, and the examination system was, of course, based solidly on the Confucian Classics and commentaries. Lawrence Kessler writes that by the end of the Kangxi emperor's reign in the early eighteenth century, "the Manchu-controlled state and the Chinese-guarded Confucian value system were harmoniously joined ... [and the] Confucian ideal of the unity of state and knowledge, under the rule of a sage-king, seemed near realization."[26]

During the Qing period, as in earlier times, one's intellectual posture was ordinarily a function of several major variables: (1) personality and family background, (2) educational experience, (3) personal and dynastic fortunes, and (4) career concerns. Political factors were especially important in determining the popularity of a certain school of thought at a particular time, but the attachment of any individual to a given point of view might well hinge on career concerns. Thus, for example, young students and gentry awaiting official appointment could be expected to emphasize Song idealism, if only because a mastery of Zhu Xi's thought brought the possibility of personal advancement. Officials, by contrast, might publicly espouse neo-Confucian moral principles only to seek administrative guidance from the School of Statecraft. And retired officials might find satisfaction in pure scholarship and the contemplative life, studying the *Yijing* and perhaps also investigating the officially disparaged but still attractive ideas of Wang Yangming, the Daoists, and even the Buddhists.

Despite the broad spectrum of Confucian thought that existed during the Qing period, we can identify certain general features that apply, more or less, to all major "schools": (1) a comparative lack of interest in metaphysics; (2) a rationalistic outlook, predicated on a belief in the intelligibility of the universe; (3) a great reverence for the past; (4) a humanistic concern with "man in society"; (5) an emphasis on morality in government and a link between personal and political values; (6) a belief in the moral perfectibility of all human beings; (7) the supreme authority of fundamental Confucian principles; and (8) a general disesteem of law.[27] Frederick Mote explains the significance of the last point:

> In a civilization like the Chinese where there are only human sources (or among
> Taoists [Daoists], "natural sources") of normative ideas, law could scarcely be expected
> to achieve the significance it possessed in other civilizations. For in all other
> civilizations it was based on the supra-rational and unchallengeable law of God, which

commanded all creatures, and states as well, to enforce its literal prohibitions. Nor in China could there be any priestly enforcers of divine commandment, or even governors enforcing divine law or civil law armed with the analogy between man and God's law.[28]

In Qing China, the ideal emphasis was on *li* (ritual, or more generally, standards of social usage) rather than law. As Confucius once remarked: "If the people are led by laws, and an attempt is made to give them uniformity by means of punishments, they will try to avoid the punishment, but have no sense of shame. If [however] they are led by virtue, and an attempt is made to give them uniformity by means of ritual, they will have a sense of shame and become good."[29]

The Confucian tradition drew upon a vast corpus of classical literature and commentaries, including the Five Classics (the *Yijing, Shijing* [Book of Poetry or Book of Songs], *Shujing* [Book of Documents or History], *Chunqiu* [Spring and Autumn Annals], and the *Liji* [Record of Ritual]); the *Zuozhuan* (Commentary of Zuo); the *Kongyang zhuan* (Commentary of Gongyang); the *Zhouli* (Rites of Zhou) and *Yili* (Etiquette and Ritual); and the Four Books (the *Lunyu* [Analects of Confucius], the *Mengzi* [Book of Mencius], the *Daxue* [Great Learning], and the *Zhongyong* [Doctrine of the Mean]).

Different schools of Confucianism sometimes emphasized different classics or commentaries. Scholars of Song Learning, for example, derived their understanding of the *Spring and Autumn Annals* from the "orthodox" *Commentary of Zuo,* while those of the New Text persuasion looked to the *Commentary of Gongyang* for inspiration and guidance (primarily because it was the only *jinwen* commentary that had survived intact from the Former Han dynasty). At the same time, "purist" *kaozheng* scholars, enamored of ritual (*li*) as an antidote to what they viewed as the "corrupt" and "debased" content of Song Learning, favored the *Record of Ritual* and *Etiquette and Ritual.* Some even enthusiastically explored the officially discouraged ideas of Xunzi, whose theory of man's innately "evil" nature stood in sharp contrast to the orthodox ideas of Mencius.[30]

Despite such differences, most Qing scholars believed that the Four Books contained the essence of Confucian thought. Fung Yu-lan considers the Four Books to be "the Bible of the Chinese people," although significantly he points out that they contain no story of creation and no mention of a heaven or hell.[31] The values contained in the Four Books were closely related. As Cheng Chung-ying has aptly remarked, the major Confucian virtues must all "be understood in relative definitions of each other ... for each supposes the rest." A careful reading of the Four Books confirms the correctness of this view. Although the relationships are not always spelled out clearly, they are no less important for their lack of systematic exposition.[32]

At the heart of the Confucian value system in late imperial times lay the Three Bonds: between ruler and minister (or, more broadly, subject); between father and son; and between husband and wife. These were the first three of the Five Relationships, which also included the relationship between older (brother) and younger (brother) and friend to friend. The concept of the Three Bonds may be traced to the influential Han scholar Dong Zhongshu, who wrote: "The relationships between sovereign and subject, father and son, and husband and wife, are all derived from the principles of *yin* and *yang*. The sovereign is *yang*, the subject is *yin*; the father is *yang*, the son is *yin*; the husband is *yang*, the wife is *yin*. … The three bonds of the Way of the [True] King may be sought in Heaven."[33]

Of these three relationships, the tie between husband and wife was considered most basic. "That male and female should live together is the greatest of human relations," asserted Mencius. The "Orderly Sequence of the Hexagrams" of the *Yijing* indicates that all other human relationships grow out of the relationship between man and wife:

> Following the existence of Heaven and Earth came the existence of all things. Following the existence of all things came the existence of male and female. Following the existence of male and female came the relationship between husband and wife. And following the relationship of husband and wife came the relationship between father and son. Following the relationship between father and son came the relationship between ruler and subject. Following the relationship between ruler and subject came the general distinction between superior and inferior. Following the distinction between superior and inferior came the arrangements of ritual and righteousness.[34]

The entire Confucian social and moral order was thus based on the "natural" relationship of husband and wife, with its assumptions of inequality, subordination, and service. As Mencius once stated, "to look upon compliance as their correct course is the rule [*dao*] for women."[35]

Some Qing scholars, notably Qian Daxin (1728–1804), believed that marriage was a human artifact rather than a natural bond, and therefore mutable. It followed, then, that divorce was not necessarily improper. Taking a similar tack, Huang Zongxi challenged the idea of "cosmological kingship" as an integral part of the Three Bonds on the grounds that the ruler-subject relationship was secular and functional and could thus be altered, depending on circumstances.[36] But neither Qian nor Huang, nor any other major Confucian thinker, could conceive of a mutable relationship between parents and children.

Filial piety (*xiao*) and its corollary, fraternal submission (*di*) lay at the very heart of Confucianism. Mencius tells us that devotion to one's parents is the greatest service and the foundation of all other services. The *Great Learning* remarks, "If one is not obedient to his parents, he will not be true to his friends," and "If one is not trusted by his friends, he will not get the confidence of his sovereign." The *Xiaojing* (Classic of Filial Piety) goes so far as to claim that the ancient Chinese sages "brought order to the world through filial piety." And the *Analects* state explicitly that *xiao* and *di* are the root of humaneness (*ren*)—the most exalted of the Five Constant Virtues of Confucianism: *ren, li* ("ritual," "propriety," or norms of social usage), *yi* ("duty" or "righteousness"), *zhi* ("humane wisdom"), and *xin* ("faithfulness").[37]

Let us examine these five cardinal virtues in greater detail, giving particular attention to the concept of *ren*. Qing Confucians considered *ren* to be a universal cosmic virtue that, in effect, generated and encompassed all the other virtues. Wing-tsit Chan's careful study of the evolution of *ren* leaves no doubt that by late imperial times the term had become all-important. *Ren*, he tells us, "precludes all evil and underlies as well as embraces all possible virtues, so much so that 'if you set your mind on *jen* [*ren*], you will be free from evil.'" Confucius tells us that *ren* means to "love human beings" (*airen*); and Mencius equates *ren* with the innate goodness of man's nature, manifest in the feeling of commiseration: the inability to bear the suffering of others. *Ren*, in the view of most Qing scholars, was the "single thread" unifying the teachings of Confucius—the one moral principle for all human actions.[38]

Much has been made of the negative thrust of the famous Confucian dictum, "Do not do to others what you would not want others to do to you." But it is clear that virtually all Confucian scholars understood this "Golden Rule" as having both a positive and negative aspect. The Qing commentator Liu Baonan (1791–1855) spoke for many in maintaining that if it is true that we must not do to others what we do not want done to ourselves, then it must also be true that "we must do to others what we want them to do to us." Further, Liu concurs with Zhu Xi and most other late-imperial thinkers in equating the principles of *zhong* (usually translated "loyalty") and *shu* ("reciprocity") as referring, respectively, to the full development of one's mind and the extension of that mind to others, thus giving a positive cast to Confucian responsibility. As the *Analects* state: "The man of *ren*, wishing to establish his own character, seeks also to establish the character of others."[39]

This did not mean, however, that all people should be treated equally. Rather, the Confucian idea of *ren* was "love with distinctions" (*ai you chadeng*), that is, love graded outward from the family and focused particularly on the virtuous. From a Confucian standpoint, it was impossible to love all people equally (*jian'ai*), as Mozi had urged, for all people were not equal, either in closeness or in social station. According to Confucians, different values were appropriate to different relationships. Thus, Mencius informs us that "between father and son, there should be affection; between sovereign and minister, righteousness; between husband and wife, attention to their separate functions; between elder and younger, proper order; and between friends, faithfulness."[40]

Ren, in the orthodox view, was the key to good government. The *Great Learning* asserts: "Yao and Shun led the kingdom with benevolence [*ren*] and the people followed them"; and again, "Never has there been a case of the sovereign loving benevolence, and the people not loving righteousness. Never has there been a case where the people have loved righteousness, and the affairs of the sovereign have not been carried to completion." Confucian government was never meant to be *by* the people, but it certainly was *for* the people, and the assumption remained that the moral cultivation of the ruler would bring peace and harmony to "all under Heaven." In the words of the *Doctrine of the Mean,*

> By honoring men of virtue and talent, the sovereign is preserved from errors of judgment. By showing affection to his relatives, there is no grumbling and resentment among his uncles and brethren. By respecting the great ministers, he is kept from errors in the practice of government. By kind and considerate treatment of the whole body of officers, they are led to make the most grateful return for his courtesies. By dealing with the mass of people as his children, they are led to exhort one another to what is good. ... By indulgent treatment of men from afar, they resort to him from all quarters.[41]

There was also, however, a more "realistic" wing of Confucian political theory, which sought administrative inspiration in less idealistic works, such as the writings of Xunzi and the *Rites of Zhou.* This latter work, which had often been cited by radical reformers in China's past, provided classical precedents for systems of equitable land distribution, public security, famine relief, arbitration, and even criminal justice. When it became necessary to reconcile the idealistic Mencian emphasis on *ren* with the harsh realities of Qing political life, scholar-officials like Yuan Shouding (1705–1782) could argue that the Qing penal code was based on the concepts of the *Rites of Zhou* but that its aim was to implement the Mencian values of humaneness and righteousness. In any case, we find many examples of Qing scholars whose idealistic Confucian values were tempered by an un-Confucian emphasis on law, rewards, and punishments.[42]

Standing between rule by moral example and rule by law, closer to the former than the latter, was rule by ritual and propriety. The *Record of Ritual* informs us that "Ceremonies [*li*] form a great instrument in the hands of the ruler. They provide the means by which to resolve what is doubtful, clarify what is abstruse, receive the spirits, examine regulations, and distinguish humaneness from righteousness. ... To govern a state without ritual would be like plowing a field without a plowshare." The seventeenth-century censor Chen Cizhi spoke for many Qing officials in asserting that "for managing the world and pacifying the people there is nothing greater than ritual." Wei Xiangshu (1617–1687) advised the early Manchu rulers: "The moral transformation of the people is the dynasty's first task, and the regulations of ritual constitute the great beginning of moral transformation."[43] Through proper ritual, the emperor not only affirmed his position as Son of Heaven and ruler of all earthly domains but he and his officials also promoted social harmony within the realm through moral example. This, at least, was the theory of Confucian government.

In Chinese ethical life, *ren* and *li* existed in a kind of creative tension, each contributing to the meaning or manifestation of the other. Tu Wei-ming considers *li* to be the "externalization" of *ren* in concrete social circumstances. Confucius once said, "If a man is not humane, what has he to do with *li?*" But in another context, the Master remarked, "To conquer the self and return to *li* is humaneness." When asked how one could achieve this object, Confucius replied, "Do not look at what is contrary to *li*; do not listen to what is contrary to *li*; do not say what is contrary to *li*; and do not make any movement contrary to *li*." The three major Chinese classics on ritual prescribed, often in minute detail, the behavior appropriate to a Confucian gentleman (*junzi*). Ritual handbooks of the Qing dynasty did the same.[44]

The massive compendium by Qin Huitian (1702–1764) entitled *Wuli tongkao* (Comprehensive Study of the Five Rituals) provides an indication of the standard categories of Chinese ceremonial practice: auspicious sacrifices, ceremonies of celebration, ceremonies of visitation, military ritual, and ceremonies of sadness. Qin devotes most of his compendium (127 *juan* and 92 *juan,* respectively) to auspicious ritual (state sacrifices, commemoration of temples, clan and family sacrifices, and so on) and ceremonies of celebration (events such as imperial weddings and state banquets down to local festivals and the marriage of commoners). Military rituals, including imperial expeditions, hunts, and formal inspections, account for only 13 *juan*—the same amount of space allotted to ceremonies of visitation, from tributary missions and audiences to daily social intercourse. Ceremonies of sadness, notably mourning ritual, account for 17 *juan* in the *Wuli tongkao.* A similar emphasis can be found in other compilations on Qing ritual, including the *Collected Statutes* of the empire.[45]

As a reading of the Four Books and other sources indicates clearly, the Chinese considered ritual and propriety to be essential to the performance of filial duties and to the overall harmony of the household. Together with music, poetry, and other forms of refinement, *li* contributed to self-cultivation and the establishment of character. Employed by the ruler and other "superior men," it encouraged respect, reverence, and right behavior at all levels of society, and followed as a standard of proper conduct, it imposed restraints on individuals and preserved social distinctions. Mencius asserts, "Without the rules of propriety and distinctions of righteousness, the high and low will be thrown into confusion." And the *Record of Ritual* states expansively:

> The rules of propriety furnish the means of determining the observances toward
> relatives, as near and remote; of settling points which may cause suspicion or doubt;
> of distinguishing where there should be agreement, and where difference; and of
> making clear what is right and what is wrong. ... To cultivate one's person and fulfill
> one's words is called good conduct. When conduct is ordered and words are in
> accordance with the *dao,* we have the substance of the rules of propriety.[46]

Ren represented the idealistic thrust of Confucianism, with its emphasis on altruism, compassion, and reciprocity, but *li* gave structure and concrete expression to *ren.*

The virtue of *yi,* usually rendered duty, righteousness, or right behavior, can only be understood in light of the preceding two Confucian values. In the most general terms it served as a unifying and ordering principle as well as a standard for moral judgment. *Yi* may be defined as appropriate behavior according to circumstance.

Like *li,* it presupposed objective and external standards of correct behavior, but like *ren,* it had a subjective, internal component. To employ a rather mundane mechanical metaphor, *yi* served as a spring controlling the tension between *ren* and *li.* It was at once a universal and particular virtue, expressing the substance of *ren* and the form of *li.* The *Analects* state that the "superior man considers righteousness to be essential. He performs it according to the rules of propriety, he brings it forth in humility, and he completes it with faithfulness." But *yi* also allows for the occasional abandonment of the rules of propriety under special circumstances. In a famous illustration, Mencius remarks that although propriety demands that men and women not touch hands in public, if a man's sister-in-law were drowning, the man who would not extend his hand to save her would be "a wolf." In this instance, *yi* mitigates *li,* but makes manifest *ren.*[47]

The Four Books define *yi* in a variety of ways. Mencius, who often discusses the term together with *ren,* contrasts *yi* and *li* ("profit"), defines courage (*yong*) as acting according to *yi,* and describes respect for elders as "the working of *yi.*" Where *ren* is associated in the Four Books with filial piety, *yi* is associated with loyalty to the ruler or fraternal submission. Where *ren* is associated with a feeling of commiseration, *yi* is associated with feelings of shame and dislike. In many respects, *yi* comes close to the idea of Confucian "conscience." Simply stated, *yi* is knowing what to do and what not to do. Mencius repeatedly emphasizes the importance of a sense of shame (*chi*) in providing moral guidance.[48]

Humane wisdom (*zhi*), the fourth of the Five Constant Virtues, was essential to the full expression of *yi.* From an orthodox Confucian standpoint, it was the only kind of knowledge worth having.[49] In various contexts, *zhi* is defined in the Four Books as the knowledge of filial piety and fraternal submission, as a feeling of approving and disapproving, and as the ability to recognize human talent. Mencius indicates that without humaneness and wisdom there can be no ritual and right behavior (*buren buzhi wuli wuyi*), which suggests that like *ren, zhi* is an internal virtue made manifest in other (external) virtues. And although to Mencius all these virtues were innate in man, the *Great Learning* indicates—and Song neo-Confucian metaphysics affirm—that some men are born with moral knowledge and others have to learn it. "Only the wise of the highest class and the stupid of the lowest class cannot be changed," the Master once said.[50]

The fifth virtue of faithfulness (*xin*) receives prominent exposure in the Four Books, often in combination with other values such as loyalty, reciprocity, and sincerity (*cheng*). Of these, the last deserves special mention. Described in the *Great Learning* as "the way of Heaven," sincerity may best be defined as being true to oneself, being consistent in word and deed, fully developing one's own nature, and extending that development to others. In this respect, *cheng* is closely akin to the concepts of loyalty (*zhong*) and reciprocity (*shu*). The *Doctrine of the Mean* tells us that "Sincerity is [the way of] self-completion. ... [It] is the beginning and ending of all things; without sincerity there would be nothing. For this reason, the superior man regards the attainment of sincerity as the most exalted thing." Further, it states, "The individual possessed of the most complete sincerity is like a spirit."[51]

How did the Confucian gentleman achieve sincerity and self-completion? The process began with the extension of knowledge and the "investigation of things." The *Great Learning* states:

> The ancients who wished to illustrate illustrious virtue throughout the world, first put their principalities in order. Wishing to put their principalities in order, they first regulated their families. Wishing to regulate their families, they first cultivated themselves. Wishing to cultivate themselves, they first rectified their hearts and minds. Wishing to rectify their hearts and minds, they first sought to be sincere in their thoughts. Wishing to be sincere in their thoughts, they first extended to the utmost their knowledge. Such extensions of knowledge lay in the investigation of things [*gewu*].[52]

The "investigation of things" was variously interpreted by Confucian scholars. Zhu Xi naturally saw it primarily as "investigating principle" (*li*); Wang Yangming viewed it as an effort to "rectify the mind"; Ling Tingkan (1757–1809), a *kaozheng* scholar, concluded that it meant the study of ritual; and Yan Yuan considered it to be "learning from actual experience and solving practical problems." But regardless of the interpretation attached to the term *gewu*, the ultimate aim of any Confucian was to develop his innate potential and extend both his knowledge and his influence. Self-improvement involved self-examination and the achievement of a balance between book study (*dushu*), meditative quiet sitting (*jingzuo*), and indulgence in ritual and the arts—especially music, poetry, painting, and calligraphy. The blend varied, of course, from school to school and from individual to individual.[53]

An examination of the Qing encyclopedia *TSJC*'s subcategory on Confucian conduct yields a wealth of information on how Confucians approached the problem of self-cultivation. In addition to the basic techniques outlined above, self-improvement could be achieved through means such as "investigating principle to the utmost," "nourishing the mind," "paying attention to fundamentals," "regulating desires," "correcting faults," and "abiding in reverence." Confucians also placed emphasis on "proper timing," the value of "personal experience" in the quest for truth, and the importance of "unifying knowledge and action."[54]

The Four Books provide numerous examples of the personal attributes of the "true gentleman." He is described as virtuous, industrious, intelligent, learned, thoughtful, open-minded, impartial, kind, just, generous, reverent, respectful, cultured, solid, straightforward, cautious, slow in speech, dignified, modest, courageous, and anxious to teach as well as learn. He "does what is proper to his station, and does not desire to go beyond this." Confucius even supplies a rough blueprint for the moral development of the sage. "At fifteen," he informs us, "I had my mind set on learning. At thirty, I stood firm. At forty, I had no doubts. At fifty, I knew the decrees of Heaven [*tianming*]. At sixty, my ear was an obedient organ [for the reception of the *dao*]. At seventy, I could follow what my heart desired, without transgressing what was right."[55]

Confucius demonstrated an abiding concern with the "mean"—the middle path of perfect harmony and equilibrium in thought, emotions, and conduct. "The superior man [*junzi*] embodies the course of the mean," said Confucius; "The petty man [*xiaoren*] acts contrary to the course of the mean." The *Doctrine of the Mean* states: "The superior man cultivates a [friendly] harmony without being weak. How firm is his strength! He stands erect in the middle, without inclining to either side." And how might the superior man determine the mean? The sage-ruler Shun provided the model. Shun questioned others, studied their words, concealed what was bad in them, and displayed what was good. "He took hold of their extremes, determined the mean, and employed it in governing the people."[56]

The example of Shun reminds us that in the Confucian view, personal sagehood was never enough. Just as the internal, subjective value of *ren* required objective manifestation in *li,* so self-cultivation required manifestation in public service. Since the goal of Confucianism was social harmony rather than personal salvation, self-realization could never be divorced from service to humanity. The Confucian imperative was "internal sagehood and external kingship." If the superior man could achieve complete sincerity and an undisturbed mind, he might, like Confucius himself, become an uncrowned king and extend his good influence far and wide.[57]

Despite a general lack of interest in metaphysics, Qing Confucians could hardly avoid considering the relationship between the moral order on earth and the great scheme, or *dao,* of the cosmos. According to orthodox neo-Confucianism, the two were one. Zhu Xi's basic assumption, in other words, was that the principle (*li*) of man's nature was his original goodness (*ren*). The *li* for all men, then, was the same. What made them different in both appearance and morality was their dissimilar endowment of "material force" (*qi*). Zhu Xi says, "Those who receive a *qi* that is clear, are the sages in whom the nature is like a pearl lying in clear, cold water. But those who receive a *qi* that is turbid, are the foolish and degenerate in whom the nature is like a pearl lying in muddy water." Long ago, Confucius had stated, "By nature, men are nearly alike, but by practice they get to be far apart"; and somewhat later, Mencius made the penetrating observation that men's innately good minds could be "injured by hunger and thirst." Xunzi, as we have seen, held that man's nature was basically evil.[58]

Orthodox neo-Confucianism, however, explained evil (*e*) as arising from selfish desires and other deviant impulses inherent in one's own physical endowment. Evil was thus a kind of moral imbalance in individuals. In the words of Cheng Hao: "All the myriad things have their opposites. When there is *yin,* there is *yang.* When there is good, there is evil. As *yang* increases, *yin* decreases, and as goodness is augmented, evil is diminished."[59] The purpose of neo-Confucian self-cultivation was to correct moral imbalance by refining one's *qi,* allowing the luster of one's *li* to shine through. Neo-Confucians believed that the mind had this transformative capacity.

A number of Qing thinkers—ranging from Wang Fuzhi, Gu Yanwu, and Huang Zongxi to Yan Yuan, Li Yong (1627–1705), and Dai Zhen—rejected the idea of a *liqi* duality, arguing that there was no "principle" apart from material force and thus no evil inherent in *qi*. They deplored Zhu Xi's attempt to distinguish man's heavenly conferred nature from his physical endowment and the way Zhu pitted "human desires" against "heavenly principle." Li Yong articulated his position this way: "The *dao* is fully realized with empathies and feelings." Dai Zhen remarked in the same spirit: "To equate the self [*ji*] with selfish desires is ... a notion the sages totally lacked." In short, to these thinkers, the metaphysical reality of nature (the *dao*) and concrete things was one. Evil arose not from man's physical endowment per se but rather from "outside" influences, such as selfishness and ignorance. To overcome evil required self-cultivation and the elimination of destructive desires.[60]

Although concepts such as *yin* and *yang*, principle and material force, and nature and concrete things continually crop up in Chinese philosophical discussions, they were by no means the only dualistic terms employed by Confucian thinkers. Neo-Confucians in particular were attracted by the terms *ti* ("substance") and *yong* ("function") to explain their ideas—including the basic notion that "principle is one, but the manifestations are many." *Ti* signifies the "inherent, enduring and fundamental (hence 'internal') qualities of a thing or situation," while *yong* refers to "its functional, fluctuating and secondary (hence 'external') manifestations."[61]

The *tiyong* formula, like the *yinyang* paradigm, could be used in a great variety of ways, and like *yin* and *yang*, the two terms generally implied mutual dependence and the superiority or precedence of one quality (*ti*) over the other (*yong*). Although Qing *kaozheng* scholars traced the *tiyong* concept directly to Chan (Zen) Buddhism (see Chapter 7), Confucians of many different intellectual orientations continued to employ it freely. At a mundane level, the *tiyong* formula might be used to distinguish between the root of a problem and its manifestations. Thus, a bureaucrat would ask, "Which ... is the proper means of ridding an area of robbery: rigorous police measures or sound economic measures so that the people 'find it unnecessary to rob for a living'?" In the realm of ethics, the *ti* of man's humaneness might be distinguished from the *yong* of his righteousness, or the *ti* of Confucian morality in general distinguished from the *yong* of government and institutions. At a higher metaphysical plane, *ti* might be equated with principle and *yong* with material force, or Heaven with *ti* and fate with *yong*.[62]

The place of Heaven (*tian*) in Chinese philosophy is a central one. Fung Yu-lan points out that the character *tian* in Chinese writing has at least five different meanings: (1) a material or physical sky, opposite the earth; (2) an anthropomorphic deity presiding over heaven; (3) an impersonal dispenser of fate; (4) the equivalent of the English word nature; and (5) an amorphous ethical entity embracing moral principles and responding to the morality of men. In neo-Confucianism, the term Heaven is used in several senses, but it is generally devoid of any personality or anthropomorphism.[63]

To most Confucians in late imperial times, Heaven represented "fullness of being and goodness," a concept equivalent to the way (*dao*) of the universe or to the idea of the Supreme Ultimate (*taiji*) in Zhu Xi's neo-Confucianism. In the orthodox view, Heaven was a self-existent moral entity that endowed all living creatures with their natures. Heaven's will was that these creatures would all act in accordance with their respective natures. Heaven had the power to express its displeasure over the actions of men by visiting upon them natural disasters and other signs, and it could even withdraw its mandate to rule if the emperor should prove immoral and thus unworthy of the throne. "Heaven sees as the people see, and Heaven hears as the people hear," said Mencius. The idea that the people had the right to rebel against oppressive rule remained at the heart of Chinese dynastic politics until the twentieth century, and echoes of it could still be heard even after the fall of the Qing dynasty in 1912.[64]

Qing Confucians, like their predecessors for centuries, saw an essential unity between Heaven, Earth, and Man. The *Doctrine of the Mean* states that he who is possessed of complete sincerity can "assist in the transforming and nourishing powers of Heaven and Earth" and thus form a triad with them. The Great Commentary of the *Yijing* remarks, "The *Changes* is a book vast and great, in which everything is completely contained. The *dao* of Heaven is in it, the *dao* of Earth is in it, and the *dao* of Man is in it." By using the *Yijing*, "Man comes to resemble Heaven and Earth, ... [and] is not in conflict with them. His wisdom embraces all things, and his *dao* brings order to the whole world; therefore he does not err. ... He rejoices in Heaven and has knowledge of fate, therefore he is free from care."[65]

The key concept here is fate (*ming*). Although the term sometimes means Heaven's mandate, nature, or man's natural endowment, Confucian "fate" is best thought of as a series, or set, of predestined situations evolving out of the natural processes of eternal cosmic change. These situations were believed to be represented by the sixty-four hexagrams of the *Yijing* and their constituent lines. By consulting the *Changes* and establishing a spiritual link with Heaven, a scholar could not only determine the nature and direction of universal change but also devise an appropriate Confucian strategy for coping with any situation. He could not only "know fate" but also "establish fate." In the words of the great Qing scholar Tang Jian (1776–1861), "He who knows fate will cultivate the Way; he who [merely] relies on fate will do harm to the Way." The Confucian belief in predestination thus did not lead to a crippling of self-reliance, although it was sometimes used to explain personal failure and adversity.[66]

All levels of traditional Chinese society evinced a concern with predestination, but not all had the luxury of time and money for leisurely study of the *Yijing* and the metaphysical principles that lay behind it. Nor did most have the education or the inclination to appreciate all the refinements of Confucian ethics. To the degree that economics allowed, commoners in Qing China tried to adhere to basic elite values in areas such as marriage, family life, and ancestor worship.[67] It is doubtful, however, that the vast majority were much attracted to philosophical Daoism, for as Joseph Levenson has remarked, "The pleasure of a flight from civilization is open only to civilized man."[68] Chinese peasants were perhaps too close to the land, too close to nature's cruel caprice.

DAOIST FLIGHT AND FANCY

For the elite, the *yang* of Confucian social responsibility was balanced by the *yin* of Daoist escape into nature. Unlike Confucianism, which for virtually all Qing scholars was a way of life, if not a living faith, Daoism—at least in its philosophical form—was essentially a state of mind. It provided an emotional and intellectual escape valve for world-weary Confucians, trammeled by social responsibility. The writings of Daoist philosophers such as Laozi and Zhuangzi were fresh and poetic, often playful, and almost always paradoxical. They admired the weak, accepted the relativity of things, advocated spiritual release, and above all sought communion with nature. The concrete symbols of Daoism were *yin*: water, the female, the child, the emptiness of the valley, and the uncarved block of wood (*pu*).[69]

Recent research, based not only on the discovery and analysis of new textual materials but also on a fundamental rethinking of the entire Chinese philosophical tradition, has produced some extraordinarily interesting scholarly studies. Chad Hansen's *A Daoist Theory of Chinese Thought* (1992) is but one fascinating example of the yield.[70] We should not, of course, be surprised to find a Daoist-inspired reevaluation of traditional Chinese philosophy, since a primary impulse of Daoism has always been to defy authority and question conventional wisdom. Nevertheless, we should keep in mind that during Qing times the prevailing understanding of Daoism was precisely of the "authoritative" sort that Hansen decries.

The essence of Daoism lay in doing what comes naturally. This meant "not striving" (*wu-wei*; lit., doing nothing). "No action is taken," Laozi asserts, "and yet nothing is left undone."[71] Sustained by this viewpoint, the Daoist "sage" declares:

> I take no action and the people of themselves are transformed.
> I love tranquility and the people of themselves become correct.
> I engage in no activity and the people of themselves become prosperous.
> I have no desires and the people of themselves become simple.[72]

This "sage" was not, however, a Confucian-style exemplar mediating between a "moral" Heaven and Earth. Indeed, the *Daode jing* (Way and Its Power), traditionally attributed to Laozi, states explicitly: "Heaven and Earth are not benevolent; they treat all things like straw dogs."[73] Nature, in this view, played no favorites; it did not discriminate in the Confucian manner.

Laozi's cosmogony and ontology were as simple as his ethics: "Reversion is the action of the *dao*. Weakness is the function of the *dao*. All things in the world come into being from being; and being comes into being from nonbeing." Zhuangzi elaborates on this point with his usual paradoxical playfulness:

There was a beginning. There was a no-beginning [before the beginning]. There was a no-no-beginning [previous to the no-beginning before the beginning]. There was being. [Similarly,] there was nonbeing [before there was being]; and there was no-nonbeing [before there was nonbeing]. There was no-no-nonbeing [before there was no-nonbeing]. Suddenly being and nonbeing appeared. And yet, between being and nonbeing, I do not know which is really being and which is really nonbeing. Just now I have said something, and yet I do not know whether what I have said really means something, or does not mean anything at all.[74]

Daoist relativity precluded absolute values of the sort embraced by Confucians. Listen, for example, to Zhuangzi discussing "right" and "wrong":

From the standpoint of preference, if we approve of anyone who is approved of by someone [at least himself], then there is no one who may not be approved of. If we condemn anyone who is condemned by someone else, then there is no one who may not be condemned. To know that [sage-king] Yao and [tyrant] Jie would each approve of himself and condemn the other, then we have a clear realization of human preference. ... Therefore it has been said, one who wishes to uphold the right and eliminate the wrong, or uphold order and eliminate disorder, must be ignorant of the great principles of the universe as well as the nature of things. One might as well try to uphold Heaven and eliminate the earth, or uphold the *yin* and eliminate the *yang*, which is clearly absurd.[75]

Such views gave Confucians fits; yet they could not help but admire Zhuangzi's insightfulness and the power of his presentation:

Whereby is the *dao* vitiated that there should be a distinction of true and false? Whereby is speech vitiated that there should be a distinction between right and wrong? ... Everything is its own self; everything is something else's other. Things do not know that they are other things' other; they only know that they are themselves. Thus it is said, the other arises out of the self, just as the self arises out of the other.[76]

And again:

It is because there is right, that there is wrong; it is because there is wrong, that there is right. ... According to the other, there is one kind of right and wrong. According to the self there is another kind of right and wrong. But really are there such distinctions as the self and the other, or are there no such distinctions? When the self and the other [or the "this" and the "that"] lose their contrariness [mutually exclusive opposition] we have the very essence of the *dao*.

He goes on to say:

The possible is possible; the impossible is impossible. The *dao* operates and things follow. Things are what they are called. What are they? They are what they are. What are they not? They are not what they are not. Everything is what it is, and everything can be what it can be. There is nothing that is not something, and there is nothing that cannot be something.

Laozi reveled in play and paradox, but he remained a child of the world, concerned with government and human affairs as well as the enjoyment and preservation of life. Thus he tells us, "In the government of the sage, he keeps their hearts empty [peaceful, pure, and free from both worry and selfish desires], fills their bellies, weakens their ambitions, and strengthens their bones." Above all, he embraces the doctrine of *wuwei*: "The more taboos and prohibitions there are in the world, the poorer the people will be. The more sharp weapons the people have, the more troubled the state will be. The more cunning and skill man possesses, the more vicious things will appear. The more laws and orders are made prominent, the more thieves and robbers there will be."[77]

Zhuangzi apparently lacked even the muted reformism of Laozi. In the words of Zhu Xi, "Laozi still wanted to do something, but Zhuangzi did not want to do anything at all. He even said that he knew what to do but just did not want to do it."[78] Predictably, Confucian commentators have excoriated him for advocating the pursuit of complete freedom. Wang Shumin's recent critical study of the *Zhuangzi*, however, argues that Zhuangzi was in fact neither egocentric nor an advocate of escapism and "libertine values."[79] His ideal was simply the "pure man," who

> alone ... associates with Heaven and Earth and spirit, without abandoning or despising things of the world. He does not quarrel over right or wrong and mingles with conventional society. ... Above he roams with the Creator [*zaowu zhe*, i.e., Nature], and below he makes friends with those who transcend life and death and beginning and end. In regard to the essential, he is broad and comprehensive, profound and unrestrained. In regard to the fundamental, he may be said to have harmonized all things and penetrated the highest level.[80]

Another of Zhuangzi's alluring visions pictured the Daoist sage

> leaning against the sun and the moon and carrying the universe under his arm, ... [blending] everything into a harmonious whole. He is unmindful of the confusion and the gloom, and equalizes the humble and the honorable. The multitude strive and toil; the sage is primitive and without knowledge. He comprehends ten thousand years as one unity, whole and simple. All things are what they are, and are thus brought together.[81]

Daoism was, then, preeminently a philosophy of "naturalness." Where Confucianism stressed others, Daoism tended to stress self. Where Confucians sought wisdom, Daoists sought blissful ignorance. Where Confucians esteemed ritual and self-control, Daoists valued spontaneity and freedom from artificial constraints. Where Confucianism stressed hierarchy, Daoists emphasized equality, and where Confucians valued refinement (*wen*), Daoists prized primitivity. What to Confucians were cosmic virtues were to Daoists simply arbitrary labels.

Laozi highlighted the essential difference between Confucianism and Taoism in claiming:

> It was when the great *dao* declined that there appeared humanity and righteousness. It was when knowledge and intelligence arose that there appeared much hypocrisy. It was when the six relations [father, son, elder brother, younger brother, husband, and wife] lost their harmony that there was talk of filial piety and paternal affection. It was when the country fell into chaos and confusion that there was talk of loyalty and trustworthiness. Banish sageliness, discard wisdom, and the people will be benefitted a hundredfold. Banish humanity, discard righteousness, and the people will return to filial piety and paternal affection. ... See the simple, embrace primitivity; reduce the self, lessen the desires.[82]

This, in brief, was the Daoist message.

There was just enough affinity between Confucianism and Daoism to ensure an enduring philosophical partnership. Both schools of thought sought inspiration and guidance in the *Yijing*, both employed *yinyang* concepts to explain their ideas, and both cherished the ideal of harmony and oneness with nature (although one posited a moral universe and the other, an amoral one). Each shared a sense of the interrelatedness of all things, and each, in its own way, advocated humility, passivity, simplicity, and the avoidance of selfish desires. Furthermore, although philosophical Daoism had no prominent proponents in late imperial times, Confucians found at least some Daoist concepts congenial to their own ideas. The *Jinsi lu*, for example, cites approvingly Zhuangzi's remark that "those who indulge in many desires have very little of the secret of Nature."[83]

In all, then, Confucianism and Daoism could easily coexist. The former gave Chinese life structure and purpose, while the latter encouraged freedom of expression and artistic creativity. Most Qing scholars had a healthy schizophrenia. As W. T. de Bary points out, many Confucians recognized that man's response to Heaven and the fulfillment of his nature were not limited to social service. He writes that in the midst of social and political engagement, there was

> a need to keep some part of ... [oneself] not subservient to the demands of state or society. To the neo-Confucian, the aesthetic and spiritual, or ... "supermoral" concerns [in the words of Tang Junyi] represent this area of freedom. Much of it was expressed in journals, lyrical poetry, prose-poetry, travel diaries written in a contemplative frame of mind, painting and calligraphy, and the appreciation of art expressed in poetic inscriptions.[84]

The inspiration of these activities was thus predominantly Daoist, even if Confucians ultimately believed the fruits of such labors to reflect moral worth.

7

Religion

Contrary to persistent Western opinion, few areas of traditional Chinese life were devoid of religious sentiment or religious ritual.[1] During the Qing period, elite and popular religious beliefs and practices intertwined to produce a vast, multicolored fabric of institutional and individual worship. A French sinologist, Henri Maspero, once described Chinese religion as encompassing "an unheard-of swarm of gods and spirits of every kind, an innumerable rabble," but Maurice Freedman, a British anthropologist, saw order behind the chaos. He argued that "all religious argument and ritual differentiation [in China] were conducted within a common language of basic conceptions, symbols, and ritual forms."[2] This common religious base encompassed the major elements of Chinese thought described in the preceding chapter, including the predominance of Confucian values, a concern with hierarchical order and social harmony, philosophical eclecticism, and the notion of *yinyang* duality.

Freedman's forceful interpretation has not gone uncontested by more recent scholars, however. A number of individuals have reiterated some version of the Maspero position, arguing, among other things, that "any unities among Chinese religious practices would be so abstract as to be meaningless." Some scholars, basing their research on contemporary Taiwan, have emphasized the way religious beliefs and practices differ not only by social class but also by geographical region. Others, using the same cultural data but somewhat different methodologies, have been at pains to show how the production of variant meanings in Chinese religion—even with respect to such fundamental questions as the nature of ghosts—reflects changing social and economic conditions.[3]

James Watson offers an inspired way of reconciling certain divergent interpretations of Chinese religion. By focusing on the historic process by which elite written accounts of worship reached downward and popular oral tales found their way upward, he reaches the following conclusion: The genius of the Qing government's approach to cultural integration was that it imposed a structure on Chinese religious life but did not dictate the content. In other words, the imperial state allowed for "a high degree of variation within an overall structure of unity."[4] He explains:

> The actual organization of temple cults devolved to local elites who had a vested interest in maintaining good relations with state officials. The system was flexible enough to allow people at all levels of the social hierarchy to construct their own representations of state-approved deities. Put another way, the state promoted symbols and not beliefs.[5]

Of course the Qing government did attempt to foster Confucian beliefs;[6] symbols, however, were far easier to monitor and manipulate. Watson concludes:

> The Chinese cultural system ... allowed for what outsiders might perceive to be chaotic local diversity. The domain of ritual, in particular, gave great scope to regional and subethnic cultural displays. The system was so flexible that those who called themselves Chinese could have their cake and eat it too: They could participate in a unified culture yet at the same time celebrate their local or regional distinctiveness.[7]

Despite the impressive uniformity and continuity in many realms of Chinese ritual, we should not assume that religious life remained constant throughout the Qing period, either in form or in content. At the top, state ceremonies, including official sacrifices, changed in accordance with the shifting beliefs and political priorities of individual emperors—sometimes with extremely serious and divisive consequences.[8] Similarly, within the empire-wide structure of institutional religion, the personal preferences of the Qing rulers exerted an enormous influence on the popularity and power of the Buddhist and Religious Daoist establishment.[9] At the same time, the outlook and actions of religious leaders—whether Chinese Muslim begs (local chieftains) in the Northwest, the Dalai Lama in Lhasa, or the Pope in Rome—often played a crucial role in the formation of imperial policy. We have seen, for instance, that the early Qing emperors were prepared to tolerate Western Christianity until papal interference made the Confucian rites a political issue (Chapter 2).[10]

At various local levels of organization, from massive "macroregions" to individual towns and villages, changing political, social, and economic conditions naturally affected the development of ritual forms and popular religious practices. For instance, gentry efforts to bolster their declining position through support of local lineage structures during the Ming-Qing transition had important implications for the conduct of Buddhist funerary rites in different parts of the country. Similarly, but with different effects, social changes, together with shifts in both popular piety and official religious policy, undermined the long-standing Ma Yuan cult later on in the Qing period.[11] Steven Sangren's microcosmic study of Daxi, Taiwan, reveals in fascinating detail the way "history and power ... played an important role in the reciprocally legitimating relationship between local and state religion and institutions in [late] imperial times."[12]

Historical circumstances also affected the writing of religious texts. Cynthia Brokaw has shown, for instance, how the content of "morality books," and the conditions of authorship of such works, changed during the seventeenth and eighteenth centuries in response to new elite concerns, such as the regulation and even containment of social mobility.[13] She describes shifts in religious ideology that "roughly followed the major developments in contemporary elite interests" during the Ming-Qing transition and into the eighteenth century, and although her study does not extend into the late Qing era, it seems evident that religion and intellectual life continued to follow parallel routes. We find, for example, that the unsettled state of China's domestic and foreign affairs during the nineteenth century gave rise to a burst of interest in "literati Buddhism"—championed by a number of leading Statecraft and New Text scholars, including Gong Zizhen, Wei Yuan, and Kang Youwei.[14]

OFFICIAL SACRIFICES

Arthur Wolf has written: "Assessed in terms of its long-range impact on the people, ... [the Chinese government] appears to have been one of the most potent governments ever known, for it created a religion in its own image. Its firm grip on the popular imagination may be one reason the imperial government survived so long despite its failings." There is much to commend this view. To a remarkable extent, the organization of traditional Chinese religion mirrored the fundamental assumptions of Chinese bureaucratic behavior. This was true not only of official state ceremonies and sacrifices, as might well be expected, but also of institutional Buddhism, Religious Daoism, and even popular religion.[15]

The Qing government, with its pervasive powers of patronage and appointment, periodically promoted and demoted various gods within its own supernatural bureaucratic establishment, called upon Buddhist and Daoist clergy to say prayers and perform sacrifices as religious agents of the state, appropriated deities from the vast pantheon of popular religion into the structure of official religion, and canonized former mortals who were either exemplars of orthodox values or whose acknowledged supernatural powers made them potentially valuable to the state. Stephan Feuchtwang has identified a kind of dialectic operating in Chinese religious life in which

> officials adopted deities from popular religion and bureaucratized them, while the [common] people worshipped gods that were like magic officials or that were magic official deities. Gods that in popular religion were fluid, whose identities flowed into one another, whose functions were potentially universal, and who were magic in their ability to metamorphose and to fuse man and nature in themselves, were in the official religion standardized and classed, minute distinctions and the separation of rites and cults keeping them apart.[16]

Qing official religion recognized three main levels of state sacrifice aside from the exclusively Manchu shamanistic observances undertaken by the Office of Ceremonial of the Imperial Household Department: (1) great sacrifices (*dasi*), (2) middle sacrifices (*zhongsi*), and (3) common sacrifices (*qunsi* or *xiaosi*). At each level, designated officials performed elaborate ceremonies in accordance with long-standing ritual prescriptions. Auspicious dates for such ceremonies were chosen well in advance after divination by the Imperial Bureau of Astronomy and deliberations involving the Board of Rites, the Court of Sacrificial Worship, and the emperor himself. These divinatory rituals and deliberations were part of the same process that yielded auspicious and inauspicious days for the imperial calendar, which was distributed to civil and military officials at the capital and in the provinces. These officials also received guidance in the form of special ceremonial handbooks.[17]

State worship at the various levels generally required ritual bathing, fasting, prostrations, prayers, and thanksgiving offerings of incense, lighted candles, precious objects, fruits, and food and wine together with music and ritual posturing or dancing.[18] These activities were believed to purify the mind and body and to please the gods. According to the Qing *Collected Statutes,* official religious ceremonies had several specific purposes. Some deities were worshipped for the simple purpose of expressing gratitude and veneration; others for the beneficial or protective influences they were supposed to exert; still others for their outstanding civil virtues and/or military services. Some spirits were worshipped for fear that they would bring calamities to the people if not suitably appeased.[19]

But behind these rather specific purposes lay more general considerations. One of these was that official religious ceremonies exemplified the cosmic order and affirmed the emperor's place within it. Another was that they reinforced status distinctions and thus protected the social order. Yet another was that they helped to undergird the prestige and political authority of the state. Undertaken by secular bureaucrats rather than a separate priestly class, these ceremonies were thus seen as powerful instruments of ideological control. The preface to one ritual handbook of the nineteenth century well illustrates the mixture of motives surrounding official religious practice. "Incense and vessels ... [i.e., ritual sacrifices] can control the gods and spirits. Jade, silk, bells and drums can reveal the rites and music. ... Awe of virtue and the passing on of merit [through worship] civilize the people and form customs." Official religion, in other words, manipulated both the gods and the people. Some officials downplayed the spiritual aspects of the rituals they performed, but they performed them nonetheless.[20]

The most awe-inspiring of the great sacrifices was the emperor's personal worship of Heaven, which took place during the winter solstice and on New Year's Day (from 1742 on). In the words of the *Record of Ritual,* "The sacrifice to Heaven [lit., Di or Shangdi] is the highest expression of reverence." As with most other Chinese ceremonies, great symbolic emphasis was placed on color, form, number, position, music, and sacrificial objects. The color of the jade and silk offerings to Heaven was blue-green, the altar was circular (*yang*) in shape, and the associated number was nine (also *yang*). Appropriately, nine pieces of music were played at the sacrifice. The emperor faced north, reversing his usual orientation. Contemporary accounts of the elaborate ritual—preceded by a dramatic imperial procession from the Forbidden City to the Temple of Heaven complex the night before—describe a solemn spectacle of awesome splendor. Attended by an entourage of imperial princes, high officials, and other state functionaries, and flanked by the spirit tablets of his ancestors and various deities of nature, the emperor paid his respects to the tablet representing Heaven with prayers and offerings—all accompanied by hymns, instrumental music, and ritual posturing undertaken by literally hundreds of performers (see Figure 7.1).[21]

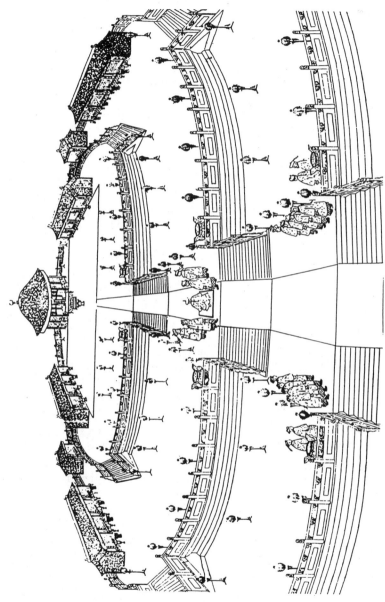

Figure 7.1   The Altar of Heaven. The Xianfeng emperor (r. 1851–1861) worshipping at the Altar of Heaven, from a Chinese painting. The central temporary shrine is to Heaven (Shangdi). The other temporary shrines house the tablets of the emperor's ancestors, the spirits of the Sun and Moon, and other deities. Source: S. W. Williams (1883), vol. 1.

The great sacrifice to Earth, also undertaken personally by the emperor, and similar in most respects to the sacrifice to Heaven, took place at a square (*yin*) altar during the summer solstice. In this ceremony, the jade and silk offerings were yellow, eight musical pieces were played, and the emperor faced south. Although the sacrifices to Heaven and Earth reflected an obvious *yinyang* symbolism, the use of the number three in the construction of the altars and in various aspects of imperial ritual, together with the importance attached to the emperor's worship of his ancestors and other notables at the Great Temple (Taimiao), indicated the symbolic unity of the three powers (*sancai*): Heaven, Earth, and Man. Another important great sacrifice at Beijing was to the Spirits of Land and Grain (*sheji*). Here too, the symbolism of number and color played a significant role: The number was five, and the colors were those associated with the five elements (*wuxing*).[22]

Middle-level sacrifices at the capital included those for local spirits of Land and Grain; the Sun; the Moon; the spirits of Wind, Rain, Thunder, Clouds, Mountains, and Rivers; the emperors of previous dynasties; the patron deity of agriculture (Xian Nong); and various sages, meritorious officials, wise men, and virtuous women. Confucius was worshipped at this middle level until 1907, when his ceremonies were elevated to the first level of great sacrifices. Provincial-level middle sacrifices included all of the spirits noted above with the exception of previous emperors and naturalistic deities. Sacrifices to Confucius and other virtuous and wise individuals took place in Temples of Civil Virtue, also called School-Temples (see Figure 7.2).[23]

Common sacrifices, conducted at every capital city from Beijing down to the district level, included ceremonies dedicated primarily to local protective deities, the most common of which were the so-called God of War (Guandi), the God of Literature (Wenchang), the Three Sovereigns (Sanhuang), the Fire God (Huoshen), the Dragon God (Longshen), and the City God (Chenghuang). Common sacrifices also were undertaken for the unworshipped dead (*li*), whose wandering spirits were presumed to be a potential threat to the community unless placated. Significantly, these "neglected spirits" were supposed to report any immoral or illegal activities to the City God, who would in turn relay this information to his Qing bureaucratic counterpart at the appropriate level for official investigation and punishment.

According to the Qing *Collected Statutes,* the deities in official religion operated in a hierarchy that paralleled exactly the administrative structure of the empire. District-level cults were subdivisions of prefectural-level cults and so on up to the imperial capital. Tablets of local spirits such as those of Land and Grain were inscribed not only with their names but also with bureaucratic designations appropriate to their respective administrative levels. Some received imperially bestowed titles of nobility or other marks of distinction as well.[24]

Of all the deities in the official pantheon, the City God occupied a position of particular importance at the district level. As a rule, each newly appointed magistrate, before assuming his official duties, secluded himself in the local City God temple overnight to report to the local deity and offer a sacrifice, which usually included an oath that he would be honest and upright. "If I govern disrespectfully," read one such

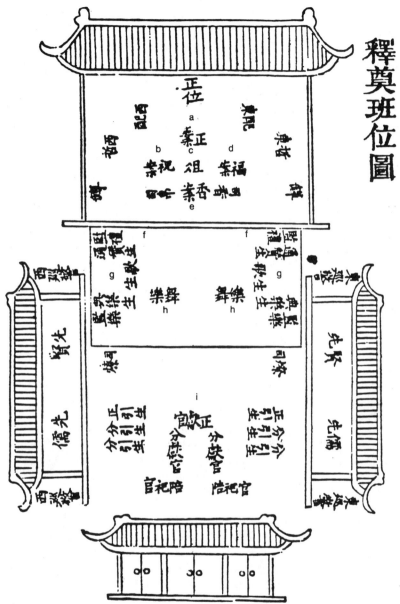

Figure 7.2 Arrangement of the Shidian Sacrifice. The shidian *ceremony was conducted to venerate Confucius and other Confucian worthies at local Temples of Civil Virtue (wenmiao). The sacrificial layout indicates the symmetry of Qing ritual fields, from the Forbidden City down to local temples and ancestral halls (see also Figure 7.6). Among the major elements in the* shidian *configuration were:* a, *the primary table;* b, *prayer table;* c, *food stand;* d, *"blessings" table;* e, *incense table;* f, *supervisors of ceremony;* g, *singers and musicians;* h, *dancers; and* i, *principal sacrificial official. Source:* JQYWL *(1871).*

sacrificial oath, "am crafty, avaricious, get my colleagues in trouble, or oppress the people, may you send down retribution upon me for three years." Other similar oaths asked for assistance in administration and for the power to fortify personal virtue.[25]

As the otherworldly equivalent of the district magistrate, the City God had responsibility for all the spirits of the local dead (including the unworshipped dead). He was also expected to cooperate with his bureaucratic counterpart in bringing peace and prosperity to his district. The following inscription on a late Ming stele expresses this charge unambiguously:

> Chenghuang temples are universally established, from the national capital to the prefectures and districts. While it is the magistrates who rule in the world of light [*yang*], it is the gods who govern in the world of shadows [*yin*]. There is close cooperation between the two authorities. When Emperor Taizu of the Ming dynasty conferred titles on the City Gods throughout the empire [in 1370], there were ranks of emperors, princes, dukes, lords and marquises. ... The god's power is effective everywhere, rewarding the good with blessing and punishing the evil with calamity, ... thus extending great benefit to man. Man prays to him for good harvests and for the avoidance of floods, droughts and pestilence.[26]

When trouble came, magistrates sought relief from the City God, as this impassioned appeal from the early Qing shows:

> O City God, both of us have duties to perform in this district: resisting disasters that may occur, offering protection in times of trouble, such things are part of the City God's spiritual realm and are part of the official's responsibilities. This year, while the workers were out in the fields but the grain had not matured, the eggs that had been laid by last year's locusts hatched out in the soil, causing almost half the wheat crops in the countryside to suffer this affliction. ... The people could not repel this calamity, so they appealed to the officials for help. The officials could not repel this calamity for the people, so they [now] pray to the City God.

The prayer ends with the suggestion that the City God anticipates the needs of the people and officials and that he sympathizes with them. Could he not, then, transmit the prayers of the people and the officials to Heaven (lit., Shangdi) in the form of a petition?[27] Like any other administrator, the City God could be appealed to by equals and inferiors, just as he could appeal to (or in fact be commanded by) a bureaucratic superior.

The bureaucratic character of the City God found expression not only in his administrative responsibilities and his role as a transmitter of messages to higher supernatural authorities but also in his physical image and surroundings. Although represented by a tablet at the open altars of official religious ceremonies, the City God was represented by an image when worshipped in his own temple. The temple itself was modeled closely along the lines of a magistrate's yamen, and the image of the City

God was dressed in official robes and usually flanked by fierce-looking secretaries and yamen runners. Furthermore, the position of City God was almost invariably occupied by the spirit of a deceased former official, appointed by the emperor for a limited term, usually three years, in regular bureaucratic fashion. As a general rule, the lower the deity in the spiritual hierarchy of official religion, the more "human" it was.[28]

Spirits such as the City God were considered powerful but not omnipotent; they had specific spheres of administrative responsibility, and like their human counterparts, they were neither infallible nor incorruptible. They could be "bribed" by mortals and punished by their superiors in either the regular or the supernatural hierarchy. It was also commonly believed that spiritual officials such as the City God had their own families, including parents, wives, concubines, and children. As with most other major religious traditions, Chinese religion in its various orthodox forms tended to reinforce gender roles and distinctions.[29]

The City God cult represented a kind of symbolic meeting point between official religion and popular religion. Official worship of the deity involved solemn, dignified ceremonies in which only officials and degree holders could participate. These activities helped legitimize the state in the eyes of the common people and preserved local status distinctions. But popular worship of the City God had no such purpose and involved no such explicit distinctions. Individuals prayed to him for any and all kinds of favors (especially good health), and the ceremonies for the City God on his "birthday" and during his thrice-yearly tours of the city were among the largest, most impressive, and most widely observed public activities in traditional Chinese community life. On these occasions, the City God temple and its environs bustled with all kinds of activity: markets; theatrical performances; the selling of food; huge crowds; the noise of firecrackers, gongs, and drums; and the burning of incense. Most of these features were not to be found in the austere ritual of official religion.[30]

It is tempting, and I think at least partially justified, to consider certain deities associated with popular religion—notably local Lords of the Earth (Tudi gong)—as supernatural subdistrict administrators. Just as town or village leaders and *baojia* or *lijia* headmen supervised subdistrict administrative units but were ultimately answerable to district magistrates, so in the supernatural subbureaucracy local Lords of the Earth oversaw discrete administrative areas but were ultimately responsible to City Gods. Like regular subdistrict administrators, these Lords of the Earth served localities rather than kinship groups, and although the vast majority were not based on decimal units, there is evidence to suggest that at least in some cases the subdistrict spiritual world could be organized along the same lines and designed for the same purposes as *baojia*. A gazetteer for the market town of Foshan in Guangdong states, for example:

> Every one hundred households constitute a neighborhood [*li*]. In each neighborhood
> is established an altar for the gods of land and grain, where annual sacrifices are
> offered in the spring and fall, with the head of the neighborhood officiating. ...

Before the feast that follows the sacrifice, one person reads a written oath: "All persons in this neighborhood agree to observe the rituals, and the strong refrain from oppressing the weak. ... Those who fail to observe the common agreement, and those committing rape, robbery, falsification, and other misdemeanors will be excluded from this organization."

This oath, and the sacrifice that followed, established a concrete link between the neighborhood social and moral order and the local spiritual establishment, illustrating the use of spiritual sanctions to enforce secular norms.[31]

The responsibilities of local Lords of the Earth, whether they were in charge of city wards, towns, villages, or subunits of these divisions, included "policing" the spirits of that area and reporting to the City God on human activities within the scope of their jurisdiction. The Lord of the Earth's human charges, for their part, appealed to him for protection and blessings and dutifully conveyed to him information regarding recent births, marriages, deaths, and other important events. Not surprisingly, Lords of the Earth were often distinguished by status within the larger community; thus, some were regarded as designated representatives of others.

The analogy between Qing sociopolitical institutions and the supernatural order may be extended further, for certain deities seem to have stood in relation to the local City God as the gentry class in Chinese society stood to the bureaucracy. Arthur Wolf points out, for example, that in modern Taiwan, where many traditional religious practices still persist, ritual specialists and close observers of temple affairs commonly distinguish two types of deities: officials (*shi*)—notably the City God and the Lord of the Earth—and "wise persons" (*fu*). The latter category is represented in the Sanxia area of the Taibei basin, for example, by several deities, including the Holy Mother in Heaven (Tianshang shengmu), also known by her imperially bestowed title Tianhou (Consort of Heaven) and her popular name Mazu, which means "grandmother" (see Figure 7.3).[32] Although the comparison is not perfect, it suggests a kind of status similarity between low-ranking deities in official religion, such as the City God, and unofficial deities who performed important social roles. And just as capable gentry members might eventually find positions in the regular bureaucracy, so might wise persons in the supernatural social order become adopted into the official pantheon. The Holy Mother in Heaven was so worshipped in Qing times.[33]

In the last analysis, as T'ung-tsu Ch'ü has demonstrated, district magistrates often found it necessary to worship a wide range of official and "unofficial" deities. According to the Qing legal code, a magistrate could be punished with eighty strokes of the bamboo for sacrificing to a deity not included in the dynasty's book of official sacrifices; but when calamity struck, the local populace often demanded that the district magistrate offer sacrifices to any god who might be of assistance. Wang Huizu informs us that during his tenure as a local Qing official, concerned residents of his district once brought more than twenty images to his yamen, demanding that he pray to them for rain. He refused on the grounds that worship of these gods was unorthodox, but he maintains that his refusal might have led to a disturbance had he not already

Figure 7.3   Temple of Tianhou. This late Qing photograph shows a temple for the Consort of Heaven. The man at the entrance is a fortune-teller; the others are idlers or perhaps beggars. Photo courtesy of the Peabody & Essex Museum, Salem, Mass.

won the people's confidence. Many other local officials are known to have succumbed to such pressure.[34]

As a general rule, a god's bureaucratic position, or at least his relationship to officials within the natural or supernatural hierarchy, meant more to most Chinese than any sectarian identification he possessed. But sectarian identifications were not insignificant, especially in the realm of nonofficial institutional religion. Before turning to the syncretism of Chinese popular religion, let us examine briefly the major features of "orthodox" Buddhism and Religious Daoism during the Qing.

BUDDHISM AND RELIGIOUS DAOISM

Of the two liturgical teachings, Buddhism had by far the greater intellectual appeal, as well as a greater institutional visibility and a larger number of both clerics and identifiable lay adherents. Although Religious Daoism enjoyed substantial imperial patronage in the late Ming period, it suffered some discrimination at the hands of the Qing emperors. Buddhism, meanwhile, proved itself remarkably adaptable to the

Chinese social and intellectual environment. Lay Buddhism flourished during the Qing precisely because, in Kristin Yü Greenblatt's words, it "did not demand a radical break from the social system in which it existed." It was, she maintains, "more activist than contemplative, more moralistic than theological, more world affirming than world rejecting."[35]

Institutional Buddhism also made compromises. One illustration of its successful adaptation to the Chinese environment in Qing times was its frequent use of names such as Baozhong si (Monastery for Honoring Loyalty [to the State]) or Huguo si (Monastery for the Protection of the State). Another illustration—particularly striking in view of the kinship-renouncing doctrine of Buddhism—was the common designation Guangxiao si (Monastery for the Glorification of Filial Piety).[36]

Despite these forms of cultural accommodation, the Qing government displayed a profound and predictable ambivalence toward Buddhism. On the one hand, as alien conquerors, the Manchus made an early decision that "their most visible religio-political image was to be Chinese and Confucian." As a result, they made a concerted effort to maintain the ideological supremacy of orthodox neo-Confucianism, with its strongly anti-Buddhist prejudices, and made no effort to impose their native shamanistic beliefs and practices on the Chinese population at large. On the other hand, the Qing rulers recognized that institutional religion, if tightly controlled, could be used to substantial political advantage. Thus they found it expedient to patronize Buddhism—especially in far-flung areas of the empire where the Buddhist (Lamaist) hierarchy was closely tied to local elite administration. In these regions, the Qing emperors generally supported Lamaism and encouraged the image of themselves in these peripheral areas as Buddhist deities. And even in China Proper, large amounts of imperial funds were periodically devoted to the publication of Buddhist books and to the construction and restoration of Buddhist monasteries and temples.[37]

There was another factor that influenced the attitude of the Qing government toward Buddhism: the personal beliefs of a number of Qing emperors and their consorts. The Shunzhi emperor, as we have already seen, was friendly with several Buddhist monks, some of whom resided in the palace. The Yongzheng emperor established a Buddhist publishing house and edited an anthology of quintessential Buddhist writings entitled *Yuxuan yulu* (Imperially Selected [Buddhist] Sayings), and his father and son (the Kangxi and Qianlong emperors, respectively) both wrote prefaces for Buddhist books as well as dedicatory inscriptions for temples and monasteries. The ultrafilial Qianlong emperor even gave his mother more than nine thousand images of Buddhist deities on her seventieth birthday. Among nineteenth-century rulers, the Empress Dowager Cixi was well known for her Buddhist beliefs and pious devotions.[38]

Although the Qing government continually worried about the seditious potential of Buddhist and other religious sects, it was relatively unconcerned with the intellectual attractiveness of Buddhist philosophy and theology. To be sure, officially endorsed neo-Confucian works such as *Reflections on Things at Hand* emphasized that "a student should forthwith get as far away from Buddhist doctrines as from licentious songs and beautiful women. Otherwise they will infiltrate him."[39] But most Qing scholars did not reject Confucianism in favor of Buddhism, especially in their active years. Only in old age, or in times of severe social unrest and uncertainty, did significant numbers of scholars gravitate toward Buddhist doctrines.

It is true that the well-known scholar Peng Shaosheng (1740–1796) abandoned a promising Confucian career in his late twenties, during the heyday of the Qing empire, to become a lay monk. Although he lived in a hotbed of anti-Buddhist *kaozheng* scholarship, and had passed the *jinshi* degree before he was twenty, Peng grew ever more attracted to Buddhism and became a disciple of the renowned cleric Shiding (1712–1778). Eventually he earned a reputation as the foremost Qing scholar in popularizing Buddhism among the laity. Yet Peng was interested not in establishing Buddhism at the expense of Confucianism, but rather in reconciling the two. As Richard Shek puts the matter, Peng dressed the Confucian sages in Buddhist garb, "portraying them as bodhisattvas with a message of salvation."[40]

Other Qing scholars found it possible to accommodate Buddhist ideas by viewing them in a Confucian light. Zhang Xuecheng, for example, advanced the rather common (and psychologically satisfying) argument that the origins of Buddhism could be found in the teachings of the *Yijing*. Further, he maintained that Buddhist mythology should not be taken lightly simply because it failed to make literal sense. "The Buddhists' description of Buddha as sixteen feet high with richly adorned, golden colored body, and their strange imaginings that no one has ever seen—the splendors of heaven, the torments of hell, the heavenly goddess scattering flowers, yakshas covered with hair—these things the Confucians criticize as absurd." But Zhang insisted that the Buddhists were simply presenting their teachings symbolically, just as the *Yijing* did in discussing things such as "dragons with dark and yellow blood." In the end, Zhang asserted, the best Buddhist writing came close to being "superior to that of the philosophers."[41]

A more down-to-earth illustration of the effort to interpret Buddhist concepts in a Confucian fashion appears in the following excerpt from a set of late Qing clan rules:

> The Buddhists say that if you want to know about previous lives, look at the sufferings of this life. If you want to know about the next life, look at what is being done in this life. This is an excellent statement. However, what the Buddhists refer to as previous lives and the lives to come stems from their theory of rebirth and transmigration of souls. I think what has happened before yesterday—the father and the ancestors—are really the previous lives, and that what will happen after today—the sons and the grandsons—are really the lives to come.[42]

In this view, at least, Buddhism and Confucianism were but two sides of the same coin of ethical conduct.

What, then, were the basic ideas of Buddhism?[43] Buddhist teachings began with the Four Noble Truths: (1) life is painful, an endless cycle of births and deaths in a transient, sorrowful world; (2) the origin of pain and sorrow is selfish desire; (3) the elimination of pain and sorrow comes with the elimination of selfish desire; and (4) the elimination of selfish desire comes with following the Eightfold Noble Path. Buddhism thus shared with both Confucianism and Daoism an abiding concern with the reduction of harmful desires.

The Eightfold Noble Path led from correct views to correct attitudes, correct speech, correct conduct, correct occupation, correct effort, correct perception and consciousness (alertness or self-examination), and correct concentration (meditation). By following Buddhist teachings as set forth in the huge corpus known as the *Tripitaka* (Chinese: *Sanzang* [Three Receptacles]) and derivative works, adherents could acquire the moral and mental discipline required to achieve Enlightenment. For the most part, Buddhist morality was based on concrete social values such as love, charity, courage, forbearance, and self-control, as well as respect for all living things, but Buddhist mental discipline was designed to demonstrate that in the end, all conceptions and distinctions were meaningless.

Buddhist Enlightenment implied a kind of transcendent understanding that permitted the perception of Ultimate Reality behind the "veil of illusion" (i.e., the false idea that a permanent or "essential" ego exists). When this perception occurs, "the ties of false sensory discrimination and of the passions (greed, envy, etc.) are broken, so that we are no longer carried along in the stream of phenomenal existence." This stream of existence and continual flux, known popularly as the wheel of life and death, was based on the idea of karmic retribution (Chinese: *yeyin*). Karma literally means "act," but the concept includes both thoughts and deeds and implies causality. According to Buddhist doctrine, the accumulated karma of each sentient being in the present as well as past existences determines the future existence of that being. Rebirths take place on several different planes (divine, human, animal, insect, etc.) depending on the net balance of "good" and "bad" karma (i.e., good or bad thoughts and deeds).

Enlightenment, then, brings about a state of oneness with Ultimate Reality (Sanskrit: *paramamartha-satya*; Chinese: *zhenti*), a break in the painful and sorrowful chain of causation that drives the everyday world of "conventional reality" (Sanskrit: *samvrti-satya*; Chinese: *suti*). In Sanskrit this state is termed *Nirvana* (Chinese: *niepan*), which literally means "extinction." Likened to the blowing out of a flame or the merging of a drop of water into an endless sea, the state (or one might say nonstate) of Nirvana was originally considered to be "incomprehensible, indescribable, inconceivable, unutterable." In the popular mind, however, it became equated with the idea of a heavenly repose. This point of view was encouraged especially by Mahayana Buddhism, a school of Indian Buddhism that developed in reaction to the austere and rather exclusive school known as Theravada, the Way of the Elders.

Although the Mahayana school considered itself to be the Great Vehicle (Chinese: *Dacheng*) of Buddhist truth, it could tolerate other belief systems, including Theravada, as "lesser truths," valid in some sense but ultimately inferior. This relativistic emphasis, a matter of expedience, made allowance for different levels of understanding both within Mahayana Buddhism and outside of its wide doctrinal sphere. Emphasizing salvation by faith and good works, Mahayana was more compassionate and other-oriented than Theravada. It involved more ritual and had a more elaborate metaphysics. Mahayana posited a universe consisting of an infinite number of spheres or realms going through an infinite number of cosmic periods. Within these realms were a myriad of heavens, hells, and assorted deities (all manifestations of the Buddha spirit or nature). Nirvana was beyond all this. Given Mahayana Buddhism's eclectic spirit, ritualism, and polytheism, it is hardly surprising that it took firm root in China and peripheral areas such as Tibet, Mongolia, Korea, Japan, and Vietnam.

There were four main Mahayanist schools in late imperial China: the Tiantai, or Lotus (Fahua), School; the Huayan (lit., Flowery Splendor) School; the Pure Land School (Jingtu); and the Chan or Meditation School, known commonly as Zen, the Japanese pronunciation of the Chinese character *chan* (meditation).[44] Indicative of both the syncretic capacity of traditional Chinese thought and the accommodating outlook of Mahayana Buddhism, the Chinese had a common saying: "The Tiantai and Huayan Schools for [metaphysical] doctrine and the Jingtu and Chan Schools for practice."[45] The scriptural common denominator of these and most other Chinese Buddhist schools was the so-called Lotus Sutra (*Miaofa lianhua jing*), a fascinating dramatic work blending elements of philosophy, theology, pageantry, and popular fable. In the fashion of the *Yijing*, the ideas of the Lotus Sutra were presented not in abstract terms but in concrete images and living symbols.[46]

The Tiantai School, which called the Lotus Sutra its own but could claim no real monopoly on it, distinguished three levels of "truth," each of which centered on the idea of *dharmas* (Chinese: *fa*), or psychosomatic "elements of existence." One level was the Truth of Emptiness—the idea that all *dharmas* were empty because they had no independent nature of their own. Another level was that of Temporary Truth, or "relative reality," in which *dharmas* had a temporary and dependent existence. In this realm, there were ten types of manifest existence, ranging from deities such as Buddhas ("enlightened ones") and bodhisattvas (enlightened ones who have postponed Nirvana to help others achieve Enlightenment) down to humans, beasts, and insects. The third level of truth was the Truth of the Mean, which said that *dharmas* were both empty and temporary and that the only reality was the Mind of Pure Nature, of which all phenomena were merely transient manifestations.[47]

The Huayan School represented the highest development of Buddhist metaphysics in China.[48] Its central cosmological notion was that all things were "coexistent, interwoven, interrelated, interpenetrating, [and] mutually inclusive." This view was basically in accordance with the outlook of Tiantai Buddhism and was also congenial with the organic character of Chinese philosophy as a whole. In fact, the Huayan School contributed substantially to the development of neo-Confucian metaphysics in the Song period. According to Huayan theory, each *dharma* possessed six characteristics in three complementary pairs: (1) universality and speciality, (2) similarity and difference, and (3) integration and disintegration. In *yinyang* fashion, each opposing characteristic implied the other.[49] As explained in the famous Chinese Buddhist analogy of the Golden Lion,

The lion represents the character of universality. The five sense organs, being various and different, represent the character of speciality. The fact that they all arise from one single cause represents the character of similarity. The fact that its eyes, ears, and so forth do not exceed their bounds represents the character of difference. Since the combination of the various organs becomes the lion, this is the character of integration. And as each of the several organs remains in its own position, this is the character of disintegration.[50]

Yet finally, when feelings were eliminated and "true substance" was revealed, everything would become an undifferentiated whole. No longer would a distinction exist between subject and object: The deceptive "self-nature" (*zixing*) of things in the conventional world would yield to a recognition that there was in the end no self-nature.[51] To quote again from the *Jinshizi zhang* (Essay on the Golden Lion),

When we look [clearly] at the lion and the gold, the two characters both perish and afflictions resulting from passions will no longer be produced. Although beauty and ugliness are displayed before the eye, the mind is as calm as the sea. Erroneous thoughts all cease, and there are no compulsions. One gets out of bondage and is free from hindrances, and forever cuts off the course of suffering. This is called entry into Nirvana.[52]

Chan Buddhism had much interest in Enlightenment but little concern with metaphysical speculation. Chan was a distinctively Chinese brand of Buddhism that had great appeal to artists and intellectuals—in part, no doubt, because of its strong affinities with philosophical Daoism.[53] Chan Buddhism stressed the "Buddha-nature" within one's own mind and regarded the regular Buddhist apparatus of scriptures, offerings, recitation of the Buddha's name, and so forth as unnecessary. Rather, it favored an intuitive approach to Enlightenment. This emphasis on a direct apprehension of Ultimate Reality through meditation can be found in Confucian terms in the thought of the great Ming scholar Wang Yangming, whose intellectual enemies considered him "a Buddhist in disguise."[54]

Meditation appealed to virtually all members of the Chinese leisured class—Confucians, Daoists, and Buddhists alike.[55] But Chan Buddhism normally required the discipline of a Chan master. The role of the master was not primarily to instruct in academic fashion but rather to prepare the mind of the disciple to intuit Ultimate Reality. Various means were employed, notably physical shock—such as shouting or beatings—and the use of puzzling sayings, stories, or conversations known as *gongan* (Japanese: *koan*; lit., public cases). The most famous *gongan* is no doubt "Listen to the sound of one hand [clapping]." Sayings of this sort were designed to jar the mind loose from its conventional moorings, to bring a recognition that Ultimate Reality could not be conceptualized or articulated. Such techniques set the stage for fruitful meditation.[56]

Although the basic goal of Chan was direct intuition of the Buddha-mind, meditation could also involve deliberations of intellect. Enlightenment might come instantly or gradually. Paradoxically, in late imperial times the "wordless doctrine" of Chan gave rise to an extensive literature of commentaries and subcommentaries explaining the cryptic sayings of past Chan masters in even more cryptic terms. During the Qing, this rather academic and somewhat fossilized form of Chan still enjoyed some influence, but in many cases it functioned more as an intellectual game of the Chinese elite than as a serious quest for Enlightenment.[57]

The most popular school of Chinese Buddhism in Qing times was the Pure Land School. On the whole, this eclectic teaching avoided both the intense mental discipline of Chan and the scriptural and doctrinal emphasis of Tiantai and Huayan. The central focus of the Pure Land School was on salvation through faith and good works. The reward was rebirth in the Western Paradise, also known as the World of Supreme Bliss, presided over by Amitabha (Chinese: Emituo Fo)—the "Buddha of Immeasurable Radiance." Chinese descriptions of this beautiful, enchanting, and serene land are as enticing as the descriptions of the bureaucratic purgatory known as the Ten Courts of Judgment are terrifying.[58]

In the view of Pure Land adherents, faith might be expressed by the mere repetition of Amitabha's name, while good works included conventional Buddhist virtues as well as the avoidance of the so-called ten evils—murder, stealing, adultery, lying, duplicity, slander, foul language, lust, anger, and false views. In the popular conception, faith in Amitabha not only offered the hope of salvation but also protection from evil spirits, wild beasts, fire, bandits, and other threats on earth. Amitabha's principal agent, the female bodhisattva Guanyin (originally a male deity, Avalokitesvara, the "Lord Who Looks Down"), proved especially popular in China as a source of protection and blessings for women and as the so-called Goddess of Fertility.[59] Other major deities in the vast Chinese Buddhist pantheon included Yaoshi Fo (the God of Medicine, identified with Bhaisajyaguru), Mile Fo (Sanskrit: Maitreya, the Buddha of the Future), Wenshu (Sanskrit: Manjusri, a bodhisattva), Puxian (Sanskrit: Samantabhadra, also a bodhisattva), and Yanwang (Sanskrit: Yama, Judge and King of Hell [i.e., the Ten Courts of Judgment]). These, however, represented only a fraction of the Buddhas, bodhisattvas, arhats (Chinese: *lohan*; disciples of Buddha), and other deities who operated in the limitless Mahayana universe.[60]

In Qing times, a number of monasteries carried on the joint practice of Chan and Pure Land Buddhism. Such establishments usually had both a meditation hall and a hall for reciting the Buddha's name. But monasteries might also permit a special form of joint practice in one hall. Holmes Welch explains: "In both sects the goal was to reduce attachment to ego. The Pure Land method of 'no stirrings in the whole mind' (*i-hsin pu-luan* [*yixin buluan*]) did not differ essentially from the Chan method of 'meditating to the point of perfect concentration' (*ch'an-ting* [*chanding*])." The eminent Chan abbot Xuyun (1840–1959) is said to have remarked, "All the Buddhas in every universe, past, present, and future, preach the same *dharma* [here meaning 'doctrine']. There is no real difference between the methods advocated by Sakyamuni [the historic Buddha] and Amitabha." For this reason, Xuyun advised some of his disciples who would have found Chan meditation too difficult to recite the Buddha's name instead.[61]

As is well known, Religious Daoism owed much to institutional Buddhism. Wing-tsit Chan goes so far as to describe it as "a wholesale imitation of Buddhism, notably in its clergy, temples, images, ceremonies and canon."[62] But despite Religious Daoism's profound cultural debt to Buddhism, it was not simply a pale reflection of the sinicized Indian import. Not only did formal Daoist ritual and symbolism differ significantly from that of institutional Buddhism, but the major thrust of Daoist religion ran counter to the conventional Buddhist emphasis on reincarnation. For all the diversity of Religious Daoist beliefs and practices, the aim was not primarily to break the chain of causation through the elimination of consciousness but rather to achieve a special kind of transcendence, manifest in the ability to know and manipulate the supernatural environment. And although Religious Daoism shared with philosophical Daoism an organic view of man and the universe, the goal of Religious Daoist ritual and personal regimen (meditative, dietary, pharmacological, gymnastic, and sexual) was not merely to find one's niche in the cosmic order but to acquire a form of cosmic power. Religious Daoism offered more than psychic release; it held the promise of longevity, invulnerability, and perhaps immortality.[63]

Two main schools of Religious Daoism flourished in late imperial times: the so-called Northern School, or Quanzhen (Complete Perfection) Sect, and the Southern School, or Zhengyi (True Unity) Sect. The Complete Perfection Sect arose during the Song dynasty in response to Chan Buddhism. Like devotees of Chan, members of this Northern School preferred the rigors of monastic discipline. Theirs was a life of celibacy, vegetarianism, and abstention from alcoholic drinks. The spiritual headquarters of the Complete Perfection Sect were located in Beijing, at the White Cloud Monastery. The True Unity Sect, which traced its spiritual origins to the Later Han period, had its headquarters on Lunghu Mountain, Jiangxi province. The hereditary Heavenly Master (Tianshi) of this Southern School, sometimes erroneously termed the Daoist "Pope," had considerable religious authority in late Ming and early Qing times, but his power was considerably curtailed thereafter. Nonetheless, the True Unity Sect enjoyed what amounted to "liturgical hegemony" among the various schools of Religious Daoism in late imperial times and continued to receive a measure of support from the Qing court.[64]

True Unity adherents lived a very different life from that of their spiritual brethren in the Complete Perfection Sect. True Unity priests were married and lived at home among the people. They were not subject to monastic discipline (except by choice), and they were allowed to eat meat and drink alcoholic beverages, except during special fasts. They relied primarily on charms and magic rather than diet for self-preservation. In fact, their principal function in traditional Chinese society was to sell charms, tell fortunes, and perform various religious ceremonies for the popular masses (see next section).

Religious Daoism, like Buddhism, had a wide variety of subsects that were at least tangentially related to one another of the major schools. Despite some liturgical and ritual differences, most Religious Daoists embraced the same basic ideas. These were distilled from the huge Daoist canon known as the *Daozang* (Receptacle of Daoism)—the Daoist counterpart to the Buddhist *Tripitaka.* Significantly, Peng Shaosheng's great-grandfather, Peng Dingqiu (1645–1689), compiled the single most important Qing dynasty publication on Daoism, which consisted of "essential excerpts" from the *Daozang.* Among the most commonly recited official scriptures in this vast and varied corpus were the *Yuhuang jing* (Jade Emperor's Classic) and the *Sanguan jing* (Three Officials' Classic), both of which were used in Complete Perfection and True Unity devotions. Although most of the scriptural, scholastic, and historical writings in the *Daozang* dealt with matters such as religious doctrine, liturgy, charms, magic, hymns, and lore, the collection also included the works of the great classical Daoist philosophers.[65]

The world view of the Religious Daoists as expressed in the *Daozang* was based in a much more explicit way than that of the Buddhists on notions of *yinyang* five-elements cosmogony and cosmology. According to one well-known formulation, derived from the *Way and Its Power* and clearly related to orthodox neo-Confucian cosmological ideas, the nameless, unmoved Prime Mover (*dao*) gives birth to the One (*taiji*, the Supreme Ultimate; or *huntun*, Primordial Chaos). This One, in turn, gives birth to the Two (the *yang* force or principle), and the Two gives birth to the Three (the *yin* force). These three forces are personified in Religious Daoism by the Three Pure Ones: (1) the Primordial Heavenly Worthy, symbol of life-giving primordial breath (*qi*); (2) the Lingbao Heavenly Worthy, symbol of the spirit (*shen*) of human beings; and (3) the Daode Heavenly Worthy, symbol of the "vital essence" (*jing*) in people. The Three Pure Ones generate the five elements (personified in the Five Rulers of traditional Chinese mythology), and from these come the myriad things of nature.[66]

A knowledge of *yinyang* and five-elements symbolism is essential to an understanding of Daoist "alchemy," which aimed not at changing base metals into gold, as in the West, but at producing physical benefits, such as strength and longevity. Since the Religious Daoists viewed the human body as a microcosm of the universe, both their meditative "internal alchemy" (*neidan*)—which included breathing exercises, sexual activity, and other forms of physical self-cultivation—and their "external alchemy" (*waidan*)—which involved the use of chemicals, drugs, and herbal medicines—were based on *yinyang* and five-elements correlations. So, in fact, was traditional Chinese medicine as a whole. Doctors and Daoists alike sought to achieve a harmonious balance of *yinyang* and five-elements influences within the body, and both assumed an integral relationship between the parts of the body and the whole. The basic principles and purposes of alchemy and acupuncture were thus essentially the same (see also Chapter 10).[67]

As was the case with Mahayana Buddhism, the value system of Religious Daoism reflected heavy Confucian influence. Indeed, all orthodox religious sects in China, and a good number of countercultural groups as well, admired the virtues of loyalty, faithfulness, integrity, duty, and filial piety. The curriculum in Buddhist and Daoist monasteries often included works from the classical canon, and Confucian values found their way to the popular masses in the form of vernacular religious tracts such as *shanshu* ("morality books") and *baojuan* ("precious scrolls").[68]

In keeping with its obsessive interest in longevity, but inspired by the Buddhist idea of karmic retribution, Religious Daoism developed an accounting system of merits (*gong*) and demerits (*guo*) that rewarded good behavior with extended life and subtracted years for evil deeds. This system, which esteemed Confucian virtues but also took into account Buddhist concern for all living creatures, found its way into Religious Daoist thought by Ming-Qing times. Like the Buddhists, the Daoists worshipped a vast number of protective deities, including not only the Three Pure Ones and the Five Rulers but also such popular gods and genies as the Jade Emperor (Yuhuang), the God of Literature (Wenchang), the Royal Mother of the West (Xiwang mu), the Eight Immortals (Baxian), and a host of spirits associated with stars and other natural objects as well as historical figures and even parts of the body.[69]

POPULAR RELIGION

These Daoist gods—like those of Buddhism and much of the official state cult—were the common property of the Chinese masses. Although some deities were clearly identified in the popular mind with either Buddhism or Daoism (or both) and others were patronized heavily by the elitist system of official religion, they all remained part of a gigantic, fluid network of national, regional, and local gods, each of whom could be supplicated by lay worshippers with no sense of disloyalty to the others.[70]

Popular Chinese divinities were known by the generic term *shen,* or "spirit." These spirits, represented by images or tablets and sometimes by both, were deified individuals, objects, or forces of nature. All possessed magical power (*ling*).[71] Some deities had their own private shrines, while others were worshipped together in temples. The significant feature of this expansive religious world, in addition to its obvious eclecticism, was its organization along functional lines. In the words of C. K. Yang,

> In popular religious life it was the moral and magical functions of the cults, and not the delineation of the boundary of religious faiths, that dominated people's consciousness. Even priests in some country temples were unable to reveal the identity of the religion to which they belonged. Centuries of mixing gods from different faiths into a common pantheon had produced a functionally oriented religious view that relegated the question of religious identity to a secondary place.[72]

Religious Daoists claimed, for instance, that the City God was their own creation, whereas frescoes depicting the Ten Courts of Judgment in the City God's temple testified to Buddhist influence, but the important point to both officials and the common people was that the City God was a local administrator with vitally important bureaucratic responsibilities.

Professor Yang has documented in detail the functional character of popular temple cults in traditional China. His survey of nearly eighteen hundred major temples in eight representative localities, although reflecting data drawn from sources published in the 1920s and 1930s, suggests patterns of distribution that probably prevailed in Qing times. Dividing these temples into five functional categories, Yang's survey yields the following information: 33.7 percent of the temples were devoted to deities associated with the well-being of the social and political order (kinship groups, local communities, and the state); 22.7 percent were devoted to the general moral order (heavenly deities and underworld authorities); 8.1 percent were devoted to economic functions (primarily patron deities of occupational groups); 1.1 percent were devoted to the preservation of health; and 3.8 percent were devoted to general and personal welfare (including "devil dispellers," "blessing deities," and unspecified gods). The remainder of the temples (30.6 percent) were monasteries and nunneries, the overwhelming majority of which (nearly 90 percent) were Buddhist.[73]

Yang emphasizes that this functional breakdown is somewhat misleading, since Chinese gods undertook a wide range of responsibilities and could be appealed to for many diverse purposes. Thus, the low percentage of temples specifically devoted to health-giving deities does not reflect lack of concern with good health. Quite the reverse was true. But the fact that most Chinese deities were believed to have the power to bestow or restore good health made functional specificity less important in this particular instance. Specific functions might be very important in individual localities, however. The Sea God (Haishen) and Holy Mother in Heaven, for example, had special significance in coastal areas. The community of Foshan, near Guangzhou (Canton), which was well known for its firecracker industry, had nearly a dozen temples devoted to the Fire God.

Overall, the most popular deities nationwide tended to be those identified with institutional religion of one kind or another.[74] But whether patronized institutionally or not, most deities were viewed in bureaucratic terms, for this was by far the most natural way for nearly everyone in Chinese society to conceive of meaningful power. The higher the god's bureaucratic status, the more powerful, although lines of authority and responsibility were not drawn as clearly in the huge popular pantheon as they were in the more orderly hierarchy of official religion.[75] Moreover, as Benjamin Schwartz reminds us, "The application of the bureaucratic metaphor to the numinous world did not *necessarily* lead to the view that the divine bureaucracy would invariably support its human counterpart."[76]

In the popular conception, as in the elite view, all gods were subordinate to, and servants of, Heaven. Characteristically, however, Heaven was personalized in the popular religious vocabulary by terms such as the Heavenly Emperor (Tiandi), the Heavenly Noble (Tiangong), and the Jade Emperor. Although popular religion was permeated with concepts and terms derived from elite culture, it was only a version of that culture, not a direct replica. Not only were abstractions such as Heaven generally personalized, but other concepts were also manipulated to conform more closely to the social outlook of commoners. Thus, whereas the elite version of nature and the cosmos emphasized harmony and order, the popular emphasis was far more on conflict and chaos. Whereas elite cosmology focused on the interaction and alternation of *yin* and *yang,* popular religion saw a constant struggle between *yang* spirits (i.e., *shen*) and malevolent *yin* spirits known as *gui* ("ghosts" or "demons").[77]

This struggle was viewed as natural and inevitable. According to a popular proverb, "Just as all things consist of *yin* and *yang,* and *yin* and *yang* are everywhere, so *shen* and *gui* are omnipresent." The struggle between *shen* and *gui* did not normally represent a titanic battle between the cosmic forces of good and evil, however. Rather, the relationship between *shen* and *gui* came to be viewed as analogous to that existing between the Qing government and disruptive elements in society such as bandits and beggars. From a popular perspective, the goal of most Chinese religious practices— whether state sacrifices or more localized rituals—was to enlist *shen* in controlling or neutralizing *gui.* The Daoist rite of "cosmic renewal" (*jiao*), for instance, was explicitly designed to "restore *yang,* that is, life, light and blessing, to its pristine state of growth, and to expel the forces of *yin,* darkness, evil and death."[78]

Gui were held responsible for all kinds of misfortune and afflictions, from accidents, illness, and death to barrenness, crop failures, and birth defects. They were believed to possess or kidnap people, to steal things, and to play tricks on people. They could remain invisible or assume a human or animal form. Although *gui* existed in seemingly endless profusion, they were associated primarily with the realm of *yin*: darkness, the ground, water, and lonely places. Many were believed to be unplacated spirits of the dead; others were considered to be inimical forces of nature. None were friendly. The supernatural world of the Chinese peasant, like the real one, could be a frightening place.[79]

Gui could be appeased by offerings of incense, food, money, or goods. They could also be repelled by various means, including the written names or images of "demon-dispelling" deities such as Zhong Kui and Jiang Taigong, amulets made of peach wood or other potent materials, paper strips with the eight trigrams or the characters for Heaven and Earth and *yin* and *yang* written on them, weapons such as swords, daggers, clubs, and spears, and various other *yang* symbols, such as loud noises, fire, blood, mirrors, and so on. Many protective objects were closely identified with the scholarly life of the Chinese elite: copies or pages from the Confucian Classics or imperial calendar, written characters, calligraphy brushes, official seals, and such.[80]

Rituals of exorcism employed numerous objects such as those mentioned above, as well as spells (*jie* or *zhu*) and written charms (*fu*). Some of these rituals could be undertaken individually or collectively by lay persons, but most involved "professional" religious agents—Buddhist and Daoist clergy, spirit mediums, sorcerers, magicians, and soothsayers—sometimes in combination. These individuals were believed to possess the special skills required to identify the source of *gui*-related problems and to devise successful strategies for their eradication.[81]

The primary means for expelling *gui* were charms written in the form of commands from superiors (*shen*) to inferiors (*gui*). Henri Doré describes these magical devices in the following terms:

> A charm is an official document, a mandate, an injunction, emanating from the god and setting to work superhuman powers who carry out the orders of the divinity. ... The charm being an official document, ... terminates in much the same manner as Chinese imperial edicts: "let the law be obeyed, let this order be respected and executed forthwith." ... The effect of the charm, as well as that of any other decree or command, depends principally on the power of him who has issued it.[82]

Although charms were generally associated with Daoist religious activity, Buddhist priests also employed them and sold them for profit. Charms could be used not only to drive away *gui* in every conceivable circumstance but also to right wrongs (such as unjust lawsuits) and to provide for the needs and interests of the deceased.

There are many colorful accounts of the activation and utilization of charms by religious agents of various sorts, but not all spiritual activities involved high drama. Public divination, for example—based on the *Yijing,* astrology, physiognomy, the dissection of characters, the casting of lots, the reading of omens, and numerous other techniques—tended to be a more somber and subdued ritual. The same was true of the popular form of geomantic divination known as *fengshui* (lit., wind and water), or "siting." *Fengshui* was predicated on the belief that *yinyang* currents of cosmic breath (*qi*), which flowed in every geographic area, influenced human fortunes. These currents, subject to various astrological influences, including "star spirits," manifested themselves in local topography. The task of a geomancer (*fengshui xiansheng*) was to calculate, on the basis of an enormous number of topographical and astrological variables, the most favorable positions to locate residences for both the living (homes, temples, businesses, official buildings, etc.) and the dead (graves).[83]

The best spot was, of course, at the proper junction of *yin* and *yang* currents. In the words of a knowledgeable nineteenth-century Western student of *fengshui,*

> The azure dragon [*yang*] must always be to the left [looking southward], and the white tiger [*yin*] to the right of any place supposed to contain a luck-bringing site. ... In the angle formed by dragon and tiger ... the luck-bringing site, the place for a tomb or dwelling, may be found. I say it *may* be found there, because, besides the conjunction of dragon and tiger, there must be there also a tranquil harmony of all the heavenly and terrestrial elements which influence that particular spot, and which is to be determined by observing the compass and its indication of the numerical proportions, and by examining the direction of the water courses.[84]

The "compass" in question was the *luopan,* an elaborate instrument about four to eight inches in diameter with a magnetic needle pointing south and a series of concentric circles arranged in symbolic sets. Jeffrey Meyer describes the prototype:

Schematically the circles of the compass begin with an inner set which deals with the center, then a group dealing with earth, then the Prior Heavens, and finally the Posterior Heavens. Represented among the circles are nearly all the Chinese symbols which are used in dealing with space and time: the trigrams and hexagrams in both the Prior and Posterior Heaven sequences, the ten stems and twelve branches, ... the five elements, *yin* and *yang,* the twenty-four directions, the nine moving stars, the six constellations, the twenty-eight asterisms (*hsiu* [*xiu*]), the four seasons and directions, the ... twenty-four fifteen-day periods of the solar year, and the seventy-two five-day divisions of the year. All these are interrelated in various combinations and thus repeated frequently in the thirty-eight circles.[85]

Geomantic compasses were not always so complex, but all assumed an integral relationship between topography and astrological configurations.

The *luopan* was often used in conjunction with popular almanacs because both were based on the fundamental assumption that certain stars and groupings of stars, in phase with *yinyang* and five-elements influences, played a crucial role in earthly affairs. This assumption was shared by all levels of Chinese society and expressed in a variety of rituals, from the worship of Heaven in official sacrifices to the ceremonies of Religious Daoism and *fengshui* divination. Thus, in practice, popular astrology—not to mention Buddhist notions of karmic retribution, Religious Daoist ideas of merits and demerits, and concepts such as the mysterious, slow-moving cosmic force known as *yunhui* ("rhythms of fate")—complicated the essentially naturalistic interpretation of fate offered by orthodox Confucians.[86]

Those who performed *fengshui* calculations consulted almanacs to determine the line on the geomantic compass that would be auspicious in a given year for the construction of a building or a grave. One could often make modifications to an environment by adding artificial elements, but if the timing was wrong, there might be no alternative but to postpone construction until a lucky year. In the meantime, of course, other buildings erected in the area might alter the *fengshui.* This complication led to much social conflict in traditional China as individuals competed for favorable geomantic influences.

Fengshui specialists had comparatively high status in traditional Chinese society despite persistent criticisms from officials and gentry. These criticisms were not, however, directed against the general theory of *fengshui,* for all levels of society accepted its basic assumptions. Rather, the literati objected to the practice of geomancy, which generated social tensions, often led to delayed burials (a serious breach of mourning ritual), and involved the manipulation of the Chinese masses by religious agents who were not part of the orthodox elite. This fear seems to have motivated much elite criticism of popular religious practice in China.[87]

Traditional Chinese homes reflected the complex religious world outlined above.[88] They were served by religious agents such as priests and geomancers and protected by a host of deities and guardian figures. The majority, at least in South China, had an altar to the household Lord of the Earth on the floor outside the door, a niche for the Heavenly Official (Tianguan) above it, and a place for the God of the

Hearth (Zaoshen) near the cooking stove. Wealth gods might be located in the hall or the main room of the house, along with Guanyin or another patron deity. But the focal point of religious life in virtually every Chinese home was the ancestral altar, located in the principal room. In Chinese society, ancestor worship was primary; individual or communal worship, only secondary. No ritual or institution did more to reinforce the solidarity of the family system than ancestor worship, and none was taken more seriously by both society and the state.[89]

The basic premise in ancestor worship was that the soul of a departed family member consisted of a *yin* component known as *po* (associated with the grave) and a *yang* component known as *hun* (associated with the ancestral tablet). According to one popular conception, these basic components became three separate "souls," each demanding ritual attention: one that went to the grave with the body, one that went to the Ten Courts of Judgment and was eventually reborn, and one that remained near the ancestral tablet on the family altar. *Po* had the potential of becoming *gui* if unplaced by sacrifices, but the spirits of one's own ancestors were not generally considered to be *gui*. One's own naturally became *shen,* assuming they received proper ritual attention.[90]

There were two universal aspects of ancestor worship in traditional China: mortuary rites (*sangli*) and sacrificial rites (*jili*). Mortuary rites involved elaborate mourning practices that differed in particulars from region to region but shared certain major features. These were, in the order they usually occurred: (1) public notification of the death through wailing and other expressions of grief; (2) the wearing of white mourning clothing by members of the bereaved family, ideally according to the five degrees of relationship (see Chapter 4); (3) ritualized bathing of the corpse; (4) the transfer of food, money, and other symbolic goods from the living to the dead; (5) the preparation and installation of a spirit tablet for the deceased; (6) the payment of ritual specialists, including Buddhist monks and Daoist priests; (7) the playing of music to accompany the corpse and settle the spirit; (8) the sealing of the corpse in an airtight coffin; and (9) the expulsion of the coffin from the community.[91]

In most regions of China, a funeral procession for the body and spirit tablet, followed by a feast for family members, marked the formal conclusion of the mourning process (see Figures 7.4 and 7.5). Burial did not always take place immediately after death, however. High-status families—including the Qing imperial household—often kept the coffin in the domestic realm for months, even years, as a mark of respect for the deceased (and perhaps to await an especially propitious time for interment according to *fengshui* calculations). In all cases, regardless of when the funeral procession and feast took place, families strained their financial resources to the limit in order to exhibit the proper measure of filial devotion (and community status) in their ritual display. Deceased children were not usually so honored, however, for their premature death was itself considered an unfilial act.[92]

Sacrificial rites consisted of daily or bimonthly devotions and anniversary services. Families burned incense every day on the domestic ancestral altar, which housed the family spirit tablets in hierarchical order (see Figures 7.6 and 7.7). In front of these

Figure 7.4   Funeral Procession. Photo courtesy of the Peabody & Essex Museum, Salem, Mass.

tablets often glowed an eternal flame, symbol of the ancestor's abiding presence within the household. Anniversary rites took place on the death date of each major deceased member of the family. Sacrificial food was offered, and living members of the family participated in the ceremony in ritual order based on age and generation. Sacrifices were also made to the ancestors during major festival periods and on important family occasions such as births and weddings (see Chapter 10). In general, these domestic devotions reflected a ritual apparatus characteristic of most other forms of Chinese religious practice.[93]

In the eyes of orthodox Confucians, ancestor worship was considered to be essentially a secular rite without religious implications. Deemed to be nothing more than the "expression of human feelings," mourning and other ritual observances expressed love and respect for the dead and at the same time cultivated the virtues of filial piety, loyalty, and faithfulness. Ancestor worship was standard means of "honoring virtue and repaying merit" (*chongde baogong*), in the stock Chinese phrase. The Confucian gentleman sacrificed to his ancestors because it was the proper thing to do; lesser men did so to "serve the spirits."[94]

This attitude was consistent with the general neo-Confucian tendency to encourage rational and secular interpretations of otherworldly phenomena. In neo-Confucian literature, for example, the popular religious terms *gui* and *shen* became expressly identified as the abstract forces of *yin* and *yang*. Official religion was justified at least

Figure 7.5   Grave. This "horseshoe"-style grave is typical of many areas in southern China. Photo courtesy of the Peabody & Essex Museum, Salem, Mass.

in part as a means of motivating the masses to perform acts of Confucian piety. Sections on religion in local gazetteers often quoted the following commentary to the *Yijing*, attributed to Confucius himself: "The sages devised guidance in the name of the gods, and [the people of] the land became obedient." Even the employment of priests, geomancers, and other religious agents by elite households could be explained away as matters of habit, female indulgence, or a kind of filial insurance for ancestors in case the popular Buddhist version of the afterlife happened to be correct.[95]

But where did neo-Confucian "rationalism" end and popular "superstition" begin? Although popular religion reflected the social landscape of its adherents, it was still in many ways "a variation of the same [elite] understanding of the world." The "Heaven" of the Chinese literati may have been remote and impersonal, but it could reward Confucian virtue and punish vice in the same spirit as the Jade Emperor and his agents. The omens and avenging ghosts of popular vernacular literature had their supernatural counterparts in the official dynastic histories. The cosmological principles of astrology and divination—not to mention many specific religious beliefs and

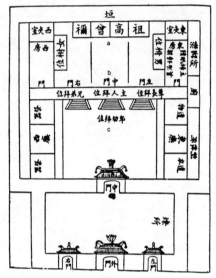

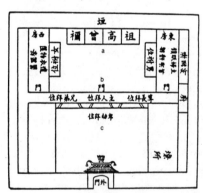

For officials of ranks four to seven

For officials of ranks one to three

For officials of ranks eight and nine

Figure 7.6   Ancestral Temples. In these diagrams, a *indicates ancestral tablets;* b, *a gate, through which the principal worshipper passes; and* c, *junior worshippers. Source: WXL (1936).*

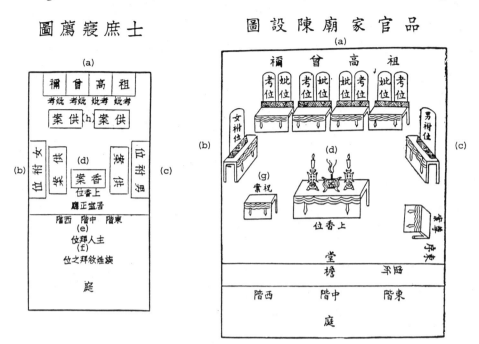

Figure 7.7 Ancestral Tablets. The inner layout of a ritually prescribed family ancestral temple (jiamiao) for the official class (right) and a more modest sacrificial shrine (qinjian) for the gentry class and commoners (left). The ancestral tablets (a), male and female, stand in front of the incense table (d), flanked by tablets representing recently deceased females (b) and males (c) situated on the right (yin) and left (yang) side of the main altar (as viewed by the ancestors), respectively. The jiamiao shows a prayer table (g), while the qinjian indicates offering tables (h), the primary worshipper (e), and the positioning of relatives in rank order (f). Although the primary focus of domestic ancestor worship remained the deceased parents and grandparents of the head of the household, a family's ancestral altar might also include tablets of nonagnatic lines that had contributed in some significant way to the well-being of the host line. Source: WXL (1936).

practices—were the same for all classes of Chinese society, as was the tendency to view the spirit world in bureaucratic terms.[96]

Furthermore, the evidence suggests strongly that in the mind of the elite, *shen* and *gui* were not always identified simply as the abstract forces of *yin* and *yang*. It may even be suggested that the ceremonial observances for official sacrifices, community religion, and domestic worship evoked many of the same emotions in the elite that they did among the common people, although the evidence is largely impressionistic. At least the sense of interlocking rituals—reinforced by common symbolic elements (architecture, written characters, colors, numbers, plants, animals, deities and culture heroes, etc.) as well as common practices (the use of music, the burning of incense and prayers, bowing and kneeling, etc.)—gave all sectors of Chinese society a sense of shared interest and common cultural purpose.[97]

There was, of course, a heterodox tradition of popular religion that was less compatible with the elite outlook. Sworn brotherhood associations of the Triad type in southern China, and folk religious sects of the White Lotus variety in the North, challenged certain Chinese social conventions and were marked by a strong millenarian emphasis. Monotheistic religious teachings such as Islam, Judaism, and Christianity also contained millenarian elements and posed a threat to the Confucian order by their devotion to a religious authority higher than the state.[98] Islam seemed especially threatening because of its large numbers of adherents and their distinctive habits. Although the Muslims accommodated themselves to the dominant culture by adopting Chinese names, speech, and dress, they nonetheless lived in segregated villages and urban neighborhoods, tended to pursue nonagricultural occupations, followed their own religious leaders, and generally eschewed the consumption of pork.[99]

Confucian scholars might criticize the specific beliefs of these religious groups on any number of grounds—the Triads, for example, because of their denial of the primacy of orthodox kinship bonds; the White Lotus sects for their messianic belief in the Eternal and Venerable Mother (Wusheng laomu); the Christians for their negative attitudes toward ancestor worship and their doctrine of original sin. But the most threatening aspect of heterodox religious traditions was their political potential, their capacity to attract and mobilize disgruntled members of Chinese society. Triad and White Lotus religious associations were closely linked with secret-society activity and popular rebellion throughout late imperial times, and during the nineteenth century, two of the most lengthy and destructive rebellions in Chinese history were inspired, respectively, by Islam and Christianity.[100]

Yet even so inconoclastic a popular movement as the Christian-inspired Taiping Rebellion (1850–1864)—which attacked Confucianism, Buddhism, and Daoism, advocated communalism and equality between men and women, and sought to eliminate long-standing social practices such as concubinage, footbinding, and ancestor worship—made many concessions to Chinese tradition in the realms of both theory and practice. The Taipings used concepts, phrases, and allusions from Confucian, Buddhist, and Daoist sources, held traditional views on the place of ritual in preserving status distinctions (including the subordination of wives to their husbands), held Confucian views on matters such as name taboos, and employed conventional symbols of imperial legitimacy in both their political institutions and public ceremonies. Even their private devotions to God (Shangdi or Tian)—the Heavenly Father (Tianfu)—bore a striking resemblance to ancestor worship down to the burning of incense before a spirit tablet in homes and offices.[101]

Undoubtedly the use of time-honored terms and concepts, sources of authority, ceremonial forms, and political symbols diminished somewhat the revolutionary impact of heterodox movements—particularly in the popular mind. It is true, of course, that even in orthodox society a tension always existed between the "ordered" realm of elite ritual (*li*) and the "disorder" of popular religious practices (*su*).[102] But the dialectic operating between the two favored order overall, as did shared ethical attitudes, philosophical concepts, and specific ritual practices. Similar cultural common denominators existed in the areas of Chinese art, literature, music, and drama.

ᴥ 8 ᴥ

Art

*Q*ing scholars considered two types of art worthwhile: that which they enjoyed but did not create, and that which they created and therefore esteemed most. The former included the work of skilled craftsmen, from elegant ancient bronzes to colorful contemporary ceramics; the latter embraced the refined arts of the brush—painting and calligraphy. Occupying a fluid middle ground were decorative textiles, often executed in exquisite detail by talented elite women. Popular art—from temple paintings and religious icons to folk crafts such as basketwork, fans, umbrellas, toys, and papercuts—remained vital and vigorous throughout the Qing period, but it was seldom taken seriously by Chinese connoisseurs.[1]

Although early Qing intellectuals stigmatized the decadent consumer society of the late Ming as a "culturally exquisite bloom which was nevertheless in some sense rotten inside" (in the words of Craig Clunas), Chinese attitudes toward connoisseurship continued to be shaped by Ming models. It may indeed have become "unfashionable," as Clunas and others have suggested, for Qing intellectuals to consume conspicuously in the Ming style, or even to talk about superfluous "things" the way Ming aesthetes did; but works on connoisseurship such as Cao Zhao's fourteenth-century *Gegu yaolun* (Essential Criteria of Antiquities) remained influential as repositories of information on Chinese art, archaeology, and authenticity throughout the Qing period.[2]

The Qing dynasty has been characterized as "an antiquarian age when, as never before, men looked back into the past." But during the first century and a half of Manchu rule there was also considerable experimentation in the arts. Part of the impetus may have been the traumatic effect of the Qing conquest, which provided loyalist painters such as Gong Xian (1620–1689) with the tortured artistic theme of "a world gone corrupt." John Henderson offers the intriguing hypothesis that the "complex deviations and distortions" of certain Qing painters, including Gong, may have been related to cosmological criticisms generated by *kaozheng* scholarship during the seventeenth and eighteenth centuries. Yet another factor, unsettling in a different way, was the rapid growth of commercial wealth, particularly in the lower Yangzi region. There, the blending of literati and merchant culture produced new fashions. The result was an enormous demand among consumers for innovative forms, colors, styles, and textures. Finally, there was the expanding foreign market for Chinese arts and crafts, especially porcelain. Although many of these goods came to be designed explicitly for export to the West, their production unquestionably influenced Chinese tastes.[3]

The Qing court's patronage of painters, calligraphers, and craftsmen naturally affected Chinese artistic developments. The Kangxi emperor began the process in earnest, but it was his grandson, the Qianlong emperor, who exerted the most profound influence. Michael Sullivan describes him rather unflatteringly as

> a voracious art collector, a niggardly and opinionated connoisseur, an unstoppable writer of inscriptions and stamper of seals who was determined, as a function of his imperial role, to leave his indelible mark upon China's artistic legacy. His seals obliterate some of the finest paintings in the imperial collection, which ... grew to such enormous size that there were few ancient masterpieces that were not gathered behind the high walls of the Forbidden City, shut away forever from the painters who might still have studied them had they remained in private hands.[4]

Financial strains during the latter part of the Qianlong reign caused the emperor to cut back on his sponsorship of the arts, however; by the end of the eighteenth century at the latest, the dominant influence on Chinese art was private patronage, together with the ever greater commercialization of production.[5]

During the nineteenth century, Qing painting lost a great deal of its vigor and vitality. Part of the problem was lack of inspiration, an unfortunate consequence of the Qianlong emperor's aggressive campaign to acquire local artworks for his imperial collection. Another difficulty was financial exigency, which diminished even further the court's support for painting, calligraphy, and craft production. Meanwhile, many "independent" Chinese artists went to one of two extremes—either surrendering to the demands of patrons and other customers for hastily produced paintings or becoming overly academic in their artistic approach. Increasingly, late Qing works were simply paintings about painting, "art-historical art." Too often the artists' inspiration "was not nature but the very tradition itself."[6]

Nonetheless, recent research has shown that the nineteenth century was not nearly as artistically sterile as it has often been portrayed. Although labor-intensive crafts such as cloisonné never achieved the same heights under private patrons that they had reached under court patronage during the eighteenth century, painting flourished among scholar-officials at the fringes of the court as well as in the provinces. During the nineteenth century, several bold regional styles either emerged for the first time or acquired new life, and cities such as Shanghai and Guangzhou (Canton) became centers of vibrant artistic activity.[7]

ATTITUDES TOWARD ART

Connoisseurship in traditional China required wealth, leisure, and education. As amateur artists, gentry scholars were expected to have a discriminating eye and to possess attractive works of art, but they were not always the most famous or successful collectors. The salt merchant An Qi (born c. 1683), for example, was the envy of all literati in the area of Tianjin. Having purchased a number of paintings and calligraphic scrolls from well-known Ming and early Qing connoisseurs, in time An became a connoisseur himself. His annotated catalogue of paintings and calligraphy, completed in 1742, was highly prized by Qing collectors for its detailed descriptions of outstanding artwork. It was reprinted twice by the noted antique collector and art patron Duanfang (1861–1911).[8]

Chinese art has long been characterized by a remarkable feeling for natural beauty, perfection of form, grace, and refinement. It is also noteworthy for its optimism, love of nature, and organic quality. As indicated in Chapter 5, much of the formal aesthetics of the Chinese elite developed out of a long-standing cognitive emphasis on *yinyang* principles and relationships. As with music, ritual, and poetry, the most exalted forms of artistic achievement in China tended to display lyrical patterns of dualistic balance, periodic rhythms, and cyclical sequences.[9]

These aesthetics had more than simply a linguistic foundation; by late imperial times they also had a cosmological one. Chinese art reflected life, which in turn reflected the order of the universe. Liu Xie's *Wenxin diaolong* (The Literary Mind and the Carving of Dragons) expresses this artistic relationship in the following way:

> *Wen,* or pattern, is a very great power indeed. It is born together with Heaven and Earth. Why do we say this? Because all color-patterns are mixed of black and yellow [the colors of Heaven and Earth], and all shape patterns are differentiated by round and square [i.e., the shapes of Heaven and Earth]. The sun and moon, like two pieces of jade, manifest the pattern of Heaven; mountains and rivers in their beauty display the pattern of Earth. These are, in fact, the *wen* of the *dao* itself. ... Man, and man alone, forms with these the "three powers" [Heaven, Earth, and Man], and he does so because he alone is endowed with spirituality [*ling*]. He is the refined essence of the five elements—indeed, the mind of the universe.[10]

In praise of the great late-Ming painter Dong Qichang (1555–1636), the *Wusheng shi shi* (History of Silent Poetry) states, "He [Dong] held the creative power of nature in his hand and was nourished by the mists and clouds. ... [It] may be said that everything in his paintings, whether clouds, peaks or stones, was made as if by the power of Heaven, his brushwork being quite unrestrained like the working of nature."[11]

Michael Sullivan has aptly remarked,

> Just as ritual, and its extension through music, poetry, and the shape and decoration of the objects used in it, was the gentleman's means of demonstrating that he was attuned to the Will of Heaven, so was aesthetic beauty felt to be what results when the artist gives sincere expression to his intuitive awareness of natural order. Beauty, therefore, is what conduces to order, harmony, [and] tranquility.

In the words of the *Record of Ritual:* "Music is [an echo of] the harmony between Heaven and Earth; ceremonies reflect the orderly distinctions [in the operations of] Heaven and Earth. From that harmony all things receive their being; to those orderly distinctions they owe the differences between them. Music has its origin in Heaven."

The goal of all elite artistic, literary, musical, and ritual activity in traditional China was thus to promote and display social and cosmic harmony.[12]

Since the *dao* of art, literature, music, and ritual was inseparable from the cosmic *dao* and the *dao* of human affairs, it followed that Chinese creative endeavor was never far removed from tradition. Like the Confucian Classics, ancient artistic models were believed to have universal and transcendent value. As Frederick Mote reminds us, in traditional China

> neither individuals nor the state could claim any theoretical authority higher or more binding than men's rational minds and the civilizing norms that those human minds had created. That is a tenuous basis of authority, and since it could not easily be buttressed by endowing it with nonrational or suprarational qualities, it had to be buttressed by the weight granted to historical experience.

In Chinese art, then, as in Chinese life, "the defining criteria for value were inescapably governed by past models, not by present experience or by future states of existence."[13]

The relationship between past and present in Chinese art (and in other areas of Chinese aesthetic and intellectual life as well) may be viewed in terms of a creative tension between the polarities of tradition and innovation, orthodoxy and individualism, structure and spontaneity, intellect and intuition, didactics and aesthetics. Different individuals responded in different ways to these competing impulses. But however such tensions were conceived, and however they were resolved, the past in Chinese imaginative endeavor remained an integral part of the Chinese present.

And how was the link established? Creative individuals sought the restoration of antiquity (*fugu*)—a fundamental neo-Confucian concern and an obsession with many Qing intellectuals. But the restoration of the past did not mean simply the slavish imitation of early literary and artistic models. Rather it involved "spiritual communication" (*shenhui*) with the ancient masters, a state in which the past and present became one in the mind of the creative individual. The greater the aesthetic or technical achievement of a Chinese writer or artist, the more he or she was thought to be in touch with the past—at once under its command and in command of it. Such spiritual communication required a total commitment on the part of the individual, body and mind.[14]

Chinese tradition thus suggested pattern, but it did not impose despotic rule. The result was a remarkable continuity of cultural style without the sacrifice of creative potential. In the words of Wen Fong, "In *fu-ku* [*fugu*] the Chinese saw history not as a long fall from grace, but as an enduring crusade to restore life and truth to art."[15] That crusade gave vitality to Chinese culture in every period, including the Qing.

Naturally enough, tradition influenced not only the artist and craftsman but also the collector and connoisseur:

> When his eye falls on the miniature porcelain tripod standing on his desk, not only does ... [he] savour the perfection of its form and glaze, but a whole train of

associations are set moving in his mind. For him, his tripod is treasured not simply for its antiquity or rarity, but because it is a receptacle of ideas, and a visible emblem of the ideals by which he lives. Indeed, although he would be gratified to know that it was the genuine Sung [Song] dynasty piece it purports to be, it would not be robbed of all its value to him if he subsequently found that it was in fact a clever imitation of the Ch'ien-lung [Qianlong] period—particularly if it bore an appropriate inscription cut in archaic characters.[16]

Even a fragment of the past was sufficient to conjure up the right kind of cultural image. The Qing collector Lu Shihua notes in his fascinating *Shuhua shuoling* (Collectors Scrapbook) that members of his circle of acquaintances would be quite content with one or two lines from a Song inscription, for "as soon as one has come to know the brush technique and the spirit of the work of the ancient artists, one can derive the rest by analogy."[17]

Books on connoisseurship, such as Cao Zhao's influential *Essential Criteria of Antiquities,* advised readers on how to determine artistic worth and detect forgeries, but they did not encourage in Qing collectors a passion for mere authenticity. Nor did they promote an inordinate attachment to individual art objects. A characteristic feature of Chinese connoisseurship in late imperial times was the trading of cultural artifacts—a Ming scroll for a Qing album, a Shang bronze for a Song ceramic. In this way, personal collections were invigorated by aesthetic variety and at the same time enriched by the scholarly associations that attached to newly acquired objects. In traditional China, prior ownership of a work of art could be as important to the collector as the work itself.[18]

The unity of cultural style in Qing China was evident not only in shared aesthetics and attitudes toward the past but also in the vocabulary of artistic, literary, and musical criticism. Terms such as *yin* and *yang, qi* (life spirit or life force), *gu* ("bone," or structure), and *shenyun* (spirit and tone, spiritual resonance, or inspired harmony) were long-standing and indispensable in the evaluation of creative work of all kinds— although each expression might have several connotations in different contexts. These critical terms suggest the thematic importance in Chinese art of life, vitality, and natural process as well as the structural importance of rhythm and balance.[19]

Chinese symbolism, too, reflected a certain unity of cultural style. Closely linked with literary symbolism, artistic symbols were drawn from several rich sources of traditional inspiration—language (including puns and stylized characters), philosophy, religion, history, popular mythology, and, of course, nature itself. Some symbols that were once meaningful had lost their original connotations by Qing times and were considered largely decorative by all but the most sophisticated connoisseurs. Other symbols, like Chinese characters themselves, held different meanings depending on context.[20] But despite these differences (and certain regional variations), the most potent abstract and concrete symbols in Chinese art (and literature) tended to be shared by all levels of society and to reflect common cultural concerns.[21]

The overwhelming majority of Chinese artistic symbols were positive. Abstract designs tended to express the harmonious patterns and processes of nature, and concrete symbols generally indicated auspicious themes of happiness and good fortune. Although most of the spiral and angular designs on ancient bronzes and pottery (and later copies) no longer had specific symbolic value by Qing times, Chinese artists continued to represent natural processes through abstract symbolism. Square-circle motifs, for example, depicted in both art and architecture the cosmic relationship between Heaven (circle, *yang*) and Earth (square, *yin*). Also popular as a cosmic symbol was the Diagram of the Supreme Ultimate (*Taiji tu*)—a motif dating from Song times that adorned a wide variety of Chinese artwork, from paintings and carved jade to primitive ceramics intended for daily use in commoner households. It consisted of a circle composed of two equal parts—one light (*yang*) and one dark (*yin*)—separated by an S-shaped line. Often this diagram was surrounded by the eight trigrams.

Plant and animal symbolism figured prominently in Chinese artwork of all kinds. The most powerful and positive animal symbol was the dragon (*long*), a composite creature with the supposed ability to change size and render itself visible or invisible at will. Associated with the east and spring, the dragon was believed to inhabit mountains and to be capable of both ascending into the heavens and living in the water. Unlike its European counterpart, the Chinese dragon symbolized benevolence, longevity, prosperity, and the renewal of life. It also served as the symbol of imperial majesty, especially when depicted with five claws on each of its four feet.

The so-called phoenix (*fenghuang*) was the *yin* equivalent of the dragon. Associated with the south and summer, it had some *yang* qualities, just as the dragon had some *yin* attributes. Like the dragon, it was a composite animal, with distinctly positive connotations. Symbolizing peace and joy, it was commonly used as the mark of an empress in imperial China.

The unicorn (*qilin*) was associated with the west and autumn. It symbolized good luck and prosperity and was believed to herald the birth of a hero or a sage. According to legend, one was seen when Confucius came into the world. Like the dragon and the phoenix, the unicorn was a composite creature, sometimes depicted with one horn, but often with two. Its predominant characteristic was goodwill and benevolence to all living things.

The tortoise (*gui*), although not a purely mythical beast in the sense of the dragon, phoenix, and unicorn, was nonetheless viewed as a supernatural animal. Associated with the north and winter, its outstanding attributes were strength, endurance, and longevity. Its symbolic importance stemmed not only from the Chinese preoccupation with longevity but also from its legendary (and historical) connection with divination. As an imperial symbol, the tortoise was often depicted with the head of a dragon.

Among more conventional creatures, the tiger was king. In general, it symbolized military prowess. The lion was viewed as the protector of all that was sacred and was particularly popular as a Buddhist symbol. Bronze, stone, and ceramic lions often stood in male-female pairs as guardians on either side of the entrance to important Chinese buildings, both secular and religious. Other large animals, such as horses and elephants (both symbolizing strength and wisdom), were also popular as guardian figures.

The deer symbolized immortality (because of its supposed ability to find a magical life-giving fungus known as *lingzhi*) and also official emoluments (because the character for deer, *lu,* sounds like another character meaning "salary"). A similar pun on the sound *yu* invested the fish with the symbolic meaning of "abundance." Yet another pun made bats (*fu*) the symbol for good luck and prosperity. The link between Chinese characters and sounds quite naturally yielded what Wolfram Eberhard describes as a "rebus-mentality."[22]

Among flying animals and other fowl, cranes symbolized longevity; swallows, success; and the quail, scholarly poverty and courage in adversity. Mandarin ducks indicated conjugal affection, whereas the wild goose conjured up feelings of sadness or longing. Roosters, hens, and chickens symbolized family prosperity. In the insect world, the cicada stood as a common symbol of fertility and rebirth. The butterfly signified joy and warmth; the dragonfly, weakness and instability.

Plant symbolism was extremely popular in late imperial China. Without doubt the most prominent symbol in this category was bamboo. Quite apart from its inherent aesthetic appeal and multifunctional role in Chinese daily life (abundantly documented in the *TSJC*), bamboo symbolized the Confucian scholar—upright, strong, and resilient yet gentle, graceful, and refined. The pine tree suggested longevity and solitude; the plum tree, fortitude and respect for old age. The willow, like the wild goose, indicated parting and sorrow, while the cassia tree, like the carp, connoted literary success. Of various popular fruits, the peach had wide-ranging significance. It symbolized marriage, spring, justice, and especially Daoist immortality. The apple signified peace (a pun on the sound *ping*); the persimmon, joy; the pomegranate, fertility. Popular flower symbols included the chrysanthemum (happiness, longevity, and integrity), the peony (love and good fortune), the plum blossom (courage and hope), the wild orchid (humility and refinement), and the lotus (purity and detachment from worldly cares)—a predominantly Buddhist symbol.

Religious symbolism was, of course, most evident in explicitly Buddhist and Religious Daoist art. Virtually all of the major Buddhas, bodhisattvas, gods, genies, and other spirits of the popular pantheon were portrayed in paintings, sculpture, carvings, ceramics, and other temple art forms. An elaborate symbolism of hand gestures (*mudra*) came to be associated with Buddhist images, in addition to the wide range of signs and objects related to specific aspects of Buddhist teaching.[23] One of the most powerful of these signs was the swastika, which symbolized the Buddha's heart and mind and served as a general indication of happiness (and sometimes immortality). Swords and other weapons denoted protection and wisdom; the conch shell, the universality of Buddhist law (*dharma*); and jewels or scepters, the granting of wishes. Similar symbols existed for Religious Daoism. For example, the Eight Immortals—all signifying longevity and good fortune—were represented by the Eight Precious Things: fans, swords, bottle gourds, castanets, flower baskets, bamboo canes, flutes, and lotus flowers.[24]

Confucian art symbolism drew its primary inspiration from history and the classics as well as from popular stories of virtuous individuals, such as the famous "Twenty-four Examples of Filial Piety" (see Chapter 10). In addition to common plant and animal symbols such as the quail and bamboo, scholars were also represented by such diverse objects as pearls, coins, books, paintings, and the rhinoceros horn. Also popular as symbols of scholarly refinement were the Chinese lute (*qin*) and the so-called Four Treasures of Literature—the writing brush, the ink stick, the grinding stone, and paper.

Indicative of both Chinese eclecticism and a penchant for combining elements into numerical categories, many artistic symbols were grouped together.[25] Combinations of two of the same symbol often indicated conjugal affection or friendship, but such pairings also reflected *yinyang* juxtapositions—aesthetic patterns in which one element was clearly "superior" to the other. Thus quail were almost invariably depicted in pairs, one with its head turned upward (*yang*) and the other with its head facing the ground (*yin*). The pairing derived from a famous line in the *Book of Poetry,* but the positioning reflected a long-standing aesthetic of unequal balance.

Plants and animals were often grouped together—the phoenix and the peony, for example, to indicate opulence; the chrysanthemum and the grouse to connote good fortune; the heron and the lotus to symbolize integrity. Larger groupings were common as well. As the Three Friends of Winter, the bamboo, plum, and pine signified enduring friendship as well as the harmony of the Three Teachings. The plum, wild orchid, bamboo, and chrysanthemum were known as the Four Gentlemen and beloved by gardeners, poets, artists, scholars, and craftsmen. The dragon, phoenix, unicorn, and tortoise were grouped together as the Four Spiritual Animals.

The Four Spiritual Animals were not the only symbols reflecting seasonal or astrological correlations. The months of the year, for example, came to be represented by flora as well as fauna. The twelve animals of the Chinese zodiac, and sometimes even the twenty-eight astral animals, were also portrayed on art objects.[26] Popular groupings of eight included not only the Daoist Immortals and their "precious" items but also the Eight Creatures (corresponding to the eight trigrams) and the Eight Buddhist Lucky Signs. The Twelve Imperial Emblems, as the name suggests, adorned items for the emperor's personal use, including clothing. The largest category of Chinese symbols was known simply as the Hundred Ancient Things, a generic designation for an indefinite number of auspicious signs and objects. In general, Confucian symbolism dominated this motif, but Buddhist, Daoist, and naturalistic symbols also figured prominently in it. Like most larger groupings of symbols, the Hundred Ancient Things appeared most commonly on Chinese craft productions.

CRAFTS

Chinese craftsmen in Qing times excelled at nearly every kind of technical art—textiles, wood and ivory carving, metalwork, lacquerware, stone sculpture, ceramics, enamels, bronzes, jades, jewelry, and glassware.[27] The Qing was also a period of technical accomplishments in areas such as architecture and landscape gardening. Not surprisingly, much of the best craftsmanship of the period was done under imperial patronage. As early as 1680 or so, the Kangxi emperor had already established workshops in the imperial palace precincts for the manufacture of porcelains, lacquerware, glass, enamel, jade, furniture, and other prized objects for court use. His grandson, the Qianlong emperor, was especially well known for his employment of skilled imperial artisans in the production of magnificent works of traditional craftsmanship.[28]

Of the many types of Chinese crafts, four may be singled out for particular attention: bronzes, jades, porcelains, and landscape gardens. All four gave special satisfaction to members of the Chinese elite, and each in its own way exhibited the major aesthetic features and symbolic elements of Chinese art discussed in the previous section.

The most highly prized bronzes in the Qing period, as in more recent times, were ancient ritual vessels of Shang and Zhou vintage. They were valued not only for their natural color and exquisite design but also for their powerful historical and ritual associations. The well-known Qing connoisseur Ruan Yuan once identified three successive stages in the evolution of Chinese attitudes toward bronze vessels: Before the Han they were symbols of privilege and power; from Han to Song times, their discovery was hailed as a portent; and from the Song dynasty onwards, "freed from superstition," they became the toys of collectors and the quarry of philologists and antiquarians. But the *Essential Criteria of Antiquities* suggests that even in late imperial times at least some members of the Chinese elite, probably a large number, considered ancient ritual vessels to provide a measure of protection against evil spirits—a function not unlike that of the more mundane charms of the so-called unenlightened masses.[29]

As indicated by Ruan Yuan, the inscriptions on ancient bronzes, together with early stone inscriptions, were of great interest to Qing antique collectors, who studied them systematically as a special class of Chinese scholarship. Some collectors, such as Chen Jieqi (1813–1884), possessed hundreds of bronzes and literally thousands of rubbings from stone inscriptions, not to mention a large number of ancient coins and other metal artifacts. Literati such as Liu Xihai (d. 1853) wrote numerous tracts on these and other antiquities, contributing to a general burst of antiquarian scholarship in the late Qing period.[30]

Qing craftsmen often sought to imitate the shape and design of Shang and Zhou bronzes, either to conform to Qing ritual specifications or out of sheer admiration for their form and style. The decorative motifs of these ancient models—particularly abstract designs such as the spiraling or curvilinear "thunder pattern" and "whorl circle"—endured in various types of Chinese art for thousands of years. The original piece-mold technique that produced them involved the transference of carved designs from one surface to another, a procedure also followed in Chinese seal carving, the carving of calligraphy in stone or wood, and, of course, the carving of printing blocks. In all these crafts, the artisan had to possess, in Wen Fong's words, "a highly refined sensitivity for the silhouetted form and a lively familiarity with, and love for, the interplay between the positive and negative design patterns." Both the zoomorphic and abstract designs of classic-style bronzes reflect a complex *yinyang* interaction between solid and void, raised and recessed, relief and intaglio, that proved invariably appealing to Chinese aesthetic sensibilities.[31]

Some Qing copies of early Chinese bronzes were deliberate forgeries, but many made no pretense of antiquity and provided the actual date of casting on the vessel. Other bronzes produced in the Qing period did not even try to approximate ancient models. Containers for practical use, decorative bells, and ornaments, as well as small religious statues, came in a wide variety of styles and shapes that often reflected more "modern" tastes.[32] Yet the aesthetic appeal of ancient bronzes, as well as their presumed protective value and their historical associations, made them highly prized throughout the ages, including the Qing period.

Ancient jades were viewed in much the same way. The Qing connoisseur Lu Shihua tells us:

> Present-day people want jades of the Three Dynasties [Xia, Shang, and Zhou] only, and require that their color be pure white, "sweet yellow," or "sweet green." Even then they are not satisfied, and insist that the "blood spots" be spread evenly over the entire surface and that the object be large and in perfect condition. If one sets his standard as high as this, he had better have a jade object newly made, and submit it to the oil treatment [*tihong you*].[33]

Michael Sullivan indicates that for most Chinese connoisseurs it was satisfying enough if jade objects were of high quality and traditional design, but there can be no doubt that antique jade was considered more valuable than new jade, not only for its use in antiquarian studies but also because it was believed to possess a much larger supply of "life force" (*qi*) or "virtue" (*de*).[34]

From Neolithic times through the Qing, jade was always highly regarded. The Chinese language is rich in words with the "jade" (*yu*) radical—expressions that convey notions of beauty, preciousness, hardness, and purity. Confucius is said to have remarked,

> The sages of old beheld in jade the reflections of every virtue. In its luster, bright yet warm, humaneness; in its compactness and strength, wisdom; in its sharp and clean edges which cause no injury, righteousness; in its use as pendants, seeming as if they would drop to the ground, propriety; in the note it emits when struck, clear and prolonged, music; by its flaws neither concealing its beauty nor its beauty concealing its flaws, loyalty; by its radiance issuing forth from within on every side, faithfulness.[35]

Jade, in other words, united in itself moral and aesthetic beauty.

In various forms, jade was used in ceremonial sacrifices, buried with the dead, displayed in homes and palaces, and worn for both decoration and protection. For official ritual purposes, it was modeled into various symbolic shapes such as the disc (*bi*) and the squared tube (*cong*)—both of which had been employed in Shang and Zhou dynasty ceremonies. Jade amulets provided protection from evil spirits and conveyed "life force," while jade musical instruments were highly esteemed both in ritual life and in daily affairs for their clear and uplifting sound. Scholars often fondled specially carved pieces of jade called *bawan,* both for the sensual pleasure it afforded and in order to refine their touch for the appreciation of fine porcelain.[36]

The Qianlong reign represented the high point of jade carving in late imperial China, in part because it was a period of great prosperity but also because vast areas of Central Asia, where much precious jade is found, were brought under imperial sway at that time. During the long and illustrious rule of the Qianlong emperor, thousands of magnificent carved jades were added to the imperial collection, some of which bore poetic inscriptions in characters that imitated the emperor's calligraphy. In the words of S. Howard Hansford, during the Qianlong period "jade was applied to countless new uses in the Forbidden City and the stately homes of nobles and officials. Though the inspiration of the designers of two thousand years earlier was rarely attained, the execution and finish left nothing to be desired and much larger works were attempted."[37] Some of these monumental jade sculptures, still on display in the Forbidden City today, stand as tall as a man.

The heyday of Qing porcelain manufacture was somewhat earlier than that of jade carving, from about 1683 to 1750, during the reign of the Kangxi emperor in particular. Of all the Chinese ceramic arts, porcelain (*ci*) stood at the apex of achievement: It was universally admired, the subject of countless essays, and a fitting topic for poetry as well. Imperial patronage was enormously important to the successful production of high-quality porcelains. Soame Jenyns has written:

> The history of Ch'ing [Qing] porcelain is in effect the history of the town of Ching-te Chen [Jingde zhen], which in turn was dominated by the presence of the imperial porcelain factory, which was situated there. Over 80 percent of the porcelains of China during the Ch'ing [Qing] period were made at this great ceramic metropolis in Kiangsi [Jiangxi], or in its immediate neighborhood; the provincial porcelain factories, with the single exception of Te-hua [Dehua] in Fukien [Fujian], producing porcelain of poor quality and negligible importance during this period.[38]

This statement perhaps undervalues local production in Qing China, but it certainly testifies to the dominant position occupied by the imperial factory.

As with bronzes and jades, Qing connoisseurs greatly admired porcelain antiques, which had a kind of dull shine, or "receded luster" (*tuiguang*). Among the most esteemed of these early porcelains, in addition to official ware (*guanyao*), was the legendary sky-blue *chai* ware, *ru* ware, and crackled *ge* ware. Qing potters excelled in the imitation of these and other types of early ceramics; expert forgers produced "receded luster" by rubbing new porcelain first with a grindstone, then with a mixture of paste and fine sand, and finally with a straw pad to obliterate the scratches. The Kangxi emperor is known to have sent to the imperial kilns at Jingde zhen rare pieces of Song dynasty *guan, chai,* and *ru* ware to be meticulously copied for imperial pleasure. The imperial kilns also continued to produce Ming-style porcelains, some of which, like the beautiful white "eggshell" bowls of the Yongle period, were executed by Qing craftsmen more flawlessly than the Ming originals.[39]

Qing potters also excelled in producing the striking multicolored Ming-style porcelains known as *sancai, wucai,* and *doucai.* The significant feature of these three types of porcelain, in addition to their vivid use of rich blues, greens, and yellows in the fashion of much architectural decoration, is their amalgamation of both popular religious and imperial symbolism, their seemingly inexhaustible range of shapes and colors (including reproductions of ancient bronzes), and their self-conscious *yinyang* juxtapositions. As with other porcelains, Qing craftsmen often inscribed *sancai, wucai,* and *doucai* pieces with reign marks other than those of the period in which they were produced, making positive identification of good copies extremely difficult.[40]

European influences found their way into the decoration of Qing porcelains for two principal reasons. One was the fact that a considerable amount of Chinese porcelain was intended for European markets in the latter half of the seventeenth century and most of the eighteenth century. The other was the general receptiveness of the imperial court to Western artistic influences during the late Ming and early Qing period. These influences can be seen not only in porcelain and other ceramics but also in some imperial architecture and court painting.[41]

Overall, however, Chinese art followed traditional models, and although some porcelains functioned as convenient vehicles for the transmission of foreign artistic influences, most conveyed a rich indigenous decorative tradition that in a real sense transcended class. Many of the highest-quality Qing porcelains were decorated with folk symbols and the bright colors of folk and religious art. It is true, however, that in several respects porcelains had a closer affinity with elite art than with the simple ceramics of commoner households. Like jades and bronzes, they were of antiquarian interest and appreciated both for their surface "feel" and melodious ring when struck. Furthermore, like paintings, many porcelains were carefully decorated with the brush, and they were categorized according to the same basic system of classification. But whereas in painting, landscape was the most popular and prestigious classification (see next section), in porcelain it was a relatively minor category.[42]

Landscape gardening, not surprisingly, sought precisely to capture the mood of a landscape painting. Although often overlooked as an art form, Chinese gardens in fact embodied the best principles of artistic expression in China, combining superb craftsmanship, complex symbolism, and the careful arrangement of aesthetic elements. During the Qing period, gardens ranged in size from the huge imperial summer palace outside Beijing known as the Yuanming yuan (Garden of Perfect Brightness), which had a seventy-mile-long walled perimeter, to tiny, cramped urban gardens only a few square feet in area and even miniature gardens planted in porcelain dishes. Members of the Chinese elite and rich merchants, of course, took special

Figure 8.1   Landscape Garden. A group of late Qing scholars with the typical trappings of elite status: long gowns, fans, and a landscape garden retreat. Photo courtesy of the Peabody & Essex Museum, Salem, Mass.

pride in constructing individualized gardens, such as Yuan Mei's famous Suiyuan in the area of Nanjing.

Chinese gardens were viewed primarily as Daoist retreats. In the words of the Qianlong emperor, "Every ... ruler, when he has returned from audience, and has finished his public duties, must have a garden in which he may stroll, look around and relax his heart. If he has a suitable place for this it will refresh his mind and regulate his emotions, but if he has not, he will become engrossed in sensual pleasures and lose his will power."[43] Access to the extensive gardens of the Forbidden City and the western section of the Imperial City in Beijing did not always distract Qing emperors from sensual indulgence, but gardens generally did provide a retreat for the world-weary Confucian—and a fitting place of rest for those of a Buddhist or Daoist inclination as well.[44]

Gardens were not always resting places, however. They also served as the focus for much elite social activity (see Figure 8.1). Although well suited for meditation and contemplation, gardens provided an ideal environment for entertaining, composing verse, and admiring art. Small wonder the expansive Prospect Garden (Daguan yuan) of the Jia family provides the setting for much of the action in the great Qing novel *Dream of the Red Chamber* (see Chapter 9). Andrew Plaks has brilliantly analyzed Cao

Xueqin's use of Prospect Garden as a microcosm of the Chinese cultural world, and indeed of the entire universe. It is true, of course, that Chinese cities—Beijing in particular—were also viewed as microcosms of the universe, but whereas the cosmological symbolism of the capital was expressed in formal patterns of geometric symmetry, in the garden it was expressed in delightful informality and irregularity. The garden recreated nature in an idealized form, but not a geometrical one.[45]

Aesthetic components of traditional Chinese gardens bore the unmistakable imprint of conscious *yinyang* duality. Buildings were deliberately interspersed with natural features; rock formations ("mountains") stood juxtaposed to water ("rivers"); light areas alternated with dark; rounded lines with angular ones; empty spaces with solids. The small led to the large, the low to the high. The Qing scholar Shen Fu, a well-known connoisseur of gardens, expressed the garden aesthetic in the following way:

> In laying out garden pavilions and towers, suites of rooms and covered walkways,
> piling up rocks into mountains, or planting flowers to form a desired shape, the aim is
> to see the small in the large, to see the large in the small, to see the real in the illusory,
> and to see the illusory in the real. Sometimes you conceal, sometimes you reveal,
> sometimes you work on the surface, sometimes in depth.[46]

Chinese gardens thus had a kind of endless, rhythmic quality. Wing-tsit Chan writes, "Almost every part [of the traditional Chinese garden] is rhythmic in expression. The winding walks, the round gate, the zigzag paths, the melody-like walls, the rockeries which are frozen music in themselves, and flowers and trees and birds are all echoes and counterpoints of rhythm." Significantly, this rhythmic quality—and often a sense of endlessness as well—found in landscape gardens was also evident in the structure of Chinese poetry and narrative prose, the flow of melody in music, the movement and sound of Chinese drama, the curved roof and other architectural elements of Chinese buildings, and, of course, in the composition of landscape paintings.[47]

The decorative symbolism of Chinese gardens followed convention. The design of gates and doorways, for example, reflected the perfection of the circle or the shape of a jar—the latter a pun on the word for "peace" (*ping*). Window grilles and other woodwork often carried stylized Chinese characters for "blessings" (*fu*), "emoluments" (*lu*), and "long life" (*shou*), as well as designs echoing ancient bronze motifs such as the "thunder pattern" and the "whorl circle." Common animal symbols included the dragon, phoenix, deer, crane, and bat. Confucian symbolism was most evident in the books contained in garden buildings and often in the names given to specific pleasure spots. Religious symbolism was comparatively muted. Buddhist or Religious Daoist statues were rare, and there was no Chinese "garden god." *Fengshui* considerations obviously affected the design of Chinese gardens, but there was an aesthetic "logic" to this geomantic system that gave it significance beyond religion.[48]

In short, the major symbolism of the landscape garden was in its natural elements and in their arrangement. Rocks were chosen primarily for their fantastic shapes (those from Lake Tai, near Suzhou, were especially admired), while flowers, shrubs, and trees reflected the basic plant symbolism noted in the previous section. Among the most common floral elements in the landscape garden were the peony, orchid, magnolia, lotus, chrysanthemum, and gardenia. Bamboo was, of course, extremely popular, as were trees such as the willow, pine, peach, plum, and pomegranate. Most of these plants were identified with specific seasons and arranged with these identifications in mind.

A sharp distinction existed between the "naturalism" of the landscape garden and the rigid functionalism of the house to which it was connected. As the garden mirrored nature, the house mirrored society. Maggie Keswick writes, "In domestic architecture the orderly succession of rooms and courtyards that make up a Chinese house have often been seen as an expression of the Chinese ideal of harmonious social relationships: formal, decorous, regular and clearly defined."[49] This rigid symmetry—and, one might add, that of other Chinese architectural structures from temples to the imperial palace itself—stood in sharp contrast to the irregularity of the landscape garden.

But despite the structural distinction between house and garden in traditional China, the two were integrally related, for the structure of the former would have been considered intolerable without the latter, and the latter would have been deemed superfluous without the former. In all, the garden was a kind of "liminal zone" linking the spiritual and earthly concerns of man. Nelson Wu puts the matter poetically: "In … eternally negative space, between reason and untarnished emotion, between the correctness of the straight lines and the effortlessness of the curve, between the measurable and the romantic infinity, lies the Chinese garden which is between architecture and landscape painting."[50]

PAINTING AND CALLIGRAPHY

Although landscapes were regarded by Qing connoisseurs as the most exalted form of traditional Chinese painting, they were by no means the only type of admired brushwork. In addition to calligraphy—which was in a special class together with landscape painting—the Chinese also esteemed paintings of religious and secular figures, buildings and palaces, birds and animals, flowers and plants, and even antique objects such as bronzes and porcelains. According to the *Essential Criteria of Antiquities,* the artists of late imperial times were especially accomplished in the painting of landscapes, trees, rocks, flowers, bamboos, birds, and fish but less skilled than their predecessors in the rendering of human figures and large animals. Folk painting in the Qing included murals in temples and other buildings, but these were generally considered to be the work of mere technicians, not true art. Significantly, even in religious temples, secular symbolism (including examples of filial piety, historical scenes, and depictions from works of fiction) tended to predominate over explicitly religious scenes or symbols.[51]

Qing painting remained delicate and decorous. Chinese artists would have been genuinely horrified by the gruesome scenes of rape, war, and destruction so prevalent in the paintings of the West; figure painters shunned the nude; still-life painters found dead objects repulsive; and landscape painters usually ignored the artistic possibilities of deserts, swamps, and other desolate places. It is true, of course, that some murals in Chinese temples depicted in graphic detail the tortures of the Ten Courts of Judgment; that there was a well-developed tradition of erotic art (*chunhua* or *chungong*) in China; and that some Qing painters—like the "Yangchow eccentric" Luo Ping (d. 1799)—went so far as to paint ghosts, skeletons, and even raging forest fires. But overall, the subject matter of Chinese painting was uplifting, if not also expressly didactic.[52]

One important function of painting throughout much of the imperial era had been moral instruction. Zhang Yanyuan, ninth-century author of the influential *Lidai minghua ji* (Record of Famous Painters of Successive Dynasties), tells us, for example, that paintings should serve as models to the virtuous and warnings to the evil. He cites the Han scholar Cao Zhi, who describes how people seeing pictures of noble rulers "look up in reverence," whereas those who see pictures of degenerate rulers "are moved to sadness." And as late as the Ming dynasty we find examples of normative judgments impinging on standards of realism. The *Essential Criteria of Antiquities* states, for instance:

> Portraits of Buddhists should show benevolence and mercy; those of Daoists, moral cultivation and salvation; those of emperors and kings, the magnificence of imperial symbols such as the sun, the dragon and the phoenix; those of barbarians, their admiration of China and their obedience; those of Confucian worthies, loyalty, sincerity, civilized behavior and righteousness.[53]

Yet in the main, by late imperial times it was less subject matter than style that inspired and uplifted the viewer of Chinese paintings. During the Qing—and in fact well before—artistic achievement came to be seen as a reflection of the artist's inner morality. Like writing and musical compositions, paintings were considered to be "prints of the heart/mind [*xin*]"—not merely a means of Confucian cultivation but also a measure of it. No critic of any consequence judged a painting solely on what he knew about the moral worth of the artist, but a scholar-critic certainly would be inclined to consider the admirable (aesthetic) qualities of a painting as an index of the artist's own admirable (Confucian) qualities. Thus, as James Cahill has remarked, "The notion of 'the man revealed in the painting' was used ... [by Chinese critics] to account for excellence in art, not to determine it." Further, Cahill indicates that the creative impulses of naturalness, spontaneity, and intuition usually attributed to Daoism and Chan Buddhism in Chinese art and literature were also part of the late imperial Confucian tradition—central, in fact, to the *wenren* (literati) aesthetic.[54]

Confucianism shaped the interpretive contours of traditional Chinese painting in yet another sense. In Song and post-Song times, neo-Confucian metaphysics provided the concept of *li* (principle), which came to be used in Chinese art criticism as both a standard for realism and a general metaphor for creative process. Painting, in the neo-Confucian view, was tantamount to an act of cosmic creation and therefore governed by the natural principles inherent in all things. The task of the painter was to attune himself to the moral mind of the universe, and in so doing, to convey the *li* of his subject matter, giving it life and vitality. The gift of the ancient masters, in the view of Wang Hui (1632–1717), was precisely their ability to "harmonize their works with those of nature."[55]

The "life" of a Chinese painting was expressed by the term *qi. Qi* literally means breath, but like *li* it acquired a metaphysical meaning ("material force") in neo-Confucianism. The constituent matter of all things, *qi* animated even "inanimate" objects. As a critical term, however, it predated neo-Confucianism by several centuries. Although no one term conveys the wide range and richness of its meanings, perhaps the best single translation of *qi* is "spirit"—as in Xie He's famous "First Law" of painting: "Spirit resonance creates life movement" (*qiyun shengdong*). Employed in this fashion, *qi* suggests the breath of Heaven, which stirs all things to life and sustains the eternal process of cosmic change. This motive power, in the words of Zhang Geng (1685–1760), was something "beyond the feeling of the brush and the effect of the ink."[56]

As early as the fifth century A.D., Chinese art critics had already begun to compare landscape painting with the symbols of the *Yijing* as a way of representing nature, and by late imperial times morality and metaphysics had become inextricably linked. In the words of the Qing critic Wang Yu: "Everybody knows that principles [*li*] and vitality [*qi*] are necessary in painting, yet they are much neglected. The important point is that the heart and character of the man should be developed; then he can express high principles and a pure vital breath. ... Although painting is only one of the fine arts, it contains the *dao*."[57]

As an expression of the fundamental order of the universe, Chinese paintings clearly had to appear "natural," and works on connoisseurship suggested numerous guidelines for artistic realism. Thus the *Essential Criteria of Antiquities* advised:

> A portrait should look as though [the person depicted] were about to speak. The folds of his wearing apparel, the trees and the rocks, should be painted with strokes similar to those in calligraphy. The folds of dresses should be large, but their rhythm subtle, and the strength of their execution gives the impression that they are fluttering and raised [by the wind]. Trees, with their wrinkled bark and their twists and knots, should show their age. Rocks should be three-dimensional and shading lines used in their depiction should produce a rugged yet mellow effect. A landscape with mountains, water, and woods and springs should present an atmosphere of placidity and vastness and should clearly show the season, the time of day, and [prevailing] weather. Rising or subsiding mists and clouds should also be depicted. The source whence a river flows as well as its destination should be clearly defined, and the water

in it should appear fluent. Bridges and roads should show the way by which people come and go, as narrow paths wind through wildernesses. Houses should face in different directions in order to avoid monotony, fish swim hither and thither, and dragons ascend or descend. Flowers and fruit should bear dew drops on all surfaces and should also indicate in which direction the wind blows. Birds and animals, poised to drink water, to pick food, to move, or to remain still, are captured in spirit, as well as form.[58]

Painting manuals such as the popular Qing handbook *Jiezi yuan huazhuan* (Mustard Seed Garden Manual) provided elaborate instructions on exactly how to paint such subject material—trees, rocks, people, buildings, flowers, bamboo, grass, insects, animals, and, of course, landscapes. The starting point, as in calligraphy (and, in fact, all of Chinese life) was self-discipline. "You must learn first to observe the rules faithfully," wrote the author-compiler of the *Mustard Seed Garden Manual,* then "afterwards modify them according to your intelligence and capacity. The end of all method is to seem to have no method." And again, "If you aim to dispense with method, learn method. If you aim at facility, work hard. If you aim for simplicity, master complexity." One began with the correct mental attitude, learned basic brushstrokes (sixteen, at first), and then progressed to more sophisticated painting techniques (see Figures 8.2–8.5).[59]

An essential part of the artist's training was the study of the ancient masters. Zhang Geng advised students not to "throw out scattered thoughts in an incoherent fashion or to make strange things in accordance with the impulses of the heart." Rather, they should "carefully follow the rules of the ancients without losing the smallest detail." After some time, they would "understand why one must be in accordance with nature," and after some more time, "why things are as they are." Local collections of paintings by great masters were of tremendous importance to painters as a source of inspiration. We know, for example, that Wang Hui's mastery of so many different artistic styles was at least in part a product of his extended trips to art centers, which enabled him to study the masterpieces of well-known collectors. Unfortunately, as we have seen, the insatiable desire of the Qing rulers to enhance the holdings of the imperial collection in Beijing took many of these masterpieces out of the hands of private collectors, denying local artists an important source of education and inspiration.[60]

In addition to viewing great works of art, aspiring students were encouraged to copy them. There were three main avenues of approach: (1) exact reproduction by tracing (*mu*); (2) direct copying (*lin*); and (3) freely interpreting in the manner of the master (*fang*). The ultimate purpose of this artistic progression was not merely to produce outer form but to capture inner essence. In the words of Fang Xun (1736–1801):

When copying ancient paintings, the foremost concern must be to grasp the ancient master's spirit of life. Testing the flavor of the work and exploring it, you will get some understanding. Then you may begin to copy. ... If it is done merely for the sake of

Figure 8.2   Sketches from the Mustard Seed Garden Manual *(A).* Top left: *the pine tree, symbol of longevity, solitude, and the* yang *power of the dragon.* Top right: *Wu Zhen's style of painting trees, copied by Shen Hao.* Bottom: *techniques of dotting leaves. Source: Sheng Chu et al., eds. (1982); see also Mai-mai Sze (1959).*

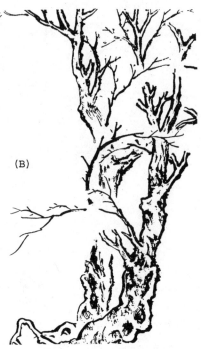

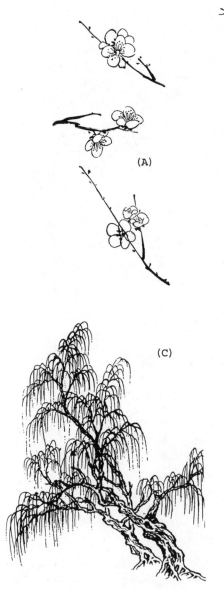

(A)

(B)

(C)

Figure 8.3 *Sketches from the* Mustard Seed Garden Manual *(B).* A. *The manual states: "The symbolism of the plum tree is determined by its* qi. *The blossoms are of the* yang *principle, that of Heaven. The wood of its trunk and branches is of the* yin *principle, that of earth. Its basic number is five, and its various parts and aspects are based on odd and even numbers. The peduncle, from which the flower issues, is a symbol of* taiji.*"* B. *The plum tree is described as having two trunks, a* yin *(lesser) trunk and a* yang *(dominant) trunk.* C. *The willow, symbol of parting. Source: Sheng Chu et al., eds. (1982); see also Mai-mai Sze (1959).*

(A)

(B)

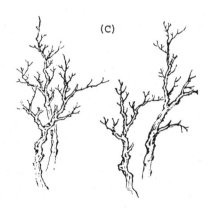

(C)

Figure 8.4   Sketches from the Mustard Seed Garden Manual *(C).* A. *Bamboo, symbol of the Confucian scholar.* B. *Figures done in the* xieyi *("writing of ideas") style.* C. *In discussing the ways of painting two trees, the manual employs a ritual vocabulary, emphasizing the relationship between old and young, dignified and modest, superior and inferior. Source: Sheng Chu et al., eds. (1982); see also Mai-mai Sze (1959).*

Figure 8.5   Sketches from the Mustard Seed Garden Manual *(D). The first three sketches show different styles of mountains.* A. *High view* (gaoyuan*).* B. *Deep view* (shenyuan*).* C. *Level view* (pingyuan*).* D. *Rocks, indicating* yin *(dark) and* yang *(light) elements. Much of the manual's discussion of painting rocks revolves around the symbolism of the family and the* Yijing. *Source: Sheng Chu et al., eds. (1982); Mai-mai Sze (1959).*

similarity [however], you had better roll up the picture and forget it at once. You may copy the whole day, yet your work will have nothing whatsoever to do with the ancient master.[61]

The eighteenth-century Qing critic Shen Zongqian wrote in a similar vein:

A student of painting must copy ancient works, just as a man learning to write must study good writing that has come down through the ages. He should put himself in a state of mind to feel as if he were doing the same painting himself. … First he should copy one artist, then branch out to copy others, and, what is more important, he should feel as if he were breathing through the work himself and should identify himself with what the artist was trying to say.[62]

Fang and Shen are discussing here the effort on the part of the painter to achieve "spiritual communication" (*shenhui*) with the ancient masters. *Shenhui,* as Tu Wei-ming has indicated, necessarily involved self-realization. Shen Zongqian put the matter this way: "The important thing in copying the ancients is that I have my own temperament. If I should forget myself to copy the ancients, I would be doing a disservice to both the ancients and myself. … The painter's concern is how to make the art of the brush his own. If this is done, then what I express is only myself, a self which is akin to the ancients." Fang Xun counseled, "When copying the ancients, you may first only worry about a lack of similarity; afterward you ought to worry about too much similarity. For, when lacking similarity, you have failed to get to the bottom of the model's style; being too similar, you have failed to achieve your own style."[63]

Discipline was a prerequisite to artistic freedom. The early nineteenth-century painter-critic Fan Ji asserted: "The beginner should imitate the ancients constantly, … [but] he must then empty himself from what he has relied on. Meanwhile, that which has fermented in him must flow out unintentionally—and for the first time he will experience the joyous sensation of freedom." On this basis, it was possible for a Qing painter like Wang Shimin (1592–1680) to produce an "original" landscape following the Ming master Dong Qichang in imitating Wang Meng's (Yuan dynasty) interpretation of the Dong Yuan (Five Dynasties–Song) manner. Imitation (*fang*) in the hands of an individual who had achieved "spiritual communication" with the great masters became "creative metamorphosis" (*bian*), not simple plagiarism. Fan Ji informs us, "If a *lin* copy shows the copyist's own manner, then it has lost the truth; if a *fang* copy fails to show one's own manner, it becomes a fake."[64]

Apart from preliminary sketches, Chinese painters seldom painted from life. They preferred instead to seek inspiration in other works or to conjure up and convey a mental image that bore no necessary relationship to a single objective reality. Meditation played a role in the creative process, as did external stimuli. Wang Yu advised preliminary concentration as well as nourishment by looking at clouds and springs, contemplating birds and flowers, strolling about humming songs, burning incense, or sipping tea. ... When the inspiration rises, spread the paper and move the brush, but stop as soon as it is exhausted; only when it rises again should you continue and complete the work. If you do it this way, the work will become alive with the moving power of Heaven.[65]

The Chinese painter was a captive of his media, but it was a creative form of bondage. Unlike Western-style oil painting, Chinese ink or watercolor on paper or silk allowed little room for trial and error; once the artist put the brush down, he or she made an irretrievable commitment—especially when using ink on paper. Thus,

when the brush touches paper, there are only differences in touch, speed, angle and direction. Too light a touch results in weakness while too heavy a touch causes clumsiness. Too much speed results in a slippery effect, too little speed drags; too much slant [of the tip of the brush] results in thinness; too perpendicular an approach in flatness; a curve may result in ragged edges and a straight line may look like one made with a ruler.[66]

Brushwork was extraordinarily important in Chinese painting, especially in late imperial times. Wen Fong writes, for example, that throughout the Ming and Qing periods, the brushwork of Chinese painting "assumed an increasingly expressive quality, eventually dominating the representational form."[67] This expressive quality, known as *xieyi* or the "writing of ideas," was a technique closely linked with calligraphy and quite distinct from the precise form of brushwork designated *gongbi* (see below). *Xieyi* required the appearance of spontaneity, but it was deliberate, preconceived, and, in fact, the product of intensive book study and calligraphic discipline. Wang Yuanqi (1642–1715) gave advice to painters that, in its essence, would apply to calligraphers as well: "When ... [one] takes up the brush he must be absolutely quiet, serene, peaceful, and collected, and shut out all vulgar emotions. He must sit down in silence before the white silk scroll, concentrate his soul and control his vital energy. He must look at the high and low, examine right and left, inside and outside the scroll, the road to enter and the road to leave."[68]

In other words, the Chinese artist had to have a fairly complete vision of the painting before beginning. Modifications could be made, of course, as the painting developed, but a unified vision was essential. Shen Zongqian wrote:

It would be a great fault to begin a picture without a preconceived plan, and then add and adjust as one goes along, with the result that the different parts do not have an organic unity. One should rather have a general idea of where the masses and connections, the light and the dark areas will be, then proceed so that one part grows out of another and the light and dark areas cooperate to build a picture. Examined closely, each section is interesting in itself; taken together, there is an organic unity.[69]

This idea of organic unity was expressed in the general term *kaihe* ("opening and closing," or "expanding and contracting"). *Kaihe* may refer to the overall layout of a painting, to the relationship of individual elements within the painting, or to the composition of the elements themselves. In each part of the painting, including every individual object, the artist had to consider beginning, ending, and beginning again. Shen Zongqian explains:

> The combined work of brush and ink depends on force of movement [*shi,* a long-standing technical term in calligraphy, sometimes translated "kinesthetic movement"]. This force refers to the movement of the brush back and forth on the paper, which carries with it and in it the opening [*kai*] and closing [*he*] movements. Where something is starting up, that is the opening movement, but with every opening movement the artist must be thinking how it will be gathered up at the end. ... The gathering up is called the closing movement, and with each closing movement the artist is already thinking where the next growth is going to arise. Thus there is always the suggestion of further development.[70]

Yinyang ideas such as *kaihe, xushi* ("void and solid"), *xiangbei* ("front and back"), and *qifu* ("rising and falling") are essential to an understanding of traditional Chinese painting. Qing handbooks and critical works repeatedly drew upon these and other concepts of complementarity and alternation to explain composition and brushstroke. Artists were encouraged to dip downward before coming up, to turn upwards before going down, to intersperse sparse with dense and dark with light, to relieve thick ink with thin, to counteract the convex with the concave, and so forth. For example, in describing the method by which to paint tree trunks and branches, the *Mustard Seed Garden Manual* advises: "Pay attention to the way the branches dispose themselves, the *yin* and *yang* of them, which are in front and which are in back, which are on the left and which are on the right; consider also the tensions created by some branches pushing forward while others seem to withdraw." In landscape painting "host" mountains required "guest" mountains, exalted trees required humble ones, and luxuriant foliage required at least some dead branches. In its most extreme form, the notion of *yinyang* complementarity was expressed in a kind of Daoist paradox: "When in your eyes you have mountains, only then can you make trees; when in your mind there is water, only then can you make mountains."[71] The term for landscape itself (*shanshui,* lit., mountains and water) suggests a basic *yinyang* relationship.

The point of *yinyang* juxtaposition in Chinese painting was not merely to create contrast, however. Primarily it was to indicate "life movement," nature's rhythm (*yun*). In their brushwork, Chinese artists attempted to recreate the endlessly alternating rise and fall, expansion and contraction, activity and quiescence of *yin* and *yang* and in so doing to come into closer harmony with the rhythmic cycles of life itself. In landscape painting, especially, Heaven dominated Earth, voids dominated solids, mountains dominated water, and movement dominated stillness, but all were integrated into a single philosophical statement reflecting the dynamism, grandeur, and limitlessness of nature.[72]

Small wonder, then, that Chinese landscape painters refused to restrict themselves (or the viewers of their works) by the use of Western-style scientific perspective. It was not that they lacked the intellectual sophistication to employ it; rather, true perspective involved a fixed point of view that was completely inimical to the purposes of the painter. An essential element of the dynamism of a Chinese landscape was the movement of both artist and viewer. Thus, "The painter ... paints and the spectator views the results from many points, never from a single position or at any one moment of time."[73] In a similar way, and for similar reasons, Chinese poets added new dimensions to the world directly perceived in their poems, and in so doing evoked a mood of infiniteness. Wang Shizhen (1634–1711) in particular was a master of the poetic "ending which doesn't end." Significantly, this "endless" quality can also be found in the best Chinese narrative literature (see Chapter 9).[74]

In the critical writing of the Qing period, scholars drew a sharp distinction between the so-called Northern School of professional and court painting (*gongbi*) and the Southern School of nonprofessional literati painting (*xieyi*). The former has been characterized as academic, representational, precise, and decorative, painted mainly in polychrome ink and on silk. The latter has been described as spontaneous, free, calligraphic, personal, and subjective, painted mainly in monochrome on paper. These distinctions—which had nothing to do with geography—were drawn by Dong Qichang in the late Ming period, and they continued to dominate Chinese art criticism for the next three hundred years.

Although based on genuine stylistic differences, Dong's system of classification was arbitrary and inconsistent, not only because it was based on certain "moral" criteria, Dong's personal preferences, and the assumed superiority of literati painting over that of professionals but also because in a very real sense all the painting of the Ming and Qing periods was academic. Furthermore, during the Qing period there were many court painters who painted beautifully in the Southern School style and many "amateur" literati who were well paid for their artistic efforts—some by the throne itself.[75]

Among the most accomplished painters of the early Qing were the Six Great Masters: the Four Wangs (Wang Shimin, Wang Hui, Wang Jian [1598–1677], and Wang Yuanqi), Wu Li (1632–1718), and Yun Shouping (1633–1690). The works of each were "academic in the best sense: skillful, decorous, and knowledgeable about both the subject and the complex history of the *wenren* tradition." Although two of the painters—Wang Hui and Wang Yuanqi—were patronized by the Kangxi emperor, the others remained loyal to the memory of the Ming dynasty and refused to serve the throne. In any case, identification with the "orthodoxy" of the Qing imperial court did not stifle creativity. Indeed, Wang Yuanqi was probably the most original of the Six Masters. His brilliant interpretations of past models and styles, and his "passion for pure form," put Wang on a plane with the best "Individualist" painters of the Qing period.[76]

The most famous and creative of the early Individualist painters were Zhu Da (also known as Bada Shanren, 1626–c. 1705), Kuncan (also known as Shiqi, c. 1610–c. 1670), Yuanji (also known as Taoji or Shitao, 1641–c. 1710), and Gong Xian.[77] Sherman Lee summarizes the distinctiveness of their work:

> Kuncan's hairy and tangled landscapes; Zhu Da's abbreviated but firm brushwork recalling that of another, earlier eccentric, Xu Wei; Yuanji's brilliant usage of wash, unusual compositions, and directly observed images, recalling the approach of Zhang Hong; and Gong Xian's deep and somber ink-play of light and shade; all justify their unusually high place in Chinese art history. The most various of the four was certainly Yuanji and that variety endears him particularly to modern critics and collectors.[78]

These "free spirits"—like the Six Great Masters and virtually all other Qing painters—acknowledged a debt to tradition. In his *Huayu lu* (Record of Talks on Painting), for example, Yuanji admits that for many years he had declared his independence of orthodox methods of painting and writing, only to discover that the way he thought was his own was actually "the *dao* of the ancients."[79]

Although Qing painting lost a certain amount of creative energy in the eighteenth century, the so-called Eight Eccentrics of Yangzhou managed to keep the Chinese art world tantalizingly off balance. Different critics have compiled variant lists of the eight, with the result that more than a dozen painters can be considered viable candidates. Among their number we may count such talented individuals as Jin Nong (1687–1764), Hua Yan (1682–c. 1755), Huang Shen (1687–c. 1768), and Luo Ping. Other possible candidates include Zheng Xie (1693–1765) and Li Shan (1686–c. 1756). These "eccentric" artists and their colleagues tended to specialize both in style and subject matter; they gravitated away from standard landscapes and inclined instead toward rocks and bamboo, flowers and birds, insects and fish, or human figures (including ghostly forms).[80]

During the nineteenth century Shanghai emerged as a major center of artistic production. There, rich patrons and wealthy consumers (including the Japanese as well as merchants from Fujian and Guangdong) encouraged an influx of artists from all over China. In addition, after 1842 foreign administrative and military control over the treaty port offered the artists relative security in which to work. Among the most distinguished painters identified with the area are Qian Du (1763–1844), Dai Xi (1801–1860), Gai Qi (1774–1829), Ren Xiong (1820–1857), Zhao Zhiqian (1829–1884), Ren Bonian (1839–1895), Ren Xun (1835–1893), and Wu Changshi (1842–1927). Most of these individuals were born in Zhejiang; the fact that they worked in Shanghai attests to the importance that city took on as an artistic center of gravity. At Guangzhou, local artists such as Xie Lansheng (1760–1831), Su Liupeng (1796–1862), and Su Renshan (1814–1850) continued the region's rich tradition of painting epitomized by the earlier work of Li Jian (1747–1798) and Liang Shu (c. 1760–1810).[81]

Chinese women artists made great strides during the Qing period. Most of them were the literate wives or concubines of Chinese scholars, and a number established their reputations in poetry as well as in painting (see Chapter 9). Some sold their art-work, and others provided instruction for friends and family or even for empresses, princesses, and concubines at court. Among the many distinguished women painters of the Qing period were Fang Weiyi (1585–1668), Liu Yin (1618–1664), Jin Yue (fl. 1665), Cai Han (1647–1686), Chen Shu (1660–1736), Yun Bing (eighteenth century), Yuexiang (eighteenth century), Fang Wanyi (eighteenth century), Qu Bingyun (1767–1810), Ma Quan (c. 1768–1848), Guan Yun (nineteenth century), and Wang Qinyun (nineteenth century).[82]

These talented painters were sustainers of inherited male traditions rather than in-novators. They have rarely been characterized by art critics as "individualistic" or "ec-centric." Although the extremely gifted artist Chen Shu was once described as sur-passing the master Ming-era flower painter Chen Shun (1483–1544) in the "vigor and originality" of her brushstrokes, she painted landscapes and other standard subjects in conventional ways, following the lead of "orthodox" painters such as Wang Shimin and Wang Hui.[83] As Marsha Weidner observes, the inventive potential of women painters "was limited by conventions designed to support the rigorously pa-triarchal social system of premodern China."[84]

Flowers were the favorite subject matter for women painters in the Qing, al-though landscapes, bamboo, and figure paintings (including, of course, paintings of the Buddhist deity Guanyin) were also popular. Conventionally, male connoisseurs disparagingly referred to women's paintings as "weak and soft." Backhanded compli-ments took forms such as the following: "[Her] brush strength is not the best, but for a woman it is remarkable."[85] Statements of this kind, which Weidner believes de-terred Western scholars from taking Chinese women painters seriously until recently, seem to reflect deeply held stereotypes more than artistic reality. We know, for in-stance, that women sometimes executed "ghost paintings" for talented male artists and that a number of highly regarded male painters, including Zhang Geng, received valuable instruction from women.[86]

Prejudices of another sort plagued the Jesuit painters who served the Qing court. Among these individuals, Guiseppe Castiglione (Lang Shining, 1688–1766), a per-sonal favorite of the Qianlong emperor, proved to be especially adept at combining the techniques of Western realism with traditional Chinese media and subject matter. Castiglione had numerous Chinese pupils, imitators, and admirers, but he and his Western colleagues exerted no lasting influence on Chinese art. The reason was that their use of shading and perspective was seen as mere craftsmanship. In the words of one admirer (Zou Yigui, 1686–1772, a talented court painter in his own right): "The student should learn something of their achievements so as to improve his own method. But their technique of strokes [i.e., brushwork] is negligible. Even if they at-tain [representational] perfection it is merely craftsmanship. Thus, foreign painting cannot be called art."[87]

Far less were foreigners able to master the intricacies of Chinese calligraphy. As a recognized art form, calligraphy predated painting, but by late imperial times the two were inseparably linked. In the words of a common proverb: "Calligraphy and painting have the same source" (*shu hua tong yuan*). Lu Shihua states simply: "Calligraphy and painting are skills [*jineng*], but they embody the great *dao*. ... The ancients achieved immortality [*buxiu*] through their calligraphy and painting." Calligraphy and painting used the same basic media, utilized many of the same brushstrokes and techniques, required the same kind of mental preparation and discipline, and were measured by the same aesthetic standards. Furthermore, both were seen as an index of the artist's morality. Lu Shihua tells us, "If the heart is right, then the brush will be right" (*xin zheng ze bi zheng*).[88]

During the Ming and Qing periods, calligraphy often adorned paintings, amplifying in various ways the artist's general philosophical statement and sometimes piquing the viewer's curiosity.[89] Poetic inscriptions might be written by the artist to indicate sources of inspiration and feelings or by subsequent owners and admirers of the work who were moved to comment upon it. Some paintings boasted a number of different colophons. Perhaps the record for inscriptions of this sort by one individual is held by the Qianlong emperor, whose enthusiasm occasionally outstripped his aesthetic judgment. He is reported to have written more than fifty inscriptions on one handscroll alone and to have placed thirteen of his seals on a single painting. In the main, however, multiple inscriptions and seals of ownership were added tastefully, and they, in turn, enriched both the emotional and artistic value of the work.[90]

Of course calligraphy stood solidly on its own as an independent art form and was universally admired as the ultimate measure of cultural refinement. In the words of the *Essential Criteria of Antiquities*: "No other art is comparable to that of calligraphy. Saints and sages of past centuries paid a great deal of attention to it, for it always has been and will forever be the means whereby civilization and the orders of government are made intelligible, while things, great or trivial, from the Six Classics to matters of daily routine, are conveyed to people." Calligraphy was ubiquitous in traditional China. It graced private homes, shops, teahouses, restaurants, temples, monasteries, official buildings, and imperial palaces. It was engraved on metal, wood, and stone and even on the face of rocks and mountains in nature. Calligraphers were in demand by all levels of Chinese society, and success in the civil-service examinations could not be achieved without a good hand—regardless of one's mastery of the classics and the "eight-legged essay."[91]

Chinese critics distinguished six basic styles of calligraphy: (1) big seal script (*dazhuan*), (2) small seal script (*xiaozhuan*), (3) clerical script (*lishu*), (4) regular or standard script (*kaishu* or *zhengshu*), (5) running script (*xingshu*), and (6) grass-style script (*caoshu*). Of these, the last two were the most susceptible to individualized interpretation. The regular script may be likened to *gongbi* in painting and the grass-style script to *xieyi,* in the sense that the former two styles demanded precision while the latter two encouraged spontaneity and freedom; all forms of Chinese calligraphy, however, left a great deal of room for creative potential (see Figure 8.6).[92]

In fact, the eighteenth century witnessed a revival of the *zhuan* and *li* styles, modifying a calligraphic tradition that had been in place for over a thousand years. As early as the fourth century A.D., the renowned calligrapher Wang Xizhi (307–365) had de-

Figure 8.6   Types of Calligraphy. These columns represent six different types of written characters. Each line reads: "There are six forms of calligraphy, called (a) zhuan, (b) li, (c) kai, (d) xing, (e) cao, and (f) song." This liushu *system differs from the system discussed in the text only in that it fails to distinguish between "big" and "small" seal script (zhuan) and adds the category* song, *which refers to the Song dynasty style of print characters. Source:* Chinese Repository 3 (May 1834–April 1835).

veloped a masterly synthesis of styles that became the basis for virtually all Chinese brushwriting until the mid-Qing period. The standard works in this tradition employed the regular, running, or "grass" styles instead of the more ancient and seemingly over-precise seal and clerical styles. But the *kaozheng* movement of the eighteenth century (see Chapter 6), which dovetailed with the Qing dynasty's ongoing effort to "restore antiquity" (*fugu*), led to a reemphasis on ancient Han and pre-Han inscriptions based on actual bronze and stone relics.

This development took two major directions. One was toward what Benjamin Elman calls a "craze" for seal designing and carving. The other was toward the reproduction of ancient calligraphic forms with modern brushes. Individualist and "eccentric" painters such as Yuanji and Jin Nong got into the act, inscribing paintings with seal script and experimenting with the simulation on paper of characters engraved on bronze and stone.[93]

Of the several outstanding calligraphers of the mid-Qing period, three deserve special mention. One was Deng Shiru (c. 1740–1805), a colorful and unconventional scholar who gravitated toward the kind of calligraphy inscribed on Qin, Han, and Three Kingdoms relics. Another was Bao Shichen (1775–1855), who not only excelled in the *kai* and *xing* styles but also experimented boldly with the *zhuan* and *li* styles, rejecting "the mechanical precision of earlier seal script styles in favor of an imposing degree of irregularity in his seal and clerical calligraphy." The third individual, Zhang Qi (1765–1833), is significant not only because he was considered the equal of Deng in the *li* style and of Bao in the *kai* and *xing* styles but also because he raised four daughters who achieved literary fame, including one of the best-known woman calligraphers (Zhang Lunying) of the dynasty.[94] Once again, it is apparent that the Qing was not simply a period of "cultural stagnation."

Many Chinese scholars have remarked on the link between calligraphy and other forms of Chinese art. Chiang Yee suggests, for example, that the style and spirit of Chinese calligraphy influenced not only painting but also sculpture, ceramics, and architecture. Similarly, Lin Yutang argues that the "basic ideas of rhythm, form and atmosphere [in calligraphy] give the different lines of Chinese art, like poetry, painting, architecture, porcelain and house decorations, an essential unity of spirit."[95] Lin's comparison of poetry and calligraphy is apt enough, but it may be extended to other types of literature, for even vernacular fiction exhibits at least some of the rhythm and "kinesthetic movement" characteristic of Chinese brushwork.

𝔐 9 𝔐

Literature

𝒯he Chinese literary tradition shared with the artistic tradition many fundamental assumptions about past models, aesthetics, ethics, and cosmology. Chinese literature was, however, much more explicitly didactic than most of Chinese art and more systematically promoted by both the Qing state and local elites as an instrument of cultural transformation. Although a great stylistic gap separated popular vernacular literature from more orthodox classical-style writings, there were certain affinities. In the first place, both kinds of literature were created by members of the scholarly elite, and both reflected elite values. Second, popular equivalents existed for nearly every kind of elite literature. Third, in truth, the elite enjoyed certain types of popular literature (such as novels) almost as much as the masses did. Thus, from the standpoint of both content and appeal, vernacular literature provides us with an especially valuable perspective on late imperial Chinese culture.

In literature, as in art, the Qing was a period of considerable vitality, especially in the realm of vernacular fiction. Material prosperity, the expansion of mass printing, and the growth of popular literacy under the Manchus produced an unprecedented demand for, and supply of, books.[1] At the same time, a consuming interest in all aspects of traditional Chinese culture led Qing scholars to produce great numbers of antiquarian studies, critical essays, histories, biographies, and gazetteers. More ambitious projects, such as encyclopedias, collections of essays, and literary anthologies, were also undertaken, both by the throne and by energetic private individuals. In theory, these works were designed to provide inspired guidance for the present and the future based on a glorious past; in practice, however, they often betrayed narrow scholarly prejudices and their compilation sometimes led to destructive factional rivalries.[2]

Intellectual trends obviously influenced literary fashions. The scholastic controversy between advocates of Han Learning and Song Learning, for example, had implications for prose style, since the former favored the revival of Han dynasty Parallel Prose (*pianwen*) and the latter, especially the Tongcheng School, esteemed the so-called Ancient Prose (*guwen*). New Text scholars, for their part, gravitated to Song-style Ancient Prose, but they also took a special interest in "lyric verse" (*ci*), which the influential Ming loyalist Chen Zilong (1608–1647)—himself an accomplished practitioner of the Parallel Prose style—invested with such power and passion. "Genres," as Benjamin Elman has aptly remarked, "were as much a part of academic debate as Confucian doctrine."[3]

Imperial politics also played a role in Chinese literary life. The Qing emperors, as guardians of official morality, naturally tried to promote certain kinds of literature and to suppress others. Pamela Crossley maintains that no ruler of China surpassed the Qianlong emperor in his ambition to dominate the literary resources of Chinese culture. This ambition took three forms: glorifying tradition, eradicating subversive works, and promoting the Manchu heritage. During the course of his reign the Qianlong emperor commissioned more than ninety scholarly works, fifteen of which dealt with the Manchu language, Manchu history, or the history of the last years of the Ming.[4]

The fluidity of social status in eighteenth-century China, the increasing lack of fit between the theoretical and practical criteria for Chinese political leadership, and the Qing elite's passive acceptance of imperial censorship all seem to have encouraged the growth of scholarly cynicism. These circumstances may also have played a role in provoking "a pessimism about the ability to achieve sagehood that hounded intellectuals of this age." Wu Peiyi describes this mood as "a deep awareness of the human proclivity to evil, an urgent need to counter this proclivity, a readiness for self-disclosure, and a deep anguish over one's wrongdoings."[5] The major literary manifestation of this apparent cynicism and pessimism was a great deal of confessional and satirical writing in the eighteenth and nineteenth centuries.

CATEGORIES OF CLASSICAL LITERATURE

Of the many great literary compilations of the Qing period, two gigantic government-sponsored projects stand out as worthy of special attention: the *Tushu jicheng* (*TSJC*) and the *Siku quanshu* (Complete Collection of the Four Treasuries; *SKQS*). We have encountered the former often in previous chapters. Commissioned during the Kangxi emperor's reign and published in final form in the early years of the Yongzheng period, the *TSJC* has been described as "the largest and most useful encyclopedia that has ever been compiled in China."[6] Orthodox in outlook, often biographical in treatment, and composed almost entirely of selected excerpts from earlier writings of various kinds, it may be considered a literary anthology as well as a convenient guide to the cultural concerns of the Qing scholarly elite.

The encyclopedia is divided into 6 main categories, 32 subcategories, and 6,109 sections. The writings comprising these sections are arranged in order according to eight major types of literature: (1) factual quotations from standard sources, arranged chronologically, if datable, or in the traditional order of the classics, histories, philosophers, and belles lettres; (2) general discussions of an orthodox nature from these four classes of literature; (3) biographies; (4) literary compositions, chosen more for style than content; (5) selected sentences, also culled out for their literary merit; (6) factual accounts, often anecdotal and of relatively less importance than the works included in the previous categories; (7) miscellaneous quotations; and (8) unorthodox material, including fiction and quotations from Buddhist and Daoist sources. Not every type of literature is included in every section, but in most cases one can find examples of types 1 or 2, 4, 6, and 7.[7]

In all, the *TSJC* consists of more than 10,000 *juan* and about 100 million characters. Of the encyclopedia's six major categories, human relations is the largest (2,604 *juan*), followed by geography (2,144), political economy (1,832), arts and sciences (1,656), literature (1,220), and heavenly phenomena (544). Of the subcategories, by far the largest is political divisions (1,544 *juan*), followed by arts and occupations (824), government service (800), clan and family names (640), classical and noncanonical writings (500), women (376), foods and commercial goods (360), ritual (348), religion (320), plants (320), mountains and rivers (320), the emperor (300), Confucian conduct (300), and military administration (300). The remaining subcategories include literature (260 *juan*), manufactures (252), animal life (192), strange phenomena (188), law and punishment (180), the study of characters (160), the earth (140), foreign states (140), the imperial household (140), astronomy and mathematics (140), the examination system (136), music (136), officialdom (120), social intercourse (120), family relationships (126), the year (116), human affairs (112), and the heavens (100).

The overlapping of these subcategories blurs the focus somewhat, but we can still see in the *TSJC* the Qing elite's preoccupation with orderly administration, scholarship, Confucian values, and family relations as well as its abiding interest in both natural and supernatural phenomena. Moreover, we can discern in the overall organization of the encyclopedia the implicit assumption that Heaven, Earth, and Man are the interrelated elements of all knowledge.

The *SKQS* ranges almost as broadly in subject matter as the *TSJC* but has a more self-conscious literary emphasis and has been more extensively studied by both Chinese and Western scholars. Intended as an imperial collection representing the best of China's magnificent literary heritage, the *SKQS* illustrates the ambivalence of the Qing rulers toward that inheritance. On the one hand, it was clearly designed by the Qianlong emperor as a monument to Manchu patronage of traditional Chinese culture. On the other, it became a device for ferreting out works that were deemed critical of the Manchus in particular or of "barbarians" in general. In the course of the so-called Literary Inquisition that took place from the early 1770s to the early 1880s, more than two thousand works were destroyed and many others suppressed or tampered with. A number of individual Chinese scholars were also punished for their allegedly "seditious" views.[8]

On the more positive side, the *SKQS* project, which began in 1772 and lasted for more than twenty years, resulted in the accumulation and transcription (in seven sets) of over 3,500 literary works in 36,500 *juan* (nearly 2.3 million pages per set). The commission in charge of the project also compiled a massive catalogue known as the *Siku quanshu zongmu tiyao* (Annotated Index of the Complete Collection of the Four Treasuries), which critically reviewed the 3,593 works mentioned above plus an additional 7,087 works of lesser quality. This catalogue, the most thorough of its kind in all of Chinese history, provides information on the size and general contents of each work as well as an overall critical evaluation. Although these evaluations were profoundly affected by *kaozheng* scholarship, they were also influenced by "Manchu sensitivities and imperial pride."[9]

Of the over 10,000 works reviewed, more than 2,000 are included in the first ten-part section on the classics (*jing*). This section begins with subsections devoted to each of the Five Classics, and these are followed by individual subsections on the *Classic of Filial Piety,* "general works," the Four Books, music, and language. By far the largest of the ten subsections is devoted to the *Yijing* (nearly 500 works).[10] The second section, on history (*shi*), comprising about 2,000 works in the catalogue, is divided into fifteen subsections. Of these, physical and political geography is the largest (nearly 600 works), followed by biographies and "personal accounts" (more than 200). Other subsections include those on the twenty-four dynastic histories, other kinds of historical records and historical criticism (including a subsection on unofficial histories and one on bronze and stone inscriptions), administrative works, official documents, and memoirs of travels in China and elsewhere.

The section on philosophers (*zi*), covering about 3,000 works in fourteen subsections, ranges widely. Although, as one might suppose, it places heavy emphasis on orthodox neo-Confucian philosophical tracts (with more than 400 works), the largest subsection is entitled simply "miscellaneous writings" (more than 850 works). It includes the works of non-Confucian philosophers such as Mozi as well as a great variety of assorted tracts, pamphlets, and collections of anecdotes. Significantly, the editors of the *SKQS* gave Mozi, who had long been discredited by orthodox Confucian philosophers, high marks for his emphasis on "temperance and the timely utilization of resources." Indeed, they went so far as to blame his lack of influence for more than two thousand years on the well-known, but in their view somewhat misguided, attack that Mencius once leveled against him.[11]

The catalogue's section on philosophers also devotes specific subsections to such diverse topics as military arts, agricultural writings, medicine, astronomy and mathematics, divination, the arts (including calligraphy, painting, seals, music, and games), repertories (including works on hobbies, connoisseurship, culinary art, and natural science), dictionaries and encyclopedias, narrative writings (including some novels), Buddhist works, and Daoist works. Of these subsections, the last is distinguished not only by the lack of mention of popular beliefs but also by its small size and certain inconsistencies in the selection of texts.[12] The final section, belles lettres (*ji*), consisting of about 3,500 works, is divided into five subsections: the elegies of Chu, collected works of individuals, general anthologies, critical treatises on literature, and songs and rhymes.[13]

An outstanding feature of many Chinese scholars in late imperial times was their astonishing productivity and literary versatility. Charles Hucker provides the example of Qian Qianyi (1582–1664), a Jiangsu dilettante "not untypical of the Ming-Ch'ing [Qing] transition era" who had a preliminary version of his collected works published in 1643 in 110 *juan*. This collection included poetry (21 *juan*), prefaces and postfaces (17), biographical and genealogical sketches (10), obituaries and epitaphs (20), funeral odes and eulogies (2), essays (6), historical annotations (5), critiques of poetry (5), memorials (2), other official documents (13), and letters and miscellany (9). To this Qian eventually added a supplement in 50 *juan*. In addition, he produced an anthology of Ming poetry in 81 *juan,* a draft history of the Ming dynasty in 100 *juan,* and annotated editions of several Buddhist texts. The Qing monarchs also aspired to such productivity and versatility—most notably the prolific, but rather pedestrian, Qianlong emperor.[14]

All such writings, and the vast majority of the works included in the *TSJC, SKQS,* and the annotated catalogue, were written in classical Chinese—the language of the scholarly elite. Popular dramas and vernacular novels, although enjoyed by the literati, were not generally included in scholarly collections for the simple reason that the classical language was considered elegant and refined (*ya*), while the written vernacular was deemed vulgar and common (*su*).[15]

Like the most exalted forms of Chinese art, classical Chinese literature was distinguished by its emphasis on rhythm and balance; its close relationship with past masters, models, and styles; the assumed link between creative genius and personal morality; and by much of the same or similar critical terminology. In both art and literature we find a concern with life (*sheng*), vitality (*qi*), spirit (*shen*), and movement (*dong*).[16] Even the rules of composition in classical literature suggest equivalents or analogues in Chinese art. Liu Dakui (1698–1780) tells us:

> Literature must, above all, attempt to be strong in vital force, but if there is no spirit to control the vital force, it will run wild, not knowing where to settle down. The spirit and the vital force are the finest essences of literature; intonation and rhythm [*yinjie*] are the somewhat coarser elements of literature; [and] diction and syntax [*zizhu*] are the coarsest elements of literature.[17]

During the Qing period there were several different conceptions of literature, all deriving from earlier theories or critical approaches. One was the notion of literature as a manifestation of the principle of the universe (the *dao*). The most influential early exponent of this point of view was Liu Xie. In Liu's view, "The *dao* is handed down in writing through the sages, and the sages make the *dao* manifest in their literary writings."[18] Yao Nai (1731–1815), a leading figure in the Tongcheng School of the Qing period, put the matter this way:

> I have heard that the *dao* of Heaven and Earth consists of nothing but the *yin* and *yang,* the gentle and strong. Literature is the finest essence of Heaven and Earth, and the manifestation of the *yin* and the *yang.* … From the philosophers of the various schools [down to the present] there has been none whose writing is not biased [in favor of either *yin* or *yang*]. If one has obtained the beauty of the *yang* and strong, then one's writing will be like thunder, like lightning, like a long wind emerging from the valley, like lofty mountains and steep cliffs, like a great river flooding, like galloping steeds. … If one has obtained the beauty of the *yin* and gentle, then one's writing will be like the sun just beginning to rise, like cool breeze, like clouds, like vapor, like mist, like secluded woods and meandering streams, like ripples, like water

gently rocking, like the sheen of pearls or jade, like the cry of a wild goose disappearing into the silent void.[19]

Yao believed that philosophical substance required literary style. Thus, in criticizing the inelegance of Mozi as an index of his philosophical errors, Yao wrote: "If the writing is insufficient, then the truth will not be clear."[20]

Some Qing scholars saw literature as a reflection of political realities. The early Qing critic Wang Wan (1624–1690), for example, discerned a close correspondence between the rise and fall of the Tang dynasty and the history of its poetry. He wrote,

> At the height [of the Tang], the ruler above exerted his energies, [and] the ministers and officials below hastened about their tasks and spoke without reserve; the administration was simple and punishments were few; the atmosphere among the people was harmonious and peaceful. Therefore, what issued forth in poetry was generally leisurely and refined. ... [By the time the dynasty declined] there was factional strife [at court] and in the country military struggle; the administration was complex and punishments were severe; the atmosphere among the people was sorrowful and bitter. Therefore, what issued forth [in poetry] was mostly sad, nostalgic, and urgent. At the very end, [poetry] became superficial and extravagant.[21]

But if there were those who viewed literature as an index of political and social circumstances, there were also those who saw in it a means of rectifying those conditions. Shen Deqian begins his *Shuoshi zuiyu* (Miscellaneous Remarks on Poetry) by observing, "The way of poetry is such that it can be used to regulate one's nature and emotions, to improve human relationships, ... to move the spirits and gods, to spread [moral] teaching in the states, and to deal with feudal lords," and in his preface to an anthology of Qing verse he maintains that poetry must "concern itself with human relationships, everyday uses, and the causes of the rise and fall [of the state] in ancient and modern times." Gu Yanwu, for his part, states succinctly, "Literature must be beneficial to the world."[22]

Aesthetic theories of literature focused primarily on the patterns of the classical language and their immediate impact on the reader. In critical writings of this sort, analogies were often drawn with other sensual experiences, including viewing art, hearing music, and eating food. But not all aesthetic theories relied on such analogies. The long-standing debate between advocates of Ancient Prose and Parallel Prose, for instance, revolved around concrete questions of style. The former was simple and forceful; the latter, elegant and allusive. Both occupied prominent positions in the Chinese classical literary tradition, but vigorous debate on their respective merits continued well into the twentieth century.[23]

Ruan Yuan was a particularly powerful proponent of Parallel Prose in the late Qing period. In contrast to Tongcheng advocates of Ancient Prose, such as Liu Dakui and Yao Nai, Ruan argued that only writings employing rhyme and parallelism could be called true literature. He thus revived the old Six Dynasties concept of literature as belles lettres rather than "plain writing." In Ruan's words,

Those engaged in literary composition, who do not concern themselves with harmonizing sounds to form rhymes or polishing words and phrases to make them go far so that what they write should be easy to recite and easy to remember, but merely use single [i.e., nonparallel] sentences to write ... [wildly], do not realize that what they write is what the ancients called "speech" [*yan*], which means "straightforward speech," or "talk" [*yu*], which means "argument," but not ... what Confucius called *wen* [embellished words, i.e., true literature].[24]

Qing scholars often employed Parallel Prose to illustrate stylistic virtuosity, but the supreme test of their literary ability was poetry (*shi*). From earliest times, poetry had been a central Chinese cultural concern. In fact, the *Shijing* (Book of Poetry) is considered by some authorities to be the single most important work in China's entire literary history. Confucius once said, "If you do not learn the *Shijing* you will not be able to converse"; and again, "[One's character is] elevated by poetry, established by ritual, and completed by music." Virtually every major type of Chinese literature—from the classics and histories to plays and novels—included substantial amounts of poetry, and few self-respecting gentlemen in Qing times lacked the ability to compose elegant verse rapidly, in any social circumstance. Moreover, in poetry as in calligraphy, the Qing period witnessed a revival of several major styles, including regulated verse (*lüshi*) and lyric verse (*ci*).[25]

Many authorities have remarked upon how well suited the classical Chinese language was for poetic expression. Even ordinary prose had an evocative, ambiguous, rhythmic quality. Poetry—which as a generic category should include not only the various types of *shi* and lyric verse but also "song-poems" (*qu*) and rhyme prose or "rhapsody" (*fu*)—gave full scope to the creative potential of the language. The grammatical flexibility of classical Chinese, as well as the multiple meanings and subtle ambiguities of each character, allowed Chinese poets to express a wide range of ideas and emotions with vividness, economy, grace, and power.[26] Grouping elements together in spatial patterns and temporal rhythms, the poet created integrated structures of meaning that, though unified, presented a kaleidoscopic series of impressions. The visual quality of the characters, enhanced by the use of calligraphy as an artistic medium, complemented the tonal and other auditory qualities of the language—all of which were exploited to great advantage in poetry. Furthermore, Chinese poetry never lost its intimate relationship with music. Even when the musical context for lyrics had been forgotten, poems were still written to be chanted, not simply read aloud. Unhappily, the visual and auditory effects that contributed so much to the richness of traditional Chinese poetry are invariably lost in translation.[27]

Four main views of Chinese poetry have been distinguished: those of the Technicians, Moralists, Individualists (or Expressionists), and Intuitionalists. Although these designations do not imply the existence of four distinct and mutually exclusive schools of literary criticism, they do suggest certain tendencies in the thinking of poets and literary critics during the late imperial period of Chinese history. A number of these tendencies stand in sharp contrast to those of Western poets and critics. Pauline

Yu has observed, for instance, that Western poets set out to "construct" a fictive world in order to embody an ideal from a higher plane of existence, and in so doing they create "ontological dichotomies"; by contrast, Chinese poets "respond" to the external world, writing in literary conventions and emphasizing "categorical correspondences" that are immanent in the world and expressed in the *Yijing*.[28]

The Technicians, as their name implies, viewed poetry primarily as a literary exercise. Their outlook was traditionalistic and frankly imitative, although rationalized on grounds that the principles of poetry embodied in the work of the great masters were, in effect, natural laws of rhythm and euphony. In the words of the Qing critic Weng Fanggang (1733–1818),

> The fundamental principles of poetic methods do not originate with oneself; they are like rivers flowing into the sea, and one must trace their sources back to the ancients. As for the infinitely varied applications of poetic methods, from such major considerations as the structural principles down to such details as the grammatical nature of a word, the tone of a syllable, and the points of continuation, transition, and development—all these one must learn from the ancients. Only so can one realize that everything is done according to rules and in consonance with the laws of music and that one cannot do as one likes to the slightest degree.[29]

This technical view of poetry placed a premium on ancient models, but it also encouraged creative stylistic manipulations, such as taking apart the characters in one line of a poem and reconstituting them (*lihe*) to form new characters in another line, or composing verse that could be read from top to bottom or from bottom to top with different meaning but equal clarity (*huiwen*).[30] Technicians also enjoyed composing poems consisting of collected lines (*jiju*) taken from past poems by different writers. Zhu Yizun (1629–1709) provides an example:

> Soft colored clouds obscured by the sun;
> Red upon red, green upon green, flowers in the park:
> How can I enhance this fine poetic feeling?
> Listen to the spring birds:
> After they've flown, the flowering branches still dance gracefully.

These lines are taken, respectively, from the poetry of Wang Wei, Wang Jian, Sikong Tu, Gu Kuang, and Wei Yingwu.[31]

Many forms of Chinese verse were highly structured, requiring careful attention to the number of lines, the number of characters in a line, the matching of tones, rhyme, and parallelism or antithesis. Antithesis was, of course, especially admired. It appeared not only in regulated verse (where it was required), four-character verse, and ancient verse (*gushi*) but also in lyric verse and song-poems, which often did not even have lines of equal length. In the best antithetical couplets, each character in the first line contrasted in tone with the corresponding character in the second. At the same time, ideally the contrasted words served the same grammatical function in each line and referred to the same categories of things.[32] A simple example drawn from the novel *Dream of the Red Chamber* should suffice:

When the sun sets, the water whitens;
When the tide rises, all the world is green.

These lines, from the brush of Wang Wei, elicit the following response from an appreciative student of his work in the novel: " 'Whitens' and 'green' at first seem like nonsense but when you start thinking about it, you realize that he *had* to use those two words in order to describe the scene exactly as it was. When you read those lines out loud, the flavor of them is so concentrated that it's as though you had an olive weighing several thousand catties [i.e., ten thousand pounds] inside your mouth."[33]

Traditional handbooks on Chinese poetry gave detailed lists of categories of objects for use in antithesis, including astronomy, geography, plants, and animals. In the hands of unskilled writers this technique could degenerate into a mere mechanical pairing of words, but when employed by the masters it became a vivid expression of *yinyang* reconciliation of opposites. In the words of the modern critic James J.Y. Liu,

At its best [antithesis] can reveal a perception of the underlying contrasting aspects of Nature and simultaneously strengthen the structure of the poem. The perfect antithetical couplet is natural, not forced, and though the two lines form a sharp contrast, they yet somehow seem to possess a strange affinity, like two people of opposite temperaments happily married, so that one might remark of the couplet, as of the couple, "What a contrast, yet what a perfect match!"[34]

The didactic view of poetry shared with the technical view a concern with tradition, and many Qing writers, such as Shen Deqian, could be described as Technicians as well as Moralists. But the fundamental purpose of poetry in the minds of the Moralists was self-cultivation and, by extension, the betterment of society. Shen wrote, for example, "To use what is poetic in poetry is commonplace; it is only when you quote from the classics, the histories, and the philosophers in poetry that you can make it different from wild and groundless writings." Naturally enough, a number of poets used their medium to criticize social customs, past and present. Listen to Gutaiqing (1799–c. 1876), concubine of a Manchu prince:

Puppets on stage let people do what they will;
Bogus tales are meant to delude doltish children.
No shreds of evidence in stories about the royal houses,
Still they charm with marvels wrought by evil genius.
  Mounted on dark-red leopards,
  Escorted by striped civets,

In fresh gowns and bright caps they fake dignity.
After the show, they are strung up high and useless;
But carved wood and pulled strings belong to another time.[35]

Individualist poets might share such sentiments, but they did not view poetry primarily as a didactic exercise. Rather, they saw it as an expression of the unfettered self. In the words of the famous Qing poet Yuan Mei (1716–1797): "Poetry is what expresses one's nature and emotion. It is enough to look no further than one's self [for the material of poetry]. If its words move the heart, its colors catch the eye, its taste pleases the mouth, and its sound delights the ear, then it is good poetry." Such diverse individuals as Yuan, his literary archenemy Zhang Xuecheng, and the noted New Text scholar Gong Zizhen shared these Individualist sentiments.[36]

Individualist poetry covered a wide range of emotional territory. Common topics included friendship and drinking, romantic love, homesickness and parting, history and nostalgia, leisure and nature. Nature themes were especially esteemed. The Qing historian Zhao Yi conveys the Daoist ideal:

I never tire in my search of solitude;
I wander aimlessly along out-of-the-way trails
Where I have never been before.
The more I change my direction, the wilder the road becomes.
Suddenly I come to the bank of a raging river;
The path breaks off, all trails vanish.
No one is there for me to ask directions:
Only a lone egret beside the tall grass, glistening white.[37]

The Intuitionalists, perhaps best represented by Wang Shizhen and Wang Fuzhi, dealt with many of the themes of the Individualists, but they advocated a more intuitive apprehension of reality (*miaowu*). Their poetry was concerned with the relationship between human emotion (*qing*) and external scene (*jing*). In the words of Wang Fuzhi, who had far greater respect for human emotions than orthodox neo-Confucianism allowed, "Although *qing* and *jing* are two in name, they are inseparable in reality. In the most inspired poetry they subtly join together, with no barrier. Good poets include *jing* in *qing* and *qing* in *jing*."[38] Further, Wang writes,

Emotion is the activity of *yin* and *yang*, and things are the products of Heaven and Earth. When the activity between *yin* and *yang* takes place in the mind, there are things produced by Heaven and Earth to respond to it from the outside. Thus, things that exist on the outside can have an internal counterpart in emotion; and where there is emotion on the inside there must be the external object [to match it].[39]

The Intuitionalists attempted, in other words, to identify the self with the object of contemplation in order to establish a form of "spiritual resonance" (*shenyun*). Although criticized by Individualists such as Yuan Mei for lacking genuine emotion, poets such as Wang Shizhen actually sought a deeper spiritual awareness, an appreciation of the interrelatedness of all things, animate and inanimate. They were concerned not simply with self-expression but with conveying a world view. We get a hint of this attitude in Wang's "Moonlit Night at Fragrant Mountain Temple":

> The bright moon appears from the east ridge,
> And the summits become still all at once.
> Melting snow still covers the ground,
> Lying in shadow before the western lodge.
> The hue of bamboos makes the solitude complete,
> As pine shadows bewitch the shimmering ripples.
> All this brilliance shines forth at once—
> A myriad of images all pure and fresh.[40]

But for all that seemed to divide the Technicians, Moralists, Individualists, and Intuitionalists, there was considerable creative overlap. We have mentioned the link between Technicians and Moralists as exemplified in Shen Deqian, but there was other common ground. Individualists such as Gong Zizhen, for example, could be highly didactic, while Intuitionalists such as Wang Shizhen paid great attention to style. Shen Deqian, for his part, stressed the quality of "spiritual resonance" that was so important to Wang, yet he also recognized the merit of "romantic" poets such as Li E (1692–1752), whose writing was characterized by originality and freedom from the stylistic standards of Wang, Zhu Yizun, and others. In fact, the best Qing poets were masters of a variety of styles and moods, as the numerous poems in Arthur Waley's delightful biography of Yuan Mei attest.[41]

On the whole, Chinese women poets, like women painters, found it necessary to employ the tools and techniques of the dominant male culture. Aside from poems written in the unique "women's script" of southwestern Hunan (see Chapter 5), women writers in the Qing were dependent on traditions they did not invent. Nonetheless, they had distinctive female voices and operated in social spaces that were part of a separate women's culture. In Charlotte Furth's words, Chinese women "found their most important audience in each other." This was particularly true in the highly developed Jiangnan area, where the exchange of verses and cross-fertilization of ideas by women writers required "a critical mass of educated women and sympathetic men, as well as publishing centers, academies and art markets."[42]

Writing primarily in the genres of *shi* and *ci*, women poets not only supplied fresh perspectives on conventional literati themes such as travel (their accounts are generally more positive than those of men) but also explored new topical and emotional territory. They wrote movingly of absent parents, friendships with women, and close mother-child relationships.[43] Consider, for example, the following poem by Gu Ruopu (1592–c. 1681), entitled "Refurbishing a Boat for My Son to Use as a Study":

> I was always conscience-stricken
> before the zeal of those ancient mothers

until I found it [the boat], at a scenic spot
beside a bridge where in other days
it used to skirt the woods
following the chaste moon (not like
those craft that cruise the mist
in search of frivolous ladies).
You have long hoped to study
in Yang Zhu's school, but now
passers-by will see the scholar Mi Fei's barge.
Don't mistake it for a pleasure boat
the way I've fixed it up
with all those old coverlets
woven of blue silk.[44]

Here, Gu, inspired (and ostensibly intimidated) by the child-rearing efforts of historical role-models such as the mother of Mencius, good-naturedly chides her eldest son for preferring Daoist self-indulgence (Yang Zhu) to Confucian scholarship—epitomized by Mi Fei, a famous Song dynasty literatus, painter, and connoisseur who maintained a large library of books and paintings on his barge so that they would always be with him, wherever he went.

By Qing times, and in fact well before, poetry and painting had become inextricably linked as the most exalted forms of elite cultural indulgence for women as well as for men. Both were "written" with brush and ink, both treated a wide variety of subject matter, and both were concerned with simplicity and stylistic balance. Furthermore, poetry and painting often inspired each other. Painters were moved to create art after reading a poem, and poets were moved to create verse after viewing a painting. Thus, we have the "eccentric" painter Zheng Xie writing the following lines to his contemporary, Bian Weiqi:

You paint the wild geese as if I could see them crying,
And on this double-threaded silk, the rustling sound of river reeds.
On the tip of your brush, how infinitely chill is the autumn wind;
Everywhere on the mountain is the sorrow of parting.[45]

In the end, the relationship between painting and poetry is perhaps best expressed in Su Dongpo's (1036–1101) famous tribute to Wang Wei, "There is painting in his poetry and poetry in his painting." Ideally, and very often in fact, the Chinese literatus in Qing times was both poet and painter.[46]

VERNACULAR LITERATURE

Although no major literary figure in China after the first century A.D. attempted to write his or her principal works in a language consonant with the spoken language, the written vernacular (*baihua wen*) still enjoyed considerable popularity throughout much of the imperial era—especially from the Tang period onward. During the Qing dynasty, a variety of vernacular works circulated widely. The popularity of these works not only reflected the growth of basic literacy in China but also contributed to this growth. (Scholars have estimated that literacy rates during the Qing reached as high as 45 percent for males and 10 percent for females.[47]) Although not as succinct, exalted, or aesthetically pleasing as classical Chinese, the vernacular was comparatively easy to learn, direct, colorful, and often extremely forceful.

Vernacular equivalents existed for many forms of elite literature. Administrative manuals advocated the modification of complex official documents for public consumption through the use of simple rhymed phrases in "nice calligraphy, easy to read." Zhang Boxing (1652–1725), as governor of Fujian in the early eighteenth century, personally wrote three different versions of the famous Sacred Edict of the Kangxi emperor: "one embellished with classical allusions for the literati, one illustrated with popular sayings for those of medium intelligence, and one with memorable jingles for the simple country folk."[48]

Almanacs, encyclopedias of daily use (*riyong leishu*), and other practical handbooks were produced in several versions to reach different reading audiences throughout the empire. "Books of convenience" (*bianshu*), often illustrated, provided specific guidance on ritual and etiquette drawn from classical sources as well as more recent works, such as Zhu Xi's paradigmatic *Jiali* (Family Ritual). Popular vernacular histories paralleled the orthodox histories of the elite, "morality books" and "precious scrolls" were the popular equivalents of philosophical tracts and the classics, and colloquial short stories served as the counterparts to Tang-style classical tales (*chuanqi*), a genre that Pu Songling (1640–1715) brought to such high levels of achievement in the early Qing period.[49]

The vast majority of vernacular writings reflected conventional elite values. These writings included such popular Buddhist and Religious Daoist tracts as the *Taishang ganying pian* (Tract of Taishang on Action and Response), the *Bufeiqian gongde li* (Meritorious Deeds at No Cost), and the *Guangshan pian gongguo ge* (Ledger of Merit and Demerit for the Spreading of Goodness). Although based on the idea of divine retribution and buttressed by other religious notions, these works employed a great deal of elite symbolism and had a decidedly ethical, this-worldly cast. To be sure, they often contained admonitions to spare animal life, to show respect to sacred images, and "not to speak ill of Buddhist and Daoist clergy"; but the importance in these tracts of family affairs, filial piety, loyalty to the ruler, obedience to the "principles of Heaven," social harmony, the avoidance of lawsuits, and even respect for paper with written characters on it indicates a decidedly Confucian point of view. Furthermore, although works such as the *Bufeiqian gongde li* classify meritorious deeds according to various social and occupational groupings, the striking feature of these works is their active promotion of the existing Confucian social hierarchy.[50]

For the most part, popular vernacular fiction reflected an elite outlook, and despite the fact that dramatic works and popular novels were generally disparaged by the Confucian literati and sometimes outlawed by the state, they were enjoyed by all sectors of Chinese society, from emperor to peasant. Drama was a particularly effective means of reaching the Chinese masses. During the late Ming and throughout the Qing, the popular theater eclipsed traditional storytelling in influence, bringing history, legends, novels, and stories to both urban centers and the countryside. Indeed, it seems evident that the bulk of popular knowledge concerning the narrative tradition in China—major heroes and villains, stock scenes, allusions, and so forth—was transmitted more on stage than through the written word. Even the Kangxi emperor's Sacred Edict was popularized most effectively by means of this medium.[51]

There were several types of Chinese drama in Qing times: the classic Yuan dynasty "variety performance" (*zaju*); the southern drama (*xiwen* or *chuanqi*); various subregional styles such as "Kunshan music" (*Kunqu*); and the late Qing hybrid interregional form known as Beijing opera (*jingxi*). Although each of these types had its own special features, all shared certain general characteristics. One such feature was a multimedia presentation, combining spoken language (both verse and prose), music (both vocal and instrumental), and acting—including mime, dance, and acrobatics.[52] Another was its nonrepresentational nature, its stress on the expression of emotion rather than the imitation of life. As James J.Y. Liu indicates,

> In nonrepresentational drama, the words spoken or sung by a character do not
> necessarily represent actual speech or even thought; they are the dramatist's means to
> make the audience imagine the feelings and thoughts of the characters as well as the
> situations in which they find themselves. When a character speaks or sings fine poetry,
> he or she is not usually represented as a poet. ... The poetry, in most cases, belongs to
> the dramatist, not the character.

Like music in a play, poetry was extremely important in conveying dramatic mood, and when read, Chinese drama tended to be measured primarily by its verse.[53]

Since Chinese playwrights were not interested in imitating life, they did not usually try to create highly individualized characters. Rather, they were concerned with portraying human types, a categorical approach to characterization abetted by Chinese stage conventions such as colorful makeup and an extraordinarily elaborate system of hand, sleeve, and facial expressions. Among the most appreciated character types were upright scholars, military men (both good and bad), heroic women, and buffoons. There was not, however, a sharp division between tragedy and comedy as such in Chinese drama, in part because theatrical convention, like much of the vernacular literary tradition, demanded happy endings or at least poetic justice.[54]

Chinese plays covered all of the thematic territory embraced by traditional Chinese fiction: sex, love, intrigue, supernatural events, religious commitment, historical and pseudo-historical episodes (civil and military), domestic dramas, murder, lawsuits, banditry, and so forth. Many dramatic themes were derived from short stories or novels. At least a few plays of the Qing period explored explicitly lesbian or bisexual themes—notably *Lianxiang ban* (The Companion Who Loved Fragrance), written by Li Yu (1611–1680), a colorful and creative playwright who was also an epicure, an inventor, and a designer of houses and gardens. According to a preface to *Lianxiang ban* written by a man named Yu Wei, the phenomenon of a beautiful girl meeting another by chance and "falling in love with her fragrance" was commonplace in Li's time. In fact, Yu indicates that the play was based on the situation in Li's own household, where his wife and concubine loved both Li and each other.[55]

In many ways Li Yu exemplified the tumultuous, uncertain times in which he lived.[56] The growing commercialization, urbanization, and monetization of China in the seventeenth century not only created new opportunities for social mobility and provided greater scope for the literary and artistic talents of both women and men but also introduced new attitudes toward friendship, love, sex, and marriage. Many of Li Yu's writings touch on these and related themes.

Although known primarily as a dramatist, Li also wrote a novel, a number of short stories (again, some of which deal explicitly with homosexual themes), and three hundred essays on topics close to his heart—all organized under a few pithy headings into such categories as writing plays, putting on plays, women and beauty, houses and gardens, food and drink, flowers and trees, health and pleasure.[57] Much of what Li wrote was witty and humorous. Patrick Hanan describes him as "the most wholehearted and versatile exponent of comedy in the history of Chinese literature—the Chinese comic specialist par excellence." Li himself once confessed: "Broadly speaking, everything I have ever written was intended to make people laugh."[58]

Of the dozen or so plays attributed to Li Yu, most are his own creation, although a few are revisions of earlier works by other playwrights, such as *Mingzhu ji* (Record of an Illustrious Pearl) by Lu Cai (1497–1537). Significantly, Li produced and directed his own plays, which were then performed for high officials by his own small troupe of concubine-actresses. According to Li Man-kuei, Li Yu's experience as a producer and director "enabled him to understand thoroughly the secret of the stage and to exemplify in practice the principles of acting and playwriting which he formulated [in his essays]."[59]

Of the numerous outstanding plays written during the Qing period, we may single out the popular drama *Taohua shan* (Peach Blossom Fan), a "southern drama" of forty scenes, for special attention. Written by a descendant of Confucius named Kong Shangren (1648–1718), *Peach Blossom Fan* ranks as one of the greatest plays in the Chinese language by virtue of its historical vision, dramatic construction, and literary quality. It is also noteworthy for its wide-ranging subject material and effective characterization. The name derives from an incident in which the heroine, Li Xiangjun, resists the advances of a wicked minister and in a defiant gesture spatters her fan with blood. A famous painter then converts the bloodstains into a peach blossom design, which serves as a vibrant metaphor for "the mixture of violence and beauty that Kong saw as lying at the heart of late Ming moral and intellectual life."[60]

Carefully structured as a historical romance, *Peach Blossom Fan* touches on many different aspects of Chinese life: personal and private, social and political, military, and even artistic. Its major characters, all actual personalities of the late Ming period, have more individuality than most Chinese dramatic characters. For example, the "hero," Hou Fangyu, is less than perfect, while the "villain," Ruan Dacheng, possesses certain admirable qualities. This attempt at balance is also evident in the dramatic story line, which alternates between scenes of sadness and joy, quiescence and activity. In these and other ways, *Peach Blossom Fan* resembles some of the great novels of the Ming and Qing periods.

The play is a moving romantic story, but it is also a basically accurate historical account, and as such, it deals with the politically sensitive subject of the fall of the Ming dynasty. It should come as no surprise, then, to find that Kong Shangren sometimes distorts the record in an apparent effort not to offend the Manchus. The loyal minister Shi Kefa, for instance, commits suicide in the play, whereas in real life he was killed by Qing forces after refusing to surrender to them. Then again, Kong has his hero renounce the world rather than take the examinations under the Manchus (as he did in fact), presumably to provide a more satisfying climax to the play. In all, Kong must have struck an effective balance, since we know that *Peach Blossom Fan* was presented at court and was also well received by the Chinese public at large.[61]

A significant feature of most Chinese dramas and short stories is their neat resolution of the plot for maximum impact. By contrast, the Chinese novel—the supreme achievement in vernacular fiction during Ming-Qing times—gives very little sense of unilinear plot development and provides no dramatic climax. The reasons for these departures from other vernacular conventions rest in the aesthetic and philosophical assumptions that underlie such works. A recent volume of translations entitled *How to Read the Chinese Novel* (1990), edited by David Rolston and based on a special genre of Chinese literature known as *dufa* (lit., how to read) books, brings together a number of valuable commentaries on the great works of Ming and Qing fiction, allowing us to see more clearly than ever before how they were understood in traditional times.[62]

The structure of the best Chinese novels is rooted in the logic of interrelated and overlapping categories—the presentation of experience in terms of *yinyang*-style juxtapositions of images, themes, situations, and personalities. Reflecting the deeply ingrained idea of existence as "ceaseless alternation and cyclical recurrence," the Chinese novel proceeds along narrative axes of change such as separation and union, prosperity and decline, sorrow and joy, elegance and baseness, movement and stillness. It also often drifts between the realms of reality and illusion. The salient point is that these dualities are complementary rather than antithetical; they do not take the form of a master dualism and are not resolved in a truly dialectical process. Instead of the kind of resolution or synthesis that might be expected in a Western novel, there is only infinite overlapping and alternation.[63]

One gains the impression of endlessness in a Chinese novel—much the same quality we have identified in landscape paintings, gardens, and certain kinds of Chinese poetry. But as in art and poetry, endlessness or purposelessness was not tantamount to meaninglessness, for there was always the assumption that the entire ground of existence is intelligible. In Andrew Plaks's words,

Any meaning in the narrative texts will tend to come not in the configurations of the individual event, or its logical relation to other events, but only in the hypothetical totality of all (or at least a good many) events. ... This sense of meaning in the overview may be partially behind the centrality of historical and pseudohistorical narrative in the Chinese tradition. The idea that an objective recounting of human events will eventually bear out its own pattern of meaning is relatively clear in historiography, and one might even say that the dimension of significance which Western narrative tends to derive from epic models of unique greatness is manifest sooner in the Chinese context in terms of the recurrent cycles, the vast overview of history.[64]

The comparison between fictional narrative and history may also be extended to the treatment of character, which in most of Chinese vernacular literature tends to be categorical. Like the evaluation of historical personalities—not to mention that of artists and writers—the tendency in Chinese narrative is to sum up the individual in vivid, economical brushstrokes. Most novelists describe their characters from the outside, focusing primarily on actions rather than ideas, but assuming an integral relationship between the two. Characterization in the best Chinese novels is more complex than in conventional historical writing, however, since in Chinese narrative the emphasis is usually on the momentary and changing attributes of character rather than on abiding or developing attributes. The central figures in novels are seldom "heroic" in the Western sense and often give the impression of inconsistency or ambivalence. Again, these features can be explained in part by the aesthetic and philosophical notion of *yinyang* alternation and complementarity, an outlook that can accommodate change and inconsistency with comparative ease.[65]

Furthermore, in keeping with the traditional Chinese emphasis on relational thinking, the character of any given individual in a novel is seldom as important as the relationship of that person to others—hence, the emphasis on groups of people acting in concert or the elaborate interplay of various individuals in a group context. Sometimes fictional characters are even depicted as composites of their acquaintances. Also important to Chinese characterization is the tension created by conflicting social roles within the framework of the Three Bonds and the Five Relationships. In narrative, as in life, a man might well be torn by the conflicting imperatives of being at once a father, a son, a husband, a minister or subject (or emperor), an elder or younger brother, and a friend.[66]

Moral dilemmas are central to the structure of Chinese novels, which, like most other forms of vernacular literature, are marked by a heavy didacticism and a strong emphasis on themes of reward and retribution. This focus reflects the Confucian idea of an inherent moral order in the universe and the principle of *bao* ("requittal" or "recompense"), which requires that a fictional tale be morally satisfying. The result is that Chinese narrative, while full of tragic situations, lacks a well-developed concept of tragedy in the Western sense.[67]

The moral world of the Chinese novel is fundamentally Confucian, but Buddhist and Daoist elements appear prominently in several major novels, and many have an explicitly supernatural dimension. Although the most esteemed values in Chinese narrative are those of loyalty, duty, filial piety, and chastity, a number of novels exhibit a "syncretic hospitality" to the transcendental doctrines of Buddhism and Daoism as well as to the universalistic ethic of the knight-errant (*xia*). Moreover, despite their Confucian tone, some of the greatest works in the Chinese narrative tradition serve as vehicles for satirizing or otherwise criticizing certain values and practices of traditional Chinese society.[68] This critical content helps account for the ambivalence of Confucian scholars toward the novel and the periodic efforts by the state in Ming-Qing times to ban a number of "novels and licentious works" (*xiaoshuo yinci*) on grounds that they were "frivolous, vulgar and untrue." Even China's greatest novel, *Dream of the Red Chamber,* was officially proscribed during a portion of the nineteenth century, although we know that the Qianlong emperor himself read and enjoyed the work in the previous century.[69]

But for all their satirical tendencies and "vulgar" content, the best novels of the Ming-Qing period enthusiastically celebrated traditional Chinese culture and provided all sectors of Chinese society with a common repository of heroes and villains. Of the many popular novels of late imperial times, several warrant at least brief discussion. Together, these works display the wide variety of Chinese narrative themes and approaches as well as the basic features of traditional fiction outlined above. All have been translated into Western languages, and all have been the subject of extensive literary criticism both in China and in the West.[70]

We may begin with the popular historical narrative *Sanguo zhi yanyi* (Romance of the Three Kingdoms)—one of the earliest, least colloquial, and least fictional of China's major novels. Reputedly written by Luo Guanzhong (c. 1330–1400), it is set in the Three Kingdoms period that followed the breakdown of the Han dynasty. The novel is full of battle and intrigue, with prominent themes of brotherhood, loyalty, personal ambition, and righteous revenge. Among the many historical characters of the novel, several have become universally known in China as either noble heroes or arch villains: Zhang Fei, the symbol of reckless courage; Guan Yu, noteworthy for his unwavering loyalty; Zhuge Liang, the brilliant strategist; and Cao Cao, the selfish and evil tyrant.[71]

A popular proverb of the Qing period advised "Let not the young read *Shuihu*; let not the old read *Sanguo*." For just as the latter novel encouraged deviousness and intrigue, so the former, *Shuihu zhuan* (Water Margin; All Men Are Brothers), encouraged rebellion against authority. For this reason, at various times in the Qing period certain versions of the novel were condemned or outlawed. Like *Romance of the Three Kingdoms, Water Margin* is full of courageous deeds and its themes center on friendship, loyalty, and revenge, as well as righteous revolt. Although traditionally attributed to Luo Guanzhong, *Water Margin* is much more colloquial and less historical than *Romance of the Three Kingdoms.* It covers a shorter time span (during the Song dynasty) and consists of a sequence of cycles rather than an "interweaving of narrative strands." Of the 108 "righteous brigands" of *Water Margin*—who represent a fascinating cross section of Chinese society—the faintly historical Song Jiang and the loyal and powerful Wu Song have become especially popular folk heroes. To this day, few Chinese are unfamiliar with the story of Wu Song's killing of the tiger.[72]

Far different in subject matter from the puritanical heroics of *Romance of the Three Kingdoms* and *Water Margin* is the debauchery of the Ming erotic novel *Jin Ping Mei* (Golden Lotus). Attributed by some to Wang Shizhen (1526–1596) and by others to Xu Wei (1521–1593), *Golden Lotus* draws upon many diverse literary sources, including *Water Margin,* vernacular short stories, classical works, plays, and popular songs. Set in the Song, it is a "novel of manners" that describes Chinese urban middle-class life in realistic detail and dwells at length on the sexual exploits of the merchant Ximen Qing. The author shows a certain ambivalence toward his characters, displaying outward disapproval of their immoral behavior but covert sympathy for their physical and emotional frustrations. Yet ultimately he opts for morality: Ximen Qing dies of sexual overindulgence, and most of the other "evil" people in the novel are punished in one way or another. Ximen Qing's son redeems his father's sins by becoming a Buddhist monk. One especially noteworthy feature of the novel is its comparatively full and sympathetic treatment of women, a sharp contrast with the negative and stereotypical views projected in *Romance of the Three Kingdoms* and *Water Margin.*[73]

Another erotic Chinese novel, written by none other than the idiosyncratic Qing dramatist Li Yu, is *Rou putuan* (Carnal Prayer Mat).[74] Like *Golden Lotus, Carnal Prayer Mat* is in part a religious allegory revolving around the theme of Buddhist redemption. It is well structured, lively, funny, sympathetic to women, and psychologically realistic. In several respects, *Carnal Prayer Mat* is an even better novel than *Golden Lotus.* It is tighter and makes more skillful use of character analogies, humor, and irony. The female character Yuxiang ("Scent"), wife of the hero, Weiyang Sheng ("Before Midnight Scholar"), provides an excellent illustration of the problem of conflicting social roles as a daughter, wife, mistress, and prostitute. She also serves as an interesting example of the interplay of individuals in a group context, since she is linked in some way to all of the major male characters in the novel with the exception of Sai Kunlun.[75]

Xiyou ji (Journey to the West; Monkey), as its title suggests, is a travel epic. The novel is based on the historic pilgrimage to India of the famous Buddhist monk Xuanzang (596–664), who made the trip by way of Central Asia between 629 and 645. But instead of the sober travel account left by the historic Xuanzang, *Journey to the West* is a comic fantasy, written by the scholar Wu Cheng'en (c. 1506–1582). It revolves around the adventures of the humorless pilgrim Sanzang ("Tripitaka," a Buddhist pun on the name Xuanzang) and his traveling companions, including the well-known magical monkey named Sun Wukong and a sensual and slothful pig called Zhu Bajie. The novel can be approached from several angles—as allegory, social and political satire, comedy, and myth. At the level of allegory, and in the popular mind, Tripitaka represents selfishness and spiritual blindness; Pigsy, gross human appetite; and Monkey, intelligence, resourcefulness, and supernatural power. Monkey is, of course, the hero of the work. The novel is full of good-natured satire, and few subjects escape the author's barbs, including the "Monkey King" himself.[76]

Another travel epic, less well known but important from both a literary and a social-psychological standpoint, is the late Qing novel *Jinghua yuan* (Flowers in the Mirror), by Li Ruzhen (c. 1763–1830). Mark Elvin describes it as "a microcosm of the educated Chinese mind around the year 1830," the time when it was published. If *Journey to the West* can be described as China's *Pilgrim's Progress,* then *Flowers in the Mirror,* also set in the Tang dynasty, is perhaps the Chinese equivalent of *Gulliver's Travels.* Like *Journey to the West, Flowers in the Mirror* is a blend of mythology and adventure, fantasy and allegory, satire and wit. By design, the viewpoints of its characters frequently differ from one another, suggesting "polarities of problems" rather than fixed positions. Although more a reflection of Confucian moral values (loyalty and filial piety) and the Daoist search for immortality than of Buddhist theology or mythology, *Flowers in the Mirror* is far from conventional. It satirizes such things as snobbery, hypocrisy, and social climbing, sharply criticizes certain Chinese social practices—particularly footbinding and concubinage—and celebrates accomplished women such as Tang Guichen (who represents literary talent), Shi Lanyan (the embodiment of morality and wisdom), and Meng Zizhi (who is witty and humorous). In the end, however, despite its trenchant social criticism, *Flowers in the Mirror* evinces obvious admiration for nearly every other aspect of traditional Chinese culture.[77]

Rulin waishi (The Scholars), by Wu Jingzi (1701–1754), is generally considered China's best satirical novel. Through his skilled use of an omniscient narrator, the author—himself an examination failure—explores the often sordid and corrupt world of the Chinese elite, underscoring both the importance of the examination system to the literati class and the many abuses of the system. In all, the novel boasts about two hundred characters, many of whom are very skillfully portrayed—sometimes with conflicting information supplied by different observers. A few scholarly figures are seen as upright and exemplary, but many more appear as imposters and hypocrites. Several critics have emphasized the autobiographical nature of the book and the author's identification with the able but highly individualistic scholar Du Shaoqing; yet even Du is satirized on occasion, as Wu Jingzi projects a consistently moral vision in the midst of vulgarity, hypocrisy, and human folly. Although often criticized for its episodic structure and apparent lack of a cohesive overall design, *The Scholars* illustrates very well the traditional Chinese emphasis on "a mass of weaving of many narrative strands" and on vast networks of human relationships.[78]

Several other novels of social criticism deserve at least passing mention, including the late Qing works *Lao Can youji* (The Travels of Lao Can) by Liu E (1857–1909) and the innovative first-person narrative entitled *Ershi nian mudu guai xianzhuang* (Bizarre Happenings Eyewitnessed over Two Decades) by Wu Woyao (1867–1910). These and other novels of the late Qing not only shed valuable light on the dynasty in decline (and on the unprecedented impact of the West during the late nineteenth and early twentieth centuries; see Chapter 11) but also represent an important transitional stage between traditional and modern fiction in China.[79]

By almost any standard, the greatest of all Chinese novels is *Honglou meng* (Dream of the Red Chamber; Dream of Red Mansions). The first 80 chapters of this massive and elegant work, commonly known as *Shihtou ji* (Story of the Stone), were written by Cao Xueqin (c. 1715–1763); the last 40 chapters are generally attributed to Gao E (fl. 1791).[80] Some versions of the full 120-chapter work consist of nearly 1,300 pages and about 700,000 words. The novel contains at least 30 major figures and some 400 minor ones representing every level of the Chinese social order. Yet, as numerous as these characters are, Fang Chao-ying rightly observes that

> they intermingle in a wonderful unity, each individual constituting an integral member of a large family group, sharing its glory and its shame, contributing to its prosperity or its ruin. Some, taking it for granted that the family fortune is irreversible, spend their days in emotional excesses or in sensual pleasures. Some, who are avaricious, contrive to profit by mismanagement of the family estate. Some foresee the dangers and so plan for their own futures; others voice warnings, but their words go unheeded. Such a panorama of complex human emotions, involving tens of masters and hundreds of servants, constitutes source-material of supreme value for a study of the social conditions in affluent households of the early Ch'ing [Qing] period.[81]

The major story line of the novel revolves around the fortunes of the Jia family and a complex love affair involving various individuals living in the family compound—notably Jia Baoyu, the "hero" (one might say anti-hero) of the book and his talented female cousins, Lin Daiyu and Xue Baochai (see Figures 9.1 and 9.2). Much of the novel is strongly autobiographical, for like Baoyu, Cao Xueqin was a sensitive, well-educated individual whose wealthy and established family experienced financial reverses and other difficulties during his lifetime. The book has several different layers of meaning, and it is written in several different literary modes—realistic, allegorical, and narrative. Like *The Scholars, Dream of the Red Chamber* is in part a critique of early Qing political and social life, and like *Flowers in the Mirror,* which was heavily influenced by Cao's brilliant narrative, it can be seen as a celebration of women.[82]

The structure of *Dream of the Red Chamber* illustrates especially well the basic organizing principle of *yinyang* complementarity and the traditional Chinese philosophical interest in relations, qualities, and states of being. As Plaks, Lucien Miller, Angelina Yee, Jing Wang, and others have indicated, much of the appeal of the novel can be found in the interpenetration or overlapping of themes of reality and illusion; the juxtaposition of Confucian and Buddhist (or Daoist) elements; contrasts between rich and poor, exalted and base; and the alternation of scenes, moods, and situations. Antithetical couplets at the beginning of many chapters, and contrasting characterizations, such as those of the frail Lin Daiyu and the robust Xue Baochai,

Figure 9.1   Characters from Dream of the Red Chamber *(A). Lin Daiyu. Source: Qi Gai (1984).*

Figure 9.2   Characters from Dream of the Red Chamber *(B). Jia Baoyu. Source: Qi Gai* (1984).

heighten the reader's sense of interpenetration, alternation, and complementary opposition.[83] Early in the novel the structural and thematic tone is set:

> There actually are some happy affairs in the Red Dust [the "real" world], it's just that
> one cannot depend on them forever. Then again, there is "discontent within bliss,
> numerous demons in auspicious affairs," a phrase of eight words all of which belong
> tightly bound together. In the twinkling of an eye, sorrow is born of utter happiness,
> men are no more, and things change. In the last analysis, it's all a dream and the
> myriad realms return to nothingness.[84]

Predictably, *Dream of the Red Chamber* ends in what Plaks describes as "narrative
lame-duck fashion." Well before the conclusion of the novel, Baoyu's family secretly
arranges for him to marry Baochai, rather than his true love, Daiyu, who dies grief
stricken on Baoyu's wedding day. A series of Jia family disasters follow, but Baoyu
eventually passes the examinations, Baochai bears him a son, and the Jia family fortunes rise again. Baoyu then decides to renounce the world and become a Buddhist
monk, thus seeking enlightenment and personal salvation after at least partially ful-
filling his Confucian responsibilities as a son and a husband. As some modern Chinese scholars have argued, the novel has a genuinely tragic dimension, but the tragedy is tempered somewhat by larger patterns of existential movement.[85]

Chinese and Western scholars alike have identified *Dream of the Red Chamber* as a
microcosm of traditional Chinese culture. In both its elaborate structure and its exquisite detail, the novel evokes a mood of completeness and authenticity. Furthermore, in a very real sense it represents the culmination of China's entire premodern
literary tradition. The novel includes every major type of Chinese literature—including philosophy, history, poetry, and fiction. We find in it quotations from Confucius
and Zhuangzi, Tang poets and Yuan dramatists. Throughout the Qing period and up
to the present, *Dream of the Red Chamber* has inspired countless plays, poems, games,
and sequels, as well as a huge body of critical scholarship.

But while the novel is a supremely accomplished example of traditional Chinese
fiction, the author reveals conventional literati prejudices throughout the work. In
chapter 42, for example, Baochai lectures Daiyu on the purpose of literature:

> A boy's proper business is to read books in order to gain an understanding of things,
> so that when he grows up he can play his part in governing the country. ... As for girls
> like you and me, ... since we can read, let us confine ourselves to good, improving
> books; let us avoid like the plague those pernicious works of fiction, which so
> undermine the character that in the end it is past reclaiming.[86]

Undoubtedly Cao Xueqin is writing a bit with tongue in cheek; but it is clear that the
author's greatest delight lies in displaying his erudition through philosophical discussions, word games, riddles, and especially classical verse. Although his characters
quote freely from such popular works as the famous thirteenth-century play *Xixiang
ji* (Romance of the Western Chamber), they spend countless hours composing po-

etry and discussing it. In fact, *Dream of the Red Chamber* provides the reader with a first-rate education in the refinements of poetic composition and appreciation.

The cultural breadth of the novel is perhaps most evident in its vivid portrayal of Chinese society. In both its psychological realism and encyclopedic scope, it is unparalleled in the history of traditional Chinese literature. As Fang Chao-ying has indicated, *Dream of the Red Chamber* sheds light on virtually every aspect of Chinese life and covers a vast social spectrum. It highlights the importance of popular religion and family ritual, the values of filial piety and respect for age and authority, and the tensions and conflicts of role fulfillment at various levels of society. In addition, it provides a wealth of detail on Chinese aesthetics, housing, clothing, food, amusements, festivals, sexual life, and popular customs. Perhaps most important, it illustrates the gap between social theory and social practice so often neglected or downplayed in official documents and other orthodox sources. With this point in mind, we may now turn our attention to Chinese daily life.

⚜ 10 ⚜

Social Life

$\mathcal{A}$s with most other realms of culture, social customs during the Qing period varied—sometimes dramatically—from region to region, time to time, and class to class. Minority groups within China added to this diversity with their own traditions. Since, however, this book is concerned primarily with recreating a Chinese-style, holistic perspective on culture, our discussion will focus on those customs identified by the Han people empire-wide as significant from the standpoint of shared symbols and values, common organizational principles, or standard ritual practices. An invaluable resource for this type of study is, of course, the "customs" (*fengsu*) sections of local gazetteers.[1]

Gazetteers record change as well as continuity. Although a full discussion of transformations over time is obviously impossible here, one or two examples may serve to illustrate certain broad trends. As we have already seen, economic developments in the seventeenth and eighteenth centuries exerted an enormously powerful influence on many aspects of Chinese life, including philosophy, religion, art, and literature. So did population growth and increased competition for scarce resources—not least, examination degrees. T'ien Ju-kang goes so far as to argue that frustration and anxiety on the part of Chinese scholars in times of uncertainty led them to give especially strong support to the neo-Confucian "chastity cult" during the Ming-Qing era. This state-sponsored cult ritually rewarded women who killed or mutilated themselves as an expression of devotion to their deceased husbands.[2]

Whatever the merits of T'ien's argument for the Ming, it seems evident that the emphasis on "chastity" in eighteenth-century China was primarily a reaction to the growing literacy and comparative freedom of women during the Ming-Qing transition. After consolidating their empire, the Manchus embarked on a combined state-elite effort to "tighten control in many areas of gender relations: more rigid rape laws, bans on pornography, legislative attacks on homosexuality, statutory support for patriarchical authority, the virtuous widow cult, and so on." One result was that for much of the Qing period Chinese women were subject to standards of fidelity and female propriety more rigid than at any previous time in Chinese history.[3]

In the midst of this growing repressiveness, Qing intellectuals vigorously debated gender roles as part of a larger but closely connected issue: the relationship between ancient "ritual teachings" (*lijiao*) and "current social practices" (*shisu*).[4] The participants in the gender debate, overwhelmingly male, cut across the intellectual spectrum of the day. They included "libertine aesthetes" like Yuan Mei, *kaozheng* philol-

245

ogists like Qian Daxin, orthodox Cheng-Zhu moralists like Zhang Xuecheng, and practical-minded Confucian activists like Chen Hongmou.[5] Few of them held consistent opinions. Yuan, for instance, argued for (and contributed to) the literary education of women, yet he defended concubinage as a reflection of the inherent inferiority of females to males. Zhang believed that men and women had the same innate intellectual gifts (he castigated Yuan for treating women as sex objects) but insisted that literate women should remain at home and have no public voice. Even Chen, for all of his well-intentioned egalitarian impulses, openly defended the female "chastity cult."[6]

Changes in Qing economic and social life did more than simply provoke vigorous theorctical debates. They also had practical consequences, not least in the realm of ritual. A well-known Chinese proverb avers: "When one is wealthy, one loves the rites." An important transformation during the Qianlong period was that public ceremonies associated with the ancestral cult began to grow ever more elaborate—at least in the provinces of Guangdong and Fujian, where powerful lineages predominated. During the late Ming and early Qing, the rites of grave worship had been confined to "recent" ancestors (up to twelve generations after death) and involved gatherings of fewer than one hundred people. By the mid-Qing, entire lineages of hundreds and even thousands of individuals began visiting the graves of their remote forebears (up to thirty generations back).[7] One can easily imagine what an impressive social spectacle this must have been.

LIFE-CYCLE RITUAL

As a general rule, the higher the social class in China, the more rigid the adherence to ritual as a matter of both Confucian responsibility and public prestige. Another factor was financial: Most elites had the advantage of indulging in costly ceremonies without undue financial hardship. An ancient Chinese proverb tells us: "Ritual and righteousness are born of adequate wealth." Nonetheless, a powerful and persistent feature of ritual life in traditional China was the effort on the part of all classes of society to put on the most impressive ceremonial displays possible, regardless of cost. One mid-nineteenth century account of rural life in South China explains:

> Poverty and death are haunting spectres of the poor. They roam through the village
> and inspire fear that is not physical but social. It is not that the villager fears death; his
> belief in Fate relieves him of that worry. But to think of his parent drawing near to the
> time of departure without funds for proper rites and burial—this is a real fear. To fail
> in the provision of rites, feasts, coffin, and funeral would be conduct most unfilial and
> condemned by social opinion.[8]

Other works, both Western and Chinese, confirm this view. John L. Buck indicates that as late as 1930, nearly 80 percent of rural credit in some areas of China was used for noneconomic purposes—primarily birth, marriage, funeral, and other ceremonies. Undoubtedly the costs were at least as high in Qing times, when, according to early Republican-era ceremonial handbooks, ritual requirements were even more rigid and elaborate.[9]

All aspects of Chinese family life were highly structured.[10] Ritual handbooks and "family instructions" provided invaluable guidance, but popular almanacs were also considered essential to the conduct of daily affairs. By virtue of their wide distribution and practical utility, almanacs were probably the most frequently used book of any kind in late imperial times. In addition to providing basic calendrical information, they supplied medical and agricultural advice, educational material for children (in the form of morality tales), and a variety of charms and divination techniques. Virtually all sectors of society employed almanacs in some way, whether for protection against evil spirits, for ethical guidance, or for advice on propitious times to undertake various domestic ritual activities such as sacrifices, prayers, marriages, and funerals. Almanacs even offered information on the best times to undertake such mundane activities as bathing, sewing, sweeping, meeting friends, taking medicine, embarking on journeys, doing business, and entering school.[11]

As indicated briefly in Chapter 7, the divinatory systems of Chinese almanacs were based on a set of interrelated cosmic variables: *yinyang/wuxing* correlations, the twenty-four directions of the compass, the twenty-eight asterisms, and so forth. Individuals fit into the cosmic order according to their date of birth, which was always carefully recorded in the form of eight characters (*bazi*), two each for the year, month, day, and hour. In the popular mind—and for many members of the elite as well—birth in a certain year identified the individual with one of twelve symbolic animals associated with the system of "earthly branches." Each of these animals, in turn, was linked with certain character traits, the qualities of *yin* or *yang,* one of the five elements, and certain stars or constellations. Quite naturally, such natal information had to be taken into account by both fortune-tellers and matchmakers.[12]

The ceremonies connected with birth in traditional China varied tremendously, but a few common denominators may be identified. Because infant mortality was so high,[13] parents almost always tried to protect their newborn children through the use of charms, prayers, and offerings. Many Chinese believed that boy babies were the special prey of evil spirits but that these evil spirits might be dissuaded if the child had an unattractive "milk name" (*naiming*). Sometimes the strategy was to give the boy a girl's name. In general, milk names were bestowed at feasts known as "full-month" (*manyue*) ceremonies, which marked the first month of life and underscored the uncertainty surrounding the child's early existence.[14]

Life was especially precarious for newborn girls, since the practice of infanticide involved them primarily. A number of astute Western observers in the late Qing period considered infanticide to be no more common in China than in Europe, but other nineteenth-century accounts—both Western and Chinese—indicate that the outlawed practice was often quite widespread, especially in times of economic hardship. Listen to You Zhi, gentry organizer of an infant-protection society in his home village near Wuxi, Jiangsu, during the mid-nineteenth century:

[When] poor families have too many children, they are often forced by practical considerations to drown the newborn infants, a practice which has already become so widespread that no one thinks it unusual. ... Not only are female infants drowned, at times even males are; not only do the poor drown their children; even the well-to-do do it. People follow each other's example, and the custom becomes more widespread day by day. There is a case where one family drowned more than ten girls in a row; there are villages where scores of girls are drowned each year. We who dwell in the country witness the crime with our own eyes—a scene too brutal to be described.[15]

Girls were considered a poor social investment in traditional China, since after years of nurture the majority of them would simply marry to become members of other households. Hard-pressed families might sell their female children into slavery or prostitution, but infants brought a low price, and many believed that it was better to destroy the child than to doom it to a life of poverty and shame. Hence such common euphemisms for infanticide as "giving [the child] away to be married" and "transmigrating [the soul of the child] to the body of someone else."[16] Furthermore, the demands of Confucian filial piety were such that the death of a baby girl might be morally justifiable if the choice for the future was between providing for one's parents and providing for one's children. A famous story in Chinese popular lore explicitly condoned and rewarded the attempt to sacrifice a child for the sake of one's parent.[17]

Filial piety had other dimensions and ramifications. While a girl child was essentially irrelevant to the question of patrilinear kinship, a boy was considered crucial for the continuation of the family line and the maintenance of ancestral sacrifices. Mencius had male children in mind when he remarked, "Of the three most unfilial things, the worst is to have no posterity." In the absence of heirs, matrilocal (uxorilocal) marriage was an option, though not a very attractive one. The other possibility was adoption. As with marriage, intermediaries of various sorts facilitated the process.

Of the several forms of adoption, the most regular and esteemed was kin-related. By law, in order to participate in family ancestral sacrifices an adopted heir had to have the same surname as the head of the household, and specific stipulations existed regarding preferential succession from various classes of nephews and grandnephews on the paternal side. In practice, however, individuals often acquired heirs with comparatively few complications simply by purchasing and adopting children outside their lineage and changing their surnames. This practice was particularly common in South China. The ceremony of adoption usually entailed a contract, a feast, and ancestral sacrifices in which the adopted son took part. Such ceremonies stood somewhere in significance between the rituals of birth and those of marriage.[18]

The stages of growth in traditional China were viewed in a variety of ways. As noted in Chapter 6, Confucius placed special stress on the ages fifteen, thirty, forty, fifty, sixty, and seventy. The "Family Regulations" chapter of the *Record of Ritual,* which discusses child-rearing practices for young males, emphasizes the ages six, ten, and thirteen and then the adult years of twenty, thirty, forty, fifty, and seventy. Predictably, females are treated in a much more cursory way, with emphasis placed on the ages ten, fifteen, and twenty. The subcategory on human affairs in the *TSJC* includes separate sections for every year of life from birth to age twenty and for each decade thereafter up to "one hundred and above." But the most common periodization in traditional times consisted of six major stages: (1) infancy, (2) the juvenile period, (3) young adulthood, (4) adulthood, (5) middle age, and (6) old age.[19]

Infancy generally lasted from birth to about three or four years old (four or five *sui* in Chinese reckoning), depending on the presence or absence of siblings and/or nursemaids. The first two years of life were a time of great indulgence; babies were fed whenever hungry, day or night, played with by the entire family, especially grandparents, and only gradually toilet trained and weaned. Elementary discipline began at about age three or four, with an effort to teach respect and obedience and an emphasis on status distinctions and devotion to parents. Didactic stories, such as the *Ershisi xiao* (Twenty-four Examples of Filial Piety), inculcated the proper attitudes in children, who also began to learn appropriate gender roles.[20]

The anecdotes in the *Twenty-four Examples of Filial Piety*, which commonly appeared in Qing almanacs, illustrate the extremes to which Chinese children were expected to go in the service of their parents. In addition to the story alluded to above, in which a man demonstrates a willingness to kill his male child in order to have enough resources to feed his aged mother, this collection includes stories about a prince (later an emperor) who attended his ailing mother relentlessly, day and night, for three years, "during which time his eyelids did not close"; a man who, even at the age of seventy, dressed up and frolicked around like a child in order to amuse his parents; a man who decided to sell himself into slavery so that he might give his father a proper burial; a child who stayed out all night on an icy river in order to procure fresh fish for his mother; a young boy who invited mosquitoes to feed on his body so that they would not disturb his sleeping parents; a woman who nourished her toothless mother-in-law with milk from her own breast; and a young man who cut flesh from his leg to use as medicine for his ill father.[21] This last story explains the surprisingly common practice known as *gegu* (lit., cutting the thigh [for one's parents]), which was institutionally rewarded by the Qing state.[22]

Discipline of Chinese children began in earnest during the juvenile period, which lasted from three or four to about fifteen or sixteen.[23] In elite households, males (and sometimes females as well) received training in the recitation of verse and the memorization of Chinese characters, followed by instruction in brushwork, and finally by schooling in the techniques of chess and the playing of musical instruments. Elite boys usually learned the skills of classical literacy through a more or less formal tutorial process, while elite girls, who also learned the "womanly" skills of embroidery and weaving, often received informal academic instruction from their mothers.[24] By the age of five or six the binding of young girls' feet usually began—both a symptom and a cause of ever more rigid sexual segregation. This crippling practice—which was

Figure 10.1   Women with Bound Feet. These two young Chinese women provide a graphic illustration of the way footbinding deformed the foot. The process involved pushing the four minor toes under the feet and at the same time compressing the front and back of the foot in order to bow the arch upward and eventually break it. Photo courtesy of the Peabody & Essex Museum, Salem, Mass.

far more widespread than generally recognized—brought both status and suffering to Chinese women (see Figures 10.1 and 10.2).[25]

Sexual segregation was never complete, as *Dream of the Red Chamber* illustrates graphically, but the cultural ideal in China remained the isolation of women in the inner apartments as much as possible (see Figure 10.3).[26] There are stories of Buddhist-oriented elite women in the Qing who expressed the wish that in their next existence they would be reborn as dogs so that they would have greater freedom. Young men, for their part, suffered from the tyranny of their fathers, who, in order to abide by explicit Confucian admonitions in the *Analects* to remain "distant," became increasingly aloof and often severe as they trained their sons in family ritual roles and proper social conduct. By contrast, the relationship between mothers and their daughters (and sometimes also their sons) was warm and close.[27]

Parental power was nearly absolute in traditional China, as the brutal beating of Jia Baoyu by his father in *Dream of the Red Chamber* makes evident. Customarily a son or grandson who assaulted or reviled a parent or grandparent could be killed with impu-

Figure 10.2   A Manchu Woman. The style of dress and lack of bound feet indicate that this woman of the late Qing period was a member of the Manchu elite. Photo courtesy of the Peabody & Essex Museum, Salem, Mass.

nity, since such acts of unfilial behavior were considered capital crimes. At an early age, Chinese children learned absolute submission to parents, grandparents, teachers, masters of trades, and other authority figures. This practice produced a strong "dependency orientation" in youths of both sexes, although in peasant households there was relatively greater equality between parents and children (and between males and females) than in elite households because all members of the family lived in close quarters and worked together in the fields as a single cooperative economic unit.[28]

Lucian Pye, among others, has written perceptively on the psychocultural implications of China's highly authoritarian approach to child rearing. "The absolute imperative of filial piety has traditionally meant that sons could never manifest in any manner the hostilities they might naturally feel toward their fathers. This denial of

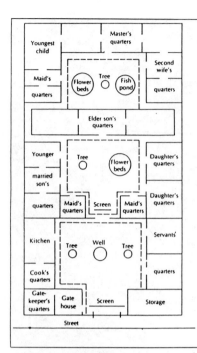

Chinese architecture, particularly of upper-class homes, accommodated the extended family. Old, large houses in Chinese cities had a series of courtyards, each of which could house one or more family units. A high wall and a large gate separated the compound from the street. Immediately inside and usually to the left was a gate house or room or two where the gate-keeper lived and slept. The rest of the first courtyard was usually given over to the servants and to stables and storerooms. The courtyard was a perfect square and in its center there was likely to be a well and maybe a tree. The passage between the first and second courtyards tended to be in line with the front gate. Just within the front gate there was likely to be a large screen or wall directly behind the gate so that when the doors were opened one did not have a direct view inward. The Chinese believed that evil spirits could move only in straight lines and thus the screen protected the living quarters from them and gave privacy and a break between living units. The second courtyard repeated the first, but on a grander scale. On both sides were two or three rooms, usually accessible only through the center room. The roof extended over the front to give a covered walkway or narrow veranda on three sides of the courtyard. This courtyard might serve as quarters for the staff and personal servants. Then depending upon the size of the total establishment, the next, or in some cases the fourth, courtyard, would be the living quarters for the junior members of the family.

Depending on the wealth and station of the family, each son and his family would occupy either a side of a courtyard or a total courtyard. Certain courtyards might also be the quarters for the master's concubines. The innermost courtyard belonged to the master. Domiciled here was the first wife and often the second and third wives, who occupied the rooms along the sides. The eldest son's courtyard would be immediately before the master's and, depending on whether he had a second wife or concubines, the second and third sons and their wives might occupy the rooms on the two sides. Questions of precedent were important. Hurt feelings could result from decisions about whether the younger son or the unmarried daughters should rank above favored concubines, the issue being less the status of the concubines and more the physical convenience of the master, who might prefer not to stumble through too many courtyards on a dark night.

Figure 10.3   House Plan. Source: "The Traditional Chinese House," pp. 96–97, from China: An Introduction, *2nd. edition, by Lucien Pye. Copyright © 1978, 1972, by Little Brown & Co., Inc. Reprinted with permission of HarperCollins Publishers, Inc.*

man's potentially strongest feelings, when combined with socialization practices such as early teasing and then steeply heightened discipline, contributed to a tendency to divorce feelings from actions and to distrust one's own affect." The result, Pye argues, is that

> the repression of aggression has been a central theme in Chinese culture, in contrast with Western civilization, whose central concern has been the repression of sexuality. The Chinese stress of etiquette, ritual, conformity; their anxieties over disorder, confusion, and collapse of hierarchy; their capacity to swing abruptly between the poles of disciplined order and explosive emotional outbursts; their sensitivity to affronts or criticism; and their need to vocalize their anxieties and tensions all suggest that the controlling of aggression is not only important but difficult. The Chinese preference for unambiguous situations and the comfort they find in well-defined hierarchical relationships are also reflections of concern over the destructive potential of human aggression.[29]

The stage of development known as young adulthood was by and large an elite phenomenon. It was a time of transition that occurred during the teenage years, before marriage. By the mid-teens, the worst of parental discipline and educational rigor had passed. Chinese males began to experience considerable freedom and to have their first sexual contacts with prostitutes or servant girls. Their sisters, however, remained confined within the home and bound by a double standard of rigid chastity.[30] In some families, the rituals of capping males and binding up the hair of females marked the formal transition to adulthood, but for the most part these ceremonies, if they took place at all, were associated in late imperial times with marriage, which normally took place from about eighteen to twenty-one years of age in the case of boys and from sixteen to eighteen with girls.[31]

The formal ceremonies of marriage brought adulthood regardless of age. Marriage was expected of every normal man and woman in Chinese society, including slaves. Indeed, the Qing legal code stipulated that slave owners were subject to criminal punishment if they neglected to find husbands for their female slaves. The purpose of marriage was to continue the male line of descent. In the words of the *Record of Ritual*: "The rites of marriage unite two [different] surnames in love, in order to maintain services in the ancestral temple and to ensure the continuation of the family line." Marriage was thus an alliance between two different families, not a matter of individual choice and mutual affection. By law, two people of the same surname could not be married, even if unrelated, and the legal principals in the match were the heads of the respective households, not the individuals to be joined in wedlock. In some cases, the wishes of the prospective bride and groom might be taken into account, but very often the choice of a marriage partner by parents or elders was arbitrary and unilateral. Baoyu's arranged marriage to Baochai rather than to Daiyu in the novel *Dream of the Red Chamber* is a tragic, but typical, example of family interests overriding personal feelings.[32]

Marriage was always a contractual affair in Qing China—by far the most important contractual relationship in traditional times. Marriage contracts might be oral or written, general or detailed, but all were surrounded by elaborate rituals that enhanced them, gave them public visibility, and symbolized their social and cosmological significance. Contracts were also associated with divorce and adoption procedures. As a rule, the smaller the economic or ritual investment in such contracts, the greater the likelihood that they would be breached.[33]

Several different forms of marriage existed in traditional China, each a product of particular social or economic circumstances. The most prestigious was the standard, or major, marriage. It involved the transfer of an "adult" bride from her natal home and her ritual rebirth in the home of her husband. This form of marriage, to be discussed in some detail below, was considered the norm, the social standard. Minor marriages followed the basic ritual pattern of major marriages, except that the bride lived in the home of her prospective husband for ten or fifteen years as a "daughter-in-law reared from childhood" (*tongyang xi* or *miaoxi*) before the actual marriage date. This arrangement was particularly common among the poor in China, but it was by no means limited to them. Another less common and less esteemed variety of marriage was uxorilocal (matrilocal), involving the transfer of a male into the household of a female as a son-in-law (a reversal of the pattern of major and minor marriages). The males involved in such matches usually came from families with several sons and entered families where there were none. The period of residence in the bride's home was variable, from a few years to a lifetime, and always carefully spelled out by contract.[34]

The distribution of major, minor, and matrilocal marriages throughout China hinged on several factors: family status, wealth, social organization (especially lineage ties), and geography. Major marriages dominated the social landscape of North China, but in many southern areas the alternative forms predominated. Arthur Wolf and Huang Chieh-shan write:

> Viewing China's marriage and adoption customs as from an earth satellite, we would probably see that minor marriages were concentrated in a continuous area along the South China coast, reaching their highest density in southern Kiangsi [Jiangxi], southwestern Fukien [Fujian], and northern Kwangtung [Guangdong]. Uxorilocal marriages would probably appear common in the same region but would achieve their highest density on the Lower Yangtze [Yangzi] Delta and in a second area of concentration on China's Western frontier. But as soon as we moved closer to our subject, we would soon discover that this view from on high concealed a great deal of local variation, variation even more marked than that between the country's major regions.[35]

A distinctive feature of family life in traditional China was the institution of concubinage. Theoretically, this ancient practice was justified by the filial imperative of producing sons to continue the male line. Often concubines (*qie*) were purchased outright from poor families by the more well-to-do, and ordinarily they did not enjoy the same status as the principal wife (*qi*).[36] As a matter of fact, upon entering her new family, a concubine usually had to participate in ceremonies designed to show her subservience to the wife. Qing law prohibited the degradation of a principal wife to the position of concubine or the elevation of a concubine to the position of principal wife. As further testimony to her inferiority, a concubine was required to observe the same degree of mourning for her master's wife as she was for his parents, his sons (by the principal wife or other concubines), and her own sons. Her sons were expected to treat the principal wife as their own mother, and by custom they were entitled to equal rights of inheritance along with the sons of the wife. Paternity was what mattered in Chinese marriages, and in divorce, the husband almost always received custody of the children.[37]

The practices of concubinage and infanticide, together with the strong social pressure on widows not to remarry as a matter of Confucian propriety, created a large pool of surplus men looking for wives—a situation that matrilocal marriage helped to reduce only in part. (About 10 percent of Chinese men probably never married, which helps explain why major marriages brought such social prestige and required such grand public display.) Although the specific customs surrounding major marriages often differed from place to place, certain practices were nearly universal.[38]

One feature of all Chinese marriages—major, minor, and matrilocal alike—was the employment of a go-between, or matchmaker. Intermediaries of this sort were essential to a great many aspects of Chinese social life, especially those involving delicate matters of "face."[39] The responsibilities of the matchmaker were extremely weighty. He or she had to take into account not only the relative social positions of the two families involved but also certain important economic and personal factors such as family wealth and individual character. Ideally, the match was expected to benefit both parties, which generally meant that the families had to be of approximately equal status and means or that one family might contribute greater status while the other contributed greater wealth. Some Qing officials, such as Chen Hongmou, deplored "viewing women as commodities" (*shi wei qihuo*), but financial considerations almost always loomed large in marriage calculations.[40]

After making discreet investigations and compiling preliminary information on all marriageable males and females in a given locality, the matchmaker was in a position to propose a match, usually to the male's family. He or she also negotiated matters such as the number and types of betrothal gifts (*pinli*) and the amount of betrothal money (*pinjin*) the groom's family would give to the bride's if the marriage deliberations went past the initial stages. The family of the bride, for its part, had to decide on the proper dowry and trousseau (*jiazhuang*) to send along at the time of transfer for exhibition at the groom's home. All these calculations were of tremendous importance to the prestige and material interests of each of the families concerned.[41]

Another universal feature of major-marriage ritual, and often a feature of other marriage arrangements as well, was the use of divination, including the frequent consultation of the ancestors by means of moonblocks. A Chinese marriage was literally "made in Heaven," and therefore the eight characters that marked the time of birth for the bride and groom had to be compatible. Ancestors were consulted at various points in the elaborate marriage process to assure their approval of the match, and diviners chose auspicious days for various ritual acts connected with the marriage. Almanacs also provided guidance on the proper times to undertake various marriage-related rituals.[42]

The stages of the marriage ritual were conventionally designated the "six rites" (*liuli*), although in Qing times certain steps in the process often merged into others.[43] The ceremonies were full of elaborate symbolism, either positive or protective. Red—the color of happiness and good fortune—was prominent in dress and decorations, including candles and lanterns, which were used even in the daytime. Firecrackers served as purifiers and signs of joy, and charms were often employed to provide additional protection for the bride. Food played an important role at various stages of the marriage ritual (as it did in most other aspects of Chinese ritual life), in the form of symbolic gifts, offerings, and ceremonial meals. "Longevity noodles," fruits, and other food items denoted marital harmony, happiness, and prosperity. Presents such as paired geese symbolized marital fidelity, and felicitous inscriptions of various sorts appeared everywhere.[44]

The first of the standard six rites was the selection of the match (*nacai*), engi-neered by the go-between after consultation with the families involved. In this and most other matters, the family of the groom normally took the initiative on advice from the matchmaker. The next step was the formal exchange of astrological infor-mation on the bride and groom (*wenming*). The third stage, called *naji,* required the ritual test of the match by means of divination. Fortune-tellers were usually em-ployed, but often the ancestors and other spirits might also be consulted. The fourth and crucial step was the betrothal (*nazheng*), for acceptance of the betrothal gifts (of-ten termed the "bride price") by the family of the bride sealed the match. Elaborate ceremonies accompanied the transfer of gifts, which were dictated by rank at the higher levels of society. Again, ancestral sacrifices usually accompanied these ceremo-nies. The fifth stage, *qingji,* involved the selection of propitious times for the transfer of the bride and related ritual activities. Here, decisions might rest with fortune-tell-ers or other sources of supernatural authority, including temple oracles.[45]

The transfer, known as "welcoming the bride" (*qinying*), was the final stage of the formal process. On the day preceding this ceremony, the groom was supposed to be "capped" and given an adult name and the bride's hair was put up in ritual fashion. Meanwhile, the groom's family had arranged to send the brightly decorated wedding chair to the wife's home, and the wife's family had her trousseau sent to his. On the day of the transfer, the bride paid solemn obeisance to her parents and ancestors, re-ceived a brief lecture on her wifely duties, and entered the gaudy red sedan chair that would take her on a noisy, ostentatious, and circuitous journey to her husband's home (see Figure 10.4). There, the bride performed various acts designed to show subservience to her husband and his family, and for the first time, perhaps—at least in many elite matches—the bride and groom actually saw each other's faces. After these ceremonies, the bridal pair reverently worshipped tablets representing Heaven and Earth, the ancestors of the groom, and the major household deities of the groom's family, especially the God of the Hearth. These activities highlighted the cosmological and familial dimensions of the match.

The transfer was, of course, marked by a banquet that, like the wedding proces-sion and display of dowry and trousseau, might well be a measure of family financial status. Often, however, the guests contributed shares (*fenzi*) to help defray costs. Lo-cal custom dictated whether the bride's family would be invited to the transfer feast, but at some point in almost all major marriages, the bride's parents were treated to a banquet and given additional gifts.[46]

When the bride visited her parents after the formal transfer, she generally did so as a guest, not as kin. Although still emotionally tied to her parents and relatives, she was now by law and custom a full-fledged member of her husband's family and bound to devote far more ritual attention to that family than to her natal family.[47] It was a difficult existence, especially at first. Except in the case of minor or matrilocal marriages, the new bride found herself in a house full of virtual strangers. In this en-vironment, the mother-in-law wielded tremendous power over her daughter-in-law, since a filial son was bound to respect his mother's wishes. Mothers were sometimes

Figure 10.4   Wedding Processions. Top: *A late Qing photograph. Photo courtesy of the Peabody & Essex Museum, Salem, Mass.* Left: *A line drawing by a Japanese visitor to China in the late eighteenth century. Source: Nakagawa (1800).*

known to force sons to divorce their wives. Small wonder then, that in the period preceding the marriage transfer, brides often wept and sang sad songs together with their friends and family.[48]

There were seven grounds for divorce in traditional China: (1) lack of offspring, (2) adultery, (3) jealousy, (4) thievery, (5) disobedience to the husband's parents, (6) incurable disease, and (7) being too talkative. In principle, a husband could not be divorced by his wife, but this was not the main reason that divorce was comparatively rare in Qing times. In the first place, there were three circumstances under which a woman could not be divorced (except in the case of adultery): (1) if she had mourned as a daughter for her husband's deceased parents, (2) if she had no family to go to, or (3) if her husband had been poor when they were married and was now rich. Often one or more of these conditions prevailed. In addition, the perennial glut of men looking for wives made the task of acquiring another virgin bride rather difficult, especially if the grounds for an earlier divorce were not very substantial. Further, to at least a degree the interests of the wife were protected by her biological parents and former kinsmen, since marriage was a family affair. Nonetheless, we know that many women found married life intolerable and either ran away or committed suicide. Others, under rather special circumstances, made a conscious choice never to marry.[49]

Aside from the self-perpetuating tyranny of the mother-in-law, another common frustration for Chinese wives, at least in elite families, was the introduction of concubines. Unlike principal spouses, concubines were usually chosen by the husband rather than his parents, and often they were selected for their beauty or their artistic, literary, and musical talents rather than for their moral character or family connections. Although ostensibly brought into the household for the purpose of producing sons to assure continuation of the line, concubines often served as little more than symbols of elite conspicuous consumption. Despite their social inferiority to the principal wife, they were often the primary object of the husband's sexual attention and thus a potential source of jealousy.[50]

We should not assume, however, that arranged marriages were devoid of romance. There is abundant evidence to indicate that in the Qing, as in earlier periods of Chinese history, love often grew out of arranged marriages. In some instances, husbands refused to remarry or committed suicide upon the death of their wives.[51] Such actions on the part of women were more problematical, however. As already indicated, devotion to one's husband after his death was not only encouraged by neo-Confucianism but also ritually rewarded by the state. The Qing government regularly honored women who refused to remarry by bestowing testimonial plaques on their families, and even by financing the construction of memorial arches and temples to them. The state also celebrated the actions of brides who committed suicide upon the death of their husbands, although at times both the Kangxi and Yongzheng emperors objected to this practice.[52] Thus, powerful social pressures that had nothing to do with conjugal love or mutual affection might influence a wife's decision to honor her husband's memory.

Nevertheless, there was great countervailing pressure on widows to remarry. For all the orthodox emphasis on women remaining "faithful" to their deceased husbands, many families did not want to provide financial support for the women who returned to them. Some, in effect, callously auctioned their youthful widowed daughters off to the highest bidder. In poor families, the economics of survival, coupled with high mortality rates, often made remarriage a necessity. Demographic data suggest that many women who were widowed before the age of thirty did, in fact, remarry, and that "chaste wives" (*jiefu*), widowed early in life and honored with plaques, arches, and official biographies, "were clearly a small minority of all widowed women."[53]

Chinese sexual life is seldom discussed but certainly important to an understanding of traditional Chinese culture. The pioneering research of R. H. Van Gulik indicates that the Chinese have long had a remarkably "healthy" attitude toward sex. Despite the rigid standards of Confucian propriety—which went so far as to condemn a husband and wife for accidentally touching hands in public (and which naturally eliminated the possibility of a Chinese tradition of social dancing)—Van Gulik argues that on the whole sexual life in traditional China was full, rich, and relatively free from the prejudices and "perversions" of the West.[54]

The Chinese drew a sharp distinction between inner (*nei*) and outer (*wai*), between what was public and what was private. In public, men were unquestionably superior to their wives, who were expected to be passive, submissive, and satisfied with few rights and privileges. In the privacy of the bedchamber, however, women often seem to have enjoyed relative sexual equality. One of the female characters in Li Yu's popular novel *Carnal Prayer Mat* articulates the idea of a woman's "sexual rights" within the framework of orthodox Confucian values (and Buddhist concepts of reincarnation):

> We behaved improperly in our previous existence and now, having been born female, we must spend all our lives in the women's quarters. Unlike men, we can't go out sightseeing or visiting friends. Sex is the one diversion we have in our lives. Surely we can't be forbidden to enjoy that! Still, we are created by Heaven and Earth for marriage, and matched with a husband by our parents; naturally it is right and proper for us to enjoy ourselves with him. ... [If] a woman does not have sex, fine, but if she is going to have sex, she should at least see that she suits herself.[55]

Detailed handbooks on sex (*fangshu*), dating from at least the Han dynasty, demonstrate a long-standing concern on the part of Chinese men with techniques explicitly designed to satisfy the sexual needs of women. Chinese erotic novels do the same. Even the popular medical tracts of late imperial times seem to have encouraged the sexual satisfaction of women—at least insofar as the aim of intercourse was to produce male children. These works emphasize that female orgasm is essential to fertility and that the gender of a child is determined by the party who had an orgasm last. Although men may simply have had their own reproductive or medical interests in mind, at least some of their beliefs worked to the sexual advantage of women.[56]

As is well known, the bound foot was an object of great erotic appeal for men in traditional China, and even women took pride in their tiny "golden lilies."[57] Historically, footbinding began in the Tang-Song period as an ironic outgrowth of the practice of wrapping the feet of dancers with colorful ribbons. During the Yuan dynasty it gradually spread from North China to the South, where it took hold primarily among the upper classes. By Qing times, the crippling practice had become widespread not only among the Chinese gentry class but also among commoners, who sought the social status footbinding implied. Even the Manchus succumbed in a sense to the fashion by wearing small attachments on the bottoms of their shoes to give the appearance of bound feet. Although footbinding was a painful process, its appeal was neither sadistic nor masochistic. Rather, it was justified as a means of keeping women at home and was admired by men for the style of walking it produced and the supposed effect this style of walking had on female sexual performance. Many passages in Chinese erotic literature dwell on the shape and mystery of the bound foot.[58]

Beyond the psychology of sexual attraction was the idea of sex as a form of physical therapy. This notion can be traced back for centuries in China. The principles were essentially the same as those of Daoist alchemy and traditional Chinese medicine. Harmony between interacting *yin* (female) and *yang* (male) influences brought physical well-being and longevity. Normally, the two essences nourished one another, except in the case of male intercourse with older women, which was commonly thought to take away *yang* essence without benefit to the man. Undoubtedly this was one reason for the traditional preference among Chinese men for youthful wives and concubines. The *Record of Ritual* stipulates, however, that men should have regular intercourse with their wives even after the latter had reached an advanced age.[59] Homosexuality was frowned upon by the state—particularly in Qing times—but widely tolerated, perhaps in part because of the long tradition of gender segregation in China and the medical/sexual assumption that the exchange of the same "essence" entailed no net loss.[60]

The Chinese obsession with good health and longevity can be seen not only in sexual practices and related therapeutic techniques but also in popular proverbs, religion, ritual symbolism, art, and literature. All traditional Chinese medical remedies—from acupuncture and acupressure to moxibustion and herbal medicine—had as their therapeutic goal the restoration of *yinyang* balance in the body.[61] Doctors were generally held in low esteem during Qing times, but the period still boasted a number of famous and able practitioners, including individuals such as Ye Gui (1666–1745) and Xu Dachun (1693–1771).[62] An extraordinary amount of attention is devoted to the section on medicine in the *TSJC*—520 *juan*—more than any other single section in the encyclopedia. Yet for all this concern with health and medicine, average life expectancy was probably not much over thirty, even in the best of times.[63] For this reason among others, the last two stages of life—middle age and old age—were times of special significance and cause for great celebration.

For most members of the Chinese elite, middle age, lasting from about forty to fifty-five, brought many satisfactions: career success, material security, and grandchildren. By the end of this period, the majority of wives had escaped domination by their mothers-in-law, only to become domineering mothers-in-law themselves. Middle age for the lower classes of Chinese society may have been somewhat less satisfying than for the elite, but a bit of property and a male heir probably provided a sufficient sense of accomplishment and security for aging commoners.[64]

Old age elicited respect and esteem from all sectors of Chinese society. Village elders in rural areas often wielded substantial power, and, as mentioned in Chapter 4, some were officially recognized as longevous commoners or longevous officials. The state-sponsored community drinking ritual known as *xiangyin jiu,* although not always regularly or properly performed, also provided a means of officially acknowledging and rewarding old age. According to statute, the ritual was supposed to be performed twice a year in various districts and departments of each province. The master of ceremonies opened the meeting of elderly guests with the expressed hope that as a result of the ritual, "seniors and juniors will maintain proper order among themselves, and elder brothers will be friendly while younger ones [will be] deferential." After the hosts and guests had emptied their first glass of wine, a local scholar would state: "The object of *xiangyin jiu* is to show proper respect for the aged and consideration for the virtuous, and to keep away the unrighteous and the perverse. Persons of advanced age and outstanding virtue are to occupy seats of honor, and others are to have places proper to their ages." Although this ceremony did not always appeal to the local scholarly elite, it was certainly tempting to "obscure townsmen and villagers who aspired to local eminence."[65]

At home, the elderly were pampered and accorded maximum deference. As the *Dream of the Red Chamber* indicates, older women often enjoyed substantial power within the family, despite the pervasive notion of the "three types of womanly dependence"—on father, husband, and son. Major birthday celebrations for men and women usually began about age fifty or so. From this point onward, such celebrations increased in size and significance, especially upon the beginning of each new decade. The sixtieth birthday held special meaning, since it marked the completion of one full sexagenary cycle (see Chapter 6).[66] Naturally enough, the concrete symbolism of birthday ceremonies centered on longevity: longevity candles, the longevity star, longevity noodles, longevity peaches or peach cakes, and the stylized character *shou* (longevity). Ancestral sacrifices were often closely associated with birthday celebrations.[67]

Longevity was also a prominent theme in funeral ceremonies. Grave clothes were designated longevity clothes, the coffin was composed of longevity boards, and the principal mourner ate longevity noodles. A "longevity portrait" of the deceased might also be displayed near the coffin, serving as an object of worship. As with the use of the auspicious color red in funerals for all that was not white (the color of mourning), the self-conscious employment of the term "longevity" in the midst of death underscores the themes of "fear-propitiation and hope supplication" that ran through so much of traditional Chinese religious life.[68]

AMUSEMENTS

Human affairs in China were not always full of fear and uncertainty. There was plenty of time for recreation, ranging from simple domestic games to huge community festivals. And despite the endless variety of Chinese amusements, certain patterns of play seem typical of China as a whole. Many of these reflect elite values and preoccupations. The general lack of physically demanding sports, for instance, can be attributed both to a concern for maintaining proper decorum and to a real fear of harming the body—an unfilial act, since the physical self was a gift of the ancestors.[69]

Nevertheless, public exhibitions of acrobatics and martial arts (*wushu*) were quite popular. Like the tradition of knight-errant literature, these performances may have provided a form of vicarious release for this predominantly civil-oriented, nonmilitary culture (*wubing di wenhua*). To be sure, even within the scholarly elite some individuals gravitated to various types of boxing and fencing as a means of cultivating their "vital force" (*qi*). Like the graceful and therapeutic posturing known as *taiji quan,* these more vigorous martial arts were predicated on the principle of *yinyang* harmonization of body and mind. But the people who displayed their strength and swordsmanship in public places were almost invariably of low social status, more likely to be linked with secret societies than with the literati class.[70]

Perhaps the Chinese preference for individual competition over team games reflects a form of recreational escape from the constraints of conventional society, since so much of Chinese social life demanded subordination of the self to the larger group and placed no real premium on individualism. The popularity of raucous festivals and risqué dramatic performances, as well as the widespread practice of teasing the bride and groom after the wedding transfer (*nao xinfang*), also suggests the periodic need to break loose, even if only temporarily, from the rigid constraints of Confucian propriety and social control.[71]

Aside from a general reluctance to engage in roughhouse and team play, there is little remarkable about most traditional Chinese games. Chinese youths ran; skipped; threw rocks; pitched coins; played with balls, shuttlecocks, tops, dolls, and other toys; kept pets (fish, birds, rabbits, kittens, etc.); and so forth. Older children and adults enjoyed watching activities such as rooster or cricket fights, and men frequented bath houses. Gambling of all kinds—from cards and dice to *majiang* (mahjong)—was popular, although often outlawed. More refined pastimes, all nature oriented, included the enjoyment of gardens, leisurely strolls (often with a caged bird), boating, swinging, and flying kites.[72] Recreational activities for women were restricted somewhat by social isolation and the practice of footbinding; but in many gentry households the women received a satisfying education in poetry and the arts (see Chapters 8 and 9). In these households, as *Dream of the Red Chamber* indicates,

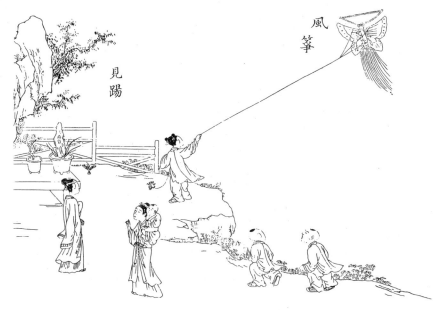

Figure 10.5   Amusements (A). Kite Flying. Source: Nakagawa (1800).

both men and women spent much of their leisure time on refinements such as the so-called Four Noble Recreations—calligraphy, painting, playing the *qin* ("lute" or "zither"), and playing *weiqi* (a popular board game) (see Figures 10.5–10.7).

Since painting and calligraphy have already been discussed at length, only the latter two recreations need be described here. The *qin* had a long and distinguished pedigree in China. For more than two thousand years it stood as the most revered Chinese musical instrument; it was celebrated in verse and inextricably linked with both friendship and moral cultivation. The term *qin* came to be associated etymologically with the similar-sounding word *jin* (to prohibit) because the instrument was believed to check evil passions; it also served as a general metaphor for marital happiness and social harmony. The rounded top and flat bottom of the *qin* symbolized the unity of Heaven and Earth, and its melodies, which pleased the ear and soothed the mind, were often descriptive of nature.

Originally composed of five strings and later of seven, the *qin* paralleled in its development the musical evolution of tone scales in Zhou times from five to seven (and eventually nine). Difficult to play and capable of many strikingly beautiful nuances, the *qin* illustrates the tremendous value attached to rhythm in classical Chinese music, the emphasis on melody rather than harmony, and the close connection between instrumental music and Chinese speech. The *qin* was, however, only one of many sophisticated musical instruments employed for ritual or recreational purposes in traditional China. The occasions ranged from grand public ceremonies and religious sacrifices to marriages, funerals, festivals, and simple domestic gatherings. S. W.

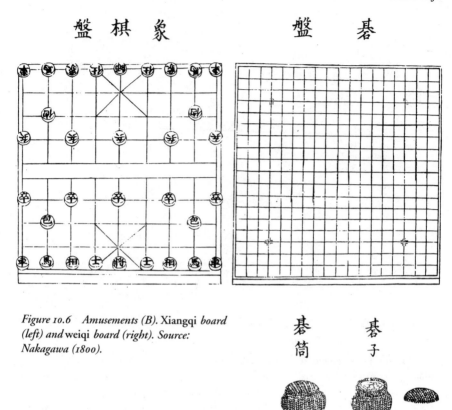

盤棋象   盤碁

Figure 10.6   Amusements (B). Xiangqi *board
(left) and* weiqi *board (right). Source:
Nakagawa (1800).*

碁   碁
筒   子

Williams observed in the nineteenth century that no people on earth made more use
of music than the Chinese.[73]

   Weiqi, known as *go* in Japanese, was (and is) played on a board with nineteen vertical and nineteen horizontal lines intersecting to form 361 tactical positions. It remained a favorite pastime of Chinese generals, statesmen, and literati from early Han
times through the Qing. Each player had about 180 men or pieces. The object of the
game was to control territory and capture, or "kill," enemy men. At first glance one
might wonder why *weiqi* was included as one of the four noble recreations of a Confucian gentleman. Painting, calligraphy, and music were, after all, aesthetically satisfying and morally uplifting, while *weiqi* was war on a game board, attack and defense, killing and capture.

   In part, the appeal of *weiqi* can be explained by the Confucian scholar's yearning
for identification with ancient China's martial heritage and with the lost tradition of
the feudal knight. But another explanation can be found in the structure and assumptions of the game itself. In the first place, like the Chinese scholar, the game of

Figure 10.7 Amusements (C). Men's Bathhouse. Source: Nakagawa (1800).

weiqi valued both intellect and intuition. Second, in *weiqi,* victory and defeat were relative, not absolute. "Victory" was based on the number of intersections dominated at the end of the game, but "defeat" was never total; a player could always save face. Furthermore, the style of play involved dispersed, yet related, nongeometric configurations rather than a single decisive tactical engagement. This emphasis on a total pattern of seemingly aimless interrelationships has been described as an "efficient, almost aesthetic, balance of forces."[74] As a creative form of competition, *weiqi* undoubtedly held much the same artistic attraction as a landscape painting, garden, poem, musical composition, or even a good novel.

Other board games were also popular in Qing times. One of these, *xiangqi,* resembled Western chess in its basic structure. Reputedly invented by King Wu of the Zhou, *xiangqi* had enduring appeal to scholars and commoners alike in China. A more recent game, *shengguan tu* (lit., advancing in officialdom), enjoyed less popularity but it is more revealing from a cultural standpoint. Leon Stover has perceptively contrasted it with the famous Parker Brothers' game Monopoly, observing that the point of the latter is the control of property and services to gain wealth, while the object of the former is to acquire rank and prestige in order to achieve financial advantage. The *shengguan tu* game board approximates the opportunity structure of the Qing bureaucratic hierarchy, with sixty-six squares for positions ranging from lowly student to grand councillor. The higher a player climbs on the official ladder (by throws of the dice), the more money can be collected from those below him. Just as

Monopoly reflects certain fundamental features of American capitalist society, so *shengguan tu* reflects traditional Chinese bureaucratic society.[75]

Social intercourse in Qing China was almost invariably a status game, played out at all levels of society. In elite circles, extraordinary attention was paid to matters of dress, salutation, demeanor, conversation, written communications (including invitations and responses), the giving of gifts, seating arrangements, food, and so forth. Figure 10.8, for example, illustrates some of the gestures of respect that were required on different occasions. Novels such as *Flowers in the Mirror* devote an enormous amount of space to discussions of ritually correct behavior, prompting Mark Elvin to observe, "It is close to impossible for a reader who has not spent years of self-induction into premodern ways of [Chinese] thought to share ... [a concern] for the almost countless specific details [of ritual and ceremony in works of this sort]."[76]

The vocabulary of Chinese social relations, like that of kinship and family protocol, was extraordinarily complex, with social distinctions that would not even occur to most non-Chinese. On formal occasions, the guest of honor always sat on the left (*yang*) side of the host, and his actions dictated the responses of the other guests. At the lower levels of society, and in relatively informal circumstances, less explicit attention was paid to status distinctions, but the distinctions were seldom forgotten. An astute mid-nineteenth century Western observer remarked, for example, "When a number of individuals are walking together, you may generally infer their age or rank or position by the order in which they naturally and almost unconsciously range themselves."[77]

Many other long-time Western residents in late Qing China have commented on the careful attention given to etiquette in all facets of Chinese social intercourse. J. H. Gray informs us that "A Chinese is seldom at a loss to know what polite observances must regulate his behaviour. Etiquette is an essential part of his education." R. F. Johnston's observations are worth quoting at length:

> [Chinese] rules of ceremony may seem, from the foreigner's point of view, too stiff and artificial, or exasperating in their pedantic minuteness. The European is inclined to laugh at social laws which indicate with preciseness when and how a mourner should wail at a funeral, what expressions a man must use when paying visits of condolence or congratulation, what clothes must be worn on different occasions, how a visitor must be greeted, how farewells are to be said, how modes of salutation are to be differentiated, and how chairs are to be sat on. ... [These] rules of Chinese etiquette may be stiff, but there is no stiffness about the Chinese gentleman—or about the illiterate Chinese peasant—when he is acting in accordance with these rules.[78]

Chinese social ritual may often have been restrictive, but to most Qing subjects it was also probably reassuring.

Food had enormous social importance in traditional China. Although in all societies food is used to create and maintain interpersonal bonds, the Chinese employed it in a particularly sophisticated way as "a marker and communicator in social

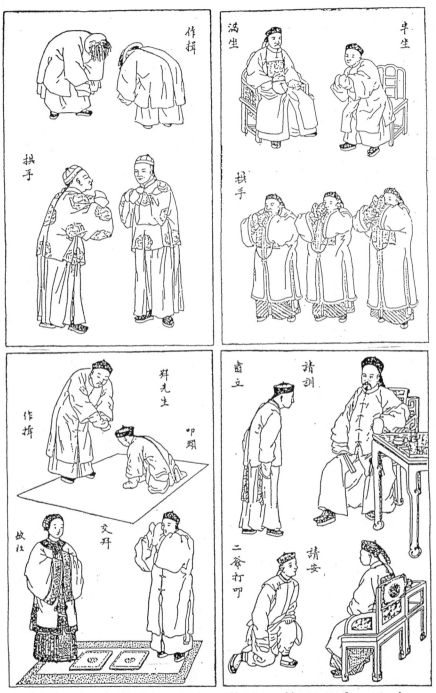

Figure 10.8   Gestures of Respect. Various forms of bowing and kowtowing from a ritual handbook. These gestures represent only a fraction of the ceremonial forms appropriate to different situations and social classes. Source: Kiong [Gong Guyu] (1906).

transactions." The bigoted but otherwise observant missionary, Arthur Smith, wrote just before the turn of the century, "If there is anything which the Chinese have reduced to an exact science, it is the business of eating." Elaborate meals were required of all major social occasions, just as sacrificial dishes were essential to the proper performance of all major forms of religious ritual.[79]

The social significance of food in China can be measured in a variety of ways. As is often noted, a common greeting in traditional China was "Have you eaten?" Food was always a fit topic for genteel conversation, as well as the subject of personal correspondence, poetry, and classical prose. A number of famous Qing scholars wrote essays on food, and much information on it appears in local gazetteers, government documents, and encyclopedias such as the *TSJC.* Vernacular literature abounds with descriptions of food, and writers such as Li Yu, Wu Jingzi, and Cao Xueqin masterfully use food motifs to describe characters, to develop or define social situations, and even to link subplots within their works. *Dream of the Red Chamber* is especially noteworthy for its elaborate descriptions of food and feasts.[80]

Food was always a good index of status in Chinese society for both gods and humans. Qing statutes specified in great detail the type, amount, and style of food for official sacrifices, just as local custom dictated the requirements for popular offerings to gods, ghosts, and ancestors. Similarly, in the human world, official regulations and popular practice indicated the proper kinds and amounts of dishes appropriate to persons of different rank and station, from the emperor down to commoners. Many Qing emperors had quite simple preferences, but, as Jonathan Spence reminds us, "the personal tastes of the emperor had little to do with the scale of culinary operations or their costs. The regulations were firm about the exact content of all major meals, which were carefully graded in accordance with their level of ritual significance."[81]

On formal occasions at the lower levels of elite society, the type and number of dishes had to be pegged to the status of the participants and the importance of the meal. Clan rules sometimes specified the number of dishes to be offered by lineage members to guests, but most commoners could not indulge in formal and elaborate meals except on special ritual occasions such as births, marriages, and funerals. *Dream of the Red Chamber* provides several indications of the gap between the eating habits of commoners and those of the elite. In discussing the price of certain dishes for a relatively small gentry party, Liu Laolao, an old countrywoman, exclaims, "It couldn't have cost less than twenty taels in all. Bless and save us! That'd keep a farmer and his family for a year." And so it might have in the early or mid-eighteenth century. Naturally enough, most peasant fare was simple and monotonous, but it was still prepared with special care. In the words of a Scottish sojourner to China in the 1850s, "The poorest classes in China seem to understand the art of preparing their food much better than the same classes at home."[82]

Despite the sharp difference between rich and poor in eating habits and the existence of a plethora of regional cooking styles, Chinese attitudes toward food were remarkably similar. The most fundamental distinction was between grains and other starches (*fan*) and vegetable or meat dishes (*cai*). A proper balance between the two was deemed necessary to a good meal—although fragrance, flavor, color, and texture also had to be harmoniously blended. *Fan* was primary; *cai* secondary. This concern with balance had a classical foundation. The *Record of Ritual* states: "In feasting and at the vernal sacrifice in the ancestral temple they had music; but in feeding the aged and at the autumnal sacrifice they had no music: these were based on the *yin* and *yang*. All drinking serves to nourish the *yang*; all eating to nourish the *yin*. ... The number of *ding* and *zu* [vessels] was odd [*yang*], and that of [the vessels] *bian* and *dou* was even [*yin*]."[83]

Foods and cooking styles were usually designated *yin* or *yang*, cold or hot, "civil" or "military." Given the holistic approach of the Chinese to good health, we should not be surprised to find that eating certain foods affected the balance of *yin* and *yang* in the body. A sore on the skin or an inexplicable fever, for example, might be blamed on overeating "hot" foods (oily, fried, or peppery items, fatty meat, and oily plants), while "cold" foods (water plants, crustaceans, and certain beans) could be blamed for producing or exacerbating a common cold. Complicating matters was the classification of Chinese food according to the five flavors—sweet, sour, bitter, pungent, and salty—which were, in turn, correlated with the five viscera, the five elements, the five seasons, and so forth. As with other aspects of traditional Chinese medicine, the variables were nearly infinite.[84]

Tea had both medicinal and gastronomical appeal. During the Qing dynasty it was no longer associated with the elaborate social ritual of the Tang period, but teahouses were very popular centers of recreation for males, and a number of individuals considered themselves connoisseurs of the national beverage. Most of the best teas were grown in South China, and although certain types were believed to be especially valuable in digesting some types of foods and ameliorating certain kinds of physical distress, the principal medical benefit of tea seems to have been the fact that it was made with boiling (and therefore sterile) water.[85]

Some alcoholic beverages had explicitly medicinal purposes, but most were valued primarily as social lubricants and closely associated with the joys of good food, friendship, and the composition of verse. The Chinese did not distinguish between true wines and starch-based spirits—both were designated *jiu*. As with tea, there were many different varieties of *jiu*, most of which were identified with locations in South China. The amount of alcohol might vary from as little as 10 percent (20 proof) to as much as 80 percent (160 proof) in these beverages, and although moderation was encouraged in drinking as well as in eating, the Chinese periodically threw caution to the wind. Drinking games were extremely popular at parties, and many members of the elite belonged to drinking clubs. The poet You Huai (1616–1696) describes drinking marathons that went on in the brothel quarter of Nanjing until "all the guests vomited and fell asleep on the ground"; but even in more refined circumstances there were numerous instances of heavy drinking by members of the elite. The lower classes of Chinese society do not seem to have acquired a special fondness for liquor, but they did prove susceptible to the curse of opium in the late eighteenth and early nineteenth centuries.[86]

Parties in traditional China often involved entertainment other than eating and drinking, composing verse, or cavorting with prostitutes. Among the elite, exhibitions of singing and dancing were popular, as were dramatic performances. Plays proved particularly appealing to the women of elite households, as we can see from a reading of *Dream of the Red Chamber*. Performances also might be staged for family and friends on festive occasions such as marriages, birthdays for the elderly, or examination successes. Apparently, the actors engaged by individual households did not always know what play they would be performing until a request was made by an honored guest. The troupe thus had to have a repertoire of several dozen plays, and some groups were known to have command of nearly a hundred.[87]

Plays were also staged in villages and towns. These performances might be sponsored by the whole community through subscription, by a segment of that community such as merchants, by a local temple, or by a private individual. In contrast to the more frequent dramatic performances of major cities, community plays were usually associated with periodic religious fairs or local festivals, which brought families and friends together for a few days of colorful and exciting entertainment, punctuated by noise and the smell of burning firecrackers and incense. Temples often sponsored plays, since they were one of the few places in traditional China that were well equipped to stage them. These performances were often held on the "birthday" of the temple's major deity and intended explicitly for the entertainment of that deity. Sacrifices usually attended the dramatic event. As Barbara Ward, David Johnson, and others have emphasized, the cumulative impact of such plays exerted a powerful influence in "the dissemination and standardization of [Chinese] culture, particularly in the sphere of ideas and values."[88]

Like local fairs and community celebrations, pilgrimages proved to be extremely popular in Qing China. The Chinese term for this sort of activity is *chaoshan jinxiang*, literally, to pay respects to a mountain. Most pilgrimage sites were located in mountainous regions, and most pilgrimages involved making contact with a resident deity enshrined in a mountain temple. Pilgrims came from all social classes. In the words of Susan Naquin and Chün-fang Yü, "Differentiated literati, imperial, clerical, and lay traditions existed together with a continuously growing set of shrines to a variety of local, regional, and national deities." With increasing ease of travel and greater political and economic integration, pilgrimage flourished in Qing times. In many parts of China, associations developed that "promoted these journeys and cared for the growing numbers of pilgrims."[89]

Countrywide annual festivals, always highlighted in popular almanacs and liturgical calendars, played an especially important role in unifying traditional Chinese culture. Almost every month a major festival occurred throughout the land, touching all classes of Chinese society directly and even cutting across ethnic lines. Many were occasions of official sacrifices, and most involved domestic ancestral sacrifices and visits to temples. Like local festivals, these national celebrations were marked by feasts and firecrackers, dramatic performances and music, fun and games. Unfortunately, the brief descriptions below convey very little of the color and pageantry surrounding such occasions.[90]

The most important annual festival in traditional China was the month-long celebration of the New Year (*yuandan*). This observance began in the twelfth lunar month. On about the twentieth day, Qing officials at every level commenced the ritual of "sealing the seals" of their yamens, in effect closing down government for a total of about four weeks. This action paralleled the shutdown of most commercial establishments during the same period. A week or so before the turn of the year, households throughout the country paid obeisance to the God of the Hearth, who, according to popular belief, ascended to Heaven to report on the family's activities during the past year to the Jade Emperor. This ceremony was taken seriously but often celebrated lightly, with sweet substances smeared on the mouth of the god's image to ensure a favorable report.

On New Year's eve, the family again sacrificed to the God of the Hearth, as well as to other household deities, and, of course, the ancestors. These ceremonies paralleled aspects of marriage ritual in symbolic significance. A family feast reaffirmed kinship ties, and the ritual of paying respect to the heads of the household in order of precedence through bowing and kowtowing served as a vivid reminder of status relationships within the family. The next day—brought in with fireworks, incense, and bursts of color—entailed visits in proper dress to friends, neighbors, relations, and superiors; gift-giving; and general merriment. Auspicious "spring couplets," written by local calligraphers on red paper, adorned residences and other buildings, bringing blessings and prosperity to families and businesses for the coming year.

The first two weeks of the New Year were devoted to various amusements, celebrations, and religious sacrifices. Ancestors and domestic gods were usually worshipped again, along with deities such as the popular God of Wealth. Officials throughout the country welcomed spring (*yingchun*) in elaborate public ceremonies designed to indicate, through the symbolism of color, what the agricultural prospects were for the coming year and to assure the best results under the circumstances. The Lantern Festival (*dengjie*) on the fifteenth day of the first month marked the end of the New Year's celebration. It was a happy time, devoted largely to the display of colorful lanterns in homes and businesses and to the entertainment of women and children. About a week later, Qing officials "opened their seals" and resumed government business.

The next major festival, Qingming (lit., Pure and Bright), took place in the third month, 106 days after the winter solstice. It was one of three important "ghost festivals" (*guijie*) in traditional China. Qingming was a time of family reunion, celebration, and devoted ancestor worship—including the sweeping of graves and offerings of food for the dead. Large-scale lineage sacrifices might also take place at this time. The *Chinese Repository* of 1832 carried an absorbing account of one such sacrifice, involving more than two thousand clan members. The prayer offered at the tomb of the founding father, taken directly from a famous ritual handbook, illustrates the purposes of the ceremony:

> Revolving years have brought again the season of Spring. Cherishing sentiments of veneration, I look up and sweep your tomb. Prostrate, I pray that you will come and be present; that you will grant to your posterity that they may be prosperous and illustrious; at this season of genial showers and gentle breezes, I desire to recompense the root of my existence, and exert myself sincerely. Always grant your safe protection. My trust is in your divine spirit. Reverently I present the fivefold sacrifice of a pig, a chicken, a duck, a goose, and a fish; also an offering of five plates of fruit; with oblations of spirituous liquors; earnestly entreating that you will come and view them.[91]

The elaborate ceremonies concluded with a massive feast in which the sacrificial foods were shared by the participants in time-honored fashion. Although most Qingming devotions were far more personal and casual than this one, all had the effect of establishing a close bond between the living and the dead.

The so-called Dragon Boat Festival (*duanyang jie,* lit., Festival of the Upright Sun) took place early in the fifth month. Although celebrated countrywide, it was especially popular in South China, where colorful and exciting boat races took place on rivers and lakes. These races, and the festival generally, commemorated the death by drowning of the famous but ill-fated Zhou dynasty scholar and poet Qu Yuan, who committed suicide in despair after losing the favor of his ruler through slander. Although a joyous occasion, the Dragon Boat Festival was surrounded by rituals designed to protect the population from evil and unhealthy influences that were believed to be especially prevalent in the fifth month. A late Ming account of the festival in Qu Yuan's home province of Hunan states:

> The current popular belief is that the boat race is held to avert misfortunes. At the end of the race, the boats carry sacrificial animals, wine, and paper coins and row straight downstream, where the animals and wine are cast into the water, the paper coins are burned, and spells are recited. The purpose of these acts is to make pestilence and premature death flow away with the water.[92]

On the seventh day of the seventh month unmarried Chinese women celebrated the Double Seventh Festival. This was "a central event in women's culture [that cut] across class boundaries throughout China." It commemorated the one time during the year when the ill-fated Weaving Maiden (Zhinü) of Chinese mythology could join her husband, the Herdsman, across the Milky Way. A play based on the Zhinü legend was usually performed, and young women made offerings to the patron deity of needlework. Preparations for the festival naturally involved sewing and embroidering. Since the Double Seventh was considered a particularly propitious day to look into the future, young girls tried to predict, through a lighthearted form of divination called "dropping the needle," whether they would be dexterous or clumsy in their work. Needle-threading competitions also took place as part of the colorful festivities.[93]

On the fifteenth day of the seventh month, various ceremonies were undertaken to honor the ancestors and placate "hungry ghosts." Graves were swept and ancestral sacrifices performed. The great Buddhist religious service known as All Souls' Day (*yulan hui*) also took place at this time. It involved the reading of sutras by the clergy to "lead those [souls] deeply engulfed in the lower world [across the sea of suffering]." Significantly, the theme of these devotions was the filial piety of a Buddhist disciple, Mu Lian (Maudgalyayana), who offered sacrifices to save his deceased mother from the torments of Hell.[94]

Exactly a month later, the Mid-Autumn Festival (*zhongqiu jie*) occurred. Among the most popular of all Chinese festivals, it involved family gatherings and feasts, the exchange of "mooncakes," offerings to the moon, ancestor worship, and the burning of incense to Heaven and Earth. Like the Lantern Festival, the Mid-Autumn Festival was especially popular with women and children. Men played a marginal role in the ceremonies, since, in the words of a popular Beijing proverb, "Men do not worship the moon, [just as] women do not sacrifice to the God of the Hearth."[95]

The Chongyang (Double *Yang*) Festival on the ninth day of the ninth month was in many parts of the country a relatively minor celebration, with little overt religious significance. It was primarily a day of hill climbing, sight-seeing, kite flying, and feasting. Contemporary Western descriptions of the festival suggest a gala mood, echoed by Chinese accounts: "Reciting poetry and drinking wine, roasting meat and distributing cakes—truly this is a time of joy."[96] In some parts of the country, however, Chongyang was marked by large-scale lineage sacrifices of the sort that occurred during the Qingming festival. Even national celebrations were not carried out with perfect uniformity throughout the country, but the similarities appear far more striking than the differences.

On the first day of the tenth month, Chinese families again worshiped their ancestors in ceremonies paralleling those of the seventh month and the Qingming festival. This celebration was known popularly as the ceremony of Sending Winter Clothes (*song hanyi*). Concern for the well-being of the ancestors was expressed at this time by inscriptions on colored paper garments or plain paper wrappers enclosing "spirit money." It was also in the tenth month that the Qing officials prepared the ritual calendar for the coming year. From this time until the New Year's preparations began in the twelfth month, there were no national festivals of any consequence—only relatively minor celebrations and a few official sacrifices. Perhaps the most widely observed ritual of the period in Chinese households was the preparation of "eighth-day gruel" (*laba zhou*) in the twelfth month, a thanksgiving ceremony designed to show gratitude for good fortune during the year.[97]

Although most Chinese festivals contributed to community solidarity and a shared sense of culture, they were not an unmixed blessing from the standpoint of either Chinese elites or the throne. This was particularly true of local religious festivals, village fairs, and pilgrimages. As crowds gathered in public places to watch entertainers, enjoy food and drink, and do business, men and women mingled more freely, fights sometimes erupted, and social discipline occasionally broke down. Gamblers, thieves, and swindlers naturally exploited the situation.[98] Especially threatening to the government was the possibility that community celebrations would serve as the recruiting grounds for secret societies. An edict of 1724 expresses this fear:

> [A] class of loafers, with neither a livelihood nor an abode, ... has come forth to usurp the name of ... [Buddhism and Daoism] and to corrupt the practical use of the same. The majority of them use [doctrines about] calamities and felicity, misfortune and happiness, to sell their foolish magic and baseless talk. They begin by cheating on goods and money to fatten themselves. Then they proceed to hold meetings for the burning of incense where males and females mingle promiscuously. Farmers and craftsmen forsake their business and trades, and engage ... in talking about miracles. Worst of all, rebellious and subversive individuals and heretical miscreants glide in among them, establish parties and form leagues by taking membership oaths. They assemble at night and disperse in daytime. They thus transgress their proper status and sin against their duty, mislead mankind and deceive the people.[99]

For the most part, the Qing authorities relied upon social pressures and the vast network of nongovernmental organs of local control to maintain or restore order in towns and villages. But penal law remained a powerful weapon in the state's arsenal, to be used with ruthless severity whenever crimes occurred that threatened the Chinese social or political system. Among these crimes, the worst were known as the "Ten Abominations": (1) rebellion against the emperor and his ritual order; (2) subversion or destruction of imperial temples, tombs, or palaces; (3) desertion or treason; (4) parricide (including the murder of a father, mother, uncle, aunt, grandfather, or grandmother); (5) the murder of three or more persons in one family; (6) lack of respect for, or improper use of, the ritual articles and implements of the emperor; (7) unfilial conduct; (8) maltreatment of relatives; (9) insubordination by inferiors toward their superiors; and (10) incest. All of these crimes bore directly on the sanctity of either the family or the state, and all were potentially punishable by death from slicing (*lingchi*)—the most severe form of punishment in the Qing code.[100]

In especially serious cases, punishment went well beyond the perpetrator. The statute on rebellion and high treason, for example, not only stipulated death by slicing for the principal offender but also the decapitation of all males in his household over the age of fifteen (including the offender's father, grandfather, sons, grandsons, brothers, and brothers' sons, as well as his maternal grandfather, father-in-law, and brothers-in-law). Further, the law provided that the rest of the family (all females and all males fifteen years of age and under) would be enslaved in the households of "meritorious ministers." This statute illustrates both the traditional emphasis on ancestral concerns as a deterrent and the pervasive principle of collective responsibility in Chinese society.[101]

Unfortunately, such draconian legal measures did not prevent crimes against the state or crimes within the family. Throughout the Qing period, rebellions repeatedly broke out, despite the harsh treatment received by the leaders of such uprisings and their families. Heterodox ritual specialists found opportunities to usurp the prerogatives of the Qing elite, and secret societies flourished. Moreover, although the state dictated severe penalties for domestic crimes, we know that among the most common cases included in the Qing dynasty's *Xing'an huilan* (Conspectus of Penal Cases) were the killing of a wife's paramour; disobedience to parents or grandparents; incest; and assault by either wives or concubines on husbands, by slaves or servants on masters, or by offspring on parents or grandparents.[102] Clearly, Chinese society was not all harmony and cooperation, even in the best of times.

Yet in all, the fabric of Confucian society wore remarkably well, strengthened by the interwoven strands of religion, law, education, and ritual. For all that divided China, much united it: a centralized system of administration; shared social attitudes and practices; a similar cosmology and world view; a common repository of ethical principles, artistic symbols, historical heroes, and literary myths; a powerful sense of unparalleled cultural development; and a universal pride in simply being "Chinese." It took the combined impact of unprecedented population pressure and Western imperialism in the nineteenth century to begin to tear this traditional garment apart, and even now it has not been completely destroyed.

❧ 11 ❧

Tradition and Modernity,
1860–1993

$\mathcal{T}$he theme of Chinese history during the past century or so has been revolutionary change.[1] Yet in the midst of China's modern transformation we can see the powerful persistence of tradition. From the late nineteenth century to the present, inherited patterns of language and perception, as well as traditional attitudes toward politics, ritual, social organization, ethics, art, and literature, have unquestionably influenced the course and speed of China's modern development. But in what particular ways? The matter is still open to debate. Consider, for example, the ongoing discussion, involving scholars throughout the world, concerning the relationship between Confucianism and modernization.[2] Although a full and systematic analysis of the complex interplay between the past and the present must await further study, this concluding chapter examines at least some of the modern manifestations and modernizing implications of China's rich, cohesive, and tenacious cultural tradition.

THE CHALLENGE OF THE WEST

In his well-known and provocative book on the late Qing reformer Wang Tao (1828–1897), Paul Cohen warns against measuring nineteenth-century China's modernization (meaning primarily technological advancement) by external standards. "Modernization," he maintains, "is not a horse race"; instead, a "much more valid way of measuring change in nineteenth century China is by internal points of reference."[3] Yet one might well argue that a horse race is exactly what modernization is. It involves the notion of competition (usually between nation states) and assumes some kind of external standard of judgment for success. Seen in this light, modernization is a cross-cultural phenomenon, as distinct from reform, which is essentially intracultural. Or, to pursue our racing metaphor, reform pits the horse against the clock (his own "best time"), while modernization stacks the horse up against other horses. In the case of nineteenth-century China, the purse was more than money or pride; it was national survival.[4]

It is true, of course, that this distinction between reform and modernization is somewhat artificial. Even if we define modernization as a special kind of externally motivated, rationally organized, technologically oriented, competitive change, it often bears a close relationship to indigenous reform. The acquisition of Western weapons by Qing officials in the 1860s, for example, was only part of a general reform program that owed its primary inspiration to the demands of the Taiping Rebellion. Qing policymakers recognized that Western guns and ships could be used as foreign policy tools as well as instruments in the suppression of the rebellion, but their priorities were overwhelmingly internal, and the *yongying* armies that used Western weapons and techniques most effectively throughout the nineteenth century developed primarily in response to an internal stimulus, within the framework of Chinese tradition and without significant Western influence.[5]

As indicated in previous chapters, "Chinese tradition" encompassed a great deal, to say the least. The intellectual heritage of Confucianism, for example, ran the gamut in the nineteenth century from the obdurate political and social conservatism of the imperial tutor Woren (d. 1871) to the highly creative synthetic philosophy of the brilliant Cantonese scholar Kang Youwei (1858–1927). Buddhism exerted considerable intellectual influence in late Qing times, and there was always a heterodox strain of millenarian thought that held out the promise of a utopian future, a "great leap" into a new age of social justice. The question facing China in the late Qing period was whether any of these ideologies had the capacity to transform the Middle Kingdom in the modern era, to effect meaningful change in the midst of unprecedented challenges.

On the whole, I am persuaded that the reformist tradition of China's Confucian heritage provided an adequate intellectual foundation for modernization based on Western standards of economic, scientific, and technological development. Certainly it sanctioned the idea of making adjustments to meet changing conditions (*biantong*) and did not prevent loyal Confucian scholar-officials in the nineteenth century from sponsoring the establishment of Western-style arsenals, shipyards, foreign-language schools, educational missions, military and naval academies, railroads and telegraphs, mines, and a wide variety of manufacturing industries. Measured solely against the baseline of China's traditional system, the reforms of the late nineteenth century were in many ways quite impressive, as Cohen, Tom Kennedy, Wang Erh-min, and many others have pointed out.[6]

But these reforms did not take place in a vacuum, and increasingly their impetus came to be external rather than internal. As foreign imperialism loomed ever larger on China's horizons, Qing policymakers could not avoid viewing their accomplishments in terms of foreign progress, including that of Meiji Japan (1868–1912). Western ideas of science, technology, and economic growth, as well as concepts such as nationalism, democracy, egalitarianism, and individualism, began to emerge as alternatives to inherited Chinese attitudes and values. The modernized West (and Japan) became the twentieth-century standard for China's progress in a world dominated by industrialization, imperialism, international competition, and rapid political and social change.[7]

The process by which the West emerged as a modernizing model for East Asia began with the imposition of the notorious "unequal treaties" on China in the period from 1842 to 1860. According to the terms of these treaties, which were imposed by force and not abrogated until 1943, the foreign powers gained the right to establish self-governing treaty-port settlements for Western residence and trade, to have access to the Chinese interior, to operate foreign ships between the treaty ports on the coast and on inland waterways, to promulgate Christianity without obstruction, to limit Chinese customs duties, and to establish formal diplomatic relations at the capital and in treaty-port areas. Westerners enjoyed immunity from Chinese law (extraterritoriality) and other nonreciprocal privileges. The entire structure was held together by the most-favored-nation clause, which brought to all the treaty powers any benefit extracted from the Chinese by one or another of the powers over time.[8]

From 1860 on, the treaty ports became conduits for the transmission of Western influences of all kinds. Foreign merchants, missionaries, diplomats, and military men collected in the port cities, bringing to China new products, ideas, practices, and skills. At the same time, these Western intruders exerted a disruptive influence on Chinese society, threatening the traditional economic system, elite prerogatives, the Chinese world order, and China's security and sovereignty. The treaty ports were both showcases for the modern West and vivid reminders of the challenge of foreign imperialism.

Contact with foreigners in treaty-port areas during the Taiping Rebellion (1850–1864) gave at least a few foresighted Chinese officials—notably Li Hongzhang (1823–1901)—the opportunity to observe firsthand the technological and organizational advantages of the West and to employ a number of Westerners in various new modernizing enterprises. Li became the leading figure in China's so-called Self-Strengthening Movement (c. 1860–1895), an effort to build China's military and economic strength in order to contend with both internal disorder and external aggression.[9]

During Li's extraordinarily long tenure as governor-general of Zhili from 1870 to 1895, new ideas penetrated much of the Middle Kingdom. The rise of Western-style Chinese newspapers, together with a growing number of Western works translated into Chinese by missionaries and by foreign employees in arsenals, shipyards, educational institutions, and the Imperial Maritime Customs Service, brought a heightened awareness of the West to China. During the first half of the nineteenth century, the majority of translated Western books and pamphlets had been religious, but during the latter part of the century, most of the translated works were in the natural, applied, and social sciences as well as in history and geography. Popular magazines such as the *Dianshizhai huabao* (Illustrated Review of the Dianshi Studio) portrayed the advantages of Western science and technology as well as the disruptive influence of foreign activity in China. By the end of the nineteenth century, the rapidly expanding Chinese periodical press had become a potent weapon in the movement for radical reform.[10]

But until the Sino-Japanese War of 1894–1895, change came slowly in China. As I have pointed out elsewhere, the outcome of the conflict perhaps causes us to place the modernizing "success" of Japan and the "failure" of China in too sharp relief. Yet it is impossible to avoid asking what went wrong with China's Self-Strengthening Movement after more than three decades of costly effort. This was, after all, precisely the question that the Chinese themselves were asking after the debacle of 1895, and the answers they produced determined in a large measure whether they would become conservative reformers like Zhang Zhidong (1837–1909), radical reformers like Kang Youwei, or revolutionaries like Sun Yat-sen (Sun Zhongshan; 1866–1925).

In retrospect, it is clear that China's modernizing problems in the late Qing period were both internal and external. On the one hand, the aggressiveness of the foreign powers in the realms of diplomacy, commerce, evangelism, and military affairs created a variety of political and economic problems. It encouraged Chinese antiforeignism and produced a natural suspicion of both Western employees and Western influences. But compounding these difficulties were China's pressing and inescapable demographic problems, the vastness and diversity of the Chinese empire, the turmoil created by the abortive millenarian movements of the Taipings and other rebel groups, and the tenacity and integration of China's traditional culture.[11] For most of the nineteenth century, the Qing dynasty seems to have been too weak militarily to protect itself from imperialism, but too strong culturally to surrender political initiative to Western-oriented modernizers.

In the realm of culture, the classical Chinese language remained the standard written medium of the Chinese elite throughout the Qing period, reinforcing long-standing attitudes, values, perceptions, and prejudices. Even if we reject the view of Marcel Granet and others that the mental world embodied in classical Chinese represents a "self-contained cultural monad hermetically sealed off from the cultural world embodied in the languages of the modern West," it is clear that the classical language—which possessed no close equivalents for concepts such as individualism, autonomy, freedom, democracy, and rights—affected the introduction of Western ideas in many ways. The preeminent translator of Western thought in the late Qing period, Yan Fu (1853–1921), refused, for example, to employ the more flexible and more widely accessible vernacular language in his renderings of Mill, Rousseau, Spencer, and others, arguing that "where language has no refinement [*ya*], the effects will not extend very far." Benjamin Schwartz argues that Yan's elegant translations "succeed on the whole in transmitting the essential thought of the Western sages," but there can be little doubt that Yan's young contemporary, Liang Qichao (1873–1929), was correct in asserting that "those who have not read many ancient books ... [find] his translations most difficult to comprehend."[12]

Schwartz himself points out that Yan resisted the use of most "standard" neologisms created by the Japanese during the early Meiji period in favor of his own renderings and that he tended to make maximum use of the traditional "allusive categories of ancient philosophic thought" in rendering Western ideas. Yan thus contributed to the general intellectual confusion of the late nineteenth and early twentieth centuries—a confusion reminiscent of the early decades of Buddhist translating activities when

> translators with different backgrounds chose different Chinese equivalents for foreign terms; translators had different degrees of knowledge of the language from which they were translating; communication among translators was infrequent; different versions

or editions of foreign works were used by different translators; [and] different stylistic preferences produced different versions of the same work.[13]

Furthermore, the ambiguity and semantic weight of many Chinese characters modified their meaning in translation, creating additional linguistic difficulties. Sun Yat-sen's use of the character *quan* for both "powers" and "rights" is one indication of the problem of ambiguity, while his employment of the classical Confucian term *minsheng* ("people's livelihood") for the concept "socialism" provides an example of the problem of semantic weight. Over time, with additional experience and the growing acceptance of precoined Japanese neologisms in the early twentieth century, Chinese translations of Western works became more uniform in usage, but it took the "literary revolution" of the New Culture Movement (c. 1915–1925), which occurred after the fall of the Qing dynasty and the rapid rise of vernacular usage, to produce a major linguistic breakthrough. And even then the power of traditional forms of expression remained strong.[14]

Yinyang and correlative thinking also proved remarkably persistent. The radical reformer Kang Youwei stated in the 1890s, for example:

> Probing into the way of Heaven, Confucius knew that everything contains polarity. He therefore employed [the concepts of] *yin* and *yang* to interpret the things of the world. ... In a human body, the back is *yin* and the front is *yang*; in a tree, its branches and trunk respectively make *yin* and *yang*; with respect to light, darkness and brightness constitute *yin* and *yang*; in color, black and white are *yin* and *yang*. ... There is not a single thing in the world that lacks *yin* and *yang*.

Kang's use of *yinyang* polarities extended into many areas of his radical reinterpretation of Confucianism, including his theory of human nature. He also used *yinyang* terminology to explain the mutual dependence of ideas and actions. He wrote, for instance,

> Square and circle, *yin* and *yang*, being and nonbeing, the unreal and the real are mutually dependent in their growth or diminution; so are the [teachings of] the sages and [those of] the Buddha. ... Regularity and expediency, *ren* [humaneness] and *yi* [right behavior], commonweal and private interest, others and self, *li* [propriety] and *zhi* [wisdom] are mutually dependent; so are "things Chinese" and "things Western."[15]

Efforts to illustrate the essential complementarity of Chinese and Western ideas were manifest in a number of other traditional formulas during the late Qing period. Among the most common dualistic distinctions was that made between the (Chinese) "moral way" (*dao*) and (Western) "manifestations" or "concrete things" (*qi*)—a polarity derived from the *Yijing*. The reformer Xue Fucheng (1838–1894) wrote, for instance:

Of the things revered in China the principle [*dao*] is foremost; of the things that Westerners understand, the manifestations [*qi*] are manifold. However, within the principle, there are at no time no manifestations, and the manifestations at their peak are in connection with the principle. Even if Yandi and Xianyuan [legendary rulers of high antiquity] were reborn into our world, they could not but immediately start work on boats and railroads, guns and cannon, and machinery; these are the natural circumstances. ... With regard to those things in which the foreigners are superior, we should not erect fences to exclude ourselves. This then means that principle and manifestations are simultaneously ready, and in this way it will not be difficult to unite [everything within] the four seas into one family.[16]

A similar dichotomy to *daoqi,* borrowed from Song neo-Confucianism, was between substance (*ti*) and function (*yong*). The *tiyong* paradigm was used in a variety of different ways by scholars in nineteenth-century China who hoped to reconcile traditional Chinese learning and new Western knowledge. Zhang Zhidong's famous formula, "Chinese learning for the substance, Western learning for the function," reflects the Sinocentric mainstream, but by the 1890s there were growing numbers of Chinese intellectuals who had come to see that the West had more to offer China than "concrete things" and that substance and function were more closely related than Zhang Zhidong was willing to admit. Nonetheless, as Chang Hao indicates, the *tiyong* approach had psychological significance, for it facilitated China's modernization without the loss of cultural identity. "Its dubious validity notwithstanding, ... [the *tiyong* formula] symbolized China's ambivalence toward the West."[17]

The Chinese search for a kind of cultural equivalence with the West in the late Qing period gave renewed impetus to the traditional effort to "find in antiquity the sanction for reform" and revived the seventeenth-century argument that new Western ideas had their inspiration or analogues in ancient Chinese thought. The *Yijing* was, of course, often cited as justification for change, and other classics served to rationalize learning from foreigners. Zhang Zhidong wrote in 1898: " 'In instruments we do not seek old ones but new.' That is the idea in the *Book of History.* 'Knowledge exists among the four barbarians.' That is the idea in the *Commentary on the Chunqiu* [Spring and Autumn Annals]. ... 'When I walk with two persons, they may serve as my teachers; I select good qualities and follow them.' That is the idea of the Confucian *Analects.*"[18] The devout Westernizer and influential translator Yan Fu, although far less committed to Chinese tradition than either Zhang Zhidong or Kang Youwei, and certainly less anxious than many of his ultraconservative contemporaries to demonstrate that all the innovations of the West had ultimately "come from the East," nonetheless often used Buddhist concepts, the symbolism of the *Yijing,* and various Confucian and Daoist sources of authority to support his views on modernizing change.[19]

The vast repository of Chinese fixed expressions (*chengyu*) provided yet another means of rationalizing Western-inspired change. The traditional phrase "viewing all [barbarians] with the same benevolence" (*yishi tongren*), for example, could be used both to justify the most-favored-nation clause of the unequal treaties and to determine policy regarding the treatment of foreign employees in the Chinese service.[20] The problem with such traditional formulations was that they often mitigated an awareness of the need for more fundamental policy changes on the part of the Qing government.

Perhaps the most vivid illustration of this problem can be found in the documentary record of China's foreign relations in the Tongzhi period (1862–1874) entitled *Chouban yiwu shimo* (A Complete Record of the Management of Barbarian Affairs), which was presented to the throne in 1880. Although this document was intended to be secret rather than public, the preface casts all of the humiliations of the Tongzhi reign—Western demands for an audience with the emperor on terms of diplomatic equality; the use of foreign troops to defend the treaty ports from the Taipings; the loss of Chinese territory to the Russians; the failure of the Alcock Convention; the establishment of an Interpreters College to train Chinese in Western languages in order to meet the needs of modern diplomacy; the belated establishment of Chinese legations abroad (related directly to a mission of apology sent by China to Great Britain after the murder of a British consular official in 1875); the limitation of Chinese customs duties; and the establishment of the Imperial Maritime Customs Administration—in terms of imperial condescension. The preface reads, in part:

> We respectfully consider that after the Tongzhi emperor came to the throne and
> stabilized the policy, … the amphibious monsters were quickly driven away and His
> Majesty's awful dignity vastly overawed everything within the imperial domain. …
> [When the barbarians returned to China] they requested to have an audience, no
> different from the Xiongnu king coming to the court of the Han dynasty. When they
> departed they wanted to join up as auxiliaries on the flanks of the imperial guard, just
> as the Uighurs assisted the Tang. They relied on the [emperor's] jade axe to mark off
> the rivers, confer their borders, and settle their boundaries. They presented cinnabar
> and turned toward civilization. How could they be aware that control-by-light-rein of
> the imperial pattern was entirely carried out according to the emperor's design? As a
> means by which speech might penetrate to all countries, the [Interpreters] College
> began to instruct in common languages. The fame of our classic books was spread
> everywhere. His Majesty proclaimed his orders to dispatch envoys abroad. … The
> merchants' customs duties were fixed, and … with the emperor's grace and rewards
> extended to them, [the foreigners] became cultivated and learned elegance and
> etiquette. Inner [Chinese] and outer [foreigners] formed one family.[21]

Even the granting of imperial audiences to Western diplomats on terms of equality after the Tongzhi emperor reached his majority could be rationalized by the notion that foreigners were simply too barbaric to be controlled by conventional Chinese rituals. In the opinion of the censor Wu Kedu, since Westerners understood only material gain and not Confucian rites, requiring them to observe Chinese ceremonies based on Confucian assumptions was as pointless as "gathering a herd of sheep, dogs, horses, and pigs in a hall and making them dance to music."[22]

Such Sinocentric attitudes were reinforced by the traditional civil-service examination system. One of the topics for the metropolitan exams in 1880 was the following quotation from the Four Books: "By indulgent treatment of men from afar they resort to him from all quarters. And by kindly cherishing the princes of states, the whole empire is brought to revere him." Such quotations, dutifully memorized by all examination candidates, perpetuated the myth of the Chinese emperor's universal kingship and encouraged China's outmoded posture of cultural condescension to foreigners.[23]

The examination system also reinforced neo-Confucian intellectual orthodoxy, which emphasized loyalty to the state and the acquisition of moral over scientific and technological knowledge. Mary Wright is correct in asserting that during the late Qing period the civil-service examinations were not always concerned exclusively with literary and scholastic questions, but even she admits that at their best the exams were "overloaded with precedent," with a premium placed on knowledge of facts rather than analysis or judgment. Chang Chung-li, for his part, goes so far as to say that the nineteenth century saw "the complete domination of the Confucian Classics in the examination questions"—a conclusion supported by abundant documentary evidence. There were, of course, Chinese criticisms of the examination system throughout the Qing period, and not all scholars embraced neo-Confucian orthodoxy; nevertheless, the basic assumption remained that Chinese scholars were moral men of broad learning who "need not be specialists" (*bubi zhuanmen mingjia*).[24]

Prior to 1895, there existed very little incentive for meaningful change in either the examinations or the Qing educational system. Education remained overwhelmingly private in nineteenth-century China, and the central government gave little support or encouragement to educational reform. Qing educational policy saw only two major innovations before the Sino-Japanese War: The government established a few Interpreters Colleges and it sent about two hundred students abroad. Most of these students were later recalled by the government because they were neglecting their traditional Chinese studies. Meanwhile, the civil-service examinations remained essentially unchanged and a powerful lure to the best minds of the empire.[25]

Even the military examination system underwent virtually no change in the nineteenth century. One important reason was the throne's fear of tampering with inherited institutions; another was its respect for ancestral precedent (*zuzong chengfa*). Time and again in late Qing China, concern over the policies of previous emperors played a key role in imperial deliberations. In the 1870s, reluctant to abandon territory conquered by an imperial ancestor (the Qianlong emperor), the throne spent vast amounts of precious revenue on the reestablishment of central government control over Chinese Central Asia instead of on maritime defense. And even after the Sino-Japanese War, Qing officials and the throne repeatedly expressed a concern for ancestral precedent in deliberations over civil and military reform.[26]

Given such cultural inertia, it should come as no surprise to find that there was very little enthusiasm for Western art, literature, or social customs in late Qing China—certainly nothing comparable to the Meiji government-sponsored wave of

Westernization that washed over Japan in the 1870s and 1880s. It is true that in some treaty-port areas the commercial middlemen known as compradors (*maiban*) proved susceptible to certain aspects of Western material culture. A few wore Western-style clothes and many lived in Western-style buildings with both Chinese and Western furnishings. Some assumed Western given names, and a number took up Western hobbies and amusements (such as watching horse races). Very few were ardent Confucians, and the majority sent their sons to study with Western tutors or to missionary-sponsored Western-style schools. But the vast majority of Chinese remained untouched by Western cultural influences during the late Qing period, particularly in rural areas, where all of the peasantry and many of the elite continued to live. The West was fundamentally a curiosity, not a source of cultural inspiration, for most Chinese.[27]

Naturally enough, the conservative Manchu government did nothing to encourage the Westernization of Chinese culture during the nineteenth century. The Manchus had, after all, originally justified their conquest in terms of the protection of China's cultural heritage. They could therefore scarcely appear to abandon traditional values, practices, and institutions without compromising their political position. China remained a combined state-and-culture in which, as John Fairbank has noted, "political power was maintained, in larger part than usual, by cultural means." Complicating the problem in the late nineteenth century was the presence of the Empress Dowager Cixi on the throne. As a female ruler who had executed a coup d'état to gain power and then manipulated the dynastic laws of succession to keep it, Cixi proved to be especially paranoid and particularly inclined to use neo-Confucian orthodoxy and the patronage of traditional Chinese culture as a means of serving personal political ends.[28]

Cixi's paranoia translated not only into a vigorous defense of orthodoxy but also into an obsessive concern with internal control. It is true that during and after the Taiping Rebellion the throne was forced to grant greater power and administrative leeway to certain loyal Chinese "regional" officials as a matter of expediency; however, it continually attempted to play these officials off against one another through the powers of appointment and the purse and by the careful manipulation and deployment of their so-called regional military forces. By and large the effort was successful, but in both the civil bureaucracy and the regular military forces of the empire, corruption and costly inefficiency continued.

In China's civil administration, the only major institutional innovations of the nineteenth century were the Zongli Yamen and the Imperial Maritime Customs Administration—both of which resulted from direct Western pressure. In reality, the former was merely an ad hoc subcommittee of the Grand Council and the latter but a subsidiary office of the former. Meanwhile, the long-standing Qing system of checks and balances discouraged initiative and often destroyed administrative continuity. Overlapping jurisdictions, dyarchy, the rule of avoidance, and the policy of frequent transfer were particularly detrimental in this regard. The throne, for its part, avoided administrative responsibility whenever possible and seldom initiated modernizing projects except those relating specifically to the Banner Armies.[29]

Despite the internally motivated military reforms of the mid-nineteenth century, the Qing army as a whole played no significant role in the modernization of Chinese society. The degenerate Banner and Green Standard forces of the empire consumed vast amounts of money but were largely untouched by Western influences, and even in the new-style *yongying* armies that assumed their military role, modernization went no further than the piecemeal acquisition of Western weapons and a certain amount of Western drill. Locally raised, armed, and trained, these "temporary" forces had little sense of either national identification or political awareness. The great majority of Chinese soldiers remained illiterate and uninformed. Within the military, as in the rest of Chinese society, the tendency for personal ties of blood, friendship, or local affinity to count for more than expertise militated against the introduction of new ideas and influences. The existence of widespread corruption and opium smoking, coupled with the lack of modern medical and other facilities, neither improved the living conditions of the average Chinese soldier nor altered his expectations.[30]

Recent research has indicated that China's nineteenth-century economy developed faster than previously thought; that neither imperialism nor landlordism was as detrimental to Chinese development as was once supposed; and that economic growth produced important social and especially political consequences.[31] Hao Yen-p'ing goes so far as to describe the economic changes as amounting to a "commercial revolution."[32] Although the Qing government did not play a particularly active role in this economic transformation, it did support limited industrialization as a means of building China's military strength. From 1860 to 1895, the state sanctioned the establishment of dozens of modernizing enterprises, including mills, mines, ironworks, and railroad and telegraph lines as well as arsenals and shipyards. But most of these activities were either undertaken by local officials or managed under the traditional formula of "government supervision and merchant operation." Such enterprises occasionally brought quick returns to certain investors, but because of bureaucratic inefficiency and corruption they discouraged reinvestment and regular growth. Private enterprises in China were notoriously weak and few in number. Commerce and agriculture developed largely on their own momentum, without the kind of systematic central government attention they received in Meiji Japan.[33]

Meanwhile, Chinese social attitudes changed slowly. In the absence of meaningful legal or administrative reform, particularistic ties of kinship, local affinity, and other forms of *guanxi* continued to loom large in various spheres of Chinese life. At the same time, conservative family values, social inequalities, and notions of collective responsibility remained firmly in place. Footbinding still received widespread customary sanction, despite its crippling effect on one-half of China's elite class and a great many other women as well.[34] The civil ethos (*wende*) of late imperial China also proved to be an obstacle to modernization. The low prestige of the military made most of the Qing elite, unlike the samurai class of Tokugawa Japan, disdainful of military affairs and unaware of the need for meaningful reform. Within the army and navy there was little incentive to acquire Western military knowledge beyond the rudiments of Western drill and tactics, and most officers continued to long for identification with the civil bureaucracy.[35]

Qing ritual practices at all levels discouraged innovation. Despite the time-honored argument that ritual must "change with the times," the state remained wed to costly traditional ceremonial practices out of fear that radical alterations or benign neglect would undermine the central government's authority. At the popular level, local religious observances, community festivals, and life-cycle ritual reinforced traditional values and status relationships while at the same time consuming great amounts of scarce capital. Meanwhile, of course, the ritual privileges of the Qing elite remained an important source of local prestige and power, and the preservation of at least the outward form of the tributary system during most of the nineteenth century blunted the throne's awareness that a new order of foreign relations had begun. In fact, the long twilight of the tributary system helps explain Beijing's lack of a sustained sense of crisis and its lingering Sinocentrism. Traditional concepts and explanations were all too effective in distorting reality.[36]

Naturally enough, China's cultural pretensions and sense of universal empire precluded the rise of modern nationalism—the identification of the individual with the nation-state and the general acceptance of a multistate system of other sovereign (and competing) national entities. The Sino-Japanese War of 1894–1895, however, shattered China's outmoded Sinocentric self-image at a single blow. This event marked the total destruction of the traditional Chinese world order by a onetime tributary. It also laid bare China's military weakness, exposed the bankruptcy of the Self-Strengthening Movement, and resulted in the loss of Chinese territory and the imposition of a costly and humiliating unequal treaty on China by the Japanese themselves. A surge of Chinese nationalism ensued, and with it, a burst of reform sentiment. Ironically, Japan now became a modernizing model for China. Even so, it took the failure of the Reform Movement of 1898 and the disastrous Boxer Rebellion of 1900 to prompt the Qing government into sponsoring meaningful reform.

REFORM, REVOLUTION, AND CHINA'S INHERITED CULTURE

The abortive reforms of 1898 resulted directly from the acceleration of foreign imperialism in the wake of the Sino-Japanese War. The so-called Scramble for Concessions on the part of the Western powers during 1897–1898, which threatened to dismember China, prompted the Guangxu emperor (r. 1875–1908) to initiate a reform movement from above with the advice and assistance of radical reformers such as Kang Youwei and Liang Qichao. At this time, the emperor's adoptive mother, the Empress Dowager Cixi, was in "retirement" at the Summer Palace outside of Beijing. Although conservative and cautious, the Empress Dowager gave her initial approval to the reform scheme, reportedly stating, "So long as you keep the ancestral tablets and do not burn them, and so long as you do not cut off your queue, I shall not inter-fere."[37]

But the reform edicts issued in the emperor's name in the period from June 11 to September 20, 1898, proved to be too threatening to Cixi and her supporters. Changes such as the abolition of sinecures and the appointment of progressives in government, the replacement of the "eight-legged essay" in the civil-service examina-tions by essays on current affairs, and the establishment of modern schools with both Western and Chinese curricula appeared too radical, and on September 21, the Empress Dowager executed a coup d'état, claiming that a serious illness had incapaci-tated the emperor. Reportedly chastising the hapless emperor for sweeping away "an-cestral institutions," Cixi rescinded virtually all the reform edicts and put a price on the head of the reformers, several of whom were executed. Kang and Liang escaped to Japan, where they continued to agitate for reform.[38]

The return of the conservatives to power happened to coincide with an upsurge of activity on the part of a secret society known as the Boxers United in Righteousness (Yihe quan), or simply the Boxers. This loose coalition of several diverse groups had in common a hostility to Westerners engendered by foreign imperialism and exacer-bated by natural disasters in North China. The Manchus, anxious to put the sectar-ian movement to their own political purposes, encouraged the Boxers to "Support the Qing and exterminate the Westerners" (*Fu Qing mieyang*). In 1900 the Boxers laid siege to foreign legations, and an eight-nation expeditionary force came in to relieve the legations in the summer of that year. The result was the occupation of Beijing by the Allied forces, the imposition of a huge indemnity on China, and a number of other destructive and demoralizing provisions stipulated in the Boxer Protocol of 1901.[39]

This humiliating event forced the Empress Dowager and her conservative sup-porters to commit themselves to fundamental reform. In the period from 1901 to 1909, a great number of reform edicts were issued. Many of these reflected the changes proposed in 1898, but several others went a great deal further. The most sig-nificant of these were: (1) the termination of the military examinations and the estab-lishment of a new, Western-style army (the Lujun); (2) the abolition of the civil-ser-vice examinations in order to encourage enrollment in new-style schools with both Western and Chinese curricula; and (3) the establishment of representative assemblies as a prelude to eventual constitutional government on the Meiji model. Debilitating practices such as footbinding were outlawed, and in 1907 the throne established a School of Ritual Studies (Lixue guan), charged with the task of selecting the best of China's "ancient and modern customs and the everyday habits of the people" and bringing them to the attention of the throne. "This," an imperial edict stated, "is proof of Our earnest desire for the preparation of the way towards the granting of a constitution and parliamentary representation to the country."[40]

The imperial reforms of the early twentieth century, designed to preserve the dy-nasty, had revolutionary consequences. Abolition of the traditional examinations, for example, dealt a staggering blow to the Confucian concept of rule by virtue and eliminated the institutional reinforcement of orthodox Confucian values. Representative government radicalized the Chinese elite, giving them a new political awareness and a new base of power. The New Army, whose officers and men were increasingly exposed to, and influenced by, nationalistic revolutionary propaganda, became a revolutionary instrument. The establishment of the School of Ritual Studies, although itself of little real importance, symbolized the erosion of the official ritual system—a process that had begun with the destruction of the Chinese world order. The pathetic effort in 1907 to elevate the worship of Confucius to the first level of state sacrifice—presumably in order to salvage the reputation of the sage (and the Manchus) after the abolition of the literary examinations—testified to the desperation of the dynasty.[41]

Despite their reform efforts, the Manchus became increasingly scorned and despised for their inability either to resist imperialism or to protect elite interests. Chinese nationalism no longer permitted alien rulers to claim legitimacy as the protectors of China's cultural heritage, for Chinese intellectuals increasingly saw the need to differentiate between politics and culture in order to achieve the modern goals of "collective achievement and dynamic growth." And despite Kang Youwei's contention that the faults of the Qing government were those of the inherited culture and not simply those of the Manchus, the cultural conservatism of the throne, its desperate attempt to maintain Manchu political supremacy, and growing Chinese fears that a vigorous anti-imperialist movement might result in foreign intervention all made the Manchus a convenient target for nationalistic advocates of republican revolution.[42] The death of the Guangxu emperor in 1908 destroyed China's best chance for a Meiji-style constitutional monarchy, and in 1911–1912, the republican revolutionaries, under Sun Yat-sen, threw out the imperial baby with the Manchu bathwater. This development created a political vacuum and a ritual void that the hastily constructed system of representative institutions could not fill. The Republic of China soon degenerated into warlordism.[43]

The warlord period, which lasted from about 1915 to 1928, witnessed the rise of the so-called New Culture Movement—an iconoclastic assault on traditional Chinese culture and a search for new values and institutions in the midst of political chaos, social unrest, widespread demoralization, and foreign imperialism. Nearly every aspect of the inherited civilization came under attack by Chinese intellectuals, including Confucian ethics and the "teachings of ritual." At the same time, the Chinese women's movement gathered momentum. The period was marked by a tremendous surge of interest in Western ideologies, science, and democracy; by experimentation with new artistic, dramatic, and literary forms; and by the development of a new national literature influenced strongly by Western themes and models. There was also a growing interest in Western fashions and amusements.[44]

The early outlook of the French-educated intellectual Chen Duxiu (1880–1942) exemplifies the vibrantly iconoclastic spirit of the New Culture Movement. Although Chen was born into an elite family and received a thorough grounding in the Confucian Classics, his experience abroad and reaction to China's deteriorating domestic situation led him to reject Chinese tradition and to embrace Western ideas. As editor of the famous and influential journal *Xin qingnian* (*La Jeunesse,* The New Youth), Chen issued a "Call to Youth" in 1915, declaring passionately that he would "much rather see the past culture of our nation [*guocui,* often translated 'national essence'] disappear than to see our race die out now because of its unfitness for living in the modern world." He urged his readers to be independent, not servile; progressive, not conservative; aggressive, not retiring; cosmopolitan, not isolationist; utilitarian, not formalistic; and scientific, not mystical. He railed against "all traditional ethics, law, scholarship, rites and customs" and scoffed at the use of *yinyang* and five-elements notions to explain natural phenomena.[45] Until his conversion to Marxism around 1920, Chen remained a leading spokesman for Western-style liberalism and a reliance on "Mr. Science" and "Mr. Democracy" for China's salvation.

The thrust of the New Culture Movement was toward what has been described as "totalistic iconoclasm." This widespread disposition to reject the past completely and to seek holistic and all-encompassing solutions to China's complex problems reflected a growing recognition that the very perfection of China's highly integrated cultural tradition now presented the nation with its most formidable modernizing problem. In the words of Chen Duxiu and Hu Shi (1891–1962), "The old literature, old politics, and old ethics have always belonged to one family; we cannot abandon one and preserve the others."[46]

To many radicals of the day, even the Chinese language was an impediment to modernization. For this reason Hu Shi spearheaded a movement to replace the classical language with the vernacular on the grounds that the old literary language merely reinforced outmoded ideas. By 1920 the vernacular had become the official medium of instruction in China's new-style schools. But Qian Xuantong, another New Culture intellectual, wanted to go further. In a letter to Chen Duxiu, he wrote:

> In an earlier essay of yours, you strongly advocated the abolition of Confucianism. Concerning this proposal of yours, I think that it is now the only way to save China. But, upon reading it, I have thought of one thing more: If you want to abolish Confucianism, then you must first abolish the Chinese language; if you want to get rid of the average person's childish, uncivilized, obstinate way of thinking, then it is all the more essential that you first abolish the Chinese language.[47]

Qian's quixotic proposal was for China to adopt Esperanto.[48]

Lin Yü-sheng explains the radical character of the New Culture movement in the following terms:

> Iconoclastic intellectuals were hardly capable of differentiating those traditional social norms and political practices that were abhorrent to them from traditional cultural symbols and values. This lack of differentiation and tendency to be monistic and holistic was affected, among other factors, by the long-term historical disposition to interlace the cultural center with a socio-political center in Chinese traditional society and by a traditional Chinese pattern of thinking in terms of association. ... The

intelligentsia in China believed in the necessary priority of cultural and intellectual change over social, political, and economic changes and not vice versa.[49]

Although the scientific spirit of the New Culture Movement attracted growing numbers of Chinese intellectuals, there were still a number of die-hard traditionalists among the educated elite. In response to the early call for "total Westernization" (*quanban Xihua*), ultraconservatives such as Gu Hongming (1857–1928) stood steadfast in defense of China's cultural tradition. Although educated in the West and able to read several foreign languages (including English, French, German, Latin, and ancient Greek), Gu maintained that Western utilitarian culture was incapable of developing the "inner mind" and that China's "spiritual civilization" was so perfect that it could not only save China but also rescue the West from its materialistic malaise. He strenuously opposed Western science and technology, defended all traditional values, and even continued to wear the Manchu queue as a sign of traditionalistic defiance.[50]

The vast majority of Chinese intellectuals, however, did not take the extremist positions of either totalistic iconoclasm or ultraconservatism. Rather, they tried to find a creative cultural balance between Chinese tradition and Western-inspired modernity. Some gravitated more toward the West, others more toward an emphasis on China's "national essence"; but even the conservatives now viewed the past from new perspectives, using new methodologies borrowed from the West. And yet, if we look at Chinese society as a whole during this period, it is clear that the New Culture Movement was essentially an urban intellectual movement that had very little impact on the rest of China. For every Western-educated radical there remained "hundreds of thousands of local leaders of secret societies, Buddhist abbots, Daoist priests, and leaders of Confucian uplift societies who continued to expound their views almost wholly in terms of categories provided by the culture of the past."[51] Traditional family values and relations of subordination, as well as the life-cycle rituals that reinforced these values and relations, remained deeply entrenched in the countryside, where about 80 percent of the people resided (as they do to this day).[52]

Furthermore, the political imperatives of Chinese nationalism, the success of the newly organized Nationalist party (Guomindang) and its Northern Expedition against the warlords in the period from 1926 to 1928, and the establishment of a new central government at Nanjing under Sun Yat-sen's successor, Chiang Kai-shek (Jiang Jieshi; 1888–1975), narrowed somewhat the parameters of discussion and debate. In politics, even among Chinese liberals, there seems to have been a "widespread tendency to appreciate democracy more as an indispensable functioning part of a modern nation state than as an institution to protect individual rights and liberties."[53] Thus nationalist impulses and the desire for a strong and rationally organized state became more important than liberal values and individualism in Chinese political and social thought. And although a battle of words still raged between advocates of "total Westernization" and those who advocated "cultural construction on a Chinese base," the Guomindang in this period of "political tutelage" and one-party rule demonstrated a clear concern with the restoration of traditional values. Although committed to rapid economic modernization and the realization of Sun Yat-sen's Three Principles of the People (nationalism, democracy, and the people's livelihood), Chiang Kai-shek's new government moved quickly to reestablish Confucianism as a kind of state-sponsored orthodoxy.[54]

As late as February 1927, the Nationalist government had ordered the abolition of official Confucian rites on the grounds that "the principles of Confucius were despotic. For more than twenty centuries they have served to oppress the people and to enslave thought. ... As to the cult of Confucius, it is superstitious and out of place in the modern world. ... China is now a Republic. These vestiges of absolutism should be effaced from the memory of citizens." But the vestiges were not effaced for long. On November 6, 1928, Chiang Kai-shek was already urging his officers to spend their leisure time studying the Four Books of Confucianism, and in 1931, the birthday of Confucius became a national holiday. By 1934, Confucius had been recanonized, and an official delegate of the national government was sent to take part in the solemn ceremonies at the Confucian temple at Qufu, birthplace of the sage. During the same year, Generalissimo Chiang inaugurated the famous New Life Movement, which called for a return to the four ancient Confucian virtues of *li* (ritual), *yi* (right behavior), *lian* (integrity), and *chi* (sense of shame). Chinese politics and culture became reunited.[55]

The New Life Movement has often been ridiculed for its overattention to minute rules of decorum and for its philosophical superficiality. In Mary Wright's words, "The whole of the neo-Restoration of the Kuomintang [Guomindang] was a dismal failure, a far sadder spectacle than the T'ung-chih [Tongzhi] Restoration it tried to copy." But the fundamental aims of the two "restorations" were different, and despite the weaknesses of the New Life Movement, it did lay the foundations for a government-sponsored approach to traditional Chinese culture that continues to this day on Taiwan. This approach considers Confucian values to be fully compatible with science and democracy and conducive to modern economic growth as well.[56] At present, traditional art and literature, and even traditional religious and ritual practices, continue to flourish alongside more "modern" aspects of material culture borrowed from the West. Like the Japanese, who now serve as a self-conscious modernizing model, the Chinese on Taiwan have evolved a dualistic culture that draws upon the traditions of both East and West in apparently judicious combination.[57]

In many respects, the Chinese Communist approach to traditional culture has been very different from that of the Guomindang. Since the founding of the party in 1921, the Chinese Communists have promoted a vision of social revolution based on the rejection of Confucianism and the implementation of Marxist-Leninist principles and practices. Although the revolutionary movement of Mao Zedong (1893–1976) grew out of the same deep patriotism and esteem for science, democracy, and social justice that had motivated Sun Yat-sen as founder of the Guomindang, Mao laid his wager on the Chinese peasantry, developing a kind of populist Marxism-Leninism that stood in sharp contrast to the urban-centered elitism that had characterized the Nationalist era. In both theory and practice, Mao emphasized the importance of ideology, human will, mass political participation, anti-imperialism, egalitarianism, social and economic reform, and above all the transformation of consciousness. He assailed Confucian beliefs as well as the popular religious practices and social rituals that seemed to encourage conservatism, waste time or money, and strengthen the position of the traditional elite.[58]

From 1949 to his death in 1976, Mao succeeded in transforming much of Chinese society. In addition to promoting Marxist-Leninist values nationwide and elevating the social position of traditionally disadvantaged groups (notably workers, peasants, women, and soldiers), Mao brought to the People's Republic a new system of economic organization that included the nationalization or collectivization of agriculture, industry, and commerce and a host of related changes in health, education, and welfare. Life expectancy nearly doubled, as did population. During the early 1950s Mao received considerable assistance from the Soviet Union, but his militantly self-reliant revolutionary approach can best be seen in the radical Great Leap Forward (1958–1960) and especially in the tumultuous Great Proletarian Cultural Revolution of 1966–1969, which hearkened back to the New Culture Movement in its self-conscious effort to "destroy the old and establish the new" (*pojiu lixin*).[59]

Yet for all his revolutionary iconoclasm, Mao did not totally reject China's heritage. As early as 1938 he wrote: "Today's China is an outgrowth of historic China. We are Marxist historicists; we must not mutilate history. From Confucius to Sun Yat-sen we must sum it up critically, and we must constitute ourselves the heirs of all that is precious in this past. ... A communist is a Marxist internationalist, but Marxism must take on a national form before it can be applied." In 1956, Mao attacked both the *tiyong* modernizing formula of the late Qing period and the notion of "total Westernization" prevalent in the New Culture era, arguing: "We must learn good things from foreign countries and also learn good things from China. ... China's art must not look more and more to the past, nor must it become more and more Western."[60]

Mao's deep sense of history and esteem for much of Chinese tradition is evident in his writings and speeches, which bristle with historical allusions and references to traditional Chinese literature. Much of Mao's discourse employs traditional terms, phrases, and metaphors. Mao even had a certain admiration for Confucius. Although he criticized the sage for his lack of revolutionary vision, disdain for physical labor, and esteem for "old rituals," Mao admired Confucius for his breadth of learning and cultural refinement. And in a publication issued during the Cultural Revolution, Mao stated, "We must not lose the Confucian tradition."

Some scholars have suggested that the Maoist concept of the transformative power of the mind resonates strongly with the traditional neo-Confucian emphasis on efficacious moral efforts (*gongfu*) and that the prominent strains of dynamism, activism, and utopianism in Mao's thought seem to be derived at least in part from the tradition of the great Ming Confucian scholar Wang Yangming. Mao's distinctive notion of "contradictions" may perhaps owe something to *yinyang* influences, and his "Great Leap" mentality hearkens back to the millenarian tradition of the Taipings and others. Certainly the persistent emphasis on ethics, self-cultivation, and small-group ritual in the People's Republic bears the strong imprint of traditional Chinese social thought.[61]

Like Chiang Kai-shek, Mao ruled in the imperial style, manipulating both factions and ritual symbolism for his own political purposes. Furthermore, in practice Mao's administration, like that of his imperial and Nationalist predecessors, displayed the familiar characteristics of authoritarianism; state supervision of political, social, and economic life; an emphasis on political morality over law; a preoccupation with ideological, artistic, and literary orthodoxy; and a clear stress on collective responsibility and mutual surveillance. Many of these tendencies were, of course, encouraged and reinforced by Marxist-Leninist ideology and practice.[62]

As an intellectual system, Maoism differed fundamentally from the ideology of both imperial China and the Guomindang. Yet it was every bit as holistic and nearly as metaphysical as Zhu Xi's neo-Confucianism had been. And while the Marxist dialectic replaced *yinyang* notions of cyclical alternation and complementary opposition as the logical underpinning of most Chinese thought, Maoist discourse continued to exhibit many time-honored features of traditional Chinese philosophical expression. Quite apart from the powerful linguistic tendency to group phrases in neat sets of four characters, and the deeply ingrained moralistic tendency to parcel out praise and blame in categorical either/or fashion, we find in much Chinese writing of the Maoist period a dogmatic formalism expressed in arbitrary groupings of elements, often organized in numerical configurations.[63]

Chinese political rhetoric in particular exhibits this tendency. If we review the various political campaigns of the Maoist era, we encounter literally dozens of formalized numerical categories embodied in slogans: There are, for instance, the "three antis" (*sanfan*), the "three highs" (*sangao*), the "three red banners" (*sanmian hongqi*), the "three histories" (*sanshi*), the "three reconciliations and one reduction" (*sanhe yishao*), the "three freedoms and one contract" (*sanzi yibao*), the "four olds" (*sijiu*), the "four firsts" (*sige diyi*), the "five histories" (*wushi*), the "five category elements" (*wulei fenzi*), and so forth. This type of classification persisted into the 1970s and beyond, as we can see from the Four Modernizations (agriculture, industry, science and technology, and national defense), the trial of the notorious Gang of Four (Jiang Qing, Mao's wife, and her three primary supporters), and the campaign known as the Five Stresses, Four Beautifications, and Three Ardent Loves (*wujiang simei sanreai*)— that is, a stress on decorum, manners, hygiene, discipline, and morals; an effort to beautify the mind, language, behavior, and the environment; and love of the motherland, socialism, and the Chinese Communist Party.[64]

The legacy of the past was even evident in the midst of Mao's devastating attack on traditional "feudal" attitudes and "bourgeois" Western influences during the Great Proletarian Cultural Revolution. To be sure, in 1966 the Chairman's overenthusiastic agents, the Red Guards, ransacked museums, temples, and private homes; destroyed ancestral tablets, ancient artifacts, old books, and works of art; and attacked citizens who dressed in the traditional fashion, followed old rituals, or pos-

sessed Buddhist and Daoist relics. But in many respects the Cultural Revolution reflected long-standing Chinese cultural predispositions. Mao himself assumed the position of an imperial-style demigod whose writings were believed to have mystical,
semi-magical power. During 1968, the cult of Mao grew to especially extravagant proportions, as Maurice Meisner has indicated:

> The writings of the Chairman were printed and distributed in ever greater volume.
> Portraits, statues, and plaster busts of Mao increased both in size and number. ... In
> households there were often "tablets of loyalty" to Mao's thought around which family
> members gathered to pay reverence. Schoolchildren no longer began the day by saying
> "good morning" but by chanting "May Chairman Mao live ten thousand times ten
> thousand years." Throughout the land exhibition halls were built to chronicle and
> commemorate the life and deeds of the Chairman, and to them came people on
> organized pilgrimages to pay homage at what the official press termed "sacred
> shrines." The test of loyalty to Mao was no longer measured by revolutionary acts
> inspired by his thought but more by the ability to recite his sayings and by the size of
> portraits that were carried in the streets or hung in homes. In 1966 the Mao cult had
> stimulated iconoclasts; in 1968 it produced icons.[65]

During the same period on Taiwan the Guomindang sponsored a Cultural Renaissance (*wenhua fuxing*) explicitly designed to preserve and foster traditional Chinese culture. In obvious response to the Cultural Revolution on the Mainland, it
called for the republication of the Confucian Classics and encouraged new writings
and translations in order to "publicize Chinese culture and build a bridge between
Chinese and Western cultures." It also promoted a revival of literature and art "based
on ethics, democracy and science" and emphasized the principles and practices of the
New Life Movement, including the "four social controls" (*li, yi, lian,* and *chi*) and the
"eight virtues" (loyalty, filial piety, benevolence, love, faithfulness, justice, harmony,
and peace). Like the New Life Movement of the 1930s, the Cultural Renaissance has
been criticized for its stress on outer form over inner substance and for its obviously
political character. Nonetheless, it offers a sharp and significant contrast to Mao's
brutally destructive effort to exorcise the "ghosts and monsters" of the past on the
Mainland.[66]

After Mao's death in 1976, there was a sharp reaction to the chaotic excesses of the
Cultural Revolution (including Mao's "cult of personality") and, from 1978 onward, a
wholehearted commitment to the Four Modernizations that continues to this day.
During this time, however, the Chinese press has carried numerous articles indicating that Mao's effort to root out "poisonous feudal influences" during the 1960s fell
far short of success and that certain traditional ideas and habits continue to plague
the People's Republic.[67]

One of the most frequent and vociferous complaints in the Chinese press is that
made against "bureaucratism" (*guanliao zhuyi*), an administrative outlook associated
with both imperial and Nationalist China and regularly denounced as rigid, dogmatic, autocratic, elitist, conservative, and often corrupt. Bureaucratism is formalism

in action (or inaction), not simply in thought or literary style. Deng Xiaoping once expressed the fear that "some of our cadres have turned into mandarins"—a remark that no one in China took lightly. But a diagnosis is not a cure, and the present leadership has found considerable resistance within the party and the bureaucracy to meaningful administrative reform. Perhaps for this reason, Chinese bureaucratism has been described by at least one high-ranking official of the People's Republic (Huang Xiang) as "far worse than any other bureaucratism in the world."[68]

In the opinion of at least some contemporary writers, "feudal" attitudes are manifest not only in bureaucratism but in other spheres of Chinese life as well, especially in the countryside. The "small producer" mentality of the peasantry has created, for instance, a deeply ingrained feudal consciousness of particularistic groupings (*bangpai yishi*) and patriarchal authority.[69] In the words of the *Red Flag*: "Because of the low level in the development of the entire society's productive forces and especially because ideology is relatively autonomous in nature, the remnants of the patriarchical system centered on the father's authority have not been purged thoroughly from society. The traditional idea, habit, and style of patriarchy are still seriously affecting people's social life."[70] Similarly, the long-standing emphasis on *guanxi* and nepotism continues to stand in the way of more rational economic and political organization in China.[71]

Inherited attitudes have surfaced in a wide variety of realms. William Hinton has indicated, for example, that the long-standing prejudice against manual labor on the part of Chinese intellectuals (which Mao tried in his own radical way to overcome) persists. He encountered tractor designers who had never been on a tractor and who were unaware of what specific needs the tractors they designed were supposed to fill. Birth-control programs in the countryside have suffered not only from ignorance on the part of the peasants but also from powerful traditional preferences for male children to continue the line and help support the family. The state's effort to curtail costly traditional rituals has also encountered serious obstacles in the rural sector. William Parish and Martin King Whyte demonstrate, for instance, that even during the period from 1969 to 1974, when the radical policies of the Gang of Four still held sway, life-cycle rituals on the old pattern were widely observed in rural South China, consuming large amounts of precious funds. In fact, they suggest that in many marriages the financial burden for the groom and his family (including payment of the traditional "bride price") has not declined in relation to family income since the establishment of the People's Republic and that it may even have increased. As in the past, poor families still find it difficult to find brides for their sons and many households go deeply into debt in order to provide a proper wedding for the sake of community face. The cost of funerals also remains high, despite official encouragement of simple ceremonies and cremation.[72]

Ironically, the "liberal" policies of Deng Xiaoping over the past decade and a half, all undertaken in the name of modernization, have helped to revivify certain aspects of traditional Chinese thought and behavior. Traditional art and literary forms are again popular, and at least a few contemporary thinkers are now openly advocating a selective revival of Confucian ideas. Buddhist temples and monasteries, first re-opened in the late 1970s along with a few Daoist temples and some Christian churches, have attracted ever-growing numbers of worshippers—young and old alike. Domestic ancestral sacrifices and other household religious devotions, severely condemned during the Cultural Revolution, have become more prominent, and re-ports in the Chinese press indicate the widespread recrudescence of so-called super-stitious practices such as geomancy, fortune-telling, and even, occasionally, witch-craft.[73]

In Fujian province, opposite Taiwan, traditional beliefs have made an especially dramatic comeback. An article in the *Wall Street Journal*, dated August 10, 1992, re-ports:

> Scattered at the edge of farm fields across the province are little temples to Tudi Gong, the land god. There's hardly a street without shops selling joss sticks and spirit money for use in appeasing ghosts. There are magnificent temples dedicated to the sea goddess Mazu … [and] nearly every home has an ancestor altar just inside the door, where offerings of food, liquor, incense and fake money are aimed at keeping the ghosts of vengeful ancestors free of vengeful notions against those left behind.

Particularly ironic in the light of Mao's concerted effort to eradicate popular religion is the presence of a small temple outside of the city of Xiamen dedicated to the Chair-man himself. In 1992 and 1993, I noticed Mao's portrait affixed to the inside of a number of car and truck windshields (serving as a Chinese-style St. Christopher's medal) and even displayed for sale in the form of a traditional-style charm in the Daoist temple known as Sanyuan gong in Guangzhou (Canton) (see Figure 11.1).

Of course there is the other, more "modern," side to Deng's cultural policies. Lan-guage reform—including the simplification of Chinese characters and the alphabet-ization of Chinese sounds (the *pinyin* system)—has continued unabated despite a considerable measure of traditionalist opposition. Greater freedom in the areas of art and literature has encouraged a surge of cosmopolitan creativity not seen since the 1950s, when the now-resurrected slogan "Let a hundred flowers bloom" was first pro-moted.[74] But the weight of tradition in matters such as stylistic imitation, as well as the long-standing tendency of the state to pass judgment on matters of intellectual and artistic orthodoxy, continues to constrain creativity and to raise troublesome questions for the Chinese leadership concerning the relationship between freedom and discipline. And, of course, the tragic Beijing Spring of 1989 reminds us of the state's willingness to use military force against its own citizens in defense of its politi-cal, social, and cultural prerogatives.[75]

At present, the balance between tradition and modernity in Taiwan appears to be much more comfortable than on the Mainland, although tensions do exist—espe-cially with the rapid growth of democracy during the past few years. Recent public opinion polls on Taiwan indicate, for instance, that in the midst of rapid political, so-cial, and economic change, citizens on the island province still embrace traditional

Figure 11.1   The Deification of Mao. A charm, consisting of Chairman Mao's photograph and a composite character indicating the "summoning of wealth," for sale in the Daoist temple known as Sanyuan gong in Guangzhou (Canton), 1992   Photo by author.

Chinese values such as loyalty, filial piety, ritual, propriety, veneration for ancestors, harmony, generosity, and submission to superiors. And yet, old-style attitudes toward agriculture, commercial development, and women are rapidly disappearing.[76] It is impossible to say what changes tomorrow may bring for Taiwan and the Mainland, but it seems evident that for a long time to come in both societies, the past will remain an integral part of the Chinese future.[77]

Appendix A:
A Note on Chinese Names

*I*n transliterating Chinese words, I have employed the *pinyin* (PY) romanization system, with the exception of a few extremely common conventions, such as Sun Yat-sen (PY: Sun Yixian) and Chiang Kai-shek (PY: Jiang Jieshi). I have also included Wade-Giles (WG) romanizations for most Chinese names and terms listed in the Index, since many scholarly books, including a number of valuable English-language reference works, have yet to be converted to the *pinyin* system.

In *pinyin* romanizations, both vowels and consonants are pronounced more or less as they are in English, with a few noteworthy exceptions: "q" sounds like the *ch* in *ch*eek; "z" sounds like the *ds* in bu*ds* (unless followed immediately by an "h," in which case the two letters together sound like the "j" in *j*ump); "x" sounds like the *sh* in *sh*eep; and "c" sounds like the *ts* in i*ts* (unless followed immediately by an "h," in which case the two letters together sound like the *ch* in *ch*eap). Thus *qing* sounds like "cheeng"; *zu* sounds like "dsoo"; *zhou* sounds like "joe"; *xing* sounds like "sheeng"; *can* sounds like "tsawn"; and *chu* sounds like "chew."

In the text, Chinese names usually appear in their original order, with the family name first. In the notes, however, I have followed Western usage for the sake of convenience and clarity. Since many Chinese scholars share the same family names, it seemed advisable to include given names for ease of reference. Most Chinese family names consist of one character, while most given names are composed of two (e.g., Gong Zizhen). The reverse is possible, however, as is the use of two characters for both surname and given name (e.g., Sima Xiangru). Polysyllabic Manchu and Mongol names are transliterated either by a single word (e.g., Nurgachi) or by a string of sounds representing the characters used to render them in Chinese (e.g., Senggelinqin—the Chinese phonetic equivalent for Senggerinchin, a Mongol name).

Emperors in the Qing dynasty are usually referred to by their reign names (*nianhao*) rather than by their personal names (which became taboo upon their accession to the throne). All reign names have felicitous meanings, but some, such as Guangxu ("Glorious Succession"), have a certain irony (see Chapter 3).

Appendix B:
Weights and Measures,
Exchange Rates, and Costs

Length

1 *cun* (inch)	=	c. 1.4 English inches
10 *cun*	=	1 *qin* (foot, c. 14.1 English inches; c. 35.6 centimeters)
10 *qin*	=	1 *chang*
180 *chang*	=	1 *li* (c. 0.333 English mile; c. 0.5 kilometer)

Weight

1 *liang* (tael)	=	c. 1.333 English ounces
16 *liang*	=	1 *jin* (catty, c. 1.333 pounds; c. 0.6 kilogram)
100 *jin*	=	1 *shi* (picul, c. 133 pounds)

Area

1 *mou*	=	c. 0.166 acre; c. 0.055 hectare

A Note on Exchange

During the Qing period, the "standard" unit of exchange was the tael (*liang*), about an ounce (c. 500 grains) of silver, usually in the form of an oval ingot, or "shoe." The paper money experiment of the Xianfeng period (1851–1861)—the first such paper issue since the early Ming dynasty—failed miserably. The value of the silver tael varied from time to time and place to place, not only because of changes in market conditions but also because of different local standards of weight and fineness. Theoretically, 1 tael was equal to 1,000 copper cash (*wen* or *li*), but in practice a tael might be worth anywhere from 1,000 up to 1,500 cash. The enormous variety in standards of currency, weight, and capacity in traditional China necessitated the employment of a great many money changers and other petty middlemen, complicating both commercial transactions and payment of taxes. For an illuminating discussion of these problems, consult Albert Feuerwerker in *CHC* (1980, vol. 11, pt. 2), pp. 40 ff.; also Morse (1908), pp. 145 ff., esp. 149–161.

A Note on Prices

Yeh-chien Wang (1972) has put together a rough price index for the Qing period. According to his data, the lowest prices were in 1682. Taking this year as a base (100), the following general patterns emerge:

Year	Index number
1646	688
1682	100
1700	130
1800	300
1815	300
1850	150
1864	500
1875	240
1885	240
1895	360
1910	600

Susan Naquin (1976, Appendix 3), provides some cost-of-living figures for North China in the 1810s:

1. Purchase price of land (cash per *mou*), northern Zhili: 6,000
2. Purchase price of land (cash per *mou*), southern Zhili:
    High-quality land, good year: 10,000
    High-quality land, bad year: 1,000
    Low-quality land, good year: 3,000–4,000
    Low-quality land, bad year: 300–400
3. Land rents in Henan (annual):
    First-grade land: 500 cash per *mou*
    Second-grade land: 400 cash per *mou*
    Third-grade land: 300 cash per *mou*
4. Wages:
    Bondservant in a prince's household: 4 taels in money and grain per month
    Regular soldier: 1.8 taels per month and 2 piculs of rice per month
    Agricultural laborer during harvest time: 100 cash per day
    Agricultural laborer during slack season: 70–80 cash per day
5. Room and Board:
    Room rent: 150–200 cash per month
    Militia soldier's food allowance: 50 cash per day
    Militia instructor's food allowance: 200 cash per day
    Regular soldier's allotment for food: 150 cash per day
6. Goods:
    Knife: 500 cash
    One foot of white cotton cloth: 100 cash
    14-year-old boy: 4,000 cash
    11-year-old boy: 1,000 cash
    Woman: 10,000 cash

According to Sidney Gamble (1943), p. 43, the wages for unskilled laborers in the area of Beijing ordinarily did not go below 60 cash per day from 1807 to 1856. From 1865 to 1871, the minimum was about 200 cash, and from 1872 to 1902, about 300 cash. Evelyn Rawski's (1979) research indicates that teachers in charitable schools averaged about 24 taels per year from 1800 to 1825 and 44 taels from 1875 to 1900. On the whole, the cost of a picul of rice seems to have fluctuated between 1.5 and 2.0 taels in the early nineteenth century, before dropping to about 1 tael by 1850. During the Taiping Rebellion the cost rose to as high as 5 or more taels per picul. See Yeh-chien Wang (1972), pp. 351–354. According to a report on provisions in the markets of Shanghai during 1849, rice was 24 cash per *jin*; wheat flour, 30 cash per *jin*; mutton and beef, about 100 cash per *jin*; chicken, 80 to 90; and ducks, 90 to 120. (*Chinese Repository,* February 1949, pp. 109–110. Cf. Jonathan Spence in Kwang-chih Chang, ed. [1977], pp. 265 ff. See also Beattie [1979], p. 137, and Chung-li Chang [1962], p. 143.)

In 1864, the exchange value of a "customs" tael in Western currency was 80 pence (6s. 8d., about US $1.65). By 1894, the value of the tael had declined to 38 pence. For a discussion of late Qing fiscal reform, consult Chuzo Ichiko in *CHC* (1980, vol. 11, pt. 2), pp. 403 ff.

Notes

REMARKS

I have cited comparatively few Chinese- or Japanese-language materials in these notes, despite many years of work on both primary and secondary sources. The main purpose of the notes is to guide nonspecialists toward available Western sources (including Chinese and Japanese works in translation) that illustrate or amplify the points I am making or lead the reader into areas of Qing culture that cannot be discussed more fully in the body of the book for lack of space (see also Bibliography).

Translations from Chinese sources (other than my own) have been modified for consistency and clarity after consulting the Chinese original. The primary change has been to render all Chinese names and terms according to the *pinyin* romanization system. In the notes, Chinese and Japanese works are generally cited only if no comparable Western-language sources of documentation or information are readily available, and the names of all Chinese authors appear in conventional Western order (given name first, then family name), regardless of whether the work cited is in Chinese or a Western language.

Finally, in the interest of brevity, I have cited only the author, and not the title, of articles included in scholarly collections—for example, Chapter 1, note 15: Arthur Wright in Gottschalk (1963), p. 39. Also, in order to keep footnotes to a minimum, I have in many cases combined several sources into a single citation. Sources for all quoted material in any one paragraph (or successive paragraphs) are listed in order, separated by a semicolon and ended by a period. If such citations give a span of relevant pages, the quoted material appears within the span.

ABBREVIATIONS

AA	*American Anthropologist*
AAR	*Asian American Review*
AH	*Art History*
AHR	*American Historical Review*
AJ	*Art Journal*
AJCA	*Australian Journal of Chinese Affairs*
AM	*Asia Major*
AQR	*Asiatic Quarterly Review*
AS	*Asian Survey*
BAOS	*Bulletin of the American Oriental Society*
BR	*Beijing Review*

BSOAS	*Bulletin of the School of Oriental and African Studies*
BSSCR	*Bulletin of the Society for the Study of Chinese Religion*
CC	*The Chinese Classics*
CHC	*The Cambridge History of China*
CHM	*Cahiers d'Histoire Mondiale*
CIAS	*Central and Inner Asian Studies*
CLEAR	*Chinese Literature: Essays, Articles, Reviews*
CNA	*China News Analysis*
CQ	*China Quarterly*
CR	*Chinese Recorder*
CSH	*Chinese Studies in History*
CSJCXB	*Congshu jicheng xinbian*
CSSH	*Comparative Studies in Society and History*
CSWT	*Ch'ing-shih wen-t'i*
DQHD	*Da Qing huidian*
DQTL	*Da Qing tongli*
EDCC	*Economic Development and Cultural Change*
ER	*Earlham Review*
FEQ	*Far Eastern Quarterly*
HJAS	*Harvard Journal of Asiatic Studies*
HR	*History of Religions*
IPQ	*International Philosophical Quarterly*
IRSH	*International Review of Social History*
JAH	*Journal of Asian History*
JAMA	*Journal of Asian Martial Arts*
JAOS	*Journal of the American Oriental Society*
JAS	*Journal of Asian Studies*
JCA	*Journal of Communication Arts*
JCCP	*Journal of Cross-Cultural Psychology*
JCFS	*Journal of Comparative Family Studies*
JCL	*Journal of Chinese Linguistics*
JCP	*Journal of Chinese Philosophy*
JCR	*Journal of Chinese Religions*
JCS	*Journal of Chinese Studies*
JEH	*Journal of Economic History*
JHI	*Journal of the History of Ideas*
JHKBRAS	*Journal of the Hong Kong Branch of the Royal Asiatic Society*
JICS	*Journal of the Institute of Chinese Studies*
JLDC	*Jiali dacheng*
JLTSJC	*Jiali tieshi jicheng*
JNCBRAS	*Journal of the North China Branch of the Royal Asiatic Society*
JOS	*Journal of Oriental Studies*
JQ	*Japan Quarterly*
JQYWL	*Huangchao jiqi yuewu lu*
JRS	*Journal of Ritual Studies*
JSH	*Journal of Social History*
JSWB	*Huangchao jingshi wenbian*

LBZL	*Qinding Libu zeli*
LIC	*Late Imperial China*
LQ	*Library Quarterly*
LYBL	*Liyi bianlan*
MAS	*Modern Asian Studies*
MC	*Modern China*
MRDTB	*Memoirs of the Research Department of the Toyo Bunko*
MS	*Monumenta Serica*
NCH	*North-China Herald*
NQCJ	*Notes and Queries on China and Japan*
OA	*Oriental Art*
PEW	*Philosophy East and West*
PFEH	*Papers on Far Eastern History*
PHR	*Pacific Historical Review*
QBLC	*Qingbai leichao*
QS	*Qingshi*
RMRB	*Renmin ribao*
SAR	*Sino-American Review*
SKQSZM	*Qinding siku quanshu zongmu*
SLR	*Stone Lion Review*
SSC	*Social Sciences in China*
TAPS	*Transactions of the American Philosophical Society*
THJ	*Tsing Hua Journal*
TP	*T'oung Pao*
TR	*Tamgang Review*
TSJC	*Qinding gujin tushu jicheng*
USCR	*U.S.-China Review*
WLTK	*Wuli tungkao*
WP	*World Politics*
WXL	*Wuxue lu*
XBZZJC	*Xinbian zhuzi jicheng*
XWXTK	*Huangchao xu wenxian tongkao*
ZDLZ	*Huangchao zhengdian leizuan*
ZWDCD	*Zhongwen da cidian*

CHAPTER 1. INTRODUCTION

1. See Berger and Luckmann (1967). On the "self-reproducing" nature of categorization, consult Sangren (1987), p. 232.

2. R. J. Smith (1987), esp. pp. 114–115; also Bell (1989).

3. R. J. Smith (1989), pp. 432–433.

4. See, for example, Zhengtong Wei (1981), esp. pp. 134–137. Wei identifies ten salient characteristics of traditional Chinese culture: isolated creation, long history, absorptive capacity, unity, conservatism, esteem of peace, feelings of local affinity, humane cosmological outlook, family and clan system, and emphasis on moral spirit. Cf. Dainian Zhang and Guanghui Jiang, eds. (1990); *RMRB* (Overseas Edition), July 29, 1985; Jiaoyu bu wenhua ju, ed. (1969); Jinjian

Zhang (1935). In English, see G. Wang et al. (1991); Godwin Chu and Yanan Ju (1991), esp. p. 74; Lung-chang Young (1988), esp. p. 40; Chinese Culture Connection (1987); Metzger (1977), esp. pp. 240–241; R. J. Smith (1989), pp. 433–435; Thomas Metzger in Cohen and Goldman, eds. (1990), esp. pp. 282–285; Dennerline (1988), passim; also note 5 below.

5. See the fascinating collection of articles on the theme of "The Changing Meaning of Being Chinese Today" in the spring 1991 issue of *Daedalus* (120, no. 2); also *CNA,* June 15, 1992.

6. On this issue, consult D. Johnson et al., eds. (1985), passim.

7. The Chinese Popular Culture Project at the University of California, Berkeley, has done an especially admirable job of exploring "folk" perspectives on China. See, for example, Po and Johnson (1992).

8. M. Cohen (1991), p. 113.

9. Ropp (1981), p. 30; Beattie (1979), pp. 18–21; Esherick and Rankin, eds. (1990), esp. p. 9; see also Tu-ki Min (1989), passim. In Johnson et al., eds. (1985), p. 59, David Johnson estimates that there were perhaps five million classically educated commoners at any given time in Qing dynasty China.

10. David Johnson in Johnson et al., eds. (1985), pp. 57–61. See also the various articles in Smith and Kwok, eds. (1993); Polachek (1992); Man-houng Lin (1991); Elman (1981, 1984, 1990); Guy (1987); Henderson (1984).

11. Esherick and Rankin, eds. (1990), p. 12. See also M. Cohen (1991), esp. pp. 113–119, 123–125.

12. An equally important but more difficult question to answer is: How did "popular" values penetrate and influence elite culture? On this issue, consult Bell (1989), pp. 48, 52–53. For evidence regarding the role of ritual and religious specialists in mediating cultural meanings, see James Hayes in D. Johnson et al., eds. (1985); also R. J. Smith (1991), passim.

13. Ping-ti Ho (1967). Pamela Crossley argues that "sinicization" is "conceptually flawed, intellectually inert and impossible to apply," since Chinese culture has itself changed constantly in response to, among other things, the "challenging and differentiating effects of aboriginal, border and heterodox cultures." As she puts the matter, "Historically it is surely true that the geographical and cultural entity of China is a totality of convergently and divergently related localisms" (Crossley 1990a). No modern scholar would quarrel with this characterization. Yet simply to speak of aboriginal, border, and heterodox cultures is to acknowledge implicitly a hegemonic, "central," and "orthodox" culture in constant tension with them. The question then becomes: What was its nature during the Qing period?

14. A. Wright (1960), pp. 234–235. Cf. Rowe (1984, 1989).

15. Arthur Wright in Gottschalk, ed. (1963), p. 39.

16. The major documentary sources for this study are mentioned in the Bibliographical Remarks. On the scholarly use (and abuse) of Chinese encyclopedias, consult Bauer (1966).

17. Arthur Wright in Gottschalk, ed. (1963), p. 39.

18. Noteworthy exceptions are Plaks (1976, 1977); Plaks, ed. (1977); Sangren (1987); Graham (1986).

19. Hawkes, trans. (1977), pp. 122–124.

20. Mu Ch'ien in Wing-tsit Chan, ed. (1986), p. 32. See also D.W.Y. Kwok in Smith and Kwok, eds. (1993); Chung-ying Cheng (1991), pp. 1–58, passim; R. J. Smith (1991), pp. 27, 51, 121–122.

21. Sangren (1987), pp. 132–140, 166–186. Plaks (1976) uses a sophisticated *yinyang* analysis with similarly good effect in the realm of literary criticism.

22. Tung-sun Chang (1952), p. 222; Yu-lan Fung (1948), pp. 355, 406; Xiaotong Fei (1992), pp. 721–779. See also Zongsan Mou in Jingxiong Wu et al., eds. (1967); Zhengtong Wei (1981), esp. pp. 58–61, 158, 233–235, 300; and the various articles in Wilson et al., eds. (1981). An excellent recent study of Chinese ethics is Ivanhoe (1990); cf. Metzger in Cohen and Goldman, eds. (1990).

23. It should be emphasized that while Confucian ethics were secular in origin, they had a decidedly sacred quality, since they were inextricably linked to cosmology throughout the imperial era. For a succinct discussion of China's "cosmological morality," consult Kwang-Ching Liu in Kwang-Ching Liu, ed. (1990), pp. 7–12. See also Zhengtong Wei (1981), pp. 50–54, 109–126; Taylor (1990), passim.

24. C. K. Yang (1961), pp. 175–176.

25. Geertz (1973), pp. 112–113.

26. See *ZWDCD*, pp. 10338 ff., on *li* and its use in various compounds. Note also the range of topics covered in the subsection on ritual administration in the *JSWB* and its supplements. M. Cohen (1991), pp. 117–118, draws a useful analytical distinction between the instrumentality of ritual and the restrictiveness of etiquette.

27. See Richard J. Smith in Kwang-Ching Liu, ed. (1990), p. 284; also Xiaotong Fei (1992), pp. 94 ff. On the development of ritual handbooks, consult Ebrey (1991); also A. Chun (1992).

28. S. W. Williams (1883), 1:424; A. Smith (1899), p. 193; Nevius (1869), p. 239. See also Gray (1878), 1:347; Wieger (1913), p. 110.

29. Geertz (1973), p. 89. See also Bell (1989), pp. 102–105. For indications of the overall social and political significance of *li* in late imperial China, consult Richard J. Smith in Kwang-Ching Liu, ed. (1990); also M. Cohen (1991); Xiaotong Fei (1992), Chapter 8. In D. Johnson et al., eds. (1985), pp. 323–324, James Watson makes the point that Chinese ritual allowed for the expression of substantial variations in outlook within an overall "structure of unity"—thus contributing significantly to cultural integration in China. See also Watson's remarks in Watson and Rawski, eds. (1988), pp. 15–18; and in Lieberthal et al., eds. (1991), pp. 368–372.

30. For a discussion of this "relational" view of culture, see Bell (1989).

31. For some historically grounded explanations, consult Bodde (1991); Elvin (1973); Ping-ti Ho (1976); Joseph Needham in Dawson, ed. (1964). See also Zhengtong Wei (1981), pp. 26–29, 35–41, 47–48, 54–58, 61, and esp. 314–315.

32. On the question of Manchu ethnicity, see Crossley (1990a); Elliot (1990). For other "ethnic" issues, consult Honig (1992), pp. 3 ff.; M. Cohen (1991), pp. 119–123; Lung-chang Young (1988); Guildin (1984); Barbara Ward in Jain, ed. (1977).

33. See the discussion in R. J. Smith (1991), p. 8.

34. See David Johnson in Johnson et al., eds. (1985).

35. For some indications of these prejudices and problems, consult Ebrey, ed. (1993); Rowe (1992); Holmgren (1981, 1984); Eastman (1988), pp. 19–33; Elvin (1984); Jochim (1988), pp. 28 ff. Elizabeth Johnson and Charlotte Furth provide particularly illuminating discussions of women's perspectives on death in Watson and Rawski, eds. (1988). See also note 36 below.

36. Recent studies of women's lives, views, and problems, in addition to those cited in note 35 above, include Stockard (1989); Siu (1989, 1990); Mann (1987, 1992); Furth (1987, 1988, 1992); Furth, ed. (1992). See also the articles by Stevan Harrall and Alison Black in Bynum et al., eds. (1986).

37. On marriage resistance as a form of "rebellion," consult Stockard (1989); Siu (1990).

38. For examples of violence, see Lipman and Harrell, eds. (1990); also Harry Lamley in Ahern and Gates, eds. (1981); Harry Lamley in Kwang-Ching Liu, ed. (1990). R. J. Smith (1993) discusses Qing efforts to curtail fighting.

39. James Watson in D. Johnson et al., eds. (1985), p. 292.

40. M. Cohen (1991), p. 114.

CHAPTER 2. THE QING INHERITANCE

1. See Junyi Tang (1981), pp. 65–74.

2. See Jagchid and Symons (1989); Barfield (1989); *CHC* (1993), vol. 6.

3. See Chapter 1, note 13, on "sinicization."

4. A. March (1974), p. 17; Jay (1990), p. 250.

5. See Crossley (1987, 1990a).

6. Guy (1987), pp. 24–25, 160–161, 203–204; Durand (1992), pt. 3.

7. See Joseph Fletcher in *CHC* (1978), vol. 10, pt. 1.

8. Leonard (1984). See also note 31 below.

9. See Joseph Fletcher in *CHC* (1978), vol. 10, pt. 1, pp. 35 ff.

10. Cressey (1955), p. 1.

11. Xiaotong Fei (1992), p. 37.

12. Ibid. pp. 38–39.

13. Myron Cohen in Graubard, ed. (1993), p. 156.

14. Xiaotong Fei (1992) provides an illuminating discussion of the social manifestations of China's rural character.

15. Fairbank (1986), p. 2.

16. On travel routes, see Brook (1988).

17. Strassberg (1983), p. 54.

18. See Elman (1981–1983).

19. Cordell Yee (1992), esp. p. 46.

20. Cited in I. Hsü (1959), pp. 43–44.

21. Elman (1981–1983), p. 5.

22. Wylie (1867), pp. 43–44; Yu-shan Han (1955), pp. 175–180.

23. Richard (1908). For more recent geographical studies, see Moser (1985); Leeming (1993).

24. See Naquin and Rawski (1987a), pp. 106–114; also Lavely et al. (1990).

25. See Chusei Suzuki and David Farquhar in Fairbank, ed. (1968), pp. 192–224; also note 40 below.

26. See Waley-Cohen (1991).

27. Cressey (1955), p. 8.

28. Dun J. Li (1978), pp. 1–28.

29. See Dodgen (1991).

30. On the Yangzi, consult Van Slyke (1988).

31. See Wills (1974, 1984); Souza (1986); Chin-keong Ng (1983); Clark (1991); Murray (1987); Knapp et al., eds. (1980).

32. See Tu-ki Min (1989); Rozman (1982); Moser (1985); Grove and Daniels, eds. (1984). Cf. Yuanqiang Song (1991).

33. Skinner (1964–1965). The summary is from Spence (1990), p. 91.

34. See Sands and Myers (1990); Little and Esherick (1989); Lavely (1989); Von Glahn (1987).

35. Naquin and Rawski (1987a).

36. Schoppa (1982); Esherick and Rankin, eds. (1990); Rankin (1986).

37. Cole (1986); Harrell (1982).

38. Esherick (1987); Sutton (1981); R. J. Smith (1991).

39. For a detailed discussion, see Naquin and Rawski (1987a), pp. 138 ff.

40. Eberhard (1982); Yin Ma, ed. (1989); Heberer (1989); Guang'an Liu (1990); Ramsey (1987), pp. 157 ff.

41. See Kwang-Ching Liu and Richard J. Smith in *CHC* (1980), vol. 11, pt. 2, pp. 211–243. See also Crossley (1990a), p. 22, on Chen Hongmou.

42. See Harry Lamley in Ahern and Gates, eds. (1981).

43. Brook (1988), pp. 3 ff.; esp. 14–19.

44. Ibid., p. 18; See also Skinner, ed. (1977), pp. 216–217; Cressey (1955), pp. 24 ff.; cf. Schran (1978).

45. See R. J. Smith (1978b), p. 9.

46. Jane Kate Leonard in Leonard and Watt, eds. (1992).

47. See Rowe (1984, 1989).

48. Skinner, ed. (1977), p. 538. See also Honig (1992), pp. 7–8; Zhengtong Wei (1981), pp. 45–49.

49. Eberhard (1965); see also Lung-chang Young (1988).

50. Eberhard (1965); see also Guildin (1984).

51. Eberhard notes little change in Chinese regional stereotypes since the Song period.

52. Spence (1975), pp. 49–50.

53. Lung-chang Young (1988), pp. 40–41.

54. Ibid.

55. Ibid., pp. 50–51; G. William Skinner in Carol Smith, ed. (1976).

56. For recent overviews, see Fairbank (1992), a chronological treatment, and Ropp, ed. (1990), a topical treatment. Note also the appropriate volumes in *CHC*.

57. Ping-ti Ho (1976); cf. Lüquan Guan (1992).

58. N. J. Girardot in Lovin and Reynolds, eds. (1985); Girardot (1976, 1983).

59. For details, see Hung Wu (1989); Allen (1981, 1991); Kwang-chih Chang (1983), pp. 2 ff.; Plaks (1976), pp. 11 ff. Cf. Derk Bodde in Kramer, ed. (1961).

60. Keightley (1978, 1988); Kwang-chih Chang (1980), pp. 335–355.

61. Ibid. (all three sources); see also Kwang-chih Chang, ed. (1986).

62. Keightley (1978, 1988); see also Keightley, ed. (1983).

63. Fairbank (1992), p. 40. For details on the early Zhou, see Hsu and Linduff, eds. (1988).

64. See Cho-yun Hsu (1965); Xueqin Li (1985); B. Watson (1989).

65. Lewis (1990), p. 95.

66. Cho-yun Hsu (1965); Xueqin Li (1985).

67. For excellent "conventional" overviews, see Schwartz (1985); Mote (1989); Graham (1989). For recent revisionist scholarship, consult C. Hansen (1992); La Fargue (1993); Roetz (1993); Peerenboom (1993); Lenk and Paul, eds. (1993).

68. Allen (1981).

69. Cf. C. Hansen (1992); Peerenboom (1993).

70. See the excellent overview of the Qin by Derk Bodde in *CHC* (1986), vol. 1; on Qin law, consult Hulsewe (1985).

71. On the "myth" of the Great Wall, and legends connecting it to the Qin, see Waldron (1990).

72. Needham and Huang (1974).

73. For an overview, see *CHC* (1986), vol. 1; also Zhongshu Wang (1982).

74. For some relevant studies, consult Bielenstein (1980); Cho-yun Hsu (1980); de Crespigny (1984); G. Young (1984); Barfield (1989); Hung Wu (1989); Powers (1992); Ames (1983).

75. See Thomsen (1988).

76. Kwang-Ching Liu in Kwang-Ching Liu, ed. (1990).

77. Vervoorn (1990); cf. Jay (1990). On the Qing dynasty's admiration of the Han synthesis, consult Metzger (1973), pp. 70–71.

78. For pertinent articles, see Albert Dien, ed. (1990); also Barfield (1989).

79. See K. Chen (1964, 1973); A. Wright (1968); Paul Demieville in *CHC* (1986), vol. 1.

80. See the article by Paul Demieville in *CHC* (1986), vol. 1; also Rolf Stein in Seidel and Welch, eds. (1979).

81. Weinstein (1987); Teiser (1988); Gregory (1991); also note 79 above. On sinicization, see Chapter 1, note 13.

82. *CHC* (1979), vol. 3, provides a comprehensive overview of the Sui-Tang period. See also A. Wright (1978); Wright and Twitchett, eds. (1973).

83. For some recent studies, consult McMullen (1988); Hartman (1986); Weinstein (1987); Verellen (1989).

84. Sullivan (1977), p. 122.

85. Hartwell (1982); see also the sources cited in note 82 above.

86. For details on continuing intellectual struggles, see Bol (1992).

87. Wechsler (1985).

88. W. Johnson, ed. (1979); Bodde and Morris (1967), pp. 3–4.

89. For an overview, consult D. Kuhn (1987); also Fairbank (1992), pp. 88–127; Haeger (1975).

90. Elvin (1973), pp. 69–90, 113–234. See also Hartwell (1982); Haeger (1975).

91. See Ebrey, trans. (1984); Hymes (1986); Hymes in Ebrey and Watson, eds. (1986); V. Hansen (1990); R. Davis (1986); McDermott (1987).

92. See Bettine Birge in de Bary and Chaffee, eds. (1989), esp. p. 431, note 72.

93. See Bol (1992); Tillman (1982); Birdwhistell (1989); K. Smith et al. (1990); Munro (1988); Hartman (1986).

94. See Joseph Needham in Dawson, ed. (1964); cf. Nathan Sivin in Daojing Hu, ed. (1982).

95. See Kang Chao (1986); Yeh-chien Wang (1990); Elvin (1973); Joseph Needham in Welskopf, ed. (1964); Eastman (1988), pp. 149–156.

96. James T.C. Liu (1988). On the examination system, see Hymes (1986); T. Lee (1985); W. W. Lo (1987); Chaffee (1985).

97. James T.C. Liu (1988), pp. 154–155; see also Hartwell (1982); Elvin (1973); Joseph Needham in Dawson, ed. (1964) and in Welskopf, ed. (1964).

98. See *CHC* (1993), vol. 6; also Barfield (1989); Hok-lam Chan (1984); Jing-shen Tao (1988); Herbert Franke in Schram, ed. (1987).

99. See Jay (1990); also W. T. de Bary and Wei-ming Tu in Hok-lam Chan and W. T. de Bary, eds. (1982).

100. de Hartog (1989); Allsen (1987); Rossabi (1988).

101. Jay (1990), pp. 259–260. See also Dardess (1983); Mote (1986).

102. See Dreyer (1982); also the articles by Edward Farmer and Romeyn Taylor in Kwang-Ching Liu, ed. (1990). For an overview of the Ming, consult *CHC* (1988), vol. 7.

103. Charles Hucker in James T.C. Liu, ed. (1970), p. 61.

104. Hucker (1975), p. 356.

105. Hao Chang in Smith and Kwok, eds. (1993). p. 24. See also W. T. de Bary's discussion of these thinkers in de Bary (1991a).

106. Dawson, ed. (1964), p. 359. On the Jesuits and their influence, see Mungello (1977, 1989); Spence (1984); J. D. Young (1983); Witek (1982); Gernet (1985); Standaert (1988).

107. Tong (1990).

108. See Wakeman (1985).

109. Ibid. See also Struve (1984, 1993); Widmer (1987); Dennerline (1981).

110. Jay (1990), pp. 261–263.

111. See the sources cited in note 106 above.

112. Frederic Wakeman in Crowley, ed. (1970), p. 1.

113. Rozman et al. (1981), p. 216.

CHAPTER 3. THE QING POLITICAL ORDER

1. Crossley (1992), p. 1482. See also Zelin (1984), p. xiv. Unless otherwise indicated, the following material is drawn from Hummel (1943–1944).

2. For a report of Kangxi's ruse, see Li Zhiting in Si Er et. al. (1986), pp. 55 ff.

3. See Spence (1975).

4. Bartlett (1991), pp. 258–259, 271; Zelin (1984), passim.

5. P. Kuhn (1990), p. 227; Zelin (1984), p. xv; Bartlett (1991), p. 264.

6. Cited in Bartlett (1991), p. 371.

7. Ibid., p. 234.

8. Zelin (1984), p. 301. See also Dodgen (1991), pp. 52–53.

9. Leonard and Watt, eds. (1992), p. 67.

10. On the late Qing succession crises, see Marianne Bastid in Schram, ed. (1987); also the fascinating "inside" articles by Rong Shidi, Xu Yipu, and Zhu Jinfu in Si Er et al. (1986), which indicate that Cixi was not responsible for the deaths of either the Tongzhi or the Guangxu emperors.

11. Kahn (1971), p. 4.

12. See Crossley (1992).

13. Spence (1975), pp. 29–59. See also Silas Wu (1970 and esp. 1970a).

14. Richard J. Smith in Kwang-Ching Liu, ed. (1990); Zito (1984, 1989).

15. See Meyer (1991).

16. James Watson in Baker and Feuchtwang, eds. (1991). Watson's analysis focuses on South China, but he suggests (p. 175) that similar concepts of the state also probably prevailed in other parts of China.

17. *Chinese Repository,* October 1832, pp. 236–238, slightly modified.

18. Bartlett (1991), p. 270.

19. Liu Guilin in Si Er et al. (1986), pp. 60 ff.

20. See note 10 above; also Xu Yipu in Si Er et al. (1986), pp. 142 ff.

21. Torbert (1978). For details on these and other Qing institutions, consult Mayers (1897); Brunnert and Hagelstrom (1911).

22. See M. Anderson (1990), pp. 291–304.

23. See Bartlett (1985); Crossley and Rawski (1993).

24. See Bartlett (1991). For Robert Hart's firsthand observations concerning the grand councillors who served in the Zongli Yamen, see R. J. Smith et al., eds. (1991), passim.

25. Bartlett (1991).

26. Mu Ch'ien (1982), p. 131.

27. Metzger (1973), Chapter 4; cf. P. Kuhn (1990), pp. 191 ff.

28. E-tu Zen Sun (1962–1963), and in Leonard and Watt, eds. (1992).

29. R. J. Smith (1991), pp. 75–76, and in Kwang-Ching Liu, ed. (1990), pp. 297–298.

30. On the importance of music, see Kaufmann (1976); DeWoskin (1982).

31. R. J. Smith (1974), pp. 127–130.

32. See Jones (1974); Shuzo Shiga (1974); Meijer (1991); Bodde and Morris (1967); also notes 33 and 34 below.

33. Ocko (1988), p. 311.

34. Alford (1984), p. 1242.

35. Lillian Li (1982). See also Will (1990); Will and Wong (1991).

36. Alford (1984), p. 1240; Lui (1978).

37. For an "inside" look at the Zongli Yamen, see R. J. Smith et al., eds. (1991), passim.

38. See Bartlett (1991), pp. 49–64, 264, 270; also P. Kuhn (1990), esp. Chapter 9.

39. See P. Kuhn (1990), pp. 203–207; Silas Wu (1970), esp. pp. 127 ff.

40. Silas Wu (1970), pp. 132–134.

41. Ibid., p. 139.

42. Zito (1989), p. 12.

43. Metzger (1973), pp. 177 ff.; Bartlett (1991), esp. pp. 103–112.

44. S. W. Williams (1883), 1:420; Ocko (1973).

45. Chu and Saywell (1984). The authors point out that more than one-quarter of all Qing governors-general had tenures that ended in demotion or dismissal—often for the misconduct or incompetence of their subordinates.

46. See the sources cited in notes 48 and 52 below.

47. Yuen-sang Leung (1990).

48. T'ung-tsu Ch'ü (1962); Watt (1972); Chu Djang, trans. (1984).

49. Ibid. (all three sources). See also Cole (1986); *CHC* (1978), vol. 10, pt. 1, pp. 111–112.

50. Kung-ch'üan Hsiao (1960); Sweeten (1976); P. Kuhn (1980).

51. Ibid. (all three sources). Cf. Bernhardt (1992).

52. Elman (1991), p. 8.

53. For details on the examination system, see ibid.; also Benjamin Elman in Elman and Woodside, eds. (forthcoming); Miyazaki (1976); Naquin and Rawski (1987a), pp. 9 ff.

54. Adam Lui (1981).

55. See Benjamin Elman in Elman and Woodside, eds. (forthcoming).

56. Wakeman (1975), pp. 20–27; also Elman (1991), pp. 14–15; Chung-li Chang (1967), pp. 123 ff.

57. See Ropp (1981), Chapters 3 and 6.

58. See Ping-ti Ho (1962), pp. 24–27, 34–38; also Mu Ch'ien (1982), pp. 134–136.

59. P. Kuhn (1990), p. 231; see also Bartlett (1991); Zelin (1984). Naquin and Rawski (1987a), pp. 10–11, view the bureaucracy primarily as a countervailing influence on the emperor.

60. Chu and Saywell (1984). During the entire Qing period, only about one-quarter of the governors-general were Han Chinese. Of these, two-thirds had the *jinshi* degree, while less than one-third of the Manchus had it.

61. Ibid., pp. 84 ff.; see also R. J. Smith (1974), pp. 131–145; Elliot (1990).

62. M. Wright (1967), Chapter 5, esp. pp. 90–91.

63. Metzger (1977), p. 207.

64. See Nathan (1976), pp. 47–58; King (1991); *CHC* (1978), vol. 10, pt. 1, pp. 114–116.

65. Nathan (1976), pp. 48–49; Zelin (1984), pp. 55 ff.; Pye (1981), pp. 138–142; Chu and Saywell (1984), p. 54; Naquin and Rawski (1987a), pp. 41, 51–53. See also the sources cited in note 66 below.

66. Metzger (1973), pp. 322–324 and notes; R. J. Smith et al., eds. (1991), pp. 20–21. See also the sources cited in note 65 above. It should be noted that "gifts" were often considered a regular part of one's salary. Consider, for example, the case of teachers discussed by Rawski (1979), p. 55.

67. Perkins (1967), pp. 487, 491–492; Rozman et al. (1981), pp. 73–77, 109–115, 130–140. Zelin (1984) documents fully the abortive Yongzheng financial reforms.

68. Metzger (1973), pp. 23 ff. See also the articles in Leonard and Watt, eds. (1992); Rozman et al. (1981), Chapter 3 and esp. pp. 205–208.

69. Cited in Balazs (1965), p. 65.

70. See Chu and Saywell (1984), pp. 12 ff., 81 ff.; Watt (1972), pp. 174–176; T'ung-tsu Ch'ü (1962), pp. 34–35.

71. Kahn (1971), p. 10.

CHAPTER 4. SOCIAL AND ECONOMIC INSTITUTIONS

1. Xiaotong Fei (1992), p. 71.

2. Ibid., pp. 60 ff., esp. p. 70.

3. Cited in Lien-sheng Yang (1969), p. 3, modified.

4. Ibid., p. 4; see also Zhang Laoshi yuekan bianji bu, ed. (1990); Naquin and Rawski (1987a), pp. 51 ff.

5. King (1991), p. 75; Skinner (1971), p. 277. See also Chapter 3, notes 63–66.

6. See Zurndorfer (1988); Madeleine Zelin in Lieberthal et al., eds. (1991); Rawski (1991); Rawski and Li, eds. (1992); Ebrey and Watson, eds. (1986).

7. Rowe (1992), p. 8.

8. Ibid. (1992), citing Susan Mann in R. Watson and Ebrey, eds. (1991).

9. See Crossley (1990).

10. Brunnert and Hagelstrom (1911), pp. 490–514; see also Garrett (1990).

11. *WXL*, Introduction: 4b; 8: 1a–116; 12: 1a–106; 13: 1a–106; 14: 1a–8b. See also Richard J. Smith in Kwang-Ching Liu, ed. (1990).

12. Chung-li Chang (1967); Ping-ti Ho (1962), esp. pp. 26–41.

13. Frederic Wakeman, Jr., in Crowley, ed. (1970), pp. 13–15. Cf. *CHC* (1978), vol. 10, pt. 1, p. 118.

14. Chung-li Chang (1962), pp. 372–378; Rozman et al. (1981), p. 122. Cf. Madeleine Zelin in Lieberthal et al., eds. (1991), pp. 46, 55.

15. Rankin (1986), pp. 109–110; *CHC* (1978), vol. 10, pt. 1, p. 112; James Polachek in Wakeman and Grant, eds. (1975).

16. Rozman et al. (1981), p. 151; Rowe (1989), pp. 29–38.

17. Ping-ti Ho (1962), pp. 20–21, 80; see also David Johnson in Johnson et al., eds. (1985).

18. See Madeleine Zelin in Lieberthal et al., eds. (1991); Eastman (1988), pp. 75–78; Spence (1990), p. 95; also Beattie (1979), esp. Chapters 1 and 3; Bernhardt (1992); Philip Huang (1985, 1990). See also notes 65 and 68 below.

19. Spence (1978), pp. 10–11, 14.

20. Madeleine Zelin in Lieberthal et al., eds. (1991), p. 33.

21. Ibid., p. 43; see also Siu (1990); Stockard (1989).

22. See David Arkush's revealing study of peasant proverbs in Kwang-Ching Liu, ed. (1990).

23. See M. Cohen (1991), esp. pp. 117–119. Gu Yanwu is quoted in Beattie (1979), p. 180, note 12.

24. Gamble (1943), p. 66. Cf. Spence (1990), p. 87, on the piecework wages of Suzhou calenderers, who received only 11 copper cash (equivalent to about one-hundredth of an ounce of silver) each for a 68-foot length of cloth that took nearly an entire day to process. See also Appendix B.

25. See Rowe (1989), pp. 36–38; also Spence (1978), pp. 121–122; Kwang-Ching Liu (1988).

26. See Mann (1987); also Madeleine Zelin in Lieberthal et al., eds. (1991), pp. 53 ff.

27. Rankin (1986), p. 7; Ping-ti Ho (1962), pp. 81–86. See also Mark Elvin in Skinner, ed. (1977), esp. p. 468.

28. Shen is cited by Ying-shih Yü in Graubard, ed. (1993), pp. 142–143.

29. Wakeman (1975), p. 51. See also Rowe (1989), pp. 56 ff.

30. Ping-ti Ho (1962), pp. 90–91, 107–111; also G. William Skinner in C. Smith, ed. (1976); Elman (1991).

31. On Qing education, consult Woodside (1983); Rawski (1979); Elman and Woodside, eds. (forthcoming); Elman (1991), esp. pp. 20–21. See also note 59 below.

32. Frederick Mote in Buxbaum and Mote, eds. (1972), pp. 13–14. See also note 31 above.

33. See K. Chen (1964), Chapter 16.

34. Ibid., p. 453; also C. K. Yang (1961), pp. 189 ff.

35. Li and Naquin (1988).

36. Mayers (1897), pp. 84–86.

37. R. J. Smith (1974), pp. 141–145.

38. R. J. Smith (1978c), pp. 15–25.

39. R. J. Smith (1974), pp. 150–157.

40. Zurndorfer (1988), pp. 152–153; Rowe (1989), p. 31. See also Honig (1992); Mi Chu Wiens in Kwang-Ching Liu, ed. (1990).

41. Bodde and Morris (1967), pp. 33, 169 ff.

42. Torbert (1978), pp. 57–58. On Cao Yin, see Spence (1966).

43. Spence (1978), pp. 123–127; Charlotte Furth in Kwang-Ching Liu, ed. (1990), pp. 202–203; Ko (1992), p. 9. Cf. Stockard (1989).

44. Holmgren (1981, 1984); Furth (1987, 1988, 1992); Mann (1992); Weidner et al., eds. (1988); Weidner, ed. (1990); Siu (1990); Rowe (1992); Ropp (1976, 1981). See also note 43 above.

45. Bodde and Morris (1967), pp. 28–29, 41, 221, 286–288, 330. See also Chapter 3, note 45.

46. Xiaotong Fei (1992), Chapter 6; R. J. Smith (1987); F. Hsu (1971).

47. M. Cohen (1991), p. 116; also Myron Cohen in Graubard, ed. (1993), pp. 161–162.

48. See Bodde and Morris (1967), passim.

49. Madeleine Zelin in Lieberthal et al., eds. (1991), esp. p. 40.

50. Charlotte Furth in Kwang-Ching Liu, ed. (1990), esp. p. 187.

51. See the articles by Jonathan Ocko and Richard J. Smith in ibid.; also Elvin (1984); Ebrey (1991).

52. C. K. Yang (1961), Chapter 2.

53. Bodde and Morris (1967), p. 139.

54. Ibid., pp. 37–38, 40–41.

55. Spence (1978), p. 138.

56. On kinship terminology, see Ebrey and Watson, eds. (1986), pp. 4–10; also Han-yi Feng (1967).

57. See Ebrey and Watson, eds. (1986); M. Cohen (1990); also Zurndorfer (1988), pp. 157–158; Beattie (1979), Chapter 4.

58. James Watson in Ebrey and Watson, eds. (1986), p. 282.

59. Beattie (1979), pp. 52, 122–123, 126, 128; Ping-ti Ho (1962), pp. 209–212; Kung-ch'üan Hsiao (1960), pp. 237–240. See also the sources cited in note 31 above.

60. See Hui-chen Wang Liu (1959); also R. J. Smith (1993); Rowe (1989), pp. 120, 276–277; Victor Mair in D. Johnson et al., eds. (1985).

61. See Hui-chen Wang Liu in Nivison and Wright, eds. (1959), pp. 17, 19–30, 37–49.

62. C. K. Yang (1961), pp. 40–43, 52–53.

63. Kung-ch'üan Hsiao (1960), Chapter 8.

64. P. Kuhn (1977, 1980).

65. Yeh-chien Wang (1974); D. Faure (1976); Chung-li Chang (1962), pp. 136–147. See also the sources cited in notes 18 above and 68 below.

66. Cited by Madeleine Zelin in Lieberthal et al., eds. (1991), p. 40. See also Naquin and Rawski (1987a), p. 230.

67. Cited in Kung-ch'üan Hsiao (1960), pp. 354–355.

68. See Jing and Luo (1978); Muramatsu (1966); Skinner (1971); also the sources cited in notes 18 above and 65 below.

69. Skinner (1964–1965); Rozman (1982).

70. Skinner (1971), pp. 272–277.

71. Ibid. Cf. Hayes (1977).

72. See the articles by G. William Skinner and Yoshonobu Shira in Skinner, ed. (1977).

73. Rankin (1986), pp. 242–243; Rowe (1989), p. 15, citing both Frederick Mote and Evelyn Rawski.

74. Rowe (1989), pp. 15–18, 83–87, 176, 345 ff. See also the articles by Arthur Wright and Frederick Mote in Skinner, ed. (1977), esp. pp. 114–117.

75. Frederick Mote in Skinner, ed. (1977). Cf. Rowe (1989), pp. 16 ff.

76. Wakeman and Grant, eds. (1975), p. 4.

77. Rankin (1986); Rowe (1989); Cole (1986).

78. See Kwang-Ching Liu (1988); Rowe (1989), Chapter 4; J. H. Smith (1987); M. Wright (1967), pp. 133 ff.

79. Fairbank (1992), p. 181.

80. Rowe (1989), pp. 174–178. See also the articles by Yoshonobu Shira, Peter Golas, Sybille van der Sprenkel, Kristopher Schipper, Tilemann Grimm, and Stephen Feuchtwang in Skinner, ed. (1977).

81. See Esherick (1987), pp. 41 ff.; also Chesneaux (1972); Kwang-Ching Liu and Richard Shek, eds. (forthcoming).

82. P. Kuhn (1980), pp. 165, 176; Wakeman (1977), p. 207.

83. Skinner, ed. (1977), p. 277.

84. See Naquin and Rawski (1987a), pp. 227 ff. Lamley (1977), p. 34, reminds us that the rise of social tensions and even violence did not always coincide with dynastic decline.

CHAPTER 5. LANGUAGE AND SYMBOLIC REFERENCE

1. See Yinxian Gao et al. (1991).
2. Norman (1988), pp. 20–21, 129.
3. Norman (1988), pp. 113, 218 ff.; Ramsey (1987), p. 217; Bartlett (1985); Crossley and Rawski (1993).
4. R. J. Smith (1991), Chapter 3, esp. p. 93.
5. Cited in De Francis (1984), p. 63. See also the discussions of dialect in Ramsey (1987), Chapter 6; Norman (1988), Chapter 8.
6. See De Francis (1950), pp. 7 ff.; Elman (1991), p. 15.
7. See Ramsey (1987), pp. 58 ff.; Bodde (1991), pp. 16–17.
8. Consult Y. K. Wong (1990), Chapters 1–3 and 7, esp. p. 166. On the use of puns and plays on words, see Miller (1975), pp. 53, 80, 153–154, 174, 251–252; also notes 19–24 below.
9. See I. Hsü (1959), pp. 55 ff., 121, and Bibliography; also Mu Qian (1937), Chapters 4 and 8; Elman (1984).
10. See Bol (1992), pp. 84–107; also Don Wyatt in Cohen and Goldman, eds. (1990).
11. Bodde (1991), pp. 21–22.
12. Cited in R. J. Smith (1978a), p. 20. See also Bodde (1991), p. 27.
13. Hummel, ed. (1943–1944), p. 22.
14. R. J. Smith (1991), p. 202. See also John Lagerway in Naundorf et al., eds. (1985).
15. The pervasive use of written instruments of this sort is extremely rare in preindustrial societies. See Madeleine Zelin in Lieberthal et al., eds. (1991), p. 40.
16. *Kangxi zidian* (1962), p. 1; cf. R. Wilhelm (1967), p. 335.
17. Creel (1936), p. 97; Chung-ying Cheng (1973), pp. 92–93; Elman (1984), pp. 213 ff.
18. See the analysis in B.K.Y. T'sou (1981).
19. C. Hansen (1992), pp. 36 ff., remarks on the importance of such "popular etymologies" in China. For some examples, see François Cheng (1982).
20. See R. J. Smith (1991), pp. 202–204, 216–218, 226–229, 250–252.
21. See Waley (1970); also Y. K. Wong (1990), p. 161; Chapter 8, note 22.
22. Lai (1969), pp. 11–12. See also R. J. Smith (1991), pp. 202–203.
23. Rolston, ed. (1990), p. 338.
24. Wang Anshi, cited in Bol (1992), p. 232.
25. Rosemont (1974), pp. 76–79.
26. See Wing-tsit Chan, trans. (1967), pp. 359–370; also Bodde (1991), pp. 35–42.
27. On classical Chinese grammar, see Ramsey (1987), Chapter 5, esp. p. 57.
28. Bodde (1991), pp. 31–42, esp. p. 34; Rosemont (1974), p. 81.
29. Bodde (1991), pp. 40–42, 55–56, 74 ff. On punctuation, consult ibid., pp. 55–64; also Rolston, ed. (1990), pp. 46–49.
30. Goodrich (1975) provides an excellent example of a traditional-style Chinese primer, organized in four-character sets. See also note 31 below.
31. Y. R. Chao (1976), p. 289. See also Bodde (1991), pp. 42–55; Granet (1934), pp. 56–82, 115–148.

32. Tung-sun Chang (1952), pp. 214–215, 222–223. See also Scharfstein, ed. (1978), pp. 20–28.

33. See Black (1989), pp. 141–159.

34. See, for example, *WXL,* Introduction: 2a; Y. K. Wong (1990), pp. 157 ff.

35. *TSJC, dian* 13, 15, 22. The reprint edition I have used provides a convenient index, pp. 2–61, which includes all major subject headings, organized by subcategories.

36. Wing-tsit Chan, trans. (1967), pp. 27, 39, 195. See also Bodde (1991), pp. 42 ff.

37. Shih, trans. (1983), pp. xlix, 368–369.

38. Ibid., p. 373.

39. See Rolston, ed. (1990), pp. 17–29; Eugene Ching in Yamagiwa, ed. (1969); Lai (1969); Ching-i Tu (1974–1975); also Baoqian Lu (1978).

40. Bodde (1991), pp. 34–35.

41. Zhengtong Wei (1981), pp. 187–189; Junyi Tang (1981), pp. 320–323; also Y. R. Chao in Egerod and Glahn, eds. (1959).

42. A. C. Graham in Dawson, ed. (1964), pp. 54–55. See also Yu-lan Fung (1948), pp. 11–14; Ying-shih Yü (1975), pp. 106–107; R. J. Smith (1991), pp. 51, 119–122, 267; Nathan Sivin in Daojing Hu, ed. (1982), esp. p. 93.

43. Hummel, ed. (1943–1944), pp. 107–108, 152–156, 276–277, 499–500; *TSJC, dian* 12 and 14.

44. See Han-yi Feng (1967); Y. R. Chao (1976), pp. 309 ff.

45. *JLDC,* pp. 17–20, 24–78; *JLTSJC* 1: 1a–17b.

46. Tung-sun Chang (1952); Yu-lan Fung (1948), p. 16; Kwang-chih Chang (1976), Chapter 7. See also C. Hansen (1992), pp. 14 ff., esp. pp. 30–32; T'sou (1981); Sung (1979); Baoqian Lu (1978).

47. For a summary of conflicting views, see Bodde (1991), pp. 90–96; also Graham (1989), Appendix 2; C. Hansen (1992), pp. 33–54; C. Hansen (1993).

48. See C. Hansen (1992), pp. 33 ff., esp. pp. 53–54; also C. Hansen (1993); François Cheng (1982); Yu-kung Kao in Murck and Fong, eds. (1991), pp. 69–71.

49. Arthur Wright in A. Wright, ed. (1953), esp. p. 287; Nakamura (1971), pp. 177–190. See also the sources cited in notes 47 and 48 above.

50. Graham (1989), esp. pp. 395–398.

51. Chung-ying Cheng (1971, 1973); C. Hansen (1992), esp. p. 52.

52. Yu-kuang Chu in Meskill, ed. (1973), p. 600; Tung-sun Chang (1952), pp. 211–217; J. Needham (1956–1992), 2: 279 ff. See also Rosemont (1974), pp. 86–88; Bodde (1991), pp. 97 ff.; Graham (1986), passim.

53. See A. C. Graham (1989), pp. 75–105, 137–170, 389–401, 406–428.

54. R. J. Smith (1991), pp. 51, 122; also the sources cited in note 52 above.

55. See Mayers (1874), pp. 293–360; also Bodde (1991), pp. 64 ff.; E. Yip (1992), passim.

56. Rosemont (1974), p. 87.

57. Tat Wei (1970), p. xxx.

58. Chung-ying Cheng (1977); see also Jullien (1989) on the "process logic" of both classical Chinese and the *Yijing.*

59. R. J. Smith (1991), pp. 93–94.

60. Toda (1963).

61. The following discussion is derived from R. J. Smith (1991), Chapter 3.

62. Yu-lan Fung (1948), p. 168. See also the illuminating discussion in Strassberg (1983), p. 88.

63. Cited in R. J. Smith (1991), p. 125.
64. Spence (1975).
65. Cited in R. J. Smith (1991), pp. 122–126.
66. Rolston, ed. (1990), p. 339. See also R. J. Smith (1991), pp. 123–124.
67. R. Wilhelm (1967), pp. 328–336.
68. See J. Needham (1956–1992), 2: 329–345.
69. Ibid., 2: 334–335.
70. Yu-lan Fung (1952), 2: 636 ff.
71. J. Needham (1956–1992), 2: 336. Cf. Nathan Sivin in Daojing Hu, ed. (1982).
72. R. J. Smith (1991), pp. 126–127.
73. Ibid., 126–129; Bodde (1991), esp. pp. 88–93.
74. Bodde (1991), pp. 82–88; see also Nathan Sivin in Daojing Hu, ed. (1982), pp. 91–93.
75. Cited in Bodde (1991), p. 88.
76. See Arthur Wright in A. Wright, ed. (1953), pp. 286–301.
77. Ibid.; also Zhengtong Wei (1981), pp. 34, 344–345, 354–355, 359; Zuobin Dong in Jingxiong Wu et al., eds. (1967), esp. pp. 78–82.

CHAPTER 6. THOUGHT

1. Zhengtong Wei (1981), pp. 31–35, 51–52, 61–67, 110. See also Chapter 1, note 20.
2. See Chapter 7, note 1, for a brief definition of "religion."
3. For an overview, see Elman (1981). The following summary discussion is based on Ying-shih Yü (1975); Wei-ming Tu (1989); Smith and Kwok, eds. (1993); Guy (1987); Polachek (1992); and Elman (1984, 1990). See also the authors cited in note 27 below.
4. Wei-ming Tu (1989), pp. 117–140; W. T. de Bary in de Bary, ed. (1975), p. 11; Metzger (1977), pp. 13–15, 50 ff. See also Elman (1991); Ying-shih Yü (1975).
5. R. J. Smith (1991), Chapter 2. On the importance of *qi* in Qing thought, see An-cho Ng in Smith and Kwok, eds. (1993).
6. Chung-ying Cheng (1991), pp. 4–39, provides an illuminating contrast between Chinese and Western cosmology and ontology. See also Smith and Kwok, eds. (1993), passim.
7. Frederick Mote in Buxbaum and Mote, eds. (1972). See also the sources cited in Chapter 2, note 59.
8. See Bodde (1991), pp. 148–172.
9. Wing-tsit Chan in de Bary, ed. (1975), pp. 561, 563. See also Smith and Kwok, eds. (1993), passim.
10. See Graham (1986); Marcel Granet in R. Needham, ed. (1973).
11. Wing-tsit Chan, ed. and trans. (1963), p. 140; Mote (1990), pp. 400–401. For the idea of hexagrams "controlling" situations, consult J. Needham (1956), 2: 288–289.
12. Mai-mai Sze (1959), p. 73; Forke (1925), pp. 207–209, 214–215.
13. Toda (1963), pt. 3.
14. See R. J. Smith (1992).
15. Bodde (1991), pp. 122–133; cf. Sivin (1966); J. Needham (1965); Fraser et al., eds. (1986).
16. My copy of the *LYBL* is dated in this fashion.
17. Yu-lan Fung (1952), 2: 469–474.
18. M. Wright (1967), Chapter 4.

19. Arthur Wright in Gottschalk, ed. (1963), p. 38, and in Skinner, ed. (1977), p. 73.

20. See Yu-shan Han (1955), pp. 196–203.

21. See Fairbank, ed. (1968); also Mancall (1984).

22. Wills (1984); Peyrefitte (1992); Hevia (1989); John Fairbank in Fairbank, ed. (1968).

23. Cited by Benjamin Schwartz in Fairbank, ed. (1968), pp. 277–278.

24. See R. J. Smith (1975).

25. Benjamin Schwartz in Fairbank, ed. (1968), pp. 277–278.

26. Ping-ti Ho (1967), p. 193; Kessler (1976), p. 169.

27. For a sampling of the recent literature on Confucianism in late imperial times, see the relevant works by Anne Birdwhistell, Alison Black, Irene Bloom, Wing-tsit Chan, Chung-ying Cheng, Julia Ching, W. T. de Bary, Benjamin Elman, Daniel Gardner, Lynn Struve, Hoyt Tillman, Wei-ming Tu; also the sources cited in note 3 above.

28. Frederick Mote in Buxbaum and Mote, eds. (1972), p. 15.

29. *CC, Analects*, p. 146; *CC, Great Learning*, p. 364.

30. See the articles by Benjamin Elman and Kai-wing Chow in Smith and Kwok, eds. (1993), passim; also Machle (1993).

31. Yu-lan Fung (1948), p. 1.

32. Chung-ying Cheng (1973), esp. p. 97; see also Hall and Ames (1987).

33. Yu-lan Fung (1948), pp. 196–197. See also Kwang-Ching Liu in Kwang-Ching Liu, ed. (1990).

34. R. Wilhelm (1967), p. 540.

35. *CC, Mencius*, p. 346.

36. Rowe (1992), p. 17; Hao Chang in Smith and Kwok, eds. (1993), esp. pp. 26–28.

37. *CC, Mencius*, pp. 264–265, 309; *CC, Great Learning*, p. 370. Ebrey, ed. (1993), pp. 64–68, provides a translation of the *Xiaojing.*

38. Wing-tsit Chan (1955), pp. 297–298, 305. See also the articles by Benjamin Elman and San-pao Li in Smith and Kwok, eds. (1993).

39. Wing-tsit Chan (1955), p. 300; *CC, Analects*, p. 194.'

40. *CC, Mencius*, pp. 150–151, 195, 241, 313–314; Chai and Chai (1967), 1: 63, 2: 92 ff., 257–260. See also *CC, Analects*, pp. 143, 147, 161, 169, 193, 208, 211, 250, 323, 354.

41. *CC, Analects*, p. 299; *CC, Mencius*, p. 307.

42. Watt (1972), pp. 96–97; *JSWB*, 54: 1; Spence (1978), p. 142. On Xunzi, see Knoblock, trans. (1988); Cua (1985); Machle (1993).

43. See Richard J. Smith in Kwang-Ching Liu, ed. (1990).

44. *CC, Mencius*, p. 356; *CC, Analects*, p. 250; *CC, Great Learning*, p. 422.

45. *WLTK*, passim.

46. *CC, Mencius*, pp. 150–151, 195, 241, 313–314; Chai and Chai (1967), 1: 63, 2: 92 ff., 257–260. See also *CC, Analects*, pp. 143, 147, 161, 169, 193, 208, 211, 250, 323, 354.

47. *CC, Analects*, p. 299; *CC, Mencius*, p. 307.

48. See Chung-ying Cheng (1972); also *CC, Mencius*, pp. 202, 251, 302, 313, 402, 456, 485, 493; *CC, Analects*, pp. 154, 170, 254, 256, 259, 265, 299, 331.

49. Statecraft scholars would argue against this sort of exclusive emphasis, of course. See Polachek (1992); also Leonard and Watt, eds. (1992).

50. *CC, Analects*, p. 318. See also *CC, Mencius*, pp. 204–205, 402, 459; *CC, Analects*, pp. 151, 204–205, 212, 225, 260, 313–314; *CC, Mencius*, p. 303.

51. *CC, Doctrine of the Mean,* pp. 395, 412–419; also *CC, Analects,* pp. 139, 141, 153, 202, 224, 256, 265, 267, 295–296, 319, 331; *CC, Mencius,* p. 303.

52. *CC, Great Learning,* pp. 257–259.

53. See Wing-tsit Chan, ed. and trans. (1963), pp. 19, 84–85, 659, 707–708; Kai-wing Chow in Smith and Kwok, eds. (1993), pp. 190–191.

54. *TSJC, dian* 22; see also Hao Chang (1971), pp. 17, 85, 273–274, 292 ff.; Ying-shih Yü (1975), pp. 105, 109, 115.

55. *CC, Analects,* pp. 146–147; also pp. 179, 251, 253, 259, 271, 273, 274, 279, 292; *CC, Mencius,* pp. 185, 265, 455, 458–459; *CC, Doctrine of the Mean,* pp. 388, 428.

56. *CC, Doctrine of the Mean,* pp. 383–384, 386, 388, 390, 391, 393, 395–396.

57. Metzger (1977) documents the tension between neo-Confucian ethical demands and human shortcomings. Cf. Hao Chang (1987).

58. Zhu Xi is cited in Yu-lan Fung (1948), p. 301; *CC, Analects,* p. 318; *CC, Mencius,* p. 465.

59. Cited in Wing-tsit Chan, ed. and trans. (1963), pp. 540–541.

60. An-cho Ng in Smith and Kwok, eds. (1993), pp. 41, 48; Benjamin Elman in ibid., p. 63; Wing-tsit Chan, ed. and trans. (1963), p. 714.

61. Gedalecia (1974); also Forke (1925), pp. 202–207; Ermin Wang (1976), pp. 51–71.

62. C. K. Yang in Nivison and Wright, eds. (1959), pp. 142–143; Wing-tsit Chan, ed. and trans. (1963), pp. 14, 141, 159, 267, 323, 344, 358, 368 369, 401, 403–404, 414–415; Yu-lan Fung (1952), 2: 363, 366, 369, 375, 619; Black (1989), pp. 94 ff.

63. Yu-lan Fung (1952), 1: 31; cf. Eno (1990); Taylor (1990).

64. *CC, Mencius,* p. 357; *CC, Doctrine of the Mean,* p. 383; also J. Needham (1956), 2: 562–564.

65. *CC, Doctrine of the Mean,* p. 416; *CC, Mencius,* pp. 119, 208–209, 359, 362, 448; also R. Wilhelm (1967), pp. 295, 351.

66. See R. J. Smith (1991), pp. 10, 14, 33, 35–36, 42, 173–174, 177 ff. on fate.

67. See San-pao Li in Smith and Kwok, eds. (1993); cf. David Arkush in Kwang-Ching Liu, ed. (1990).

68. See the discussion in Levenson (1964).

69. Wing-tsit Chan, ed. and trans. (1963), pp. 136–210, offers an excellent selection of Daoist writings.

70. See C. Hansen (1992); also Peerenboom (1993); Lenk and Paul, eds. (1993); Roetz (1993); La Fargue (1993); Kohn, ed. (1993).

71. Wing-tsit Chan, ed. and trans. (1963), p. 162, modified.

72. Ibid., p. 167, modified.

73. Ibid., p. 141, modified.

74. de Bary et al., eds. (1964), 1: 70, modified.

75. Ibid., 1: 69, modified.

76. Ibid.

77. Wing-tsit Chan, ed. and trans. (1963), pp. 141–142.

78. Ibid., pp. 177–178.

79. Mote (1990), p. 399; cf. Allinson (1989).

80. Wing-tsit Chan, ed. and trans. (1963), pp. 177–178.

81. de Bary et al., eds. (1964), 1: 71, modified.

82. Wing-tsit Chan, ed. and trans. (1963), pp. 148–149.

83. Wing-tsit Chan, trans. (1967), p. 274; see also Spence (1975), p. 97.

84. W. T. de Bary in de Bary, ed. (1975), pp. 10, 94.

CHAPTER 7. RELIGION

1. Religion refers here to "transactions" between humans and designated spirits that take such cultural forms as sacrifice, prayer, and some kinds of divination. See Romeyn Taylor in Kwang-Ching Liu, ed. (1990), p. 128. These transactions may be distinguished from the rather more amorphous (but no less powerful) "spiritual" beliefs that were central to Confucianism. See the discussion in R. J. Smith (1991), pp. 25–27, 52, 65–66, 95, 108–110, 118, 119; also Chapter 6, note 63.

2. Maspero is cited in Thompson (1979), p. 55. See Maurice Freedman in A. Wolf, ed. (1974), pp. 37 ff. Cf. Stephan Feuchtwang in Baker and Feuchtwang, eds. (1991), esp. pp. 148 ff.

3. For a review of the recent literature, see Bell (1989).

4. James Watson in Lieberthal et al., eds. (1991), p. 74.

5. James Watson in D. Johnson et al., eds. (1985), p. 323.

6. See Feuchtwang (1992), pp. 8–9; Evelyn Rawski in Watson and Rawski, eds. (1988); R. J. Smith (1993).

7. James Watson in Lieberthal et al., eds. (1991), p. 74.

8. See E. T. Williams (1913), pp. 15–17, 21–23; cf. the essays by Edward Farmer and Romeyn Taylor in Kwang-Ching Liu, ed. (1990).

9. See, for instance, K. Chen (1964), pp. 449 ff.

10. On the Dalai Lama, see ibid., esp. p. 450. On begs, consult Kwang-Ching Liu and Richard J. Smith in *CHC* (1980), vol. 11, pt. 2.

11. See Brook (1989); Sutton (1989).

12. Sangren (1987), p. 231.

13. Brokaw (1991), pp. 157 ff., esp. pp. 162, 232–233.

14. See Sin-Wai Chan (1985).

15. Arthur Wolf in Wolf, ed. (1974), p. 145.

16. Stephan Feuchtwang in Skinner, ed. (1977), p. 607.

17. R. J. Smith (1988); Zito (1984, 1989); Richard J. Smith in Kwang-Ching Liu, ed. (1990).

18. Bartlett (1991), p. 253, notes that Qing emperors washed their hands before handling memorials that dealt with important state sacrifices.

19. Stephan Feuchtwang in Skinner, ed. (1977), pp. 591–593.

20. Ibid. On the emperor's powerful awareness of a spiritual presence, see the *Chinese Repository,* October 1832, pp. 236–238.

21. See the illuminating account in E. T. Williams (1913); cf. Zito (1989); Meyer (1991), passim.

22. For an overview, see Stephan Feuchtwang in Skinner, ed. (1977); also the sources cited in note 21 above.

23. Stephan Feuchtwang in Skinner, ed. (1977).

24. Ibid. See also T'ung-tsu Ch'ü (1962), pp. 164–165.

25. Stephan Feuchtwang in Skinner, ed. (1977), p. 601.

26. C. K. Yang (1961), pp. 156–157.

27. Cited in Spence (1978), pp. 49–50.

28. See, for example, R. F. Johnston (1910), pp. 364–374; Gray (1878), 1: 118–119. Instances of the Chinese cursing their gods are not uncommon. See A. Smith (1899), p. 160.

29. On gender issues, see Sangren (1987), pp. 74, 135–136, 148–156, 183–184, 198; also the articles by Alison Black and Stevan Harrall in Bynum et al., eds. (1986); Barbara Reed in Cabezon, ed. (1985).

30. See Stephan Feuchtwang in Skinner, ed. (1977); Zito (1987).

31. C. K. Yang (1961), pp. 98–99. On Tudi gong, see Arthur Wolf in Wolf, ed. (1974).

32. See Arthur Wolf in Wolf, ed. (1974); Thompson, ed. (1973), pp. 196–201.

33. James Watson in D. Johnson et al., eds. (1985).

34. T'ung-tsu Ch'ü (1962), p. 165; Balazs (1965), pp. 63–64; R. F. Johnston (1910), pp. 134–135.

35. Kristin Greenblatt in de Bary, ed. (1975), pp. 131–132.

36. C. K. Yang (1961), p. 281.

37. K. Chen (1964), pp. 441 ff.; Farquhar (1978), p. 33.

38. Farquhar (1978), p. 33; E. T. Williams (1913), p. 12.

39. Wing-tsit Chan, trans. (1967), p. 283.

40. Richard Shek in Smith and Kwok, eds. (1993).

41. Nivison (1966), pp. 76, 126–127.

42. Cited by Hui-chen Wang Liu in Nivison and Wright, eds. (1959), pp. 71–72.

43. For a sampling of early Buddhist writings, consult de Bary et al., eds. (1964), 1: 266–286. On Buddhist apocrypha, see Buswell, ed. (1990).

44. For overviews of these schools, see de Bary et al., eds. (1964), 1: 309–368.

45. Ibid., 1: 292.

46. Wing-tsit Chan (1969), pp. 438 ff.

47. See Wing-tsit Chan, ed. and trans. (1963), pp. 398–400; also Swanson (1989).

48. See the articles by John McRae and Robert Gimello in Gimello and Gregory, eds. (1983); also Odin (1982).

49. Wing-tsit Chan, ed. and trans. (1963), p. 407.

50. Ibid.

51. Smith (1987).

52. Wing-tsit Chan, ed. and trans. (1963), pp. 413–414.

53. On early Chan, consult McRae (1987) and the articles by Jeffrey Broughton, Luis Gomez, and John McRae in Gimello and Gregory, eds. (1983). See also B. Faure (1991, 1993).

54. On Wang, consult Wei-ming Tu (1976); Ching (1976); de Bary (1991), Chapter 6.

55. See Wei-ming Tu in Gregory, ed. (1987).

56. On the complexity of Chan Buddhist approaches to enlightenment, consult Gregory, ed. (1987).

57. See E. Zurcher in Dawson, ed. (1964). pp. 73–79.

58. See Wieger (1913), pp. 345–391, for descriptions and illustrations of the Ten Courts of Judgment and ibid., pp. 397–398, for descriptions and illustrations of the Western Paradise.

59. Consult Barbara Reed in Cabezon, ed. (1985).

60. Reichelt (1934), pp. 174–199.

61. Welch (1967), pp. 398 ff.

62. Wing-tsit Chan (1969), p. 419.

63. Saso (1978, 1991); Kohn, ed. (1989, 1993); Lagerwey (1987); Seidel and Welch, eds. (1979); Dean (1993).

64. Saso (1978), pp. 52 ff.

65. On Religious Daoist writings, see Bolz (1987).

66. Saso (1978), pp. 5–7, 52 ff.

67. See the sources cited in Chapter 10, notes 56, 61, 62.

68. See Brokaw (1991); Tadao Sakai in de Bary, ed. (1970), pp. 341–362.

69. K. Chen (1964), pp. 436–439; also Ching-lang Hou in Seidel and Welch, eds. (1979).

70. See Stephan Feuchtwang (1992); also Overmyer (1986).

71. See Sangren (1987) on *ling*.

72. C. K. Yang (1961), p. 25.

73. Ibid., pp. 7–10.

74. Ibid. See also the discussion by Stephan Feuchtwang in Baker and Feuchtwang, eds. (1991).

75. C. K. Yang (1961), pp. 10–15.

76. Schwartz (1985), p. 379.

77. See Daniel Overmyer in Reynolds and Ludwig, eds. (1980).

78. The quotation is from Plopper (1926), p. 78. Weller (1987) makes the important point that concepts of *gui* changed over time in response to changing social and economic conditions.

79. See Daniel Overmyer in Reynolds and Ludwig, eds. (1980), p. 164.

80. See De Groot (1912), pp. 4–28.

81. See the discussion in R. J. Smith (1991), passim; also De Groot (1912), pp. 35–59.

82. Doré (1914–1933), 3: iii–vi.

83. See the discussion in R. J. Smith (1991), Chapter 4.

84. Cited in Thompson (1979), pp. 22–23.

85. Meyer (1978), pp. 148–155.

86. R. J. Smith (1991), Chapter 4.

87. Ibid., pp. 72–73, 231–233.

88. On Chinese homes, see Knapp (1986, 1989, 1990).

89. See Watson and Rawski, eds. (1988), passim; also Maurice Freedman in Skinner, ed. (1979), pp. 296–312.

90. Thompson (1979), Chapter 3; C. K. Yang (1961), pp. 40–43, 52–53; Doré (1914–1933), 4: 417 ff.

91. James Watson in Watson and Rawski, eds. (1988), pp. 12–15.

92. Ibid.

93. See Richard J. Smith in Kwang-Ching Liu, ed. (1990); also note 90 above.

94. C. K. Yang in Fairbank, ed. (1957), p. 276.

95. Ibid., p. 227; see also Welch (1967), pp. 181–185; Brook (1989). Paper (1985), p. 3, offers the intriguing suggestion that in China "aesthetic activity … became an alternative mode of religiosity for the traditional elite."

96. See Richard J. Smith in Kwang-Ching Liu, ed. (1990).

97. M. Cohen (1991), esp. pp. 117–123; R. J. Smith (1991), pp. 265–266; Sangren (1987), pp. 191 ff.

98. See Liu and Shek, eds. (forthcoming); Esherick (1987); Naquin and Rawski (1987a), pp. 134–137, 166–167, 191–193; Ebrey, ed. (1993), pp. 318–322.

99. Naquin and Rawski (1987), pp. 185–186.

100. On the Taipings, see Richard Bohr in Liu and Shek, eds. (forthcoming); on Islam in China, consult Israeli (1980); Leslie (1986); Kwang-Ching Liu and Richard J. Smith in *CHC* (1980), vol. 11, pt. 2.

101. Richard J. Smith in Kwang-Ching Liu, ed. (1990).
102. Ibid.; also A. Chun (1992); Ebrey (1991), esp. pp. 11, 49, 216 ff.

CHAPTER 8. ART

1. For an overview of Qing material culture see Naquin and Rawski (1987a), pp. 72 ff.
2. Clunas (1991), esp. p. 169; Elman (1984), p. 189.
3. Sullivan (1977), p. 230; Sullivan (1979), p. 139; Henderson (1984), pp. 227–234; Naquin and Rawski (1987a), pp. 64–79, esp. p. 77.
4. Sullivan (1979), p. 140. On patronage, see Daphne Rosenzweig in Chu-tsing Li, ed. (1989); Chou and Brown (1985).
5. Brown and Chou (1992), p. 14. See also Chu-tsing Li, ed. (1989), section 3.
6. Sullivan (1977), pp. 216–219, 233–236.
7. See the essays by Ginger Tong, Ginger Cheng-hsi Hsu, and Stella Yu Lee in Chu-tsing Li, ed. (1989); also Brown and Chou (1992), pp. 17–21, 40–42, 102–109, 240–247, 282–284.
8. Hummel, ed. (1943–1944), pp. 11–13, 780–782.
9. See Saussy (1993); Plaks, ed. (1977); Shih, trans. (1983), pp. 353–359; Yu-kung Kao in Murck and Fong, eds. (1991), esp. pp. 64 ff. on "lyric aesthetics."
10. Shih, trans. (1983), p. 13, modified. See also Paper (1985); Mungello (1969).
11. Mungello (1969), p. 379.
12. Michael Sullivan in Dawson, ed. (1964), p. 178; Chai and Chai (1967), 2: 98–100. On the link between music and aesthetics, see DeWoskin (1982); Shih, trans. (1983), pp. 353–359; also Yu-kung Kao in Murck and Fong, eds. (1991).
13. Frederick Mote in C. Murck, ed. (1976), p. 6.
14. See the essays by Wei-ming Tu and Wen Fong in ibid.
15. Wen Fong in C. Murck, ed. (1976), p. 93.
16. Michael Sullivan in Dawson, ed. (1964), p. 206.
17. Van Gulik, trans. (1958), pp. 59–60.
18. Michael Sullivan in Dawson, ed. (1964), pp. 207–210.·
19. See Christian Murck, Frederick Mote, and James J.Y. Liu in C. Murck, ed. (1976), esp. pp. 17–18. For other important artistic expressions, see Clunas (1991), Chapter 3.
20. See Eberhard (1986), esp. pp. 66, 87.
21. Ibid, passim; see also C.A.S. Williams (1941); Yetts (1912); Burling and Burling (1953); Yu-ho Ecke Tseng (1977); Berlinger (1986). The following discussion is based primarily on these sources.
22. Eberhard (1986), pp. 7–16. See also Chapter 5, notes 20–21.
23. For examples of *mudras,* see Thompson, ed. (1973), pp. 97 ff.
24. Eberhard (1986), pp. 91–92. See also Jochim (1986), pp. 92–101.
25. Eberhard (1986), pp. 91–92.
26. On the animals of the zodiac, see R. J. Smith (1991), pp. 189, 193.
27. See Yu-ho Ecke Tseng (1977) and Berlinger (1986) on popular crafts.
28. Sullivan (1977), p. 252.
29. W. Watson (1962), p. 15; David (1971), p. 12.
30. On Chen and Liu, consult Hummel, ed. (1943–1944), pp. 520–521; also Elman (1984), pp. 188 ff.
31. See Wen Fong (1980), esp. pp. 30–31.

32. Smolen (1980). On forgeries, consult Van Gulik, trans. (1958), pp. 50, 77 n. 21.

33. Van Gulik, trans. (1958), pp. 50, 76 n. 20.

34. Michael Sullivan in Dawson, ed. (1964), p. 180.

35. Hansford (1950), p. 31. Cf. Chai and Chai (1967), 2: 464.

36. Hansford (1969), p. 24.

37. Ibid., p. 16.

38. Jenyns (1965), p. 2. For new scholarship on Chinese ceramics, consult Kerr (1986) and Huwayama, ed. (1992).

39. Van Gulik, trans. (1958), p. 51; Jenyns (1965), pp. 70, 72 ff.

40. Legeza (1980).

41. Sullivan (1977), pp. 247–249. See also Chou and Brown (1985); Steinhardt (1990).

42. See Hansford (1961), pp. 74–75.

43. See Keswick (1978); R. S. Johnston (1991); Tun-chen Liu (1993). On the Suiyuan, consult Waley (1970), pp. 47–48, 69–70.

44. Cited in Keswick (1978), p. 60.

45. On Prospect Garden as a social and literary focus, see Plaks (1976), pp. 146 ff. On the symmetry and symbolism of Beijing, consult Meyer (1991); Steinhardt (1990).

46. Cited in Keswick (1978), pp. 196–197.

47. Wing-tsit Chan in Inn and Lee, eds. (1940), esp. pp. 31–32. See also Yu-kung Kao in Murck and Fong, eds. (1991).

48. On the aesthetics of *fengshui,* see R. J. Smith (1991), Chapter 4.

49. Keswick (1978), pp. 12–14. On the household module, consult Emily Ahern in Wilson, ed. (1979), pp. 155 ff.; Sung-hsin Wang in A. Wolf, ed. (1974), pp. 183 ff.; Knapp (1986, 1989, 1990).

50. Cited in Keswick (1978), pp. 198–199.

51. David (1971), p. 29; Eberhard (1971), pp. 15 ff.

52. Rowley (1970), pp. 9–10, 20; Beurdeley et al., eds. (1969).

53. David (1971), pp. 14–15; James Cahill in A. Wright, ed. (1960), pp. 117–118, 130. See also Silbergeld (1982, 1987).

54. James Cahill in A. Wright, ed. (1960), pp. 117–118.

55. Siren (1937), pp. 195, 209; Mungello (1969).

56. Siren (1937), p. 215.

57. Ibid., p. 209.

58. David (1971), pp. 14–15.

59. Mai-mai Sze (1959), pp. 115, 130–131, 133–153. See also Rowley (1970); Silbergeld (1982).

60. Fu and Fu (1973), p. 12; Siren (1937), p. 217.

61. Loehr (1970), pp. 35–36.

62. Yutang Lin (1967), p. 198.

63. Ibid, p. 200. See also Loehr (1970), p. 36; Wei-ming Tu in C. Murck, ed. (1976), pp. 10–15; Van Gulik, trans. (1958), pp. 34–40.

64. Loehr (1970), p. 36. On lines of transmission, see Wen Fong (1971).

65. Siren (1937), p. 210.

66. Yutang Lin (1967), p. 165; see also Siren (1937), pp. 206–207.

67. Wen Fong (1971), p. 283. See also Silbergeld (1982); Mote and Chu, eds. (1988); Gong Qi in Murck and Fong, eds. (1991); So Kam Ng (1992).

68. Siren (1937), pp. 208–209; see also the sources cited in the previous note.

69. Yutang Lin (1967), p. 169. Cf. Shih, trans. (1983), pp. xli–xlviii.

70. Yutang Lin (1967), pp. 175–176.

71. Mai-mai Sze (1959), pp. 157, 325–328; Rowley (1970), pp. 8, 13–14, 17, 42, 47, 51–55, 93; Silbergeld (1982), esp. pp. 56–57. Cf. So Kam Ng (1992).

72. Mungello (1969), esp. pp. 381–382.

73. Mai-mai Sze (1959), p. 107. See also Yutang Lin (1967), pp. 39–42, 69–80; Rowley (1970), pp. 64–67; Wen Fong (1971), pp. 282–283.

74. See Yu-kung Kao and Tsu-lin Mei in C. Murck, ed. (1976), esp. p. 132; also Andrew Plaks in Plaks, ed. (1977), p. 338.

75. See Wai-Kam Ho in C. Murck, ed. (1976); Sullivan (1979), pp. 131–134.

76. Sherman Lee in Rogers and Lee, eds. (1988), p. 28.

77. For a stimulating recent study of Zhu Da, consult Wang and Barnhart (1990).

78. Sherman Lee in Rogers and Lee, eds. (1988), p. 28.

79. Mai-mai Sze (1959), p. 5; see also Sullivin (1977), pp. 238–244; Cahill (1982).

80. See the articles by Wen Fong and James Cahill in Murck and Fong, eds. (1991).

81. See Stella Yu Lee in Chu-tsing Li, ed. (1989); Rogers and Lee, eds. (1988), pp. 200–204; Brown and Chou (1992).

82. See Weidner et al., eds. (1988); Weidner, ed. (1990), passim; Brown and Chou (1992), p. 20; Ko (1992), p. 17; Widmer (1992), p. 139; Hummel, ed. (1943–1944), pp. 99, 278, 324, 386, 431, 566, 685–686, 841.

83. Ellen Johnston Laing in Weidner, ed. (1990), pp. 93–94; also Marsha Weidner in ibid., esp. pp. 130–133.

84. Marsha Weidner in Weidner et al., eds. (1988), p. 13.

85. Ibid., p. 26.

86. Ibid., p. 94; Marsha Weidner in Weidner, ed. (1990), p. 148.

87. Cited in Sullivan (1979), p. 142.

88. Van Gulik, trans. (1958), p. 34.

89. See, for example, the articles by Gong Qi, Jonathan Chaves, Chao-shen Chiang, Wen Fong, and James Cahill in Murck and Fong, eds. (1991).

90. Sullivan (1979), pp. 15–17, 30 ff.; Kahn (1971), p. 136.

91. David (1971), p. 201; Yee Chiang (1973), pp. 225–239. See also the articles cited in note 89 above.

92. See Yee Chiang (1973).

93. Elman (1984), pp. 28, 191–199.

94. Hummel, ed. (1943–1944), pp. 25–26, 610–611, 715–716. See also ibid., p. 278, on Wang Zhaoyuan (1763–1851), another talented woman calligrapher of the Qing period.

95. Yee Chiang (1973), Chapter 1; Yutang Lin (1935), pp. 290–297.

CHAPTER 9. LITERATURE

1. Rawski (1979); see also the articles by David Johnson and Evelyn Rawski in D. Johnson et al., eds. (1985).

2. See Guy (1987), esp. p. 204.

3. Elman (1981), p. 13. On Ming loyalist writing, see Widmer (1987).

4. Crossley (1992), p. 1480; Guy (1987), p. 163.

5. Cited in Naquin and Rawski (1987a), p. 67; cf. Pei-yi Wu (1990); Vinograd (1992).

6. Teng and Biggerstaff (1971), p. 95.

7. Ibid., pp. 95–96.

8. Guy (1987), pp. 157–204.

9. Ibid., p. 201.

10. For an excellent comparative discussion of classical commentary in China and the West, consult Henderson (1991).

11. Guy (1987), pp. 150–152; also Elman (1984), pp. 76–78.

12. Guy (1987), pp. 111–115.

13. See Wieger (1927), pp. 759–766, for a convenient inventory. Wylie (1867) may be considered a kind of *SKQSZM* in miniature.

14. Hucker (1975), pp. 386–387; cf. Wylie (1867), pp. 234 ff.

15. See the discussion in Bol (1992), pp. 84–107; also Hanan (1981), p. 15.

16. See the articles by Gong Qi and Yu-kung Kao in Murck and Fong, eds. (1991); also Shih, trans. (1983), pp. 522–523, 533–535.

17. James J.Y. Liu (1975), pp. 44, 96–97.

18. Shih, trans. (1983), p. 19.

19. James J.Y. Liu (1975), p. 45.

20. Cited in Guy (1987), p. 150.

21. James J.Y. Liu (1975), p. 66.

22. Ibid., pp. 115, 135.

23. Ibid., pp. 99–105.

24. Ibid., pp. 21, 26–27, 82, 88, 104.

25. *CC, Analects,* p. 211. For some recent translations of Qing poetry, consult Lo and Schultz, eds. (1986); also Chaves, ed. (1986); Panda Books (1986). On the problems of translation, see Owen (1985, 1988); P. Yu (1987); Van Zoeren (1991); James J.Y. Liu (1988).

26. See James J.Y. Liu (1988), p. 56, on the principle of "saying more by saying less." Cf. Van Zoeren (1991).

27. See Wai-lim Yip (1976), pp. 1–22; cf. P. Yu (1987).

28. P. Yu (1987), pp. 17 ff.

29. James J.Y. Liu (1966), p. 80.

30. See the example from Su Dongpo cited in Wai-lim Yip (1976), p. 3.

31. Liu and Lo, eds. (1975), pp. 478–479.

32. Y. K. Wong (1990), pp. 157 ff., esp. p. 160; also Lai (1969); note 34 below.

33. Hawkes, trans. (1973–1979), 2: 459.

34. James J.Y. Liu (1966), pp. 149–150. See also note 32 above.

35. Ibid., pp. 65–69; Liu and Lo, eds. (1975), pp. 497–498. See also Spence (1975), p. 117.

36. James J.Y. Liu (1975), pp. 70–76.

37. Liu and Lo, eds. (1975), p. 491.

38. Siu-kit Wong in Rickert, ed. (1978), pp. 130–131, 140; see also Black (1989), pp. 242 ff.

39. Siu-kit Wong in Rickert, ed. (1978), pp. 130–131, 140.

40. Liu and Lo, eds. (1975), p. 480.

41. Shirleen Wong (1975), p. 71; James J.Y. Liu (1966), p. 75; Waley (1970), passim.

42. Furth, ed. (1992), Introduction, esp. pp. 2–5; Ko (1992), esp. p. 33.

43. For examples, see Robertson (1992); also Irving Yucheng Lo in Weidner et al., eds. (1988).

44. Robertson (1992), pp. 86–87.

45. Liu and Lo, eds. (1975), p. 487.

46. See Chaves (1993).

47. On hierarchies of literacy, consult David Johnson in Johnson et al., eds. (1985), pp. 36–38, 42–43, 55–57.

48. Spence (1968), p. 5.

49. For examples of these genres see Ebrey (1991); Chun (1992); R. J. Smith in Kwang-Ching Liu, ed. (1990); Brokaw (1991); Zeitlin (1993).

50. See Brokaw (1991); also Tadeo Sakai in de Bary, ed. (1970), pp. 341–362; Eberhard (1967), esp. pp. 117–125.

51. See Mackerras (1972); Ward (1979); Barbara Ward in Jain, ed. (1977), pp. 190 ff. Cf. Victor Mair in D. Johnston et al., eds. (1985).

52. See Tao-Ching Hsu (1985); Bell Yung (1989); Mackerras (1972).

53. James J.Y. Liu (1979), p. 86. See also the sources cited in note 52 above.

54. See the details in Tao-Ching Hsu (1985), passim; also Rushan Qi in Jingxiong Wu et al., eds. (1967).

55. Hanan (1988), pp. 15–16.

56. This is the general theme of Chang and Chang (1992).

57. For an analysis of his essays, see Hanan (1988), Chapter 8, esp. pp. 196–197.

58. Hanan (1988), p. 1.

59. Hummel, ed. (1943–1944), pp. 495–497. Hanan (1988), pp. 15 ff., provides a summary of Li's plays.

60. Spence (1990), p. 64; for a translation, consult Chen and Acton, trans. (1976).

61. James J.Y. Liu (1979), pp. 109–110; Struve (1987).

62. Rolston, ed. (1990).

63. See Plaks (1976, 1977, 1987); also Plaks in Rolston, ed. (1990).

64. Plaks (1977), p. 42.

65. Andrew Plaks in Plaks, ed. (1977), pp. 340–343; Hanan (1981), p. 20; Robert Ruhlman in A. Wright, ed. (1964), pp. 127 ff.

66. Plaks (1976), pp. 61–71.

67. Andrew Plaks in Plaks, ed. (1977), p. 349; Hanan (1981), p. 27.

68. See the emphasis on irony in Plaks (1987).

69. Robert Ruhlmann in A. Wright, ed. (1964), esp. p. 126; Miller (1975), p. 264.

70. For some recent works on Chinese narrative, see Plaks (1987); McMahon (1988a); Shelly Hsueh-lun Chang (1990); Rolston, ed. (1990); Wai-yee Li (1993).

71. Roberts, trans. (1991); see also Peter Li in Plaks, ed. (1977).

72. Shapiro, trans. (1981); see also Peter Li in Plaks, ed. (1977).

73. The title *Jin Ping Mei* is based on the names of three female characters. Egerton, trans. (1939). See also David Roy in Plaks, ed. (1977) and esp. Carlitz (1986).

74. Hanan (1988) assumes Li Yu is the author; Chang and Chang (1992) argue otherwise.

75. F. Kuhn, trans. (1963); Hanan (1988), Chapter 6, esp. pp. 123–137.

76. Waley, trans. (1944); A. Yu, trans. (1977–1983). On allegory in *Xiyou ji,* see Andrew Plaks in Plaks, ed. (1977); also Bantly (1989).

77. Tai-yi Lin, trans. (1966); Elvin (1991); C. T. Hsia in Plaks, ed. (1977); Brandauer (1977).

78. Yang and Yang, trans. (1957); Ropp (1981), esp. Chapter 6; also Shuen-fu Lin in Plaks, ed. (1977).

79. See Shadick, trans. (1952); Shih-shun Liu, trans. (1975); Dolezelova-Velingerova, ed. (1980); Ts'un-yan Liu, ed. (1984).

80. Yang and Yang, trans. (1978). Hawkes, trans. (1973–1979), renders the first 80 chapters; Minford, trans. (1979–1987), renders the last 40 chapters.

81. Hummel, ed. (1943–1944), p. 738.

82. See Plaks (1976); Andrew Plaks in Plaks, ed. (1977), esp. pp. 281–282; cf. Brandauer (1977); Elvin (1991).

83. Plaks (1976); Miller (1975); Andrew Plaks in Rolston, ed. (1990); A. Yee (1990); Jing Wang (1992).

84. Miller (1975), p. 56.

85. Andrew Plaks in Plaks, ed. (1977), pp. 334–339, esp. p. 338.

86. Hawkes, trans. (1973–1979), 2: 334.

CHAPTER 10. SOCIAL LIFE

1. For examples of recent works based largely on gazetteer materials, consult R. J. Smith (1991); Sutton (1981); Lung-chang Young (1988); Ju-k'ang T'ien (1988).

2. Ju-k'ang T'ien (1988). See also notes 52 and 53 below.

3. Ropp (1976), esp. pp. 20–21; Fang Fu Ruan (1991), pp. 97–98; Rowe (1992); Van Gulik (1961), pp. 123, 264–265, 285–287, 335.

4. See R. J. Smith (1991); Kai-wing Chow in Smith and Kwok, eds. (1993); Ebrey (1991), esp. pp. 188–201.

5. Rowe (1992), p. 9.

6. Nivison (1966), pp. 265–266. Cf. Rowe (1992), passim.

7. Xiaotong Fei (1992), p. 99; James Watson in Ebrey and Watson, eds. (1986), p. 280.

8. Tianhua Mou (1977), pp. 649–650; Baker (1979), p. 39. See also A. Smith (1899), p. 191; Walshe (1906), pp. 212–213.

9. Buck (1937), pp. 462 ff.; James Hayes in D. Johnson et al., eds. (1985); M. Cohen (1991), pp. 117–119.

10. For a fascinating re-creation of daily life in traditional China, see Lowe (1983). Cf. Saari (1990).

11. See R. J. Smith (1992).

12. Walshe (1906), pp. 192 ff., esp. p. 202. See also note 42 below.

13. Of the Kangxi emperor's fifty-five children, twenty-two died before the age of four. See Naquin and Rawski (1987a), p. 107; also note 63 below.

14. See Waltner (1986); Baker (1979), pp. 28–29; also notes 19–26 below.

15. Ebrey, ed. (1993), pp. 313–317, slightly modified; cf. Naquin and Rawski (1987a), pp. 108, 110. See also the fascinating tract translated in the *Chinese Repository,* January 1848, pp. 11–16.

16. Ebrey, ed. (1993), p. 313.

17. From the *Ershisi xiao.* See below, note 21.

18. Waltner (1990).

19. Chai and Chai (1967), 1: 476–479; *TSJC, dian* 38. The six major stages are discussed in M. Levy (1949). On childhood socialization in the Qing, consult Saari (1990); Headland (1901, 1914); Doolittle (1865), 1: 113 ff., 452 ff.

20. Waltner (1986), esp. pp. 684–687; Rowe (1992), pp. 25–29. See also note 21 below.

21. I. Chen (1920), pp. 33–60. For some revealing nineteenth-century Western perspectives on filial piety in general and the *Ershisi xiao* in particular, consult Doolittle (1865), 1: 452–459; *JNCBRAS,* n.s., 20 (1885): 115–144.

22. See the appendix to Ju-k'ang T'ien (1988); also Key Rey Chong (1990), pp. 93–94, 115–120, 164–166.

23. On the legal status of children at this stage, see Waltner (1986), pp. 679–684. For details on child-rearing, consult the sources cited in note 19 above.

24. See the schedule in Ko (1992), p. 24.

25. For a graphic description of the process, consult Fairbank (1992), pp. 173–176. See also note 58 below.

26. Rowe (1992); Ko (1992); Ropp (1976). On classical sanction for the isolation of women, see Chai and Chai (1967), 1: 479.

27. See Ko (1992), pp. 25–28. Mothers also tried to establish close relationships with their sons and were often accused of "spoiling" them. Consult Rowe (1992), p. 25; also Eastman (1988), pp. 28–29.

28. See Metzger (1977), pp. 19–20, and notes; also note 29 below.

29. Pye (1981), p. 137. See also note 28 above.

30. Rowe (1992), pp. 22–25.

31. Naquin and Rawski (1987a), pp. 108–109; cf. Eastman (1988), p. 248, n. 9.

32. Chai and Chai (1967), 2: 248–434; Baker (1979), pp. 32–33, 42–43, 116–117.

33. See R. Watson and Ebrey, eds. (1991), passim.

34. For variations, consult James Watson in Ebrey and Watson, eds. (1986), pp. 284–285; also Diana Martin in Baker and Feuchtwang, eds. (1991); Wolf and Huang (1980); Stockard (1989).

35. Wolf and Huang (1980), Chapter 21, esp. p. 335.

36. For a valuable discussion of marriage terminology, see R. Watson and Ebrey, eds. (1991), pp. 7–8.

37. David Buxbaum in Buxbaum and Mote, eds. (1972), esp. pp. 216–217; also Baker (1979), pp. 35–36.

38. See Wolf and Huang (1980); also R. Watson and Ebrey, eds. (1991). For contemporary Western accounts, consult Doolittle (1865), 1: 65 ff.; Gray (1878), 1: 191 ff.; Walshe (1906), pp. 108 ff.; S. W. Williams (1883), 1: 785 ff. See also note 49 below.

39. See Richard J. Smith in Kwang-Ching Liu, ed. (1990).

40. Rowe (1992), p. 16.

41. On these issues, consult Patricia Ebrey's Introduction and Rubie Watson's Afterword in R. Watson and Ebrey, eds. (1991), esp. pp. 5–8, 17–20, 353 ff.

42. See R. J. Smith (1991, 1992).

43. See Ebrey (1991).

44. See Maurice Freedman in Skinner, ed. (1979), pp. 266–268, on marriage symbolism. For colorful illustrations, consult Hong Kong Urban Council (1986).

45. See R. J. Smith (1991); Ebrey (1991); Chun (1992).

46. See the sources cited in note 38 above. On "shares," consult A. Smith (1899), pp. 179 ff.

47. An exception was the extremely localized marriage practice known as *buluojia*. See Siu (1990).

48. Baker (1979), pp. 46–47, 125 ff.

49. See Spence (1978). On divorce and its limitations, consult Wolf and Huang (1980), Chapter 13; Baker (1979), pp. 129–130. For various kinds of marriage resistance, consult Marjorie Topley in A. Wolf, ed. (1978); Siu (1990); Stockard (1989).

50. Ropp (1981), pp. 124, 138–140, 145–146, 148.

51. Ibid., pp. 146–147; R. F. Johnston (1910), pp. 219, 243–245; Macgowan (1912), pp. 249, 255–256.

52. See Ju-k'ang T'ien (1988); Elvin (1984); Susan Mann in R. Watson and Ebrey, eds. (1991); Ropp (1976); Ebrey, ed. (1993), pp. 253–255.

53. Telford (1986), p. 126.

54. Van Gulik (1961); Fang Fu Ruan (1991); Wile, ed. (1992). Cf. Bodde (1991), pp. 270 ff.; Furth (1992), esp. p. 15. For a revealing perspective on Chinese sexual attitudes and anxieties, see H. Levy (1974).

55. Cited in Hanan (1988), p. 121.

56. See Harper (1987); Wile, ed. (1992); Fang Fu Ruan (1991); Furth (1992), esp. pp. 33–34.

57. See Ko (1992), esp. pp. 10–13.

58. M. Cohen (1991), pp. 120–121; H. Levy (1966). See also note 25 above.

59. Van Gulik (1961); also Fang Fu Ruan (1991), esp. pp. 12 ff. Furth (1992) provides a useful corrective to Van Gulik.

60. On homosexuality in China, consult Hinsch (1990); also Fung Fu Ruan (1991), pp. 107 ff.

61. On theories of Chinese medicine, consult Unschuld (1985, 1986, 1988); also Porkert (1988).

62. *TSJC, dian* 17. See also Wong and Wu (1936), p. 22; Macgowan (1912), Chapter 14; A. Leung (1987); Hummel, ed. (1943–1944), pp. 322–324, 902–903.

63. See the demographic statistics in Naquin and Rawski (1987a), pp. 106–114.

64. For Western perspectives on Chinese home life, consult Macgowan (1912), Chapter 19; S. W. Williams (1883), 1: 724 ff.; Doolittle (1865), 1: 113 ff.; R. F. Johnston (1910), pp. 112 ff., 135 ff.; Nevius (1869), p. 237. Such foreign observers often remark on the lack of privacy in Chinese homes compared to Western homes—a contrast also evident today.

65. Kung-ch'üan Hsiao (1960), pp. 205–220.

66. Mann (1987). See the revealing edict issued to commemorate the sixtieth birthday of the Daoguang emperor's mother in the *Chinese Repository.*

67. Baker (1979), pp. 31–32.

68. Thompson (1979), p. 50. See also Richard J. Smith in Kwang-Ching Liu, ed. (1990).

69. Yutang Lin (1935), p. 177.

70. On China's "a-military culture," consult R. J. Smith (1974), pp. 124–125. On boxing, see Naquin (1976), pp. 30–32, 106–107; Esherick (1987), pp. 38, 45–66, 209–214, 333–340; Burkhardt (1953–1958), 2: 88–94; Rowe (1989), p. 240.

71. Wieger (1913), pp. 508–509; Doolittle (1865), 1: 90; S. W. Williams (1883), 1: 788.

72. Headland (1901, 1906); Bryson (1886), Chapters 5 and 6; Ting, ed. (1990), esp. pp. 39–47; Cutter (1989); Culin (1972); Lowe (1982), passim.

73. S. W. Williams (1883), 2: 104. On the *qin,* see Wen-ying Hsu (1978). On Chinese music generally, consult DeWoskin (1982); Kaufmann (1976); Wiant (1965).

74. S. Boorman (1969), Chapter 1. On noted Qing players, consult Hummel, ed. (1943–1944), pp. 63, 70, 528.

75. Stover (1974), pp. 215–225.

76. Elvin (1991), p. 43. See also Richard J. Smith in Kwang-Ching Liu, ed. (1990); Walshe (1906); Kiong (1906); Gray (1878), esp. 1: 342 ff.

77. Nevius (1869), pp. 239–240.

78. R. F. Johnston (1910), pp. 170–171. See also Gray (1878), 1: 347 ff.

79. Kwang-chih Chang, ed. (1977); E. Anderson (1988); Simoons (1991); F. T. Cheng (1954).

80. See the essays by Frederick Mote and Jonathan Spence in Kwang-chih Chang, ed. (1977).

81. Jonathan Spence in Kwang-chih Chang, ed. (1977), p. 282. See also Stuart Thompson in Watson and Rawski, eds. (1988); Arthur Wolf in Wolf, ed. (1974), pp. 176 ff.

82. Jonathan Spence in Kwang-chih Chang, ed. (1977), pp. 267, 275–277; Hawkes, trans. (1973–1979), 2: 265.

83. Kwang-chih Chang, ed. (1977), p. 48; see also pp. 7–8, 10, 227–234, 272–275.

84. Ibid., pp. 10, 228.

85. Ibid, pp. 308–341.

86. Ibid., p. 278. On opium, consult Jonathan Spence in Wakeman and Grant, eds. (1975).

87. See Doolittle (1865), 2: 296–297; Macgowan (1912), Chapter 16; also Chapter 9, notes 51–55.

88. See Naquin and Rawski (1987a), pp. 60–62; Barbara Ward in Jain, ed. (1977); also the articles by David Johnson, Tanaka Issei, and Barbara Ward in D. Johnson et al., eds. (1985).

89. Naquin and Yü, eds. (1992), p. 19.

90. For convenient overviews, consult Stepanchuk and Wong (1991); Bodde (1965); Wieger (1913), pp. 405–441.

91. Cited in Stover (1974), pp. 207–209 (slightly modified). Cf. *Chinese Repository,* July 1849, p. 378.

92. Cited in Ebrey, ed. (1993), pp. 208–209.

93. See Ko (1992), p. 21, n. 8; Stockard (1989), pp. 41 ff.; M. Robertson (1992), pp. 95–96.

94. Bodde (1965), p. 61. See also D. Johnson, ed. (1989).

95. Bodde (1965), pp. 64, 98.

96. Ibid., p. 69.

97. Ibid., pp. 75–76.

98. See Esherick (1987), esp. pp. 63 ff.

99. Cited in C. K. Yang (1961), p. 195. See also pp. 84–85.

100. See Boulais (1924), pp. 28–30; Bodde and Morris (1967), pp. 76–112. Bodde (1969) provides a fascinating firsthand account of prison life by the well-known scholar-official Fang Bao (1668–1749).

101. Bodde and Morris (1967), p. 286. See also Dau-lin Hsu (1970–1971).

102. See the papers by Jonathan Ocko and Richard J. Smith in Kwang-Ching Liu, ed. (1990); also Bodde and Morris (1967), pp. 162–163, 271–275; Meijer (1991), passim.

CHAPTER 11. TRADITION AND MODERNITY, 1860–1993

1. The literature on twentieth-century China is vast. For some relevant overviews and useful bibliographical leads, consult *CHC* (1983, 1986, 1987, and 1991), vols. 12–15; Dreyer (1993); Pye (1988); Scalapino and Yu (1985); Meisner (1986); Eastman (1988); Spence (1990); I. Hsü (1990).

2. See Rozman, ed. (1991); Jochim (1992).

3. P. Cohen (1974), p. 4.

4. R. J. Smith (1976, 1978c). For an illuminating Chinese perspective, see Zhengtong Wei (1981), pp. 315–336.

5. R. J. Smith (1974).

6. P. Cohen (1974); T. Kennedy (1974); Ermin Wang (1976).

7. On Japan as a modernizing model, see Chuzo Ichiko and Marius Jansen in *CHC* (1980), vol. 11, pt. 2.

8. John Fairbank in *CHC* (1978), vol. 10, pt. 1, provides an instructive overview of the unequal treaty system.

9. See Chu and Liu, eds. (1993).

10. Britton (1933).

11. R. J. Smith (1974, 1976, 1978, 1978b, 1978c, 1981).

12. Schwartz (1964), pp. 94–95. See also M. Cohen (1991), p. 127; Erh-min Wang in Smith and Kwok, eds. (1993), p. 213.

13. Arthur Wright in A. Wright, ed. (1953), p. 293.

14. Ibid., pp. 294 ff.; De Francis (1950); Tse-tsung Chow (1960), esp. Chapter 11; Perry Link in Graubard, ed. (1993), pp. 195–196.

15. Kung-ch'üan Hsiao (1975), pp. 145–146, 150, 155–157; San-pao Li (1978), pp. 115–116, 119, 162 ff.

16. H. Wilhelm (1951), p. 58.

17. Ermin Wang (1976), pp. 51–71, 80–81; Hao Chang in *CHC* (1980), vol. 11, pt. 2, p. 201.

18. Teng and Fairbank, eds. (1979), p. 171.

19. Schwartz (1964), pp. 50 ff.

20. R. J. Smith (1978b), pp. 162–163, 194.

21. Cited by John K. Fairbank in Fairbank, ed. (1968), p. 265 (slightly modified).

22. Cited in R. J. Smith (1981a), p. 102.

23. Ibid., p. 101. For context, consult Chapter 6, note 41.

24. M. Wright (1967), pp. 83–84; Chung-li Chang (1967), pp. 176 ff. See also Benjamin Elman in Elman and Woodside, eds. (forthcoming).

25. See Biggerstaff (1961).

26. R. J. Smith (1978c), p. 19.

27. Rankin (1986), pp. 242–243. Cf. R. J. Smith (1976).

28. See John Fairbank in Fairbank, ed. (1968), p. 273. On Cixi, consult Kwang-Ching Liu in Cohen and Schrecker, eds. (1976). Cf. Kwong (1984).

29. R. J. Smith (1976, 1978c).

30. Ibid. (both sources); also Kwang-Ching Liu and Richard J. Smith in *CHC* (1980), vol. 11, pt. 2.

31. See Rankin (1986); Fewsmith (1985); D. Faure (1989); Philip Huang (1985, 1990); Bernhardt (1992); Myers (1991); R. Bin Wong (1992).

32. Yen-p'ing Hao (1986).

33. See the sources cited in note 30 above.

34. Ermin Wang (1977), pp. 122–124; Elizabeth Croll in Goodman, ed. (1990); *NCH*, October 2, 1896.

35. R. J. Smith (1978c), p. 31.

36. R. J. Smith (1981, 1981a); also Richard J. Smith in Kwang-Ching Liu, ed. (1990).

37. Cited in I. Hsü (1990), p. 377.

38. See Kwong (1984).

39. Esherick (1987).

40. Brunnert and Hagelstrom (1911), pp. 129–130; cf. *NCH*, July 19, 1907.

41. See Richard J. Smith in Kwang-Ching Liu, ed. (1990).

42. On the theme of anti-Manchuism, consult Laitinen (1990); Shimada (1990); Young-tsu Wong (1989); Crossley (1990); Dikotter (1992).

43. On the political process that led to warlordism, consult M. Wright, ed. (1968); Schoppa (1982); Rankin (1986); Eto and Schiffrin, eds. (1984); Bergere (1989). See also the sources cited in note 42 above and note 44 below.

44. On the New Culture Era, consult Tse-tsung Chow (1960); Schwarcz (1986, 1991); Wen-Hsin Yeh (1990); also the articles by Evelyn Rawski, Leo Lee, Michael Hunt, and Lloyd Eastman in Lieberthal et al., eds. (1991). For different perspectives on the women's movement in China, see Kay Ann Johnson (1983); Siu (1989); Ono (1989); Key Rey Chow (1991); Kennedy, trans. (1993).

45. Teng and Fairbank (1979), pp. 239–245; R. J. Smith (1991), p. 274.

46. Tse-tsung Chow (1960), p. 289.

47. Cited in Ramsey (1987), p. 3. See also Perry Link in Graubard, ed. (1993), pp. 195–196.

48. On language reform in modern China, consult De Francis (1984), Chapters 14 and 15; Ramsey (1987), Chapter 1; Norman (1988), Chapter 10.

49. Yü-sheng Lin (1979), p. 29.

50. Hung-ming Ku (1956); see also de Bary et al., eds. (1964), 2: 184 ff.

51. Benjamin Schwartz in Schwartz, ed. (1972), p. 4. See also Ying-shih Yü in Graubard, ed. (1993), p. 147.

52. See, for example, Kulp (1925); also Duara (1988); M. Cohen (1991).

53. Hao Chang (1971), p. 305. See also Nathan (1985).

54. M. Wright (1967), pp. 303 ff.; Eastman (1974). Cf. Wen-Hsin Yeh (1990).

55. M. Wright (1967), p. 304; R. J. Smith (1993).

56. M. Wright (1967), pp. 304–312; cf. Gold (1986); Sutter (1988); Hung-mao Tien (1989); Jochim (1992).

57. See V. Shen (1993); also the sources cited in note 56 above.

58. See Dirlik (1989); Meisner (1986); Schram (1969, 1974, 1989).

59. See the overview by Thomas Bernstein in Lieberthal et al., eds. (1991). See also Schwartz, ed. (1972); Dittmer and Chen (1982).

60. Schram (1969), p. 172; Schram (1974), p. 88. See Sivin (1987) on the distinctive place of traditional Chinese medicine in contemporary China.

61. See R. J. Smith (1981, 1989, 1993).

62. R. J. Smith (1989).

63. R. J. Smith (1981). See also Dittmer and Chen (1982); Kaidi Zhan (1992).

64. For details, consult R. J. Smith (1981, 1989, 1993).

65. Meisner (1986), pp. 363–364.

66. Tozer (1970).

67. See, for example, R. J. Smith (1981), p. 10.

68. Ibid.

69. See Longji Sun (1987), pp. 133 ff.; Zehou Li (1988), pp. 339 ff.

70. Cited in Kwang-Ching Liu (1981), p. 315.

71. See R. J. Smith (1989); King (1991).

72. Parish and Whyte (1978), Chapter 13, esp. pp. 252–260. See also R. J. Smith (1981, 1989); James Watson in Lieberthal et al., eds. (1991); Madsen et al., eds. (1989).

73. R. J. Smith (1989); Pas, ed. (1989); Jochim (1992). See also *CNA*, August 1, 1991, and June 15, 1992.

74. Mayching Kao, ed. (1988); J. Cohen (1987).

75. See Wasserstrom and Perry, eds. (1992), passim.

76. See the data in G. Wang et al. (1991), esp. p. 74.

77. R. J. Smith (1989). Cf. the somewhat different conclusion offered by Chu and Ju (1991). The influential Mainland philosopher Li Zehou advocates a reversal of Zhang Zhidong's famous modernizing formula (see note 17 above). Consult Zehou Li (1988), pp. 351–358.

Bibliography

REMARKS

In the hope that this book will be of value not only as an interpretive synthesis but also as a research tool, I have included a number of references in Chinese and Japanese, as well as Western languages, in the Bibliography. For a more complete listing of relevant works, consult Tung-li Yuan (1958); Hucker (1962); Chun-shu Chang (1971); Kamachi et al. (1975); Ling (1975); Nathan (1973); Skinner and Hsieh, eds. (1973); Teng and Biggerstaff (1971); Wilkinson (1973); Tsien and Cheng (1978); and Seaman, ed. (1993). The *Bibliography of Asian Studies,* published annually by the Association for Asian Studies, provides a comprehensive listing of recent Western-language publications on China (and other parts of Asia).

Among the documentary materials used most frequently in this study are the *TSJC, SKQSZM, XWXTK, QBLC,* and the *JSWB* and its supplements. Particularly helpful in the study of Qing ritual have been the *WXL, WLTK, DQTL, DQHD, LBZL, JLDC, JLTSJC,* and related works. Nakagawa (1800) provides a unique, fascinating, and abundantly illustrated Japanese perspective on eighteenth-century China.

Secondary works in Chinese on traditional Chinese culture abound. The 1980s produced a torrent of Mainland publications on the subject as a result of what the Chinese described at the time as "culture fever" (*wenhua re*). During this period, Fudan University in Shanghai published a series of volumes under the general title *Zhongguo wenhua yanjiu jikan* (Collected Papers on Research into Chinese Culture). At about the same time, the Chinese People's University of Beijing sponsored a number of publications under the general heading *Chuantong wenhua yu xiandai wenhua congshu* (A Collection of Works on Traditional and Modern Culture). Meanwhile, on Taiwan, Taibei's *Shibao* (Times) produced a great many books on traditional Chinese culture under the general title *Wenhua Zhongguo congshu* (A Collection of Works on Cultural China).

Longji Sun's controversial book on the "deep structure" of Chinese culture, first published in 1983, helped feed China's culture fever. See R. J. Smith (1989). Recent works of special interest are Tai Gu et al. (1990); Dainian Zhang and Guanghui Jiang, eds. (1990); and Shanghai guji chuban she, ed. (1987). Older but still valuable studies of Chinese thought and culture include Zhengtong Wei (1981); Junyi Tang (1981); Guang Luo (1981); Baojian Lu (1978); E. Wang (1977); Zhonghua wenhua fuxing yundong tuixing weiyuan hui (1974); Yiyuan Li and Guoshu Yang, eds. (1973); Mu Qian (1937, 1968, 1970); Jiaoyu bu wenhua ju, ed. (1969); Deli Cui and Douxing Liao (1968); Tang Tao (1968); Jingxiong Wu et al., eds. (1967); Haiguang Yin (1966); Yizheng Liu (1964); Dengyuan Chen (1956); Gaoyong Chen (1937); Youjiong Yang (1945); Jinjian Zhang (1935); and Dongfang zazhi she (1925).

Zichen Zhang (1985) provides an excellent (though rather ideological) general survey of Chinese popular customs that includes both topical and chronological discussions. Other useful Chinese-language works on popular culture include Fulan Zhong (1989); Ying Zhou (1988); Licheng Guo (1984); and Zhiwan Liu (1974).

Among the many Chinese-language periodicals devoted to various aspects of Chinese culture, the following are representative: *Zhongguo wenhua yuekan* (The Chinese Culture Monthly; Donghai University, Taiwan); *Wenhua yanjiu* (Cultural Research), produced by the Chinese People's University in Beijing; *Zhongguo wenhua fuxing yuekan* (The Chinese Cultural Renaissance Monthly), published in Taiwan; and the *Jiuzhou xuekan* (Chinese Culture Quarterly; Hong Kong).

Of the many recent reference works on Chinese culture in Japanese and Chinese, at least three should be mentioned here. Hihara, ed. (1984) offers a comprehensive encyclopedia of Chinese thought, broken down by topics and arranged according to the *kana* syllabary. This work contains more than 1,400 entries that cover not only individuals, books, doctrines, and concepts but also topics such as calligraphy, social institutions, and offices. Zhongguo ge minzu zongjiao yu shenhua da cidian bianshen weiyuan hui, ed. (1990), provides a wide-ranging discussion of terms, concepts, and practices relating to the folk beliefs, legends, and practices of China's many ethnic groups, including the Han. Not surprisingly, the section on Han customs is by far the largest and most complete. Cheng Ren (1991) focuses on popular "taboos" (*jinji*) in China. The book is divided into twenty-one different categories, including human affairs, gender, marriage, birth and nurture, clothing, food and drink, residence, travel, speech, sacrifices, and so on. The book also contains a large section on various ways to avert misfortune (charms and firecrackers, for example).

For the Qing period, still-useful Chinese references include Fengchen Ma (1935); *QS*; and Yishan Xiao (1967). No comparable works exist in English, although Pao-chao Hsieh (1925) offers a generally reliable institutional overview. See also E-tu Zen Sun (1961). Recent Western-language surveys focusing primarily or substantially on the Qing dynasty include: Smith and Kwok, eds. (1993); Spence (1990); Lui (1990); I. Hsü (1990); Eastman (1988); Naquin and Rawski (1987a); *CHC* (vols. 10 and 11); and Feuerwerker (1976). For some broad-ranging Western-language introductions to traditional Chinese culture, see Hook, ed. (1991); Bodde (1991); Ropp, ed. (1990); Y. K. Wong (1990); R. J. Smith (1978, 1978a); Dawson (1978); Council of the Chinese Cultural Renaissance (1977); Stover and Stover (1976); Scharfstein (1974); Stover (1974); Moore, ed. (1967); and Chi-pao Cheng, ed. (1964). An extremely useful academic journal on Qing history is *LIC*, formerly *CSWT*. In addition to its valuable articles, research notes, and reviews, this journal provides periodic updates (and occasional translations) of Japanese scholarship on Qing China.

Among the most informative contemporary accounts of the late Qing period by Westerners are: J. F. Davis (1846); Meadows (1856); Doolittle (1865); Nevius (1869); Gray (1878); S. W. Williams (1883); Bryson (1886); Martin (1897); Parker (1899); A. Smith (1899); Walshe (1906); R. F. Johnston (1910); Macgowan (1912); Wieger (1913); and Headland (1914). Hummel, ed. (1943–1944) contains biographies, or at least a mention, of most of the Chinese referred to in the text.

Adkins, Curtis, and Yang, Winston, eds. (1980). *Critical Essays on Chinese Fiction* (Hong Kong).

Ahern, Emily (1982). *Chinese Ritual and Politics* (New York and Cambridge, Eng.).

Ahern, Emily, and Gates, Hill, eds. (1981). *The Anthropology of Taiwanese Society* (Stanford).

Alford, William P. (1984). "Of Arsenic and Old Laws: Looking Anew at Criminal Justice in Late Imperial China," *California Law Review* 72.

Alitto, Guy (1979). *The Last Confucian* (Berkeley).

———. (1984). "Ch'ing Local History Projects," *CSWT* 5, 1 (June).

Allen, Sarah (1981). *The Heir and the Sage: Dynastic Legend in Early China* (San Francisco).

———. (1991). *The Shape of the Turtle: Myth, Art, and Cosmos in Early China* (Albany).

Allinson, Robert E. (1989). *Chuang-Tzu for Spiritual Transformation* (Albany).

———, ed. (1989). *Understanding the Chinese Mind* (Oxford).

Allsen, Thomas T. (1987). *Mongol Imperialism: The Policies of the Grand Qan Mongke in China, Russia, and the Islamic Lands, 1251–1259* (Berkeley).

Ames, Roger (1983). *The Art of Rulership: A Study in Ancient Chinese Political Thought* (Honolulu).

Anderson, E. N. (1988). *The Food of China* (New Haven and London).

Anderson, Mary (1990). *Hidden Power: The Palace Eunuchs of Imperial China* (Buffalo).

Baker, Hugh (1979). *Chinese Family and Kinship* (London).

Baker, Hugh, and Feuchtwang, Stephan, eds. (1991). *An Old State in a New Setting: Studies in the Social Anthropology of China* (Oxford).

Balazs, Etienne (1964). *Chinese Civilization and Bureaucracy* (New Haven).

———. (1965). *Political Theory and Administrative Reality* (London).

Bantly, Francisca Cho (1989). "Buddhist Allegory in the *Journey to the West*," *JAS* 48, 3 (August).

Barfield, Thomas J. (1989). *The Perilous Frontier: Nomadic Empires and China* (Oxford).

Bartlett, Beatrice S. (1985). "Book of Revelations: The Importance of the Manchu Language Archival Record Books for Research," *LIC* 6, 2 (December).

———. (1991). *Monarchs and Ministers: The Grand Council in Mid-Ch'ing China (1723–1820)* (Berkeley).

Bauer, Wolfgang (1966). "The Encyclopedia in China," *CHM* 9, 3.

Beattie, Hilary (1979). *Land and Lineage in China* (Cambridge, Eng.).

Bell, Catherine (1989). "Religion and Chinese Culture: Toward an Assessment of 'Popular Religion,'" *HR* 29, 1.

Berger, Peter, and Luckmann, Thomas (1967). *The Social Construction of Reality* (New York).

Bergere, Marie-Claire (1989). *The Golden Age of the Chinese Bourgeoisie* (Cambridge, Eng.).

Berlinger, Nancy (1986). *Chinese Folk Art* (Boston).

Bernhardt, Kathryn (1992). *Rents, Taxes, and Peasant Resistance: The Lower Yangzi Region, 1840–1850* (Stanford).

Beurdeley, Michel, et al., eds. (1969). *Chinese Erotic Art* (Rutland, Vt.; translated by Diana Imber).

Bielenstein, Hans (1980). *The Bureaucracy of Han Times* (Cambridge, Eng.).

Biggerstaff, Knight (1961). *The Earliest Modern Government Schools in China* (Ithaca, N.Y.).

Birch, Cyril, ed. (1974). *Studies of Chinese Literary Genres* (Berkeley).

Birdwhistell, Anne (1989). *Transition to Neo-Confucianism* (Stanford).

Black, Alison Harley (1989). *Man and Nature in the Philosophical Thought of Wang Fu-chih* (Seattle).

Bloom, Alfred (1981). *The Linguistic Shaping of Thought: A Study in the Impact of Language on Thinking in China and the West* (Hillsdale, N.J.).

Bloom, Irene, ed. and trans. (1987). *Knowledge Painfully Acquired: The K'un-chih chi of Lo Ch'in-shun* (New York).

Bodde, Derk (1965). *Annual Customs and Festivals in Peking* (Hong Kong).

————. (1969). "Prison Life in Eighteenth Century Peking," *JAOS* 89, 2 (April–June).

————. (1991). *Chinese Thought, Society, and Science: The Intellectual and Social Background of Science and Technology in Pre-Modern China* (Honolulu).

Bodde, Derk, and Morris, Clarence (1967). *Law in Imperial China* (Cambridge, Mass.).

Bol, Peter K. (1992). *"This Culture of Ours": Intellectual Transition in T'ang and Sung China* (Stanford).

Bolz, Judith (1987). *A Survey of Taoist Literature: Tenth to Seventeenth Century* (Berkeley).

Bond, M. H., ed. (1986). *The Psychology of the Chinese People* (Oxford).

————. (1991). *Beyond the Chinese Face: Insights from Psychology* (Hong Hong, Oxford, and New York).

Boorman, Howard (1966). "Mao Tse-tung as Historian," *CQ* 28 (October–December).

Boorman, Scott (1969). *The Protracted Game* (New York).

Boulais, Guy (1924). *Manuel du code chinois* (Shanghai).

Brandauer, Frederick (1977). "Women in the Ching-hua yüan," *JAS* 36, 4 (August).

Brandt, Loren (1989). *Commercialization and Agricultural Development: Central and Eastern China, 1870–1937* (Cambridge, Eng.).

Britton, Roswell (1933). *The Chinese Periodical Press, 1800–1912* (Shanghai).

Brokaw, Cynthia (1991). *The Ledgers of Merit and Demerit: Social Change and Moral Order in Late Imperial China* (Princeton).

Brook, Timothy (1988). *Geographical Sources of Ming-Qing History* (Ann Arbor).

————. (1989). "Funerary Ritual and the Building of Lineages in Late Imperial China," *HJAS* 49.

Brown, Claudia, and Chou, Ju-hsi (1992). *Transcending Turmoil: Painting at the Close of China's Empire, 1796–1911* (Phoenix).

Brunnert, H. S., and Hagelstrom, V. V. (1911). *Present Day Political Organization of China* (Foochow).

Bryson, M. I. (1886). *Home Life in China* (New York).

Buck, John L. (1937). *Land Utilization in China* (Nanking).

Burkhardt, V. R. (1953–1958). *Chinese Creeds and Customs* (Hong Kong), 3 vols.

Burling, Judith, and Burling, Arthur (1953). *Chinese Art* (New York).

Bush, Susan, and Murck, Christian, eds. (1983). *Theories of the Arts in China* (Princeton).

Buswell, Robert E., ed. (1990). *Chinese Buddhist Apocrypha* (Honolulu).

Buxbaum, David, ed. (1967). *Traditional and Modern Legal Institutions in Asia and Africa* (Leiden).

Buxbaum, David, and Mote, Frederick, eds. (1972). *Transition and Permanence* (Hong Kong).

Bynum, Carolyn, et al., eds. (1986). *Gender and Religion: On the Complexity of Symbols* (Boston).

Cabezon, José, ed. (1985). *Buddhism, Sexuality, and Gender* (Albany).

Cahill, James (1982). *The Compelling Image: Nature and Style in Seventeenth Century Chinese Painting* (Cambridge, Mass.).

Cantoniensis [pseud.] (1868). "Cost of Living Among the Chinese," *NQCJ* 1 (January) and 2, 2 (February).

Carlitz, Katherine (1986). *The Rhetoric of Chin P'ing Mei* (Bloomington, Ind.).

CC (1893–1895). James Legge. *The Chinese Classics* (London and Oxford).

Chaffee, John W. (1985). *The Thorny Gates of Learning in Sung China* (Cambridge, Eng.).

Chai, Ch'u, and Chai, Winberg (1967). *Li-chi* (New Hyde Park, N.Y., reprint of James Legge's translation of the *Liki,* originally printed in The Sacred Books of the East, Oxford, 1885).

Chan, Albert (1982). *The Glory and Fall of the Ming Dynasty* (Norman, Okla.).

Chan, Hok-lam (1984). *Legitimation in Imperial China: Discussions Under the Jurchen Chin Dynasty* (Seattle).

Chan, Hok-lam, and de Bary, William T., eds. (1982). *Yuan Thought: Chinese Thought and Religion Under the Mongols* (New York).

Chan, Sin-Wai (1985). *Buddhism in Late Ch'ing Political Thought* (Boulder, Colo.).

Chan, Wing-tsit (1955). "The Evolution of the Confucian Concept *Jen,*" *PEW* 4.

———, ed. and trans. (1963). *A Source Book in Chinese Philosophy* (Princeton).

———, trans. (1967). *Reflections on Things at Hand* (New York).

———. (1969). *Neo-Confucianism, Etc.* (Hanover, N.H.).

———, ed. (1986). *Neo-Confucian Terms Explained (The Pei-hsi tzu-i)* (New York).

———, ed. (1989). *Chu Hsi: New Studies* (Honolulu).

Chang, Chun-shu (1971). *Premodern China: A Bibliographical Introduction* (Ann Arbor).

Chang, Chun-shu, and Chang, [Shelly] Hsueh-lun (1973). "The World of P'u Sung-ling's *Liao-chai chih-i,*" *JICS* 6, 2.

———. (1992). *Crisis and Transformation in Seventeenth-Century China* (Ann Arbor).

Chang, Chung-li (1962). *The Income of the Chinese Gentry* (Seattle).

———. (1967). *The Chinese Gentry* (Seattle).

Chang, Chung-yuan (1963). *Creativity and Taoism* (New York).

Chang, Hao (1971). *Liang Ch'i-ch'ao and Intellectual Transition in China, 1890–1907* (Cambridge, Mass.).

———. (1987). *Chinese Intellectuals in Crisis: Search for Order and Meaning (1890–1911)* (Berkeley).

Chang, Kwang-chih (1976). *Early Chinese Civilization* (Cambridge, Mass.).

———, ed. (1977). *Food in Chinese Culture* (New Haven and London).

———. (1980). *Shang Civilization* (New Haven).

———. (1983). *Art, Myth and Ritual* (Cambridge, Mass.).

———. (1986). *The Archaeology of Ancient China* (New Haven).

———, ed. (1986). *Studies of Shang Archaeology: Selected Papers from the International Conference on Shang Civilization* (New Haven).

Chang, Shelly Hsueh-lun (1990). *History and Legend: Ideas and Images in the Ming Historical Novels* (Ann Arbor).

Chang, Tung-sun (1952). "A Chinese Philosopher's Theory of Knowledge," *Etc.* 9, 3 (Spring).

Chao, Kang (1981). "New Data on Land Ownership Patterns in Ming-Ch'ing China," *JAS* 40, 4 (August).

———. (1986). *Man and Land in Chinese History: An Economic Analysis* (Stanford).

Chao, Y. R. (1976). *Aspects of Chinese Sociolinguistics* (Stanford).

Chaves, Jonathan, ed. (1986). *The Columbia Book of Later Chinese Poetry: Yuan, Ming, and Ch'ing Dynasties (1279–1911)* (New York).

———. (1993). *Singing of the Source: Nature and God in the Poetry of the Chinese Painter Wu Li* (Honolulu).

CHC (1978–1991). Denis Twitchett and John K. Fairbank, general eds. *The Cambridge History of China* (Cambridge, Eng.). Vols. 1 (Ch'in-Han, 1986); 3 (Sui-T'ang, part 1, 1979); 6 (Alien Regimes and Border States, 1993); 7 (Ming, part 1, 1988); 10 (Late Ch'ing, part 1, 1978); 11

(Late Ch'ing, part 2, 1980); 12 (Republican China, part 1, 1983); 13 (Republican China, part 2, 1986); 14 (The People's Republic, part 1, 1987); 15 (The People's Republic, part 2, 1991).

Chen, Dengyuan (1956). *Zhongguo wenhua shi* (History of Chinese Culture; Taibei).

Chen, Gaoyong (1937). *Zhongguo wenhua wenti yanjiu* (Research on Problems of Chinese Culture; Shanghai).

Chen, Guofu, and Peihao, Jin (1964). *Tongli xinbian* (A New Edition of the Comprehensive Rituals; Taibei).

Chen, Ivan (1920). *The Book of Filial Duty* (London).

Chen, Kenneth (1964). *Buddhism in China* (Princeton).

———. (1973). *The Chinese Transformation of Buddhism* (Princeton).

Chen, Shih-hsiang, and Acton, Harold, trans. (1976). *The Peach Blossom Fan* (Berkeley and Los Angeles).

Cheng, Chi-pao, ed. (1964). *Symposium on Chinese Culture* (New York).

Cheng, Chung-ying (1971). "Aspects of Classical Chinese Logic," *IPQ* 11, 2 (June).

———. (1971a). *Tai Chen's Inquiry into Goodness* (Honolulu).

———. (1972). "On Yi as a Universal Principle of Specific Application in Confucian Morality," *PEW* 22, 3 (July).

———. (1973). "A Generative Unity: Chinese Language and Chinese Philosophy," *THJ*, n.s., 10, 1 (June).

———. (1977). "Chinese Philosophy and Symbolic Reference," *PEW* 27, 3 (July).

———. (1991). *New Dimensions of Confucian and Neo-Confucian Philosophy* (Albany).

Cheng, F. T. (1954). *Musings of a Chinese Gourmet* (London).

Cheng, François (1982). *Chinese Poetic Writing* (Bloomington, Ind.; translated by Donald Riggs and Jerome Seaton).

Cheng, Lucie, et al., comps. (1978). *Women in China: Bibliography of Available English Language Materials* (Berkeley).

Cheng, Te-k'un (1957). "Yin-Yang Wu-Hsing and Han Art" *HJAS* 20.

———. (1975). "New Light on Shang China," *Antiquity* 49.

Chesneaux, Jean (1971). "The Modern Relevance of *Shui-hu chuan*," *PFEH* 3 (March).

———. (1972). *Popular Movements and Secret Societies in China, 1840–1950* (Stanford).

Chiang, Yee (1973). *Chinese Calligraphy* (Cambridge, Mass.).

Ch'ien, Mu (1982). *Traditional Government in Imperial China: A Critical Analysis* (Hong Kong and New York; translated by Chün-tu Hsüeh and George O. Totten).

Chinese Culture Connection (1987). "Chinese Values and the Search for Culture-Free Dimensions of Culture," *JCCP* 18, 2 (June).

Ching, Julia (1976). *To Acquire Wisdom* (New York).

———, ed. and trans. (1987). *The Records of Ming Scholars* (Honolulu).

Chong, Key Ray (1990). *Cannibalism in China* (Wakefield, N.H.).

Chou, Ju-hsi, and Brown, Claudia (1985). *The Elegant Brush: Chinese Painting Under the Qianlong Emperor, 1735–1795* (Phoenix).

Chow, Key Rey (1991). *Women and Chinese Modernity: The Politics of Reading Between East and West* (Minneapolis and Oxford).

Chow, Tse-tsung (1960). *The May Fourth Movement* (Stanford).

Chu, Godwin, and Ju, Yanan (1991). "Emerging New Chinese Culture," *JCA* 12 (Spring).

Chu, Raymond, and Saywell, William (1984). *Career Patterns in the Ch'ing Dynasty: The Office of Governor-general* (Ann Arbor).

Chu, Samuel, and Liu, Kwang-Ching, eds. (1993). *Li Hung-chang and China's Early Moderniza-tion* (Armonk, N.Y.).

Chu, Sheng, et al., eds. (1982). *Jiezi yuan huazhuan* (The Mustard Seed Garden Painting Manual; Beijing).

Ch'ü, T'ung-tsu (1962). *Local Government in China Under the Ch'ing* (Cambridge, Mass.).

———. (1972). *Han Social Structure* (Seattle; edited by Jack Dull).

Chun, Allen (1992). "The Practice of Tradition in the Writing of Custom, or Chinese Marriage from *Li* to *Su*," *LIC* 13, 2 (December).

Clark, Hugh (1991). *Community, Trade and Networks: Southern Fujian Province from the Third to the Thirteenth Century* (Cambridge, Eng.).

Clunas, Craig (1991). *Superfluous Things: Material Culture and Social Status in Early Modern China* (Cambridge, Eng.).

Cohen, Joan Lebold (1987). *The New Chinese Painting: 1949–1986* (New York).

Cohen, Myron (1990). "Lineage Organization in North China," *JAS* 49, 3 (August).

———. (1991). "Being Chinese: The Peripheralization of Traditional Identity," *Daedalus* 120, 2 (Spring).

Cohen, Paul (1974). *Between Tradition and Modernity* (Cambridge, Mass.).

———. (1984). *Discovering History in China: American Historical Writings on the Recent Chinese Past* (New York).

Cohen, Paul, and Goldman, Merle, eds. (1990). *Ideas Across Cultures: Essays on Chinese Thought in Honor of Benjamin I. Schwartz* (Cambridge, Mass.).

Cohen, Paul, and Schrecker, John, eds. (1976). *Reform in Nineteenth Century China* (Cambridge, Mass.).

Cole, James H. (1986). *Shaohsing: Competition and Cooperation in Nineteenth-Century China* (Tucson).

Council for Cultural Planning and Development (1986). *The Traditional Art of Chinese Woodblock Prints* (Taipei).

Council of the Chinese Cultural Renaissance (1977). *An Introduction to Chinese Culture* (Taipei).

Covell, Ralph (1986). *Confucius, the Buddha, and Christ: A History of the Gospel in Chinese* (Maryknoll, N.Y.).

Creel, H. G. (1936). "On the Nature of Chinese Ideography," *TP* 32.

———. (1970). *The Origins of Statecraft in China* (Chicago).

Cressey, George (1955). *Land of the Five Hundred Million* (New York).

Croll, Elizabeth (1980). *Feminism and Socialism in China* (New York).

Crossley, Pamela Kyle (1987). "*Manzhou yuanliu kao* and the Formalization of the Manchu Heritage," *JAS* 46, 4 (November).

———. (1990). *Orphan Warriors: The Manchu Generations and the End of the Qing World* (Princeton).

———. (1990a). "Thinking About Ethnicity in Early Modern China," *LIC* 11, 2 (June).

———. (1992). "The Rulerships of China," *AHR* 97, 5 (December).

Crossley, Pamela Kyle, and Rawski, Evelyn (1993). "A Profile of the Manchu Language in Ch'ing History," *HJAS* 53, 1 (June).

Crowley, James, ed. (1970). *Modern East Asia* (New York).

CSJCXB (1986). Xinwenfeng guban gongsi bianji bu, ed. *Congshu jicheng xinbian* (A New Edition of the Collectanea; Taibei).

Cua, A. S. (1979). "Dimensions of Li (Propriety)," *PEW* 29, 4 (October).

―――. (1985). *Ethical Argumentation: A Study in Hsun Tzu's Moral Epistemology* (Honolulu).

Cui, Deli, and Liao, Douxing (1968). *Zhongguo wenhua gailun* (Introduction to Chinese Culture; Taibei).

Culin, Stewart (1972). *Chinese Games with Dice and Dominoes* (Seattle; reprint).

Cutter, Robert Joe (1989). *The Brush and the Spur: Chinese Culture and the Cockfight* (Hong Kong).

Dardess, John (1973). *Conquerors and Confucians* (New York).

―――. (1983). *Confucianism and Autocracy* (Berkeley).

David, Percival (1971). *Chinese Connoisseurship* (New York and Washington, D.C.).

Davis, J. F. (1846). *The Chinese* (London).

Davis, Richard L. (1986). *Court and Family in Sung China, 960–1279: Bureaucratic Success and Kinship Fortunes for the Shih of Ming-chou* (Durham).

Dawson, Raymond, ed. (1964). *The Legacy of China* (Oxford).

―――. (1978). *The Chinese Experience* (London).

Dean, Kenneth (1993). *Taoist Ritual and Popular Cults of Southeast China* (Princeton).

de Bary, W. T., ed. (1970). *Self and Society in Ming Thought* (New York).

―――, ed. (1975). *The Unfolding of Neo-Confucianism* (New York).

―――, ed. (1981). *Neo-Confucian Orthodoxy and the Learning of the Mind-and-Heart* (New York).

―――. (1983). *The Liberal Tradition in China* (New York).

―――. (1989). *The Message of the Mind in Neo-Confucian Thought* (New York).

―――. (1991). *The Trouble with Confucianism* (Cambridge, Mass.).

―――. (1991a). *Learning for One's Self: Essays on the Individual in Neo-Confucian Thought* (New York).

de Bary, W. T., and Bloom, Irene, eds. (1979). *Principle and Practicality* (New York).

de Bary, W. T., and Chaffee, John W., eds. (1989). *Neo-Confucian Education: The Formative Stage* (Berkeley).

de Bary, W. T., et al., eds. (1964). *Sources of Chinese Tradition* (New York and London), 2 vols.

de Crespigny, Rafe (1984). *Northern Frontier: The Policies and Strategies of the Later Han Empire* (Canberra).

De Francis, John (1950). *Nationalism and Language Reform in China* (Princeton).

―――. (1984). *The Chinese Language: Fact and Fantasy* (Honolulu).

De Groot, J.J.M. (1892–1910) *The Religious System of China* (Leiden), 5 vols.

―――. (1903). *Sectarianism and Religious Persecution in China* (Amsterdam).

―――. (1912). *The Religion of the Chinese* (New York and London).

de Hartog, Leo (1989). *Genghis Khan: Conqueror of the World* (New York).

Dennerline, Jerry (1981). *The Chia-ting Loyalists: Confucian Leadership and Social Change in Seventeeth Century China* (New Haven and London).

―――. (1988). *Qian Mu and the World of Seven Mansions* (New Haven and London).

DeWoskin, Kenneth (1982). *A Song for One or Two: Music and the Concept of Art in Early China* (Ann Arbor).

Dien, Albert, ed. (1990). *State and Society in Early Medieval China* (Hong Kong).

Dikotter, Frank (1992). *The Discourse of Race in Modern China* (London).

Dirlik, Arif (1989). *The Origins of Chinese Communism* (Oxford).

Dittmer, Lowell, and Chen, Ruoxi (1982). *Ethics and Rhetoric of the Chinese Cultural Revolution* (Berkeley).

Djang, Chu, trans. (1984). *A Complete Book Concerning Happiness and Benevolence: Fu-hui ch'üan-shu, a Manual for Local Magistrates in Seventeenth-Century China*, by Huang Liu-hung (Tucson).

Dodgen, Randall A. (1991). "Hydraulic Evolution and Dynastic Decline: The Yellow River Conservancy, 1796–1855," *LIC* 12, 2 (December).

Dolezelova-Velingerova, Milena (1980). *The Chinese Novel at the Turn of the Century* (Toronto and Buffalo).

Dongfang zazhi she, ed. (1923). *Mixin yu kexue* (Superstition and Science; Shanghai).

Dongfang zazhi she (1925). *Zhongguo wenhua shehui* (Chinese Society and Culture; Shanghai).

Doolittle, Justus (1865). *Social Life of the Chinese* (New York).

Doré, Henri (1914–1933). *Researches into Chinese Superstitions* (Shanghai; translated by M. Kennelly), 6 vols.

Douglas, Robert K. (1882). *China* (London).

DQHD (1911). *Da Qing huidian* (Collected Statutes of the Qing Dynasty; Beijing).

DQTL (1759). Lai Bao. *Da Qing tongli* (Imperially Endorsed Comprehensive Rituals of the Qing Dynasty; Beijing).

Drake, Fred W. (1975). *China Charts the World: Hsü Chi-yü and His Geography of 1848* (Cambridge, Mass.).

Dreyer, Edward L. (1982). *Early Ming China: A Political History, 1355–1435* (Stanford).

Dreyer, June [Teufel] (1976). *China's Forty Millions* (Cambridge, Mass.).

―――. (1993). *China's Political System: Modernization and Tradition* (New York).

Duara, Prasenjit (1988). *Culture, Power, and the State: Rural North China, 1900–1942* (Stanford).

Durand, Pierre-Henri (1992). *Lettrés et Pouvoirs: Un procès littéraire dans la Chine impériale* (Paris).

Eastman, Lloyd (1974). *The Abortive Revolution* (Cambridge, Mass.).

―――. (1988). *Family, Fields, and Ancestors: Constancy and Change in China's Social and Economic History, 1550–1949* (Oxford).

Eber, Irene, ed. (1986). *Confucianism: The Dynamics of Tradition* (New York).

Eberhard, Wolfram (1965). "Chinese Regional Stereotypes," *AS* 5, 12 (December).

―――. (1967). *Guilt and Sin in Traditional China* (Berkeley and Los Angeles).

―――. (1971). *Moral and Social Values of the Chinese* (Taipei).

―――. (1982). *China's Minorities: Yesterday and Today* (Belmont, Calif.).

―――. (1986). *A Dictionary of Chinese Symbols* (London and New York).

Ebrey, Patricia B. (1983). "Types of Lineages in Ch'ing China: A Re-examination of the Chang Lineage of T'ung-ch'eng," *CSWT* 4, 9 (June).

―――, trans. (1984). *Family and Property in Sung China: Yuan Tsai's Precepts for Social Life* (Princeton).

―――. (1991). *Confucianism and Family Rituals in Imperial China* (Princeton).

―――, trans. (1991). *Chu Hsi's Family Rituals* (Princeton).

―――, ed. (1993). *Chinese Civilization and Society* (New York and London).

Ebrey, Patricia B., and Watson, James, eds. (1986). *Kinship Organization in Late Imperial China, 1000–1940* (Berkeley).

Egerod, Soren, and Glahn, Else, eds. (1959). *Studia Serica Karlgren Dedicata* (Copenhagen).

Egerton, Clement, trans. (1939). *The Goldon Lotus* (London).

Elliot, Mark (1990). "Bannerman and Townsman: Ethnic Tension in Nineteenth-Century Jiangnan," *LIC* 11, 2 (June).

Elman, Benjamin (1979). "The Hsueh-hai T'ang and the Rise of New Text Scholarship in Canton," *CSWT* 4, 2 (December).

———. (1981). "Ch'ing Dynasty 'Schools' of Scholarship," *CSWT* 4, 6.

———. (1981–1983). "Geographical Research in the Ming-Ch'ing Period," *MS* 35.

———. (1984). *From Philosophy to Philology: Intellectual and Social Aspects of Change in Late Imperial China* (Cambridge, Mass.).

———. (1990). *Classicism, Politics, and Kinship: The Ch'ang-chou School of New Text Confucianism in Late Imperial China* (Berkeley).

———. (1991). "Political, Social, and Cultural Reproduction via Civil Service Examinations in Late Imperial China," *JAS* 50, 1 (February).

Elman, Benjamin, and Woodside, Alexander, eds. (forthcoming). *Education and Society in Late Imperial China* (Berkeley).

Elvin, Mark (1973). *The Pattern of the Chinese Past* (Stanford).

———. (1984). "Female Virtue and the State in China," *Past and Present* 104.

———. (1991). "The Inner World of 1830," *Daedalus* 120, 2 (Spring).

Endicott-West, Elizabeth (1989). *Mongolian Rule in China: Local Administration in the Yuan Dynasty* (Cambridge, Mass.).

Eno, Robert (1990). *The Confucian Creation of Heaven: Philosophy and the Defense of Ritual Mastery* (Albany).

Er, Si, et al. (1986). *Inside Stories from the Forbidden City* (Beijing; translated by Zhao Shuhan).

Esherick, Joseph (1981). "Number Games: A Note on Land Distribution in Prerevolutionary China," *MC* 7, 4 (October).

———. (1987). *The Origins of the Boxer Uprising* (Berkeley).

Esherick, Joseph, and Rankin, Mary, eds. (1990). *Chinese Local Elites and Patterns of Dominance* (Berkeley).

Eto, Shinkichi, and Schiffrin, Harold, eds. (1984). *The 1911 Revolution: Interpretive Essays* (Tokyo).

Evans, John C. (1992). *Tea in China: The History of China's National Drink* (New York).

Fairbank, John K., ed. (1957). *Chinese Thought and Institutions* (Chicago).

———. (1965). *Ch'ing Documents: An Introductory Syllabus* (Cambridge, Mass.).

———, ed. (1968). *The Chinese World Order* (Cambridge, Mass.).

———. (1986). *The Great Chinese Revolution: 1800–1985* (New York).

———. (1992). *China: A New History* (Cambridge, Mass.).

Fairbank, John K., and Teng, Ssu-yü (1940). "On the Types and Uses of Ch'ing Documents," *HJAS* 5.

Farmer, Edward (1976). *Early Ming Government* (Cambridge, Mass.).

Farquhar, David (1978). "Emperor as Bodhisattva in the Governance of the Ch'ing Dynasty," *HJAS* 38, 1 (June).

Faure, Bernard (1991). *The Rhetoric of Immediacy: A Cultural Critique of Chan/Zen Buddhism* (Princeton).

———. (1993). *Chan Insights and Oversights: An Epistemological Critique of the Chan Tradition* (Princeton).

Faure, David (1976). "Land Tax Collection in Kiangsu Province in the Late Ch'ing Period," *CSWT* 3, 6 (December).

_____. (1989). *The Rural Economy of Pre-Liberation China: Trade Expansion and Peasant Livelihood in Jiangsu and Guangdong, 1870–1937* (Oxford).

_____. (1990). "What Made Foshan a Town? The Evolution of Rural-Urban Identities in Ming-Qing China," *LIC* 11, 2 (December).

Fei, Xiaotong (1992). *From the Soil: The Foundations of Chinese Society* (Berkeley, Los Angeles, and Oxford; translated by Gary G. Hamilton and Wang Zheng).

Feng, Han-yi (1967). *The Chinese Kinship System* (Cambridge, Mass.).

Feuchtwang, Stephan (1992). *The Imperial Metaphor: Popular Religion in China* (London and New York).

Feuerwerker, Albert (1976). *State and Society in Eighteenth Century China* (Ann Arbor).

Fewsmith, Joseph (1985). *Party, State, and Local Elites in Republican China: Merchant Organizations and Politics in Shanghai, 1890–1930* (Honolulu).

Fong, Wen (1969). "Towards a Structuralist Analysis of Chinese Landscape Painting," *AJ* 28, 4 (Summer).

_____. (1971). "How to Understand Chinese Painting," *TAPS* 115, 4 (August).

_____. (1980). *The Great Bronze Age of China* (New York).

Forke, Alfred (1925). *The World Conception of the Chinese* (London).

Fraser, J. T., et al., eds. (1986). *Time, Science, and Society in China and the West* (Amherst, Mass.).

Freedman, Maurice (1966). *Chinese Lineage and Society* (London).

_____. (1975). "Sinology and the Social Sciences," *Ethnos* 40.

_____. (1979). *The Study of Chinese Society* (Stanford).

Fu, Marilyn, and Fu, Shen (1973). *Studies in Connoisseurship* (Princeton).

Fung, Yu-lan (1948). *A Short History of Chinese Philosophy* (New York; edited by Derk Bodde).

_____. (1952). *A History of Chinese Philosophy* (Princeton; translated by Derk Bodde), 2 vols.

Furth, Charlotte, ed. (1976). *The Limits of Change* (Cambridge, Mass.).

_____. (1987). "Concepts of Pregnancy, Childbirth, and Infancy in Ch'ing Dynasty China," *JAS* 46, 1 (February).

_____. (1988). "Androgynous Males and Deficient Females: Biology and Gender Boundaries in Sixteenth- and Seventeenth-Century China," *LIC* 9, 2 (December).

_____. (1992). "Rethinking Van Gulik: Sexuality and Reproduction in Traditional Chinese Medicine." Unpublished paper for the conference on "Engendering China," Harvard University and Wellesley College, February 7–9, 1992.

_____, ed. (1992). "Symposium on Poetry and Women's Culture in Late Imperial China," *LIC* 13, 1 (June).

Gamble, Sidney (1943). "Daily Wages of Unskilled Chinese Laborers, 1807–1902," *FEQ* 3, 1 (November).

Gang, Tianyu (1987). *Tangtu mingsheng tuhui* (Collected Illustrations of Famous Scenery in the Land of the Tang [China]; Beijing reprint).

Gai, Qi (1984). *Honglou meng tuyong* (Illustrated Songs from Dream of the Red Chamber; Beijing reprint).

Gao, Yinxian, et al. (1991). *Nüshu—shijie weiyi di nuxing wenzi* (Women's Writing—The Only Female Script in the World; Taipei).

Gardner, Daniel (1986). *Chu Hsi and the Ta-hsueh: Neo-Confucian Reflection on the Confucian Canon* (Cambridge, Mass.).

———, trans. (1990). *Learning to Be a Sage: Selections from the Conversation of Master Chu, Arranged Topically* (Berkeley).

Garrett, Valery M. (1990). *Mandarin Squares* (Hong Kong, Oxford, and New York).

Gedalecia, David (1974). "Excursion into Substance and Function," *PEW* 24, 4 (October).

Geertz, Clifford (1973). *The Interpretation of Cultures* (New York).

Gernet, Jacques (1985). *China and the Christian Impact: A Conflict of Cultures* (Cambridge, Eng.).

Gerstlacker, Anna, et al., eds. (1985). *Women and Literature in China* (Bochum).

Gimello, Robert, and Gregory, Peter, eds. (1983). *Studies in Ch'an and Hua-yen* (Honolulu).

Girardot, N. J. (1976). "The Problem of Creation Mythology in the Study of Chinese Religion," *HR* 15, 4 (May).

———. (1983). *Myth and Meaning in Early Taoism* (Berkeley).

Gold, Thomas B. (1986). *State and Society in the Taiwan Miracle* (Armonk, N.Y.).

Goodman, David, ed. (1990). *China and the West: Ideas and Activists* (Manchester and New York).

Goodrich, L. Carrington (1975). *Fifteenth Century Illustrated Chinese Primer* (Hong Kong).

Gottschalk, Louis, ed. (1963). *Generalization in the Writing of History* (Chicago).

Graham, A. C. (1986). *Yin-Yang and the Nature of Correlative Thinking* (Singapore).

———. (1989). *Disputers of the Tao: Philosophical Argument in Ancient China* (LaSalle, Ill.).

Granet, Marcel (1934). *La pensée chinoise* (Paris).

Graubard, Stephen R., ed. (1993). *China in Transformation* (Cambridge, Mass.).

Gray, John H. (1878). *China* (London).

Gregory, Peter, ed. (1987). *Sudden and Gradual: Approaches to Englightenment in Chinese Thought* (Honolulu).

———. (1991). *Tsung-mi and the Sinification of Buddhism* (Princeton).

Grove, Linda, and Daniels, Christian, eds. (1984). *State and Society in China: Japanese Perspectives on Ming-Qing Social and Economic History* (Tokyo).

Gu, Tai, et al. (1990). *Zhongguo chuantong wenhua qiguan* (The Wonders of Traditional Chinese Culture; Jilin).

Guan, Lüquan (1992). "Zhonghua wen hua di baorong xing yu minzu di ningju" (The Accommodating Nature of Chinese Culture and the Consolidation of the People), *Zhongguo wenhua yuekan* 155 (September).

Guildin, Gregory (1984). "Seven-Veiled Ethnicity: A Hong Kong Chinese Folk Model," *JCS* 1, 2.

Guisso, Richard, and Johannesen, Stanley (1981). *Women in China: Current Directions in Historical Scholarship* (Youngstown, N.Y.).

Guo, Licheng (1984). *Zhongguo minsu shihua* (Historical Discussions of Chinese Customs; Taibei).

Guy, R. Kent (1987). *The Emperor's Four Treasuries: Scholars and the State in the Late Ch'ien-lung Era* (Cambridge, Mass.).

Haeger, John (1975). *Crisis and Prosperity in Sung China* (Tucson).

Hall, David L., and Ames, Roger T. (1987). *Thinking Through Confucius* (Albany).

Han, Yu-shan (1955). *Elements of Chinese Historiography* (Hollywood, Calif.).

Hanan, Patrick (1981). *The Chinese Vernacular Story* (Cambridge, Mass.).

———. (1988). *The Invention of Li Yu* (Cambridge, Mass.).

Handlin, Joanna (1983). *Action in Late Ming Thought: The Reorientation of Lu K'un and Other Scholar Officials* (Berkeley).

Hansen, Chad (1983). *Language and Logic in Ancient China* (Ann Arbor).

———. (1992). *A Daoist Theory of Chinese Thought: A Philosophical Interpretation* (Oxford).

———. (1993). "Chinese Ideographs and Western Ideas," *JAS* 52, 2 (May).

Hansen, Valerie (1990). *Changing Gods in Medieval China, 1127–1276* (Princeton).

Hansford, Howard (1950). *Chinese Jade Carving* (London).

———. (1961). *A Glossary of Chinese Art and Archaeology* (London).

———. (1969). *Jade, Essence of Hills and Streams* (New York).

Hao, Yen-p'ing (1970). *The Comprador in Nineteenth Century China* (Cambridge, Mass.).

———. (1986). *The Commercial Revolution in Nineteenth-Century China* (Berkeley).

Harper, Donald (1987). "The Sexual Arts of Ancient China as Described in a Manuscript of the Second Century B.C.," *HJAS* 47.

Harrell, Stevan (1982). *Ploughshare Village: Culture and Context in Taiwan* (Seattle).

Harrell, Stevan, et al. (1985). "Lineage Genealogy: The Genealogical Records of the Qing Imperial Lineage," *LIC* 6, 2 (December).

Hartman, Charles (1986). *Han Yü and the T'ang Search for Unity* (Princeton).

Hartwell, Robert (1982). "Demographic, Political, and Social Transformations of China, 750–1550," *HJAS* 42, 2 (December).

Hawkes, David, trans. (1973–1979). *The Story of the Stone* (Harmondsworth, Eng.), 3 vols. See also under Minford (1979–1987).

Hayes, James (1977). *The Hong Kong Region, 1850–1911* (Hamden, Conn.).

He, Lin (1988). *Wenhua yu rensheng* (Culture and Life; Beijing; revision of 1946 edition).

Headland, Isaac T. (1901). *The Chinese Boy and Girl* (New York).

———. (1906). "Chinese Children's Games," *JNCBRAS*, n.s., 37.

———. (1914). *Home Life in China* (London).

Heberer, Thomas (1989). *China and Its National Minorities: Autonomy or Assimilation?* (New York; translated by Michael Vale).

Hegel, Robert (1981). *The Novel in Seventeenth Century China* (New York).

Hegel, Robert, and Hessney, Richard C., eds. (1985). *Expressions of Self in Chinese Literature* (New York).

Henderson, John B. (1984). *The Development and Decline of Chinese Cosmology* (New York).

———. (1991). *Scripture, Canon, and Commentary: A Comparison of Confucian and Western Exegesis* (Princeton).

Hevia, James L. (1989). "A Multitude of Lords: Qing Court Ritual and the Macartney Embassy of 1793," *LIC* 10, 2 (December).

Hihara, Toshikuni, ed. (1984). *Chugoku shiso jiten* (Dictionary of Chinese Thought; Tokyo).

Hinsch, Bret (1990). *Passions of the Cut Sleeve: The Male Homosexual Tradition in China* (Berkeley).

Ho, David Yau-fai, et al., eds. (1989). *Chinese Patterns of Behavior: A Sourcebook of Psychological and Psychiatric Studies* (New York; Westport, Conn.; and London).

Ho, Peng Yoke (1986). *Li, Qi and Shu: An Introduction to Science and Civilization in China* (Hong Kong).

Ho, Ping-ti (1959). *Studies on the Population of China, 1368–1953* (Cambridge, Mass.).

———. (1962). *The Ladder of Success in Imperial China* (New York).

_____ . (1967). "The Significance of the Ch'ing Period in Chinese History," *JAS* 26, 2 (February).

_____ . (1976). *The Cradle of the East* (Chicago).

Holmgren, Jennifer (1981). "Myth, Fantasy, or Scholarship: Images of the Status of Women in Traditional China," *AJCA* 6.

_____ . (1984). "The Economic Foundations of Virtue," *AJCA* 13.

Hong Kong Urban Council (1986). *Local Traditional Chinese Wedding* (Hong Kong).

Honig, Emily (1992). *Creating Chinese Ethnicity: Subei People in Shanghai, 1850–1980* (New Haven).

Hook, Brian, ed. (1991). *The Cambridge Encyclopedia of China* (Cambridge, Eng.).

Hsia, C. T. (1968). *The Classic Chinese Novel* (New York).

Hsiao, Kung-ch'üan (1960). *Rural China* (Seattle).

_____ . (1975). *A Modern China and a New World* (Seattle).

_____ . (1979). *A History of Chinese Political Thought* (Princeton; translated by Frederick Mote).

_____ . (1979a). *Compromise in Imperial China* (Seattle).

Hsieh, Jih-chang, and Chuang, Ying-chang, eds. (1985). *The Chinese Family and Its Ritual Behavior* (Taipei).

Hsieh, Pao-chao (1925). *The Government of China (1644–1911)* (Baltimore).

Hsu, Cho-yun (1965). *Ancient China in Transition* (Stanford).

_____ . (1980). *Han Agriculture* (Seattle and London).

Hsu, Cho-yun, and Linduff, Katheryn, eds. (1988). *Western Chou Civilization* (New Haven).

Hsu, Dau-lin (1970–1971). "The Myth of the Five Human Relationships of Confucius," *MS* 29.

Hsu, Francis L.K. (1971). "Filial Piety in Japan and China," *JCFS* 2, 1 (Spring).

_____ . (1981). *Americans and Chinese: Passage to Differences* (Honolulu).

Hsü, Immanuel C.Y. (1959). *Intellectual Trends in the Ch'ing Period* (Cambridge, Mass.).

_____ . (1990). *The Rise of Modern China* (New York).

Hsu, Tao-Ching (1985). *The Chinese Conception of the Theatre* (Seattle and London).

Hsu, Wen-ying (1978). *The Ku-Ch'in* (Los Angeles).

Hu, Daojing, ed. (1982). *Explorations in the History of Science and Technology in China* (Shanghai).

Huang, Pei (1974). *Autocracy at Work, A Study of the Yung-cheng Period, 1723–1735* (Bloomington, Ind.).

Huang, Philip C.C. (1985). *The Peasant Economy and Social Change in North China* (Stanford).

_____ . (1990). *The Peasant Family and Rural Development in the Yangzi Delta, 1350–1988* (Stanford).

Huang, Ray (1988). *China: A Macro History* (Armonk, N.Y.).

Hucker, Charles (1962). *China: A Critical Bibliography* (Tucson).

_____ . (1966). *The Censorial System of Ming China* (Stanford).

_____ . (1969). *Chinese Government in Ming Times, 1368–1644* (New York).

_____ . (1975). *China's Imperial Past* (Stanford).

_____ . (1985). *A Dictionary of Official Titles in Imperial China* (Stanford).

Hulsewe, A.F.P. (1985). *Remnants of Ch'in Law* (Leiden).

Hummel, Arthur, ed. (1943–1944). *Eminent Chinese of the Ch'ing Period* (Washington, D.C.).

Huwayama, George, ed. (1992). *New Perspectives on the Art of Ceramics in China* (Los Angeles).

Hymes, Robert P. (1986). *Statesmen and Gentlemen: The Elite of Fu-chou, Chiang-hsi, in Northern and Southern Sung* (Cambridge, Eng.).

Idema, W. L. (1985). *The Dramatic Oeuvre of Chu Yu-tun (1379–1439)* (Leiden).

Inn, Henry, and Lee, S. C., eds. (1940). *Chinese Homes and Gardens* (Honolulu).

Israeli, Raphael (1980). *Muslims in China: A Study in Cultural Confrontation* (Atlantic Highlands, N.J.).

Ivanhoe, Philip (1990). *Ethics in the Confucian Tradition: The Thought of Mencius and Wang Yang-ming* (Atlanta).

Jackson, J. H., trans. (1937). *Water Margin* (Shanghai).

Jagchid, Sechin, and Symons, Van Jay (1989). *Peace, War and Trade Along the Great Wall: Nomadic Chinese Interaction Through Two Millennia* (Bloomington, Ind.).

Jain, Ravindra, ed. (1977). *Text and Context* (Philadelphia).

Jansen, Marius (1969). *Changing Japanese Attitudes Toward Modernization* (Princeton).

Jay, Jennifer W. (1990). *A Change in Dynasties: Loyalism in Thirteenth-Century China* (Bellingham, Wash.).

Jen, Yu-wen (1973). *The Taiping Revolutionary Movement* (New Haven and London).

Jenyns, Soame (1965). *Later Chinese Porcelains* (London).

Jiaoyu bu wenhua ju, ed. (1969). *Zhonghua wenhua zhi tezhi* (The Special Characteristics of Chinese Culture; Taibei).

Jin, Kaicheng (1980). "Artistic Recreation of the Unique Characteristics of Things," *SSC* 3.

Jing, Su, and Luo, Lun (1978). *Landlord and Labor in Late Imperial China* (Cambridge, Mass.; translated by Endymion Wilkinson).

JLDC (1975). Lü Zizhen. *Jiali dacheng* (Great Collection of Family Rituals; Taibei reprint).

JLTSJC (1842). Chen Mingsheng. *Jiali tieshi jicheng* (Collection of Family Rituals and Writing Models).

Jochim, Christian (1979). "The Imperial Audience Ceremonies of the Ch'ing Dynasty," *BSSCR* 7 (Fall).

———. (1986). *Chinese Religions: A Cultural Perspective* (Englewood Cliffs, N.J.).

———. (1988). " 'Great' and 'Little,' 'Grid' and 'Group'; Defining the Poles of the Elite-Popular Continuum in Chinese Religion," *JCR* 16.

———. (1992). "Confucius and Capitalism: Views of Confucianism in Works on Confucianism and Economic Development," *JCR* 20.

Johnson, David, ed. (1989). *Ritual Opera, Operatic Ritual: "Mu-lien Rescues His Mother" in Chinese Popular Culture* (Berkeley).

Johnson, David, et al., eds. (1985). *Popular Culture in Late Imperial China* (Berkeley).

Johnson, Kay Ann (1983). *Women, the Family, and Peasant Revolution in China* (Chicago).

Johnson, Linda Cooke, ed. (1993). *Cities of Jiangnan in Late Imperial China* (Ithaca).

Johnson, Wallace, ed. and trans. (1979). *The T'ang Code*, vol. 1, *General Principles* (Princeton).

Johnston, R. F. (1910). *Lion and Dragon in Northern China* (London).

Johnston, R. Stewart (1991). *Scholar Garden of China: A Study and Analysis of the Spatial Design of the Chinese Private Garden* (Cambridge, Eng.).

Jones, William (1974). "Studying the Ch'ing Code—The Ta Ch'ing Lü Li," *The American Journal of Comparative Law* 22.

Jordan, David K. (1972). *Gods, Ghosts and Ancestors: The Folk Religion of a Taiwanese Village* (Berkeley).

Jordan, David K., and Overmyer, Daniel L. (1986). *The Flying Phoenix: Aspects of Chinese Sectarianism in Taiwan* (Princeton).

JQYWL (1871). *Huangchao jiqi yuewu lu* (Record of the Qing Dynasty's Sacrificial Implements, Music and Dances; Beijing).

JSWB (1826). He Changling. *Huangchao jingshi wenbian* (The Qing Dynasty's Writings on Statecraft; Shanghai).

Jullien, François (1989). *Proces ou Création: Une introduction a la pensée des lettrés chinois: Essai de problématique interculturelle* (Paris).

Kahn, Harold (1967). "The Politics of Filiality," *JAS* 26, 2 (February).

———. (1971). *Monarchy in the Emperor's Eyes* (Cambridge, Mass.).

Kamachi, Noriko, et al., eds. (1975). *Japanese Studies of Modern China Since 1953* (Cambridge, Mass.).

Kangxi zidian (1962). (The Kangxi Dictionary; Taibei reprint).

Kao, Mayching, ed. (1988). *Twentieth-Century Chinese Painting* (Hong Kong, Oxford, and New York).

Kaufmann, Walter (1976). *Musical References in the Chinese Classics* (Detroit).

Keightley, David N. (1978). "The Religious Commitment: Shang Theology and the Genesis of Chinese Political Culture," *HR* 17, 3 (February–May).

———, ed. (1983). *The Origins of Chinese Civilization* (Berkeley).

———. (1988). "Archaeology and Mentality: The Making of China," *Representations* 18 (Spring).

Kennedy, Thomas (1974). "Self-Strengthening," *CSWT* 3, 1 (November).

———, trans. (1993). *Testimony of a Confucian Woman: The Autobiography of Mrs. Nie Zeng Jifen, 1852–1942* (Athens, Ga., and London).

Kerr, Rose (1986). *Chinese Ceramics: Porcelain of the Qing Dynasty, 1644–1911* (London).

Kessler, Lawrence (1976). *K'ang-hsi and the Consolidation of Ch'ing Rule, 1661–1684* (Chicago).

Keswick, Maggie (1978). *The Chinese Garden* (New York).

King, Ambrose (1991). "Kuan-hsi and Network Building: A Sociological Interpretation," *Daedalus* 120, 2 (Spring).

Kiong, Simon [Gong Guyu] (1906). *Quelques mots sur la politesse chinoise* (Shanghai).

Kleinman, Arthur, and Lin, T. Y., eds. (1981). *Normal and Abnormal Behavior in Chinese Culture* (Dordrecht, Boston, and London).

Knapp, Ronald G. (1986). *China's Traditional Rural Architecture: A Cultural Geography of the Common House* (Honolulu).

———. (1989). *China's Vernacular Architecture: House Form and Culture* (Honolulu).

———. (1990). *The Chinese House: Craft, Symbol, and the Folk Tradition* (Hong Kong, Oxford, and New York).

———, ed. (1992). *Chinese Landscapes: The Village as Place* (Honolulu).

Knapp, Ronald G., et al., eds. (1980). *China's Island Frontier: Studies in the Historical Geography of Taiwan* (Honolulu).

Knoblock, John, trans. (1988). *Xunzi: A Translation and Study of the Complete Works,* vol. 1 (Stanford).

Knoerle, Jeanne (1972). *"The Dream of the Red Chamber": A Critical Study* (Bloomington, Ind., and London).

Ko, Dorothy (1992). "Pursuing Talent and Virtue: Education and Women's Culture in Seventeenth- and Eighteenth-Century China," *LIC* 13, 1 (June).

Kohn, Livia, ed. (1989). *Taoist Meditation and Longevity Techniques* (Ann Arbor).

—————, ed. (1993). *The Taoist Experience: An Anthology* (Ithaca).

Kramer, S. N., ed. (1961). *Mythologies of the Ancient World* (New York).

Ku, Hung-ming (1956). *The Spirit of the Chinese People* (New York).

Ku, Yangjie (1980). "The Feudal Clan System Inherited from the Song and Ming Periods," *SSC,* 3.

Kuhn, Dieter (1987). *Die Song-Dynastie (960 bis 1279)* (Weinheim).

Kuhn, Franz, trans. (1963). *Jou Pu Tuan* (New York; translated by Richard Martin).

Kuhn, Philip (1977). "Origins of the Taiping Vision," *CSSH* 19, 3 (July).

—————. (1980). *Rebellion and Its Enemies in Late Imperial China* (Cambridge, Mass.).

—————. (1990). *Soulstealers: The Chinese Sorcery Scare of 1768* (Cambridge, Mass.).

Kulp, Daniel H. (1925). *Country Life in South China* (New York).

Kwong, Luke S.K. (1984). *A Mosaic of the Hundred Days: Personalities, Politics, and Ideas of 1898* (Cambridge, Mass.).

La Fargue, Michael (1993). *Tao and Method: A Reasoned Approach to the Tao Te Ching* (Ithaca).

Lagerwey, John (1987). *Taoist Ritual in Chinese Society and History* (New York).

Lai, T. C. (1969). *Chinese Couplets* (Hong Kong).

—————. (1970). *A Scholar in Imperial China* (Hong Kong).

Laitinen, Kauko (1990). *Chinese Nationalism in the Late Qing Dynasty: Zhang Binglin as an Anti-Manchu Propagandist* (London).

Lamley, Harry (1977). "Hsieh-tou, The Pathology of Violence in South-east China," *CSWT* 3, 7 (November).

Lancashire, David, ed. (1982). *Chinese Essays on Religion and Faith* (Taipei).

Langlois, John, ed. (1981). *China Under Mongol Rule* (Princeton).

Lau, D. C. (1963). "On Mencius' Use of the Method of Analogy in Argument," *AM,* n.s., 10, 2.

Lavely, William (1989). "The Spatial Approach to Chinese History: Illustrations from North China and the Upper Yangzi," *JAS* 48, 1 (February).

Lavely, William, et al. (1990). "Chinese Demography: The State of the Field," *JAS* 49, 4 (November).

LBZL (1845). *Qinding Libu zeli* (Imperially Endorsed Regulations of the Board of Rites).

Le Blanc, Charles (1985). *Huai-nan Tzu: Philosophical Synthesis in Early Han Thought* (Hong Kong).

LeBlanc, Charles, and Blader, Susan (1987). *Chinese Ideas About Nature and Society* (Hong Kong).

Le Blanc, Charles, and Borei, Dorothy, eds. (1982). *Essays on Chinese Civilization* (Princeton).

Lee, Robert (1989). *France and the Exploitation of China: A Study in Economic Imperialism* (Hong Kong).

Lee, Thomas H.C. (1985). *Government Education and Examinations in Sung China* (New York).

Leeming, Frank (1993). *The Changing Geography of China* (Oxford).

Legeza, Laszlo (1980). "Ming and Ch'ing Imperial Tou-ts'ai and Wu-Ts'ai Porcelains," *AA* (January–February).

Lenk, Hans, and Paul, Gregor, eds. (1993). *Epistemological Issues in Classical Chinese Philosophy* (Ithaca).

Leonard, Jane Kate (1984). *Wei Yuan and China's Rediscovery of the Maritime World* (Cambridge, Mass.).

Leonard, Jane Kate, and Watt, John, eds. (1992). *To Achieve Security and Wealth: The Qing Imperial State and the Economy, 1644–1911* (Ithaca).

Leslie, Donald D. (1986). *Islam in Traditional China: A Short History to 1800* (Canberra).

Leung, Angela Ki Che (1987). "Organized Medicine in Ming-Qing China: State and Private Medical Institutions in the Lower Yangzi Region," *LIC* 8, 1 (June).

Leung, Yuen-sang (1990). *The Shanghai Taotai: Linkage Man in a Changing Society, 1843–1890* (Honolulu).

Levenson, Joseph (1964). "The Humanistic Disciplines," *JAS* 23, 4 (August).

Levenson, Joseph, and Schurmann, Franz (1970). *China: An Interpretive History* (New Haven and London).

Levius, John (1936). *The Foundations of Chinese Musical Art* (Peiping).

Levy, Howard (1966). *Chinese Footbinding* (New York).

———. (1974). *Chinese Sex Jokes in Traditional Times* (Taipei).

Levy, Marion (1949). *The Family Revolution in Modern China* (New York).

———. (1953). "Contrasting Factors in the Modernization of China and Japan," *EDCC* 2 (October).

———. (1962). "Some Aspects of 'Individualism' and the Problem of Modernization in China and Japan," *EDCC* 10, 3 (April).

Lewis, Mark E. (1990). *Sanctioned Violence in Early China* (Albany).

Li, Chu-tsing, ed. (1989). *Artists and Patrons: Some Social and Economic Aspects of Chinese Painting* (Lawrence, Kans.).

Li, Chu-tsing, and Watt, James C.Y., eds. (1987). *The Chinese Scholar's Studio* (New York).

Li, Dun J. (1978). *The Ageless Chinese* (New York).

Li, Lillian (1982). "Introduction: Food, Famine and the Chinese State," *JAS* 41, 4 (August).

Li, Lillian, and Rawski, Thomas, eds. (1992). *Chinese History in Economic Perspective* (Berkeley and Los Angeles).

Li, San-pao (1978). "K'ang Yu-wei's Iconoclasm" (Ph.D. dissertation, University of California, Davis).

Li, Thomas Shiyu, and Naquin, Susan (1988). "The Baoming Temple: Religion and the Throne in Ming and Qing China," *HJAS* 48, 1.

Li, Wai-yee (1993). *Enchantment and Disenchantment: Love and Illusion in Chinese Literature* (Princeton).

Li, Xueqin (1985). *Eastern Zhou and Qin Civilizations* (New Haven; translated by K. C. Chang).

Li, Yiyuan, and Yang, Guoshu, eds. (1973). *Zhongguo ren di xingge* (The Character of the Chinese People; Taibei).

Li, Zehou (1988). *Li Zehou ji* (The Collected Works of Li Zehou; Harbin).

Lieberthal, Kenneth, et al., eds. (1991). *Perspectives on Modern China: Four Anniversaries* (Armonk, N.Y.).

Lin, Man-houng (1991). "Two Social Theories Revealed: Statecraft Controversies Over China's Monetary Crisis, 1808–1854," *CSWT* 12, 2 (December).

Lin, Qing (1886). *Hongxue yinyuan tuji* (Illustrated Record of Goose-Snow Destiny; Shanghai).

Lin, Tai-yi, trans. (1966). *Flowers in the Mirror* (Berkeley and Los Angeles).

Lin, Yü-sheng (1979). *The Crisis of Chinese Consciousness* (Madison, Wis., and London).

Lin, Yutang (1935). *My Country and My People* (New York).

———. (1967). *The Chinese Theory of Art* (London).

Ling, Scott K. (1975). *Bibliography of Chinese Humanities: 1941–1972* (Taipei).

Lipman, Jonathan, and Harrell, Stevan, eds. (1990). *Violence in China: Essays in Culture and Counterculture* (Ithaca).

Little, Daniel (1985). *Understanding Peasant China: Case Studies in the Philosophy of Social Science* (New Haven and London).

Little, Daniel, and Esherick, Joseph (1989). "Testing the Testers," *JAS* 48, 1 (February).

Liu, Guang'an (1990). "A Short Treatise on the Ethnic Legislation of the Qing Dynasty," *SSC* 4 (Winter).

Liu, Hui-chen Wang (1959). *The Traditional Chinese Clan Rules* (Locust Valley, N.Y.).

Liu, James J.Y. (1966). *The Art of Chinese Poetry* (Chicago and London).

––––––. (1975). *Chinese Theories of Literature* (Chicago).

––––––. (1979). *Essentials of Chinese Literary Art* (Stanford).

––––––. (1988). *Language—Paradox—Poetics: A Chinese Perspective* (Princeton).

Liu, James T.C., ed. (1970). *Traditional China* (Englewood Cliffs, N.J.).

––––––. (1988). *China Turning Inward: Intellectual-Political Changes in the Early Twelfth Century* (Cambridge, Mass.).

Liu, Kwang-Ching (1981). "World View and Peasant Rebellion," *JAS* 40, 2 (February).

––––––. (1988). "Chinese Merchant Guilds: An Historical Inquiry," *PHR* 57, 1 (February).

––––––, ed. (1990). *Orthodoxy in Late Imperial China* (Berkeley).

Liu, Kwang-Ching, and Shek, Richard, eds. (forthcoming). *Heterodoxy in Late Imperial China* (Berkeley).

Liu, Shih-shun, trans. (1975). *Vignettes from the Late Ch'ing* (Hong Kong).

Liu, Ts'un-yan, ed. (1984). *Chinese Middlebrow Fiction from the Ch'ing and Early Republican Eras* (Hong Kong).

Liu, Tun-chen (1993). *Chinese Classical Gardens of Suzhou* (New York; translated by Chen Lixian).

Liu, Wu-chi, and Lo, Irving, eds. (1975). *Sunflower Splendor* (Washington, D.C., and London).

Liu, Yizheng (1964). *Zhongguo wenhua shi* (History of Chinese Culture; Taibei).

Liu, Zhiwan (1974). *Zhongguo minjian xinyang lunji* (A Collection of Essays on Chinese Folk Beliefs; Taibei).

Lo, Irving Yucheng, and Schultz, William, eds. (1986). *Waiting for the Unicorn: Poems and Lyrics of China's Last Dynasty, 1644–1911* (Bloomington, Ind.).

Lo, Winston W. (1987). *An Introduction to the Civil Service of Sung China, with Emphasis on Its Personnel Administration* (Honolulu).

Loehr, Max (1970). "Art-Historical Art," *OA* 16 (Spring).

Loewe, Michael (1982). *Chinese Ideas of Life and Death* (London).

Lovin, Robin, and Reynolds, Frank, eds. (1985). *Cosmogony and Ethical Order: New Studies in Comparative Ethics* (Chicago and London).

Lowe, H. Y. [Lu, Xingyuan] (1983). *The Adventures of Wu* (Princeton).

Lu, Baoqian (1978). *Qingdai sixiang shi* (History of Qing Thought; Taibei).

Lui, Adam Y.C. (1970). "The Ch'ing Civil Service: Promotions, Demotions, Transfers, Leaves, Dismissals and Retirements," *JOS* 8.

––––––. (1974). "The Imperial College (*Kuo-tzu-chien*) in the Early Ch'ing (1644–1795)," *PFEH* 10.

––––––. (1974a). "Syllabus of the Provincial Examination (*hsiang-shih*) Under the Early Ch'ing (1644–1795)," *MAS* 8.

———. (1978). *Chinese Censors and the Alien Emperor, 1644–1660* (Hong Kong).

———. (1981). *The Hanlin Academy* (Hamden, Conn.).

———. (1990). *Ch'ing Institutions and Society* (Hong Kong).

Luo, Guang (1981). *Zhongguo zhexue sixiang shi: Qingdai* (Taibei).

Luo, Ming (1984). "The General State of Qing Historical Research in Recent Years [in the People's Republic of China]," *CSWT* 5, 2 (December; translated by Lynn Struve).

LYBL (1911). Zhou Liang. *Liyi bianlan* (A Guide to Ritual and Etiquette).

Ma, Fengchen (1935). *Qingdai xingzheng zhidu yanjiu cankao shumu* (Annotated Bibliography for Research into the Administrative System of the Qing Dynasty; Beiping).

Ma, Yin, ed. (1989). *China's Minority Nationalities* (Beijing).

Ma, Yong, et al., eds. (1988). *Zhong Xi wenhua xin renshi* (New Understandings of Chinese and Western Culture; Shanghai).

Macgowan, John (1912). *Men and Manners of Modern China* (London).

Machle, Edward (1993). *Nature and Heaven in the Xunzi* (Albany).

Mackerras, Colin (1972). *The Rise of Peking Opera, 1770–1870* (Oxford).

Madsen, Richard, et al., eds. (1989). *Unofficial China: Essays in Popular Culture and Thought* (Boulder, Colo.).

Mair, Victor (1989). *T'ang Transformation Texts: A Study of the Buddhist Contribution to the Rise of Vernacular Fiction and Drama in China* (Cambridge, Mass.).

Mancall, Mark (1984). *China at the Center: Three Hundred Years of Foreign Policy* (New York).

Mann, Susan (1987). *Local Merchants and the Chinese Bureaucracy, 1750–1950* (Stanford).

———. (1987a). "Widows in the Kinship, Class and Community Structures of Qing Dynasty China," *JAS* 46, 1 (February).

———. (1992). "Fuxue (Women's Learning) by Zhang Xuecheng (1738–1801): China's First History of Women's Culture," *LIC* 13, 1 (June).

———. (1992a). Review of Ju-k'ang T'ien (1988), *HJAS* 52, 1.

March, Andrew (1974). *The Idea of China: Myth and Theory in Geographic Thought* (London and Vancouver).

March, Benjamin (1935). *Some Technical Terms of Chinese Painting* (Baltimore).

March, Tamar, ed. (1987). *Interpreting the Humanities, 1986* (Princeton).

Marks, Robert B. (1991). "Rice Prices, Food Supply, and Market Structure in Eighteenth-Century South China," *LIC* 12, 2 (December).

Marshall, Robert (1993). *Storm from the East: From Genghis Khan to Kubilai Khan* (Berkeley).

Martin, W.A.P. (1897). *A Cycle of Cathay* (Edinburgh and London).

Maspero, Henri (1981). *Taoism and Chinese Religion* (Amherst, Mass.; translated by Frank Kierman, Jr.).

Mayers, William (1874). *The Chinese Reader's Manual* (Shanghai).

———. (1897). *The Chinese Government* (London).

McDermott, Joseph (1987). Review of Ebrey, trans. (1984), *HJAS* 47, 1.

McKnight, Brian (1992). *Law and Order in Sung China* (Cambridge, Eng.).

McMahon, Keith (1988). "A Case for Confucian Sexuality: The Eighteenth-Century Novel, *Yesou Puyan*," *LIC* 9, 2 (December).

———. (1988a). *Causality and Containment in Seventeenth-Century Chinese Fiction* (Leiden).

McMullen, David (1988). *State and Scholars in T'ang China* (Cambridge, Eng.).

McRae, John R. (1987). *The Northern School and the Formation of Early Ch'an Buddhism* (Honolulu).

Meadows, Thomas T. (1856). *The Chinese and Their Rebellions* (London).

Meijer, M[arinus] J. (1981). "The Price of a P'ai-lou," *TP* 67.

_____. (1991). *Murder and Adultery in Late Imperial China: A Study of Law and Morality* (Leiden).

Meisner, Maurice (1986). *Mao's China and After* (New York and London).

Meng, Sen (1977). *Qingdai shi* (A History of the Qing Dynasty; Taibei).

Meskill, John, ed. (1973). *An Introduction to Chinese Civilization* (Toronto).

Metzger, Thomas (1973). *The Internal Organization of Ch'ing Bureaucracy* (Cambridge, Mass.).

_____. (1977). *Escape from Predicament* (New York).

Meyer, Jeffrey (1978). "Feng-shui of the Chinese City," *HR* 18, 2 (November).

_____. (1991). *The Dragons of Tiananmen* (Columbia, S.C.).

Michael, Franz (1966, 1972). *The Taiping Rebellion* (Seattle), 3 vols.

Miller, Lucien (1975). *Masks of Fiction in Dream of the Red Chamber* (Tucson).

Min, Tu-ki (1989). *National Polity and Local Power: The Transformation of Late Imperial China* (Cambridge, Mass.; edited by Philip Kuhn and Timothy Brook).

Minford, John, trans. (1979–1987). *The Story of the Stone* (Harmondsworth, Eng.), vols. 4–5. See also Hawkes (1973–1979).

Miyazaki, Ichisada (1976). *China's Examination Hell* (New York and Tokyo; translated by Conrad Schirokauer).

Moore, Charles, ed. (1967). *The Chinese Mind* (Honolulu).

Morse, H. B. (1908). *The Trade and Administration of the Chinese Empire* (Shanghai).

Moser, Leo (1985). *The Chinese Mosaic: The Peoples and Provinces of China* (Boulder, Colo.).

Mote, Frederick (1986). Review of Dardess (1983), *HJAS* 46, 1.

_____. (1989). *Intellectual Foundations of China* (New York).

_____. (1990). Review of Schwartz (1985), *HJAS* 50, 1.

Mote, Frederick, and Chu, Hung-lam (1988). *Calligraphy and the East Asian Book* (Princeton).

Mou, Tianhua (1977). *Chengyu dian* (Dictionary of Fixed Expressions; Taipei).

Mungello, David (1969). "Neo-Confucianism and Wen-jen Aesthetic Theory," *PEW* 19, 4 (October).

_____. (1977). *Leibnitz and Confucianism* (Honolulu).

_____. (1989). *Curious Land: Jesuit Accommodation and the Origins of Sinology* (Honolulu).

Munro, Donald J. (1988). *Images of Human Nature: A Sung Portrait* (Princeton).

Muramatsu, Yuji (1966). "A Documentary Study of Chinese Landlordism in the Late Ch'ing and Early Republican Kiangnan," *BSOAS* 29, 3.

Murck, Alfreda, and Fong, Wen C., eds. (1991). *Words and Images: Chinese Poetry, Calligraphy and Painting* (Princeton).

Murck, Christian, ed. (1976). *Artists and Traditions* (Princeton).

Murray, Dian (1987). *Pirates of the South China Coast, 1790–1810* (Stanford).

Myers, Ramon (1980). *The Chinese Economy, Past and Present* (Belmont, Calif.).

_____. (1991). "How Did the Modern Chinese Economy Develop?—A Review Article," *JAS* 50, 3 (August).

Nakagawa, Chūei (1800). *Shinzoku kibun* (A Record of Qing Customs).

Nakamura, Hajime (1971). *Ways of Thinking of Eastern Peoples* (Honolulu; translated by Philip Wiener).

Nakayama, Shigeru, and Sivin, Nathan, eds. (1973). *Chinese Science* (Cambridge, Mass., and London).

Naquin, Susan (1976). *Millenarian Rebellion in China* (New Haven and London).

Naquin, Susan, and Rawski, Evelyn (1987). "Topics for Research in Ch'ing History," *LIC* 8, 1 (June).

———. (1987a). *Chinese Society in the Eighteenth Century* (New Haven).

Naquin, Susan, and Yü, Chün-fang, eds. (1992). *Pilgrims and Sacred Sites in China* (Berkeley and Los Angeles).

Nathan, Andrew (1973). *Modern China, 1841–1972* (Ann Arbor).

———. (1976). *Peking Politics, 1918–1923: Factionalism and the Failure of Constitutionalism* (Berkeley, Los Angeles, and London).

———. (1985). *Chinese Democracy* (New York).

Naundorf, Gert, et al., eds. (1985). *Religion und Philosophie in Ostasien* (Wurzberg).

Needham, Joseph (1956–1992). *Science and Civilisation in China* (Cambridge, Eng.).

———. (1965). *Time and Eastern Man* (London).

———. (1976). *Moulds of Understanding* (London).

Needham, Joseph, and Huang, Ray (1974). "The Nature of Chinese Society—A Technical Interpretation," *JOS* 12, 1–2.

Needham, Rodney, ed. (1973). *The Right and the Left: Essays on Dual Symbolic Classification* (Chicago).

Nevius, John (1869). *China and the Chinese* (New York).

Ng, Chin-keong (1983). *Trade and Society: The Amoy Network on the China Coast, 1683–1735* (Singapore).

Ng, So Kam (1992). *Styles and Techniques of Chinese Painting* (Seattle).

Ng, Vivien W. (1987). "Ideology and Sexuality: Rape Laws in Qing China," *JAS* 46, 1 (February).

———. (1990). *Madness in Late Imperial China: From Illness to Deviance* (Norman, Okla.).

Nivison, David (1956). "Communist Ethics and Chinese Tradition," *FEQ* 16, 1 (November).

———. (1966). *The Life and Thought of Chang Hsüeh-ch'eng (1738–1801)* (Stanford).

Nivison, David, and Wright, Arthur, eds. (1959). *Confucianism in Action* (Stanford).

Norman, Jerry (1988). *Chinese* (Cambridge, Eng.).

Ocko, Jonathan (1973). "The British Museum's Peking Gazette," *CSWT* 2, 9 (January).

———. (1983). *Bureaucratic Reform in Provincial China* (Cambridge, Mass., and London).

———. (1988). "I'll take it all the way to Beijing: Capital Appeals in the Qing," *JAS* 47, 2 (May).

Odin, Steve (1982). *Process Metaphysics and Hua-yen Buddhism* (Albany).

Ono, Kazuko (1989). *Chinese Women in a Century of Revolution, 1850–1950* (Stanford; translated by Joshua Fogel).

Overmyer, Daniel (1976). *Folk Buddhist Religion* (Cambridge, Mass.).

———. (1986). *Religions of China: The World as a Living System* (New York).

Owen, Stephen (1985). *Traditional Chinese Poetry and Poetics: Omens of the World* (Madison, Wis.).

———. (1986). *Remembrances: The Experience of the Past in Classical Chinese Literature* (Cambridge, Mass.).

———. (1988). Review of Chaves, ed. (1986), and Lo and Schultz, eds. (1986), *HJAS* 48, 1.

Panda Books (1986). *Poetry and Prose of the Ming and Qing* (Beijing).

Paper, Jordan (1985). " 'Riding on a White Cloud': Aesthetics as Religion in China," *Religion* 15.

Parish, William, and Whyte, Martin K. (1978). *Village and Family in Contemporary China* (Chicago and London).

Parker, E. H. (1899). *Chinese Customs* (Shanghai).

Pas, Julian F., ed. (1989). *The Turning of the Tide: Religion in China Today* (Oxford).

Peerenboom, R. P. (1993). *Law and Morality in Ancient China: The Silk Manuscripts of Huang-Lao* (Ithaca).

Perdue, Peter (1987). *Exhausting the Earth: State and Peasant in Hunan, 1500–1850* (Cambridge, Mass.).

Perkins, Dwight (1967). "Government as an Obstacle to Industrialization," *JEH* 27, 4 (December).

Perry, Elizabeth J., and Harrell, Stevan, eds. (1982). "Symposium: Syncretic Sects in Chinese Society," *MC* 8, 3 (July and October).

Perry, John C., and Smith, Bardwell L., eds. (1976). *Essays on T'ang Society: The Interplay of Social, Political, and Economic Forces* (Leiden).

Peyrefitte, Alain (1992). *The Immobile Empire* (New York; translated by Jon Rothschild).

Plaks, Andrew (1976). *Archetype and Allegory in the Dream of the Red Chamber* (Princeton).

———. (1977). "Conceptual Models in Chinese Narrative Theory," *JCP* 4.

———, ed. (1977). *Chinese Narrative* (Princeton).

———. (1987). *The Four Masterworks of the Ming Novel* (Princeton).

Plopper, Clifford (1926). *Chinese Religion Seen Through the Proverb* (Shanghai).

Po, Sung-nien, and Johnson, David (1992). *Domesticated Deities and Auspicious Emblems: The Iconography of Everyday Life in Village China* (Berkeley).

Polachek, James M. (1992). *The Inner Opium War* (Cambridge, Mass.).

Porkert, Manfred (1988). *Chinese Medicine* (New York; translated by Mark Howson).

Powers, Martin (1992). *Art and Political Expression in Early China* (New Haven).

Pye, Lucian (1978). *China: An Introduction* (Boston).

———. (1981). *The Dynamics of Chinese Politics* (Cambridge, Mass.).

———. (1988). *The Mandarin and the Cadre: China's Political Cultures* (Ann Arbor).

QBLC (1916). Xu Ke. *Qingbai leichao* (Classified Collection of Anecdotes from the Qing Dynasty; Shanghai).

Qian, Hao, et al. (1981). *Out of China's Earth* (New York and Beijing).

Qian, Mu (1937). *Zhongguo jin sanbai nian xueshu shi* (History of the Past Three Hundred Years of Chinese Scholarship; Shanghai).

———. (1968). *Zhonghua wenhua shijiang* (Ten Lectures on Chinese Culture; Taibei).

———. (1970). *Zhonghua wenhua congtan* (Collected Notes on Chinese Culture; Taibei).

Qiu Jun, ed. (1701). *Zhuzi jiali* (Master Zhu's Family Rituals).

QS (1961). Qingshi bianzuan weiyuan hui, ed. *Qingshi* (History of the Qing Dynasty; Taibei).

Ramsey, S. Robert (1987). *The Languages of China* (Princeton).

Rankin, Mary (1986). *Elite Activism and Political Transformation in China, Zhejiang Province, 1865–1911* (Stanford).

Ratchnevsky, Paul (1989). *Chinggis Khan: His Life and Legacy* (Oxford; translated by Thomas Haining).

Rawski, Evelyn (1979). *Education and Popular Literacy in Ch'ing China* (Ann Arbor).

———. (1991). "Research Themes in Ming-Qing Socioeconomic History—The State of the Field," *JAS* 50, 1 (February).

Rawski, Thomas, and Li, Lillian, eds. (1992). *Chinese History in Economic Perspective* (Berkeley and Los Angeles).

Reichelt, Karl (1934). *Truth and Tradition in Chinese Buddhism* (Shanghai; translated by Katrina Bugge).

Ren, Cheng (1991). *Zhongguo minjian jinji* (Popular Taboos in China; Beijing).

Reynolds, Frank, and Ludwig, Theodore, eds. (1980). *Transitions and Transformations in the History of Religions* (Leiden).

Richard, L. (1908). *Comprehensive Geography of the Chinese Empire and Dependencies* (Shanghai; translated by M. Kennelly).

Rickert, Adele, ed. (1978). *Chinese Approaches to Literature from Confucius to Liang Ch'i-chao* (Princeton).

Rickett, W. Allyn (1985). *Guanzi: Political, Economic, and Philosophical Essays from Early China*, vol. 1 (Princeton).

Roberts, Moss, trans. (1991). *Three Kingdoms: A Historical Novel* (Berkeley).

Robertson, Maureen (1992). "Voicing the Feminine: Constructions of the Gendered Subject in Lyric Poetry by Women of Medieval and Late Imperial China," *LIC* 13, 1 (June).

Roetz, Heiner (1993). *Confucian Ethics of the Axial Age* (Ithaca).

Rogers, Howard, and Lee, Sherman E., eds. (1988). *Masterworks of Ming and Qing Painting from the Forbidden City* (Lansdale, Pa.).

Rolston, David L., ed. (1990). *How to Read the Chinese Novel* (Princeton).

Ronan, Charles, and Oh, Bonnie B.C., eds. (1988). *East Meets West: The Jesuits in China, 1582–1773* (Chicago).

Ropp, Paul (1976). "The Seeds of Change," *Signs* 2, 1 (Autumn).

———. (1981). *Dissent in Early Modern China* (Ann Arbor).

———, ed. (1990). *Heritage of China: Contemporary Perspectives on Chinese Civilization* (Berkeley).

Rosemont, Henry, Jr. (1974). "On Representing Abstractions in Archaic Chinese," *PEW* 24, 1 (January).

———, ed. (1984). *Explorations in Early Chinese Cosmology* (Chico, Calif.).

———, ed. (1991). *Chinese Texts and Philosophical Contexts* (La Salle, Ill.).

Rossabi, Morris, ed. (1983). *China Among Equals* (Berkeley).

———. (1988). *Khubilai Khan: His Life and Times* (Berkeley).

Rowe, William T. (1984). *Hankow: Commerce and Society in a Chinese City, 1796–1889* (Stanford).

———. (1989). *Hankow: Conflict and Community in a Chinese City, 1796–1895* (Stanford).

———. (1992). "Women and the Family in Mid-Qing Social Thought: The Case of Chen Hongmou," *LIC* 13, 2 (December).

Rowley, George (1970). *Principles of Chinese Painting* (Princeton).

Rozman, Gilbert (1982). *Population and Marketing Settlements in Ch'ing China* (Cambridge, Eng.).

———, ed. (1991). *The East Asian Region: Confucian Heritage and Its Modern Adaptation* (Princeton).

Rozman, Gilbert, et al. (1981). *The Modernization of China* (New York and London).

Ruan, Fang Fu (1991). *Sex in China: Studies in Sexology in Chinese Culture* (New York and London).

Ruitenbeek, Klaas (1993). *Carpentry and Building in Late Imperial China* (Leiden and New York).

Saari, Jon (1990). *Legacies of Childhood: Growing up Chinese in a Time of Crisis, 1890–1920* (Cambridge, Mass.).

Sands, Barbara, and Myers, Ramon (1990). "Economics and Macroregions: A Reply to Our Critics," *JAS* 49, 2 (May).

Sangren, P. Steven (1987). *History and Magical Power in a Chinese Community* (Stanford).

Saso, Michael (1978). *The Teachings of Taoist Master Chuang* (New Haven and London).

———. (1978a). "What is the *Ho-t'u?*" *HR* 17, 3 (February–May).

———. (1991). *Blue Dragon White Tiger: Taoist Rites of Passage* (Honolulu).

Saussy, Haun (1993). *The Problem of a Chinese Aesthetic* (Stanford).

Scalapino, Robert, and Yu, George T. (1985). *Modern China and Its Revolutionary Process: Recurrent Challenges to the Traditional Order, 1850–1920* (Berkeley and Los Angeles).

Scharfstein, Ben-Ami (1974). *The Mind of China* (New York).

———, ed. (1978). *Philosophy East/Philosophy West* (Oxford).

Schoppa, R. Keith (1982). *Chinese Elites and Political Change: Zhejiang Province in the Early Twentieth Century* (Cambridge, Mass.).

Schram, Stuart (1969). *The Political Thought of Mao Tse-tung* (New York).

———. (1974). *Chairman Mao Talks to the People* (New York).

———, ed. (1987). *Foundations and Limits of State Power in China* (London).

———. (1989). *The Thought of Mao Tse-tung* (Cambridge, Eng.).

Schran, Peter (1978). "A Reassessment of Inland Communications in Late Ch'ing China," *CSWT* 3, 10 (November).

Schuyler, Cammann (1990). "The Eight Trigrams: Variants and Their Uses," *HR* 29, 4 (May).

Schwarcz, Vera (1986). *The Chinese Enlightenment: Intellectuals and the Legacy of the May Fourth Movement of 1919* (Berkeley).

———. (1991). "No Solace from Lethe: History, Memory, and Cultural Identity in Twentieth-Century China," *Daedalus* 120, 2 (Spring).

Schwartz, Benjamin (1964). *In Search of Wealth and Power* (Cambridge, Mass.).

———, ed. (1972). *Reflections on the May Fourth Movement* (Cambridge, Mass.).

———. (1985). *The World of Thought in Ancient China* (Cambridge, Mass.).

Seaman, Gary, ed. (1993). *Chinese Religion: Publications in Western Languages, 1981 Through 1992* (Tucson; compiled by Laurence Thompson).

Seidel, Anna, and Welch, Holmes, eds. (1979). *Facets of Taoism: Essays in Chinese Religion* (New Haven).

Shadick, Harold, trans. (1952). *The Travels of Lao Ts'an* (Ithaca, N.Y.).

Shanghai guji chuban she, ed. (1987). *Zhongguo wenhua shi sanbai ti* (Three Hundred Questions Concerning China's Cultural History; Shanghai).

Shapiro, Sidney, trans. (1981). *Outlaws of the Marsh* (Peking and Bloomington, Ind.).

Shen, Fuwei (1985). *Zhong Xi wenhua jiaoliu shi* (A History of Sino-Western Cultural Interaction; Shanghai).

Shen, Vincent (1993). "Creativity as Synthesis of Contrasting Wisdoms: An Interpretation of Chinese Philosophy in Taiwan Since 1949," *PEW* 43, 2 (April).

Shiga, Shuzo (1974). "Criminal Procedure in the Ch'ing Dynasty," *MRDTB* 32, 1.

Shih, Vincent (1967). *The Taiping Ideology* (Seattle).

———, trans. (1983). *The Literary Mind and the Carving of Dragons* (Hong Kong).

Shimada, Kenji (1990). *Pioneer of the Chinese Revolution: Zhang Binglin and Confucianism* (Stanford; translated by Joshua Fogel).

Silbergeld, Jerome (1982). *Chinese Painting Style* (Seattle and London).

———. (1987). "Chinese Painting Studies in the West: A State-of-the-Field Article," *JAS* 46, 4 (November).

Simoons, Frederick (1991). *Food in China: A Cultural and Historical Inquiry* (Boca Raton).

Siren, Oswald (1937). *The Chinese on the Art of Painting* (Peiping).

Siu, Helen (1989). *Agents and Victims in South China: Accomplices in Rural Revolution* (New Haven).

———. (1990). "Where Were the Women? Rethinking Marriage Resistance and Regional Culture in South China," *LIC* 11, 2 (December).

Sivin, Nathan (1966). "Chinese Conceptions of Time," *ER* 1.

———. (1987). *Traditional Medicine in Contemporary China* (Ann Arbor).

———. (1988). "Science and Medicine in Imperial China: The State of the Field," *JAS* 47, 1 (February).

Skinner, G. William (1964–1965). "Marketing and Social Structure in Rural China," *JAS* 24, 1 (November 1964); 24, 2 (February 1965); 24, 3 (May 1965).

———. (1971). "Chinese Peasants and the Closed Community," *CSSH* 13, 3 (July).

———, ed. (1977). *The City in Late Imperial China* (Stanford).

———, ed. (1979). *The Study of Chinese Society* (Stanford).

Skinner, G. William, and Hsieh, Winston, eds. (1973). *Modern Chinese Society: An Analytical Bibliography* (Stanford; one volume on Western-language sources, one on Chinese sources, and one on Japanese sources).

SKQSZM (1970). Ji Yun. *Qinding siku quanshu zongmu* (Index to the Imperially Endorsed Complete Collection of the Four Treasuries; Taibei reprint).

Smith, Arthur (1899). *Village Life in China* (New York).

———. (1914). *Proverbs and Common Sayings from the Chinese* (Shanghai).

Smith, Carol, ed. (1976). *Regional Analysis* (New York).

Smith, Joanna Handlin (1987). "Benevolent Societies: The Reshaping of Charity During the Late Ming and Early Ch'ing," *JAS* 46, 2 (May).

Smith, Kidder, et al. (1990). *Sung Dynasty Uses of the I Ching* (Princeton).

Smith, Richard J. (1974). "Chinese Military Institutions in the Mid-Nineteenth Century, 1850–1860," *JAH* 8, 2.

———. (1975). "The Employment of Foreign Military Talent," *JHKBRAS* 15.

———. (1976). "Reflections on the Comparative Study of Modernization in China and Japan," *JHKBRAS* 16.

———. (1978). "An Approach to the Study of Traditional Chinese Culture," *Chinese Culture* 19, 2 (June).

———. (1978a). *Traditional Chinese Culture,* Rice University Studies, vol. 65 (Houston).

———. (1978b). *Mercenaries and Mandarins* (Millwood, N.Y.).

———. (1978c). "The Reform of Military Education in Late Ch'ing China, 1842–1895," *JHKBRAS* 18.

———. (1981). "Tradition and Modernization," *USCR* 5, 6 (November–December).

———. (1981a). "China's Early Reach Westward: The Burlingame Mission, 1867–1870," *Sino-American Relations* 7, 3 (Autumn).

_____ . (1987). "China and the West: Some Comparative Possibilities," *Liberal Education* 73, 4 (September–October).

_____ . (1988). "A Note on Qing Dynasty Calendars," *LIC* 9, 1.

_____ . (1989). "The Future of Chinese Culture," *Futures* (October).

_____ . (1991). *Fortune-tellers and Philosophers: Divination in Traditional Chinese Society* (Boulder, Colo., and Oxford).

_____ . (1992). *Chinese Almanacs* (Hong Kong and Oxford).

_____ . (1993). "Ritual and Rhetoric, Past and Present." Paper for the conference on Traditional Institutions and Values in Contemporary China, Honolulu (May 20–22).

Smith, Richard J., and Kwok, D.W.Y., eds. (1993). *Cosmology, Ontology and Human Efficacy: Essays in Chinese Thought* (Honolulu).

Smith, Richard J., et al., eds. (1991). *Robert Hart and China's Early Modernization: His Journals, 1863–1866* (Cambridge, Mass.).

Smolen, Elwyn (1980). "Chinese Bronzes of the Ming Dynasty," *Arts of Asia* (January–February).

Solomon, Richard (1971). *Mao's Revolution and the Chinese Political Culture* (Berkeley, Los Angeles, and London).

Song, Yuanqiang (1991). "The Study of Regional Socio-Economic History in China: Retrospect and Prospects," *LIC* 12, 1 (June).

Souza, George B. (1986). *The Survival of Empire: Portuguese Trade and Society in China and the South China Sea, 1630–1754* (Cambridge, Eng.).

Spence, Jonathan (1966). *Ts'ao Yin and the K'ang-hsi Emperor* (New Haven).

_____ . (1968). "Chang Po-hsing and the K'ang-hsi Emperor," *CSWT* 1, 8 (May).

_____ . (1975). *Emperor of China* (New York).

_____ . (1978). *The Death of Woman Wang* (New York).

_____ . (1980). *To Change China* (Middlesex, Eng.).

_____ . (1984). *The Memory Palace of Matteo Ricci* (New York).

_____ . (1990). *The Search for Modern China* (New York and London).

Spence, Jonathan, and Wills, John, eds. (1980). *From Ming to Ch'ing* (New Haven and London).

Standaert, Nicholas (1988). *Yang Tingyun, Confucian and Christian in Late Ming China: His Life and Thought* (Leiden).

Steinhardt, Nancy Shatzman (1990). *Chinese Imperial City Planning* (Honolulu).

Stepanchuk, Carol, and Wong, Charles (1991). *Mooncakes and Hungry Ghosts: Festivals of China* (San Francisco).

Stockard, Janice (1989). *Daughters of the Canton Delta, Marriage Patterns and Economic Strategies in South China, 1860–1930* (Stanford).

Stover, Leon (1974). *The Cultural Ecology of Chinese Civilization* (New York).

Stover, Leon, and Stover, Takeko (1976). *China: An Anthropological Perspective* (Pacific Palisades, Calif.).

Strassberg, Richard E. (1983). *The World of K'ung Shang-jen: A Man of Letters in Early Ch'ing China* (New York).

Struve, Lynn (1977). " 'The Peach Blossom Fan' as Historical Drama," *Renditions* 8 (Autumn).

_____ . (1984). *Southern Ming, 1644–1662* (New Haven).

_____ . (1988). "Huang Zongxi in Context: A Reappraisal of His Major Writings," *JAS* 47, 3 (August).

————. (1993). *Voices from the Ming-Qing Cataclysm* (New Haven).

Sullivan, Michael (1977). *The Arts of China* (Berkeley).

————. (1979). *Symbols of Eternity* (Stanford).

Sullivan, Michael, et al. (1965). *The Arts of the Ch'ing Dynasty* (London).

Sun, E-tu Zen (1961). *Ch'ing Administrative Terms* (Cambridge, Mass.).

————. (1962–1963). "The Board of Revenue in Nineteenth Century China," *HJAS* 24.

Sun, Longji (1987). *Zhongguo wenhua di shenceng jiegou* (The Deep Structure of Chinese Culture; Hong Kong; 2d ed.).

Sung, Margaret (1979). "Chinese Language and Culture," *JCL* 7.

Sutter, Robert G. (1988). *Taiwan: Entering the 21st Century* (New York and London).

Sutton, Donald (1981). "Pilot Surveys of Chinese Shamans, 1875–1945: A Spatial Approach to Social History," *JSH* 15, 1.

————. (1989). "A Case of Literati Piety: The Ma Yuan Cult from High-Tang to High-Qing," *CLEAR* 11.

Swanson, Paul (1989). *Foundations of T'ien-t'ai Philosophy: The Flowering of the Two Truths Theory in Chinese Buddhism* (Berkeley).

Sweeten, Alan (1976). "The Ti-pao's Role in Local Government as Seen in Fukien Christian 'Cases,' 1863–1869," *CSWT* 3, 6 (December).

Sze, Mai-mai (1959). *The Way of Chinese Painting* (New York).

Tang, Junyi (1981). *Zhongguo wenhua zhi jingshen jiazhi* (The Spiritual Value of Chinese Culture; Taibei).

Tanigawa, Michio (1985). *Medieval Chinese Society and the Local "Community"* (Berkeley and Los Angeles; translated by Joshua A. Fogel).

Tao, Jing-shen (1988). *Two Sons of Heaven: Studies in Sung-Liao Relations* (Tucson).

Tao, Tang (1968). *Zhongguo wenhua kailun* (Introduction to Chinese Culture; Taibei).

Taylor, Rodney (1990). *The Religious Dimensions of Confucianism* (Albany).

Teiser, Stephen (1988). *The Ghost Festival in Medieval China* (Princeton).

Telford, Ted A. (1986). "Survey of Social Demographic Data in Chinese Genealogies," *LIC* 7, 2 (December).

Teng, Ssu-yü, and Biggerstaff, Knight (1971). *An Annotated Bibliography of Selected Chinese Reference Works* (Cambridge, Mass.).

Teng, Ssu-yü, and Fairbank, John K., eds. (1979). *China's Response to the West* (Cambridge, Mass., and London).

ter Haar, B. J. (1992). *The White Lotus Teachings in Chinese Religious History* (Leiden).

Thompson, Laurence, ed. (1973). *The Chinese Way in Religion* (Encino, Calif., and Belmont, Calif.).

————. (1979). *Chinese Religion* (Belmont, Calif.).

————. (1980). "Taiwanese Temple Arts and Cultural Integrity," *BSSCR* 8 (Fall).

————. (1981). "Popular and Classical Modes of Ritual in a Taiwanese Temple," *BSSCR* 9 (Fall).

Thomsen, Rudi (1988). *Ambition and Confucianism* (Aarhus, Denmark).

Tien, Hung-mao (1989). *The Great Transition: Political and Social Change in the Republic of China* (Stanford).

T'ien, Ju-k'ang (1988). *Male Anxiety and Female Chastity: A Comparative Study of Chinese Ethical Values in Ming-Qing Times* (Leiden).

Tikhvinsky, S. L. (1983). *Manzhou Rule in China* (Moscow; translated by David Skvirsky).

Tillman, Hoyt (1982). *Utilitarian Confucianism* (Cambridge, Mass., and London).

Ting, Joseph Sun-pao, ed. (1990). *Children of the Gods: Dress and Symbolism in China* (Hong Kong).

Toda, Toyosaburo (1963). "Shincho ekigaku Kanken" (On Studies of the Yijing in the Qing Dynasty), *Hiroshima daigaku bungakubu kiyo* 22, 1 (March).

Tong, James (1990). *Disorder Under Heaven: Collective Violence in the Ming Dynasty* (Stanford).

Topley, Marjorie, ed. (1967). *Some Traditional Chinese Ideas and Conceptions in Hong Kong Social Life Today* (Hong Kong).

Torbert, Preston (1978). *The Ch'ing Imperial Household Department* (Cambridge, Mass.).

Tozer, Warren (1970). "Taiwan's 'Cultural Renaissance,'" *CQ* 43 (July–September).

Tregear, T. R. (1965). *A Geography of China* (Chicago).

Tseng, Yu-ho Ecke (1977). *Chinese Folk Art* (Honolulu).

Tsien, Tsuen-hsuin (1952). "A History of Bibliographical Classification in China," *LQ* 22, 4 (October).

Tsien, Tsuen-hsuin, and Cheng, James (1978). *China: An Annotated Bibliography of Bibliographies* (Boston).

TSJC (1977). Chen Menglei et al. *Qinding gujin tushu jicheng* (Complete Collection of Writings and Illustrations, Past and Present, Imperially Endorsed; Taibei reprint).

T'sou, B.K.Y. (1981). "A Sociolinguistic Analysis of the Logographic Writing System of the Chinese," *JCL* 9, 1 (January).

Tu, Ching-i (1974–1975). "The Chinese Examination Essay: Some Literary Considerations," *MS* 31.

Tu, Wei-ming (1976). *Neo-Confucian Thought in Action* (Berkeley).

––––––. (1989). *Way, Learning, and Politics: Essays on the Confucian Intellectual* (Singapore).

––––––. (1991). "Cultural China: The Periphery as the Center," *Daedalus* 120, 2 (Spring).

Twitchett, Denis (1983). *Printing and Publishing in Medieval China* (New York).

Unschuld, Paul U. (1985). *Medicine in China: A History of Ideas* (Berkeley).

––––––. (1986). *Medicine in China: A History of Pharmaceutics* (Berkeley).

––––––. (1988). *Introductory Readings in Classical Chinese Medicine* (Dordrecht, Boston, and London).

Van Gulik, Robert H., trans. (1958). *Scrapbook for Chinese Collectors* (Beirut).

––––––. (1961). *Sexual Life in Ancient China* (Leiden).

Van Slyke, Lyman (1988). *Yangtze: Nature, History, and the River* (Reading, Mass.).

Van Zoeren, Steven (1991). *Poetry and Personality: Reading, Exegesis, and Hermeneutics in Traditional China* (Stanford).

Verellen, Franciscus (1989). *Du Guangting (850–933). Taoiste de cour a la fin de la Chine médiévale* (Paris).

Vervoorn, Aat (1990). *Men of the Cliffs and Caves: The Development of the Chinese Eremitic Tradition to the End of the Han Dynasty* (Hong Kong).

Vinograd, Richard (1992). *Boundaries of the Self: Chinese Portraits, 1600–1900* (Cambridge, Eng.).

Viraphol, Sarasin (1977). *Tribute and Profit: Sino-Siamese Trade, 1652–1853* (Cambridge, Mass.).

von Glahn, Richard (1987). *The Country of Streams and Grottoes: Expansion and Settlement, and the Civilizing of the Sichuan Frontier in Song Times* (Cambridge, Mass.).

Wakeman, Frederic, Jr. (1972). "The Price of Autonomy: Intellectuals in Ming and Ch'ing Politics," *Daedalus* 101, 2 (Spring).

———. (1973). *History and Will* (Berkeley, Los Angeles, and London).

———. (1975). *The Fall of Imperial China* (New York).

———. (1977). "Rebellion and Revolution," *JAS* 36, 2 (February).

———. (1985). *The Great Enterprise: The Manchu Restoration of Imperial Order in Seventeenth-Century China* (Berkeley).

Wakeman, Frederic, Jr., and Grant, Carolyn, eds. (1975). *Conflict and Control in Late Imperial China* (Berkeley).

Waldron, Andrew (1990). *The Great Wall of China: From History to Myth* (Cambridge, Eng.).

Waley, Arthur, trans. (1944). *Monkey* (New York).

———. (1970). *Yüan Mei* (Stanford).

Waley-Cohen, Joanna (1991). *Exile in Mid-Qing China: Banishment to Xinjiang, 1758–1820* (New Haven and London).

Walshe, Gilbert (1906). *Ways That Are Dark* (Shanghai).

Waltner, Ann (1986). "The Moral Status of the Child in Late Imperial China: Childhood in Ritual and Law," *Social Research* 53, 4 (Winter).

———. (1990). *Getting an Heir: Adoption and Construction of Kinship in Late Imperial China* (Honolulu).

Wang, Ermin (1976). *Zhongguo jindai sixiang shilun* (Historical Discussion of Recent Chinese Thought; Taibei).

———. (1977). *Wan Qing zhengzhi sixiang shilun* (Historical Discussion of Late Qing Political Thought; Taibei).

Wang, Fangyu, and Barnhart, Richard (1990). *Master of the Lotus Garden: The Life and Art of Bada Shanren (1626–1705)* (New Haven).

Wang, Georgette, et al. (1991). "Cultural Value Survey in Taiwan," *JCA* 12 (Spring).

Wang, Jing (1992). *The Story of Stone: Intertextuality, Ancient Chinese Stone Lore, and the Stone Symbolism in Dream of the Red Chamber* (Durham, N.C., and London).

Wang, Shu'nan (1935). *Zhongguo changji shi* (History of Prostitution in China; Shanghai).

Wang, Yeh-chien (1972). "The Secular Trend of Prices During the Ch'ing Period (1644–1911)," *JICS* (December).

———. (1974). *Land Taxation in Imperial China, 1750 1911* (Cambridge, Mass.).

———. (1990). Review of Kang Chao (1981), *HJAS* 50, 1.

Wang, Zhongshu (1982). *Han Civilization* (New Haven and London; translated by K. C. Chang).

Ward, Barbara (1979). "Not Merely Players: Drama, Art and Ritual in Traditional China," *Man*, n.s., 14 (March).

Wasserstrom, Jeffrey, and Perry, Elizabeth, eds. (1992). *Popular Protest and Political Culture in Modern China* (Boulder, Colo., San Francisco, and Oxford).

Watson, Burton (1962). *Early Chinese Literature* (New York and London).

———. (1989). *The Tso Chuan: Selections from China's Oldest Narrative History* (New York).

Watson, James, and Rawski, Evelyn, eds. (1988). *Death Ritual in Late Imperial and Modern China* (Berkeley).

Watson, Rubie S., and Ebrey, Patricia B., eds. (1991). *Marriage and Inequality in Chinese Society* (Berkeley).

Watson, William (1962). *Ancient Chinese Bronzes* (London).

Watt, John (1972). *The District Magistrate in Late Imperial China* (New York and London).

Wechsler, Howard (1985). *Offerings of Jade and Silk: Ritual and Symbol in the Legitimation of the T'ang Dynasty* (New Haven).

Wei, Tat (1970). *An Exposition of the I-ching* (Taipei).

Wei, Zhengtong (1981). *Zhongguo wenhua gailun* (A [Critical] Introduction to Chinese Culture; Taibei).

Weidner, Marsha, ed. (1990). *Flowering in the Shadows: Women in the History of Chinese and Japanese Painting* (Honolulu).

Weidner, Marsha, et al., eds. (1988). *Views from a Jade Terrace: Chinese Women Artists, 1300–1912* (Indianapolis and New York).

Weinstein, Sidney (1987). *Buddhism Under the T'ang* (New York).

Welch, Holmes (1967). *The Practice of Chinese Buddhism, 1900–1950* (Cambridge, Mass.).

Weller, Robert (1987). *Unities and Diversities in Chinese Religion* (Seattle).

Welskopf, Elizabeth, ed. (1964). *Neue Betrage zur Geschichte der alten Welt* (Berlin).

Weng, Wan-go (1978). *Chinese Painting and Calligraphy* (New York).

Werner, E.T.C. (1961). *A Dictionary of Chinese Mythology* (New York).

Whyte, Martin K. (1974). *Small Groups and Political Rituals in China* (Berkeley).

Wiant, Bliss (1965). *The Music of China* (Hong Kong).

Wichmann, Elizabeth (1991). *Listening to Theatre: The Aural Dimension of Beijing Opera* (Honolulu).

Widmer, Ellen (1987). *The Margins of Utopia: Shui-hu hou-chuan and the Literature of Ming Loyalism* (Cambridge, Mass.).

———. (1989). "The Epistolary World of Female Talent in Seventeenth-Century China," *LIC* 10, 2 (December).

Wieger, L. (1913). *Moral Tenets and Customs in China* (Hokien).

———. (1927). *A History of the Religious Beliefs and Philosophical Opinions in China* (Peking).

Wile, Douglas, ed. (1992). *Art of the Bedchamber: The Chinese Sexual Yoga Classics Including Women's Solo Meditation Texts* (Albany).

Wilhelm, Hellmut (1951). "The Problem of Within and Without, A Confucian Attempt in Syncretism," *JHI* 12, 1 (January).

Wilhelm, Richard (1967). *The I Ching or Book of Changes* (Princeton; translated by C. F. Baynes).

Wilkinson, Endymion (1973). *The History of Imperial China: A Research Guide* (Cambridge, Mass.).

Will, Pierre-Etienne (1990). *Bureaucracy and Famine in Eighteenth-Century China* (Stanford).

Will, Pierre-Etienne, and Wong, R. Bin (1991). *Nourish the People: The State Civilian Granary System in China, 1650–1850* (Ann Arbor).

Williams, C.A.S. (1941). *Outlines of Chinese Symbolism and Art Motives* (Shanghai).

Williams, E. T. (1913). "The State Religion of China During the Manchu Dynasty," *JNCBRAS* 46.

Williams, Samuel W. (1883). *The Middle Kingdom* (New York).

Wills, John E. (1974). *Peppers, Guns, and Parleys: The Dutch East India Company and China, 1622–1681* (Cambridge, Mass.).

———. (1979). "State Ceremonial in Late Imperial China," *BSSCR* 7 (Fall).

———. (1984). *Embassies and Illusions: Dutch and Portuguese Envoys to K'ang-hsi, 1666–1687* (Cambridge, Mass.).

Wilson, Richard, ed. (1979). *Value Change in Chinese Society* (New York).

Wilson, Richard, et al., eds. (1981). *Moral Behavior in Chinese Society* (New York).

Witek, John (1982). *Controversial Ideas in China and in Europe: A Biography of Jean-Francois Foucquet (1665–1741)* (Rome).

WLTK (1880). Qin Huitian. *Wuli tongkao* (Comprehensive Examination of the Five Rituals; Shanghai).

Wolf, Arthur, ed. (1974). *Religion and Ritual in Chinese Society* (Stanford).

———, ed. (1978). *Studies in Chinese Society* (Stanford).

Wolf, Arthur, and Huang, Chieh-shan (1980). *Marriage and Adoption in China, 1843–1945* (Stanford).

Wolf, Margery (1985). *Revolution Postponed: Women in Contemporary China* (Stanford).

Wong, K. Chimin, and Wu, Lien-teh (1936). *A History of Chinese Medicine* (Shanghai).

Wong, R. Bin (1992). "Chinese Economic History and Development: A Note on the Myers-Huang Exchange," *JAS* 51, 3 (August).

Wong, Shirleen (1975). *Kung Tzu-chen* (Boston).

Wong, Y. K. (1990). *Unlocking the Chinese Heritage* (Singapore).

Wong, Young-tsu (1989). *The Search for Modern Nationalism: Zhang Binglin and Revolutionary China, 1869–1936* (Oxford).

Woodside, Alexander (1983). "Some Mid-Qing Theorists of Popular Schools: Their Innovations, Inhibitions, and Attitudes Toward the Poor," *MC* 9.

Wright, Arthur, ed. (1953). *Studies in Chinese Thought* (Chicago).

———. (1960). "The Study of Chinese Civilization," *JHI* 21, 2 (April–June).

———, ed. (1960). *The Confucian Persuasion* (Stanford).

———, ed. (1964). *Confucianism and Chinese Civilization* (New York).

———. (1968). *Buddhism in Chinese History* (New York).

———. (1978). *The Sui Dynasty* (New York).

Wright, Arthur, and Twitchett, Denis, eds. (1973). *Perspectives on the T'ang* (New Haven).

Wright, Mary (1967). *The Last Stand of Chinese Conservatism* (New York).

———, ed. (1968). *China in Revolution* (New Haven and London).

Wu, Hung (1989). *The Wu Liang Shrine* (Stanford).

Wu, Jingxiong, et al., eds. (1967). *Zhongguo wenhua lunji* (Collected Writings on Chinese Culture; Taibei).

Wu, Pei-yi (1990). *The Confucian's Progress: Autobiographical Writings in Traditional China* (Princeton).

Wu, Silas (1970). *Communication and Imperial Control in China* (Cambridge, Mass.).

———. (1970a). "Emperors at Work," *THJ*, n.s., 8, 1–2 (August).

———. (1979). *Passage to Power* (Cambridge, Mass., and London).

WXL (1936). Wu Rongguang. *Wuxue lu* (A Record of My Studies; Shanghai reprint).

Wylie, Alexander (1867). *Notes on Chinese Literature* (Shanghai).

XBZZJC (1974). Shijie shuju bianji bu, ed. *Xinbian zhuzi jicheng* (New Edition of the Collection on Philosophical Writings; Taibei).

Xiao, Yishan (1967). *Qingdai tongshi* (Comprehensive History of the Qing Dynasty; Taibei).

XWXTK (1935). Liu Jinzao. *Huangchao xu wenxian tongkao* (Supplement to the Encyclopedic Examination of the Historical Records of the Qing Dynasty; Shanghai reprint).

Yamagiwa, Joseph, ed. (1969). *Papers of the C.I.C. Far Eastern Language Institute* (Ann Arbor).

Yang, C. K. (1961). *Religion in Chinese Society* (Berkeley).

Yang, Hsien-yi, and Yang, Gladys, trans. (1957). *The Scholars* (Peking).

_____, trans. (1978). *A Dream of Red Mansions* (Peking).

Yang, Lien-sheng (1969). *Excursions in Sinology* (Cambridge, Mass.).

Yang, Winston, et al., eds. (1978). *Classical Chinese Fiction* (Boston).

Yang, Youjiong (1945). *Zhongguo wenhua shi* (History of Chinese Culture; Taibei).

Yee, Angelina C. (1990). "Counterpoise in *Honglou meng,*" *HJAS* 50, 2.

Yee, Cordell D.K. (1992). "A Cartography of Introspection: Chinese Maps as Other Than European," *Asian Art,* 5, 4 (Fall).

Yeh, Wen-Hsin (1990). *The Alienated Academy: Culture and Politics in Republican China, 1919–1937* (Cambridge, Mass.).

Yetts, W. Percival (1912). *Symbolism in Chinese Art* (Leiden).

Yin, Haiguang (1966). *Zhongguo wenhua de zhanwang* (The Outlook for Chinese Culture; Taibei).

Yip, Evelyn (1992). *Chinese Numbers* (Singapore).

Yip, Wai-lim (1976). *Chinese Poetry* (Berkeley and Los Angeles).

Young, Gregory (1984). *Three Generals of the Later Han* (Canberra).

Young, John D. (1983). *Confucianism and Christianity: The First Encounter* (Hong Kong).

Young, Lung-chang (1988). "Regional Stereotypes in China," *CSH* 21, 4 (Summer).

Yu, Anthony, trans. (1977–1983). *The Journey to the West* (Chicago), 4 vols.

Yu, Pauline (1987). *The Reading of Imagery in the Chinese Poetic Tradition* (Princeton).

Yü, Ying-shih (1975). "Some Preliminary Observations on the Rise of Ch'ing Confucian Intellectualism," *THJ,* n.s., 11, 1–2 (December).

Yüan, Tung-li (1958). *China in Western Literature* (New Haven).

Yung, Bell (1989). *Cantonese Opera: Performance as Creative Process* (Cambridge, Eng.).

ZDLZ (1903). Xi Yufu, ed. *Huangchao zhengdian leizuan* (Classified Documents on the Administrative Institutions of the Dynasty).

Zeitlin, Judith T. (1993). *Historian of the Strange: Pu Songling and the Chinese Classical Tale* (Stanford).

Zelin, Madeleine (1984). *The Magistrate's Tael: Rationalizing Fiscal Reform in Eighteenth Century Ch'ing China* (Berkeley).

Zen, Sophia, ed. (1969). *Symposium on Chinese Culture* (New York).

Zhan, Kaidi (1992). *The Strategies of Politeness in the Chinese Language* (Berkeley).

Zhang, Dainian, and Jiang, Guanghui, eds. (1990). *Zhongguo wenhua chuantong duihua* (Dialogues on China's Cultural Tradition; Beijing).

Zhang, Dechang (1970). *Qingji yige jingguan di shenghuo* (The Life of a Metropolitan Official in the Late Qing Period; Hong Kong).

Zhang, Jinjian (1935). "Zhongguo wenhua zhi tezhi" (The Special Characteristics of Chinese Culture), *Wenhua jianshe* 1, 6 (March).

Zhang Laoshi yuekan bianji bu, ed. (1990). *Zhongguo ren di renqing yu mianzi* (The Human Feelings and Face of the Chinese People; Beijing).

Zhang, Rucheng (1723). *Jiali huitong* (Compendium on Family Ritual; Changzhou).

Zhang, Zichen (1985). *Zhongguo minsu yu minsu xue* (Chinese Folklore and Folklore Studies; Hangzhou).

Zhong, Fulan (1989). *Zhongguo minsu liubian* (Changes in Chinese Popular Customs; Hong Kong).

Zhongguo ge minzu zongjiao yu shenhua da cidian bianshen weiyuan hui, ed. (1990). *Zhongguo ge minzu zongjiao yu shenhua da cidian* (A Great Dictionary of the Religions and Myths of the Various Nationalities of China; Beijing).

Zhonghua shuju (1915). *Qingchao quanshi* (Complete History of the Qing Dynasty; Shanghai).

Zhonghua wenhua fuxing yundong tuixing weiyuan hui (1974). *Zhonghua wenhua gaishu* (Chinese Culture: A General Narration; Taibei).

Zhou, Ying (1988). "Fengjian mixin yu qunzhong wenhua" (Feudal Superstition and Mass Culture), *Qunzhong wenhua* 5.

Zhu, Xi (1979). *Zhouyi benyi* (The Basic Meaning of the Zhou Changes; Taibei reprint).

Zito, Angela (1984). "Re-presenting Sacrifice: Cosmology and the Editing of Texts," *CSWT* 5, 2 (December).

————. (1987). "City Gods, Filiality, and Hegemony in Late Imperial China," *MC* 13, 3.

————. (1989). "Grand Sacrifice as Text/Performance: Ritual Writing in Eighteenth Century China" (Ph.D. dissertation, University of Chicago).

Zunz, Oliver, ed. (1985). *Reliving the Past: The Worlds of Social History* (Chapel Hill).

Zurndorfer, Harriet (1988). "A Guide to the 'New' Chinese History: Recent Publications Concerning Chinese Social and Economic Development Before 1800," *IRSH* 33.

ZWDCD (1968). Zhang, Qiyun, ed. *Zhongwen da cidian* (Great Dictionary of Chinese Terms; Taibei).

About the Book and Author

*T*he Qing dynasty (1644–1912)—a crucial bridge between "traditional" and "modern" China—was a period remarkable for its expansiveness and cultural sophistication. In this extensively revised and expanded edition of his highly regarded book, Richard J. Smith shows how the Chinese of the Qing dynasty viewed the world; how their outlook was expressed in their institutions, material culture, and customs; and how China's preoccupation with order, unity, and harmony contributed to the remarkable cohesiveness and continuity of traditional Chinese civilization. In addition to offering a new and challenging interpretation of Chinese culture as a whole, he provides a fresh perspective on a wide variety of topics, from gender issues, philosophy, religion, and mythology to language, aesthetics, and symbolism. He also examines a number of important but too-often neglected aspects of traditional Chinese daily life, including divination, food, music, sexual practices, festivals, child-rearing, and games.

Based on the author's careful rethinking of certain themes and arguments presented in the first edition, this revised version of *China's Cultural Heritage* also draws heavily upon the enormous body of new scholarship on Chinese history and culture that has appeared in the past decade. Although focused primarily on the Qing dynasty, the book not only sheds valuable light on the distant past but also helps us to understand China's contemporary problems of modernization. A concluding chapter systematically explores the legacy of traditional Chinese culture to the twentieth century.

Richard J. Smith is professor of history, director of Asian Studies, and former Master of Hanszen College at Rice University, Houston, Texas. He is also an adjunct professor at the Center for Asian Studies at the University of Texas at Austin. He has written several books on late imperial China, including *Fortune-tellers and Philosophers: Divination in Traditional Chinese Society* (Westview Press, 1991). Smith is the recipient of nine teaching awards, including the Minnie Stevens Piper Professorship and the George R. Brown Certificate of Highest Merit.

Index

Although this book employs the increasingly popular *pinyin* (PY) system of transliterating Chinese sounds, the Wade-Giles (WG) system is still used in many scholarly publications on China (see Appendix A). I have therefore included WG equivalents in parentheses after the PY entry for commonly cited or otherwise familiar proper names. For example: Mao, Zedong (Mao, Tse-tung). Place names and the names of individuals mentioned only in passing do not appear in the index. As a rule, romanized equivalents for standard translations of Chinese terms (e.g., governor, district magistrate, etc.) appear only on first citation in the text and have not been included in the index. By contrast, most romanized Chinese book titles are listed as such in the index, since the translations of these titles (at least one of which appears on first citation in the text) vary so widely in Western-language writings on China.

Acupuncture, 173, 260. *See also* Medicine
Administration. *See* Government
Adoption, 248, 253
Aesthetics, 113–114, 189–191, 195–196, 200, 201, 202, 203–204, 210–212, 223–224, 226–227, 234–235, 243, 264, 265. *See also* Balance; Endlessness; Yinyang
Agriculture. *See* Land system; Peasantry
Alchemy, 126, 173
Alcoholic beverages, 261, 269–270
Allen, Sarah, 30
All Souls' Day, 273
Almanacs, 135, 231, 247, 270
Altar of Heaven, 158, 159
Amitabha Buddha, 171
Amusements. *See* Festivals; Games; Parties
An, Lushan (An, Lu-shan), 33, 34
An, Qi, 188–189
Analects. See Lunyu
Ancestor worship, 28, 88–92, 179–181, 184, 261, 270, 271–272
Ancient prose, 219, 224
Annam (Vietnam), 16, 128, 137, 169
Architecture, 200–201, 217. *See also* Forbidden City; Houses
Arhat, 171
Artisans (gong), 79
Audiences, imperial, 55–57
Authoritarianism, 86–87, 251–252, 294. *See also* Family system; Hierarchy

Autocracy, 28, 29, 34, 36, 37, 44–45, 47, 63, 83, 158. *See also* Emperors; Government

Balance
    as an aesthetic principle, 113–114, 189, 190, 195, 196, 200, 201, 210–212, 223, 224–225, 226–227, 234, 264
    in government, 31, 44, 67
    in intellectual life, 131
    in society, 67, 95, 99
Ban, Gu (Pan, Ku), 27, 124
Banner Army, 51, 62, 63, 71, 83–84, 286
Banner Office, 51
Bao. *See* Reciprocity
Bao, Shichen (Pao, Shih-ch'en), 217
Baojia, 59, 92, 163. *See also* Local control
Baoming Temple, 83
Barbarians, 11–12, 26, 32, 36–37, 137–138. *See also* Foreign relations
Bartlett, Beatrice, 48
Beijing Gazette. See Jingbao
Beijing Spring (1989), 297
Bian, Weiqi (Pien, Wei-ch'i), 230
Bisexuality. *See* Sexual life
Board of Civil Appointments, 51–52
Board of Music, 52
Board of Punishments, 53–54
Board of Revenue, 52, 54
Board of Rites, 52, 157
Board of War, 53

Board of Works, 54
Bodde, Derk, 104, 116, 127
Bodhisattvas, 169, 171
Bondservants, 85
Book of Changes. See Yijing
Book of History. *See Shujing*
Book of Poetry. *See Shijing*
Boxer Rebellion, 288
Brokaw, Cynthia, 156
Bronzes, 194, 195–196
Buddhism, 4–5, 32–33, 44, 82–83, 88, 91, 127, 133, 134, 135, 139, 156, 165–172, 174, 175, 177, 179, 184, 192, 193, 194, 199, 202, 220, 222, 231, 235–236, 242, 250, 259, 274, 280, 282, 297. *See also* Mahayana Buddhism; Theravada Buddhism
Bufeiqian gongde li, 231
Bureau of Astronomy, 52, 157,
Bureaucracy, 6, 30–31, 36, 47–48, 63, 66, 71, 73, 132, 157, 162, 163–164, 175, 176, 183, 295–296, 314(n59). *See also* Government; Hierarchy

Cahill, James, 202
Cai, Han, 214
Cai, Wan, 85
Calendar, 52, 137, 157–158
Calligraphy, 106, 201, 214–217
Cao, Cao (Ts'ao Ts'ao), 236
Cao, Xueqin (Ts'ao Hsueh-ch'in), 187, 199–200, 239, 242, 268
Cao, Zhao, 187, 191
Cao, Zhi, 202
Carnal Prayer Mat. See Rou putuan
Categorization, xiii, 1, 2, 3–4, 15, 67, 117, 136, 157, 160, 175, 193–194, 220–222, 232, 294. *See also* Correlations; Culture; Encyclopedias
Censorate, 54–55
Ceramics, 197–198
Chan, Wing-tsit, 142, 172, 200
Chancery of Memorials, 55
Chang, Hao, 38, 282
Chang, Kwang-chih, 117
Chang, Tung-sun, 5, 117, 119
Chan (Zen) School of Buddhism, 170–171, 172
Chao, Y. R., 112
Charitable enterprises. *See* Welfare
Charms, 176, 247, 297
Chastity, cult of, 245–246, 258–259
Checks and balances, 63–64. *See also* Bureaucracy
Chen, Bin, 56
Chen, Cizhi, 143
Chen, Duxiu (Ch'en, Tu-hsiu), 289, 290
Chen, Hongmou, 246, 255
Chen, Jieqi (Ch'en, Chieh-ch'i), 195
Chen, Shu (Ch'en, Shu), 85, 214

Chen, Shun (Ch'en Shun), 214
Chen, Zilong, 219
Cheng, Chung-ying, 107, 118, 119, 140
Cheng, Hao (Ch'eng, Hao), 35, 147
Cheng, Yi (Ch'eng, I), 35, 125
Chiang, Yee, 217
Chiang Kai-shek (Jiang Jieshi), 291, 292, 294
Children, 247–253, 271, 273, 331(n13)
Chinese Communism, 292–297
Chinese names, 299. *See also* Pinyin transliteration system
Chineseness, definitions of, xi, 1, 275, 307–308(n4). *See also* Culture; Han people; Sinocentrism
Chinese Turkestan, 16–18
Chinggis Khan, 37
Chongyang Festival. *See* Double Yang Festival
Chouban yiwu shimo, 283
Christianity, 133, 135, 156, 184, 279. *See also* Jesuits; Missionaries
Chu, Yu-kuang, 118
Ch'ü, T'ung-tsu, 164
Chufen zeli, 52
Chunqiu, 110, 140
Ci. *See* Lyric Verse
Cities, 34, 95–96. *See also* Urban-rural relations
City God (Chenghuang), 160–163, 174–175
Cixi. *See* Empress Dowager
Clans, 19, 90–92, 93, 97
Classical literature, 220–230, 231
Classic of Filial Piety. See Xiaojing
Classification. *See* Categorization
Clunas, Craig, 187
Cognition, 4
Cohen, Joanna Waley, 18
Cohen, Myron, 2, 9, 93
Cohen, Paul, 277, 278
Cole, James, 22
Collective responsibility, 86, 90–91, 97–98, 274, 294. *See also* Baojia; Clans; Guilds; Lijia
Commentary of Gongyang. See Gongyang zhuan
Commentary of Zuo. See Zuozhuan
Communism. *See* Chinese Communism
Concubinage, 184, 238. *See also* Marriage
Confucian Classics. *See* Five Classics; Four Books
Confucianism, 5, 30–31, 33, 35, 37–38, 91, 129–131, 136, 139–149, 166, 167, 176, 184, 202–203, 231–232, 238, 259, 277, 278, 289
compared with Daoism, 152–153
and modernization, 277, 278, 292, 293, 294
See also Confucius; Ethics
Confucius, 24, 30, 120, 142, 143, 144, 145, 147, 181, 192, 196, 225, 248, 289, 292, 293
personal qualities of, 146
sacrifices to, 160, 289, 292

views on stages of moral development, 146–147
See also Confucianism

Contracts, 87–88, 93, 97, 248, 253, 254, 318(n15)

Cooking, 268–269. *See also* Food

Corporate organization. *See* Clans; Collective
responsibility; Guilds; Secret societies

Correlations, 118–120, 132–133, 173, 226, 294

Corruption, 43, 63, 65–66, 286. *See also* Bureaucracy;
Guanxi; Particularism

Cosmogony. *See* Creation myths

Cosmology, 44–45, 96, 132–134, 148–149, 177–178, 181,
189–190, 203, 247, 255, 275. *See also* Dao;
Heaven; Metaphysics; *Yijing*; Yinyang

County magistrate. *See* District magistrate

Courage (yong), 145

Court of Banqueting, 52

Court of Colonial Affairs, 16, 22, 55

Court of Revision, 54

Court of Sacrificial Worship, 52, 157

Court of State Ceremonial, 52

Crafts, 187, 188, 194–201. *See also* Bronzes; Ceramics;
Gardens; Jade

Creation myths, 27, 133, 134, 140

Creel, H. G., 107

Crossley, Pamela, 220

Cultural Renaissance, 295

Cultural Revolution, 293, 294, 295, 297

Culture, xi–xiii, 1–4, 9, 27–28, 36, 82, 96, 99, 104,
115–118, 127–128, 156, 185, 191, 200, 238, 242–
243, 275, 277, 291, 292, 295
changes in, 1, 9, 285, 289–291, 297–298
constructions of, xii, 307(n4)
definitions of, 1, 3
literature on, 305, 339–340
See also Categorization; Chineseness; Integration;
Sinocentrism; Wen

Customary fees (lougui), 43. *See also* Corruption

Dai, Liang (Tai, Liang), 37

Dai, Xi, 213

Dai, Zhen, 103, 104, 148

Dalai Lama, 156. *See also* Lamaism

Dao (The Way) 118, 133, 147, 150, 151, 152, 153, 173,
190, 203, 213, 215, 223, 281, 282. *See also*
Cosmology

Daode Heavenly Worthy, 173

Daode jing, 115, 134, 150, 173. *See also* Laozi

Daoguang (Tao-kuang) Emperor, 43, 47

Daoism, 30, 31, 129, 134, 139, 149, 150–153, 173, 199,
220, 222, 235, 235–236, 238
compared with Confucianism, 152–153

Daotai. *See* Intendant

Daozang, 173

Da Qing huidian, 54, 144, 160

Da Qing lüli, 53–54, 143, 253, 274–275. *See also* Law

Dardess, John, 37

Daxue, 140, 141, 142, 145, 147, 149

de Bary, W. T., 131, 153

Demeaned people, 71, 84–85

Democracy, 288–289, 290, 291–292, 297

Deng, Shiru, 217

Deng, Xiaoping, 296, 297

Department of the Imperial Bodyguard, 51

"Dependency orientation," 251–252. *See also*
Authoritarianism

Desires, 147, 148, 150, 152, 153, 168

Dharmas (fa), 169

Dialects, 101, 102–104

Dibao (constable), 59

Director of Education, 57–58

Discipline, 204–205, 209

District magistrate, 58–59

Diversity, xi–xii, 8, 9, 11, 18–23, 24–26 *See also*
Integration; Order and disorder; Unity and
disunity

Divination, 109, 121–122, 177–178, 247, 255, 256, 272,
297

Divorce, 253, 254, 258

Doctors. *See* Medicine

Domestic life. *See* Life-cycle ritual

Dong, Qichang, 189, 209, 212

Dong, Yuan, 209

Dong, Zhongshu (Tung Chung-shu), 31, 141

Dorgon, 41

Double Seventh Festival, 272–272

Double Yang Festival, 273

Dragon Boat Festival, 272

Dragon God, 160

Drama, 231–234, 270, 271

Dream of the Red Chamber. See Honglou meng

Du, Shaoqing, 238

Duan, Yucai, 103

Duanfang, 189

Eberhard, Wolfram, 25, 193

Ebrey, Patricia, 35

Economic change, 29, 31, 34–35, 36, 37–38, 39, 70, 71,
78, 80, 81, 187, 233, 245, 286, 292, 293, 297–298

Economic organization (Qing dynasty), 52, 65–66,
70, 75–82, 97–98, 127. *See also* Land system;
Merchants; Monopolies; Taxation

Education, 2, 60, 82, 90–91, 103, 250–251, 275, 284–
285, 288, 290, 308(n9). *See also* Examination
system; Literacy

Eight Eccentrics of Yangchow, 213, 214, 216

Eightfold Noble Path, 168

Eight Immortals, 174, 194

Eight Lucky Signs, 194

Eight Precious Things, 193

Eight Virtues, 295

Elites, 1–2, 3, 8, 73–75, 84, 88, 89, 91, 93–95, 176, 179, 180–181, 195, 198, 219, 220, 231, 249, 250, 258, 260, 261, 286, 293, 308(n12). *See also* Gentry

Elman, Benjamin, 60, 216, 219

Elvin, Mark, 238, 266

Emituo Fo. *See* Amitabha Buddha

Emperors, 41–49, 192. *See also under* individual reign titles (e.g. Kangxi Emperor)

Empress Dowager (Cixi), 44, 48, 166, 285, 287–288

Empresses, 48, 192

Encyclopedias, 219, 220–221, 231, 308(n16). *See also Tushu jicheng*

Endlessness (as an aesthetic principle), 200, 212, 234

Enlightenment (in Buddhism), 168

Erlitou, 27

Ershi nian mudu guai xianzhuang, 238

Ershisi xiao, 194, 248, 249

Erya, 115

Esherick, Joseph, 2, 22

Ethics, 3, 5–6, 67, 91, 117, 136, 149, 153, 158, 164, 168, 171, 173, 196, 202, 219, 227, 231, 235–236, 238, 247, 259, 288, 292, 294, 309(n23). *See also* Aesthetics; Buddhism; Confucianism; Religious Daoism

Ethnic minorities. *See* Minorities

Etiquette and Ritual. See Yili

Eunuchs, 50

Examination system, 33, 37, 59–63, 81–82, 84, 90, 114, 215, 238, 242, 245, 270, 284, 288, 289. *See also* Education

Fairbank, John K., 13, 44, 98, 138, 285

Faithfulness (xin), 145

Family ritual, 88 *See also Jiali*; Ritual

Family system, 48, 86–90, 115–116, 124, 163, 179–180, 221. *See also* Ancestor worship; Clans; Marriage

Fan, Ji, 209

Fang, Chao-ying, 239, 243

Fang, Wanyi, 214

Fang, Weiyi, 214

Fang, Xun, 204

Fangyu shuzheng, 104

Fate, 149, 178. *See also* Divination; Karma

Fei, Xiaotong, 13, 69

Feng, Youlan. *See* Fung, Yu-lan

Fengshui. *See* Geomancy

Festivals, 243, 270–274

Feuchtwang, Stephen, 157

Feudalism, 28–29

Filial piety (xiao), 141–142, 145, 166, 202, 231, 243, 248, 249, 250–253, 274. *See also*

Authoritarianism; *Ershisi xiao*; Family system; Three Bonds; *Xiaojing*

Finance Commissioner, 57

Fire God, 160, 175

First Emperor (King Zheng), 30

Five Classics, 60, 61, 110, 140, 222

Five Constant Virtues, 142. *See also* Faithfulness; Humaneness; Righteousness, Ritual; Wisdom

Five elements, agents, or activities (wuxing), 24–25, 132–133, 173. *See also* Cosmology

Five Relationships, 138, 140–141, 235

Five Rulers, 27, 173, 174

Five Stresses and Four Points of Beauty, 294

Fletcher, Joseph, 12

Flowers in the Mirror. See Jinghua yuan

Fong, Wen, 190, 195–196, 210

Food, 118, 176, 224, 243, 255, 261, 266–269. *See also* Cooking

Footbinding, 184, 238, 249–250, 260, 262, 286, 288

Forbidden City, 45–46, 197, 199

Foreign relations, 12, 32, 36, 137–138. *See also* Barbarians; Inner Asia

Four Books, 60, 61, 110, 140–149, 222, 292

Four Gentlemen, 194

Four Modernizations, 294

Four Noble Truths, 167–168

Four Social Controls, 292, 295

Four Spiritual Animals, 194

Four Treasures. See Siku quanshu

Four Wangs, 212

Freedman, Maurice, 155

Fu. *See* Rhapsody

Fu, Xi (Fu, Hsi), 27

Fugu (restoration of antiquity), 190, 216. *See also* Tradition-mindedness

Fung, Yu-lan, 5, 117

Furth, Charlotte, 229

Gai, Qi, 213

Gamble, Sidney, 79

Games, 262, 264–266

Gao, E (Kao, E), 239

Gao, Yihan, 55

Gardens, 198–199

Gazetteers, 26, 245

Geertz, Clifford, 7

Gegu yaolun, 187, 191, 195, 201, 202, 203, 215

Gentry, 1–2, 6, 59, 73–75, 81, 84, 95, 99–100, 164, 260

Genghis Khan. *See* Chinggis Khan

Geography, 11, 12, 14–15, 117, 221, 222. *See also* Maps; Stereotypes

Geomancy (fengshui), 177–178, 179, 200

God of Literature (Wenchang), 160, 174

God of the Hearth (Zaoshen), 179

"God of War." *See* Guandi; Guan, Yu
God of Wealth (Caishen), 271
Gong, Xian (Kung, Hsien), 187, 213
Gong, Zizhen (Kung, Tzu-chen), 130, 157, 228, 229
Gongan (koan), 170
Gongfu, 293
Gongyang zhuan, 140
Government, 55–59, 70, 142–143, 285–286. *See also*
      Autocracy; Emperors; Local control; Manchus
Governor, 57, 64
Governor-general, 57, 64
Graham, A. C., 115, 118
Grand Canal, 23–24, 43
Grand Council, 51, 54, 55, 285
Grand Secretariat, 51, 55
Granet, Marcel, 280
Gray, J. H., 266
Great Learning. See Daxue
Great Proletarian Cultural Revolution. *See* Cultural
      Revolution
Great Wall, 18
Greenblatt, Kristin Yü, 166
Green Standard Army, 53, 64, 83–84, 286
Gu, Hongming (Ku, Hung-ming), 291
Gu, Ruopu, 229–230
Gu, Yanwu (Ku, Yen-wu), 39, 103–104, 127, 130, 148,
      224
Gu, Zuyu (Ku, Tsu-yü), 14–15
Guan, Yu (Kuan, Yü), 236. *See also* Guandi
Guandi ("God of War"), 160
Guangshan pian gongguo ge, 231
Guangxu (Kuang-hsü), Emperor, 44, 48, 287–288,
      289
Guanxi, 64–65, 69–70, 74, 286, 296. *See also*
      Bureaucracy; Corruption; Particularism
Guanyin (Goddess of Mercy), 171, 214
Gui (yin spirits), 176, 177, 179, 180, 183. *See also*
      Spirits
Guilds, 79, 97–98
Guliang zhuan,
Guomindang (Kuomintang), 291, 292. *See also*
      Republic of China; Taiwan
Gutaiqing, 227

Hall of Preserving Harmony, 60
Hall of Supreme Harmony, 56
Han, Yu, 35
Hanan, Patrick, 233
Han dynasty, 31–32, 137
Hang, Shijun, 116
Han Learning, 130–131, 134, 219
Hanlin Academy, 60
Han people (Hanren), 11–12, 22, 31, 36, 254. *See also*
      Chineseness

Hansen, Chad, 118, 150
Hansen, Valerie, 35
Hansford, S. Howard, 197
Hao, Chang, 38, 282
Hao, Yen-p'ing, 286
Harmony, 5, 113, 129, 132–133, 189, 231. *See also*
      Balance; Integration
Harrell, Stevan, 22
Hartwell, Robert, 127
Hayes, James, 95
Heaven, 29, 47, 134, 149, 150, 158–159, 162, 175–176,
      181. *See also* Cosmology; Dao
Heavenly Emperor (Tiandi), 175
Heavenly Father (Tianfu), 184
Heavenly Noble (Tiangong), 175
Heavenly Official (Tianguan), 178
Henderson, John, 187
Heresy, 99. *See also* Heterodoxy
Heshen (Ho-shen), 42, 43, 65
Heterodoxy, 39, 99–100, 184, 274–275
Hetu, 122
Hexagrams, 102, 118–127
Hierarchy, 4, 71–86, 116, 143–144, 164, 165, 175, 243,
      252, 261, 268, 271, 295–296, 330(n47). *See also*
      Authoritarianism; Elites; Yinyang
Hinton, William, 296
History, 26–27, 136–137, 139, 232, 235, 293. *See also*
      Mythology
Ho, Ping-ti, 22, 81, 139
Holy Mother in Heaven. *See* Tianhou
Homosexuality. *See* Sexual life
Hong, Taiji, 38–39, 41
Honglou meng, 4, 110, 125, 199–200, 227, 236, 239–
      243, 250, 251, 253, 261, 268
Hou, Fangyu (Hou, Fang-yü), 234
Houses, 201, 243, 252. *See also* Architecture; Gardens
Hu, Shi (Hu, Shih), 290
Hua, Yan (Hua, Yen), 213
Huang, Chao, 14, 34
Huang, Chieh-shan, 254
Huang, Gongwang (Huang, Kung-wang), 14
Huang, Liuhong, 89
Huang, Shen, 213
Huang, Xiang, 296
Huang, Zongxi, 39, 130, 148
Huangdi. *See* Yellow Emperor
Huayan School of Buddhism, 169–170, 171
Huayu lu, 213
Hucker, Charles,
Hui, Dong (Hui, Tung), 134–135
Humaneness (ren), 114, 142–144, 145
Humane wisdom (zhi), 145
Human feelings, 69–70
Hun (yang aspect of the soul), 179

Hymes, Robert, 35

Imperial Clan Court, 51
Imperial Household Department, 49–50, 71
Imperialism, 275, 278–280, 283, 287
Imperial Maritime Customs Administration, 279, 283, 285
Individualists
    painters, 213, 214, 216
    poets, 228, 229
Infanticide, 247–248, 249
Inner Asia, 16–18, 44, 55, 64. *See also* Mongolia; Tibet
Institutions. *See* Bureaucracy; Government
Integration, xii–xiii, 2, 9, 11, 16, 18, 22–23, 26, 55, 63, 95–97, 99, 101, 127–128, 131, 155–156, 184, 185, 270, 275, 280, 290–291, 309(n29). *See also* Balance; Harmony; Order and disorder
Intendent (daotai), 58
Intermediaries (marriage brokers, middlemen, etc.), 80, 255
Interpreter's Colleges, 283
Intuition, 115, 170. *See also* Logic; Meditation
Intuitionalists, 228–229
Investigation of things (gewu), 146
Islam, 133, 135, 156, 184

Jade, 196–197
Jade Emperor, 174, 175, 181
Japan, 81, 101, 128, 137, 169, 213, 278, 279, 280, 281, 284–285, 286, 287, 288, 292
Jay, Jennifer, 37
Jenyns, Soame, 197
Jesuits, 38, 39, 127. *See also* Christianity; Missionaries
Jia, Baoyu (Chia, Pao-yü), 125, 239, 241, 242, 250, 253
Jiali, 231. *See also* Family ritual
Jiang, Taigong (Chiang T'ai-kung), 176
Jiang Jieshi. *See* Chiang Kai-shek
Jiao (rite of renewal), 176
Jiaqing (Chia-ch'ing) Emperor, 42–43, 83
Jiezi yuan huazhuan, 124, 204, 206–208, 211
Jin, Nong, 213, 216
Jin, Yue, 214
Jingbao, 57
Jinghua yuan, 238, 239, 266
Jin Ping Mei, 237
Jinshizi zhang, 170
Jinsi lu, 113–114, 120, 132, 153, 166–167
Johnson, David, 8, 270
Johnston, R. F., 266
Journey to the West ("Monkey"). *See Xiyou ji*
Judaism, 133, 135, 184
Judicial Commissioner, 57

Kang, Youwei (K'ang, Yu-wei), 130, 157, 278, 281, 287, 288, 289
Kangxi (K'ang-hsi), Emperor, 2, 25–26, 41–42, 45, 50, 56, 124, 139, 166, 188, 197, 198
Kangxi zidian, 106, 107, 108, 110
Kanji, 101
Kaozheng School. *See* School of Evidential Research
Karma, 168, 174
Kennedy, Tom, 278
Kessler, Lawrence, 139
Keswick, Maggie, 201
Kinship. *See* Ancestor worship; Clans; Family system
Kites, 262, 263
Kong, Shangren (K'ung, Shang-jen), 13, 233, 234
Korea, 128, 137
Kubilai Khan. *See* Qubilai Khan
Kuhn, Philip, 63, 99
Kuncan (K'un-ts'an), 213

Lamaism, 166. *See also* Dalai Lama
Landlordism, 77–78, 93, 99–100
Landscape Garden. *See* Gardens
Land system, 31, 36, 37, 75, 78, 82, 92–93. *See also* Landlordism; Peasantry
Lang, Shining (Lang, Shih-ning; Castiglione, Guiseppe), 214
Language, 3, 101–108, 127–128, 223–226, 229, 230–231, 280–281, 282–283, 290, 294, 297. *See also* Dialects; Logic; Manchu language; Symbolism; Wen; Women's script; Word play; Writing; *Yijing*
Lantern Festival, 271, 273
Lao Can youji, 238
Laozi (Lao-tzu), 30, 150, 151, 152, 153. *See also Daode jing*
Law, 34, 53–54, 67, 87, 89, 139, 143, 253, 254, 274–275, 294. *See also Da Qing lüli*; Punishments
Lee, Sherman, 213
Legalism, 30–31, 131
Leonard, Jane Kate, 12, 43
Levenson, Joseph, 149
Lewis, Mark, 29
Li (etiquette, propriety, ritual, etc.). *See* Ritual
Li (principles), 134, 147, 148, 203. *See also* Cosmology; School of Principle
Li (unworshipped dead), 160, 162
Li, E, 229
Li, Gong (Li Kung), 130
Li, Hongzhang (Li, Hung-chang), 279
Li, Jian, 213
Li, Jiannong, 42
Li, Lianying (Li, Lien-ying), 50
Li, Man-kuei, 233
Li, Ruzhen (Li, Ju-chen), 238

Li, Shan, 213
Li, Suzhen, 85
Li, Yong, 148
Li, Yu (Li, Yü), 232–233, 237, 259, 268
Li, Zhaole (Li, Chao-lo), 14–15
Li, Zhi (Li Chih), 38
Li, Zicheng (Li, Tzu-ch'eng), 39
Liang, Qichao (Liang, Ch'i-ch'ao), 130, 280, 287
Liang, Shu, 213
Liang, Zhangju (Liang, Chang-chü), 115
Liangxiang ban, 232
Lidai minghua ji, 202
Life-cycle ritual, 246–262. *See also* Children;
    Domestic life
Liji, 6, 140, 143, 144, 248–249, 253, 260, 269
Lijia (taxation system), 59, 163
Lijin. *See* Likin
Likin (Lijin), 80
Lin, Daiyu (Lin, Tai-yü), 239, 242, 253
Lin, Puqing (Lin, P'u-ch'ing), 85
Lin, Yü-sheng, 290
Lin, Yutang, 217
Lineages. *See* Clans
Ling, Tingkan, 146
Lingbao Heavenly Worthy, 173
Literacy, 2, 219, 231
Literary Inquisition, 221
Literary Mind and the Carving of Dragons, The. See
    Wenxin diaolong
Literature. *See* Classical literature; Drama; Narrative
    literature; Poetry; *Siku quanshu; Tushu jicheng;*
    Vernacular literature
Liu, Baonan (Liu, Pao-nan), 142
Liu, Dakui (Liu, Ta-k'uei), 223, 224
Liu, E (Liu, O), 238
Liu, Hui-chen Wang,
Liu, James J. Y., 227, 232
Liu, James T. C., 36
Liu, Kwang-Ching, 32
Liu, Laolao ("Granny Liu"), 110, 268
Liu, Xianting (Liu, Hsien-t'ing), 14–15
Liu, Xie (Liu, Hsieh), 114, 189, 223
Liu, Xihai (Liu, Hsi-hai), 195
Liu, Yiming, 124
Liu, Yin, 214
Liuqiu (Ryukyu) Islands, 137
Local control, 58–59, 163–164. *See also* Baojia; Clans;
    Lijia
Localism, xii, 8, 13, 24, 64; 99, 155–156, 245, 332(n47)
Logic, 115, 118–120, 136. *See also* Correlations
Longevity, 172–173, 192, 193, 200, 255, 260, 261–262
Longhua sect, 99
Lords of the Earth. *See* Tudi gong
Lotus Sutra. See Miaofa lianhua jing

Lougui. *See* Customary fees
Loyalty (zhong), 32, 37, 39, 55, 142, 145, 231
Lu, Cai, 233
Lu, Shihua (Lu, Shih-hua), 191, 196, 215
Lu, Xiangshan (Lu, Hsiang-shan), 35,
Lü, Liuliang (Lü, Liu-liang), 39
Lunyu, 110, 140, 141, 142, 145, 250. *See also* Confucius
Luo, Guanzhong (Lo, Kuan-chung), 236, 237
Luo, Ping (Lo, P'ing), 202, 213
Luopan (geomantic compass), 177
Luoshu, 122
Lüshi. *See* Regulated Verse
Lyric Verse, 219, 225

Ma, Quan, 214
Ma Yuan cult, 156
Macartney, Lord George, 138
Mahayana Buddhism, 168–169. *See also* Chan School
    of Buddhism; Huayan School of Buddhism;
    Lamaism; Pure Land School of Buddhism;
    Tiantai School of Buddhism
Mainland China. *See* People's Republic of China
Maitreya Buddha ("Buddha of the Future), 171
Majiang (Mahjong), 262
Manchu language, 51, 101–102, 220
Manchus, 12, 16, 36, 38–39, 44–45, 48–49, 62, 63–64,
    101–102, 139, 143, 157, 220, 221, 245, 260, 285,
    288, 289, 315(n60). *See also* Qing dynasty
Mandarin dialect, 102. *See also* Dialects
Mandate of Heaven, 29, 47, 149
Mao, Zedong (Mao, Tse-tung), 292, 293, 294, 295,
    297, 298
Maps, 14
Marketing communities, 94–95. *See also* Merchants
Marriage, 141, 253–258, 259–260, 270, 296. *See also*
    Concubinage; Family system
Martial arts, 262. *See also* Boxer Rebellion; Taiji quan
Maspero, Henri, 155
Matchmakers. *See* Intermediaries; Marriage
Mean, Doctrine of the. See Zhongyong
Medicine, 173, 247, 259, 260–261, 269. *See also*
    Alchemy; Sexual life
Meditation, 146, 168, 170–173. *See also* Chan School
    of Buddhism
Meisner, Maurice, 295
Memorials, 55
Mencius, 30, 104, 141, 142, 143, 145, 149, 147, 222, 248
    mother of, 230
    See also Mengzi
Meng, Zizhi, 238
Mengzi, 140
Merchants, 79–81, 94–95, 188–189, 198–199
Merits and demerits (gongguo), 174

Metaphysics, 121, 134, 139, 145, 147–149, 169, 203. *See also* Cosmology
Metzger, Thomas, 67
Meyer, Jeffrey, 177–178
Mi, Fei, 230
Miaofa lianhua jing, 169
Mid-Autumn Festival, 273
Military organization, 16–17, 51, 52–53, 64, 83–84, 278, 284, 285–286, 287, 288, 289. *See also* Banner Army; Green Standard Army; Tuanlian; Yong; Yongying
Militia. *See* Tuanlian
Miller, Lucien, 239
Ming dynasty, 37–38
Mingshi, 136
Minorities, 22–23
Missionaries, 38, 39, 127. *See also* Jesuits
Modernization, 277–278, 279, 285, 286, 287–298
Mongolia, 12, 15, 16, 17, 18, 22, 55, 169
Mongols, 15, 16, 36–37, 62
Monkey King. *See* Sun, Wukong
Monopolies, 97–98
Monopoly (game), 265
Moralists, 227–228
Morality. *See* Ethics
Morality books (shanshu), 156, 174
Mote, Frederick, 82, 190
Mourning, 86–87, 89, 116, 261–262. *See also* Ancestor worship
Mozi (Mo-tzu), 30, 142, 222, 224
Mu, Lian, 273
Murray, Dian, 21
Music, 52, 158, 184, 189, 200, 202, 222, 224, 225, 232, 263–264. *See also* Aesthetics; Drama
Mythology, 27, 30, 125, 275. *See also* Creation myths

Naquin, Susan, 22, 270
Narrative literature, 234–243
Nathan, Andrew, 65
Nationalism, 287, 289
Nature, 131, 149–150, 198–201, 202–204, 211–212, 228–229. *See also* Dao
Needham, Joseph, 119, 126–127
Nevius, John, 7
New Culture Movement, 281, 289–291
New Life Movement, 292
New Text School, 31–32, 130, 131, 140, 157, 219
New Year's Festival, 271
Ng, Chin-keong, 21
Nianer shi zhaji, 136
Nirvana, 32, 168
Northern School (of painting; gongbi), 210, 212, 215
Novels, 234–243
Nü, Gua (Nü, Wa), 27

Numerical categories, 119, 121, 160, 193–194, 294. *See also* Correlations; Logic
Nurgachi, 38–39
Nüshu. *See* Women's script

Oboi, 41
Ocko, Jonathan, 54
Office of Ceremonial, 49–50
Office of the Privy Purse, 49–51
Office of Transmission,
Official sacrifices. *See* State sacrifices
Old Text School, 31–32, 130, 131
Order and disorder, xiii, 8–9, 16, 99–100, 155, 185, 274, 275. *See also* Heterodoxy; Orthodoxy; Rebellion; Unity and disunity
Orthodoxy, 37, 83, 99, 139, 166, 184, 212, 213, 214, 216, 220, 222, 243, 245, 246, 259, 292, 294, 297, 308(n13). *See also* Heterodoxy

Painting, 124, 187, 188, 201–214, 215, 230
Pan, Gu (P'an, Ku), 27, 133
Parallel Prose, 219, 224, 225
Parish, William, 296
Particularism, 65, 70, 296. *See also* Confucianism; Family system; Guanxi; Localism; Personal relations
Parties, 74, 199, 270
Patriarchy, 250–253, 296. *See also* Authoritarianism; "Dependency orientation;" Family system; Hierarchy
"Peach Blossom Fan." *See Taohua shan*
Peasantry, 1–2, 13, 75–79, 99–100, 149–150, 176, 292–293, 296. *See also* Landlordism; Land system
Peng, Shaosheng (P'eng, Shao-sheng), 167
People's Republic of China, 293, 294, 295, 296, 297, 298
Perkins, Dwight, 66
Personal relations, 64–65, 69–70, 74, 87–88. *See also* Guanxi; Particularism
Philosophy. *See* Buddhism; Confucianism; Daoism; Thought
Pilgrimages, 270, 273
Pinyin transliteration system, xii, 297, 299 *See also* Chinese names
Plaks, Andrew, 199–200, 234–235, 239, 242
Po (yin aspect of the soul), 179
Poetry, 74, 109, 114, 115, 215, 225–230, 228, 229, 232, 242–243, 270, 273
Polarities, 112–114, 122–124, 226–227, 234, 238, 239, 242. *See also* Balance; Correlations; *Yijing*; Yinyang
Political organization. *See* Bureaucracy; Government; Manchus

Popular religion, 155–156, 163, 174–184. *See also* Gui; Shen; Spirits

Population, 15–16, 245, 275

Porcelain. *See* Ceramics

Precious scrolls (baojuan), 174

Prices and exchange rates, 301–303

Primordial Heavenly Worthy, 173

Printing, 35, 219. *See also* Literacy

Prospect Garden, 199–200

Prostitution, 84, 88, 253

Proverbs and "fixed expressions," 114–115. *See also* Language

Pu, Songling (P'u, Sung-ling), 231

Punishments, 89–90, 91, 274–275. *See also* Law

Puns. *See* Word Play

Pure Land School of Buddhism, 171–172

Pusa. *See* Bodhisattvas

Pye, Lucian, 251

Qi (cosmic breath), 12, 203

Qi (material force), 147, 148, 203

Qi (spirit, vitality or "life force" in art), 191, 197, 203, 217, 223

Qi ("vital force" in the body), 162

Qian, Daxin (Ch'ien, Ta-hsin), 115, 246

Qian, Dian (Ch'ien Tien), 116

Qian, Du, 213

Qian, Qianyi (Ch'ien, Ch'ien-i), 222–223

Qian, Xuantong, 290

Qianlong (Ch'ien-lung), Emperor, 2, 15, 42, 83, 138, 166, 188, 199, 214, 215, 220, 223, 236

Ten Great Campaigns of, 15, 197

Qianzi wen, 60

Qin (Ch'in) dynasty,

Qin ("zither"), 263

Qin, Huitian (Ch'in, Hui-t'ien), 144

Qin, Liangyu, 85

Qin, Nong (Ch'in, Nung),

Qing, Prince, 44

Qing dynasty, 2, 38–33, 83, 139, 157. *See also* Emperors; Manchus

Qing Legal Code. *See Da Qing lüli*

Qingming Festival, 271–272, 273

Qingshi gao, 136

Qu. *See* Song-poems

Qu, Bingyun, 214

Qu, Yuan (Ch'ü, Y'üan), 24, 272

Quanzhen (Ch'üan-chen) sect, 172

Qubilai Khan, 37

Queue (bianzi), 39, 288

Rankin, Mary, 2, 22

Rawski, Evelyn, 22

Rebellion, 31, 32, 33, 34, 35, 39, 43, 99, 274–275. *See also* Taiping Rebellion

Reciprocity (shu), 142, 145

Reciprocity or requital (bao), 65, 69, 235. *See also* Guanxi; Human feelings

Red Guards, 294

Reflections on Things at Hand. See Jinsi lu

Regulated Verse, 225

Relational thinking, 118–120. *See also* Correlations

Religion, definition of, 323 (n1)

Religious Daoism, 5, 32–33, 82–83, 91, 149, 150, 165, 172–174, 177, 179, 184, 193, 194, 202, 220, 222, 231, 235–236, 274, 297. *See also* Quanzhen sect; Zhengyi sect

Ren, Bonian, 213

Ren, Xiong, 213

Ren, Xun, 213

Renqing. *See* Human feelings

Republic of China, 289, 291–292, 295, 297–298. *See also* Taiwan

Rhapsody, 225

Rhythms of fate (yunhui), 178

Righteousness (yi; also duty or "conscience"), 114, 144–145

Ritual, 6–7, 32, 45, 52, 56–57, 60, 69, 79, 88, 92, 98, 131, 137, 138, 140, 158–165, 179, 180, 183, 184, 189, 195, 196, 197, 243, 245, 246–247, 252, 255–256, 261, 266, 283, 287, 288, 289–290, 293, 296, 309(nn 26, 29)

as a philosophical value, 143–144, 145, 189, 292

See also Ancestor worship; Family ritual; State sacrifices

Rolston, David, 234

Romance of the Three Kingdoms. See Sanguo zhi yanyi

"Romance of the Western Chamber." *See Xixiang ji*

Rosemont, Henry, 119

Rou putuan, 237, 259

Rowe, William, 95–96

Royal Mother of the West, 174

Ruan, Dacheng, 234

Ruan, Yuan (Juan, Yüan), 114, 131, 195, 224–225

Rulin waishi, 238, 239

Runners, 58, 59

Sacred Edict, 8, 91, 231, 232

Sai, Kunlun (Sai, K'un-lun), 237

Sangang. *See* Three Bonds

Sangren, Stephen, 5, 156

Sanguan jing, 173

Sanguo zhi yanyi, 236, 237

Sanzang, 168

Sanzi jing, 112

Scholars, The. See Rulin waishi

School of Evidential Research, 129–130, 131, 140, 146, 148, 167, 216, 222, 245–246
School of Names, 30
School of Principle, 129, 131, 140, 147, 149, 219. *See also* Zhu, Xi
School of Ritual Studies, 288
School of Statecraft, 130, 131, 139, 157
School of the Mind, 38. *See also* Wang, Yangming
School Temples, 160
Schools. *See* Education; School Temples
Schoppa, Keith, 22
Schwartz, Benjamin, 138, 175, 280
Science, 35, 39, 125–127, 278, 279, 289, 290, 292, 294, 295
Secret societies, 97–99, 184–185, 275
Self-strengthening Movement, 279
Sending Winter Clothes Festival, 273
Sexual life, 70–71, 173, 202, 232–233, 245, 246, 249–250, 253, 258, 259–260. *See also* Concubinage; Prostitution
Shangdi, 158. *See also* Heaven
Shang dynasty, 28, 195, 196
Shao, Yong (Shao, Yung), 35, 135
Shek, Richard, 167
Shen (yang spirits), 176, 177, 179, 180, 183
Shen, Deqian (Shen, Te-ch'ien), 224, 227, 229
Shen, Fu, 200
Shen, Gua (Shen, Kua), 35, 127
Shen, Nong (Shen, Nung), 27, 125
Shen, Yao, 81
Shen, Zongqian (Shen, Tsung-ch'ien), 210, 211
Shengguan tu, 265–266
Shenhui, 190, 204, 209
Shenshi. *See* Gentry
Shi, Kefa (Shih, K'o-fa), 234
Shi, Lanyan (Shih, Lan-yen), 238
Shi, Xiangyun (Shih, Hsiang-yün), 4
Shichao shengxun, 67
Shiding, 167
Shijing, 114, 225
Shitou ji, 239. *See also Honglou meng*
Shoppa, Keith, 22
Shu. *See* Reciprocity
Shuhua shuoling, 191
Shuihu zhuan, 125, 236, 237
Shujing, 103, 140, 282
Shun, 27, 125, 142, 147
Shunzhi (Shun-chih), Emperor, 41, 166
Shuoshi cuiyu, 224
Shuowen jiezi, 106, 108, 112
Sikong, Tu (Ssu-k'ung, T'u),
Siku quanshu, 220, 221–222, 223
Siku quanshu zongmu tiyao, 222
Sima, Guang (Ssu-ma, Kuang), 35

Sima, Qian (Ssu-ma, Ch'ien), 124, 136
Sima, Xiangru (Ssu-ma Hsiang-ju), 24
Sincerity (cheng), 145–146
Sinicization, 2, 11, 33, 127, 308(n13). *See also* Chineseness; Sinocentrism
Sinocentrism, 11–12, 13, 16, 39–40, 128, 137–138, 283–284. *See also* Barbarians; Chineseness; Tributary system
Sino-Japanese War (1894–1895), 279, 287
Six Boards, 51–55, 58
Six Dynasties period, 32–33
Six Great Masters of the Qing, 212
Skinner, G. William, 21–22, 24, 26
SKQS. *See Siku quanshu*
Slaves, 85, 253. *See also* Bondservants
Smith, Arthur H., 7, 268
Social life, 199, 266–274. *See also* Festivals; Games; Life-cycle ritual
Social tensions, 9, 92, 93, 98–100, 178, 184, 274–275
Song (Sung) dynasty, 34
Song, Jiang (Sung, Chiang), 236
Song Learning. *See* School of Principle
Song-poems, 225
Southern School (of painting; xieyi), 210, 212, 215
Spence, Jonathan, 89, 268
Spirits, 5, 158, 174–184, 95. *See also* Gui; Shen
Spirits of Land and Grain (sheji), 160
Spirituality, 120, 121, 130, 146, 149, 173, 189, 190, 195, 223, 291. *See also* Cosmology; Divination; Three Powers; *Yijing*
State sacrifices, 133, 157–163
Status. *See* Hierarchy
Stereotypes, 24–26
Story of the Stone. See Shitou ji
Stover, Leon, 265
Su, Dongpo (Su, Tung-p'o), 35, 230
Su, Liupeng, 213
Su, Renshan, 213
Subdistrict administration. *See* Baojia; Tuanlian
Sui dynasty, 33
Sui Garden, 199
Sullivan, Michael, 33, 188, 189, 196
Sun, E-tu Zen, 52
Sun, Wukong (Sun, Wu-k'ung; "Monkey"), 237
Sun, Yat-sen (Sun Zhongshan), 116, 280, 281, 289, 292
Supreme Ultimate. *See* Taiji
Su Shi. *See* Su Dongpo
Sutton, Donald, 22
Symbolic reference, 101, 102, 118–127. *See also* Symbolism; *Yijing*
Symbolism, 150, 160, 167, 183, 184, 189, 191–194, 195–196, 200–201, 232, 236, 237, 238, 255, 261–262, 271, 275

T'ien, Ju-kang, 245
Taiji, 62, 134, 192
Taiji quan, 262
Taiji tu, 192
Taiping Rebellion, 93, 184, 279, 285
Taishang ganying pian, 231
Taiwan, 295, 297–298. *See also* Republic of China
Tang, Guichen (T'ang, Kuei-ch'en), 238
Tang, Jian (T'ang, Chien), 149
Tang, Junyi, 153
Tang (T'ang) dynasty, 33–34, 137, 224
Taohua shan, 233–234
Taxation, 92–93. *See also* Lijia
Tea, 269
Technicians, 226–227
Technology, 35–36. *See also* Science
Temple of Heaven complex, 158–159
Ten Abominations, 274
Tenantry, 77–78. *See also* Land system; Landlords
Ten Courts of Judgment (Hell), 171, 174, 324(n58)
Theravada Buddhism, 168–169
Thought, basic patterns of, 29–30, 118–120, 131–138.
    See also Language; Logic
Three Bonds, 6, 138, 140–141, 235
Three Courts of High Adjudicature, 54
Three Friends of Winter, 194
Three Powers (Heaven, Earth and Man), 149, 189. *See
    also* Cosmology; Spirituality
Three Principles of the People, 292
Three Pure Ones, 173, 174
Three Sovereigns, 119, 160
Three Teachings, 119, 129. *See also* Buddhism;
    Confucianism; Daoism
Tian. *See* Heaven
Tianhou (Tianshang shengmu; Mazu), 5, 164, 175,
    297
Tianming. *See* Mandate of Heaven
Tiantai School of Buddhism, 169, 171
Tibet, 12, 15, 16, 17, 18, 22, 55, 169. *See also* Lamaism
Time, 135–136
Tiyong formula, 148, 282, 293
Toda, Toyosaburo, 120
Tongcheng School, 129, 223
Tongzhi (T'ung-chih), Emperor, 44, 48
Tongzhi Restoration, 136, 283, 292
Tradition-mindedness, 48–49, 91–92, 96, 131, 136,
    139–140, 187, 188, 190–191, 195, 198, 204, 209–
    210, 216, 219, 226, 282–286, 287, 291, 293, 294,
    295, 296–298. *See also* Fugu
Treaty of Nanjing (1842), 138
Triads, 99, 184
Tributary system, 137–138
Trigrams, 121, 124, 126
Tripitaka (Sanzang; literary character), 237

Tripitaka. See Sanzang
TSJC. *See* Tushu jicheng
Tu, Wei-ming, 131, 143
Tuanlian, 59
Tudi gong (Lords of the Earth), 13, 98, 163–164, 178,
    297
Tushu jicheng (TSJC), 3–4, 6–7, 14, 39, 113, 116, 117,
    146, 193, 194, 220–221, 223, 249, 260, 268
"Twenty-Four Examples of Filial Piety." *See Ershisi
    xiao*

Unequal treaties, 278–279
Unity and disunity, 29, 31, 32, 155–156, 184–185, 273,
    274–275, 309(n29). *See also* Integration; Order
    and disorder
Urban-rural relations, 34, 95–96, 99–100, 292. *See also*
    Marketing communities

van Gulik, R. H., 259
Vernacular literature, 230–243
Voltaire, François, 38
Von Bell, Adam Schall, 41

Wakeman, Frederic, 74, 81, 99
Waley, Arthur, 229
Wang, Anshi (Wang, An-shih), 35
Wang, Duan (Wang, Tuan), 85
Wang, Erh-min, 278
Wang, Fuzhi (Wang, Fu-chih), 39, 120, 148, 228–229
Wang, Gen (Wang Ken), 38
Wang, Hui, 204, 212, 214
Wang, Huizu (Wang, Hui-tsu), 67, 164
Wang, Ji (Wang Chi), 38
Wang, Jian (Wang, Chien), 212
Wang, Jing, 239
Wang, Kui (Wang, K'uei), 126
Wang, Mang, 31–32, 33
Wang, Meng, 209
Wang, Qinyun, 214
Wang, Shimin (Wang, Shih-min), 209, 212, 214
Wang, Shizhen (Wang, Shih-chen), 212, 228–229, 237
Wang, Shumin, 152
Wang, Tao (Wang, T'ao), 277
Wang, Wan, 224
Wang, Wei, 226, 227, 230
Wang, Xizhi (Wang Hsi-chih), 215–216
Wang, Yangming (Wang, Yang-ming), 38, 139, 146,
    293
Wang, Yu (Wang, Yü), 209
Wang, Yuanqi (Wang, Yüan-ch'i), 210, 212
Ward, Barbara, 270
Warlordism,
Water Margin. See Shuihu zhuan
Watson, James, 9, 155–156

Way, The. *See* Dao
Way and Its Power, The. See Daode jing
Weber, Eugen, 9
Wei, Xiangshu (Wei, Hsiang-shu), 143
Wei, Yingwu (Wei, Ying-wu), 226
Wei, Yuan, 130, 157
Weidner, Marsha, 214
Weights and measures, 301
Weiqi (go), 264–265
Weiyang Sheng, 237
Welch, Holmes, 171
Welfare, 82, 90–91, 97, 98
Wen (culture, literature, patterns), 3, 189. *See also*
    Language
Wen, King, 28
Wen, Tong, 125
Wenchang. *See* God of Literature
Weng, Fanggang (Weng, Fang-kang), 226
Wenxin diaolong, 114, 189. *See also* Liu, Xie
Western influence and "Westernization," 278, 279,
    280, 281, 282, 284–285, 286, 287, 289, 290, 291–
    292, 293. *See also* Imperialism; Missionaries;
    Modernization
Western Paradise, 171, 324(n58)
Whitehead, Alfred North, 120
White Lotus sect, 99, 184
Whyte, Martin King, 296
Williams, S. W., 7, 263–264
Wills, John, 21, 138
Wisdom, 145
Wolf, Arthur, 157, 164, 254
Women, 8–9, 60, 70–712, 78, 85–86, 90, 117, 119, 124,
    141, 163, 181, 187, 213–214, 229–230, 233, 238,
    239, 242–243, 245–246, 247–248, 249, 251, 253,
    256, 257–261, 271–272, 273
Women's script, 101, 229
Word play, 103, 109–110, 119, 193, 200, 242
Woren (Wo-jen), 278
Wright, Arthur, 127, 136
Wright, Mary, 284, 292
Writing, 105–115. *See also* Calligraphy
Wu, Changshi, 213
Wu, Cheng'en (Wu, Ch'eng-en), 237
Wu, Jingzi (Wu, Ching-tzu), 238, 268
Wu, Kedu (Wu, K'o-tu), 283
Wu, King, 28
Wu, Li, 212
Wu, Nelson, 201
Wu, Peiyi, 220
Wu, Sangui (Wu, San-kuei), 39
Wu, Song (Wu Sung), 237
Wu, Woyao (Wu, Wo-yao), 238
Wudi (Wu-ti), Emperor, 31

Wujiang simei. *See* Five Stresses and Four Points of
    Beauty
Wuli tongkao, 144
Wusheng shi shi, 189

Xia (Hsia) dynasty, 27. *See also* Mythology
Xianfeng (Hsien-feng) Emperor, 43–44, 48
Xiangqi, 265
Xiangyin jiu ritual, 261
Xiannong,
Xiao. *See* Filial piety
Xiaojing, 112, 141
Xie, He (Hsieh, Ho), 203
Xie, Lansheng, 213
Ximen, Qing (Hsi-men, Ch'ing), 237
Xin. *See* Faithfulness
Xin (Hsin) dynasty, 31
Xing'an huilan, 275
Xingli jingyi, 129
Xinjiang, 18
Xin qingnian, 290
Xixiang ji, 242
Xiyou ji, 124–125, 237, 238
Xu, Dachun (Hsü, Ta-ch'un), 260
Xu, Shirong, 102
Xu, Wei (Hsü, Wei), 213
Xuantong (Hsuan-t'ung) Emperor, 44
Xuanzang (Hsüan-tsang), 237
Xue, Baochai (Hsüeh, Pao-ch'ai), 239, 240, 242, 253
Xue, Fucheng (Hsüeh, Fu-ch'eng), 281–282
Xunzi (Hsün-tzu), 30, 140, 147
Xuyun (Hsü-yün), 171–172

Yamen (office), 58
Yan, Fu (Yen, Fu), 280, 282
Yan, Ruoju, 130
Yan, Yuan (Yen, Yüan), 130, 146, 148
Yang, C. K., 174, 175
Yang, Weizhen (Yang, Wei-chen), 37
Yangtze River. *See* Yangzi River
Yangzi River, 23
Yao (sage hero), 27, 125, 142
Yao, Nai, 223–224
Ye, Gui (Yeh, Kuei), 260
Yee, Angelina, 239
Yehenala. *See* Empress Dowager
Yellow Emperor, 27, 125
Yellow River, 19–20, 23–24
Yi. *See* Righteousness
Yihe quan. *See* Boxer Rebellion
Yijing, 101, 102, 103, 105, 106, 114, 118, 119, 120–127,
    139, 140, 141, 149, 153, 167, 222, 226, 281, 282.
    See also Divination; Hexagrams; Trigrams
Yili, 6, 140

Yinxue wushu, 104

Yinyang, 4–5, 6, 14, 28, 112, 113, 114, 119, 121–124, 126, 129, 132, 134–135, 141, 147–148, 150, 155, 162, 169, 173, 176, 177, 178, 179, 180, 183, 191, 192, 194, 196, 200, 211–212, 223–224, 227, 228, 234, 235, 239, 247, 260, 262, 266, 269, 281, 290, 293, 294, 308(n21). *See also* Balance; Polarities

Yong ("braves"), 84

Yongying ("brave battalions"), 84, 278, 286

Yongzheng (Yung-cheng) Emperor, 2, 42, 65, 166

You, Huai (Yu, Huai), 269

You, Zhi (Yu, Chih), 247

Yu (Yü), 27

Yu, Chün-fang, 270

Yu, Pauline, 225–226

Yü, Ying-shih, 131

Yuan dynasty, 36–37, 81

Yuan, Mei, 228, 245–246

Yuan, Shouding (Yüan, Shou-ting), 143

Yuanji, 213, 216

Yuhuang jing, 173

Yun, Shouping (Yün, Shou-p'ing), 212

Yunhui. *See* Rhythms of fate

Yuxiang, 237

Yuxuan yulu, 166

Zelin, Madeline, 43

Zen. *See* Chan School of Buddhism

Zeng, Guofan (Tseng, Kuo-fan), 131

Zha, Siting, 106

Zhang, Boxing (Chang, Po-hsing), 231

Zhang, Fei (Chang, Fei), 236

Zhang, Geng (Chang, Keng), 204, 214

Zhang, Lunying, 217

Zhang, Qi (Chang, Qi), 217

Zhang, Xinzhi, 125

Zhang, Xuecheng (Chang, Hsueh-ch'eng), 124, 167, 228, 246

Zhang, Zai (Chang, Tsai), 35

Zhang, Zhidong (Chang, Chih-tung), 280, 282

Zhao, Yi (Chao, I), 136, 228

Zhao, Zhiqian, 213

Zheng, Xie (Cheng, Hsieh), 213, 230

Zheng, Zhen, 115

Zhengyi (Cheng-i) sect, 172

Zhi. *See* Wisdom.

Zhinü ("Weaving Maiden"), 272

Zhong, Kui (Chung K'uei), 176

Zhongyong, 140, 145, 147, 149

Zhou (Chou), Duke of, 28

Zhou, Dunyi (Chou, Tun-i), 35, 124

Zhou (Chou) dynasty, 28–30

Zhou li, 6, 140, 143

Zhu, Bajie ("Pigsy"), 237

Zhu, Da (Chu, Ta), 213

Zhu, Xi (Chu, Hsi), 35, 129, 139, 142, 146, 147, 148, 149, 152, 231, 294

Zhu, Yizun (Chu, I-tsun), 226, 229

Zhu, Yuanzhang (Chu, Yüan-chang), 99

Zhuan, Xu (Chuan, Hsu), 27

Zhuangzi (Chuang-tzu), 30, 150, 151, 152, 153

Zhuangzi, 152

Zhuge, Liang (Chu-ko, Liang), 236

Zito, Angela, 57

Zongli Yamen, 55

Zou, Yan (Tsou, Yen), 30

Zou, Yigui (Tsou, I-kuei), 214

Zuozhuan, 140, 282